Function Reference

Microsoft EXCEL

Spreadsheet with Business Graphics and Database
Version 4.0 for Apple® Macintosh® Series or Windows™ Series

Document Number XL26298-1292
Printed in the United States of America.

Contents

Welcome

Welcome to the *Microsoft Excel Function Reference,* a complete description of Microsoft Excel's worksheet and macro functions. This book is for users of Microsoft® Excel for Windows™ and Microsoft® Excel for the Macintosh.

The *Function Reference* is divided into five sections. The first section reviews the differences between worksheet and macro functions, shows how the information for each function is organized, and explains the conventions used in this manual.

The second section lists the changed worksheet and macro functions in Microsoft Excel version 4.0, and gives a brief description of each.

The third section lists worksheet functions by category.

The fourth section lists macro functions by category and points out functions that are available only in specific operating environments.

The fifth section describes all of Microsoft Excel's functions in alphabetic order.

If You Are New to Functions

If you are new to functions, first read the following section, "About Functions." To learn how to enter worksheet functions into formulas, see "Entering a Formula" in Chapter 5 in Book 1 of the *Microsoft Excel User's Guide.* For information about how to create and use macros, see Chapters 6 through 8 in Book 2 of the *Microsoft Excel User's Guide*.

If You Are Familiar with Functions

If you are familiar with functions, read "How Function Descriptions Are Organized" in the following section, "About Functions."

About Functions

In Microsoft Excel, functions are calculation tools that you can use to perform decision-making, action-taking, and value-returning operations automatically. Microsoft Excel provides a wide variety of functions that perform many different types of calculations.

Microsoft Excel has two types of functions: worksheet functions and macro functions. You can use worksheet functions on both worksheets and macro sheets. For example, the worksheet function COS returns the cosine of an angle; you usually use COS on a worksheet, but you can also use it on a macro sheet.

Some functions are available only on macro sheets and are instructions you use in macros to perform actions. Many macro functions also accept and return values. Functions on a macro sheet are calculated only when the associated macro is run. Macro functions are identified in this book by the heading "Macro Sheets Only."

Function Categories

In Microsoft Excel, functions are organized by category, as shown in the following table. These categories appear in the Paste Function dialog box. To see the Paste Function dialog box, choose the Paste Function command from the Formula menu.

Category	Action
Financial	Performs financial actions on values
Date & Time	Returns chronological information
Math & Trig	Performs mathematical actions on values
Statistical	Performs statistical actions on values

Category	Action
Lookup & Reference	Manipulates references, cells, ranges, and positions, or returns information from one of these
Database	Returns information about a database
Text	Performs actions on text values
Logical	Returns logical values
Information	Returns information about parts of the Microsoft Excel environment
Commands	Performs actions equivalent to choosing commands or tools
Customizing	Customizes Microsoft Excel
Macro Control	Controls macro execution
DDE/External	Performs actions on objects that are not part of Microsoft Excel
Engineering	Performs engineering calculations on values

Worksheet Functions

You use worksheet functions on worksheets and macro sheets to calculate and return values based on information you provide. Worksheet functions take a value or values, perform some operation on them, and return a value or values. Functions on a worksheet are calculated as soon as you enter them.

Online Help for Worksheet Functions

Microsoft Excel includes a directory of worksheet functions as part of the online Help system. To use the online directory, choose the Contents command from the Help menu or press F1 (in Microsoft Excel for Windows) or choose the Help command from the Window menu (in Microsoft Excel for the Macintosh), and then select Worksheet Functions from the list of Help topics. If you are using Apple system software version 7.0 or later and you have a 13-inch or larger monitor, access Help by choosing Microsoft Excel Help from the Help menu.

Macro Functions

Microsoft Excel's macro language contains more than 400 macro functions. You can use macros to automate anything you do manually, such as choosing commands, selecting options in dialog boxes, entering data on worksheets, and changing the current selection. You can also use the macro language to create custom functions that perform specialized calculations.

Command-Equivalent Functions

Using a command-equivalent function is the same as choosing a particular command from one of the Microsoft Excel menus. For example, using the FILE.DELETE function is like choosing the Delete command from the File menu. The arguments to a command-equivalent function correspond to the option buttons, check boxes, text boxes, and list boxes associated with that command. Instead of being listed in the Commands category, some functions that carry out commands are listed in categories that are more appropriate to their function. For example, the SET.DATABASE function is part of the Database category, even though it is equivalent to the Set Database command on the Data menu.

Option buttons are represented by number values. For example, in the Alignment dialog box, seven option buttons represent the seven horizontal alignment options. In the ALIGNMENT macro function, you select one of the options by specifying a number from 1 to 7 corresponding to those buttons. To see the Alignment dialog box, choose the Alignment command from the Format menu.

Check boxes are represented by logical values. If an argument is TRUE, Microsoft Excel selects the check box; if FALSE, Microsoft Excel clears the check box. If an argument is omitted, the current state of the check box is usually not changed.

Text boxes are represented by text values.

List boxes are represented by number or text values. You can make a choice from a list of items in a list box. You either specify a number (for example, to select a color in the Display dialog box) or text (for example, to select a format in the Number dialog box).

Dialog-Box Functions

Every command that displays a dialog box has a dialog-box form of the command-equivalent function. The dialog-box form has the same name as the command-equivalent function, but its name is followed by a question mark. This form displays a dialog box while the macro is running. The dialog box remains on the screen until you select the options you want. After you close the dialog box by choosing the OK or Cancel button, the macro continues to run. In dialog-box functions, all arguments are optional.

Other Action-Equivalent Functions

Action-equivalent functions correspond to actions you take without choosing a command, such as selecting a cell (the SELECT function), scrolling through a window (the HSCROLL and VSCROLL functions), or using a tool on a toolbar (the PROMOTE and DEMOTE functions). Action-equivalent functions are included in the Commands category.

Customizing Functions

You can use customizing functions to carry out actions that can be performed only by macros, such as creating custom menus, commands, tools, toolbars, and dialog boxes.

Other Macro Functions

There are two kinds of macro functions that do not perform actions: macro control functions and information functions.

Macro Control Functions

You can use macro control functions to direct how your command macros run. Macro control functions can create loops, redirect macro execution to other cells, and control how Microsoft Excel receives and returns information from functions. For example, you can use the FOR and NEXT functions to create a loop to repeat an operation a specified number of times.

Information Functions

Information functions return or manipulate information about almost every detail of your Microsoft Excel working environment. You can use them to get information about cells, objects, windows, documents, and many other Microsoft Excel items. You can design macros that decide what actions to perform based on the values returned by these functions.

How Function Descriptions Are Organized

To help you find information, function descriptions in the fifth section, "Function Reference," follow a template consisting of some or all of the following parts:

- **Name**   The name of the function as you type it into Microsoft Excel.

- **Return value**   What the function returns, or what command or action the function performs, and suggestions for using the function.

- **Syntax**   The name of the function, including all required and optional arguments in the correct order.

- **Arguments**   A description of each argument in the order of the function's syntax.

- **Remarks**   General information, notes, and tips to make using the function easier.

- **Examples**   Examples showing how to use the function.

- **Related functions**   A list of related functions with short descriptions.

Conventions in This Manual

- In the syntax line, required arguments are **bold** and optional arguments are not bold. Whether they are required or optional, all arguments are *italic*.

- In text, whether they are required or optional, all arguments are *italic* and not bold. For more information about required and optional arguments, see "Syntax of Functions" later in this section.

- Function and macro formula examples are shown in a different font. For example, this is a macro formula from the ACTIVATE function: `ACTIVATE("MACRO1.XLM",1)`.

- Argument names use underline characters between words; for example, *num_chars* is an argument name.

- Macro and cell names use no punctuation between words; for example, SalesTotals is a cell name.

- In procedures, anything you type is shown in **bold.**

- Functions are shown without the equal sign (=). Remember to type an equal sign at the beginning of every formula, but not before functions in nested formulas. For example, type **=SUM(3,8)** but type **=SUM(3,(PRODUCT(2,4)))**

Note   The illustrations in this book may look slightly different from their appearance on your screen.

Syntax of Functions

Every function description includes a syntax line. For example, the syntax line for the LEFT function looks like this:

LEFT(***text,****num_chars*)

In the syntax line, the function's name and required arguments are bold; optional arguments are not bold.

If you do not provide required arguments to a function, you will not be able to enter the function in a cell. In the preceding example, the argument *text* is bold, and therefore it is required. *Num_chars* is not bold and therefore is optional, so either of the following is allowed:

```
LEFT("Hiram",2)
LEFT("Corley")
```

LEFT() is not allowed, because *text* is a required argument.

When an argument is followed by an ellipsis (…), you can have more than one argument of that data type. You can have up to 30 arguments for some functions, as long as the total number of characters in the formula does not exceed 1024. Also, no individual string can be larger than 255 characters. For example, here is the syntax for the MAX function:

MAX(***number1,****number2,…*)

Any of the following formulas would be allowed:

```
MAX(26)
MAX(26,31)
MAX(26,31,29)
```

Functions with an empty set of parentheses after the name take no arguments, although you must include the parentheses in order for Microsoft Excel to recognize the function.

In descriptive text, all argument names appear in plain *italic* (not bold) so that it's easier to see them. For example, the CELL function has one required argument and one optional argument. Syntax is shown as:

CELL(***info_type,****reference*)

When we talk about the *info_type* and *reference* arguments in text, however, both arguments are italic and not bold. Use the format in the syntax line to determine whether an argument is required or optional.

Tip   If you are typing a function and you cannot remember the argument list, press CTRL+A (in Microsoft Excel for Windows) or CONTROL+A (in Microsoft Excel for the Macintosh) after you have typed the equal sign, function name, and opening parenthesis. This pastes the argument list and the closing parenthesis for the function. For example, if you are entering a formula that contains the PMT function, type **=PMT(** and then press CTRL+A or CONTROL+A. Microsoft Excel pastes the argument list and closing parenthesis.

Argument Names

Many argument names tell you what kind of information to use as the argument. For example, in the function LEFT(*text,num_chars*), the first argument must be text, and the second argument must be a number.

If the abbreviation *num, ref,* or *logical* appears in the name of the argument, that argument must be a number, a reference, or a logical value, respectively. Similarly, the words *number, reference, logical, text,* and *array* in the name of an argument specify that the argument must be of that data type. *Value* means that the argument can be anything that results in a single value. That value can be a number, text, logical, or error value.

Note Not every argument name specifies the argument's data type. For functions with many arguments, adding the data-type abbreviations makes the syntax listing too long to read easily. For these functions, the data type for each argument is specified in the argument description.

Using Arguments

Arguments are the information that a function uses to produce a new value or perform an action. Arguments are always located to the right of the function name and are enclosed in parentheses. Most arguments are expected to be of a certain data type. The argument you give should be either the appropriate type or another type that Microsoft Excel can convert to the appropriate type. For more information about how Microsoft Excel converts argument types, see "Converting Data Types" later in this section.

An argument can be anything that produces a desired data type. For example, the SUM function, which adds its arguments, can take from 1 to 30 arguments. You can give the SUM function any of the following four kinds of arguments, which produce a number or numbers:

- A value that is a number, such as:
  SUM(1,10,100)

- A formula that results in a number, such as:
  SUM(0.5+0.5,AVERAGE(5,5),10^2)

  Using a function as an argument to a function, as in the preceding example, is called nesting functions. In this example, the AVERAGE function is an argument to the SUM function. You can nest up to seven levels of functions in a formula.

- A reference to a cell or range of cells that contains a number or a formula that results in a number, such as:
  SUM(A1,A2)
  SUM(A1:A5)

  The second preceding example is equivalent to the formula SUM(A1,A2,A3,A4,A5). An advantage of using the range form is that the argument A1:A5 counts as only one argument, while the other form counts as five arguments. If you wanted to add more than 30 numbers, you would have to use the range form, because you can only use 30 arguments with this function.

- A name that refers to a value, a formula, or a cell or range containing a value or formula, such as:
  SUM(AdjustingValue,Inflation)

Types of Arguments

A function's arguments can be any of the following:

- Numbers
- Text
- Logical values
- Error values
- References
- Arrays

You can also use the reference and array types of arguments to provide numbers, text, logical values, and error values to a function.

Numbers   Examples of numbers are 5.003, 0, 150.286, and –30.05. Numbers without decimals are called integers. Examples of integers are 5, 0, 150, and –30. Numbers are accurate to 15 digits.

Text   Examples of text are "a", "Word", "w/punc.", or "". Text values used in formulas must be enclosed in double quotation marks. If the text itself contains quotation marks, use two double quotation marks for each double quotation mark in the text. For example, to find the length in characters for this text— in the "good" old days—enter the formula:

```
LEN("in the ""good"" old days")
```

Text values can be a maximum of 255 characters long including quotation marks. A text constant that contains no characters is written as "" and is called "empty text."

Note   If text used as an argument is not enclosed in quotation marks, Microsoft Excel assumes it is a name and tries to replace it with the value that the name refers to. If the unquoted text is not a name, and therefore has no associated value, Microsoft Excel returns the #NAME? error value.

Logical values   The logical values are TRUE and FALSE. Logical arguments can also be statements, such as B10>20, that evaluate to TRUE or FALSE.

Error values   Examples of error values are #DIV/0!, #N/A, #NAME?, #NULL!, #NUM!, #REF!, and #VALUE!.

References   Examples of references are $A$10, A10, $A10, A$10, R1C1, or R[10]C[–10]. References can refer to single cells, ranges, or multiple selections, and can be relative, absolute, or mixed. When you use a reference as an argument that is supposed to be a number, text, error value, or logical value, the contents of the cells specified by the reference are used as the argument.

For information about references in macro functions, see Chapter 7, in Book 2 of the *Microsoft Excel User's Guide*.

- Functions that return references display the value contained in the reference instead of the reference. To use the reference itself in a macro formula, use the REFTEXT function to convert the reference to a text string.

- To supply a multiple selection as a single reference argument, enclose the reference in a second set of parentheses, for example:

```
SELECT(("R1C1:R2C2,R3C3:R4C4"))
```

Arrays   An example of an array is {1,2,3;4,5,6}. Microsoft Excel converts arrays in three ways:

- Some worksheet functions (AND, AVERAGE, COUNT, COUNTA, MAX, MIN, OR, STDEV, STDEVP, SUM, VAR, and VARP) can take from 1 to 30 arguments, all of the same data type. If an array is used as an argument to one of those functions, each element of the array produces a single result. For example, SUM({1,2,3;4,5,6}) has one element and produces one result, 21. This operates just as if you had entered the formula SUM(A1:C2) on the following worksheet.

	A	B	C
1	1	2	3
2	4	5	6
3			

- If the formula is an array formula, the function acts on each element of the array and produces an array result. Each element of the array is evaluated as if it were a separate and unique value used as the argument. For example, the ABS function takes a single number as an argument and returns the absolute value of the number. You can use an array as the argument to ABS: the array formula {=ABS({1,–2,3;–4,5,–6})} equals {1,2,3;4,5,6}.

- If the formula is not an array formula and an array argument is not expected, the function takes the first element of the array and ignores the rest. For example, if the following formula is not entered as an array formula, then: ABS({1,-2,3;-4,5,-6}) equals 1.

If the formula requires an array as the argument and you use a single value, Microsoft Excel creates an array from the value. For example, the following formula compares a single value, the text SALES.XLS, with a three-item array returned by the DOCUMENTS function:

OR("SALES.XLS"=DOCUMENTS())

To evaluate the formula, Microsoft Excel converts the single value SALES.XLS into an array of the same size as the one returned by the DOCUMENTS function, as follows:

OR({"SALES.XLS","SALES.XLS","SALES.XLS"}=
{"Chart1","Macro1","SALES.XLS"})

The two arrays shown in the function are in effect evaluated as follows:

SALES.XLS = Chart1 returns FALSE

SALES.XLS = Macro1 returns FALSE

SALES.XLS = SALES.XLS returns TRUE

Microsoft Excel evaluates each element in the first array against the corresponding element in the second array. Since one of the formulas in the example evaluates to TRUE, and since the OR function returns TRUE if any of its arguments returns TRUE, the function returns TRUE.

For more information about arrays, see "Creating and Using an Array Formula" in Chapter 5 in Book 1 of the *Microsoft Excel User's Guide*.

Tip For any data type, you can always use a name that refers to the desired data type as an argument. You can also use another function that returns the desired data type as an argument.

If you work with a large number of complicated formulas, you may want to convert some of them to custom functions. For information about custom functions, see Chapter 5 in Book 2 of the *Microsoft Excel User's Guide.*

Converting Data Types

If you use an argument that does not produce the correct data type for a function, Microsoft Excel tries to convert the argument to the required data type. For example, the LEN function takes one text argument and returns the number of characters in that argument; LEN("abc") is equal to 3. If you enter the formula LEN(1202) in a cell, Microsoft Excel internally converts the number 1202 to the text value "1202". The formula LEN(1202) is therefore equal to 4.

Numbers, text, and logical values are converted as shown in the following table.

If an argument should be	Result
A number, but is given as text	Microsoft Excel tries to convert the text to a number. If the text is in any standard number, date, time, or currency format, it is interpreted as if the quotation marks weren't there, just as in the VALUE function.
A number, but is given as a logical value	TRUE is converted to 1, and FALSE is converted to 0.
Text, but is given as a number	The number is treated as text (as if it were enclosed in quotation marks).
Text, but is given as a logical value	TRUE is converted to " TRUE", and FALSE is converted to "FALSE".
Logical, but is given as a number	Any number other than 0 is TRUE, and 0 is FALSE.
Logical, but is given as text	Only the text "TRUE" and "FALSE" are converted. Any other text is ignored.

Using Commas in a List of Arguments

You must separate individual arguments with commas, but be careful not to type extra commas. If you use a comma to hold a place for an argument, but you don't enter the argument, Microsoft Excel substitutes the default value for that argument, unless the argument is required. For example, for a worksheet function that takes three arguments, if you enter (,arg2,arg3) as the arguments, Microsoft Excel substitutes an appropriate value for *arg1*. If you enter (*arg1,,*), it substitutes appropriate values for *arg2* and *arg3*.

In worksheet functions, particularly in functions that count the number of arguments before calculating, extra commas will affect the count of arguments and therefore the way the function is calculated. For example, AVERAGE(1,2,3,4,5) returns 3, but AVERAGE(,,1,2,3,4,5) returns 2.14. In macro functions, extra commas act as placeholders for arguments and generally have no effect.

For most arguments, the value substituted for an omitted argument is 0, FALSE, or "" (empty text), depending on what the data type of the argument should be. For omitted *reference* arguments, the default value is usually the active cell or selection.

For example, in the DISPLAY function (equivalent to the Display command on the Options menu), if you omit the first three arguments and specify TRUE for the fourth, the state of the first three check boxes in the Display dialog box remains unchanged. If an omitted argument is assumed to be some other value, the description of the argument will tell you so.

Note If you are using a reference as an argument and that reference uses a comma as a union operator, enclose the reference in parentheses. The AREAS function, for example, takes one argument: a reference. If you try to enter the formula AREAS(A1,C1), Microsoft Excel interprets A1 and C1 as two separate arguments and displays the "Too many arguments" message. The correct form would be AREAS((A1,C1)). For information about reference operators, see Chapter 8 in Book 1 of the *Microsoft Excel User's Guide*.

Changed Functions by Category

This section lists changed functions in the categories described in the first section, "About Functions."

Command Functions

ACTIVATE.NEXT(*workbook_text*)

ACTIVATE.PREV(*workbook_text*)
These functions can now be used with workbooks.

ALIGNMENT(*horiz_align,wrap,vert_align, orientation*)
The new *vert_align* and *orientation* arguments allow you to control the vertical alignment and orientation of text. The *horiz_align* argument adds new options to the former *type_num* argument.

ARRANGE.ALL(*arrange_num,active_doc, sync_horiz,sync_vert*)
The new arguments allow you to specify what windows to arrange, how to arrange them, and whether or not to turn vertical or horizontal synchronization on.

CALCULATION(***type_num,****iter,max_num, max_change,update,precision,date_1904, calc_save,save_values,alt_expr,alt_form*)
The new *alt_expr* and *alt_form* arguments allow you to control use of Alternate Expression Evaluation and Alternate Formula Entry.

COLUMN.WIDTH(*width_num,reference,standard, type_num,standard_num*)
The new *standard_num* argument allows you to specify the standard column width for all of the columns in a document.

COPY(*from_reference,to_refererence*)
The new arguments allow you to specify a range of cells to copy from and paste to.

CREATE.DIRECTORY(*path_text*)
This function was formerly included as an add-in in the Microsoft Excel Library and is now part of Microsoft Excel.

CREATE.OBJECT(***obj_type,ref_1,****x_offset1, y_offset1,ref_2,x_offset2,y_offset2,text,fill*)

CREATE.OBJECT(***obj_type,ref_1,****x_offset1, y_offset1,ref_2,x_offset2,y_offset2,xy_series, fill,gallery_num,type_num*)
The new arguments allow you to create and edit the new object types in Microsoft Excel version 4.0.

CUT(*from_reference,to_reference*)
The new arguments allow you to specify a range of cells to cut from and paste to.

DATA.SERIES(*rowcol,type_num,date_num, step_value,stop_value,trend*)
The new *trend* argument allows you to generate a linear or exponential trend with DATA.SERIES.

DEFINE.NAME(***name_text,****refers_to,macro_type, shortcut_text,hidden,category*)
The new *category* argument allows you to specify a built-in or custom category in the Paste Function dialog box in which to display custom functions.

FORMAT.MAIN(***type_num,****view,overlap, gap_width,vary,drop,hilo,angle,gap_depth, chart_depth,up_down,series_line,labels*)
The new *series_line*, *up_down*, and *labels* arguments correspond to new dialog box options.

FORMAT.OVERLAY*(type_num,view,overlap,*
gap_width,vary,drop,hilo,angle,series_dist,
series num,up down,series_line,labels)
The new *series_line, up_down,* and *labels*
arguments correspond to new dialog box
options.

FREEZE.PANES*(logical,col_split,row_split)*
This function now allows you to specify the
column or the row at which you want to split the
active window.

LIST.NAMES*( )*
This function now pastes the category assigned
to custom functions.

MOVE*(x_pos,y_pos,window_text)*
The MOVE function is converted to the more
powerful WINDOW.MOVE command in
Microsoft Excel version 4.0.

NEW*(type_num,xy_series,add_logical)*
The *type_num* argument now accepts
information for creating a workbook.

NOTE*(add_text,cell_ref,start_char,num_chars)*
Using the empty text, "", as an argument deletes
any note text but reserves any associated sound.

OPEN*(file_text,update_links,read_only,*
delimiter_num,prot_pwd,write_res_pwd,
ignore_rorec,file_origin,custom_text)
The new *custom_text* argument allows you to
specify a custom delimiter to be used when
opening text files.

PAGE.SETUP*(head,foot,left,right,top,bot,hdng,*
grid,h_cntr,v_cntr,orient,paper_size,scale,
pg_num,pg_order,bw_cells)

PAGE.SETUP*(head,foot,left,right,top,bot,size,*
h_cntr,v_cntr,orient,paper_size,scale,pg_num)
The new *pg_num, pg_order,* and *bw_cells*
arguments correspond to new options in the
Page Setup dialog box.

PARSE*(parse_text,destination_ref)*
The new *destination_ref* argument allows you to
specify a range of cells into which to place the
result of the PARSE.

PASTE*(to_reference)*
This function now allows you to specify a range
of cells into which to paste the contents of the
Clipboard.

PASTE.SPECIAL*(paste_num,operation_num,*
skip_blanks,transpose)
The new *format* argument for the worksheet
form of this function allows you to specify how
complex clipboard data is pasted.

RUN*(reference,step)*
Now supports Auto_Activate and
Auto_Deactivate macros.

SAVE.AS*(document_text,type_num,prot_pwd,*
backup,write_res_pwd,read_only_rec)
Now supports the Microsoft Excel version 3.0
file format.

SEND.MAIL*(recipients,subject,return_receipt)*
This function is now available for Microsoft
Excel for Windows.

SET.PRINT.TITLES*(titles_for_columns_ref,*
titles_for_rows_ref)
The new arguments allow you to specify ranges
of rows and columns to use as the print titles
area.

SOLVER.OPTIONS*(max_time,iterations,precision,*
assume_linear,step_thru,estimates,derivatives,
search,int_tolerance,scaling)
The *int_tolerance* and *scaling* arguments correspond to new options in the Solver Options
dialog box.

SOLVER.SAVE*(save_area)*
This function now saves all of the information
if just one cell is specified as the save range.
Previously, you had to specify the precise range
location and size.

WORKGROUP*(name_array)*
This function is now equivalent to the new
Group Edit command on the Options menu.

Lookup & Reference Functions

TEXTREF(*text,a1*)
This function can now be used on multiple selections.

Macro Control Functions

VOLATILE(*logical*)
The new *logical* argument allows you to specify whether or not the function is volatile.

Customizing Functions

ADD.COMMAND(*bar_num,menu,command_ref, position*)
This function now allows you to add commands to shortcut menus.

ALERT(*message_text,type_num,help_ref*)
The new *help_ref* argument allows you to specify custom help for Alert messages.

DIALOG.BOX(*dialog_ref*)
This function now supports dialog box features new to Microsoft Excel version 4.0.

INPUT(*message_text,type_num,title_text,default, x_pos,y_pos,help_ref*)
The *help_ref* argument lets you use a custom help topic with input dialog boxes.

ON.DATA(*document_text,macro_text*)
This function now can be used with Publish and Subscribe in Microsoft Excel for the Macintosh when using system software version 7.0 or later.

ON.WINDOW(*window_text,macro_text*)
This function is now compatible with the new Auto_Activate and Auto_Deactivate macros.

Information Functions

CALLER( )
This function now supports the new ON.ENTRY and ON.DOUBLECLICK macro functions. CALLER also returns information about the tool or menu command chosen.

DOCUMENTS(*type_num,match_text*)
The new *match_text* argument allows you to specify what document names you want returned by the function. You can include wildcards as part of the *match_text* argument.

GET.CELL(*type_num,reference*)
This function now returns new types of information about the formatting and contents of the specified cells.

GET.DOCUMENT(*type_num,name_text*)
This function now returns new types of information about the formatting and contents of the specified document.

GET.OBJECT(*type_num,object_id_text,start_num, count_num*)
This function now returns new types of information about the formatting and type of the specified object.

GET.WINDOW(*type_num,window_text*)
This function now returns new types of information about the formatting and contents of the specified window.

GET.WORKSPACE(*type_num*)
This function now returns new types of information about the workspace.

NAMES(*document_text,type_num,match_text*)
The new *match_text* argument allows you to specify what names you want returned.

SELECTION( )
This function now returns information about selected chart items and new worksheet objects.

WINDOWS(*type_num,match_text*)
The new *match_text* argument allows you to specify the name or names of windows you want the WINDOWS function to return.

DDE/External Functions

CREATE.PUBLISHER(*file_text,appearance,size, formats*)

The new *formats* argument allows you to specify the type of file format used to create the Edition file.

EDITION.OPTIONS(*edition_type,edition_name, reference,**option**,appearance,size,formats*)

The new *appearance, size,* and *formats* arguments allow you to control the appearance of the published item and file format of the published file.

Worksheet Functions Listed by Category

This section lists worksheet functions in the categories described in the first section, "About Functions." An asterisk (*) following a function name means that the function is new to Microsoft Excel version 4.0. A dagger (†) following a function name means that you must install one of the macro add-in files located in the Library directory in order to use the function. For information about which add-in file to install, see the function's complete description in the fifth section, "Function Reference." For more information, see "Managing Add-in Commands and Functions" in Chapter 4 in Book 2 of the *Microsoft Excel User's Guide.*

Engineering Functions

BESSELI*(x,n)* *†
Returns the modified Bessel function $I_n(x)$.

BESSELJ*(x,n)* *†
Returns the Bessel function $J_n(x)$.

BESSELK*(x,n)* *†
Returns the modified Bessel function $K_n(x)$.

BESSELY*(x,n)* *†
Returns the Bessel function $Y_n(x)$.

BIN2DEC*(number)* *†
Converts a binary number to decimal.

BIN2HEX*(number,places)* *†
Converts a binary number to hexadecimal.

BIN2OCT*(number,places)* *†
Converts a binary number to octal.

COMPLEX*(real_num,i_num,suffix)* *†
Converts real and imaginary coefficients into a complex number.

CONVERT*(number,from_unit,to_unit)* *†
Converts a number from one measurement system to another.

DEC2BIN*(number,places)* *†
Converts a decimal number to binary.

DEC2HEX*(number,places)* *†
Converts a decimal number to hexadecimal.

DEC2OCT*(number,places)* *†
Converts a decimal number to octal.

DEGREES*(angle_in_radians)* *†
Converts radians to degrees.

DELTA*(number1,number2)* *†
Tests whether two numbers are equal.

ERF*(lower_limit,upper_limit)* *†
Returns the error function.

ERFC*(x)* *†
Returns the complementary error function.

GESTEP*(number,step)* *†
Tests whether a number is greater than a threshold value.

HEX2BIN*(number,places)* *†
Converts a hexadecimal number to binary.

HEX2DEC*(number)* *†
Converts a hexadecimal number to decimal.

HEX2OCT*(number,places)* *†
Converts a hexadecimal number to octal.

IMABS*(inumber)* *†
Returns the absolute value (modulus) of a complex number.

IMAGINARY*(inumber)* *†
Returns the imaginary coefficient of a complex number.

---

*   New function in Microsoft Excel version 4.0.

†   To use this function, you must install one of the add-in macros.

IMARGUMENT(*inumber*) *†
Returns the argument θ, an angle expressed in radians, such that:
$$x + yi = |x + yi| \times e^{i\theta} = |x + yi|(\cos \theta + i \sin \theta)$$

IMCONJUGATE(*inumber*) *†
Returns the complex conjugate of a complex number.

IMCOS(*inumber*) *†
Returns the cosine of a complex number.

IMDIV(*inumber1,inumber2*) *†
Returns the quotient of two complex numbers.

IMEXP(*inumber*) *†
Returns the exponential of a complex number.

IMLN(*inumber*) *†
Returns the natural logarithm of a complex number.

IMLOG10(*inumber*) *†
Returns the base-10 logarithm of a complex number.

IMLOG2((*inumber*) *†
Returns the base-2 logarithm of a complex number.

IMPOWER(*inumber,number*) *†
Returns a complex number raised to an integer power.

IMPRODUCT(*inumber1,inumber2*) *†
Returns the product of two complex numbers.

IMREAL(*inumber*) *†
Returns the real coefficient of a complex number.

IMSIN(*inumber*) *†
Returns the sine of a complex number.

IMSQRT(*inumber*) *†
Returns the square root of a complex number.

IMSUB(*inumber1,inumber2*) *†
Returns the difference of two complex numbers.

IMSUM(*inumber1,inumber2,number3,...*) *†
Returns the sum of complex numbers.

OCT2BIN(*number,places*) *†
Converts an octal number to binary.

OCT2DEC(*number*) *†
Converts an octal number to decimal.

OCT2HEX(*number,places*) *†
Converts an octal number to hexadecimal.

RADIANS(*angle_in_degrees*) *†
Converts degrees to radians.

SQRTPI(*number*) *†
Returns the square root of (*number* x π).

Financial Functions

ACCRINT(*issue,settlement,coupon,par,frequency, basis*) *†
Returns the accrued interest for a security that pays periodic interest.

ACCRINTM(*issue,maturity,coupon,par,basis*) *†
Returns the accrued interest for a security that pays interest at maturity.

COUPDAYBS(*settlement,maturity,frequency,basis*) *†
Returns the number of days from the beginning of the coupon period to the settlement date.

COUPDAYS(*settlement,maturity,frequency,basis*) *†
Returns the number of days in the coupon period that contains the settlement date.

COUPDAYSNC(*settlement,maturity,frequency, basis*) *†
Returns the number of days from the settlement date to the next coupon date.

COUPNCD(*settlement,maturity,frequency,basis*) *†
Returns the next coupon date after the settlement date.

COUPNUM(*settlement,maturity,frequency, basis*) *†
Returns the number of coupons payable between the settlement date and maturity date.

---

*   New function in Microsoft Excel version 4.0.

†   To use this function, you must install one of the add-in macros.

COUPPCD*(settlement,maturity,frequency,basis)* *†
Returns the previous coupon date before the settlement date.

CUMIPMT*(rate,nper,pv,start_period,end_period, type)* *†
Returns the cumulative interest paid between two periods.

CUMPRINC*(rate,nper,pv,start_period,end_period, type)* *†
Returns the cumulative principal paid on a loan between two periods

DB*(cost,salvage,life,period,month)*
Returns the depreciation of an asset for a specified period using the fixed-declining balance method.

DDB*(cost,salvage,life,period,factor)*
Returns the depreciation of an asset for a specified period using the double-declining balance method.

DISC*(settlement,maturity,pr,redemption,basis)* *†
Returns the discount rate for a security.

DOLLARDE*(fractional_dollar,fraction)* *†
Converts a dollar price, expressed as a fraction, into a dollar price, expressed as a decimal number.

DOLLARFR*(decimal_dollar,fraction)* *†
Converts a dollar price, expressed as a decimal number, into a dollar price, expressed as a fraction.

DURATION*(settlement,maturity,coupon,yld, frequency,basis)* *†
Returns the annual duration of a security with periodic interest payments.

EFFECT*(nominal_rate,npery)* *†
Returns the effective annual interest rate.

FV*(rate,nper,pmt,pv,type)*
Returns the future value of an investment.

FVSCHEDULE*(principal,schedule)* *†
Returns the future value of an initial principal after applying a series of compound interest rates.

INTRATE*(settlement,maturity,investment, redemption,basis)* *†
Returns the interest rate for a fully invested security.

IPMT*(rate,per,nper,pv,fv,type)*
Returns the interest payment for an investment for a given period.

IRR*(values,guess)*
Returns the internal rate of return for a series of cash flows.

MDURATION*(settlement,maturity,coupon,yld, frequency,basis)* *†
Returns the Macauley modified duration for a security with an assumed par value of $100.

MIRR*(values,finance_rate,reinvest_rate)*
Returns the internal rate of return where positive and negative cash flows are financed at different rates.

NOMINAL*(effect_rate,npery)* *†
Returns the annual nominal interest rate.

NPER*(rate,pmt,pv,fv,type)*
Returns the number of periods for an investment.

NPV*(rate,value1,value2,...)*
Returns the net present value of an investment based on a series of periodic cash flows and a discount rate.

ODDFPRICE*(settlement,maturity,issue, first_coupon,rate,yld,redemption,frequency, basis)* *†
Returns the price per $100 face value of a security with an odd first period.

ODDFYIELD*(settlement,maturity, first_coupon,rate,pr,redemption,frequency, basis)* *†
Returns the yield of a security with an odd first period.

---

*   New function in Microsoft Excel version 4.0.

†   To use this function, you must install one of the add-in macros.

ODDLPRICE(*settlement,maturity,last_coupon,rate,*
yld,redemption,frequency,basis) *†
Returns the price per $100 face value of a
security with an odd last period.

ODDLYIELD(*settlement,maturity,last_coupon,rate,*
pr,redemption,frequency,basis) *†
Returns the yield of a security with an odd last
period.

PMT(*rate,nper,pv,fv,type*)
Returns the periodic payment for an annuity.

PPMT(*rate,per,nper,pv,fv,type*)
Returns the payment on the principal for an
investment for a given period.

PRICE(*settlement,maturity,rate,yld,redemption,*
frequency,basis) *†
Returns the price per $100 face value of a
security that pays periodic interest.

PRICEDISC(*settlement,maturity,discount,*
redemption,basis) *†
Returns the price per $100 face value of a
discounted security.

PRICEMAT(*settlement,maturity,issue,rate,yld,*
basis) *†
Returns the price per $100 face value of a
security that pays interest at maturity.

PV(*rate,nper,pmt,fv,type*)
Returns the present value of an investment.

RATE(*nper,pmt,pv,fv,type,guess*)
Returns the interest rate per period of an annuity.

RECEIVED(*settlement,maturity,investment,*
discount,basis) *†
Returns the amount received at maturity for a
fully invested security.

SLN(*cost,salvage,life*)
Returns the straight-line depreciation of an asset
for one period.

SYD(*cost,salvage,life,per*)
Returns the sum-of-years' digits depreciation of
an asset for a specified period.

TBILLEQ(*settlement,maturity,discount*) *†
Returns the bond-equivalent yield for a Treasury
bill.

TBILLPRICE(*settlement,maturity,discount*) *†
Returns the price per $100 face value for a
Treasury bill.

TBILLYIELD(*settlement,maturity,pr*) *†
Returns the yield for a Treasury bill.

VDB(*cost,salvage,life,start_period,end_period,*
factor,no_switch)
Returns the depreciation of an asset for a
specified or partial period using a declining
balance method.

XIRR(*values,dates,guess*) *†
Returns the internal rate of return for a schedule
of cash flows.

XNPV(*rate,values,dates*) *†
Returns the net present value for a schedule of
cash flows.

YIELD(*settlement,maturity,rate,pr,redemption,*
frequency,basis) *†
Returns the yield on a security that pays periodic
interest.

YIELDDISC(*settlement,maturity,pr,redemption,*
basis) *†
Returns the annual yield for a discounted
security. For example, a treasury bill.

YIELDMAT(*settlement,maturity,issue,rate,pr,*
basis) *†
Returns the annual yield of a security that pays
interest at maturity.

---

*   New function in Microsoft Excel version 4.0.

†   To use this function, you must install one of the add-in
macros.

Date & Time Functions

DATE*(year,month,day)*
Returns the serial number of a particular date.

DATEVALUE*(date_text)*
Converts a date in the form of text to a serial number.

DAY*(serial_number)*
Converts a serial number to a day of the month.

DAYS360*(start_date,end_date)*
Calculates the number of days between two dates based on a 360-day year.

EDATE*(start_date,months)* *†
Returns the serial number of the date that is the indicated number of months before or after the start date.

EOMONTH*(start_date,months)* *†
Returns the serial number of the last day of the month before or after a specified number of months.

HOUR*(serial_number)*
Converts a serial number to an hour.

MINUTE*(serial_number)*
Converts a serial number to a minute.

MONTH*(serial_number)*
Converts a serial number to a month.

NETWORKDAYS*(start_date,end_date,holidays)* *†
Returns the number of whole workdays between two dates.

NOW*( )*
Returns the serial number of the current date and time.

SECOND*(serial_number)*
Converts a serial number to a second.

TIME *(hour,minute,second)*
Returns the serial number of a particular time.

TIMEVALUE*(time_text)*
Converts a time in the form of text to a serial number.

TODAY*( )*
Returns the serial number of today's date.

WEEKDAY*(serial_number)*
Converts a serial number to a day of the week.

WORKDAY*(start_date,days,holidays)* *†
Returns the serial number of the date before or after a specified number of workdays.

YEAR*(serial_number)*
Converts a serial number to a year.

YEARFRAC*(start_date,end_date,basis)* *†
Returns the year fraction representing the number of whole days between *start_date* and *end_date*.

Information Functions

CELL*(info_type,reference)*
Returns information about the formatting, location, or contents of a cell.

ERROR.TYPE*(error_val)* *
Returns a number corresponding to an error type.

INFO*(type_text)*
Returns information about the current operating environment.

ISBLANK*(value)*
Returns TRUE if the value is blank.

ISERR*(value)*
Returns TRUE if the value is any error value except #N/A.

ISERROR*(value)*
Returns TRUE if the value is any error value.

ISEVEN*(number)* *†
Returns TRUE if the number is even.

ISLOGICAL*(value)*
Returns TRUE if the value is a logical value.

---

*   New function in Microsoft Excel version 4.0.

†   To use this function, you must install one of the add-in macros.

ISNA(*value*)
Returns TRUE if the value is the #N/A error value.

ISNONTEXT(*value*)
Returns TRUE if the value is not text.

ISNUMBER(*value*)
Returns TRUE if the value is a number.

ISODD(*number*) *†
Returns TRUE if the number is odd.

ISREF(*value*)
Returns TRUE if the value is a reference.

ISTEXT(*value*)
Returns TRUE if the value is text.

N(*value*)
Returns the value converted to a number.

NA( )
Returns the error value #N/A.

TYPE(*value*)
Returns a number indicating the data type of a value.

Math & Trig Functions

ABS(*number*)
Returns the absolute value of a number.

ACOS(*number*)
Returns the arccosine of a number.

ACOSH(*number*)
Returns the inverse hyperbolic cosine of a number.

ASIN(*number*)
Returns the arcsine of a number.

ASINH(*number*)
Returns the inverse hyperbolic sine of a number.

ATAN(*number*)
Returns the arctangent of a number.

ATAN2(*x_num,y_num*)
Returns the arctangent from *x*- and *y*-coordinates.

ATANH(*number*)
Returns the inverse hyperbolic tangent of a number.

BASE(*number,target_base,precision*) *†
Converts a base-10 number into another base.

CEILING(*number,significance*) *
Rounds a number up to the nearest integer.

COMBIN(*number,number_chosen*) *
Returns the number of combinations for a given number of objects.

COS(*number*)
Returns the cosine of a number.

COSH(*number*)
Returns the hyperbolic cosine of a number.

EVEN(*number*) *
Rounds a number up to the nearest even integer.

EXP(*number*)
Returns *e* raised to the power of a given number.

FACT(*number*)
Returns the factorial of a number.

FACTDOUBLE(*number*) *†
Returns the double factorial of a number.

FLOOR(*number,significance*) *
Rounds a number down, toward zero.

GCD(*number1,number2,...*) *†
Returns the greatest common divisor.

INT(*number*)
Rounds a number down to the nearest integer.

LCM(*number1,number2,...*) *†
Returns the least common multiple.

LN(*number*)
Returns the natural logarithm of a number.

LOG(*number,base*)
Returns the logarithm of a number to a specified base.

---

*   New function in Microsoft Excel version 4.0.

†   To use this function, you must install one of the add-in macros.

LOG10(*number*)
Returns the base-10 logarithm of a number.

MDETERM(*array*)
Returns the matrix determinant of an array.

MINVERSE(*array*)
Returns the matrix inverse of an array.

MMULT(*array1,array2*)
Returns the matrix product of two arrays.

MOD(*number,divisor*)
Returns the remainder from division.

MROUND(*number,multiple*) *†
Returns a number rounded to the desired multiple.

MULTINOMIAL(*number1,number2,...*) *†
Returns the multinomial of a set of numbers.

ODD(*number*) *
Rounds a number up to the nearest odd integer.

PI( )
Returns the value π.

PRODUCT(*number1,number2,...*)
Multiplies its arguments.

QUOTIENT(*numerator,denominator*) *†
Returns the integer portion of a division.

RAND( )
Returns a random number between 0 and 1.

RANDBETWEEN(*bottom,top*) *†
Returns a random number between the numbers you specify.

ROUND(*number,num_digits*)
Rounds a number to a specified number of digits.

SERIESSUM(*x,n,m,coefficients*) *†
Returns the sum of a power series based on the formula:

$$SERIES(x, n, m, a) = a_1 x^n + a_2 x^{(n+m)}$$
$$+ a_3 x^{(n+2m)} + ... + a_i x^{(n+(i-1)m)}$$

SIGN(*number*)
Returns the sign of a number.

SIN(*number*)
Returns the sine of the given angle.

SINH(*number*)
Returns the hyperbolic sine of a number.

SQRT(*number*)
Returns a positive square root.

SQRTPI(*number*) *†
Returns the square root of (*number* * π).

SUM(*number1,number2,...*)
Adds its arguments.

SUMPRODUCT(*array1,array2,array3,...*)
Returns the sum of the products of corresponding array components.

SUMSQ(*number1,number2,...*) *
Returns the sum of the squares of the arguments.

SUMX2MY2(*array_x,array_y*) *
Returns the sum of the difference of squares of corresponding values in two arrays.

SUMX2PY2(*array_x,array_y*) *
Returns the sum of the sum of squares of corresponding values in two arrays.

SUMXMY2(*array_x,array_y*) *
Returns the sum of squares of differences of corresponding values in two arrays.

TAN(*number*)
Returns the tangent of a number.

TANH(*number*)
Returns the hyperbolic tangent of a number.

TRUNC(*number,num_digits*)
Truncates a number to an integer.

---

*   New function in Microsoft Excel version 4.0.

†   To use this function, you must install one of the add-in macros.

Statistical Functions

AVEDEV(*number1,number2,...*) *
Returns the average of the absolute deviations of data points from their mean.

AVERAGE(*number1,number2,...*)
Returns the average of its arguments.

BETADIST(*x,alpha,beta,A,B*) *
Returns the cumulative beta probability density function.

BETAINV(*probability,alpha,beta,A,B*) *
Returns the inverse of the cumulative beta probability density function.

BINOMDIST(*number_s,trials,probability_s, cumulative*) *
Returns the individual term binomial distribution.

CHIDIST(*x,degrees_freedom*) *
Returns the one-tailed probability of the chi-squared (χ^2) distribution.

CHIINV(*probability,degrees_freedom*) *
Returns the inverse of the chi-squared (χ^2) distribution.

CHITEST(*actual_range,expected_range*) *
Returns the test for independence.

CONFIDENCE(*alpha,standard_dev,size*) *
Returns a confidence interval for a population.

CORREL(*array1,array2*) *
Returns the correlation coefficient between two data sets.

COUNT(*value1,value2,...*)
Counts how many numbers are in the list of arguments.

COUNTA(*value1,value2,...*)
Counts how many values are in the list of arguments.

COVAR(*array1,array2*) *
Returns covariance, the average of the products of paired deviations.

CRITBINOM(*trials,probability_s,alpha*) *
Returns the smallest value for which the cumulative binomial distribution is less than or equal to a criterion value.

DEVSQ(*number1,number2,...*) *
Returns the sum of squares of deviations.

EXPONDIST(*x,lambda,cumulative*) *
Returns the exponential distribution.

FDIST(*x,degrees_freedom1,degrees_freedom2*) *
Returns the *F* probability distribution.

FINV(*probability,degrees_freedom1, degrees_freedom2*) *
Returns the inverse of the *F* probability distribution.

FISHER(*x*) *
Returns the Fisher transformation.

FISHERINV(*y*) *
Returns the inverse of the Fisher transformation.

FORECAST(*x,known_y's,known_x's*) *
Returns a value along a linear trend.

FREQUENCY(*data_array,bins_array*)) *
Returns a frequency distribution as a vertical array.

FTEST(*array1,array2*) *
Returns the result of an *F*-test.

GAMMADIST(*x,alpha,beta,cumulative*) *
Returns the gamma distribution.

GAMMAINV(*probability,alpha,beta*) *
Returns the inverse of the gamma cumulative distribution.

GAMMALN(*x*) *
Returns the natural logarithm of the gamma function, $\Gamma(x)$.

GEOMEAN(*number1,number2,...*) *
Returns the geometric mean.

---

*   New function in Microsoft Excel version 4.0.

†   To use this function, you must install one of the add-in macros.

GROWTH(*known_y's,known_x's,new_x's,const*)
Returns values along an exponential trend.

HARMEAN(*number1,number2...*) *
Returns the harmonic mean.

HYPGEOMDIST(*sample_s,number_sample, population_s,number_population*) *
Returns the hypergeometric distribution.

INTERCEPT(*known_y's,known_x's*) *
Returns the intercept of the linear regression line.

KURT(*number1,number2,...*) *
Returns the kurtosis of a data set.

LARGE(*array,k*) *
Returns the *k*-th largest value in a data set.

LINEST(*known_y's,known_x's,const,stats*)
Returns the parameters of a linear trend.

LOGEST(*known_y's,known_x's,const,stats*)
Returns the parameters of an exponential trend.

LOGINV(*probability,mean,standard_dev*) *
Returns the inverse of the lognormal distribution.

LOGNORMDIST(*x,mean,standard_dev*) *
Returns the lognormal distribution.

MAX(*number1,number2,...*)
Returns the maximum value in a list of arguments.

MEDIAN(*number1,number2,...*)
Returns the median of the given numbers.

MIN(*number1,number2,...*)
Returns the minimum value in a list of arguments.

MODE(*number1,number2,...*) *
Returns the most common value in a data set.

NEGBINOMDIST(*number_f,number_s, probability_s*) *
Returns the negative binomial distribution.

NORMDIST(*x,mean,standard_dev,cumulative*) *
Returns the normal cumulative distribution.

NORMINV(*probability,mean,standard_dev*) *
Returns the inverse of the normal cumulative distribution.

NORMSDIST(*z*) *
Returns the standard normal cumulative distribution.

NORMSINV(*probability*) *
Returns the inverse of the standard normal cumulative distribution.

PEARSON(*array1,array2*) *
Returns the Pearson product moment correlation coefficient.

PERCENTILE(*array,k*) *
Returns the *k*-th percentile of values in a range.

PERCENTRANK(*array,x,significance*) *
Returns the percentage rank of a value in a data set.

PERMUT(*number,number_chosen*) *
Returns the number of permutations for a given number of objects.

POISSON(*x,mean,cumulative*) *
Returns the Poisson probability distribution.

PROB(*x_range,prob_range,lower_limit, upper_limit*) *
Returns the probability that values in a range are between two limits.

QUARTILE (*array,quart*) *
Returns the quartile of a data set.

RANK(*number,ref,order*)) *
Returns the rank of a number in a list of numbers.

RSQ(*known_y's,known_x's*) *
Returns the r^2 value of the linear regression line.

SKEW(*number1,number2,...*) *
Returns the skewness of a distribution.

---

*   New function in Microsoft Excel version 4.0.

†   To use this function, you must install one of the add-in macros.

SLOPE(*known_y's,known_x's*) *
Returns the slope of the linear regression line.

SMALL(*array,k*) *
Returns the *k*-th smallest value in a data set.

STANDARDIZE(*x,mean,standard_dev*) *
Returns a normalized value.

STDEV(*number1,number2,...*)
Estimates standard deviation based on a sample.

STDEVP(*number1,number2,...*)
Calculates standard deviation based on the entire population.

STEYX(*known_y's,known_x's*) *
Returns the standard error of the predicted *y*-value for each *x* in the regression.

TDIST(*x,degrees_freedom,tails*) *
Returns the Student's *t*-distribution.

TINV(*probability,degrees_freedom*) *
Returns the inverse of the Student's *t*-distribution.

TREND(*known_y's,known_x's,new_x's,const*)
Returns values along a linear trend.

TRIMMEAN(*array,percent*) *
Returns the mean of the interior of a data set.

TTEST(*array1,array2,tails,type*) *
Returns the probability associated with a Student's *t*-Test.

VAR(*number1,number2,...*)
Estimates variance based on a sample.

VARP(*number1,number2,...*)
Calculates variance based on the entire population.

WEIBULL(*x,alpha,beta,cumulative*) *
Returns the Weibull distribution.

ZTEST(*array,x*) *
Returns the two-tailed *P*-value of a *z*-test.

Lookup & Reference Functions

ADDRESS(*row_num,column_num,abs_num,a1, sheet_text*)
Returns a reference as text to a single cell in a worksheet.

AREAS(*reference*)
Returns the number of areas in a reference.

CHOOSE(*index_num,value1,value2,...*)
Chooses a value from a list of values.

COLUMN(*reference*)
Returns the column number of a reference.

COLUMNS(*array*)
Returns the number of columns in a reference.

FASTMATCH(*lookup_value,lookup_array, match_type*)†
Returns the relative position of an element in an array that matches the specified value.

HLOOKUP(*lookup_value,table_array, row_index_num*)
Looks in the top row of an array and returns the value of the indicated cell.

INDEX(*reference,row_num,column_num, area_num*)

INDEX(*array,row_num,column_num*)
Uses an index to choose a value from a reference or array.

INDIRECT(*ref_text,a1*)
Returns a reference indicated by a text value.

LOOKUP(*lookup_value,lookup_vector, result_vector*)

LOOKUP(*lookup_value,array*)
Looks up values in a vector or array.

---

* New function in Microsoft Excel version 4.0.

† To use this function, you must install one of the add-in macros.

MATCH(*lookup_value,lookup_array,match_type*)
Looks up values in a reference or array.

OFFSET(*reference,rows,cols,height,width*)
Returns a reference offset from a given reference.

ROW(*reference*)
Returns the row number of a reference.

ROWS(*array*)
Returns the number of rows in a reference.

TRANSPOSE(*array*)
Returns the transpose of an array.

VLOOKUP(*lookup_value,table_array, col_index_num*)
Looks in the first column of an array and moves across the row to return the value of a cell.

Database Functions

CROSSTAB(*label,expression*) *†

CROSSTAB(*label,"Columns:",columns_array*) *†

CROSSTAB(*label,"Rows:",rows_array*) *†

CROSSTAB(*label,"Summary:",values_array, create_outline,create names,multiple_values*) *†
Defines the structure and content of a cross-tabulation table.

DAVERAGE(*database,field,criteria*)
Returns the average of selected database entries.

DCOUNT(*database,field,criteria*)
Counts the cells containing numbers from a specified database and criteria.

DCOUNTA(*database,field,criteria*)
Counts nonblank cells from a specified database and criteria.

DGET(*database,field,criteria*)
Extracts from a database a single record that matches the specified criteria.

DMAX(*database,field,criteria*)
Returns the maximum value from selected database entries.

DMIN(*database,field,criteria*)
Returns the minimum value from selected database entries.

DPRODUCT(*database,field,criteria*)
Multiplies the values in a particular field of records that match the criteria in a database.

DSTDEV(*database,field,criteria*)
Estimates the standard deviation based on a sample of selected database entries.

DSTDEVP(*database,field,criteria*)
Calculates the standard deviation based on the entire population of selected database entries.

DSUM(*database,field,criteria*)
Adds numbers in a database.

DVAR(*database,field,criteria*)
Estimates variance based on a sample from selected database entries.

DVARP(*database,field,criteria*)
Calculates variance based on the entire population of selected database entries.

Text Functions

CHAR(*number*)
Returns the character specified by the code *number*.

CLEAN(*text*)
Removes all nonprintable characters from text.

CODE(*text*)
Returns a numeric code for the first character in a text string.

DOLLAR(*number,decimals*)
Converts a number to text, using currency format.

EXACT(*text1,text2*)
Checks to see if two text values are identical.

---

*   New function in Microsoft Excel version 4.0.

†   To use this function, you must install one of the add-in macros.

FIND(*find_text,within_text,*start_at_num)
Finds one text value within another (case-sensitive).

FIXED(*number,decimals,no_comma*)
Formats a number as text with a fixed number of decimals.

LEFT(*text,*num_chars)
Returns the leftmost characters from a text value.

LEN(*text*)
Returns the number of characters in a text string.

LOWER(*text*)
Converts text to lowercase.

MID(*text,start_num,num_chars*)
Returns a specific number of characters from a text string starting at the position you specify.

PROPER(*text*)
Capitalizes the first letter in each word of a text value.

REPLACE(*old_text,start_num,num_chars, new_text*)
Replaces characters within text.

REPT(*text,number_times*)
Repeats text a given number of times.

RIGHT(*text,*num_chars)
Returns the rightmost characters from a text value.

SEARCH(*find_text,within_text,*start_num)
Finds one text value within another (not case-sensitive).

SUBSTITUTE(*text,old_text,new_text, instance_num*)
Substitutes new text for old text in a text string.

T(*value*)
Converts its arguments to text.

TEXT(*value,format_text*)
Formats a number and converts it to text.

TRIM(*text*)
Removes spaces from text.

UPPER(*text*)
Converts text to uppercase.

VALUE(*text*)
Converts a text argument to a number.

Logical Functions

AND(*logical1,logical2,...*)
Returns TRUE if all its arguments are TRUE.

FALSE( )
Returns the logical value FALSE.

IF(*logical_test,value_if_true,value_if_false*)
Specifies a logical test to perform.

NOT(*logical*)
Reverses the logic of its argument.

OR(*logical1,logical2,...*)
Returns TRUE if any argument is TRUE.

TRUE( )
Returns the logical value TRUE.

DDE/External Functions

CALL(*register_id,argument1,...*)

CALL(*module_text,procedure,type_text, argument1,...*)

CALL(*file_text,resource,type_text,argument1,...*)
Calls a procedure in a dynamic link library or code resource.

Note This function appears when you choose All in the Paste Function dialog box when a worksheet is the active sheet. It appears when you choose DDE/External from the Paste Function dialog box when a macro sheet is the active sheet.

---

*   New function in Microsoft Excel version 4.0.

†   To use this function, you must install one of the add-in macros.

Macro Functions Listed by Category

This section lists macro functions in the categories described in the first section, "About Functions." An asterisk (*) following a function name means the function is new to Microsoft Excel version 4.0. A dagger (†) following a function name means that you must install one of the macro add-in files located in the Library directory in order to use the function. For information about which add-in file to install, see the function's complete description in the fifth section, "Function Reference." For more information, see "Managing Add-in Commands and Functions" in Chapter 4 in Book 2 of the *Microsoft Excel User's Guide*.

Statistical Functions

ANOVA1*(inprng,outrng,grouped,labels,alpha)* *†
Performs single-factor analysis of variance.

ANOVA2*(inprng,outrng,sample_rows,alpha)* *†
Performs two-factor analysis of variance with replication.

ANOVA3*(inprng,outrng,labels,alpha)* *†
Performs two-factor analysis of variance without replication.

DESCR*(inprng,outrng,grouped,labels,summary, ds_large,ds_small,confid)* *†
Generates descriptive statistics for data in the input range.

EXPON*(inprng,outrng,damp,stderrs,chart)* *†
Predicts a value based on the forecast for the prior period.

FTESTV*(inprng1,inprng2,outrng,labels)* *†
Performs a two-sample *F*-test.

HISTOGRAM*(inprng,outrng,binrng,pareto,chartc, chart)* *†
Calculates individual and cumulative percentages for a range of data and a corresponding range of data bins.

MCORREL*(inprng,outrng,grouped,labels)* *†
Returns the correlation coefficient of two or more data sets that are scaled to be independent of the unit of measurement.

MCOVAR*(inprng,outrng,grouped,labels)* *†
Returns the covariance between two or more data sets.

MOVEAVG*(inprng,outrng,interval,stderrs,chart)* *†
Returns values along a moving average trend.

PTTESTM*(inprng1,inprng2,outrng,labels,alpha, difference)* *†
Performs a paired two-sample Student's *t*-Test for means.

PTTESTV*(inprng1,inprng2,outrng,labels,alpha)* *†
Performs a two-sample Student's *t*-Test, assuming unequal variances.

RANDOM*(outrng,variables,points,**distribution**, seed,**from,to**)* *†

RANDOM*(outrng,variables,points,**distribution**, seed,**probability**)* *†

RANDOM*(outrng,variables,points,**distribution**, seed,**probability,trials**)* *†

RANDOM*(outrng,variables,points,**distribution**, seed,**from,to,step,repeat_num,repeat_seq**)* *†

RANDOM(*outrng,variables,points,**distribution,
seed,inprng***) *†
Fills a range with independent random or
patterned numbers drawn from one of several
distributions.

RANKPERC(*inprng,outrng,grouped,labels*) *†
Returns a table that contains the ordinal and
percent rank of each value in a data set.

REGRESS(*inpyrng,inpxrng,constant,labels,confid,
soutrng,residuals,sresiduals,rplots,lplots,**routrng,**
nplots,**poutrng***) *†
Performs multiple linear regression analysis.

TTESTM(***inprng1,inprng2,outrng,**labels,alpha,
difference*) *†
Performs a two-sample Student's *t*-Test for
means, assuming equal variances.

ZTESTM(***inprng1,inprng2,outrng,**labels,alpha,
difference,**var1,var2***) *†
Performs a two-sample *z*-test for means,
assuming variances.

Engineering Functions

FOURIER(***inprng,outrng,**inverse*) *†
Performs a Fourier transform.

SAMPLE(***inprng,outrng,method,rate***) *†
Samples data.

Command Functions

Chart menu	Function
Add Arrow	ADD.ARROW
Add Legend	LEGEND
Add Overlay	ADD.OVERLAY
Attach Text	ATTACH.TEXT
Axes	AXES
Calculate Now	CALCULATE.NOW
Delete Arrow	DELETE.ARROW
Delete Overlay	DELETE.OVERLAY
Edit Series	EDIT.SERIES

Chart menu	Function
Gridlines	GRIDLINES
Select Chart	SELECT.CHART
Select Plot Area	SELECT.PLOT.AREA

Control menu	Function
Close	CLOSE
Maximize (application)	APP.MAXIMIZE
Maximize (window)	WINDOW.MAXIMIZE
Minimize (application)	APP.MINIMIZE
Minimize (window)	WINDOW.MINIMIZE
Move (application)	APP.MOVE
Move (document)	MOVE
Move (window)	WINDOW.MOVE
Restore (application)	APP.RESTORE
Restore (window)	WINDOW.RESTORE
Size (application)	APP.SIZE
Size (window)	WINDOW.SIZE

Data menu	Function
Consolidate	CONSOLIDATE
Delete	DATA.DELETE
Extract	EXTRACT
Find	DATA.FIND
Form	DATA.FORM
Parse	PARSE
Series	DATA.SERIES
Set Criteria	SET.CRITERIA
Set Database	SET.DATABASE
Set Extract	SET.EXTRACT
Sort	SORT
Table	TABLE

---

*   New function in Microsoft Excel version 4.0.

†   To use this function, you must install one of the add-in
macros.

Edit menu	Function
Clear	CLEAR
Copy	COPY
Copy Chart	COPY.CHART
Copy Picture	COPY.PICTURE
Copy Tool Face	COPY.TOOL
Create Publisher	CREATE.PUBLISHER
Cut	CUT
Delete	EDIT.DELETE
Fill Down	FILL.DOWN
Fill Group	FILL.GROUP
Fill Left	FILL.LEFT
Fill Right	FILL.RIGHT
Fill Up	FILL.UP
Insert	INSERT
Insert Object	INSERT.OBJECT
Paste	PASTE
Paste Link	PASTE.LINK
Paste Picture	PASTE.PICTURE
Paste Picture Link	PASTE.PICTURE.LINK
Paste Special	PASTE.SPECIAL
Repeat	EDIT.REPEAT
Undo	UNDO

File menu	Function
Close	FILE.CLOSE
Close All	CLOSE.ALL
Delete	FILE.DELETE
Exit	QUIT
Links	CHANGE.LINK
Links	LINKS
Links	OPEN.LINKS
Links	UPDATE.LINK
New	NEW
Open	OPEN

File menu	Function
Open Mail	OPEN.MAIL
Page Setup	PAGE.SETUP
Print	PRINT
Print Preview	PRINT.PREVIEW
Quit	QUIT
Save	SAVE
Save As	SAVE.AS
Save Workbook	SAVE.WORKBOOK
Send Mail	SEND.MAIL

Format menu	Function
3-D View	VIEW.3D
Alignment	ALIGNMENT
AutoFormat	FORMAT.AUTO
Border	BORDER
Bring To Front	BRING.TO.FRONT
Cell Protection	CELL.PROTECTION
Column Width	COLUMN.WIDTH
Font	FORMAT.FONT
Group	GROUP
Legend	FORMAT.LEGEND
Main Chart	FORMAT.MAIN
Number	DELETE.FORMAT
Number	FORMAT.NUMBER
Object Placement	PLACEMENT
Object Properties	OBJECT.PROPERTIES
Object Protection	OBJECT.PROTECTION
Overlay	FORMAT.OVERLAY
Patterns	PATTERNS
Row Height	ROW.HEIGHT
Scale	SCALE
Send To Back	SEND.TO.BACK
Style	APPLY.STYLE
Text	FORMAT.TEXT
Ungroup	UNGROUP

Formula menu	Function
Apply Names	APPLY.NAMES
Create Names	CREATE.NAMES
Define Name	DEFINE.NAME
Find	FORMULA.FIND
Goal Seek	GOAL.SEEK
Goto	FORMULA.GOTO
Note	NOTE
Outline	OUTLINE
Paste Function	FORMULA
Paste Name	LIST.NAMES
Replace	FORMULA.REPLACE
Scenario Manager	SCENARIO.ADD
Select Special	SELECT.LAST.CELL
Select Special	SELECT.SPECIAL
Show Active Cell	SHOW.ACTIVE.CELL

Gallery menu	Function
3-D Area	GALLERY.3D.AREA
3-D Bar	GALLERY.3D.BAR
3-D Column	GALLERY.3D.COLUMN
3-D Line	GALLERY.3D.LINE
3-D Pie	GALLERY.3D.PIE
3-D Surface	GALLERY.3D.SURFACE
Area	GALLERY.AREA
Bar	GALLERY.BAR
Column	GALLERY.COLUMN
Combination	COMBINATION
Line	GALLERY.LINE
Pie	GALLERY.PIE
Preferred	PREFERRED
*Radar	GALLERY.RADAR
Set Preferred	SET.PREFERRED
XY (Scatter)	GALLERY.SCATTER

Macro menu	Function
Assign To Object	ASSIGN.TO.OBJECT
Assign To Tool	ASSIGN.TO.TOOL
Resume	RESUME
Run	RUN

Options menu	Function
Calculate Document	CALCULATE.DOCUMENT
Calculate Now	CALCULATE.NOW
Calculation	CALCULATION
Calculation	PRECISION
Color Palette	COLOR.PALETTE
Color Palette	EDIT.COLOR
Display	DISPLAY
Group Edit	WORKGROUP
Protect Document	PROTECT.DOCUMENT
Remove Page Break	REMOVE.PAGE.BREAK
Set Page Break	SET.PAGE.BREAK
Set Print Area	SET.PRINT.AREA
Set Print Titles	SET.PRINT.TITLES
Spelling	SPELLING
Toolbars	SHOW.TOOLBAR
Workspace	SHOW.INFO
Workspace	WORKSPACE

Window menu	Function
Arrange	ARRANGE.ALL
Hide	HIDE
Freeze Panes	FREEZE.PANES
New Window	NEW.WINDOW
Show Clipboard	SHOW.CLIPBOARD
Show Info	SHOW.INFO
Split	SPLIT
Unhide	UNHIDE
View	VIEW.SHOW
Zoom	ZOOM

Information Functions

ACTIVE.CELL( )
Returns the reference of the active cell.

CALLER( )
Returns the reference of the calling function.

DIRECTORIES(*path_text*) †
Returns an array of all subdirectories or subfolders in the specified path.

DIRECTORY(*path_text*)
Sets the current drive and directory to a specified path.

DOCUMENTS(*type_num,match_text*)
Returns the names of the specified open documents.

FILE.EXISTS(*path_text*) †
Tests for the existence of a file, directory, or folder.

FILES(*directory text*)
Returns the filenames in the specified directory or folder.

GET.BAR( )

GET.BAR(*bar_num,menu,command*)
Returns the name or position number of menu bars, menus, and commands.

GET.CELL(*type_num,reference*)
Returns information about the specified cell.

GET.CHART.ITEM(*x_y_index,point_index, item_text*)
Returns information about a chart item.

GET.DEF(*def_text,document_text,type_num*)
Returns a name matching a definition.

GET.DOCUMENT(*type_num,name_text*)
Returns information about a document.

GET.FORMULA(*reference*)
Returns the contents of a cell.

GET.LINK.INFO(*link_text,type_num,type_of_link, reference*)
Returns information about a link.

GET.NAME(*name_text*)
Returns the definition of a name.

GET.NOTE(*cell ref,start char,num chars*)
Returns characters from a note.

GET.OBJECT(*type_num,object_id_text,start_num, count_num*)
Returns information about an object.

GET.TOOL(*type_num,bar_id,position*) *
Returns information about a tool or tools on a toolbar.

GET.TOOLBAR(*type_num,bar_id*) *
Retrieves information about a toolbar.

GET.WINDOW(*type_num,window_text*)
Returns information about a window.

GET.WORKBOOK(*type_num,name_text*) *
Returns information about a workbook document.

GET.WORKSPACE(*type_num*)
Returns information about the workspace.

LAST.ERROR( )
Returns the reference of the cell where the last error occurred.

LINKS((*document_text,type_num*)
Returns the name of all linked documents.

NAMES(*document_text,type_num,match_text*)
Returns the names defined in a document.

REPORT.GET(*type_num,report_name*) *
Returns information about reports defined for the active document.

SCENARIO.GET(*type_num*) *
Returns the specified information about the scenarios defined on your worksheet.

SELECTION( )
Returns the reference of the selection.

---

*   New function in Microsoft Excel version 4.0.

†   To use this function, you must install one of the add-in macros.

SLIDE.GET(*type_num,name_text,slide_num*) *
Returns information about a slide or slide show.

SOLVER.GET(***type_num,sheet_name***) *
Returns information about the current settings for Solver.

VIEW.GET(***type_num,****view_name*) *
Returns an array of all of the views in the active document.

WINDOWS(*type_num,match_text*)
Returns the names of all open windows.

Lookup & Reference Functions

ABSREF(*ref_text,reference*)
Returns the absolute reference of a range of cells to another range.

DEREF(*reference*)
Returns the value of the cells in the reference.

EVALUATE(*formula_text*) *
Evaluates a formula or expression that is in the form of text and returns the result.

FORMULA.CONVERT(***formula_text,from_a1,***
to_a1,to_ref_type,rel_to_ref)
Changes the reference style and type.

REFTEXT(*reference,a1*)
Converts a reference to text.

RELREF(***reference,rel_to_ref***)
Returns a relative reference.

TEXTREF(*text,a1*)
Converts text to a reference.

Database Functions

CROSSTAB.CREATE(*rows_array,columns_array,*
values_array,*create_outline,create_names,*
multiple_values,auto_drilldown,new_sheet) *†
Creates a cross-tabulation table.

CROSSTAB.DRILLDOWN( ) *†
Returns the records in the active result table in a cross-tabulation table.

CROSSTAB.RECALC(*rebuild*) *†
Recalculates an existing cross-tabulation table.

DATA.DELETE( )
Deletes data that match the current criteria.

DATA.FIND(*logical*)
Finds records in a database.

DATA.FINDNEXT()

DATA.FIND.PREV( )
Finds next or previous matching record in a database.

DATA.FORM( )
Displays the data form.

EXTRACT( )
Copies database records that match the criteria into a separate extract range.

SET.CRITERIA( )
Defines the name Criteria for the selected range on the active sheet.

SET.DATABASE( )
Defines the name Database for the selected range on the active sheet.

SET.EXTRACT( )
Defines the name Extract for the selected range on the active sheet.

Other Command Functions

A1.R1C1(***logical***)
Displays A1 or R1C1 references.

ACTIVATE(*window_text,pane_num*)
Switches to a window.

---

*   New function in Microsoft Excel version 4.0.

†   To use this function, you must install one of the add-in macros.

ACTIVATE.NEXT(*workbook_text*)

ACTIVATE.PREV(*workbook_text*)
Switches to the next or previous window, respectively, or switches to the next or previous document in a workbook.

CANCEL.COPY(*render_logical*)
Cancels the copy marquee.

CHART.WIZARD(*long,**ref**,gallery_num,type_num, plot_by,categories,ser_titles,legend,title,x_title, y_title,z_title*) *
Creates and formats a chart.

CONSTRAIN.NUMERIC(*numeric_only*)
Constrains handwriting recognition to numbers and punctuation only.

CREATE.DIRECTORY(***path_text***)
Creates a directory or folder.

CREATE.OBJECT(***object_type,ref_1,***x_offset1, y_offset1,***ref_2,***x_offset2,y_offset2,text,fill*)

CREATE.OBJECT(***object_type,ref_1,***x_offset1, y_offset1,***ref_2,***x_offset2,y_offset2,***array,***fill*)

CREATE.OBJECT(***object_type,ref_1,***x_offset1, y_offset1,***ref_2,***x_offset2,y_offset2,xy_series, fill,gallery_num,type_num*)
Creates an object.

CUSTOMIZE.TOOLBAR?(*category*) *
Displays the Customize Toolbar dialog box.

DELETE.DIRECTORY(***path_text***)
Deletes an empty directory.

DELETE.FORMAT(***format_text***)
Deletes a number format.

DEMOTE(*row_col*)
Demotes the selection in an outline.

DUPLICATE( )
Makes a copy of an object.

EXTEND.POLYGON(*array*) *
Adds vertices to a polygon.

FILL.AUTO(*destination_ref,copy_only*) *
Copies cells or automatically fills a selection.

FORMAT.AUTO(*format_num,number,font, alignment,border,pattern,width*) *
Formats the selected range of cells from a built-in gallery of formats.

FORMAT MOVE(***x_offset,y_offset,***reference*)
Moves the selected object.

FORMAT.SHAPE(***vertex_num,insert,***reference, x_offset,y_offset*) *
Inserts, moves, or deletes vertices of the selected polygon.

FORMAT.SIZE(*x_off,y_off,**reference***) *

FORMAT.SIZE(*width,height*) *
Sizes an object.

FORMULA(***formula_text,***reference*)

FORMULA(***formula_text***)
Enters values into a cell or range or onto a chart.

FORMULA.ARRAY(***formula_text,***reference*)
Enters an array.

FORMULA.FILL(***formula_text,***reference*)
Enters a formula in the specified range.

FULL(*logical*)
Changes the size of the active window.

HIDE.OBJECT(*object_id_text,hide*)
Hides an object.

HLINE(*num_columns*)
Horizontally scrolls through the active window by columns.

HPAGE(*num_windows*)
Horizontally scrolls through the active window one window at a time.

HSCROLL(*position,col_logical*)
Horizontally scrolls through a document by percentage or by column number.

---

* New function in Microsoft Excel version 4.0.

† To use this function, you must install one of the add-in macros.

LINE.PRINT(*command,file,append*) *

LINE.PRINT(*command,setup_text,leftmarg, rightmarg,topmarg,botmarg,pglen,formatted*) *

LINE.PRINT(*command,setup_text,leftmarg, rightmarg,topmarg,botmarg,pglen,wait,autolf, port,update*) *
Prints the active document using methods compatible with those of Lotus 1-2-3.

OBJECT.PROPERTIES(*placement_type, print_object*) *
Determines an object's relationship to underlying cells.

PROMOTE(*rowcol*)
Promotes the selection in an outline.

REPORT.DEFINE(*report_name, views_scenarios_array, pages_logical*) *†
Creates or replaces a report definition.

REPORT.DELETE(*report_name*) *†
Removes a report definition from the active document.

REPORT.PRINT(*report_name,copies_num, show_print_dlg_logical*) *†
Prints a report.

RESUME(*type_num*) *
Resumes a paused macro.

SAVE.WORKBOOK(*document_text,type_num, prot_pwd,backup,write_res_pwd, read_only_rec*) *
Saves the workbook to which the active document belongs.

SCENARIO.ADD(*scen_name,value_array*) *†
Defines the specified values as a scenario.

SCENARIO.CELLS(*changing_ref*) *†
Defines the changing cells for a model on your worksheet.

SCENARIO.DELETE(*scen_name*) *†
Deletes the specified scenario.

SCENARIO.SHOW(*scen_name*) *†
Recalculates a model using the specified scenario and displays the result.

SCENARIO.SHOW.NEXT( ) *†
Recalculates a model using the next scenario and displays the result.

SCENARIO.SUMMARY(*result_ref*) *†
Generates a table summarizing the results of all the scenarios for the model on your worksheet.

SELECT(*selection,active_cell*)

SELECT(*object_id_text,replace*)

SELECT(*item_text,single_point*)
Selects a cell, worksheet object, or chart item.

SELECT.END(*direction_num*)
Selects the last cell in a range.

SHOW.CLIPBOARD( )
Displays the contents of the Clipboard in a new window.

SHOW.DETAIL(*rowcol,rowcol_num,expand*)
Expands or collapses a portion of an outline

SHOW.LEVELS(*row_level,col_level*)
Displays a specific number of levels of an outline.

SLIDE.COPY.ROW( ) *†
Copies the selected slides, each of which is defined on a single row, onto the Clipboard.

SLIDE.CUT.ROW( ) *†
Cuts the selected slides and pastes them onto the Clipboard.

SLIDE.DEFAULTS(*effect_num,speed_num, advance_rate_num,soundfile_text*) *†
Specifies the default values for the active slide show document.

SLIDE.DELETE.ROW( ) *†
Deletes the selected slides.

SLIDE.EDIT(*effect_num,speed_num, advance_rate_num,soundfile_text*) *†
Changes the attributes of the selected slide.

---

* New function in Microsoft Excel version 4.0.

† To use this function, you must install one of the add-in macros.

SLIDE.PASTE(*effect_num,speed_num, advance_rate_num,soundfile_text*) *†
Pastes the contents of the Clipboard onto a slide.

SLIDE.PASTE.ROW( ) *†
Pastes previously cut or copied slides onto the current selection.

SLIDE.SHOW(*initialslide_num,repeat_logical, dialogtitle_text,allownav_logical, allowcontrol_logical*) *†
Starts the slide show in the active document.

SOLVER.ADD(*cellref,relation,formula*)†
Adds a constraint to the current problem.

SOLVER.CHANGE(*cellref,relation,formula*)†
Changes the right side of an existing constraint.

SOLVER.DELETE(*cellref,relation,formula*)†
Deletes an existing constraint.

SOLVER.FINISH(*keepfinal,reportarray*)†
Allows you to specify whether or not you want to keep the results and where you want the array to be placed.

SOLVER.LOAD(*load_area*)†
Allows you to load a model.

SOLVER.OK(*setcell,max_min_val,value_of, by_changing*)†
Specifies options in the Solver dialog box.

SOLVER.OPTIONS(*max_time,iterations,precision, assume_linear,step_thru,estimates,derivatives, search,int_tolerance,scaling*)†
Specifies available options in the Solver dialog box.

SOLVER.RESET( )†
Erases all cell selections and restraints from the Solver dialog box.

SOLVER.SAVE(*save_area*)†
Specifies a cell range in which to save the current problem specification.

SOLVER.SOLVE(*user_finish,show_ref*)†
Solves the current problem.

SOUND.NOTE(*cell_ref,erase_snd*) *†
Records or erases sound from cell notes.

SOUND.NOTE(*cell_ref,file_text,resource*) *†
Imports sound from another file.

SOUND.PLAY(*cell_ref,file_text,resource*) *†
Plays the sound from a cell note or a file.

SPLIT(*col_split,row_split*)
Splits a window.

TEXT.BOX(*add_text,object_id_text,start_num, num_chars*)
Replaces text in a text box.

UNLOCKED.NEXT( )

UNLOCKED.PREV( )
Goes to the next or previous unlocked cell.

VIEW.DEFINE(*view_name, print_settings_log, row_col_log*) *†
Creates or replaces a view.

VIEW.DELETE(*view_name*) *†
Removes a view from the active document.

VIEW.SHOW(*view_name*) *†
Shows a view.

VLINE(*num_rows*)
Vertically scrolls through the active window by rows.

VPAGE(*num_windows*)
Vertically scrolls through the active window one window at a time.

VSCROLL(*position,row_logical*)
Vertically scrolls through a document by percentage or row number.

WINDOW.MAXIMIZE(*window_text*) *
Maximizes a window.

WINDOW.MINIMIZE(*window_text*) *
Minimizes a window.

WINDOW.MOVE(*x_pos,y_pos,window_text*) *
Moves a window.

---

* New function in Microsoft Excel version 4.0.

† To use this function, you must install one of the add-in macros.

WINDOW.RESTORE*(window_text)* *
Restores a window to its previous size.

WORKBOOK.ACTIVATE*(sheet_name, new_window_logical)* *
Activates the specified workbook document.

WORKBOOK.ADD*(name_array,dest_book, position_num)* *
Adds the specified document to the specified workbook.

WORKBOOK.COPY*(name_array,dest_book, position_num)* *
Copies one or more documents from their current workbook into another workbook.

WORKBOOK.MOVE*(name_array,dest_book, position_num)* *
Moves one or more documents from one workbook to another workbook or to another position in the same workbook.

WORKBOOK.OPTIONS*(sheet_name, workbook_name,bound_logical)* *
Changes the settings of a workbook document.

WORKBOOK.SELECT*(name_array, active_name)* *
Selects the specified documents in a workbook.

ZOOM*(magnification)* *
Enlarges or reduces a document in the active window.

Macro Control Functions

ARGUMENT*(name_text,data_type_num)*

ARGUMENT*(name_text,date_type_num,**reference**)*
Passes an argument to a macro.

BREAK*( )*
Interrupts a FOR–NEXT, FOR.CELL–NEXT, or WHILE–NEXT loop.

ELSE*( )*
Specifies an action to take if an IF function returns FALSE.

ELSE.IF*(logical_test)*
Specifies an action to take if an IF or another ELSE.IF function returns FALSE.

END.IF*( )*
Ends a group of macro functions started with an IF statement.

FOR*(**counter_text,start_num,end_num,**step_num)*
Starts a FOR–NEXT loop.

FOR.CELL*(**ref_name,**area_ref,skip_blanks)*
Starts a FOR.CELL–NEXT loop.

GOTO*(reference)*
Directs macro execution to another cell.

HALT*(cancel_close)*
Stops all macros from running.

IF*(logical_test)*
Specifies an action to take if a logical test is TRUE.

NEXT*( )*
Ends a FOR–NEXT, FOR.CELL–NEXT, or WHILE–NEXT loop.

PAUSE*(no_tool)* *
Pauses a macro.

RESTART*(level_num)*
Removes return addresses from the stack.

RESULT*(type_num)*
Specifies the data type a custom function returns.

RETURN*(value)*
Ends the currently running macro.

SET.NAME*(**name_text,**value)*
Defines a name as a value.

SET.VALUE*(reference,values)*
Sets the value of a cell on a macro sheet

STEP*( )*
Turns on macro single-stepping.

---

* New function in Microsoft Excel version 4.0.

† To use this function, you must install one of the add-in macros.

VOLATILE*(logical)*
Makes custom functions recalculate automatically.

WAIT*(serial_number)*
Pauses a macro.

WHILE*(logical_test)*
Starts a WHILE–NEXT loop.

Customizing Functions

ADD.BAR*(bar_num)*
Adds a menu bar.

ADD.COMMAND*(bar_num,menu,command_ref, position)*
Adds a command to a menu.

ADD.MENU*(bar_num,menu_ref,position)*
Adds a menu to a menu bar.

ADD.TOOL*(bar_id,position,tool_ref)* *
Adds one or more tools to a toolbar.

ADD.TOOLBAR*(bar_name,tool_ref)* *
Creates a new toolbar with the specified tools.

ALERT*(message_text,type_num,help_ref)*
Displays a dialog box and a message.

APP.TITLE*(text)* *
Changes the title of the application workspace.

ASSIGN.TO.TOOL*(bar_id,position,macro_ref)* *
Assigns a macro to a tool.

BEEP*(tone_num)*
Sounds a tone

CANCEL.KEY*(enable,macro_ref)*
Disables macro interruption.

CHECK.COMMAND*(bar_num,menu,command, check)*
Adds or deletes a check mark to or from a command.

COPY.TOOL*(bar_id,position)* *
Copies a tool face to the Clipboard.

CUSTOM.REPEAT*(macro_text,repeat_text, record_text)*
Specifies a macro to run when the Repeat command is chosen from the Edit menu.

CUSTOM.UNDO*(macro_text,undo_text)*
Specifies a macro to run to undo a custom command.

DELETE.BAR*(bar_num)*
Deletes a menu bar.

DELETE.COMMAND*(bar_num,menu,command)*
Deletes a command from a menu.

DELETE.MENU*(bar_num,menu)*
Deletes a menu.

DELETE.TOOL*(bar_id, position)* *
Deletes a tool from a toolbar.

DELETE.TOOLBAR*(bar_name)* *
Deletes custom toolbars.

DIALOG.BOX*(dialog_ref)*
Displays a custom dialog box.

DISABLE.INPUT*(logical)*
Blocks all input to Microsoft Excel.

ECHO*(logical)*
Controls screen updating.

ENABLE.COMMAND*(bar_num,menu,command, enable)*
Enables or disables a menu or custom command.

ENABLE.TOOL*(bar_id,position,enable)* *
Enables or disables a tool on a toolbar.

ENTER.DATA*(logical)* *
Turns Data Entry mode on and off.

ERROR*(enable_logical,macro_ref)*
Specifies what action to take if an error is encountered while a macro is running.

---

* New function in Microsoft Excel version 4.0.

† To use this function, you must install one of the add-in macros.

HELP(*help_ref*)
Displays a custom Help topic.

INPUT(*message_text,*type_num,title_text,default,
x_pos,y_pos,help_ref)
Displays a dialog box for user input.

MESSAGE(*logical,*text)
Displays a message in the status bar.

MOVE.TOOL(*from_bar_id,from_bar_position,*
to_bar_id,to_bar_position,copy,width) *
Moves or copies a tool from one toolbar to
another.

ON.DATA(*document_text,macro_text*)
Runs a macro when data is sent to Microsoft
Excel by another application.

ON.DOUBLECLICK(*sheet_text,macro_text*) *
Runs a macro when you double-click any cell or
object on the specified document or double-click
any item on the specified chart.

ON.ENTRY(*sheet_text,macro_text*) *
Runs a macro when data is entered.

ON.KEY(*key_text,*macro_text)
Runs a macro when a specified key is pressed.

ON.RECALC(*sheet_text,macro_text*)
Runs a macro when a document is recalculated.

ON.TIME(*time,macro_text,*tolerance,insert_logical)
Runs a macro at a specific time.

ON.WINDOW(*window_text,macro_text*)
Runs a macro when you switch to a window.

PASTE.TOOL(*bar_id,position*) *
Pastes a tool face from the Clipboard to a
specified position on a toolbar.

PRESS.TOOL(*bar_id,position,down*) *
Formats a tool so that it appears either normal or
depressed into the screen.

RENAME.COMMAND(*bar_num,menu,command,*
name_text)
Changes the name of a command or menu.

RESET.TOOL(*bar_id,position*) *
Resets a tool to its original tool face.

RESET.TOOLBAR(*bar_id*) *
Resets a built-in toolbar to its initial default
setting.

SAVE.TOOLBAR(*bar_id,filename*) *
Saves one or more toolbar definitions to a
specified file.

SHOW.BAR(*bar_num*)
Displays a menu bar.

SHOW.TOOLBAR(*bar_id,visible,dock,x_pos,*
y_pos,width) *
Hides or displays a toolbar.

WINDOW.TITLE(*text*) *
Changes the title of the active window.

Text Functions

SPELLING.CHECK(*word_text,custom_dic,*
ignore_uppercase)
Checks the spelling of a word.

DDE/External Functions

APP.ACTIVATE(*title_text,wait_logical*)
Switches to another application.

EDIT.OBJECT(*verb_num*)
Starts the application associated with the
selected object and makes the object available
for editing or other actions.

EDITION.OPTIONS(*edition_type,edition_name,*
reference,option,appearance,size,formats)
Sets publisher and subscriber options.

EMBED(*object_type,item*)
Displayed in the formula bar when an embedded
object is selected.

---

*   New function in Microsoft Excel version 4.0.

†   To use this function, you must install one of the add-in
       macros.

EXEC(*program_text,*window_num)

EXEC(*program_text,*background,
   preferred_size_only)
   Starts another application.

EXECUTE(*channel_num,execute_text*)
   Carries out a command in another application.

FCLOSE(*file_num*)
   Closes a text file.

FOPEN(*file_text,*access_num)
   Opens a file with the type of permission
   specified.

FPOS(*file_num,*position_num)
   Sets the position in a text file.

FREAD(*file_num,*num_chars)
   Reads characters from a text file.

FREADLN(*file_num*)
   Reads a line from a text file.

FSIZE(*file_num*)
   Returns the size of a text file.

FWRITE(*file_num,text*)
   Writes characters to a text file.

FWRITELN(*file_num,text*)
   Writes a line to a text file.

INITIATE(*app_text,topic_text*)
   Opens a channel to another application.

INSERT.OBJECT(*object_class*)
   Creates an embedded object whose source data
   is supplied by another application and places it
   on Microsoft Excel's object layer.

POKE(*channel_num,item_text,data_ref*)
   Sends data to another application.

REGISTER(*module_text,*procedure,type_text,
   function_text,argument_text,macro_type,
   category,shortcut_text)

REGISTER(*file_text,*resource,type_text,
   function_text,argument_text,macro_type,
   category,shortcut_text)
   Registers a code resource.

REGISTER.ID(*module_text,procedure,*type_text) *

REGISTER.ID(*file_text,resource,*type_text) *
   Returns the register ID of the resource.

REQUEST(*channel_num,item_text*)
   Returns data from another application.

SEND.KEYS(*key_text,*wait_logical)
   Sends a key sequence to an application.

SET.UPDATE.STATUS(*link_text,status,
   type_of_link*)
   Controls the update status of a link.

SUBSCRIBE.TO(*file_text,format_num*)
   Inserts contents of an edition into the active
   document.

TERMINATE(*channel_num*)
   Closes a channel to another application.

UNREGISTER(*register_id*)

UNREGISTER(*module_text*)

UNREGISTER(*file_text*)
   Removes a registered code resource from
   memory.

Differences Due to Operating Environment

Most of the information in this book applies to all
users of Microsoft Excel. However, there are some
functions that are not supported by both Microsoft
Excel for the Macintosh and Microsoft Excel for
Windows. You can create macros for use in another
operating environment using macro functions that
are not supported by your current operating environment. The macro functions will be accepted by the
macro sheet when you type them but will return
error values when you try to run them in the
unsupported environment.

---

*   New function in Microsoft Excel version 4.0.

†   To use this function, you must install one of the add-in
    macros.

The following functions in Microsoft Excel for Windows are not supported by Microsoft Excel for the Macintosh:

- APP.MAXIMIZE
- APP.MINIMIZE
- APP.MOVE
- APP.RESTORE
- APP.SIZE
- PRINTER.SETUP
- SEND.KEYS

The following function in Microsoft Excel for the Macintosh is not supported by Microsoft Excel for Windows:

- OPEN.MAIL

The following functions are only supported by Microsoft Excel for the Macintosh if you are using system software version 7.0 or later:

- APP.ACTIVATE
- EXEC
- EXECUTE
- INITIATE
- ON.DATA
- POKE
- REQUEST
- TERMINATE

The following functions are only supported by Microsoft Excel for the Macintosh if you are using system software version 7.0 or later. They are not supported by Microsoft Excel for Windows:

- CREATE.PUBLISHER
- SUBSCRIBE.TO

The following function is only available in Microsoft® Windows for Pen Computing:

- CONSTRAIN.NUMERIC

Function Reference

A1.R1C1

Macro Sheets Only

Displays row and column headings and cell references in either the R1C1 or A1 reference style. A1 is the Microsoft Excel default reference style.

Syntax

A1.R1C1(*logical*)

Logical   is a logical value specifying which reference style to use. If *logical* is TRUE, all worksheets and macro sheets use A1 references; if FALSE, all worksheets and macro sheets use R1C1 references.

Example

The following macro formula displays an alert box asking you to choose either A1 or R1C1 reference style. This is useful in an Auto_Open macro if several persons who prefer different reference styles must maintain the same worksheet.

```
A1.R1C1(ALERT("Click OK for A1 style;
Cancel for R1C1",1))
```

ABS

Returns the absolute value of a number. The absolute value of a number is the number without its sign.

Syntax

ABS(*number*)

Number   is the real number of which you want the absolute value.

Examples

ABS(2)   equals 2

ABS(-2)   equals 2

If A1 contains –16, then:

SQRT(ABS(A1))   equals 4

Related Functions

Function	Description
IMABS	Returns the absolute value (modulus) of a complex number
SIGN	Returns the sign of a number

ABSREF

Macro Sheets Only

Returns the absolute reference of the cells that are offset from a reference by a specified amount. You should generally use OFFSET instead of ABSREF. This function is provided for users who prefer to supply a relative reference in text form.

Syntax

ABSREF(*ref_text,reference*)

Ref_text   specifies a position relative to *reference*. Think of *ref_text* as "directions" from one range of cells to another.

- *Ref_text* must be an R1C1-style relative reference in the form of text, such as "R[1]C[1]".

- *Ref_text* is considered relative to the cell in the upper-left corner of *reference*.

Reference   is a cell or range of cells specifying a starting point that *ref_text* uses to locate another range of cells. *Reference* can be an external reference.

Remarks

- If you use ABSREF in a function or operation, you will usually get the values contained in the reference instead of the reference itself because the reference is automatically converted to the contents of the reference.

- If you use ABSREF in a function that requires a reference argument, then Microsoft Excel does not convert the reference to a value.

- If you want to work with the actual reference, use the REFTEXT function to convert the active-cell reference to text, which you can then store or manipulate (or convert back to a reference with TEXTREF). See the third example following.

Examples

ABSREF("R[-2]C[-2]",C3) equals $A$1

ABSREF(RELREF(A1,C3),D4) equals $B$2

REFTEXT(ABSREF("R[-2]C[-2]:R[2]C[2]", C3:G7),TRUE) equals
REFTEXT(ABSREF("R[-2]C[-2]:R[2]C[2]", C3),TRUE) equals "$A$1:$E$5"

In Microsoft Excel for Windows, if the document in the active window is named FINANCE.XLS:

ABSREF("R[-2]C[-2]",FINANCE.XLS!C3) equals FINANCE.XLS!$A$1

In Microsoft Excel for the Macintosh, if the document in the active window is named FINANCE:

ABSREF("R[-2]C[-2]",FINANCE!C3) equals FINANCE!$A$1

Related Functions

Function	Description
OFFSET	Returns a reference offset from a given reference
RELREF	Returns a relative reference

ACCRINT

Returns the accrued interest for a security that pays periodic interest.

If this function is not available, you must install the Analysis ToolPak add-in macro. For more information, see "Managing Add-in Commands and Functions" in Chapter 4 in Book 2 of the *Microsoft Excel User's Guide*.

Syntax

ACCRINT(*issue,first_interest,settlement,rate, par,frequency,basis*)

Issue is the security's issue date, expressed as a serial date number.

First_interest is the security's first interest date, expressed as a serial date number.

Settlement is the security's settlement date, expressed as a serial date number.

Rate is the security's annual coupon rate.

Par is the security's par value. If you omit *par*, ACCRINT uses $1000.

Frequency is the number of coupon payments per year. For annual payments, *frequency* = 1; for semi-annual, *frequency* = 2; for quarterly, *frequency* = 4.

Basis is the type of day count basis to use.

Basis	Day count basis
0 or omitted	30/360
1	Actual/actual
2	Actual/360
3	Actual/365

Remarks

- *Issue, first_interest, settlement, frequency,* and *basis* are truncated to integers.

- If *issue, first_interest,* or *settlement* is not a valid serial date number, ACCRINT returns the #NUM! error value.

- If *coupon* ≤ 0 or if *par* ≤ 0, ACCRINT returns the #NUM! error value.

- If *frequency* is any number other than 1, 2, or 4, ACCRINT returns the #NUM! error value.

- If *basis* < 0 or if *basis* > 3, ACCRINT returns the #NUM! error value.

- If *issue* ≥ *settlement*, ACCRINT returns the #NUM! error value.

Example

A Treasury bond has the following terms:

February 28, 1991 issue date
May 1, 1991 settlement date
August 31, 1991 first interest date
10.0% semiannual coupon
$1000 par value
30/360 basis

The accrued interest (in the 1900 Date System) is:

```
ACCRINT(33297,33481,33359,0.1,1000,
2,0) equals 16.94444
```

Related Functions

Function	Description
ACCRINTM	Returns the accrued interest for a security that pays interest at maturity
DATE	Returns the serial number of a particular date

ACCRINTM

Returns the accrued interest for a security that pays interest at maturity.

If this function is not available, you must install the Analysis ToolPak add-in macro. For more information, see "Managing Add-in Commands and Functions" in Chapter 4 in Book 2 of the *Microsoft Excel User's Guide*.

Syntax

ACCRINTM(*issue,settlement,rate,par,basis*)

Issue   is the security's issue date, expressed as a serial date number.

Settlement   is the security's maturity date, expressed as a serial date number.

Rate   is the security's annual coupon rate.

Par   is the security's par value. If you omit *par*, ACCRINTM uses $1000.

Basis   is the type of day count basis to use.

Basis	Day count basis
0 or omitted	30/360
1	Actual/actual
2	Actual/360
3	Actual/365

Remarks

- *Issue, settlement,* and *basis* are truncated to integers.

- If any argument is non-numeric, ACCRINTM returns the #VALUE! error value.

- If *issue* or *settlement* is not a valid serial date number, ACCRINTM returns the #NUM! error value.

- If *rate* ≤ 0 or if *par* ≤ 0, ACCRINTM returns the #NUM! error value.

- If *basis* < 0 or if *basis* > 3, ACCRINTM returns the #NUM! error value.

- If *issue* ≥ *settlement*, ACCRINTM returns the #NUM! error value.

Example

A note has the following terms:

April 1, 1991 issue date
June 15, 1991 maturity date
10.0% coupon
$1000 par value
Actual/365 basis

The accrued interest (in the 1900 Date System) is:

```
ACCRINTM(33329,33404,0.1,1000,3)
```
equals 20.54795

Related Functions

Function	Description
ACCRINT	Returns the accrued interest for a security
DATE	Returns the serial number of a particular date

ACOS

Returns the arccosine of a number. The arccosine is the angle whose cosine is *number*. The returned angle is given in radians in the range 0 to π.

Syntax

ACOS(*number*)

Number   is the cosine of the angle you want and must be from –1 to 1.

If you want to convert the result from radians to degrees, multiply it by 180/PI( ).

Examples

ACOS(-0.5) equals 2.094395 ($2\pi/3$ radians)

ACOS(-0.5)*180/PI() equals 120 (degrees)

Related Functions

Function	Description
COS	Returns the cosine of a number
PI	Returns the value π

ACOSH

Returns the inverse hyperbolic cosine of *number*. *Number* must be greater than or equal to 1. The inverse hyperbolic cosine is the value whose hyperbolic cosine is *number*, so ACOSH(COSH(*number*)) equals *number*.

Syntax

ACOSH(*number*)

Examples

ACOSH(1) equals 0

ACOSH(10) equals 2.99323

Related Functions

Function	Description
ASINH	Returns the inverse hyperbolic sine of a number
ATANH	Returns the inverse hyperbolic tangent of a number
COSH	Returns the hyperbolic cosine of a number

ACTIVATE

Macro Sheets Only

Switches to a window if more than one window is open, or a pane of a window if the window is split and its panes are not frozen. Switching to a pane is useful with functions such as VSCROLL, HSCROLL, and GOTO, which operate only on the active pane.

Syntax

ACTIVATE(*window_text,pane_num*)

Window_text   is text specifying the name of a window to switch to: for example, "Sheet1" or "Sheet1:2".

- If a document is displayed in more than one window and *window_text* does not specify which window to switch to, the first window containing that document is switched to.

- If *window_text* is omitted, the active window is not changed.

Pane_num   is a number from 1 to 4 specifying which pane to switch to. If *pane_num* is omitted and the window has more than one pane, the active pane is not changed.

Pane_num	Activates
1	Upper-left pane. If the window is not split, this is the only pane. If the window is split only horizontally, this is the upper pane. If the window is split only vertically, this is the left pane.
2	Upper-right pane. If the window is split only vertically, this is the right pane. If the window is split only horizontally, an error occurs.
3	Lower-left pane. If the window is split only horizontally, this is the lower pane. If the window is split only vertically, an error occurs.
4	Lower-right pane. If the window is split into only two panes either vertically or horizontally, an error occurs.

Examples

In Microsoft Excel for Windows, the following macro formula switches to the upper pane of a horizontally split window in a macro sheet called MACRO1.XLM:

```
ACTIVATE("MACRO1.XLM",1)
```

The following macro formula switches to a chart called CHART3.XLC:

```
ACTIVATE("CHART3.XLC")
```

In Microsoft Excel for the Macintosh, the following macro formula switches to the upper pane of a horizontally split window in a macro sheet called MACRO1:

```
ACTIVATE("MACRO1",1)
```

The following macro formula switches to a chart called SALESCHART:

```
ACTIVATE("SALESCHART")
```

Related Functions

Function	Description
ACTIVATE.NEXT and ACTIVATE.PREV	Switches to the next or previous window respectively, or switches to the next or previous document in a workbook
DOCUMENTS	Returns the names of the specified open documents
FREEZE.PANES	Freezes the panes of a window so that they do not scroll
ON.WINDOW	Runs a macro when you switch to a window
SPLIT	Splits a window
WINDOWS	Returns the names of all open windows

ACTIVATE.NEXT
ACTIVATE.PREV

Macro Sheets Only

Switches to the next or previous window, respectively, or switches to the next or previous document in a workbook.

Syntax

ACTIVATE.NEXT(*workbook_text*)
ACTIVATE.PREV(*workbook_text*)

Workbook_text　is the name of the workbook for which you want to activate a window.

- If *workbook_text* is specified, ACTIVATE.NEXT and ACTIVATE.PREV are equivalent to pressing ALT+PAGE DOWN and ALT+PAGE UP (in Microsoft Excel for Windows) or OPTION+PAGE DOWN and OPTION+PAGE UP (in Microsoft Excel for the Macintosh). These functions switch to the next and previous sheets, respectively.

- If *workbook_text* is omitted, these functions are equivalent to pressing CTRL+F6 or CTRL+SHIFT+F6 (in Microsoft Excel for Windows) or COMMAND+M or COMMAND+SHIFT+M (in Microsoft Excel for the Macintosh). These functions switch to the next and previous windows, respectively.

Related Functions

Function	Description
ACTIVATE	Switches to a window
ON.WINDOW	Runs a macro when you switch to a window

ACTIVE.CELL

Macro Sheets Only

Returns the reference of the active cell in the selection as an external reference.

Syntax

ACTIVE.CELL( )

Remarks

- If an object is selected, ACTIVE.CELL returns the #N/A error value.

- If a chart window is active, ACTIVE.CELL returns the #REF! error value.

- If you use ACTIVE.CELL in a function or operation, you will usually get the value contained in the active cell instead of its reference, because the reference is automatically converted to the contents of the reference. See the third example following.

- If you use ACTIVE.CELL in a function that requires a reference argument, then Microsoft Excel does not convert the reference to a value.

- If you want to work with the actual reference, use the REFTEXT function to convert the active-cell reference to text, which you can then store or manipulate (or convert back to a reference with TEXTREF). See the second example following.

Tip Use the following macro formula to verify that the current selection is a cell or range of cells:

```
=ISREF(ACTIVE.CELL( ))
```

Examples

The following macro formula assigns the name Sales to the active cell:

```
SET.NAME("Sales",ACTIVE.CELL())
```

In this example, note that "Sales" refers to a cell on the active worksheet, but the name itself exists only in the macro sheet's list of names. In other words, the preceding formula does not define a name on the worksheet.

The following macro formula puts the reference of the active cell into the cell named Temp:

```
FORMULA("="&REFTEXT(ACTIVE.CELL()),"Temp")
```

The following macro formula checks the contents of the active cell. If the cell contains only the letter "c" or "s", the macro branches to an area named FinishRefresh:

```
IF(OR(ACTIVE.CELL()="c",ACTIVE.CELL()="s"),
GOTO(FinishRefresh))
```

In Microsoft Excel for Windows, if the document in the active window is named SALES.XLS and A1 is the active cell, then:

```
ACTIVE.CELL()  equals SALES.XLS!$A$1
```

In Microsoft Excel for the Macintosh, if the document in the active window is named SALES 1 and A1 is the active cell, then:

```
ACTIVE.CELL()  equals SALES 1!$A$1
```

Related Functions

Function	Description
OFFSET	Returns a reference offset from a given reference
SELECT	Selects a cell, worksheet object, or chart item

ADD.ARROW

Macro Sheets Only

Equivalent to choosing the Add Arrow command from the Chart menu or clicking the chart arrow tool. Adds an arrow to the active chart. If a chart is not the active document, displays an error value. For detailed information about the Add Arrow command, see online Help.

Syntax

ADD.ARROW( )

Remarks

After you create an arrow with ADD.ARROW, the arrow remains selected, so you can use the arrow form of the PATTERNS function to format the arrow and the FORMAT.MOVE and FORMAT.SIZE functions to change the position and size of the arrow.

Related Functions

Function	Description
CREATE.OBJECT	Creates an object
DELETE.ARROW	Deletes the selected arrow
FORMAT.MOVE	Moves the selected object
FORMAT.SIZE	Changes the size of the selected object
PATTERNS	Changes the appearance of the selected object

ADD.BAR

Macro Sheets Only

Creates a new menu bar and returns the bar ID number. Use the bar ID number to identify the menu in functions that display and add menus and commands to the menu bar. You can also use ADD.BAR to restore a built-in menu bar with its original menus and commands.

Syntax

ADD.BAR(*bar_num*)

Bar_num   is the number of a built-in menu bar that you want to restore. Use ADD.BAR(*bar_num*) to restore an unaltered version of a built-in menu bar after you have made changes to the menu bar's menus and commands. See ADD.COMMAND for a list of ID numbers for built-in menu bars.

Important   Restoring a built-in menu bar will remove menus and commands added by other macros. Use ADD.COMMAND and ADD.MENU to restore individual commands and menus.

Remarks

ADD.BAR just creates a new menu bar; it does not display it. Use SHOW.BAR to display a menu bar. The argument to the SHOW.BAR function should be the number returned by ADD.BAR or a reference to the cell containing ADD.BAR.

You can define up to 15 custom menu bars at one time, in addition to the six built-in Microsoft Excel menu bars and three shortcut menus. If you carry out an ADD.BAR function when more than 15 custom menu bars are already defined, Microsoft Excel returns the #VALUE! error value.

For information about custom menus, see "Creating a Custom Menu" in Chapter 8 in Book 2 of the *Microsoft Excel User's Guide.*

Example

The following formula creates a new menu bar and returns a bar ID number:

```
ADD.BAR()
```

Related Functions

Function	Description
ADD.COMMAND	Adds a command to a menu
ADD.MENU	Adds a menu to a menu bar
DELETE.BAR	Deletes a menu bar
SHOW.BAR	Displays a menu bar

ADD.COMMAND

Macro Sheets Only

Adds a command to a menu. ADD.COMMAND returns the position number on the menu of the added command. Use ADD.COMMAND to add one or more custom menu commands to a menu on a built-in or custom menu bar. You can also use ADD.COMMAND to restore a deleted built-in command to its original menu. For more information about using custom menu bars, menus, and commands, see Chapter 8 in Book 2 of the *Microsoft Excel User's Guide*.

Syntax

ADD.COMMAND(*bar_num,menu,command_ref, position*)

Bar_num   is a number corresponding to a menu bar or a type of shortcut menu to which you want to add a command.

- *Bar_num* can be the ID number of a built-in or custom menu bar. The ID number of a custom menu bar is the number returned by the ADD.BAR function.

- *Bar_num* can also refer to a type of shortcut menu; use *menu* to identify the specific shortcut menu.

The ID numbers of the built-in menu bars and the types of shortcut menus are listed in the following tables. Short menus are abbreviated versions of the normal Microsoft Excel menus. To turn on short menus, use the SHORT.MENUS function.

Bar_num	Built-in menu bar
1	Worksheet and macro sheet
2	Chart
3	Null (the menu displayed when no documents are open)

Bar_num	Built-in menu bar
4	Info
5	Worksheet and macro sheet (short menus)
6	Chart (short menus)

Bar_num	Shortcut menu
7	Cell, toolbar, and workbook
8	Object
9	Chart

Menu   is the menu to which you want the new command added.

- *Menu* can be either the name of a menu as text or the number of a menu.

- If *bar_num* is 1 through 6, menus are numbered starting with 1 from the left of the menu bar.

- If *bar_num* is 7, 8, or 9, *menu* refers to a built-in shortcut menu. The combination of *bar_num* and *menu* determines which shortcut menu to modify, as shown in the following table.

Bar_num	*Menu*	Shortcut menu
7	1	Toolbars
7	2	Toolbar tools
7	3	Workbook paging icons
7	4	Cells (worksheet)
7	5	Column selections
7	6	Row selections
7	7	Workbook items
7	8	Cells (macro sheet)
8	1	Drawn or imported objects
8	2	Buttons
8	3	Text boxes
9	1	Chart series
9	2	Chart text
9	3	Chart plot area and walls
9	4	Entire charts

Bar_num	Menu	Shortcut menu
9	5	Chart axes
9	6	Chart gridlines
9	7	Chart floor and arrows
9	8	Chart legends

Note Any commands that you add to the toolbar tools shortcut menu will be dimmed.

Command_ref is an array or a reference to an area on the macro sheet that describes the new command or commands.

- *Command_ref* must be at least two columns wide. The first column specifies command names; the second specifies macro names. Optional columns can be specified for shortcut keys (in Microsoft Excel for the Macintosh), status bar messages, and custom Help topics, in that order.

- *Command_ref* is similar to *menu_ref* in ADD.MENU. For more information about *command_ref,* see the description of *menu_ref* in ADD.MENU.

- *Command_ref* can be the name, as text, of a previously deleted built-in command that you want to restore. You can also use the value returned by the DELETE.COMMAND formula that deleted the command.

Position specifies the placement of the new command.

- *Position* can be a number indicating the position of the command on the menu. Commands are numbered from the top of the menu starting with 1.

- *Position* can be the name of an existing command, as text, above which you want to add the new command.

- If *position* is omitted, the command is added to the bottom of the menu.

- For the toolbar shortcut menu (*bar_num* 7, *menu* 1) and the shortcut menu for workbook paging icons (*bar_num* 7, *menu* 3), you cannot add commands to the middle of the toolbar name list or the middle of the workbook contents list.

Tip In general, use menu and command names rather than numbers for arguments. The numbers assigned to menus and commands change as you add and delete menus and commands. Using names ensures that your menu and command macro functions always refer to the correct items.

Example

The following macro formula adds the command described in cells G16:J16 to the bottom of the worksheet cells shortcut menu:

```
ADD.COMMAND(7,4,G16:J16)
```

Also see the example for SHOW.BAR.

Related Functions

Function	Description
ADD.BAR	Adds a menu bar
ADD.MENU	Adds a menu to a menu bar
ADD.TOOL	Adds one or more tools to a toolbar
ADD.TOOLBAR	Creates a toolbar with the specified tools
DELETE.COMMAND	Deletes a command from a menu
ENABLE.COMMAND	Enables or disables a menu or custom command
GET.TOOLBAR	Retrieves information about a toolbar
RENAME.COMMAND	Changes the name of a command or menu

ADD.MENU

Macro Sheets Only

Adds a menu to a menu bar. Use ADD.MENU to add a custom menu to a built-in or custom menu bar. You can also use ADD.MENU to restore built-in menus you have deleted with DELETE.MENU. ADD.MENU returns the position number in the menu bar of the new menu.

Syntax

ADD.MENU(*bar_num,menu_ref,position*)

Bar_num   is the menu bar to which you want a menu added. *Bar_num* can be the ID number of a built-in or custom menu bar. See ADD.COMMAND for a list of ID numbers for built-in menu bars.

Menu_ref   is an array or a reference to an area on the macro sheet that describes the new menu or the name of a deleted built-in menu you want to restore.

- *Menu_ref* must be made up of at least two rows and two columns of cells. The upper-left cell of *menu_ref* specifies the menu title, which is displayed in the menu bar. In the following example, the range A3:E10 is a valid *menu_ref*.

	A	B	C	D	E
1	Menu or command name	Macro name	Shortcut key	Status bar	Help topics
2			Macintosh only		
3	Reports				
4	Weekly Report	WeeklyRept		Prints weekly report	Help!35
5	Monthly Report	MonthlyRept		Prints monthly report	Help!36
6	Quarterly Report	QuartRept		Prints quarterly report	Help!37
7	-				
8	Custom Report	CustomRpt		Create a custom report	Help!38
9	-				
10	Remove Menu	RemoveMen		Removes Reports menu	Help!39

- The rest of the first column indicates the names of the commands. The corresponding rows in the second column give the names of the macros that run when the commands are chosen.

- You can also specify status-bar text and Help topics in *menu_ref*. In Microsoft Excel for the Macintosh, you can specify shortcut keys in *menu_ref*. For more information about creating custom menus, see Chapter 8 in Book 2 of the *Microsoft Excel User's Guide*.

Position   specifies the placement of the new menu. *Position* can be the name of a menu, as text, or the number of a menu. Menus are numbered from left to right starting with 1. Menus are added to the left of the position specified.

- If *position* is omitted, the menu is added to the end of the menu bar.

- If there is already a menu at *position*, that menu is shifted to the right and the new menu is added in its place.

- If you are using ADD.MENU to restore a deleted built-in menu, you can use the *position* argument to put it back in its original place on the menu bar. For example, to restore the Data menu on the worksheet and macro sheet menu bar, use *position* 5. If *position* is omitted, the menu is added to the right of the last menu restored.

For more information about custom menus, see Chapter 8 in Book 2 of the *Microsoft Excel User's Guide*.

Example

The following macro formula adds a new menu to the end of the worksheet menu bar, where A10:B15 is the *menu_ref* describing the menu:

```
ADD.MENU(1,A10:B15)
```

Also see the example for SHOW.BAR.

Related Functions

Function	Description
ADD.COMMAND	Adds a command to a menu
DELETE.MENU	Deletes a menu
ENABLE.COMMAND	Enables or disables a menu or custom command

ADD.OVERLAY

Macro Sheets Only

Equivalent to choosing the Add Overlay command from the Chart menu (full menus). Adds an overlay to a 2-D chart. If the active chart already has an overlay, ADD.OVERLAY takes no action and returns TRUE. For detailed information about the Add Overlay command, see online Help.

Syntax

ADD.OVERLAY( )

Related Functions

Function	Description
ADD.ARROW	Adds an arrow to a chart
LEGEND	Adds a legend to a chart

ADD.TOOL

Macro Sheets Only

Adds one or more tools to a toolbar. For information about customizing toolbars, see "Displaying and Customizing Toolbars" in Chapter 4 in Book 2 of the *Microsoft Excel User's Guide*.

Syntax

ADD.TOOL(*bar_id,position,tool_ref*)

Bar_id is either a number from 1 to 9 specifying one of the built-in toolbars or the name of a custom toolbar.

Bar_id	Built-in toolbar
1	Standard
2	Formatting
3	Utility
4	Chart
5	Drawing
6	Excel 3.0
7	Macro
8	Macro recording
9	Macro paused

Position specifies the position of the tool within the toolbar. *Position* starts with 1 at the left side (if horizontal) or at the top (if vertical).

Tool_ref is either a number specifying a built-in tool or a reference to an area on the macro sheet that defines a custom tool or set of tools (or an array containing this information). For a complete list of built-in tools and their corresponding numbers, see "Displaying and Customizing Toolbars" in Chapter 4 in Book 2 of the *Microsoft Excel User's Guide.*

For customized tools, the following example shows the components of a tool reference area on a macro sheet and defines custom tools. The range A1:II4 is a valid *tool_ref*. Row 1 refers to a built-in tool. Row 2 defines a gap. For this illustration, values are displayed instead of formulas so that text can wrap in cells.

	A	B	C	D	E	F	G	H
	Tool_id	Macro	Down	Enabled	Face	Help_text	Balloon_text	Help_topics
1	14							
2	0							
3	201	ShiftCells	TRUE	TRUE	Picture 1	Move selected cells right one cell	Use the Shift Cells Right tool to move the selected cells to the right.	Help!40
4	202	Multiply	TRUE	TRUE	Picture 2	Multiply a column or row of numbers	Use the Multiply tool to multiply a column or row of numbers	Help!41
5								

- *Tool_id* is a number associated with the tool. A zero specifies a gap on the toolbar. To specify a custom tool, use a name, or a number between 201 and 231. For a complete list of built-in tools and their corresponding numbers, see "Displaying and Customizing Toolbars" in Chapter 4 in Book 2 of the *Microsoft Excel User's Guide*.

- *Macro* is the name of, or a quoted R1C1-style reference to, the macro you want to run when the tool is clicked.

- *Down* is a logical value specifying the default image of the tool. If *down* is TRUE, the tool appears depressed into the screen; if FALSE or omitted, it appears normal (up).

- *Enabled* is a logical value specifying whether the tool can be used. If *enabled* is TRUE, the tool is enabled; if FALSE, it is disabled.

- *Face* specifies a face associated with the tool. *Face* must be a reference to a picture-type object, for example "Picture 1". If *face* is omitted, Microsoft Excel uses the default face for the tool.

- *Help_text* is the text, if any, that you want displayed in the status bar when the tool is selected.

- *Balloon_text* is the balloon help text, if any, associated with the tool. *Balloon_text* is available only in Microsoft Excel for the Macintosh using system software version 7.0 or later.

- *Help_topics* is a reference to a topic in a Help file, in the form "filename!topic_number". *Help_topics* must be text. If *help_topics* is omitted, HELP displays the Contents topic for Microsoft Excel Help.

To indicate that a particular component of *tool_ref* is not used, clear the contents of the corresponding cell.

Remarks

- If you do not want to reserve a section of your macro sheet to define the tools, you can use an array as the *tool_ref* argument as shown in the following syntax:

  ADD.TOOL(*bar_id,position,{tool_id$_1$,macro$_1$, down$_1$,enabled$_1$,face$_1$,help_text$_1$,balloon_text$_1$, help_topics$_1$;tool_id$_2$,macro$_2$,down$_2$,enabled$_2$, face$_2$,help_text$_2$,balloon_text$_2$,help_topics$_2$;...}*)

- Picture objects can be created with the camera tool or pasted in from another application. In Microsoft Excel for Windows, the graphic object must be either a Windows bitmap or picture object. In Microsoft Excel for the Macintosh, the object must be a picture object.

Examples

The following macro formula adds a tool to Toolbar5. The cell range B6:I6 contains *tool_ref*.

```
ADD.TOOL("Toolbar5",6,B6:I6)
```

The following macro formula adds the New Macro Sheet tool to the fifth position on the Standard toolbar:

```
ADD.TOOL(1,5,6)
```

Related Functions

Function	Description
ADD.COMMAND	Adds a command to a menu
ADD.TOOLBAR	Creates a toolbar with the specified tools
DELETE.TOOL	Deletes a tool from a toolbar
DELETE.TOOLBAR	Deletes custom toolbars
RESET.TOOLBAR	Resets a built-in toolbar to its default initial setting

ADD.TOOLBAR

Macro Sheets Only

Creates a new toolbar with the specified tools. For more information about customizing toolbars, see "Displaying and Customizing Toolbars" in Chapter 4 in Book 2 of the *Microsoft Excel User's Guide*.

Syntax

ADD.TOOLBAR(*bar_name,tool_ref*)

Bar_name   is a text string identifying the toolbar you want to create.

Tool_ref   is either a number specifying a built-in tool or a reference to an area on the macro sheet that defines a custom tool or set of tools (or an array containing this information). For a complete list of built-in tools and their corresponding numbers, see "Displaying and Customizing Toolbars" in Chapter 4 in Book 2 of the *Microsoft Excel User's Guide*.

For a complete description of *tool_ref*, see ADD.TOOL.

Remarks

If you create a toolbar without tools, use ADD.TOOL to add them. Use SHOW.TOOLBAR to display the toolbar.

Example

The following macro formula creates Toolbar9 with one tool in it. The cell range B7:I7 contains *tool_ref*.

```
ADD.TOOLBAR("Toolbar9",B7:I7)
```

Related Functions

Function	Description
ADD.TOOL	Adds a tool to a toolbar
DELETE.TOOL	Deletes a tool from a toolbar
DELETE.TOOLBAR	Deletes custom toolbars
RESET.TOOLBAR	Resets a built-in toolbar to its default initial setting
SHOW.TOOLBAR	Hides or displays a toolbar

ADDRESS

Creates a cell address as text, given specified row and column numbers.

Syntax

ADDRESS(*row_num,column_num,abs_num,a1, sheet_text*)

Row_num   is the row number to use in the cell reference.

Column_num   is the column number to use in the cell reference.

Abs_num   specifies the type of reference to return.

Abs_num	Returns this type of reference
1 or omitted	Absolute
2	Absolute row; relative column
3	Relative row; absolute column
4	Relative

A1   is a logical value that specifies the A1 or R1C1 reference style. If *a1* is TRUE or omitted, ADDRESS returns an A1 style reference; if FALSE, ADDRESS returns an R1C1-style reference.

Sheet_text   is text specifying the name of the worksheet or macro sheet to be used as the external reference. If *sheet_text* is omitted, no sheet name is used.

Examples

ADDRESS(2,3) equals "$C$2"

ADDRESS(2,3,2) equals "C$2"

ADDRESS(2,3,2,FALSE) equals "R2C[3]"

ADDRESS(2,3,2,FALSE,"SHEET1.XLS") equals "SHEET1.XLS!R2C3"

ADDRESS(2,3,2,FALSE,"EXCEL SHEET") equals "'EXCEL SHEET'!R2C3"

Related Functions

Function	Description
ACTIVE.CELL	Returns the reference of the active cell
COLUMN	Returns the column number of a reference
OFFSET	Returns a reference offset from a given reference
ROW	Returns the row number of a reference
SELECTION	Returns the reference of the selection

ALERT

Macro Sheets Only

Displays a dialog box and message and waits for you to choose a button. Use ALERT instead of MESSAGE if you want to interrupt the flow of a macro and force the user to make a choice or to notice an important message.

Syntax

ALERT(*message_text,type_num,help_ref*)

Message_text   is the message displayed in the dialog box.

Type_num   is a number from 1 to 3 specifying which type of dialog box to display. If you omit *type_num*, it is assumed to be 2.

- If *type_num* is 1, ALERT displays a dialog box containing the OK and Cancel buttons. Choose a button to continue or cancel an action. ALERT returns TRUE if you choose the OK button and FALSE if you choose the Cancel button. See the last example below.

- If *type_num* is 2 or 3, ALERT displays a dialog box containing an OK button. Choose the button to continue, and ALERT returns TRUE. The only difference between specifying 2 or 3 is that ALERT displays a different icon on the left side of the dialog box as shown in the examples below. So, for example, you could use 2 for notes or to present general information, and 3 for errors or warnings.

Help_ref   is a reference to a custom online Help topic in a text file, in the form "filename! topic_number".

- If *help_ref* is present, a Help button appears in the lower-right corner of the alert message. Choosing the Help button starts Help and displays the specified topic.

- If *help_ref* is omitted, no Help button appears.

- *Help_ref* must be given in text form.

For more information about custom Help topics, see HELP in this manual and "Creating a Custom Help Topic" in Chapter 8 in Book 2 of the *Microsoft Excel User's Guide*.

Note   In Microsoft Excel for the Macintosh, the ALERT dialog box is not a movable window.

Examples

The following dialog boxes show the results of using ALERT with *type_num* 1, 2, and 3. The first and fourth examples include a Help button.

In Microsoft Excel for Windows, the following macro formulas display these three dialog boxes.

```
ALERT("Are you sure you want to delete this
item?",1,"CUSTHELP.DOC!101")
```

```
ALERT("The number should be between 1 and
100",2)
```

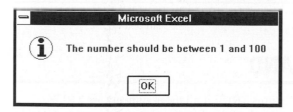

```
ALERT("Your debits and credits are not
equal; do not end this transaction.",3)
```

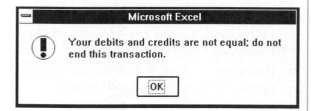

In Microsoft Excel for the Macintosh, the following macro formulas display these three dialog boxes.

```
ALERT("Are you sure you want to delete this
item?",1,"Custom Help!101")
```

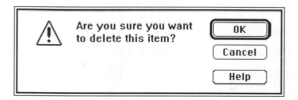

```
ALERT("The number should be between 1 and
100",2)
```

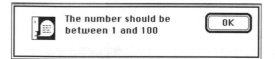

```
ALERT("Your debits and credits are not
equal; do not end this transaction.",3)
```

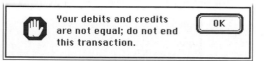

A common use of the ALERT function is to give the user a choice of two actions. The following macro formula in an Auto_Open macro asks which reference style to use when the worksheet is opened.

```
A1.R1C1(ALERT("Click OK for A1 style;
Cancel for R1C1",1))
```

Also see the examples for ARGUMENT, SHOW.CLIPBOARD, and the macro sheet-only form of the IF function.

Related Functions

Function	Description
INPUT	Displays a dialog box for user input
MESSAGE	Displays a message in the status bar

ALIGNMENT

Macro Sheets Only

Equivalent to choosing the Alignment command from the Format menu. Aligns the contents of the selected cells. For detailed information about the Alignment command, see online Help.

Syntax

ALIGNMENT(*horiz_align,wrap,vert_align, orientation*)
ALIGNMENT?(*horiz_align,wrap,vert_align, orientation*)

Horiz_align is a number from 1 to 7 specifying the type of horizontal alignment, as shown in the following table. If *horiz_align* is omitted, horizontal alignment does not change.

Horiz_align	Horizontal alignment
1	General
2	Left
3	Center
4	Right
5	Fill
6	Justify
7	Center across selection

Wrap is a logical value corresponding to the Wrap Text check box in the Alignment dialog box. If *wrap* is TRUE, Microsoft Excel selects the check box and wraps text in cells; if FALSE, Microsoft Excel clears the check box and does not wrap text. If *wrap* is omitted, wrapping does not change.

Vert_align is a number from 1 to 3 specifying the vertical alignment of the text. If *vert_align* is omitted, vertical alignment does not change.

Vert_align	Vertical alignment
1	Top
2	Center
3	Bottom

Orientation is a number from 0 to 3 specifying the orientation of the text. If *orientation* is omitted, text orientation does not change.

Orientation	Text orientation
0	Horizontal
1	Vertical
2	Upward
3	Downward

Example

The following macro formula centers text horizontally and vertically with an upward orientation:

```
ALIGNMENT(3,FALSE,2,2)
```

Related Function

Function	Description
FORMAT.TEXT	Formats a worksheet text box or a chart text item

AND

Returns TRUE if all the arguments are TRUE; returns FALSE if one or more arguments is FALSE.

Syntax

AND(*logical1*,*logical2*,...)

Logical1, logical2,... are 1 to 30 conditions you want to test that can be either TRUE or FALSE.

- The arguments should be logical values or arrays or references that contain logical values.

- If an array or reference argument contains text or empty cells, those values are ignored.

- If the specified range contains no logical values, AND returns the #VALUE! error value.

Examples

AND(TRUE,TRUE) equals TRUE

AND(TRUE,FALSE) equals FALSE

AND(2+2=4,2+3=5) equals TRUE

If B1:B3 contains the values TRUE, FALSE, and TRUE, then:

AND(B1:B3) equals FALSE

If B4 contains a number between 1 and 100, then:

AND(1<B4,B4<100) equals TRUE

Suppose you want to display B4 if it contains a number strictly between 1 and 100, and you want to display a message if it is not. If B4 contains 104, then:

IF(AND(1<B4,B4<100),B4,"The value is out of range.") equals "The value is out of range."

If B4 contains 50, then:

```
IF(AND(1<B4,B4<100),B4,"The value is
out of range.") equals 50
```

Related Functions

Function	Description
NOT	Reverses the logic of its argument
OR	Returns TRUE if any argument is TRUE

ANOVA1

Macro Sheets Only

Performs single-factor analysis of variance, which tests the hypothesis that means from several samples are equal. For more information, see "Analyzing Statistical or Engineering Data" in Chapter 1 in Book 2 of the *Microsoft Excel User's Guide*.

If this function is not available, you must install the Analysis ToolPak add-in macro. For more information, see "Managing Add-in Commands and Functions" in Chapter 4 in Book 2 of the *Microsoft Excel User's Guide.*

Syntax

ANOVA1(*inprng,outrng,grouped,labels,alpha*)

Inprng is the input range.

Outrng is the first cell (the upper-left cell) in the output table.

Grouped is a text character that indicates whether the data in the input range is organized by row or column.

- If *grouped* is "C" or omitted, then the data is organized by column.

- If *grouped* is "R", then the data is organized by row.

Labels is a logical value that describes where the labels are located in the input range, as shown in the following table:

Labels	Grouped	Labels are in
TRUE	"C"	First row of the input range.
TRUE	"R"	First column of the input range.
FALSE or omitted	(ignored)	No labels. All cells in the input range are data.

Alpha is the significance level at which to evaluate critical values for the F statistic. If omitted, *alpha* is 0.05.

Related Functions

Function	Description
ANOVA2	Performs two-factor analysis of variance with replication
ANOVA3	Performs two-factor analysis of variance without replication

ANOVA2

Macro Sheets Only

Performs two-factor analysis of variance with replication. For more information, see "Analyzing Statistical or Engineering Data" in Chapter 1 in Book 2 of the *Microsoft Excel User's Guide*.

If this function is not available, you must install the Analysis ToolPak add-in macro. For more information, see "Managing Add-in Commands and Functions" in Chapter 4 in Book 2 of the *Microsoft Excel User's Guide.*

ANOVA2(*inprng,outrng,sample_rows,alpha*)

Inprng is the input range. The input range should contain labels in the first row and column.

Outrng is the first cell (the upper-left cell) in the output table.

Sample_rows is the number of rows in each sample.

Alpha is the significance level at which to evaluate critical values for the F statistic. If omitted, *alpha* is 0.05.

Related Functions

Function	Description
ANOVA1	Performs single-factor analysis of variance
ANOVA3	Performs two-factor analysis of variance without replication

ANOVA3

Macro Sheets Only

Performs two-factor analysis of variance without replication. For more information, see "Analyzing Statistical or Engineering Data" in Chapter 1 in Book 2 of the *Microsoft Excel User's Guide*.

If this function is not available, you must install the Analysis ToolPak add-in macro. For more information, see "Managing Add-in Commands and Functions" in Chapter 4 in Book 2 of the *Microsoft Excel User's Guide*.

Syntax

ANOVA3(***inprng,outrng,****labels,alpha*)

Inprng is the input range.

Outrng is the first cell (the upper-left cell) in the output table.

Labels is a logical value.

- If *labels* is TRUE, then the first row and column of the input range contain labels.

- If *labels* is FALSE or omitted, all cells in *inprng* are considered data. Microsoft Excel will then generate the appropriate data labels for the output table.

Alpha is the significance level at which to evaluate critical values for the F statistic. If omitted, *alpha* is 0.05.

Related Functions

Function	Description
ANOVA1	Performs single-factor analysis of variance
ANOVA2	Performs two-factor analysis of variance with replication

APP.ACTIVATE

Macro Sheets Only

Switches to an application. Use APP.ACTIVATE to switch to another application that is already running or that you have started by using EXEC.

Syntax

APP.ACTIVATE(*title_text,wait_logical*)

Important Microsoft Excel for the Macintosh requires system software version 7.0 or later for this function.

Title_text is the name of an application as displayed in its title bar.

- If *title_text* is omitted, APP.ACTIVATE switches to Microsoft Excel.

- If *title_text* is not a currently running application, APP.ACTIVATE returns the #VALUE! error value and interrupts the macro.

- *Title_text* is not necessarily the name of the application file. Use the text that appears in the title bar of the application, which might include the name of the open document and path information.

- In Microsoft Excel for the Macintosh, *title_text* can also refer to the Process Serial Number (PSN) that is returned by an EXEC function.

Wait_logical is a logical value determining when to switch to the application specified by *title_text*.

- If *wait_logical* is TRUE, Microsoft Excel waits to be switched to before switching to the application specified by *title_text*.

- If *wait_logical* is FALSE or omitted, Microsoft Excel immediately switches to the application specified by *title_text*.

Remarks

If you are running an application using Microsoft Excel macros, and you want to switch to a third application without switching to Microsoft Excel first, use FALSE as the *wait_logical* argument. With FALSE, you can use the application *title_text* without having to switch to Microsoft Excel first.

Examples

In Microsoft Excel for Windows, this macro formula switches to the Control Panel application as soon as you switch to Microsoft Excel:

```
APP.ACTIVATE("CONTROL PANEL",TRUE)
```

The following macro formula switches to Microsoft® Word, which is currently displaying the document MONTHRPT.DOC:

```
APP.ACTIVATE("MICROSOFT WORD -
MONTHRPT.DOC")
```

In Microsoft Excel for the Macintosh, the following macro formula switches to Microsoft Word:

```
APP.ACTIVATE("MICROSOFT WORD")
```

Tip Use an IF statement with APP.ACTIVATE to run an EXEC function if the application you want to switch to is not yet running.

Related Functions

The first five functions following are only for Microsoft Excel for Windows.

Function	Description
APP.MAXIMIZE	Maximizes the Microsoft Excel application window
APP.MINIMIZE	Minimizes the Microsoft Excel application window
APP.MOVE	Moves the Microsoft Excel application window

Function	Description
APP.RESTORE	Restores the Microsoft Excel application window
APP.SIZE	Changes the size of the Microsoft Excel application window
EXEC	Starts another application

APP.MAXIMIZE

Macro Sheets Only

Equivalent to choosing the Maximize command from the Control menu for the application window. Maximizes the Microsoft Excel window. For detailed information about the Maximize command, see online Help.

Syntax

APP.MAXIMIZE( )

Note This function is only for Microsoft Excel for Windows. You can use this function in macros created with Microsoft Excel for the Macintosh, but it will return the #N/A error value.

Related Functions

Function	Description
APP.ACTIVATE	Switches to an application
APP.MINIMIZE	Minimizes the Microsoft Excel application window
APP.MOVE	Moves the Microsoft Excel application window
APP.RESTORE	Restores the Microsoft Excel application window
APP.SIZE	Changes the size of the Microsoft Excel application window

APP.MINIMIZE

Macro Sheets Only

Equivalent to choosing the Minimize command from the Control menu for the application window. Minimizes the Microsoft Excel window. For detailed information about the Minimize command, see online Help.

Syntax

APP.MINIMIZE( )

Note This function is only for Microsoft Excel for Windows. You can use this function in macros created with Microsoft Excel for the Macintosh, but it will return the #N/A error value.

Related Functions

Function	Description
APP.ACTIVATE	Switches to an application
APP.MAXIMIZE	Maximizes the Microsoft Excel application window
APP.MOVE	Moves the Microsoft Excel application window
APP.RESTORE	Restores the Microsoft Excel application window
APP.SIZE	Changes the size of the Microsoft Excel application window

APP.MOVE

Macro Sheets Only

Equivalent to choosing the Move command from the Control menu for the application window. Moves the Microsoft Excel window. In Microsoft Excel for Windows, APP.MOVE returns the #VALUE! error value if the application window is already maximized. For detailed information about the Move command, see online Help.

Syntax

APP.MOVE(x_num,y_num)
APP.MOVE?(x_num,y_num)

Note This function is only for Microsoft Excel for Windows. You can use this function in macros created with Microsoft Excel for the Macintosh, but it will return the #N/A error value.

X_num specifies the horizontal position of the Microsoft Excel window measured in points from the left edge of your screen to the left side of the Microsoft Excel window.

Y_num specifies the vertical position of the Microsoft Excel window measured in points from the top edge of your screen to the top of the Microsoft Excel window.

APP.MOVE?, the dialog-box form of the function, doesn't display a dialog box. Instead, it is equivalent to pressing ALT SPACEBAR, M or to dragging the title bar with the mouse. With APP.MOVE?, you can move the window with the keyboard or mouse. If you specify *x_num* and/or *y_num* in the dialog-box form of the function, the window is moved according to the specified coordinates, and you are left in move mode.

Example

The following macro formula moves the Microsoft Excel window 25 points from the left edge of your screen and 18 points from the top edge of your screen:

```
APP.MOVE(25,18)
```

Related Functions

Function	Description
APP.ACTIVATE	Switches to an application
APP.MAXIMIZE	Maximizes the Microsoft Excel application window
APP.MINIMIZE	Minimizes the Microsoft Excel application window

Function	Description
APP.RESTORE	Restores the Microsoft Excel application window
APP.SIZE	Changes the size of the Microsoft Excel application window

APP.RESTORE

Macro Sheets Only

Equivalent to choosing the Restore command from the Control menu for the application window. Restores the Microsoft Excel window to its previous size and location. For detailed information about the Restore command, see online Help.

Syntax

APP.RESTORE( )

Note This function is only for Microsoft Excel for Windows. You can use this function in macros created with Microsoft Excel for the Macintosh, but it will return the #N/A error value.

Related Functions

Function	Description
APP.ACTIVATE	Switches to an application
APP.MAXIMIZE	Maximizes the Microsoft Excel application window
APP.MINIMIZE	Minimizes the Microsoft Excel application window
APP.MOVE	Moves the Microsoft Excel application window
APP.SIZE	Changes the size of the Microsoft Excel application window

APP.SIZE

Macro Sheets Only

Equivalent to choosing the Size command from the Control menu for the application window. Changes the size of the Microsoft Excel window. For detailed information about the Size command, see online Help.

Syntax

APP.SIZE(x_num, y_num)
APP.SIZE?(x_num, y_num)

Note This function is only for Microsoft Excel for Windows. You can use this function in macros created with Microsoft Excel for the Macintosh, but it will return the #N/A error value.

X_num specifies the width of the Microsoft Excel window in points.

Y_num specifies the height of the Microsoft Excel window in points.

APP.SIZE?, the dialog-box form of the function, doesn't display a dialog box. Instead, it is equivalent to pressing ALT, SPACEBAR, S or to dragging a window border with the mouse. Using APP.SIZE?, you can size the window with the keyboard or mouse. If you specify x_num and/or y_num in the dialog-box form of the function, the window is sized according to the specified coordinates, and you are left in size mode.

Related Functions

Function	Description
APP.ACTIVATE	Switches to an application
APP.MAXIMIZE	Maximizes the Microsoft Excel application window
APP.MINIMIZE	Minimizes the Microsoft Excel application window
APP.MOVE	Moves the Microsoft Excel application window
APP.RESTORE	Restores the Microsoft Excel application window

APP.TITLE

Macro Sheets Only

Changes the title of the Microsoft Excel application workspace to the title you specify. The title appears at the top of the application window and in the Microsoft Windows Task List. Use APP.TITLE to control the application title when you're using Microsoft Excel to create a custom application. This function does not affect Microsoft Excel for the Macintosh.

Syntax

APP.TITLE*(text)*

Text is the title you want to assign to the Microsoft Excel application workspace. If *text* is omitted, it is restored to Microsoft Excel.

Remarks

- The custom application, followed by the individual document title, will appear in the application title bar if the document is maximized.

- APP.TITLE does not affect DDE communications. You will still refer to the application as "Excel".

Example

The following macro formula changes the title of the Microsoft Excel workspace to Monthly Inventory:

```
APP.TITLE("Monthly Inventory")
```

Related Function

Function	Description
WINDOW.TITLE	Changes the title of the active window

APPLY.NAMES

Macro Sheets Only

Equivalent to choosing the Apply Names command from the Formula menu. Replaces definitions with their respective names. If no names are defined in the current selection, APPLY.NAMES returns the #VALUE! error value. Use APPLY.NAMES to replace references and values in formulas with names. For detailed information about the Apply Names command, see online Help.

Syntax

APPLY.NAMES*(name_array,ignore,use_rowcol, omit_col,omit_row,order_num,append_last)*
APPLY.NAMES?*(name_array,ignore,use_rowcol, omit_col,omit_row,order_num,append_last)*

Name_array is the name or names to apply as text elements in an array.

- To give more than one name as the argument, you must use an array. For example:

  ```
  APPLY.NAMES({"DataRange",
  "CriteriaRange"})
  ```

- If the names indicated by the argument *name_array* have already replaced all of the appropriate references or values, the #VALUE! error value is returned.

The next four arguments correspond to check boxes and options in the Apply Names dialog box. Arguments that correspond to check boxes are logical values. If an argument is TRUE, Microsoft Excel selects the check box; if FALSE, Microsoft Excel clears the check box.

Ignore corresponds to the Ignore Relative/Absolute check box.

Use_rowcol corresponds to the Use Row And Column Names check box. If *use_rowcol* is FALSE, the next two arguments are ignored.

Omit_col corresponds to the Omit Column Name If Same Column check box.

Omit_row corresponds to the Omit Row Name If Same Row check box.

Order_num determines which range name is listed first when a cell reference is replaced by a row-oriented and a column-oriented range name, as shown in the following table.

Order_num	Order of range names
1	Row Column
2	Column Row

Append_last determines whether the names most recently defined are also replaced.

- If *append_last* is TRUE, Microsoft Excel replaces the definitions of the names in *name_array* and also replaces the definitions of the last names defined.

- If *append_last* is FALSE or omitted, Microsoft Excel replaces the definitions of the names in *name_array* only.

Example

The following macro formula applies the names SalesOne, SalesTwo, and SalesThree:

```
APPLY.NAMES({"SalesOne","SalesTwo",
"SalesThree"},TRUE,TRUE,FALSE,TRUE,1,FALSE)
```

Related Functions

Function	Description
CREATE.NAMES	Creates names automatically from text labels on a worksheet
DEFINE.NAME	Defines a name on the active worksheet or macro sheet
LIST.NAMES	Lists names and their associated information

APPLY.STYLE

Macro Sheets Only

Equivalent to choosing the Style command from the Format menu, selecting a style, and choosing the OK button. Applies a previously defined style to the current selection. For detailed information about the Style command, see online Help.

Syntax

APPLY.STYLE(*style_text*)
APPLY.STYLE?(*style_text*)

Style_text is the name, as text, of a previously defined style. If *style_text* is not defined, APPLY.STYLE returns the #VALUE! error value and interrupts the macro. If *style_text* is omitted, the Normal style is applied to the selection.

Examples

The following macro formula applies a style named Titles to the current selection:

```
APPLY.STYLE("Titles")
```

To apply a style that exists for a particular cell to another range, use the GET.CELL function, with 40 as the *type_num* argument, to return the name of the style, as shown in the following macro.

	A	B	C
1	Names	Formulas	Comments
2			
3		GetStyle	
4	Style	=GET.CELL(40)	Gets style name
5		=SELECT("NewTitles")	Selects a new range
6		=APPLY.STYLE(Style)	Applies style to selection
7		=RETURN()	

Related Functions

Function	Description
DEFINE.STYLE	Defines a cell style
DELETE.STYLE	Deletes a cell style
MERGE.STYLES	Imports styles from another document into the active document

AREAS

Returns the number of areas in a reference. An area is a range of contiguous cells or a single cell.

Syntax

AREAS(*reference*)

Reference is a reference to a cell or range of cells and can refer to multiple areas. If you want to specify several references as a single argument, then you must include extra sets of parentheses so that Microsoft Excel will not interpret the comma as a field separator. See the second example following.

Tip This function is useful in a macro for testing whether or not a reference is a nonadjacent selection. See the fourth example following.

Examples

AREAS(B2:D4) equals 1

AREAS((B2:D4,E5,F6:I9)) equals 3

If the name Prices refers to the areas B1:D4, B2, and E1:E10, then:

AREAS(Prices) equals 3

The following macro formula branches to an error routine if the current selection is not contiguous:

IF(AREAS(SELECTION())>1,GOTO(Error))

Related Functions

Function	Description
ADDRESS	Returns a reference as text to a single cell in a worksheet
CELL	Returns information about the formatting, location, or contents of a cell
COLUMN	Returns the column number of a reference
COLUMNS	Returns the number of columns in a reference

Function	Description
INDEX	Uses an index to choose a value from a reference or array
ROW	Returns the row number of a reference
ROWS	Returns the number of rows in a reference

ARGUMENT

Macro Sheets Only

Describes the arguments used in a custom function, which is a type of macro, or in a subroutine. A custom function or subroutine must contain one ARGUMENT function for each argument in the macro itself. There are two forms of the ARGUMENT function. In the first form, only *name_text* is required; in the second form, only *reference* is required. Use the first form if you want to store the argument as a name. Use the second form if you want to store the argument in a specific cell or cells.

For more information about custom functions and subroutines, see Chapter 5 and Chapter 7 in Book 2 of the *Microsoft Excel User's Guide*.

Syntax 1

For name storage

ARGUMENT(*name_text,data_type_num*)

Syntax 2

For cell storage

ARGUMENT(*name_text,data_type_num,reference*)

Name_text is the name of the argument or of the cells containing the argument. *Name_text* is required if you omit *reference*.

Data_type_num is a number that determines what type of values Microsoft Excel accepts for the argument. The following table lists the possible data types.

Data_type_num	Type of value
1	Number
2	Text
4	Logical
8	Reference
16	Error
64	Array

- *Data_type_num* can be a sum of the preceding different numbers to allow for more than one possible type of data. For example, if *data_type_num* is 7, which is the sum of 1, 2, and 4, then the value can be a number, text, or logical value.

- *Data_type_num* is an optional argument. If you omit *data_type_num*, it is assumed to be 7.

- If the value that is passed to the function macro is not of the type specified by *data_type_num*, Microsoft Excel first attempts to convert it to the specified type. If the value cannot be converted, the macro returns the #VALUE! error value.

Reference is the cell or cells in which you want to store the argument's value.

- If you specify *reference*, the value that is passed to ARGUMENT is entered as a constant in the specified cell, and *name_text* becomes an optional argument because you can refer to the cell with either *reference* or *name_text*.

- If you omit *reference*, *name_text* is defined on the macro sheet and refers to the value that is passed to ARGUMENT. Once *name_text* is defined, you can use it in formulas. See the first example following.

Remarks

- Custom functions and subroutines can accept from 1 to 29 arguments.

- If a macro contains an ARGUMENT function and you omit the corresponding argument in the function that starts the macro, the macro uses the #N/A error value as the value of the argument.

Examples

The following custom function calculates profit; each argument must be a number.

	A	B	C
1	*Names*	*Formulas*	*Comments*
2			
3		**PROFIT**	Calculates profit
4		**CalculateProfit**	
5		=RESULT(1)	Returns a number
6		=ARGUMENT("UnitsSold",1)	Defines the three
7		=ARGUMENT("UnitCost",1)	arguments
8		=ARGUMENT("UnitPrice",1)	
9	TotalProfit	=UnitsSold*(UnitPrice–UnitCost)	Computes the profit
10		=RETURN(TotalProfit)	Returns the profit

The following lines in a macro ask if you want to open a document. If you do, cell B25 calls a subroutine to make sure the document is available. The entire subroutine is shown, although only the last few lines of the calling macro are shown.

	A	B	C
22	OpenYes	=ALERT("Open another document?",1)	
23		=IF(OpenYes)	If OK, the macro continues
24	DocToOpen	=INPUT("Enter the document to open",2)	
25		=CheckDocument(DocToOpen)	Calls subroutine
26		=END.IF()	
27		=RETURN()	
28			
29			
30		**CheckDocument**	Checks for errors
31		=ARGUMENT("NameOfDoc")	
32		=ERROR(TRUE,ErrorOccurs)	Adds custom ALERT
33		=OPEN(NameOfDoc)	Tries to open document
34		=GOTO(End)	If successful, macro ends
35	ErrorOccurs	=ALERT(""""&NameOfDoc&"""" did not open;	Otherwise, error message
36	End	=RETURN()	

Following is the complete formula in cell B35:

```
=ALERT(""""""&NameOfDoc&"""""" did not open; it
may not be in the current directory or
folder",2)
```

Related Function

Function	Description
RESULT	Specifies the data type a custom function returns

ARRANGE.ALL

Macro Sheets Only

Equivalent to choosing the Arrange command from the Window menu. Rearranges open windows and icons and resizes open windows. Also synchronizes scrolling of windows of the active document. For detailed information about the Arrange command, see online Help.

Syntax

ARRANGE.ALL(*arrange_num,active_doc, sync_horiz,sync_vert*)
ARRANGE.ALL?(*arrange_num,active_doc, sync_horiz,sync_vert*)

Arrange_num is a number from 1 to 6 specifying how to arrange the windows.

Arrange_num	Result
1 or omitted	Tiled (also used to arrange icons)
2	Horizontal
3	Vertical
4	None
5	Horizontally arranges and sizes the windows based on the position of the active cell.
6	Vertically arranges and sizes the windows based on the position of the active cell.

If you want to change whether the windows are synchronized for scrolling but not how they are arranged, make sure *arrange_num* is 4.

Active_doc is a logical value specifying which windows to arrange. If *active_doc* is TRUE, Microsoft Excel arranges only windows on the active document; if FALSE or omitted, all open windows are arranged.

Sync_horiz is a logical value corresponding to the Sync Horizontal check box.

- If *sync_horiz* is TRUE, Microsoft Excel selects the check box and synchronizes horizontal scrolling.

- If *sync_horiz* is FALSE or omitted, Microsoft Excel clears the check box, and windows will not be synchronized when you scroll horizontally.

- This argument is used only when *active_doc* is TRUE.

Sync_vert is a logical value corresponding to the Sync Vertical check box.

- If *sync_vert* is TRUE, Microsoft Excel selects the check box and synchronizes vertical scrolling.

- If *sync_vert* is FALSE or omitted, Microsoft Excel clears the check box, and windows will not be synchronized when you scroll vertically.

- This argument is used only when *active_doc* is TRUE.

Note If arguments are omitted in the dialog box form of this function, the default values are the previous settings, if any; otherwise the default values are as described above.

Remarks

- After arranging windows, the top or leftmost window is active.

- In Microsoft Excel for Windows, if all windows are minimized, ARRANGE.ALL ignores its arguments, if any, and arranges the corresponding icons horizontally along the bottom of the workspace.

Tip You can use synchronized horizontal or vertical scrolling when you need to scroll while viewing macro formulas in one window and corresponding macro values in another window of the same macro sheet.

Related Function

Function	Description
ACTIVATE	Switches to a window

ASIN

Returns the arcsine of a number. The arcsine is the angle whose sine is *number*. The returned angle is given in radians in the range $-\pi/2$ to $\pi/2$.

Syntax

ASIN(*number*)

Number is the sine of the angle you want and must be from -1 to 1.

To express the arcsine in degrees, multiply the result by $180/\text{PI}(\ )$.

Examples

ASIN(-0.5) equals -0.5236 ($-\pi/6$ radians)

ASIN(-0.5)*180/PI() equals 30 (degrees)

Related Functions

Function	Description
ASINH	Returns the inverse hyperbolic sine of a number
PI	Returns the value π
SIN	Returns the sine of the given angle

ASINH

Returns the inverse hyperbolic sine of *number*. The inverse hyperbolic sine is the value whose hyperbolic sine is *number*, so ASINH(SINH(*number*)) equals *number*.

Syntax

ASINH(*number*)

Examples

ASINH(-2.5) equals -1.64723

ASINH(10) equals 2.998223

Related Functions

Function	Description
ACOSH	Returns the inverse hyperbolic cosine of a number
ATANH	Returns the inverse hyperbolic tangent of a number
SINH	Returns the hyperbolic sine of a number

ASSIGN.TO.OBJECT

Macro Sheets Only

Equivalent to choosing the Assign To Object command from the Macro menu. Assigns a macro to be run when an object is clicked with the mouse. For detailed information about the Assign To Object command, see online Help.

Syntax

ASSIGN.TO.OBJECT(*macro_ref*)
ASSIGN.TO.OBJECT?(*macro_ref*)

Macro_ref is the name of, or a reference to, the macro you want to run when the object is clicked. If *macro_ref* is omitted, Microsoft Excel no longer runs the previously specified macro (ASSIGN.TO.OBJECT is turned off).

Remarks

- If an object is not selected, ASSIGN.TO.OBJECT returns the #VALUE! error value and interrupts the macro.

- To change the macro assigned to an object, select the object and use ASSIGN.TO.OBJECT again, using the reference to the new macro as *macro_ref*. The previous macro is replaced with the new macro.

Examples

In Microsoft Excel for Windows, the following macro formula assigns the macro MakeGroup on the macro sheet WORKGRP.XLM to the selected object :

ASSIGN.TO.OBJECT(WORKGRP.XLM!MakeGroup)

In Microsoft Excel for the Macintosh, the following macro formula assigns the macro MakeGroup on the macro sheet GROUPS to the selected object :

```
ASSIGN.TO.OBJECT(GROUPS!MakeGroup)
```

Related Functions

Function	Description
CREATE.OBJECT	Creates an object
RUN	Runs a macro

ASSIGN.TO.TOOL

Macro Sheets Only

Equivalent to choosing the Assign To Tool command from the Macro menu or from the Tools shortcut menu. Assigns a macro to be run when a tool is clicked with the mouse. For detailed information about the Assign To Tool command, see online Help.

Syntax

ASSIGN.TO.TOOL(*bar_id,position,macro_ref*)

Bar_id   specifies the number or name of a toolbar to which you want to assign a macro. For more information about *bar_id*, see ADD.TOOL.

Position   specifies the position of the tool within the toolbar. *Position* starts with 1 at the left side (if horizontal) or at the top (if vertical).

Macro_ref   is the name of, or a reference to, the macro you want to run when the tool is clicked. If *macro_ref* is omitted, Microsoft Excel no longer runs the previously specified macro. After cancelling the macro, if the tool is a built-in tool, Microsoft Excel performs the normal default action when the tool is clicked. If the tool is a custom tool, Microsoft Excel displays the Assign To Tool dialog box when the tool is clicked.

Example

The following macro formula assigns the macro ShiftData to the tool in position 3 on Toolbar5:

```
ASSIGN.TO.TOOL("Toolbar5",3,ShiftData)
```

Related Functions

Function	Description
ADD.TOOL	Adds one or more tools to a toolbar
GET.TOOL	Returns information about a tool or tools on a toolbar

ATAN

Returns the arctangent of a number. The arctangent is the angle whose tangent is *number*. The returned angle is given in radians in the range $-\pi/2$ to $\pi/2$.

Syntax

ATAN(*number*)

Number   is the tangent of the angle you want.

To express the arctangent in degrees, multiply the result by 180/PI( ).

Examples

`ATAN(1)` equals 0.785398 ($\pi/4$ radians)

`ATAN(1)*180/PI()` equals 45 (degrees)

Related Functions

Function	Description
ATAN2	Returns the arctangent from *x*- and *y*-coordinates
ATANH	Returns the inverse hyperbolic tangent of a number
PI	Returns the value π
TAN	Returns the tangent of a number

ATAN2

Returns the arctangent of the specified *x*- and *y*-coordinates. The arctangent is the angle from the *x*-axis to a line containing the origin (0,0) and a point with coordinates (*x_num,y_num*). The angle is given in radians between $-\pi$ and π, excluding $-\pi$.

Syntax

ATAN2(*x_num,y_num*)

X_num   is the *x*-coordinate of the point.

Y_num   is the *y*-coordinate of the point.

If both *x_num* and *y_num* are 0, ATAN2 returns the #DIV/0! error value.

To express the arctangent in degrees, multiply the result by 180/PI( ).

Remarks

- A positive result represents a counterclockwise angle from the *x*-axis; a negative result represents a clockwise angle.

- ATAN2(*a,b*) equals ATAN(*b/a*), except that *a* can equal 0 in ATAN2.

Examples

ATAN2(1,1) equals 0.785398 (π/4 radians)

ATAN2(-1,-1) equals –2.35619 (–3π/4 radians)

ATAN2(-1,-1)*180/PI() equals –135 (degrees)

Related Functions

Function	Description
ATAN	Returns the arctangent of a number
ATANH	Returns the inverse hyperbolic tangent of a number
PI	Returns the value π
TAN	Returns the tangent of a number

ATANH

Returns the inverse hyperbolic tangent of *number*. *Number* must be between –1 and 1 (excluding –1 and 1). The inverse hyperbolic tangent is the value whose hyperbolic tangent is *number*, so ATANH(TANH(*number*)) equals *number*.

Syntax

ATANH(*number*)

Examples

ATANH(0.76159416) equals 1, approximately

ATANH(-0.1) equals –0.10034

Related Functions

Function	Description
ACOSH	Returns the inverse hyperbolic cosine of a number
ASINH	Returns the inverse hyperbolic sine of a number
TANH	Returns the hyperbolic tangent of a number

ATTACH.TEXT

Macro Sheets Only

Equivalent to choosing the Attach Text command from the Chart menu. Attaches text to certain parts of the selected chart. Use ATTACH.TEXT with the FORMULA function to attach text as a title or as a label for an axis, plot area, or data point. For detailed information about the Attach Text command, see online Help.

Syntax

ATTACH.TEXT(*attach_to_num,series_num, point_num*)
ATTACH.TEXT?(*attach_to_num,series_num, point_num*)

Attach_to_num   specifies which item on a chart to attach text to. *Attach_to_num* is different for 2-D and 3-D charts. *Attach_to_num* values for 2-D charts are shown in the following table.

Attach_to_num	Attaches text to
1	Chart title
2	Value (*y*) axis
3	Category (*x*) axis
4	Series and data point
5	Overlay value (*y*) axis
6	Overlay category (*x*) axis

Attach_to_num values for 3-D charts are shown in the following table.

Attach_to_num	Attaches text to
1	Chart title
2	Value (*z*) axis
3	Series (*y*) axis
4	Category (*x*) axis
5	Series and data point

Series_num   specifies the series number if *attach_to_num* specifies a series or data point. If *attach_to_num* specifies a series or data point and *series_num* is omitted, the macro is interrupted.

Point_num   specifies the number of the data point, but only if you specify a series number. *Point_num* is required if *series_num* is specified, unless the chart is an area chart.

Remarks

When you record adding an axis title or a chart title with the Attach Text command from the Chart menu, Microsoft Excel records both an ATTACH.TEXT function to attach the text and a FORMAT.FONT function to make the text bold.

Example

The following macro attaches text to the selected chart.

	A	B	C
1	Names	Formulas	Comments
2			
3		**AddLabels**	Adds labels to a chart
4	X_Label	=INPUT("Enter x-axis label",2)	
5		=ATTACH.TEXT(3)	
6		=FORMULA(X_Label)	Labels the x-axis
7	Y_Label	=INPUT("Enter y-axis label",2)	
8		=ATTACH.TEXT(2)	
9		=FORMULA(Y_Label)	Labels the y-axis
10	TitleText	=INPUT("Enter a title",2)	
11		=ATTACH.TEXT(1)	
12		=FORMULA(TitleText)	Gives the chart a title
13		=RETURN()	

AVEDEV

Returns the average of the absolute deviations of data points from their mean. AVEDEV is a measure of the variability in a data set.

Syntax

AVEDEV(*number1*,*number2*,...)

Number1, number2,...   are 1 to 30 arguments for which you want the average of the absolute deviations. You can also use a single array or a reference to an array instead of arguments separated by commas.

Remarks

- The arguments should be numbers, or names, arrays, or references that contain numbers.

- If an array or reference argument contains text, logical values, or empty cells, those values are ignored; however, cells with the value zero are included.

- The equation for average deviation is:

$$\frac{1}{n}\sum|x - \bar{x}|$$

AVEDEV is influenced by the unit of measurement in the input data.

Example

AVEDEV(4,5,6,7,5,4,3) equals 1.020408

Related Functions

Function	Description
DEVSQ	Returns the sum of squares of deviations
STDEV	Estimates standard deviation based on a sample
STDEVP	Calculates standard deviation based on the entire population
VAR	Estimates variance based on a sample
VARP	Calculates variance based on the entire population

AVERAGE

Returns the average (arithmetic mean) of the arguments.

Syntax

AVERAGE(*number1,number2,…*)

Number1, number2,…   are 1 to 30 numeric arguments for which you want the average.

Remarks

- The arguments should be numbers, or names, arrays, or references that contain numbers.

- If an array or reference argument contains text, logical values, or empty cells, those values are ignored; however, cells with the value zero are included.

Tip   When averaging cells, keep in mind the difference between empty cells and those containing the value zero, especially if you have cleared the Zero Values check box in the Display dialog box. Empty cells are not counted, but zero values are. To see the Display dialog box, choose the Display command from the Options menu.

Examples

If A1:A5 is named Scores and contains the numbers 10, 7, 9, 27, and 2, then:

AVERAGE(A1:A5) equals 11

AVERAGE(Scores) equals 11

AVERAGE(A1:A5,5) equals 10

AVERAGE(A1:A5) equals
SUM(A1:A5)/COUNT(A1:A5) equals 11

If C1:C3 is named OtherScores and contains the numbers 4, 18, and 7, then:

AVERAGE(Scores,OtherScores) equals 10.5

Also see the sixth example for REFTEXT.

Related Functions

Function	Description
DAVERAGE	Returns the average of selected database entries
GEOMEAN	Returns the geometric mean
HARMEAN	Returns the harmonic mean
MEDIAN	Returns the median of the given numbers
MODE	Returns the most common value in a data set
TRIMMEAN	Returns the mean of the interior of a data set

AXES

Macro Sheets Only

Equivalent to choosing the Axes command from the Chart menu. Controls whether the axes on a chart are visible. There are two syntax forms of this function. Syntax 1 is for 2-D charts; syntax 2 is for 3-D charts. For detailed information about the Axes command, see online Help.

Syntax 1

For 2-D charts

AXES(*x_main,y_main,x_over,y_over*)
AXES?(*x_main,y_main,x_over,y_over*)

Syntax 2

For 3-D charts

AXES(*x_main,y_main,z_main*)
AXES?(*x_main,y_main,z_main*)

Arguments are logical values corresponding to the check boxes in the Chart Axes dialog box.

- If an argument is TRUE, Microsoft Excel selects the check box and displays the corresponding axis.

- If an argument is FALSE, Microsoft Excel clears the check box and hides the corresponding axis.

- If an argument is omitted, the display of that axis is unchanged.

X_main   corresponds to the category (*x*) axis on the main chart.

Y_main   corresponds to the value (*y*) axis on the main chart.

Z_main   corresponds to the value (*z*) axis on the 3-D main chart.

X_over   corresponds to the category (*x*) axis on the overlay chart.

Y_over   corresponds to the value (*y*) axis on the overlay chart.

If a 2-D chart has no overlay, only the first two arguments are used.

Examples

The following macro formula displays the category (*x*) axis and value (*y*) axis on the selected 2-D chart:

AXES(TRUE,TRUE,FALSE,FALSE)

The following macro formula hides the category (*x*) axis on the selected 3-D chart:

AXES(FALSE,TRUE,TRUE)

Related Function

Function	Description
GRIDLINES	Controls whether chart gridlines are visible

BASE

Returns, as text, the equivalent of a base-10 number in another base.

If this function is not available, you must install the Add-in Functions add-in macro. For more information, see "Managing Add-in Commands and Functions" in Chapter 4 in Book 2 of the *Microsoft Excel User's Guide*.

Syntax

BASE(***number***,*target_base,precision*)

Number   is a base-10 number.

Target_base   is the base you want to convert the number into. It must be an integer between 2 and 36. If *target_base* is omitted, BASE returns a base-16 number.

Precision   specifies the number of digits you want after the decimal in the returned base. It must be a positive integer. If *precision* is omitted, it is assumed to be 0, and BASE returns an integer.

Examples

BASE(256,8) equals 400

BASE(299.875,7,5) equals 605.6061

Related Functions

Function	Description
BIN2DEC	Converts a binary number to decimal
DEC2BIN	Converts a decimal number to binary
DEC2HEX	Converts a decimal number to hexadecimal
HEX2DEC	Converts a hexadecimal number to decimal
RADIANS	Converts degrees to radians

BEEP

Macro Sheets Only

Sounds a tone. Use BEEP to signal a message, a dialog box, or the end of a macro, or whenever you need to get the user's attention.

Syntax

BEEP(*tone_num*)

Tone_num is a number from 1 to 4 specifying the tone to be played.

- On most computers, all numbers produce the same sound—the sound that you hear when an error occurs or when you click outside some dialog boxes.

- If *tone_num* is omitted, it is assumed to be 1.

Remarks

- With a Macintosh, you can control the volume of the tone by using the Control Panel desk accessory.

- With Microsoft® Windows™ version 3.0 or later, you can turn off the tone by using the Control Panel.

Related Functions

Function	Description
ALERT	Displays a dialog box and a message
MESSAGE	Displays a message in the status bar

BESSELI

Returns the modified Bessel function $I_n(x)$, which is equivalent to the Bessel function J_n evaluated for purely imaginary arguments.

If this function is not available, you must install the Analysis ToolPak add-in macro. For more information, see "Managing Add-in Commands and Functions" in Chapter 4 in Book 2 of the *Microsoft Excel User's Guide*.

Syntax

BESSELI *(x,n)*

X is the value at which to evaluate the function.

N is the order of the Bessel function. If *n* is not an integer, it is truncated.

Remarks

- If *x* is non-numeric, BESSELI returns the #VALUE! error value.

- If *n* is non-numeric, BESSELI returns the #VALUE! error value.

- If $n < 0$, BESSELI returns the #NUM! error value.

- The *n*-th order modified Bessel function of the variable *x* is:

$$I_n(x) = (i)^{-n} J_n(ix)$$

Example

BESSELI(1.5,1) equals 0.981666

Related Functions

Function	Description
BESSELJ	Returns the Bessel function $J_n(x)$
BESSELK	Returns the modified Bessel function $K_n(x)$
BESSELY	Returns the Bessel function $Y_n(x)$

BESSELJ

Returns the Bessel function $J_n(x)$.

If this function is not available, you must install the Analysis ToolPak add-in macro. For more information, see "Managing Add-in Commands and Functions" in Chapter 4 in Book 2 of the *Microsoft Excel User's Guide*.

Syntax

BESSELJ *(x,n)*

X is the value at which to evaluate the function.

N is the order of the Bessel function. If *n* is not an integer, it is truncated.

Remarks

- If *x* is non-numeric, BESSELJ returns the #VALUE! error value.

- If *n* is non-numeric, BESSELJ returns the #VALUE! error value.

- If *n* < 0, BESSELJ returns the #NUM! error value.

- The *n*-th order Bessel function of the variable *x* is:

$$J_n(x) = \sum_{k=0}^{\infty} \frac{(-1)^k}{k!\,\Gamma(n+k+1)} \left(\frac{x}{2}\right)^{n+2k}$$

where:

$$\Gamma(n+k+1) = \int_0^{\infty} e^{-x} x^{n+k} dx$$

is the Gamma function.

Example

BESSELJ(1.9,2) equals 0.329926

Related Functions

Function	Description
BESSELI	Returns the modified Bessel function $I_n(x)$
BESSELK	Returns the modified Bessel function $K_n(x)$
BESSELY	Returns the Bessel function $Y_n(x)$

BESSELK

Returns the modified Bessel function $K_n(x)$, which is equivalent to the Bessel functions J_n and Y_n evaluated for purely imaginary arguments.

If this function is not available, you must install the Analysis ToolPak add-in macro. For more information, see "Managing Add-in Commands and Functions" in Chapter 4 in Book 2 of the *Microsoft Excel User's Guide*.

Syntax

BESSELK*(x,n)*

X is the value at which to evaluate the function.

N is the order of the function. If *n* is not an integer, it is truncated.

Remarks

- If *x* is non-numeric, BESSELK returns the #VALUE! error value.

- If *n* is non-numeric, BESSELK returns the #VALUE! error value.

- If *n* < 0, BESSELK returns the #NUM! error value.

- The *n*-th order modified Bessel function of the variable *x* is:

$$K_n(x) = \frac{\pi}{2} i^{n+1} [J_n(ix) + iY_n(ix)]$$

where J_n and Y_n are the *J* and *Y* Bessel functions, respectively.

Example

BESSELK(1.5,1) equals 0.277388

Related Functions

Function	Description
BESSELJ	Returns the Bessel function $J_n(x)$
BESSELY	Returns the Bessel function $Y_n(x)$
BESSELI	Returns the modified Bessel function $I_n(x)$

BESSELY

Returns the Bessel function $Y_n(x)$, which is also called the Weber function or the Neumann function.

If this function is not available, you must install the Analysis ToolPak add-in macro. For more information, see "Managing Add-in Commands and Functions" in Chapter 4 in Book 2 of the *Microsoft Excel User's Guide.*

Syntax

BESSELY*(x,n)*

X is the value at which to evaluate the function.

N is the order of the function. If *n* is not an integer, it is truncated.

Remarks

- If *x* is non-numeric, BESSELY returns the #VALUE! error value.

- If *n* is non-numeric, BESSELY returns the #VALUE! error value.

- If *n* < 0, BESSELY returns the #NUM! error value.

- The *n*-th order Bessel function of the variable *x* is:

$$Y_n(x) = \lim_{v \to n} \frac{J_v(x) \cos(v\pi) - J_{-v}(x)}{\sin(v\pi)}$$

where:

$$J_{-n}(x) = (-1)^n J_n(x)$$

Example

BESSELY(2.5,1) equals 0.145918

Related Functions

Function	Description
BESSELJ	Returns the Bessel function $J_n(x)$
BESSELK	Returns the modified Bessel function $K_n(x)$
BESSELI	Returns the modified Bessel function $I_n(x)$

BETADIST

Returns the cumulative beta probability density function. The cumulative beta probability density function is commonly used to study variation in the percentage of something across samples, such as the fraction of the day people spend watching television.

Syntax

BETADIST*(x,alpha,beta,A,B)*

X is the value at which to evaluate the function over the interval $A \le x \le B$.

Alpha is a parameter to the distribution.

Beta is a parameter to the distribution.

A is an optional lower bound to the interval of *x*.

B is an optional upper bound to the interval of *x*.

Remarks

- If any argument is non-numeric, BETADIST returns the #VALUE! error value.

- If *alpha* ≤ 0 or *beta* ≤ 0, BETADIST returns the #NUM! error value.

- If $x < A$, $x > B$, or $A = B$, BETADIST returns the #NUM! error value.

- If you omit values for *A* and *B*, BETADIST uses the standard cumulative beta distribution, so that $A = 0$ and $B = 1$.

Example

BETADIST(2,8,10,1,3) equals 0.685471

Related Function

Function	Description
BETAINV	Returns the inverse of the cumulative beta probability density function

BETAINV

Returns the inverse of the cumulative beta probability density function. That is, if *probability* = BETADIST(*x*,…), then BETAINV(*probability*,…) = *x*. The cumulative beta distribution can be used in project planning to model probable completion times given an expected completion time and variability. For example, a project might take three days to complete, plus or minus a day, and you want to know the probability that it will take less than three days.

Syntax

BETAINV(*probability,alpha,beta,A,B*)

Probability is a probability associated with the beta distribution.

Alpha is a parameter to the distribution.

Beta is a parameter to the distribution.

A is an optional lower bound to the interval of *x*.

B is an optional upper bound to the interval of *x*.

Remarks

- If any argument is non-numeric, BETAINV returns the #VALUE! error value.

- If *alpha* ≤ 0 or *beta* ≤ 0, BETAINV returns the #NUM! error value.

- If *probability* ≤ 0 or *probability* > 1, BETAINV returns the #NUM! error value.

- If $x < A$, $x > B$, or $A = B$, BETAINV returns the #NUM! error value.

- If you omit values for *A* and *B*, BETAINV uses the standard cumulative beta distribution, so that $A = 0$ and $B = 1$.

- BETAINV uses an iterative technique for calculating the function. Given a probability value, BETAINV iterates until the result is accurate to within $\pm 3 \times 10^{-7}$. If BETAINV does not converge after 100 iterations, the function returns the #N/A error value.

Example

BETAINV(0.685471,8,10,1,3) equals 2

Related Function

Function	Description
BETADIST	Returns the cumulative beta probability density function

BIN2DEC

Converts a binary number to decimal.

If this function is not available, you must install the Analysis ToolPak add-in macro. For more information, see "Managing Add-in Commands and Functions" in Chapter 4 in Book 2 of the *Microsoft Excel User's Guide*.

Syntax

BIN2DEC(*number*)

Number is the binary number you want to convert. *Number* may not contain more than 10 characters (10 bits). The most significant bit of *number* is the sign bit. The remaining 9 bits are magnitude bits. Negative numbers are represented using two's-complement notation.

Remarks

- If *number* is not a valid binary number, or if *number* contains more than 10 characters (10 bits), BIN2DEC returns the #NUM! error value.

Examples

BIN2DEC(1100100) equals 100

BIN2DEC(1111111111) equals –1

Related Functions

Function	Description
DEC2BIN	Converts a decimal number to binary
HEX2BIN	Converts a hexadecimal number to binary
OCT2BIN	Converts an octal number to binary

BIN2HEX

Converts a binary number to hexadecimal.

If this function is not available, you must install the Analysis ToolPak add-in macro. For more information, see "Managing Add-in Commands and Functions" in Chapter 4 in Book 2 of the *Microsoft Excel User's Guide*.

Syntax

BIN2HEX(*number,places*)

Number is the binary number you want to convert. *Number* may not contain more than 10 characters (10 bits). The most significant bit of *number* is the sign bit. The remaining 9 bits are magnitude bits. Negative numbers are represented using two's-complement notation.

Places is the number of characters to use. If *places* is omitted, BIN2HEX uses the minimum number of characters necessary. *Places* is useful for padding the return value with leading 0s (zeros).

Remarks

- If *number* is not a valid binary number, or if *number* contains more than 10 characters (10 bits), BIN2HEX returns the #NUM! error value.

- If *number* is negative, BIN2HEX ignores *places* and returns a 10-character hexadecimal number.

- If BIN2HEX requires more than *places* characters, it returns the #NUM! error value.

- If *places* is not an integer, it is truncated.

- If *places* is non-numeric, BIN2HEX returns the #VALUE! error value.

- If *places* is negative, BIN2HEX returns the #NUM! error value.

Examples

BIN2HEX(11111011,4) equals 00FB

BIN2HEX(1110) equals E

BIN2HEX(1111111111) equals FFFFFFFFFF

Related Functions

Function	Description
DEC2BIN	Converts a decimal number to binary
HEX2BIN	Converts a hexadecimal number to binary
OCT2BIN	Converts an octal number to binary

BIN2OCT

Converts a binary number to octal.

If this function is not available, you must install the Analysis ToolPak add-in macro. For more information, see "Managing Add-in Commands and Functions" in Chapter 4 in Book 2 of the *Microsoft Excel User's Guide*.

Syntax

BIN2OCT(*number,places*)

Number is the binary number you want to convert. *Number* may not contain more than 10 characters (10 bits). The most significant bit of *number* is the sign bit. The remaining 9 bits are magnitude bits. Negative numbers are represented using two's-complement notation.

Places is the number of characters to use. If *places* is omitted, BIN2OCT uses the minimum number of characters necessary. *Places* is useful for padding the return value with leading 0s (zeros).

Remarks

- If *number* is not a valid binary number, or if *number* contains more than 10 characters (10 bits), BIN2OCT returns the #NUM! error value.

- If *number* is negative, BIN2OCT ignores *places* and returns a 10-character octal number.

- If BIN2OCT requires more than *places* characters, it returns the #NUM! error value.

- If *places* is not an integer, it is truncated.

- If *places* is non-numeric, BIN2OCT returns the #VALUE! error value.

- If *places* is negative, BIN2OCT returns the #NUM! error value.

Examples

BIN2OCT(1001,3) equals 011

BIN2OCT(01100100) equals 144

BIN2OCT(1111111111) equals 7777777777

Related Functions

Function	Description
DEC2BIN	Converts a decimal number to binary
HEX2BIN	Converts a hexadecimal number to binary
OCT2BIN	Converts an octal number to binary

BINOMDIST

Returns the individual term binomial distribution probability. Use BINOMDIST in problems with a fixed number of tests or trials, when the outcomes of any trial are only success or failure, when trials are independent, and when the probability of success is constant throughout the experiment. For example, BINOMDIST can calculate the probability that two of the next three babies born are male.

Syntax

BINOMDIST(*number_s,trials,probability_s, cumulative*)

Number_s is the number of successes in *trials*.

Trials is the number of independent trials.

Probability_s is the probability of success on each trial.

Cumulative is a logical value that determines the form of the function. If *cumulative* is TRUE, then BINOMDIST returns the cumulative distribution function, which is the probability that there are at most *number_s* successes; if FALSE, it returns the probability mass function, which is the probability that there are *number_s* successes.

Remarks

- *Number_s* and *trials* are truncated to integers.

- If *number_s, trials,* or *probability_s* is non-numeric, BINOMDIST returns the #VALUE! error value.

- If *number_s* < 0 or *number_s* > *trials*, BINOMDIST returns the #NUM! error value.

- If *probability_s* < 0 or *probability_s* > 1, BINOMDIST returns the #NUM! error value.

- The binomial probability mass function is:

$$b(x; n, p) = \binom{n}{x} p^x (1-p)^{n-x}$$

where:

$$\binom{n}{x}$$

is COMBIN(*n,x*).

The binomial cumulative distribution function is:

$$B(x; n, p) = \sum_{y=0}^{x} b(y; n, p)$$

Example

The flip of a coin can only result in heads or tails. The probability of the first flip being heads is 0.5, and the probability of exactly 6 of 10 flips being heads is:

`BINOMDIST(6,10,0.5,FALSE)` equals 0.205078

Related Functions

Function	Description
COMBIN	Returns the number of combinations for a given number of objects
CRITBINOM	Returns the smallest value for which the cumulative binomial distribution is less than or equal to a criterion value
FACT	Returns the factorial of a number
HYPGEOMDIST	Returns the hypergeometric distribution
NEGBINOMDIST	Returns the negative binomial distribution

Function	Description
PERMUT	Returns the number of permutations for a given number of objects
PROB	Returns the probability that values in a range are between two limits

BORDER

Macro Sheets Only

Equivalent to choosing the Border command from the Format menu. Adds a border to the selected cell, range of cells, or object. For detailed information about the Border command, see online Help.

Syntax

BORDER*(outline,left,right,top,bottom,shade, outline_color,left_color,right_color,top_color, bottom_color)*
BORDER?*(outline,left,right,top,bottom, shade,outline_color,left_color,right_color,top_color, bottom_color)*

Outline, left, right, top, and *bottom* are numbers from 0 to 7 corresponding to the line styles in the Border dialog box, as shown in the following table.

Argument	Line type
0	No border
1	Thin line
2	Medium line
3	Dashed line
4	Dotted line
5	Thick line
6	Double line
7	Hairline

Note For compatibility with earlier versions of Microsoft Excel, TRUE and FALSE values for the above arguments create a thin border or no border, respectively.

Shade corresponds to the Shade check box in the Border dialog box.

Outline_color, left_color, right_color, top_color, and *bottom_color* are numbers from 1 to 16 corresponding to the Color box in the Border dialog box. Zero corresponds to automatic color.

Example

The following macro formula puts a dashed line around the top, bottom, left, and right of each cell in the selection, using color 5 for the left and right and color 10 for the top and bottom.

```
BORDER(0,3,3,3,3,,,5,5,10,10)
```

Related Function

Function	Description
PATTERNS	Changes the appearance of the selected object

BREAK

Macro Sheets Only

Interrupts a FOR–NEXT, a FOR.CELL–NEXT, or a WHILE–NEXT loop. If BREAK is encountered within a loop, that loop is terminated and the macro proceeds to the statement following the NEXT statement at the end of the current loop. For information about looping, see Chapter 7 in Book 2 of the *Microsoft Excel User's Guide.*

Syntax

BREAK( )

Example

Use BREAK to test for conditions not anticipated by the FOR or WHILE statement. For example, the following macro uses BREAK nested in an IF statement to exit a WHILE–NEXT loop when a certain value is encountered.

	A	B	C
1	Names	Formulas	Comments
2			
3		ExitLoop	
4		=SET.VALUE(Counter,1)	Initializes Counter to 1
5		=WHILE(Counter<10)	Begins WHILE–NEXT loop
6	Counter	=Counter+INT(RAND()*5)	Increments Counter
7		=ProcessCounter(Counter)	Runs subroutine
8		=IF(Counter=8,BREAK())	If Counter = 8, break
9		=NEXT()	Ends WHILE–NEXT loop
10		=RETURN()	Ends the macro

Related Functions

Function	Description
FOR	Starts a FOR–NEXT loop
FOR.CELL	Starts a FOR.CELL–NEXT loop
NEXT	Ends a FOR–NEXT, FOR.CELL–NEXT, or WHILE–NEXT loop
WHILE	Starts a WHILE–NEXT loop

BRING.TO.FRONT

Macro Sheets Only

Equivalent to choosing the Bring To Front command from the Format menu. Puts the selected object or objects on top of all other objects. For example, if some worksheet objects are covering part of an embedded chart, you can select the chart and use BRING.TO.FRONT to display the chart on top of the worksheet objects. For detailed information about the Bring To Front command, see online Help.

Syntax

BRING.TO.FRONT( )

If the selection is not an object or a group of objects, BRING.TO.FRONT returns the #VALUE! error value.

Related Function

Function	Description
SEND.TO.BACK	Sends selected objects behind other objects

CALCULATE.DOCUMENT

Macro Sheets Only

Equivalent to choosing the Calculation command from the Options menu and then choosing the Calc Document button. Calculates only the active document.

Syntax

CALCULATE.DOCUMENT( )

Remarks

If the active document is a chart, CALCULATE.DOCUMENT returns the #VALUE! error value.

Related Functions

Function	Description
CALCULATE.NOW	Calculates all open documents immediately
CALCULATION	Controls calculation settings

CALCULATE.NOW

Macro Sheets Only

Equivalent to choosing the Calculation command from the Options menu and then choosing the Calc Now button. Calculates all open documents. Use CALCULATE.NOW to calculate all open documents when calculation is set to manual. For detailed information about the Calculation command, see online Help.

Syntax

CALCULATE.NOW( )

Related Functions

Function	Description
CALCULATE.DOCUMENT	Calculates the active document only
CALCULATION	Controls calculation settings

CALCULATION

Macro Sheets Only

Equivalent to choosing the Calculation command from the Options menu. Use CALCULATION to control when and how formulas in open documents are calculated. For detailed information about the Calculation command, see online Help.

Syntax

CALCULATION(*type_num,iter,max_num, max_change,update,precision,date_1904,calc_save, save_values,alt_exp,alt_form*)
CALCULATION?(*type_num,iter,max_num, max_change,update,precision,date_1904,calc_save, save_values,alt_exp,alt_form*)

Arguments correspond to check boxes and options in the Calculation dialog box. Arguments that correspond to check boxes are logical values. If an argument is TRUE, Microsoft Excel selects the check box; if FALSE, Microsoft Excel clears the check box.

Type_num   is a number from 1 to 3 indicating the type of calculation.

Type_num	Type of calculation
1	Automatic
2	Automatic except tables
3	Manual

Iter corresponds to the Iteration check box. The default is FALSE.

Max_num is the maximum number of iterations. The default is 100.

Max_change is the maximum change of each iteration. The default is 0.001.

Update corresponds to the Update Remote References check box. The default is TRUE.

Precision corresponds to the Precision As Displayed check box. The default is FALSE.

Date_1904 corresponds to the 1904 Date System check box. The default is FALSE in Microsoft Excel for Windows and TRUE in Microsoft Excel for the Macintosh.

Calc_save corresponds to the Recalculate Before Save check box. If *calc_save* is FALSE, the document is not recalculated before saving when in manual calculation mode. The default is TRUE.

Save_values corresponds to the Save External Link Values check box. The default is TRUE.

Alt_exp corresponds to the Alternate Expression Evaluation check box.

- If *alt_exp* is TRUE, Microsoft Excel uses a set of rules compatible with that of Lotus 1-2-3 when calculating formulas. Text is treated as 0; TRUE and FALSE are treated as 1 and 0; and certain characters in database criteria ranges are interpreted the same way Lotus 1-2-3 interprets them. For more information, see "Controlling Calculation" in Chapter 5 in Book 1 of the *Microsoft Excel User's Guide*.

- If *alt_exp* is FALSE or omitted, Microsoft Excel calculates normally.

Alt_form corresponds to the Alternate Formula Entry check box.

- This argument is available only in Microsoft Excel for Windows.

- If *alt_form* is TRUE, Microsoft Excel accepts formulas entered in Lotus 1-2-3 style. For more information, see "Entering a Formula" in Chapter 5 in Book 1 of the *Microsoft Excel User's Guide*.

- If *alt_form* is FALSE or omitted, Microsoft Excel only accepts formulas entered in Microsoft Excel style.

Note Microsoft Excel for Windows and Microsoft Excel for the Macintosh use different date systems as their default. For more information, see NOW.

Remarks

Use GET.DOCUMENT to return the current calculation settings for your document. For more information, see GET.DOCUMENT.

Related Functions

Function	Description
CALCULATE.DOCUMENT	Calculates the active document only
CALCULATE.NOW	Calculates all open documents immediately

CALL

Calls a procedure in a dynamic link library (DLL) or code resource. There are two syntax forms of this function. Use syntax 1 only with a previously registered code resource. Use syntax 2a or 2b, which use arguments from the REGISTER function, to simultaneously register and call a code resource.

For more information about DLLs and code resources, see the Appendix, "Using the CALL and REGISTER Functions."

Important This function is provided for advanced users only. If you use the CALL function incorrectly, you could cause errors that will require you to restart your computer.

Syntax 1

Used with REGISTER

CALL(*register_id,argument1,...*)

Syntax 2a

Used alone (in Microsoft Excel for Windows)

CALL(*module_text,procedure,type_text, argument1,...*)

Syntax 2b

Used alone (in Microsoft Excel for the Macintosh)

CALL(*file_text,resource,type_text, argument1,...*)

Register_id   is the value returned by a previously executed REGISTER or REGISTER.ID function.

Argument1,...   are the arguments to be passed to the procedure.

Module_text or *file_text*   is quoted text specifying the name of the dynamic link library (DLL) that contains the procedure (in Microsoft Excel for Windows) or the name of the file that contains the code resource (in Microsoft Excel for the Macintosh).

Procedure or *resource*   is text specifying the name of the function in the DLL (in Microsoft Excel for Windows) or the name of the code resource (in Microsoft Excel for the Macintosh). In Microsoft Excel for Windows, you can also use the ordinal value of the function from the EXPORTS statement in the module-definition file (.DEF). In Microsoft Excel for the Macintosh, you can also use the resource ID number. The ordinal value or resource ID number should not be in the form of text.

Type_text   is text specifying the data type of the return value and the data types of all arguments to the DLL or code resource. The first letter of *type_text* specifies the return value. The codes you use for *type_text* are described in detail in the Appendix, "Using the CALL and REGISTER Functions." For stand-alone DLLs or code resources (XLLs), you can omit this argument.

Example   Syntax 1

In Microsoft Excel for Windows, the following macro formula registers the GetTickCount function from Microsoft Windows. GetTickCount returns the number of milliseconds that have elapsed since Microsoft Windows was started.

```
REGISTER("User","GetTickCount","J")
```

Assuming that this REGISTER function is in cell A5, after your macro registers GetTickCount, you can use the CALL function to return the number of milliseconds that have elapsed:

```
CALL(A5)
```

Example   Syntax 2a

On a worksheet, you can use the following CALL formula (syntax 2a) to call the GetTickCount function:

```
CALL("User","GetTickCount","J!")
```

The ! in the *type_text* argument forces Microsoft Excel to recalculate the CALL function every time the worksheet recalculates. This updates the elapsed time whenever the worksheet recalculates.

Tip   You can use optional arguments to the REGISTER function to assign a custom name to a function. This name will appear in the Paste Function dialog box, and you can call the function by using its custom name in a formula. For more information, see REGISTER.

Related Functions

Function	Description
REGISTER	Registers a code resource
REGISTER.ID	Returns the register ID of the resource
UNREGISTER	Removes a registered code resource from memory

CALLER

Macro Sheets Only

Returns information about the cell, range of cells, command on a menu, tool on a toolbar, or object that called the macro that is currently running. Use CALLER in a subroutine or custom function whose behavior depends on the location, size, name, or other attribute of the caller.

Syntax

CALLER( )

Remarks

- If the custom function is entered in a single cell, CALLER returns the reference of that cell.

- If the custom function was part of an array formula entered in a range of cells, CALLER returns the reference of the range.

- If CALLER appears in a macro called by an Auto_Open, Auto_Close, Auto_Activate, or Auto_Deactivate macro, it returns the name of the calling sheet.

- If CALLER appears in a macro called by a command on a menu, it returns a horizontal array of three elements including the command's position number, the menu number, and the menu bar number.

- If CALLER appears in a macro called by an assigned-to-object macro, it returns the object identifier.

- If CALLER appears in a macro called by a tool on a toolbar, it returns a horizontal array containing the position number and the toolbar name.

- If CALLER appears in a macro called by an ON.DOUBLECLICK or ON.ENTRY function, CALLER returns the name of the chart object identifier or cell reference, if applicable, to which the ON.DOUBLECLICK or ON.ENTRY macro applies.

- If CALLER appears in a macro that was run manually, or for any reason not described above, it returns the #REF! error value.

Examples

If the custom function MACROS!VALUEONE is entered in cell B3 on a worksheet named SALES, the nested CALLER function returns the following values.

Nested function	Returns
COLUMN(CALLER())	2
COLUMNS(CALLER())	1
GET.CELL(1,CALLER())	SALES!$B$3
ROW(CALLER())	3
ROWS(CALLER())	1

If the same custom function was entered into an array in cells B2:C3, the following values would be returned.

Nested function	Returns
COLUMN(CALLER())	2
COLUMNS(CALLER())	2
ROW(CALLER())	2
ROWS(CALLER())	2

Related Functions

Function	Description
COLUMN	Returns the column number of a reference
COLUMNS	Returns the number of columns in a reference
GET.BAR	Returns the name or position number of menu bars, menus, and commands
GET.CELL	Returns information about the specified cell
ROW	Returns the row number of a reference
ROWS	Returns the number of rows in a reference

CANCEL.COPY

Macro Sheets Only

Equivalent to pressing ESC in Microsoft Excel for Windows or ESC or COMMAND+PERIOD in Microsoft Excel for the Macintosh to cancel the marquee after you copy or cut a selection.

Syntax

CANCEL.COPY*(render_logical)*

Render_logical   is a logical value that, if TRUE, places the contents of the Excel Clipboard on the Clipboard or, if FALSE or omitted, does not place them on the Clipboard. *Render_logical* is available only in Microsoft Excel for the Macintosh.

CANCEL.KEY

Macro Sheets Only

Disables macro interruption, or specifies a macro to run when a macro is interrupted. Use CANCEL.KEY to control what happens when a macro is interrupted.

Syntax

CANCEL.KEY*(enable,macro_ref)*

Enable   specifies whether the macro can be interrupted by pressing ESC in Microsoft Excel for Windows or ESC or COMMAND+PERIOD in Microsoft Excel for the Macintosh.

If *enable* is	Then
FALSE	Pressing ESC or COMMAND+PERIOD does not interrupt a macro
TRUE and *macro_ref* is omitted	Pressing ESC or COMMAND+PERIOD interrupts a macro
TRUE and *macro_ref* is specified	*Macro_ref* runs when ESC or COMMAND+PERIOD is pressed

Macro_ref   is a reference to a macro, as a cell reference or a name, that runs when *enable* is TRUE and ESC or COMMAND+PERIOD is pressed.

Remarks

CANCEL.KEY affects only the macro that is currently running. Once the macro is stopped by a RETURN or HALT function, ESC or COMMAND+PERIOD is reactivated.

Examples

The following macro formula prevents the macro from being interrupted by pressing ESC or COMMAND+PERIOD:

```
CANCEL.KEY(FALSE)
```

The following macro formula reactivates ESC or COMMAND+PERIOD to cancel macro execution:

```
CANCEL.KEY(TRUE)
```

The following line in a macro named CheckCancel runs CheckCancel when ESC or COMMAND+PERIOD is pressed:

```
CANCEL.KEY(TRUE,CheckCancel)
```

Related Functions

Function	Description
ERROR	Specifies an action to take if an error occurs while a macro is running
ON.KEY	Runs a macro when a specified key is pressed
ON.TIME	Runs a macro at a specified time

CEILING

Returns *number* rounded up to the nearest multiple of *significance*. For example, if you want to avoid using pennies in your prices and your product is priced at $4.42, use the formula =CEILING(4.42,0.05) to round prices up to the nearest nickel.

Syntax

CEILING(*number,significance*)

Number   is the value you want to round.

Significance   is the multiple to which you want to round.

Remarks

- If either argument is non-numeric, CEILING returns the #VALUE! error value.

- Regardless of the sign of *number*, a value is rounded up when adjusted away from zero. If *number* is an exact multiple of *significance*, no rounding occurs.

- If *number* and *significance* have different signs, CEILING returns the #NUM! error value.

Examples

CEILING(2.5,1) equals 3

CEILING(-2.5,-2) equals -4

CEILING(-2.5,2) equals #NUM!

CEILING(1.5,0.1) equals 1.5

CEILING(0.234,0.01) equals 0.24

Related Functions

Function	Description
EVEN	Rounds a number up to the nearest even integer
FLOOR	Rounds a number down, toward zero
INT	Rounds a number down to the nearest integer
ODD	Rounds a number up to the nearest odd integer
ROUND	Rounds a number to a specified number of digits
TRUNC	Truncates a number to an integer

CELL

Returns information about the formatting, location, or contents of the upper-left cell in a reference.

Syntax

CELL(*info_type,reference*)

Info_type   is a text value that specifies what type of cell information you want. The following list shows the possible values of *info_type* and the corresponding results.

Info_type	Returns
"address"	Reference of the first cell in *reference,* as text.
"col"	Column number of the cell in *reference.*
"color"	1 if the cell is formatted in color for negative values; otherwise returns 0.
"contents"	Contents of the upper-left cell in *reference.*
"filename"	Filename (including full path) of the file that contains *reference,* as text. Returns empty text ("") if the worksheet that contains *reference* has not yet been saved.
"format"	Text value corresponding to the number format of the cell. The text values for the various formats are shown in the following table. Returns "–" at the end of the text value if the cell is formatted in color for negative values. Returns "()" at the end of the text value if the cell is formatted with parentheses for positive or all values.
"parentheses"	1 if the cell is formatted with parentheses for positive or all values; otherwise returns 0.
"prefix"	Text value corresponding to the "label prefix" of the cell. Returns single quotation mark (') if the cell contains left-aligned text, double quotation mark (") if the cell contains right-aligned text, caret (^) if the cell contains centered text, backslash (\) if the cell contains fill-aligned text, and empty text ("") if the cell contains anything else.

Info_type	Returns
"protect"	0 if the cell is not locked, and 1 if the cell is locked
"row"	Row number of the cell in *reference*.
"type"	Text value corresponding to the type of data in the cell. Returns "b" for blank if the cell is empty, "l" for label if the cell contains a text constant, and "v" for value if the cell contains anything else.
"width"	Column width of the cell rounded off to an integer. Each unit of column width is equal to the width of one character in the currently selected font size.

Reference   is the cell that you want information about.

- If *reference* is omitted, it is assumed to be the active cell.

- If *reference* is a nonadjacent selection, CELL returns the #VALUE! error value.

The following list describes the text values CELL returns when *info_type* is "format" and *reference* is a cell formatted with a built-in number format.

If the Microsoft Excel format is	CELL returns
General	"G"
0	"F0"
#,##0	",0"
0.00	"F2"
#,##0.00	",2"
$#,##0_);($#,##0)	"C0'
$#,##0_);[Red]($#,##0)	"C0–"
$#,##0.00_);($#,##0.00)	"C2"
$#,##0.00_);[Red]($#,##0.00)	"C2 "
0%	"P0"
0.00%	"P2"
0.00E+00	"S2"
# ?/? or # ??/??	"G"
m/d/yy or m/d/yy h:mm or mm/dd/yy	"D4"

If the Microsoft Excel format is	CELL returns
d-mmm-yy or dd-mmm-yy	"D1"
d-mmm or dd-mmm	"D2"
mmm-yy	"D3"
mm/dd	"D5"
h:mm AM/PM	"D7"
h:mm:ss AM/PM	"D6"
h:mm	"D9"
h:mm:ss	"D8"

If the *info_type* argument in the CELL formula is "format", and if the cell is formatted later with a custom format, then you must recalculate the worksheet to update the CELL formula. For more information about formats, see Chapter 7 in Book 1 of the *Microsoft Excel User's Guide*.

Remarks

The CELL function is provided for compatibility with other spreadsheet programs. If you need to use cell information in a macro, GET.CELL provides a broader set of attributes.

Examples

CELL("row",A20) equals 20

If B12 has the format "d-mmm", then:

CELL("format",B12) equals "D2"

If the active cell contains TOTAL, then:

CELL("contents") equals "TOTAL"

Related Function

Function	Description
GET.CELL	Returns information about the specified cell

CELL.PROTECTION

Macro Sheets Only

Equivalent to choosing the Cell Protection command from the Format menu. Allows you to control cell protection and display. For detailed information about the Cell Protection command, see online Help.

Arguments are logical values corresponding to check boxes in the Cell Protection dialog box. If an argument is TRUE, Microsoft Excel selects the check box; if FALSE, Microsoft Excel clears the check box. If an argument is omitted and the setting has been previously changed from the defaults, the setting is not changed.

Syntax

CELL.PROTECTION(*locked,hidden*)
CELL.PROTECTION?(*locked,hidden*)

Locked   corresponds to the Locked check box. The default is TRUE.

Hidden   corresponds to the Hidden check box. The default is FALSE.

Remarks

Options selected in the Cell Protection dialog box or with the CELL.PROTECTION function are activated only when the Protect Document command is chosen from the Options menu or the PROTECT.DOCUMENT function is used to select protection.

Examples

The following macro formula locks the selected cells when the Protect Document command is chosen from the Options menu:

```
CELL.PROTECTION(TRUE)
```

The following macro formula unlocks and hides the selected cells when the Protect Document command is chosen:

```
CELL.PROTECTION(FALSE,TRUE)
```

Related Functions

Function	Description
PROTECT.DOCUMENT	Controls protection for the active document
SAVE.AS	Saves a document and allows you to specify the name, file type, password, backup file, and location of the document

CHANGE.LINK

Macro Sheets Only

Equivalent to choosing the Change button in the Links dialog box, which appears when you choose the Links command from the File menu. Changes a link from one supporting document to another. For more information about the Links command, see online Help.

Syntax

CHANGE.LINK(*old_text,new_text,type_of_link*)
CHANGE.LINK?(*old_text,new_text,type_of_link*)

Old_text   is the path of the link from the active dependent document you want to change.

New_text   is the path of the link you want to change to.

Type_of_link   is the number 1 or 2 specifying what type of link you want to change.

Type_of_link	Link document type
1 or omitted	Microsoft Excel link
2	DDE link

Remarks

The document whose links you want to change must be active when this function is calculated.

Examples

In Microsoft Excel for Windows, the following macro formula changes the link on the active document from SALESET.XLS in the current directory to SALESWE.XLS in the EXCEL directory:

```
CHANGE.LINK("SALESET.XLS",
"C:\EXCEL\SALESWE.XLS")
```

In Microsoft Excel for the Macintosh, the following macro formula changes the link on the active document from SALES EAST in the current folder to SALES WEST in the HARD DRIVE:EXCEL folder:

```
CHANGE.LINK("SALES EAST","HARD
DRIVE:EXCEL:SALES WEST")
```

In Microsoft Excel for Windows, the following macro formula changes the DDE link on the active document from Winword|'C:\DOC1.DOC'!DDE_LINK1 to DOC2.DOC:

```
CHANGE.LINK
("Winword|'C:\DOC1.DOC'!DDE_LINK1",
"Winword|'C:\DOC2.DOC'!DDE_LINK1",2)
```

Related Functions

Function	Description
GET.LINK.INFO	Returns information about a link
OPEN.LINKS	Opens specified supporting documents
SET.UPDATE.STATUS	Controls the update status of a link
UPDATE.LINK	Updates a link to another document

CHAR

Returns the character corresponding to the code *number*. Use CHAR to translate code numbers you might get from files on other types of computers into characters.

Syntax

CHAR(*number*)

Number   is a number between 1 and 255 specifying which character you want. The character is from the character set used by your computer.

Operating environment	Character set
Macintosh	Macintosh character set
Windows	ANSI

Examples

```
CHAR(65)  equals "A"
CHAR(33)  equals "!"
```

Related Functions

Function	Description
CODE	Returns a numeric code for the first character in a text string

CHART.WIZARD

Macro Sheets Only

Equivalent to choosing the ChartWizard tool on the standard or chart toolbar. Formats a chart. It is generally easier to use the macro recorder to enter this function on your macro sheet. For detailed information about the ChartWizard tool, see online Help.

Syntax

CHART.WIZARD*(long,**ref,**gallery_num,type_num, plot_by,categories,ser_titles,legend,title,x_title, y_title,z_title)*
CHART.WIZARD?*(long,ref,gallery_num, type_num,plot_by,categories,ser_titles,legend, title,x_title,y_title,z_title)*

Long is a logical value that determines which type of ChartWizard tool CHART.WIZARD is equivalent to.

- If *long* is TRUE or omitted, CHART.WIZARD is equivalent to using the five-step ChartWizard tool.

- If *long* is FALSE, CHART.WIZARD is equivalent to using the two-step ChartWizard tool, and *gallery_num, type_num, legend*, and the last four arguments are ignored.

Ref is a reference to the range of cells on the active worksheet that contains the source data for the chart, or the object identifier of the chart if it has already been created.

Gallery_num is a number from 1 to 14 specifying the type of chart you want to create.

Gallery_num	Chart
1	Area
2	Bar
3	Column
4	Line
5	Pie
6	Radar
7	XY (scatter)
8	Combination
9	3-D area
10	3-D bar
11	3-D column
12	3-D line
13	3-D pie
14	3-D surface

Type_num is a number identifying a formatting option. The formatting options are shown in the dialog box of the Gallery command that corresponds to the type of chart you're creating. The first formatting option in any gallery is 1. For a complete list of galleries, see "Changing the Chart Type or Format" in Chapter 12 in Book 1 of the *Microsoft Excel User's Guide*.

Plot_by is the number 1 or 2 and specifies whether the data for each data series is in rows or columns. 1 specifies rows; 2 specifies columns. If *plot_by* is omitted, Microsoft Excel uses the appropriate value for the chart you're creating.

Categories is the number 1 or 2 and specifies whether the first row or column contains a list of x-axis labels, or data for the first data series. 1 specifies x-axis labels; 2 specifies the first data series. If *categories* is omitted, Microsoft Excel uses the appropriate value for the chart you're creating.

Ser_titles is the number 1 or 2 and specifies whether the first column or row contains series titles, or data for the first data point in each series. 1 specifies series titles; 2 specifies the first data point. If *ser_titles* is omitted, Microsoft Excel uses the appropriate value for the chart you're creating.

Legend is the number 1 or 2 and specifies whether to include a legend. 1 specifies a legend; 2 specifies no legend. If *legend* is omitted, Microsoft Excel does not include a legend.

For the following arguments, if an argument is omitted or is empty text (""), no title is specified.

Title is text that you want to use as a chart title.

X_title is text that you want to use as an x-axis title.

Y_title is text that you want to use as a y-axis title.

Z_title is text that you want to use as a z-axis title.

Remarks

If you are using the macro recorder, Microsoft Excel records a CREATE.OBJECT function when the chart is created and a CHART.WIZARD function when the chart is formatted.

Related Functions

Function	Description
CREATE.OBJECT	Creates an object
FORMAT.MAIN	Formats a main chart
FORMAT.OVERLAY	Formats an overlay chart

CHECK.COMMAND

Macro Sheets Only

Adds or removes a check mark to or from a command name on a menu. A check mark beside a command indicates that the command has been chosen.

Syntax

CHECK.COMMAND(*bar_num,menu, command,check*)

Bar_num is the menu bar containing the command. *Bar_num* can be the ID number of a built-in or custom menu bar.

Menu is the menu containing the command. *Menu* can be either the name of a menu as text or the number of a menu. Menus are numbered starting with 1 from the left of the screen.

Command is the command you want to check. *Command* can be the name of the command as text or the number of the command; the first command on a menu is in position 1.

Check is a logical value corresponding to the check mark. If *check* is TRUE, Microsoft Excel adds a check mark to the command; if FALSE, Microsoft Excel removes the check mark.

Remarks

The check mark doesn't affect execution of the command. Microsoft Excel automatically adds and deletes check marks to some commands, such as the name of the active document in the Window menu. If you have assigned a check mark to a built-in command that Microsoft Excel automatically changes in response to the user's actions, the check mark will be added or removed as appropriate, and any check marks you have added or deleted with CHECK.COMMAND will be ignored.

Example

The following macro formula adds a check mark to the Sales command on the Weekly menu on a custom menu bar created by the ADD.BAR function in a cell named Reports:

```
CHECK.COMMAND(Reports,"Weekly","Sales",
TRUE)
```

Related Functions

Function	Description
ADD.COMMAND	Adds a command to a menu
DELETE.COMMAND	Deletes a command from a menu
ENABLE.COMMAND	Enables or disables a menu or custom command
RENAME.COMMAND	Changes the name of a command or menu

CHIDIST

Returns the one-tailed probability of the chi-squared (χ^2) distribution. The χ^2 distribution is associated with a χ^2 test. Use the χ^2 test to compare observed and expected values. For example, a genetic experiment might hypothesize that the next generation of plants will exhibit a certain set of colors. By comparing the observed results with the expected ones, you can decide if your original hypothesis is valid.

Syntax

CHIDIST*(x,degrees_freedom)*

X is the value at which you want to evaluate the distribution.

Degrees_freedom is the number of degrees of freedom.

Remarks

- If either argument is non-numeric, CHIDIST returns the #VALUE! error value.

- If *x* is negative, CHIDIST returns the #NUM! error value.

- If *degrees_freedom* is not an integer, it is truncated.

- If *degrees_freedom* < 1 or *degrees_freedom* ≥ 10^{10}, CHIDIST returns the #NUM! error value.

Example

CHIDIST(18.307,10) equals 0.050001

Related Functions

Function	Description
CHIINV	Returns the inverse of the χ^2 distribution
CHITEST	Returns the test for independence

CHIINV

Returns the inverse of the chi-squared (χ^2) distribution. If *probability* = CHIDIST(*x,...*), then CHIINV(*probability,...*) = *x*. Use the χ^2 distribution to compare observed results with expected ones to decide if your original hypothesis is valid.

Syntax

CHIINV*(probability,degrees_freedom)*

Probability is a probability associated with the χ^2 distribution.

Degrees_freedom is the number of degrees of freedom.

Remarks

- If either argument is non-numeric, CHIINV returns the #VALUE! error value.

- If *probability* < 0 or *probability* > 1, CHIINV returns the #NUM! error value.

- If *degrees_freedom* is not an integer, it is truncated.

- If *degrees_freedom* < 1 or *degrees_freedom* ≥ 10^{10}, CHIINV returns the #NUM! error value.

CHIINV uses an iterative technique for calculating the function. Given a probability value, CHIINV iterates until the result is accurate to within $\pm 3 \times 10^{-7}$. If CHIINV does not converge after 100 iterations, the function returns the #N/A error value.

Example

CHIINV(0.05,10) equals 18.30703

Related Functions

Function	Description
CHIDIST	Returns the one-tailed probability of the χ^2 distribution
CHITEST	Returns the test for independence

CHITEST

Returns the test for independence. CHITEST returns the value from the chi-squared (χ^2) distribution for the statistic and the appropriate degrees of freedom. You can use χ^2 tests to determine if hypothesized results are verified by an experiment.

Syntax

CHITEST*(actual_range,expected_range)*

Actual_range is the range of data that contains observations to test against expected values.

Expected_range is the range of data that contains the ratio of the product of row totals and column totals to the grand total.

Remarks

- If *actual_range* and *expected_range* have a different number of data points, CHITEST returns the #N/A error value.

- If either argument contains a single row or column, CHITEST returns the #NUM! error value.

- The χ^2 test first calculates a χ^2 statistic and then sums the differences of actual values from the expected values.

The χ^2 statistic is:

$$\chi^2 = \sum_{i=1}^{r} \sum_{j=1}^{c} \frac{\left(A_{ij} - E_{ij}\right)^2}{E_{ij}}$$

where:

A_{ij} = actual frequency in the *i-th* row, *j-th* column

E_{ij} = expected frequency in the *i-th* row, *j-th* column

r = number or rows

c = number of columns

CHITEST returns the probability for a χ^2 statistic and degrees of freedom, *df,* where $df = (r - 1)(c - 1)$.

Example

	A	B	C
1	Actual		
2		Men	Women
3	Agree	58	35
4	Neutral	11	25
5	Disagree	10	23
6			
7	Expected		
8		Men	Women
9	Agree	45.35	47.65
10	Neutral	17.56	18.44
11	Disagree	16.09	16.91

The χ^2 statistic for the data above is 16.16957 with 2 degrees of freedom.

`CHITEST(B3:C5,B9:C11)` equals 0.000308

Related Functions

Function	Description
CHIDIST	Returns the one-tailed probability of the χ^2 distribution
CHIINV	Returns the inverse of the χ^2 distribution

CHOOSE

Uses *index_num* to return a value from the list of value arguments. Use CHOOSE to select one of up to 29 values based on the index number. For example, if *value1* through *value7* are the days of the week, CHOOSE returns one of the days when a number between 1 and 7 is used as *index_num*.

Syntax

CHOOSE(*index_num,value1,*value2,...)

Index_num   specifies which value argument is selected. *Index_num* must be a number between 1 and 29, or a formula or reference to a cell containing a number between 1 and 29.

- If *index_num* is 1, CHOOSE returns *value1*; if it is 2, CHOOSE returns *value2*; and so on.

- If *index_num* is less than 1 or greater than the number of the last value in the list, CHOOSE returns the #VALUE! error value.

- If *index_num* is a fraction, it is truncated to the lowest integer before being used.

Value1, value2,...   are 1 to 29 value arguments from which CHOOSE selects a value or an action to perform based on *index_num*. The arguments can be numbers, cell references, defined names, formulas, macro functions, or text. For information about using value arguments, see "Converting Data Types" in the first section, "About Functions."

Remarks

- If you are using CHOOSE in a macro, the *value* arguments can be GOTO functions or action-taking functions. For example, the following formulas are allowed in a macro, where Level is a name referring to a value or a cell containing a value between 1 and 3:

```
CHOOSE(Level,GOTO(Begin),GOTO(Intermed),
GOTO(Adv))
```

```
CHOOSE(Level,ACTIVATE.NEXT(),
ACTIVATE.PREV())
```

- If *index_num* is an array, every *value* is evaluated when CHOOSE is executed. If some of those *value* arguments are action-taking functions, all the actions are taken. For example, the following formula opens both a new worksheet and a new chart:

```
CHOOSE({1,2},NEW(1),NEW(2))
```

- The *value* arguments to CHOOSE can be range references as well as single values. For example, the formula:

```
SUM(CHOOSE(2,A1:A10,B1:B10,C1:C10))
```

evaluates to:

```
SUM(B1:B10)
```

which then returns a value based on the values in the range B1:B10.

The CHOOSE function is evaluated first, returning the reference B1:B10. The SUM function is then evaluated using B1:B10, the result of the CHOOSE function, as its argument.

Examples

```
CHOOSE(2,"1st","2nd","3rd","Finished")
```
equals "2nd"

```
SUM(A1:CHOOSE(3,A10,A20,A30))
```
equals SUM(A1:A30)

If A10 contains 4, then:

```
CHOOSE(A10,"Nails","Screws","Nuts",
"Bolts")
```
equals "Bolts"

If A10–3 equals 3, then:

```
CHOOSE(A10-3,"1st","2nd","3rd",
"Finished")
```
equals "3rd"

If SalesOld is a name defined to refer to the value 10,000, then:

```
CHOOSE(2,SalesNew,SalesOld,
SalesBudget)
```
equals 10,000

Related Function

Function	Description
INDEX	Uses an index to choose a value from a reference or an array

CLEAN

Removes all nonprintable characters from *text*. Use CLEAN on text imported from other applications which contains characters that may not print with your operating system. For example, you can use CLEAN to remove some low-level computer code that is frequently at the beginning and end of data files and cannot be printed.

Syntax

CLEAN*(text)*

Text   is any worksheet information from which you want to remove nonprintable characters.

Example

Since CHAR(7) returns a nonprintable character:

```
CLEAN(CHAR(7)&"text"&CHAR(7))
```
equals "text"

Related Functions

Function	Description
CHAR	Returns the character specified by the code number
TRIM	Removes spaces from text

CLEAR

Macro Sheets Only

Equivalent to choosing the Clear command from the Edit menu. Clears formulas, formats, notes, or all of these from the active worksheet or macro sheet. Clears formulas, formats, or chart items from the active chart. For detailed information about the Clear command, see online Help.

Syntax

CLEAR(*type_num*)
CLEAR?(*type_num*)

Type_num   is a number from 1 to 4 specifying what to clear. Only values 1, 2, and 3 are valid if the selected item is a chart.

On a worksheet or macro sheet, or if an entire chart is selected, the following occurs.

Type_num	Clears
1	All
2	Formats (if a chart, clears the chart format or clears pictures)
3	Formulas (if a chart, clears all data series)
4	Notes (including sound notes; this does not apply to charts)

On a chart, if a single point or an entire data series is selected, the following occurs.

Type_num	Clears
1	Selected series
2	Format in the selected point or series

If *type_num* is omitted, the default values are set as shown in the following table.

Active document	Type_num
Worksheet	3
Macro sheet	3
Chart (with no selection)	1
Chart (with item selected)	Deletes the selected item

Example

The following macro formula clears cell contents from the selected range of cells in a worksheet or macro sheet without affecting formats or notes:

```
CLEAR(3)
```

Related Function

Function	Description
EDIT.DELETE	Removes cells from a sheet

CLOSE

Macro Sheets Only

Closes the active window. In Microsoft Excel for Windows, CLOSE is equivalent to choosing the Close command from the Document Control menu. In Microsoft Excel for the Macintosh, CLOSE is equivalent to clicking the close box.

Syntax

CLOSE(*save_logical*)

Save_logical   is a logical value that specifies whether to save the file before closing the window.

Save_logical	Result
TRUE	Saves the file
FALSE	Does not save the file
Omitted	If you've made changes to the file, displays a dialog box asking if you want to save the file

Remarks

- If you close a workbook that contains an unbound sheet, Microsoft Excel saves the changes if *save_logical* is TRUE, but does not close the window.

- Users of Microsoft Excel versions earlier than 3.0 should note that if the macro sheet containing the function is the active sheet, CLOSE now closes the macro sheet.

- If you make any changes to the contents of a workbook, such as which documents are included, their order, whether or not they are bound, and so on, then that information will be saved regardless of the *save_logical* value.

Note   When you use the CLOSE function, Microsoft Excel does not run any Auto_Close macros before closing the document.

Example

The following macro closes all windows, except the main window in the active document. If only one window is open in the document, the macro takes no action.

	A	B	C
1	*Names*	*Formulas*	*Comments*
2			
3		**CloseExtraWindows**	Closes all extra windows
4	Windows	=GET.DOCUMENT(13)	Number of open windows
5		=IF(Windows>1)	
6		=FOR("Counter",1,Windows–1)	Loops for all windows but one
7		=CLOSE()	
8		=NEXT()	
9		=END.IF()	
10		=RETURN()	

Related Functions

Function	Description
CLOSE.ALL	Closes all unprotected windows
FILE.CLOSE	Closes the active document
SAVE	Saves the active document

CLOSE.ALL

Macro Sheets Only

Equivalent to choosing the Close All command from the File menu. Closes all protected and unprotected windows and all hidden windows. If unsaved changes have been made to the document in one or more windows, a message is displayed asking if you want to save the document. For detailed information about the Close All command, see online Help.

Syntax

CLOSE.ALL( )

Related Functions

Function	Description
CLOSE	Closes the active window
FILE.CLOSE	Closes the active document
QUIT	Ends a Microsoft Excel session
SAVE	Saves the active document

CODE

Returns a numeric code for the first character in a text string. The returned code corresponds to the character set used by your computer.

Syntax

CODE(*text*)

Operating environment	Character set
Macintosh	Macintosh character set
Windows	ANSI

Text   is the text for which you want the code of the first character.

Examples

CODE("A") equals 65

CODE("Alphabet") equals 65

The following macro returns the numeric code for each character in a string of text and places the codes in successive cells in the same column.

	A	B	C
1	*Names*	*Formulas*	*Comments*
2			
3		**CharacterCodes**	Returns codes for text
4	TextString	=INPUT("Enter your text:",2)	
5		=FOR("Counter",1,LEN(TextString))	Iterates for each character
6	CharCode	=CODE(MID(TextString,Counter,1))	Code of current character
7		=FORMULA(CharCode)	Places code in active cell
8		=SELECT(OFFSET(ACTIVE.CELL(),1,0))	Continues with next cell
9		=NEXT()	
10		=RETURN()	

Also see the example for FREAD.

Related Function

Function	Description
CHAR	Returns the character specified by the code number

COLOR.PALETTE

Macro Sheets Only

Equivalent to choosing a file from the Copy Colors From box in the Color Palette dialog box, which appears when you choose the Color Palette command from the Options menu. Copies a color palette from an open document to the active document. Use COLOR.PALETTE to share color palettes between documents. For detailed information about the Color Palette command, see online Help.

Syntax

COLOR.PALETTE(*file_text*)
COLOR.PALETTE?(*file_text*)

File_text   is the name of a document, as a text string, that you want to copy a color palette from. The document specified by *file_text* must be open, or COLOR.PALETTE returns the #VALUE! error value and interrupts the macro. If *file_text* is empty text (""), then COLOR.PALETTE sets colors to the default values.

Examples

In Microsoft Excel for Windows, the following macro formula copies the color palette from a document named MASTER.XLS to the active document:

```
COLOR.PALETTE("MASTER.XLS")
```

In Microsoft Excel for the Macintosh, the following macro formula copies the color palette from a document named MASTER to the active document:

```
COLOR.PALETTE("MASTER")
```

Related Function

Function	Description
EDIT.COLOR	Defines a color on the color palette

COLUMN

Returns the column number of the given reference.

Syntax

COLUMN(*reference*)

Reference   is the cell or range of cells for which you want the column number.

- If *reference* is omitted, it is assumed to be the reference of the cell in which the COLUMN function appears.

- If *reference* is a range of cells and if COLUMN is entered as a horizontal array, COLUMN returns the column numbers of *reference* as a horizontal array.

- *Reference* cannot refer to multiple areas.

Examples

COLUMN(A3) equals 1

When entered as an array in any three horizontally contiguous cells:

COLUMN(A3:C5) equals {1,2,3}

If COLUMN is entered in C5, then:

`COLUMN()` equals `COLUMN(C5)` equals 3

Related Functions

Function	Description
COLUMNS	Returns the number of columns in a reference
ROW	Returns the row number of a reference

COLUMN.WIDTH

Macro Sheets Only

Equivalent to choosing the Column Width command from the Format menu. Changes the width of the columns in the specified reference. For detailed information about the Column Width command, see online Help.

Syntax

COLUMN.WIDTH(*width_num,reference,standard, type_num,standard_num*)
COLUMN.WIDTH?(*width_num,reference, standard,type_num,standard_num*)

Width_num   specifies how wide you want the columns to be in units of one character of the font corresponding to the Normal cell style. *Width_num* is ignored if *standard* is TRUE or if *type_num* is provided.

Reference   specifies the columns for which you want to change the width.

- If *reference* is specified, it must be either an external reference to the active worksheet, such as !$A:$C or !Database, or an R1C1-style reference in the form of text, such as "C1:C3", "C[–4]:C[–2]", or "Database".

- If *reference* is a relative R1C1-style reference in the form of text, it is assumed to be relative to the active cell.

- If *reference* is omitted, it is assumed to be the current selection.

Standard   is a logical value corresponding to the Use Standard Width check box in the Column Width dialog box.

- If *standard* is TRUE, Microsoft Excel sets the column width to the currently defined standard (default) width and ignores *width_num*.

- If *standard* is FALSE or omitted, Microsoft Excel sets the width according to *width_num* or *type_num*.

Type_num   is a number from 1 to 3 corresponding to the Hide, Unhide, or Best Fit button, respectively, in the Column Width dialog box.

Type_num	Action taken
1	Hides the column selection by setting the column width to 0
2	Unhides the column selection by setting the column width to the value set before the selection was hidden
3	Sets the column selection to a best-fit width, which varies from column to column depending on the length of the longest data string in each column

Standard_num   specifies how wide the standard width is, and is measured in points. If *standard_num* is omitted, the standard width setting remains unchanged.

Remarks

- Changing the value of *standard_num* changes the width of all columns except those that have been set to a custom value.

- If any of the argument settings conflict, such as when *standard* is TRUE and *type_num* is 3, Microsoft Excel uses the *type_num* argument and ignores any arguments that conflict with *type_num*. See the following third example.

- If you are recording a macro while using a mouse and you change column widths by dragging the column border, Microsoft Excel records the references of the columns using R1C1-style references in the form of text.

Examples

If the range C1:E50 is selected, the following macro formula changes the width of columns C through E to 15:

```
COLUMN.WIDTH(15)
```

Each of the following macro formulas changes the width of columns C and D to the best fit. The first formula uses A1-style references; the second uses R1C1-style references.

```
COLUMN.WIDTH(,!$C:$D,,3)
COLUMN.WIDTH(,"C3:C4",TRUE,3)
```

The following macro formula hides the selected columns:

```
COLUMN.WIDTH(,,,1)
```

Related Function

Function	Description
ROW.HEIGHT	Changes the heights of rows

COLUMNS

Returns the number of columns in an array or reference.

Syntax

COLUMNS(*array*)

Array   is an array or array formula, or a reference to a range of cells for which you want the number of columns.

Examples

```
COLUMNS(A1:C4)  equals 3
```

```
COLUMNS({1,2,3;4,5,6})  equals 3
```

The following macro formula returns the number of columns in a contiguous selection:

```
COLUMNS(SELECTION())
```

If the selection is not contiguous, the following macro formula returns the number of columns in a particular area (specified by AreaNum) of the selection. An "area" is a contiguous region within a nonadjacent selection, so a nonadjacent selection consists of multiple areas.

```
COLUMNS(INDEX(SELECTION(),,,AreaNum))
```

Related Functions

Function	Description
COLUMN	Returns the column number of a reference
ROWS	Returns the number of rows in a reference

COMBIN

Returns the number of ways that *number_chosen* objects can be selected from *number* objects, without regard for order. Use COMBIN to determine the total possible number of groups for a given number of objects.

Syntax

COMBIN(*number,number_chosen*)

Number   is the number of objects.

Number_chosen   is the number of objects in each combination.

Remarks

- Numeric arguments are truncated to integers.

- If either argument is non-numeric, COMBIN returns the #NAME? error value.

- If *number* < 0, *number_chosen* < 0, or *number* < *number_chosen,* COMBIN returns the #NUM! error value.

- A combination is any set or subset of objects, regardless of their internal order. Combinations are distinct from permutations, for which the internal order is significant.

- The number of combinations is as follows, where *number* = n and *number – chosen* = k:

$$\binom{n}{k} = \frac{P_{k,n}}{k!} = \frac{n!}{k!(n-k)!}$$

where:

Example

Suppose you want to form a two-person team from eight candidates and you want to know how many possible teams can be formed. COMBIN(8,2) equals 28 teams.

Related Functions

Function	Description
BINOMDIST	Returns the individual term binomial distribution
CRITBINOM	Returns the smallest value for which the cumulative binomial distribution is less than or equal to a criterion value
FACT	Returns the factorial of a number
HYPGEOMDIST	Returns the hypergeometric distribution
NEGBINOMDIST	Returns the negative binomial distribution
PERMUT	Returns the number of permutations for a given number of objects

COMBINATION

Macro Sheets Only

Equivalent to choosing the Combination command from the Gallery menu that is available when a chart is the active document. Changes the format of the active chart to the combination format you select from the gallery. For detailed information about the Combination command, see online Help.

Syntax

COMBINATION(*type_num*)
COMBINATION?(*type_num*)

Type_num   is a number corresponding to the chart number in the Combination dialog box.

Example

The following macro formula formats both the main chart and overlay chart as line charts:

```
COMBINATION(3)
```

Related Functions

Function	Description
FORMAT.MAIN	Formats a main chart
FORMAT.OVERLAY	Formats an overlay chart

COMPLEX

Converts real and imaginary coefficients into a complex number of the form $x + yi$ or $x + yj$.

If this function is not available, you must install the Analysis ToolPak add-in macro. For more information, see "Managing Add-in Commands and Functions" in Chapter 4 in Book 2 of the *Microsoft Excel User's Guide.*

Syntax

COMPLEX(*real_num,i_num,suffix*)

Real_num is the real coefficient of the complex number.

I_num is the imaginary coefficient of the complex number.

Suffix is the suffix for the imaginary component of the complex number. If omitted, *suffix* is assumed to be "i".

Note All complex number functions accept "i" and "j" for *suffix*, but neither "I" nor "J". Using uppercase results in the #NUM! error value. All functions that accept two or more complex numbers require that all suffixes match.

Remarks

■ If *real_num* is non-numeric, COMPLEX returns the #VALUE! error value.

■ If *i_num* is non-numeric, COMPLEX returns the #VALUE! error value.

■ If *suffix* is not text, COMPLEX returns the #VALUE! error value.

■ If *suffix* is neither "i" nor "j", COMPLEX returns the #VALUE! error value.

Examples

COMPLEX(3,4) equals 3 + 4i

COMPLEX(3,4,"j") equals 3 + 4j

COMPLEX(0,1) equals i

COMPLEX(1,0) equals 1

Related Functions

Related functions include other complex number functions such as IMABS, IMAGINARY, IMREAL, and so on.

CONFIDENCE

Returns the confidence interval for a population mean. The confidence interval is a range on either side of a sample mean. For example, if you order a product through the mail, you can determine, with a particular level of confidence, the earliest and latest the product should arrive.

Syntax

CONFIDENCE*(alpha,standard_dev,size)*

Alpha is the significance level used to compute the confidence level. The confidence level equals $100(1 - alpha)\%$, or in other words, an *alpha* of 0.05 indicates a 95% confidence level.

Standard_dev is the population standard deviation for the data range, and is assumed to be known.

Size is the sample size.

Remarks

■ If any argument is non-numeric, CONFIDENCE returns the #VALUE! error value.

■ If *alpha* ≤ 0 or *alpha* ≥ 1, CONFIDENCE returns the #NUM! error value.

■ If *standard_dev* ≤ 0, CONFIDENCE returns the #NUM! error value.

■ If *size* is not an integer, it is truncated.

■ If *size* < 1, CONFIDENCE returns the #NUM! error value.

■ If we assume *alpha* equals 0.05, we need to calculate the area under the standard normal curve that equals $(1 - alpha)$, or 95%. This value is ± 1.96. The confidence interval is therefore:

$$\bar{x} \pm 1.96\left(\frac{\sigma}{\sqrt{n}}\right)$$

Example

Suppose we observe that, in our sample of 50 commuters, the average length of travel to work is 30 minutes with a population standard deviation of 2.5. We can be 95 percent confident that the population mean is in the interval:

$$30 \pm 1.96\left(\frac{2.5}{\sqrt{50}}\right)$$

or:

$30 \pm \text{CONFIDENCE}(0.05, 2.5, 50),$

$= 30 \pm 0.692951$ minutes,

$= 29.3$ to 30.7 minutes.

Related Function

Function	Description
ZTEST	Returns the two-tailed *P*-value of a *z*-test

CONSOLIDATE

Macro Sheets Only

Equivalent to choosing the Consolidate command from the Data menu. Consolidates data from multiple ranges on multiple worksheets into a single range on a single worksheet. For detailed information about the Consolidate command, see online Help.

Syntax

CONSOLIDATE(*source_refs,function_num, top_row,left_col,create_links*)
CONSOLIDATE?(*source_refs,function_num, top_row,left_col,create_links*)

Source_refs are external references to areas on other worksheets that contain data to be consolidated on the destination worksheet. *Source_refs* must be in text form and include the full path of the file and the cell reference or named ranges on the worksheet to be consolidated. *Source_refs* must be given as an array, for example: {"SHEET!IncomeOne","SHEET2!IncomeTwo"}

To add or delete *source_refs* from an existing consolidation on a worksheet, reuse the CONSOLIDATE function, specifying the new *source_refs.*

Function_num is a number from 1 to 11 that specifies one of the 11 functions you can use to consolidate data. If *function_num* is omitted, the SUM function, number 9, is used. The functions and their corresponding numbers are listed in the following table.

Function_num	Function
1	AVERAGE
2	COUNT
3	COUNTA
4	MAX
5	MIN
6	PRODUCT
7	STDEV
8	STDEVP
9	SUM
10	VAR
11	VARP

The following arguments correspond to text boxes and check boxes in the Consolidate dialog box. Arguments that correspond to check boxes are logical values. If an argument is TRUE, Microsoft Excel selects the check box; if FALSE, Microsoft Excel clears the check box.

Top_row corresponds to the Top Row check box. The default is FALSE.

Left_col corresponds to the Left Column check box. The default is FALSE.

If *top_row* and *left_col* are both FALSE or omitted, the data is consolidated by position.

Create_links corresponds to the Create Links To Source Data check box.

Remarks

- If you use the CONSOLIDATE function with no arguments and there is a consolidation on the active worksheet, Microsoft Excel reconsolidates, using the sources, function, and position attributes used to create the existing consolidation.

- If you use the CONSOLIDATE function with no arguments and there is no consolidation on the active worksheet, the function returns the #VALUE! error value.

- For more information about consolidation, see Chapter 11 in Book 1 of the *Microsoft Excel User's Guide*.

Examples

The following macro formula reconsolidates an existing consolidation on the active worksheet:

```
CONSOLIDATE()
```

If there is no consolidation on the active worksheet, a message is displayed and the function returns the #VALUE! error value.

In Microsoft Excel for Windows, the following macro formula consolidates data from the ranges $A$10:$F$25 on the worksheets SALES.XLS and SALESWES.XLS using the SUM function and the categories in both the top row and left column:

```
CONSOLIDATE({"C:\EXCEL\SALES.XLS!R10C1:
R25C6","C:\EXCEL\SALESWES.XLS!R10C1:
R25C6"},9,TRUE,TRUE)
```

In Microsoft Excel for the Macintosh, the following macro formula consolidates data from the ranges named Income on the worksheets named SALES WEST and SALES EAST using the COUNTA function and the categories in the top row only:

```
CONSOLIDATE({"'HARD DRIVE:EXCEL:FINANCIALS:
SALES WEST'!Income","'HARD DRIVE:
EXCEL:FINANCIALS:SALES EAST'!Income"},
3,TRUE,FALSE)
```

Related Functions

Function	Description
CHANGE.LINK	Changes supporting worksheet links
LINKS	Returns the names of all linked documents
OPEN.LINKS	Opens specified supporting documents
UPDATE.LINK	Updates a link to another document

CONSTRAIN.NUMERIC

Macro Sheets Only

Equivalent to choosing the Constrain Numeric tool, which you can find by selecting the Formula tools category in the Toolbar Customize dialog box. Constrains handwriting recognition to numbers and punctuation only. Use this function in a macro to improve the accuracy of handwriting recognition when the user is entering a series of numbers or formulas. For detailed information about the Constrain Numeric tool, see online Help.

Note This function is only available if you are using Microsoft Windows for Pen Computing.

Syntax

CONSTRAIN.NUMERIC(*numeric_only*)

Numeric_only is a logical value that turns the numeric constraint on or off. If *numeric_only* is TRUE, only numbers and digits are recognized; if FALSE, all characters are recognized as usual; if omitted, the numeric constraint is toggled.

Remarks

When the numeric constraint is on, Microsoft Excel recognizes only the following symbols:

0 1 2 3 4 5 6 7 8 9 $ # @ % ( ) − + = { } : < > , ? |

Tip Use GET.WORKSPACE(45) to make sure you're running Microsoft Windows for Pen Computing.

CONVERT

Converts a number from one measurement system to another. For example, CONVERT can translate a table of distances in miles to a table of distances in kilometers.

If this function is not available, you must install the Analysis ToolPak add-in macro. For more information, see "Managing Add-in Commands and Functions" in Chapter 4 in Book 2 of the *Microsoft Excel User's Guide.*

Syntax

CONVERT(*number,from_unit,to_unit*)

Number   is the value in *from_units* to convert.

From_unit   is the units for *number.*

To_unit   is the units for the result.

CONVERT accepts the following text values for *from_unit* and *to_unit*:

Weight and mass	From_unit or to_unit
Gram	"g"
Slug	"sg"
Pound mass (avoirdupois)	"lbm"
U (atomic mass unit)	"u"
Ounce mass (avoirdupois)	"ozm"

Distance	From_unit or to_unit
Meter	"m"
Statute mile	"mi"
Nautical mile	"Nmi"
Inch	"in"
Foot	"ft"
Yard	"yd"
Angstrom	"ang"

Time	From_unit or to_unit
Year	"yr"
Day	"day"
Hour	"hr"
Minute	"mn"
Second	"sec"

Pressure	From_unit or to_unit
Pascal	"p"
Atmosphere	"at"

Force	From_unit or to_unit
Newton	"N"
Dyne	"dy"
Pound force	"lbf"

Energy	From_unit or to_unit
Joule	"J"
Erg	"e"
Thermodynamic calorie	"c"

Energy	From_unit or to_unit
IT calorie	"cal"
Electron volt	"ev"
Horsepower-hour	"hh"
Watt-hour	"wh"
Foot-pound	"flb"
BTU	"btu"

Power	From_unit or to_unit
Horsepower	"h"
Watt	"w"

Magnetism	From_unit or to_unit
Tesla	"T"
Gauss	"ga"

Temperature	*From_unit* or *to_unit*
Degree Celsius	"cel"
Degree Fahrenheit	"fah"
Degree Kelvin	"kel"

Liquid measure	*From_unit* or *to_unit*
Teaspoon	"tsp"
Tablespoon	"tbs"
Fluid ounce	"oz"
Cup	"cup"
Pint	"pt"
Quart	"qt"
Gallon	"gal"
Liter	"lt"

The following abbreviated unit prefixes can be prepended to any metric *from_unit* or *to_unit*.

Prefix	Multiplier	Abbreviation
exa	1E+18	"E"
peta	1E+15	"P"
tera	1E+12	"T"
giga	1E+09	"G"
mega	1E+06	"M"
kilo	1E+03	"k"
deka	1E+01	"e"
deci	1E–01	"d"
centi	1E–02	"c"
milli	1E–03	"m"
micro	1E–06	"u"
nano	1E–09	"n"
pico	1E–12	"p"
femto	1E–15	"f"
atto	1E–18	"a"

Remarks

- If the input data types are incorrect, CONVERT returns the #VALUE! error value.
- If the unit does not exist, CONVERT returns the #N/A error value.
- If the unit does not support an abbreviated unit prefix, CONVERT returns the #N/A error value.
- If the units are in different groups, CONVERT returns the #N/A error value.
- Unit names and prefixes are case-sensitive.

Examples

CONVERT(1.0,"lbm","kg") equals 0.453592

CONVERT(68,"fah","cel") equals 20

CONVERT(2.5,"ft","sec") equals #N/A

Related Functions

Related functions include all base conversion functions such as BIN2DEC, BIN2HEX, BIN2OCT, HEX2BIN, OCT2BIN, and so on.

COPY

Macro Sheets Only

Equivalent to choosing the Copy command from the Edit menu. Copies and pastes data or objects. For detailed information about the Copy command, see online Help.

Syntax

COPY(*from_reference,to_reference*)

From_reference is a reference to the cell or range of cells you want to copy. If *from_reference* is omitted, it is assumed to be the current selection.

To_reference is a reference to the cell or range of cells where you want to paste what you have copied.

- *To_reference* should be a single cell or an enlarged multiple of *from_reference*. For example, if *from_reference* is a 2 by 4 rectangle, *to_reference* can be a 4 by 8 rectangle.

- *To_reference* can be omitted so that you can subsequently paste using the PASTE, PASTE.LINK, or PASTE.SPECIAL functions.

Examples

COPY() defines the selection to be copied when you use one of the PASTE functions.

The following macro formula copies cells on the active worksheet from $A$4:$C$6 to a range whose upper-left corner is cell $T$7:

COPY(!$A$4:$C$6,!$T$7)

Related Functions

Function	Description
CUT	Cuts or moves data or objects
PASTE	Pastes cut or copied data
PASTE.SPECIAL	Pastes specific components of copied data

COPY.CHART

Macro Sheets Only

Equivalent to choosing the Copy Chart command from the Edit menu in Microsoft Excel for the Macintosh version 1.5 or earlier. This function is included only for macro compatibility. You can copy a chart with the COPY.PICTURE function by omitting the *appearance_num* argument.

Syntax

COPY.CHART*(size_num)*

Related Function

Function	Description
COPY.PICTURE	Creates a picture of the current selection for use in another program

COPY.PICTURE

Macro Sheets Only

Equivalent to choosing the Copy Picture command from the Edit menu. The Copy Picture command appears if you hold down SHIFT while choosing the Edit menu. It copies a chart or range of cells to the Clipboard as a graphic. Use COPY.PICTURE to create an image of the current selection or chart for use in another program. For detailed information about the Copy Picture command, see online Help.

Syntax

COPY.PICTURE*(appearance_num,size_num, type_num)*
COPY.PICTURE?*(appearance_num,size_num, type_num)*

Remarks

Graphics are created differently on screen and on a printer. Thus, the printed picture may look different from the one on screen.

Appearance_num is a number describing how to copy the picture.

Appearance_num	Action
1 or omitted	Copies a picture as closely as possible to the picture displayed on your screen
2	Copies what you would see if you printed the selection

Size_num is a number describing how to copy the picture and is only available if the current selection is a chart.

Size_num	Action
1 or omitted	Copies the chart in the same size as the window on which it is displayed
2	Copies what you would see if you printed the chart

Type_num is a number specifying the format of the picture. This argument is available only in Microsoft Excel for Windows.

Type_num	Format of the picture
1 or omitted	Picture
2	Bitmap

Related Functions

Function	Description
COPY	Copies and pastes data or objects
CUT	Cuts or moves data or objects
PASTE	Pastes cut or copied data
PASTE.PICTURE.LINK	Pastes a linked picture of the currently copied area
PASTE.SPECIAL	Pastes specific components of copied data

COPY.TOOL

Macro Sheets Only

Equivalent to selecting a tool and choosing the Copy Tool Face command from the Edit menu. Copies a tool face to the Clipboard. For detailed information about the Copy Tool Face command, see online Help.

Syntax

COPY.TOOL(*bar_id,position*)

Bar_id specifies the number or name of a toolbar from which you want to copy the tool face. For detailed information about *bar_id,* see ADD.TOOL.

Position specifies the position of the tool within the toolbar. *Position* starts with 1 at the left side (if horizontal) or at the top (if vertical).

Example

The following macro formula copies the tool face from the tool in position 3 on toolbar MyToolbar.

```
COPY.TOOL("MyToolbar",3)
```

Related Functions

Function	Description
ADD.TOOL	Adds one or more tools to a toolbar
GET.TOOL	Returns information about a tool or tools on a toolbar
PASTE.TOOL	Pastes a tool face from the Clipboard to a specified position on a toolbar

CORREL

Returns the correlation coefficient of the *array1* and *array2* cell ranges. Use the correlation coefficient to determine the relationship between two properties. For example, you can examine the relationship between a location's average temperature and the use of air conditioners.

Syntax

CORREL(*array1,array2*)

Array1 is a cell range of values.

Array2 is a second cell range of values.

Remarks

- The arguments should be numbers, or names, arrays, or references that contain numbers.

- If an array or reference argument contains text, logical values, or empty cells, those values are ignored; however, cells with the value zero are included.

- If *array1* and *array2* have a different number of data points, CORREL returns the #N/A error value.

- If either *array1* or *array2* are empty, or if σ (the standard deviation) of their values equals zero, CORREL returns the #DIV/0! error value.

Microsoft Excel Function Reference

- The equation for the correlation coefficient is:

$$\rho_{x,y} = \frac{Cov(X,Y)}{\sigma_x \cdot \sigma_y}$$

where:

$$-1 \le \rho_{xy} \le 1$$

and:

$$Cov(X,Y) = \frac{1}{n} \sum_{i=1}^{n} (x_i - \mu_x)(y_i - \mu_y)$$

Example

CORREL({3,2,4,5,6},{9,7,12,15,17}) equals 0.997054

Related Functions

Function	Description
COVAR	Returns covariance, the average of the products of paired deviations
FISHER	Returns the Fisher transformation
FISHERINV	Returns the inverse of the Fisher transformation
MCORREL	Returns the correlation coefficient of two or more data sets
MCOVAR	Returns the covariance between two or more data sets

COS

Returns the cosine of the given angle.

Syntax

COS(*number*)

Number is the angle in radians for which you want the cosine. If the angle is in degrees, multiply it by PI()/180 to convert it to radians.

Examples

COS(1.047) equals 0.500171

COS(60*PI()/180) equals 0.5, the cosine of 60 degrees

Related Functions

Function	Description
ACOS	Returns the arccosine of a number
COSH	Returns the hyperbolic cosine of a number
PI	Returns the value π

COSH

Returns the hyperbolic cosine of *number*.

Syntax

COSH(*number*)

The formula for the hyperbolic cosine is:

$$COSH(z) = \frac{e^z + e^{-z}}{2}$$

Examples

COSH(4) equals 27.30823

COSH(EXP(1)) equals 7.610125, where EXP(1) is e, the base of the natural logarithm.

Related Functions

Function	Description
ACOSH	Returns the inverse hyperbolic cosine of a number
SINH	Returns the hyperbolic sine of a number
TANH	Returns the hyperbolic tangent of a number

COUNT

Counts how many numbers are in the list of arguments. Use COUNT to get the number of entries in a number field in a range or array of numbers.

Syntax

COUNT(*value1,value2,...*)

Value1, value2,... are 1 to 30 arguments that can contain or refer to a variety of data types, but only numbers are counted.

- Arguments that are numbers, null, logical values, dates, or text representations of numbers are counted; arguments that are error values or text that cannot be translated into numbers are ignored.

- If an argument is an array or reference, only numbers in that array or reference are counted. Empty cells, logical values, text, or error values in the array or reference are ignored.

Examples

	A	B	C	D
1				
2				
3	Sales			
4	12/8/90			
5				
6	19			
7	22.34			
8				
9	#DIV/0!			

In the preceding worksheet:

COUNT(A6:A7) equals 2

COUNT(A4:A7) equals 3

COUNT(A2,A6:A9,"Twelve",5) equals 3

COUNT(A1:A9,,"2"), where "2" is a text representation of a number, equals 5

COUNT(0,1,TRUE,"three",4..6.6666,700..9,#DIV/0!) equals 8

Related Functions

Function	Description
AVERAGE	Returns the average of its arguments
COUNTA	Counts how many values are in the list of arguments
DCOUNT	Counts the cells containing numbers from a specified database and criteria
DCOUNTA	Counts nonblank cells from a specified database and criteria
SUM	Adds its arguments

COUNTA

Counts the number of nonblank values in the list of arguments. Use COUNTA to count the number of cells with data in a range or array.

Syntax

COUNTA(*value1,value2,...*)

Value1, value2,... are 1 to 30 arguments representing the values you want to count. In this case, a value is any type of information, including empty text ("") but not including empty cells. If an argument is an array or reference, empty cells within the array or reference are ignored.

Examples

	A	B	C	D
1				
2				
3	Sales			
4	12/8/90			
5				
6	19			
7	22.34			
8				
9	#DIV/0!			

In the preceding worksheet:

COUNTA(A6:A7) equals 2

COUNTA(A4:A7) equals 3

COUNTA(A3,A6:A9) equals 4

`COUNTA(A1:A9)` equals 5

`COUNTA(1,,1)` equals 3

`COUNTA(A4:A7,10)` equals 4

Related Functions

Function	Description
AVERAGE	Returns the average of its arguments
COUNT	Counts how many numbers are in the list of arguments
DCOUNT	Counts the cells containing numbers from a specified database and criteria
DCOUNTA	Counts nonblank cells from a specified database and criteria
PRODUCT	Multiplies its arguments
SUM	Adds its arguments

COUPDAYBS

Returns the number of days from the beginning of the coupon period to the settlement date.

If this function is not available, you must install the Analysis ToolPak add-in macro. For more information, see "Managing Add-in Commands and Functions" in Chapter 4 in Book 2 of the *Microsoft Excel User's Guide.*

Syntax

COUPDAYBS(*settlement,maturity,frequency,basis*)

Settlement   is the security's settlement date, expressed as a serial date number.

Maturity   is the security's maturity date, expressed as a serial date number.

Frequency   is the number of coupon payments per year. For annual payments, *frequency* = 1; for semi-annual, *frequency* = 2; for quarterly, *frequency* = 4.

Basis   is the type of day count basis to use.

Basis	Day count basis
0 or omitted	30/360
1	Actual/actual

Basis	Day count basis
2	Actual/360
3	Actual/365

Remarks

- All arguments are truncated to integers.

- If any argument is non-numeric, COUPDAYBS returns the #VALUE! error value.

- If *settlement* or *maturity* is not a valid serial date number, COUPDAYBS returns the #NUM! error value.

- If *frequency* is any number other than 1, 2, or 4, COUPDAYBS returns the #NUM! error value.

- If *basis* < 0 or if *basis* > 3, COUPDAYBS returns the #NUM! error value.

- If *settlement* ≥ *maturity,* COUPDAYBS returns the #NUM! error value.

Example

A bond has the following terms:

January 25, 1991 settlement date
November 15, 1992 maturity date
Semiannual coupon
Actual/actual basis

The number of days from the beginning of the coupon period to the settlement date (in the 1900 Date System) is:

`COUPDAYBS(33263,33923,2,1)` cquals 71

Related Functions

Function	Description
COUPDAYS	Returns the number of days in the coupon period that contains the settlement date
COUPDAYSNC	Returns the number of days from the settlement date to the next coupon date
COUPNCD	Returns the next coupon date after the settlement date

Function	Description
COUPNUM	Returns the number of coupons payable between the settlement date and maturity date
COUPPCD	Returns the previous coupon date before the settlement date
DATE	Returns the serial number of a particular date

COUPDAYS

Returns the number of days in the coupon period that contains the settlement date.

If this function is not available, you must install the Analysis ToolPak add-in macro. For more information, see "Managing Add-in Commands and Functions" in Chapter 4 in Book 2 of the *Microsoft Excel User's Guide.*

Syntax

COUPDAYS(*settlement,maturity,frequency,basis*)

Settlement is the security's settlement date, expressed as a serial date number.

Maturity is the security's maturity date, expressed as a serial date number.

Frequency is the number of coupon payments per year. For annual payments, *frequency* = 1; for semi-annual, *frequency* = 2; for quarterly, *frequency* = 4.

Basis is the type of day count basis to use.

Basis	Day count basis
0 or omitted	30/360
1	Actual/actual
2	Actual/360
3	Actual/365

Remarks

- All arguments are truncated to integers.

- If any argument is non-numeric, COUPDAYS returns the #VALUE! error value.

- If *settlement* or *maturity* is not a valid serial date number, COUPDAYS returns the #NUM! error value.

- If *frequency* is any number other than 1, 2, or 4, COUPDAYS returns the #NUM! error value.

- If *basis* < 0 or if *basis* > 3, COUPDAYS returns the #NUM! error value.

- If *settlement* ≥ *maturity,* COUPDAYS returns the #NUM! error value.

Example

A bond has the following terms:

January 25, 1991 settlement date
November 15, 1992 maturity date
Semiannual coupon
Actual/actual basis

The number of days in the coupon period that contains the settlement date (in the 1900 Date System) is:

COUPDAYS(33263,33923,2,1) equals 181

Related Functions

Function	Description
COUPDAYBS	Returns the number of days from the beginning of the coupon period to the settlement date
COUPDAYSNC	Returns the number of days from the settlement date to the next coupon date
COUPNCD	Returns the next coupon date after the settlement date
COUPNUM	Returns the number of coupons payable between the settlement date and maturity date
COUPPCD	Returns the previous coupon date before the settlement date
DATE	Returns the serial number of a particular date

COUPDAYSNC

Returns the number of days from the settlement date to the next coupon date.

If this function is not available, you must install the Analysis ToolPak add-in macro. For more information, see "Managing Add-in Commands and Functions" in Chapter 4 in Book 2 of the *Microsoft Excel User's Guide.*

Syntax

COUPDAYSNC(*settlement,maturity,frequency, basis*)

Settlement   is the security's settlement date, expressed as a serial date number.

Maturity   is the security's maturity date, expressed as a serial date number.

Frequency   is the number of coupon payments per year. For annual payments, *frequency* = 1; for semi-annual, *frequency* = 2; for quarterly, *frequency* = 4.

Basis   is the type of day count basis to use.

Basis	Day count basis
0 or omitted	30/360
1	Actual/actual
2	Actual/360
3	Actual/365

Remarks

- All arguments are truncated to integers.

- If any argument is non-numeric, COUPDAYSNC returns the #VALUE! error value.

- If *settlement* or *maturity* is not a valid serial date number, COUPDAYSNC returns the #NUM! error value.

- If *frequency* is any number other than 1, 2, or 4, COUPDAYSNC returns the #NUM! error value.

- If *basis* < 0 or if *basis* > 3, COUPDAYSNC returns the #NUM! error value.

- If *settlement* ≥ *maturity,* COUPDAYSNC returns the #NUM! error value.

Example

A bond has the following terms:

January 25, 1991 settlement date
November 15, 1992 maturity date
Semiannual coupon
Actual/actual basis

The number of days from the beginning of the coupon period to the settlement date (in the 1900 Date System) is:

COUPDAYSNC(33263,33923,2,1) equals 110

Related Functions

Function	Description
COUPDAYBS	Returns the number of days from the beginning of the coupon period to the settlement date
COUPDAYS	Returns the number of days in the coupon period that contains the settlement date
COUPNCD	Returns the next coupon date after the settlement date
COUPNUM	Returns the number of coupons payable between the settlement date and maturity date
COUPPCD	Returns the previous coupon date before the settlement date
DATE	Returns the serial number of a particular date

COUPNCD

Returns the next coupon date after the settlement date.

If this function is not available, you must install the Analysis ToolPak add-in macro. For more information, see "Managing Add-in Commands and Functions" in Chapter 4 in Book 2 of the *Microsoft Excel User's Guide.*

Syntax

COUPNCD(*settlement,maturity,frequency,basis*)

Settlement is the security's settlement date, expressed as a serial date number.

Maturity is the security's maturity date, expressed as a serial date number.

Frequency is the number of coupon payments per year. For annual payments, *frequency* = 1; for semi-annual, *frequency* = 2; for quarterly, *frequency* = 4.

Basis is the type of day count basis to use.

Basis	Day count basis
0 or omitted	30/360
1	Actual/actual
2	Actual/360
3	Actual/365

Remarks

- All arguments are truncated to integers.

- If any argument is non-numeric, COUPNCD returns the #VALUE! error value.

- If *settlement* or *maturity* is not a valid serial date number, COUPNCD returns the #NUM! error value.

- If *frequency* is any number other than 1, 2, or 4, COUPNCD returns the #NUM! error value.

- If *basis* < 0 or if *basis* > 3, COUPNCD returns the #NUM! error value.

- If *settlement* ≥ *maturity,* COUPNCD returns the #NUM! error value.

Example

A bond has the following terms:

January 25, 1991 settlement date
November 15, 1992 maturity date
Semiannual coupon
Actual/actual basis

The next coupon date after the settlement date (in the 1900 Date System) is:

COUPNCD(33263,33923,2,1) equals 33373 or May 15, 1991

Related Functions

Function	Description
COUPDAYBS	Returns the number of days from the beginning of the coupon period to the settlement date
COUPDAYS	Returns the number of days in the coupon period that contains the settlement date
COUPDAYSNC	Returns the number of days from the settlement date to the next coupon date
COUPNUM	Returns the number of coupons payable between the settlement date and maturity date
COUPPCD	Returns the previous coupon date before the settlement date
DATE	Returns the serial number of a particular date

COUPNUM

Returns the number of coupons payable between the settlement date and maturity date, rounded up to the nearest whole coupon.

If this function is not available, you must install the Analysis ToolPak add-in macro. For more information, see "Managing Add-in Commands and Functions" in Chapter 4 in Book 2 of the *Microsoft Excel User's Guide.*

Syntax

COUPNUM(*settlement,maturity,frequency,basis*)

Settlement is the security's settlement date, expressed as a serial date number.

Maturity is the security's maturity date, expressed as a serial date number.

Frequency is the number of coupon payments per year. For annual payments, *frequency* = 1; for semi-annual, *frequency* = 2; for quarterly, *frequency* = 4.

Basis is the type of day count basis to use.

Basis	Day count basis
0 or omitted	30/360
1	Actual/actual
2	Actual/360
3	Actual/365

Remarks

- All arguments are truncated to integers.

- If any argument is non-numeric, COUPNUM returns the #VALUE! error value.

- If *settlement* or *maturity* is not a valid serial date number, COUPNUM returns the #NUM! error value.

- If *frequency* is any number other than 1, 2, or 4, COUPNUM returns the #NUM! error value.

- If *basis* < 0 or if *basis* > 3, COUPNUM returns the #NUM! error value.

- If *settlement* ≥ *maturity,* COUPNUM returns the #NUM! error value.

Example

A bond has the following terms:

January 25, 1991 settlement date
November 15, 1992 maturity date
Semiannual coupon
Actual/actual basis

The number of coupon payments (in the 1900 Date System) is:

COUPNUM(33263,33923,2,1) equals 4

Related Functions

Function	Description
COUPDAYBS	Returns the number of days from the beginning of the coupon period to the settlement date
COUPDAYS	Returns the number of days in the coupon period that contains the settlement date
COUPDAYSNC	Returns the number of days from the settlement date to the next coupon date
COUPNCD	Returns the next coupon date after the settlement date
COUPPCD	Returns the previous coupon date before the settlement date
DATE	Returns the serial number of a particular date

COUPPCD

Returns the previous coupon date before the settlement date.

If this function is not available, you must install the Analysis ToolPak add-in macro. For more information, see "Managing Add-in Commands and Functions" in Chapter 4 in Book 2 of the *Microsoft Excel User's Guide.*

Syntax

COUPPCD(*settlement,maturity,frequency,basis*)

Settlement is the security's settlement date, expressed as a serial date number.

Maturity is the security's maturity date, expressed as a serial date number.

Frequency is the number of coupon payments per year. For annual payments, *frequency* = 1; for semi-annual, *frequency* = 2; for quarterly, *frequency* = 4.

Basis is the type of day count basis to use.

Basis	Day count basis
0 or omitted	30/360
1	Actual/actual
2	Actual/360
3	Actual/365

Remarks

- All arguments are truncated to integers.

- If any argument is non-numeric, COUPPCD returns the #VALUE! error value.

- If *settlement* or *maturity* is not a valid serial date number, COUPPCD returns the #NUM! error value.

- If *frequency* is any number other than 1, 2, or 4, COUPPCD returns the #NUM! error value.

- If *basis* < 0 or if *basis* > 3, COUPPCD returns the #NUM! error value.

- If *settlement* ≥ *maturity,* COUPPCD returns the #NUM! error value.

Example

A bond has the following terms:

January 25, 1991 settlement date
November 15, 1992 maturity date
Semiannual coupon
Actual/actual basis

The previous coupon date before the settlement date (in the 1900 Date System) is:

COUPPCD(33263,33923,2,1) equals 33192 or November 15, 1990

Related Functions

Function	Description
COUPDAYBS	Returns the number of days from the beginning of the coupon period to the settlement date
COUPDAYS	Returns the number of days in the coupon period that contains the settlement date
COUPDAYSNC	Returns the number of days from the settlement date to the next coupon date
COUPNCD	Returns the next coupon date after the settlement date
COUPNUM	Returns the number of coupons payable between the settlement date and maturity date
DATE	Returns the serial number of a particular date

COVAR

Returns covariance, the average of the products of deviations for each data point pair. Use covariance to determine the relationship between two data sets. For example, you can examine whether greater income accompanies greater levels of education.

Syntax

COVAR(*array1,array2*)

Array1 is the first cell range of integers.

Array2 is the second cell range of integers.

Remarks

- The arguments should be numbers, or names, arrays, or references that contain numbers.

- If an array or reference argument contains text, logical values, or empty cells, those values are ignored; however, cells with the value zero are included.

- If *array1* and *array2* have a different number of data points, COVAR returns the #N/A error value.

- If either *array1* or *array2* are empty, COVAR returns the #DIV/0! error value.

- The covariance is:

$$Cov(X,Y) = \frac{1}{n} \sum_{i-1}^{n} (x_i - \mu_x)(y_i - \mu_y)$$

Example

```
COVAR({3,2,4,5,6},{9,7,12,15,17})
equals 5.2
```

Related Functions

Function	Description
CORREL	Returns the correlation coefficient between two data sets
FISHER	Returns the Fisher transformation
FISHERINV	Returns the inverse of the Fisher transformation
MCORREL	Returns the correlation coefficient of two or more data sets
MCOVAR	Returns the covariance between two or more data sets

CREATE.DIRECTORY

Macro Sheets Only

Creates a directory or folder.

If this function is not available, you must load FILEFNS.XLA from the Library directory (in Microsoft Excel for Windows) or File Functions from the Macro Library folder (in Microsoft Excel for the Macintosh) in the directory or folder where you installed Microsoft Excel. For more information, see "Managing Add-in Commands and Functions" in Chapter 4 in Book 2 of the *Microsoft Excel User's Guide.*

Syntax

CREATE.DIRECTORY*(path_text)*

Path_text is the name of the directory or folder you want created inside the current one, or the path location and name for a new directory or folder.

Examples

In Microsoft Excel for Windows, the following macro formula creates a directory named SALEWEST in the current directory:

```
CREATE.DIRECTORY("SALEWEST")
```

The following macro formula creates a directory named SALEWEST in the directory C:\WORD\REPORTS:

```
CREATE.DIRECTORY("C:\WORD\REPORTS\
SALEWEST")
```

In Microsoft Excel for the Macintosh, the following macro formula creates a folder named AUGUST SALES in the current folder:

```
CREATE.DIRECTORY("AUGUST SALES")
```

The following macro formula creates a folder named AUGUST SALES in the folder HARD DISK:WORD:REPORTS:

```
CREATE.DIRECTORY("HARD DISK:WORD:REPORTS:
AUGUST SALES")
```

Related Functions

Function	Description
DELETE.DIRECTORY	Deletes an empty directory
DIRECTORIES	Returns an array of all subdirectories or subfolders in the specified path
FILE.EXISTS	Tests for the existence of a file, directory, or folder

CREATE.NAMES

Macro Sheets Only

Equivalent to choosing the Create Names command from the Formula menu (full menus). Use CREATE.NAMES to quickly create names from text labels on a worksheet. For detailed information about the Create Names command, see online Help.

Arguments are logical values corresponding to check boxes in the Create Names dialog box. If an argument is TRUE, Microsoft Excel selects the check box; if FALSE or omitted, Microsoft Excel clears the check box.

Syntax

CREATE.NAMES*(top,left,bottom,right)*
CREATE.NAMES?*(top,left,bottom,right)*

Top　corresponds to the Top Row check box.

Left　corresponds to the Left Column check box.

Bottom　corresponds to the Bottom Row check box.

Right　corresponds to the Right Column check box.

Remarks

The cell containing the label text that Microsoft Excel uses to create the names is not included in the resulting named range.

Examples

	A	B	C	D
1		Jan	Feb	Mar
2	Apples			
3	Oranges			
4	Bananas			

In the preceding worksheet, when A1:D4 is selected, CREATE.NAMES(TRUE,TRUE) creates the following named ranges:

Jan	$B$2:$B$4
Feb	$C$2:$C$4
Mar	$D$2:$D$4
Apples	$B$2:$D$2
Oranges	$B$3:$D$3
Bananas	$B$4:$D$4

	A	B	C	D	E
1		Jan	Feb	Mar	
2	Apples				Macintosh
3	Oranges				Navel
4	Bananas				Brazilian

In the preceding worksheet, when A1:E4 is selected, CREATE.NAMES(TRUE,TRUE,,TRUE) creates the same names as the previous example, plus:

Macintosh	$B$2:$D$2
Navel	$B$3:$D$3
Brazilian	$B$4:$D$4

Related Functions

Function	Description
APPLY.NAMES	Replaces references and values with their corresponding names
DEFINE.NAME	Defines a name on the active worksheet or macro sheet
DELETE.NAME	Deletes a name
FORMULA.GOTO	Selects a named area or reference on any open document

CREATE.OBJECT

Macro Sheets Only

Draws an object on a worksheet or macro sheet and returns a value identifying the object created. It is generally easier to use the macro recorder to enter this function on your macro sheet.

Syntax 1

Lines, rectangles, ovals, arcs, pictures, text boxes, and buttons

CREATE.OBJECT(*obj_type,**ref1**,x_offset1, y_offset1,**ref2**,x_offset2,y_offset2,text,fill*)

Syntax 2

Polygons

CREATE.OBJECT(*obj_type,**ref1**,x_offset1, y_offset1,**ref2**,x_offset2,y_offset2,**array**,fill*)

Syntax 3

Embedded charts

CREATE.OBJECT(*obj_type,**ref1**,x_offset1, y_offset1,**ref2**,x_offset2,y_offset2,xy_series, fill,gallery_num,type_num*)

Obj_type is a number from 1 to 10 specifying the type of object to create.

Obj_type	Object
1	Line
2	Rectangle
3	Oval
4	Arc
5	Embedded chart
6	Text box
7	Button
8	Picture (created with the camera tool)
9	Closed polygon
10	Open polygon

Ref1 is a reference to the cell from which the upper-left corner of the object is drawn, or from which the upper-left corner of the object's bounding rectangle is defined.

X_offset1 is the horizontal distance from the upper-left corner of *ref1* to the upper-left corner of the object or to the upper-left corner of the object's bounding rectangle. *X_offset1* is measured in points. A point is 1/72nd of an inch. If *x_offset1* is omitted, it is assumed to be 0.

Y_offset1 is the vertical distance from the upper-left corner of *ref1* to the upper-left corner of the object or to the upper-left corner of the object's bounding rectangle. *Y_offset1* is measured in points. If *y_offset1* is omitted, it is assumed to be 0.

Ref2 is a reference to the cell from which the lower-right corner of the object is drawn, or from which the lower-right corner of the object's bounding rectangle is defined.

X_offset2 is the horizontal distance from the upper-left corner of *ref2* to the lower-right corner of the object or to the lower-right corner of the object's bounding rectangle. *X_offset2* is measured in points. If *x_offset2* is omitted, it is assumed to be 0.

Y_offset2 is the vertical distance from the upper-left corner of *ref2* to the lower-right corner of the object or to the lower-right corner of the object's bounding rectangle. *Y_offset2* is measured in points. If *y_offset2* is omitted, it is assumed to be 0.

Text specifies the text that appears in a text box or button. If *text* is omitted for a button, the button is named "Button *n*", where *n* is a number. If *object_type* is not 6 or 7, *text* is ignored.

Fill is a logical value specifying whether the object is filled or transparent. If *fill* is TRUE, the object is filled; if FALSE, the object is transparent; if omitted, the object is filled with an applicable pattern for the object being created.

Array is an *n* by 2 array of values, or a reference to a range of cells containing values, that indicate the position of each vertex in a polygon, relative to the upper-left corner of the polygon's bounding rectangle.

- A vertex is a point that is defined by a pair of coordinates in one row of *array*.

- If the polygon contains many vertices, one array may not be sufficient to define it. If the number of characters in the formula exceeds 1024, you must include one or more EXTEND.POLYGON functions. If you're recording a macro, Microsoft Excel automatically records EXTEND.POLYGON functions as needed. For more information, see EXTEND.POLYGON.

Xy_series is a number from 0 to 3 that specifies how data is arranged in a chart and corresponds to options in the First Row/Column Contains dialog box.

Xy_series	Result
0	Displays a dialog box if the selection is ambiguous
1 or omitted	First row/column is the first data series
2	First row/column contains the category (*x*) axis labels
3	First row/column contains the *x*-values; the created chart is an xy (scatter) chart

- *Xy_series* is ignored unless *obj_type* is 5 (chart).

- If you want more control over how the data is arranged, use the *plot_by*, *categories*, and *ser_titles* arguments to the CHART.WIZARD function. For more information, see CHART.WIZARD.

Gallery_num   is a number from 1 to 14 specifying the type of embedded chart you want to create.

Gallery_num	Chart
1	Area
2	Bar
3	Column
4	Line
5	Pie
6	Radar
7	XY (scatter)
8	Combination
9	3-D area
10	3-D bar
11	3-D column
12	3-D line
13	3-D pic
14	3-D surface

Type_num   is a number identifying a formatting option for a chart. The formatting options are shown in the dialog box of the Gallery command that corresponds to the type of chart you're creating. The first formatting option in any gallery is 1. For a complete list of galleries, see "Changing the Chart Type or Format" in Chapter 12 in Book 1 of the *Microsoft Excel User's Guide*.

Remarks

- CREATE.OBJECT returns the object identifier of the object it created. Object identifiers include text describing the object, such as "Text" or "Oval", and a number indicating the order in which the object was created. For example, CREATE.OBJECT returns "Oval 3" after creating an oval that is the third object on the document.

- If the offsets are not specified, the object is drawn from the upper-left corner of *ref1* to the upper-left corner of *ref2*.

- If the object is not a picture and either *ref1* or *ref2* is omitted, CREATE.OBJECT returns the #VALUE! error value and does not create the object.

- If a chart is active, CREATE.OBJECT returns the #VALUE! error value.

- CREATE.OBJECT also selects the object.

- You must use the COPY function before the CREATE.OBJECT function to create a chart or a picture.

Tip   To assign a macro to an object, use the ASSIGN.TO.OBJECT function immediately after creating the object.

Related Functions

Function	Description
ASSIGN.TO.OBJECT	Assigns a macro to an object
EXTEND.POLYGON	Adds vertices to a polygon
FORMAT.MOVE	Moves the selected object
FORMAT.SHAPE	Inserts, moves, or deletes vertices of the selected polygon
FORMAT.SIZE	Sizes an object
GET.OBJECT	Returns information about an object

Function	Description
OBJECT.PROPERTIES	Determines an object's relationship to underlying cells
TEXT.BOX	Replaces text in a text box

CREATE.PUBLISHER

Macro Sheets Only

Equivalent to choosing the Create Publisher command from the Edit menu. Publishes the selected range or chart to an edition file for use by other Macintosh applications. For detailed information about the Create Publisher command, see online Help.

Important This function is only available if you are using Microsoft Excel for the Macintosh with system software version 7.0 or later.

Syntax

CREATE.PUBLISHER(*file_text,appearance,size, formats*)
CREATE.PUBLISHER?(*file_text,appearance,size, formats*)

File_text is a text string to be used as the name of the new file that will contain the selected data. If *file_text* is omitted, Microsoft Excel uses the format "<DocumentName> Edition #*n*", where DocumentName is the name of the document from which the publisher is being created, Edition indicates that the file is an edition file, and *n* is a unique integer.

For example, if you omit *file_text* and are publishing a selection from a worksheet named Seasonal, and it is your third publisher from that document in the current work session, the default name of the publisher would be "Seasonal Edition #3".

Appearance specifies whether the selection is to be published as shown on screen or as shown when printed. The default value for *appearance* is 1 if the selection is a sheet and 2 if the selection is a chart.

Appearance	Selection is published
1	As shown on screen
2	As shown when printed

Size specifies the size at which to publish a chart. *Size* is only available if a chart is to be published.

Size	Chart is published
1 or omitted	As shown on screen
2	As shown when printed

Formats is number specifying what file format or formats CREATE.PUBLISHER should use when it creates the Edition file.

Formats	File format
1	PICT
2	BIFF
4	RTF
8	VALU

- You can also use the sum of the allowable file formats for *formats*. For example, a value of 6 specifies BIFF and RTF.

- If *formats* is omitted and the document is a worksheet, *formats* is assumed to be 15 (all formats); if the document is a chart, *formats* is assumed to be 1 (PICT).

Examples

The following macro formula publishes the current selection, as shown on screen, to an edition file called MARCH DATA EDITION 1:

```
CREATE.PUBLISHER("MARCH DATA EDITION 1",1)
```

The following macro formula publishes the active chart to an edition file called MARCH SALES CHART, with the appearance and size as shown on screen:

```
CREATE.PUBLISHER("MARCH SALES CHART",1,1)
```

Related Functions

Function	Description
EDITION.OPTIONS	Sets publisher and subscriber options
GET.LINK.INFO	Returns information about a link
SUBSCRIBE.TO	Inserts contents of an edition into the active document
UPDATE.LINK	Updates a link to another document

CRITBINOM

Returns the smallest integer k for which the cumulative binomial distribution function is greater than or equal to the criterion value *alpha*. Use this function for quality assurance applications. For example, use CRITBINOM to determine the greatest number of defective parts that are allowed to come off an assembly line run without rejecting the entire lot.

Syntax

CRITBINOM(*trials,probability_s,alpha*)

Trials   is the number of Bernoulli trials.

Probability_s   is the probability of a success on each trial.

Alpha   is the criterion value.

Remarks

- If any argument is non-numeric, CRITBINOM returns the #VALUE! error value.

- If *trials* is not an integer, it is truncated.

- If *trials* < 0, CRITBINOM returns the #NUM! error value.

- If *probability_s* is < 0 or *probability_s* > 1, CRITBINOM returns the #NUM! error value.

- If *alpha* < 0 or *alpha* > 1, CRITBINOM returns the #NUM! error value.

Example

CRITBINOM(6,0.5,0.75) equals 4

Related Functions

Function	Description
BINOMDIST	Returns the individual term binomial distribution
COMBIN	Returns the number of combinations for a given number of objects
FACT	Returns the factorial of a number
HYPGEOMDIST	Returns the hypergeometric distribution
NEGBINOMDIST	Returns the negative binomial distribution
PERMUT	Returns the number of permutations for a given number of objects
PROB	Returns the probability that values in a range are between two limits

CROSSTAB

Defines the structure and content of a cross-tabulation table. It is generally easier to use the Crosstab Wizard to create the cross-tabulation table and to enter the necessary CROSSTAB formulas. Once the table is created, you can modify it by editing the CROSSTAB formulas. For more information, see "Reporting Database Information in a Crosstab Table" in Chapter 10 in Book 1 of the *Microsoft Excel User's Guide*.

If this function is not available, you must install the Crosstab add-in macro. For more information, see "Managing Add-in Commands and Functions" in Chapter 4 in Book 2 of the *Microsoft Excel User's Guide*.

Syntax 1

For defining row and column headings of the cross-tabulation table

CROSSTAB(*label,expression*)

Syntax 2

For defining columns in the cross-tabulation table

CROSSTAB(*label,"Columns:",columns_array*)

Syntax 3

For defining rows in the cross-tabulation table

CROSSTAB(*label,"Rows:",rows_array*)

Syntax 4

For defining summaries in the cross-tabulation table

CROSSTAB(*label,"Summary:",values_array, create_outline,create_names,multiple_values, auto_drilldown)*

Label is text that you want displayed in the cell containing the CROSSTAB formula. *Label* is not used by the cross-tabulation table. If *label* is omitted, *expression* determines the value displayed in the cell.

Expression is a name, formula, or other information that is used to compute the cross-tabulation table. *Expression* varies depending on the type of data in the table.

"Columns:", "Rows:", and *"Summary:"* are literal text values which you must enter as shown in the syntax lines.

For the descriptions of the remaining arguments, see CROSSTAB.CREATE.

Related Function

Function	Description
CROSSTAB.CREATE	Creates a cross-tabulation table

CROSSTAB.CREATE

Macro Sheets Only

Equivalent to choosing the Crosstab command from the Data menu. Creates a cross-tabulation table. The dialog-box form of this function activates the Crosstab Wizard. It is generally easier to use the macro recorder to enter this function on your macro sheet. For detailed information about the Define Crosstab command, see online Help. For more information about cross-tabulation tables, see "Reporting Database Information in a Crosstab Table" in Chapter 10 in Book 1 of the *Microsoft Excel User's Guide*.

If this function is not available, you must install the Crosstab add-in macro. For more information, see "Managing Add-in Commands and Functions" in Chapter 4 in Book 2 of the *Microsoft Excel User's Guide*.

Syntax

CROSSTAB.CREATE(*rows_array,columns_array, values_array,create_outline,create_names, multiple_values,auto_drilldown,new_sheet*)

CROSSTAB.CREATE?( )

Rows_array is a two-dimensional array that specifies a set of fields that appears in each row of the cross-tabulation table.

The following example shows the components of a rows array on a macro sheet. The range A3:E4 is a valid *rows_array*.

	A	B	C	D	E
1	Field_name	Grouping_index	From	To	Subtotals
2					
3	Product	0	FALSE	FALSE	YNNNNNN
4	Country	0	BELGIUM	USA	YNNNNNN
5					

- *Field_name* specifies a field name as text or a reference to a cell to be included in the cross-tabulation field.

- *Grouping_index* indicates how to group date values and numeric values. The following table lists *grouping_index* for date values. For numeric fields, *grouping_index* is the size of the group. For text fields, or to specify no grouping, use 0.

Grouping_index	Description
0	No grouping or text field
1	Group by days
2	Group by weeks
3	Group by months
4	Group by 30-day periods
5	Group by quarters
6	Group by years

- *From* is a value that specifies the starting field for the cross-tabulation table. *From* is a numeric value for a numeric field, a text string for a character field, or a serial number or date enclosed in quotation marks for a date field. Entering FALSE specifies starting at the minimum possible value for this field.

- *To* is a value that specifies the ending field for the cross-tabulation table. *To* is a numeric value for a numeric field, a text string for a character field, or a serial number or date enclosed in quotation marks for a date field. Entering FALSE specifies ending at the maximum possible value for this field.

- *Subtotals* is a string of seven characters. Each character represents a type of subtotal. To request a type of subtotal, set the corresponding character to Y. To skip a type of subtotal, set the corresponding character to N. The following table lists types of subtotals and their corresponding position within the seven-character string.

Character position	Type of subtotal
1	Sum
2	Count
3	Average
4	Minimum
5	Maximum
6	Standard deviation
7	Variance

Columns_array is a two-dimensional array that specifies a set of fields that appears in each column of the cross-tabulation table.

The following example shows the components of a columns array on a macro sheet. The range A3:E3 is a valid *columns_array*.

	A	B	C	D	E
1	Field_name	Grouping_index	From	To	Subtotals
2					
3	DATE	5	="1/1/90"	="12/31/91"	YNNNNNN
4					

The descriptions of the *field_name*, *grouping_index*, *from*, *to*, and *subtotals* elements within *columns_array* are the same as those for *rows_array*.

Values_array is a two-dimensional array that specifies each field that appears as a value field.

The following example shows the components of a values array on a macro sheet. The range A3:D3 is a valid *values_array*.

	A	B	C	D
1	Field_label	Summary_ expression	Display_items	Use_all_values
2				
3	Units Sold	SUM(SALES)	YNNNN	FALSE
4				
5				

- *Field_label* specifies a label for the summary field.

- *Summary_expression* is a text string that specifies the expression, including an aggregation operator, to compute.

- *Display_items* is a string of five characters that specifies desired display values. To specify a display value, set the corresponding character to Y. To omit a display value, set the corresponding character to N. The following table lists *display_items* values.

Character position	Type of display
1	Values
2	Row percent
3	Column percent
4	Total percent
5	Index

- *Use_all_values* is a logical value that specifies what values to use when calculating subtotals and percentages.

    If *use_all_values* is TRUE, CROSSTAB.CREATE uses any table values that it needs, including values outside the *from* and *to* range, even though those values will not appear in the resulting cross-tabulation table.

    If *use_all_values* is FALSE, CROSSTAB.CREATE uses only values that appear in the final cross-tabulation table.

Create_outline is a logical value that, if TRUE, creates an outline for the cross-tabulation table, or, if FALSE, does not create an outline for the table.

Create_names is a logical value that, if TRUE, creates names for the values from the table, or, if FALSE, does not create names for the values. You can use names to reference rows and columns, so that formulas are independent of position.

Multiple_values is a numerical value that specifies how to handle multiple summaries. The following table lists *multiple_values* values.

Multiple_values	Description
1	Inner columns
2	Outer columns
3	Inner rows
4	Outer rows

Auto_drilldown is a logical value that, if TRUE, places drilldown formulas in the result cells, or, if FALSE, does not place drilldown formulas in the result cells.

New_sheet is a logical value that, if TRUE, creates the cross-tabulation table on a new sheet, or, if FALSE, creates the cross-tabulation table on the existing sheet.

Related Functions

Function	Description
CROSSTAB	Defines the structure and content of a cross-tabluation table
CROSSTAB.DRILLDOWN	Returns the records in the active result cell in a cross-tabulation table

CROSSTAB.DRILLDOWN

Macro Sheets Only

Equivalent to double-clicking a cell that contains a summary value in a cross-tabulation table. Performs a database query to retrieve the records that are summarized in the cell.

If this function is not available, you must install the Crosstab add-in macro. For more information, see "Managing Add-in Commands and Functions" in Chapter 4 in Book 2 of the *Microsoft Excel User's Guide*.

Syntax

CROSSTAB.DRILLDOWN( )

Remarks

CROSSTAB.DRILLDOWN returns TRUE if successful or #N/A if the active cell is not in a cross-tabulation table or does not contain a summary value.

Related Function

Function	Description
CROSSTAB.CREATE	Creates a cross-tabulation table

CROSSTAB.RECALC

Macro Sheets Only

Equivalent to choosing the Recalculate Existing Crosstab command from the Data menu and then choosing the Recalculate Existing Crosstab button. Recalculates an existing cross-tabulation table.

If this function is not available, you must install the Crosstab add-in macro. For more information, see "Managing Add-in Commands and Functions" in Chapter 4 in Book 2 of the *Microsoft Excel User's Guide*.

Syntax

CROSSTAB.RECALC(*rebuild*)

Rebuild is a logical value that specifies the type of recalculation you want to perform.

- If *rebuild* is TRUE, CROSSTAB.RECALC recreates the cross-tabulation table from row, column, and value definitions. With this option, you can update the cross-tabulation table to reflect changes in the database.

- If *rebuild* is FALSE or omitted, CROSSTAB.RECALC recalculates the cross-tabulation table with its current layout and elements.

Related Functions

Function	Description
CROSSTAB.CREATE	Creates a cross-tabulation table
CROSSTAB.DRILLDOWN	Returns the records in the active result cell in a cross-tabulation table

CUMIPMT

Returns the cumulative interest paid on a loan between *start_period* and *end_period*.

If this function is not available, you must install the Analysis ToolPak add-in macro. For more information, see "Managing Add-in Commands and Functions" in Chapter 4 in Book 2 of the *Microsoft Excel User's Guide*.

Syntax

CUMIPMT(*rate,nper,pv,start_period,end_period, type*)

Rate is the interest rate.

Nper is the total number of payment periods.

Pv is the present value.

Start_period is the first period in the calculation. Payment periods are numbered beginning with 1.

End_period is the last period in the calculation.

Type is the timing of the payment.

Type	Timing
0	Payment at the end of the period
1	Payment at the beginning of the period

Remarks

- Make sure that you are consistent about the units you use for specifying *rate* and *nper*. If you make monthly payments on a four-year loan at 12% annual interest, use 12%/12 for *rate* and 4*12 for *nper*. If you make annual payments on the same loan, use 12% for *rate* and 4 for *nper*.

- *Nper, start_period, end_period,* and *type* are truncated to integers.

- If any argument is non-numeric, CUMIPMT returns the #VALUE! error value.

- If *rate* ≤ 0, *nper* ≤ 0, or *pv* ≤ 0, CUMIPMT returns the #NUM! error value.

- If *start_period* < 1, *end_period* < 1, or *start_period* > *end_period,* CUMIPMT returns the #NUM! error value.

- If *type* is any number other than 0 or 1, CUMIPMT returns the #NUM! error value.

Example

A home mortgage loan has the following terms:

Interest rate, 9.00% per annum (*rate* = 9.00% ÷ 12 = 0.0075)
Term, 30 years (*nper* = 30 x 12 = 360)
Present value, $125,000

The total interest paid in the second year of payments (periods 13 through 24) is:

CUMIPMT(0.0075,360,125000,13,24,0) equals –11135.23

The interest paid in a single payment, in the first month, is:

CUMIPMT(0.0075,360,125000,1,1,0) equals –937.50

Related Function

Function	Description
CUMPRINC	Returns the cumulative principal paid on a loan between two periods

CUMPRINC

Returns the cumulative principal paid on a loan between *start_period* and *end_period*.

If this function is not available, you must install the Analysis ToolPak add-in macro. For more information, see "Managing Add-in Commands and Functions" in Chapter 4 in Book 2 of the *Microsoft Excel User's Guide.*

Syntax

CUMPRINC(*rate,nper,pv,start_period,end_period, type*)

Rate is the interest rate.

Nper is the total number of payment periods.

Pv is the present value.

Start_period is the first period in the calculation. Payment periods are numbered beginning with 1.

End_period is the last period in the calculation.

Type is the timing of the payment.

Type	Timing
0	Payment at the end of the period
1	Payment at the beginning of the period

Remarks

- Make sure that you are consistent about the units you use for specifying *rate* and *nper.* If you make monthly payments on a four-year loan at 12% annual interest, use 12%/12 for *rate* and 4*12 for *nper.* If you make annual payments on the same loan, use 12% for *rate* and 4 for *nper.*

- *Nper, start_period, end_period,* and *type* are truncated to integers.

- If any argument is non-numeric, CUMPRINC returns the #VALUE! error value.

- If *rate* ≤ 0, *nper* ≤ 0, or *pv* ≤ 0, CUMPRINC returns the #NUM! error value.

- If *start_period* < 1, *end_period* < 1, or *start_period* > *end_period,* CUMPRINC returns the #NUM! error value.

- If *type* is any number other than 0 or 1, CUMPRINC returns the #NUM! error value.

Example

A home mortgage loan has the following terms:

Interest rate, 9.00% per annum (*rate* = 9.00% ÷ 12 = 0.0075)
Term, 30 years (*nper* = 30 x 12 = 360)
Present value, $125,000

The total principal paid in the second year of payments (periods 13 through 24) is:

CUMPRINC(0.0075,360,125000,13,24,0) equals −934.1071

The principal paid in a single payment, in the first month, is:

CUMPRINC(0.0075,360,125000,1,1,0) equals −68.27827

Related Function

Function	Description
CUMIPMT	Returns the cumulative interest paid on a loan between two periods

CUSTOM.REPEAT

Macro Sheets Only

Allows custom commands to be repeated using the Repeat tool or the Repeat command on the Edit menu. Also allows custom commands to be recorded using the macro recorder.

Syntax

CUSTOM.REPEAT(*macro_text,repeat_text, record_text*)

Macro_text   is the name of, or a reference to, the macro you want to run when the Repeat command is chosen. If *macro_text* is omitted, no repeat macro is run, but the custom command can still be recorded.

Repeat_text   is the text you want to use as the repeat command on the Edit menu (for example, "Repeat Reports") You can omit *repeat_text* and *macro_text* if you only want to record the formula specified by *record_text* when using the macro recorder.

Record_text   is the formula you want to record. For example, if the user chooses a command named Run Reports in Macro 1, the *record_text* argument would be "=Macro1!RunReports( )", where RunReports is the name of the macro called by the Run Reports command.

- References in *record_text* must be in R1C1 format.

- If *record_text* is omitted, the macro recorder records normally (a RUN function with the first cell of the macro as its argument).

- If you are not recording a macro, *record_text* is ignored.

Tip   Place CUSTOM.REPEAT at the end of the macro you will want to repeat. If you place it before the end, then the macro formulas that follow CUSTOM.REPEAT may interfere with the desired effects of CUSTOM.REPEAT. The Repeat tool and the Repeat command continue to change as you choose subsequent commands that can be repeated.

Example

The following macro formula specifies that the macro RepeatReport on the REPEAT.XLM macro sheet will be run when the Repeat Report command is chosen:

CUSTOM.REPEAT("REPEAT.XLM!RepeatReport", "Repeat Report")

Also see the example for CUSTOM.UNDO.

Related Function

Function	Description
CUSTOM.UNDO	Specifies a macro to run to undo a custom command

CUSTOM.UNDO

Macro Sheets Only

Creates a customized Undo tool and Undo or Redo command on the Edit menu for custom commands.

Syntax

CUSTOM.UNDO(*macro_text,undo_text*)

Macro_text   is the name of, or an R1C1-style reference to, the macro you want to run when the Undo command is chosen. *Macro_text* can be the name or cell reference of a macro.

Undo_text   is the text you want to use as the Undo command.

Example

The following macro function, which multiplies the active cell times 100, supports Undo, Redo, and Repeat, just as most built-in commands do.

	B	C
1	*Formulas*	*Comments*
2		
3	**Times100**	
4	=SET.NAME("Mcell",ACTIVE.CELL())	Names active cell "Mcell"
5	=FORMULA.GOTO(Mcell)	Activates Mcell
6	=FORMULA(Mcell*100)	Mcell * 100
7	=CUSTOM.UNDO("UndoMult","&Undo Times100")	Sets custom undo
8	=CUSTOM.REPEAT("Times100","&Repeat Times100")	Sets custom repeat
9	=RETURN()	
10		
11	**UndoMult**	
12	=FORMULA.GOTO(Mcell)	Activates Mcell
13	=FORMULA(Mcell/100)	Divides Mcell by 100
14	=CUSTOM.UNDO("R5C2","Redo (&u) Times100")	Sets custom redo
15	=RETURN()	

Tip   Use CUSTOM.UNDO directly after the macro functions you want to be able to repeat, because other macro functions following CUSTOM.UNDO might reset the Undo command.

CUSTOMIZE.TOOLBAR

Macro Sheets Only

Equivalent to choosing the Toolbars command from the Options menu and choosing the Customize button. Displays the Customize Toolbar dialog box. This function has a dialog-box syntax only.

Syntax

CUSTOMIZE.TOOLBAR?*(category)*

Category   is a number from 1 to 10 that specifies which category of tools you want displayed in the dialog box. If omitted, the previous setting is used.

Category	**Category of tools**
1	File
2	Edit
3	Formula
4	Formatting (nontext)
5	Text formatting
6	Drawing
7	Macro
8	Charting
9	Utility
10	Custom

Related Functions

Function	**Description**
ADD.TOOLBAR	Creates a new toolbar with the specified tools
SHOW.TOOLBAR	Hides or displays a toolbar

CUT

Macro Sheets Only

Equivalent to choosing the Cut command from the Edit menu. Cuts or moves data or objects. For detailed information about the Cut command, see online Help.

Syntax

CUT*(from_reference,to_reference)*

From_reference   is a reference to the cell or range of cells you want to cut. If *from_reference* is omitted, it is assumed to be the current selection.

To_reference is a reference to the cell or range of cells where you want to paste what you have cut.

- *To_reference* should be a single cell or an enlarged multiple of *from_reference*. For example, if *from_reference* is a 2 by 4 rectangle, *to_reference* can be a 4 by 8 rectangle.

- *To_reference* can be omitted so that you can paste *from_reference* later using the PASTE or PASTE.SPECIAL functions.

Remarks

The following information may be helpful if you're having problems with CUT updating references in unexpected ways. When you move cells using CUT, formulas that referred to *from_reference* will refer to *to_reference*, and formulas that referred to *to_reference* may return #REF! error values. However, if *from_reference* or *to_reference* contains references that are calculated at runtime (for example, CUT(ACTIVE.CELL(),!B1)), then Microsoft Excel does not update those references when the CUT function is run, so no error values are returned.

Examples

CUT() defines a selection that will be moved when you use one of the PASTE functions.

The following macro formula cuts cells from $A$4:$C$6 on the active worksheet and pastes them to a range whose upper-left corner is cell $T$7:

CUT(!$A$4:$C$6,!$T$7)

Related Functions

Function	Description
COPY	Copies and pastes data or objects
PASTE	Pastes cut or copied data

DATA.DELETE

Macro Sheets Only

Equivalent to choosing the Delete command from the Data menu (full menus). Deletes data that matches the current criteria in the current database. For detailed information about the Delete command, see online Help.

In the dialog-box form, DATA.DELETE?, Microsoft Excel displays a message warning you that matching records will be permanently deleted, and you can approve or cancel. In the plain form, DATA.DELETE, matching records are deleted without any message being displayed.

Syntax

DATA.DELETE( )
DATA.DELETE?( )

DATA.FIND

Macro Sheets Only

Equivalent to choosing the Find and Exit Find commands from the Data menu. Selects records in the database range which match criteria in the criteria range. For detailed information about the Find command, see online Help.

Syntax

DATA.FIND(*logical*)

Logical is a logical value that specifies whether to enter or exit the Data Find mode. If *logical* is TRUE, Microsoft Excel carries out the Find command; if FALSE, Microsoft Excel carries out the Exit Find command.

Related Functions

Function	Description
DATA.FIND.NEXT	Finds next matching record in a database
DATA.FIND.PREV	Finds previous matching record in a database

DATA.FIND.NEXT
DATA.FIND.PREV

Macro Sheets Only

Equivalent to pressing the DOWN ARROW or UP ARROW key after the Find command has been chosen from the Data menu. Finds the next or previous matching record in a database. If the function cannot find a matching record, it returns the logical value FALSE. For detailed information about the Find command, see online Help.

Syntax

DATA.FIND.NEXT( )
DATA.FIND.PREV( )

Related Function

Function	Description
DATA.FIND	Enters or exits Data Find mode

DATA.FORM

Macro Sheets Only

Equivalent to choosing the Form command from the Data menu. Displays the data form. For detailed information about the Form command, see online Help.

If no database is defined on the active sheet, DATA.FORM returns the #VALUE! error value and interrupts the macro.

Syntax

DATA.FORM( )

Remarks

You can create custom data forms by using the Dialog Editor to design a data entry dialog box and then naming the dialog-box definition table "Data_form" on the worksheet containing the database you want to use with the data form. You do not need to include the OK and Close buttons in your custom data form, because the data form includes its own buttons.

For more information about data forms, see Chapter 9 in Book 1 of the *Microsoft Excel User's Guide.*

DATA.SERIES

Macro Sheets Only

Equivalent to choosing the Series command from the Data menu. Use DATA.SERIES to enter an interpolated or incrementally increasing or decreasing series of numbers or dates on a worksheet or macro sheet. For detailed information about the Series command, see online Help.

Syntax

DATA.SERIES(*rowcol,type_num,date_num, step_value,stop_value,trend*)
DATA.SERIES?(*rowcol,type_num,date_num, step_value,stop_value,trend*)

Rowcol   is a number that specifies where the series should be entered. If *rowcol* is omitted, the default value is based on the size and shape of the current selection.

Rowcol	Enter series in
1	Rows
2	Columns

Type_num   is a number from 1 to 4 that specifies the type of series.

Type_num	Type of series
1 or omitted	Linear
2	Growth
3	Date
4	AutoFill

Date_num is a number from 1 to 4 that specifies the date unit of the series, as shown in the following table. To use the *date_num* argument, the *type_num* argument must be 3.

Date_num	Date unit
1 or omitted	Day
2	Weekday
3	Month
4	Year

Step_value is a number that specifies the step value for the series. If *step_value* is omitted, it is assumed to be 1.

Stop_value is a number that specifies the stop value for the series. If *stop_value* is omitted, DATA.SERIES continues filling the series until the end of the selected range.

Trend is a logical value corresponding to the Trend check box. If *trend* is TRUE, Microsoft Excel generates a linear or exponential trend; if FALSE or omitted, Microsoft Excel generates a standard data series.

Remarks

- If you specify a positive value for *stop_value* that is lower than the value in the active cell of the selection, DATA.SERIES takes no action.

- If *type_num* is 4 (AutoFill), Microsoft Excel performs an AutoFill operation just as if you had filled the selection by dragging the fill selection handle or had used the FILL.AUTO macro function. For more information, see "Filling a Range of Adjacent Cells" in Chapter 6 in Book 1 of the *Microsoft Excel User's Guide*.

Related Function

Function	Description
FILL.AUTO	Copies cells or automatically fills a selection

Database Functions

This section describes the 12 worksheet functions used for Microsoft Excel database calculations. For information about database structure and criteria, see Chapter 10 in Book 1 of the *Microsoft Excel User's Guide*. Each of these functions, referred to collectively as D*function*, uses three arguments: *database*, *field*, and *criteria*. These arguments refer to the worksheet ranges that are used in the database function.

The following illustration shows a sample database and criteria range.

	A	B	C	D
1	Name	Species	Age	Value
2				>500
3	Name	Species	Age	Value
4	Paul	Mallard	2.6	5
5	Wally	Wombat	2	650
6	Jo	Sun Bear	2	700
7	John	Crow	2.2	150
8	Steve	Carp	2.5	100
9	Lesley	White Tiger	2	1000
10	Dayle	Puffin	1.5	50

The *database* is the range A3:D10; the *fields* are Name, Species, Age, and Value; and the *criteria* are listed in cells A1:D2. To average the ages of all animals that are worth more than $500, you could use the DAVERAGE function as follows:

```
DAVERAGE(A3:D10,"Age",A1:D2)
```

Syntax

D*function*(*database,field,criteria*)

Database is the range of cells that make up the database.

- A Microsoft Excel database is a contiguous range of cells organized into records (rows) and fields (columns). The *database* reference can be entered as a cell range, or as a name assigned to a range.

- If you use the Set Database command from the Data menu on a selected range of cells, Microsoft Excel automatically names the range Database. For example, if you had selected the range A3:D10 in the example above and chosen the Set Database command, you could use:

```
DAVERAGE(Database,"Age",A1:D2)
```

Tips

- You can use any range that includes field headings at the top of each row of data as the *database* argument. This is useful if you want to perform D*function* calculations on more than one range of data on a worksheet.

- Remember that when you use a name as an argument, the name should not be enclosed in double quotation marks. When you use a field heading, you must use double quotation marks.

Field indicates which field is used in the function. Database fields are columns of data with an identifying field name in the first row. The *field* argument can be given as text, such as "Age" or "Value" in the example above, or as a field number: 1 for the first field (Name, in the example above), 2 for the second (Species), and so on.

Criteria is the range of cells that contains the database criteria. The *criteria* reference can be entered as a cell range, such as A1:D2 in the example above, or as a name assigned to a range. If you use the Set Criteria command from the Data menu on a selected range of cells, Microsoft Excel automatically names the range Criteria. For example, if you had selected the range A1:D2 in the example above and chosen the Set Criteria command, you could use this formula:

```
DAVERAGE(A3:D10,"Age",Criteria)
```

Tips

- You can use any range for the *criteria* argument, as long as it includes at least one field name and at least one cell for specifying a criteria comparison value.

- For example, if the range G1:G2 contains the field heading Income in G1 and the amount 10,000 in G2, you could define the range as MatchIncome and use that name as the *criteria* argument in your database functions.

- To perform an operation on an entire column in a database, enter a blank line below the field names in the criteria range.

Examples

The following illustration shows a sample database of employee records. Each row contains information about one employee. The database is defined as A3:E8, and the criteria are defined as A1:E2.

	A	B	C	D	E
1	Name	Hire Date	Age	Sex	Income
2		>1/1/84			
3	Name	Hire Date	Age	Sex	Income
4	Andrews, Jane	5/6/79	42	F	$17,000
5	Brown, Jessica	6/7/85	21	F	$39,000
6	Miller, Jim	12/1/70	64	M	$38,000
7	Sebring, Dave	9/23/84	34	M	$18,000
8	Smith, Cindy	2/1/83	34	F	$21,000

`DAVERAGE(Database,"Income",Criteria)` equals $28,500, the average income for employees hired after 1/1/84 (Jessica Brown and Dave Sebring).

`DAVERAGE(Database,3,Criteria)` equals 27.5, the average age for employees hired after 1/1/84.

`DCOUNT(Database,"Income",Criteria)` equals 2. This function looks at the records of employees hired after 1/1/84 and counts how many of the Income fields in those records contain numbers.

DCOUNT(Database,"Name",Criteria) equals 0. This function looks at the records of employees hired after 1/1/84 and counts how many of the Name fields in those records contain numbers.

DCOUNTA(Database,"Income",Criteria) equals 2. This function looks at the records of employees hired after 1/1/84 and counts how many of the Income fields in those records are not blank.

DMAX(Database,"Income",Database) equals $39,000, the maximum income value.

DMIN(Database,5,Criteria) equals $18,000, the minimum income for employees hired after 1/1/84.

The following illustration shows a database for a small orchard. Each record contains information about one tree. The database is defined as A1:E7, and the criteria are defined as A9:F11.

	A	B	C	D	E	F
1	Tree	Height	Age	Yield	Profit	
2	Apple	18	20	14	$105.00	
3	Pear	12	12	10	$96.00	
4	Cherry	13	14	9	$105.30	
5	Apple	14	15	10	$75.00	
6	Pear	9	8	8	$76.80	
7	Apple	8	9	6	$45.00	
8						
9	Tree	Height	Age	Yield	Profit	Height
10	Apple	>10				<16
11	Pear					

DSUM(Database,"Profit",A9:A10) equals $225.00, the total profit from apple trees.

DSUM(Database,"Profit",A9:F10) equals $75.00, the total profit from apple trees with a height between 10 and 16.

DPRODUCT(Database,"Yield",A9:F10) equals 10, the product of the yields from apple trees with a height between 10 and 16.

DAVERAGE(Database,3,Database) equals 13, the average age of all trees in the database.

DAVERAGE(Database,"Yield",A9:A11) equals 9.6, the average yield for apple and pear trees.

DSTDEV(Database,"Yield",A9:A11) equals 2.97, the estimated standard deviation in the yield of apple and pear trees if the data in the database is only a sample of the total orchard population.

DSTDEVP(Database,"Yield",A9:A11) equals 2.65, the true standard deviation in the yield of apple and pear trees if the data in the database is the entire population.

DVAR(Database,"Yield",A9:A11) equals 8.8, the estimated variance in the yield of apple and pear trees if the data in the database is only a sample of the total orchard population.

DVARP(Database,"Yield",A9:A11) equals 7.04, the true variance in the yield of apple and pear trees if the data in the database is the entire orchard population.

DGET(Database,"Yield",Criteria) returns the #NUM! error value because more than one record meets the criteria.

Related Functions

AVERAGE, COUNT, COUNTA, MAX, MIN, PRODUCT, STDEV, STDEVP, SUM, VAR, and VARP perform the same operations as the corresponding database functions. However, they operate on their lists of arguments instead of on selected database entries.

DATE

Returns the serial number of a particular date. For more information about serial numbers, see NOW.

Syntax

DATE(*year,month,day*)

Year   is a number from 1900 to 2078 in Microsoft Excel for Windows or 1904 to 2078 in Microsoft Excel for the Macintosh. To specify a year in the range 1920 to 2019, you can give the last two digits of the year. To specify a year before 1920 or after 2019, give all four digits of the year.

Month is a number representing the month of the year. If *month* is greater than 12, then *month* adds that number of months to the first month in the year specified. For example, DATE(90,14,2) returns the serial number representing February 2, 1991.

Day is a number representing the day of the month. If *day* is greater than the number of days in the month specified, then *day* adds that number of days to the first day in the month. For example,

DATE(91,1,35) returns the serial number representing February 4, 1991.

Note Microsoft Excel for Windows and Microsoft Excel for the Macintosh use different date systems as their default. For more information, see NOW.

Remarks

The DATE function is most useful in formulas where *year*, *month*, and *day* are formulas, not constants.

Examples

Using the 1900 Date System (the default in Microsoft Excel for Windows), DATE(91,1,1) equals 33239, the serial number corresponding to January 1, 1991.

Using the 1904 Date System (the default in Microsoft Excel for the Macintosh), DATE(91,1,1) equals 31777, the serial number corresponding to January 1, 1991.

The following example uses the 1900 Date System.

	A	B	C	D
1	Date of Sales			
2	Month	Day	Year	Term (in days)
3	1	24	91	90
4				

In the preceding worksheet, to find the due date for a bill due 90 days from 1/24/91, use: DATE(C3,A3,B3+D3), which equals 33352. The date corresponding to serial number 33352 is April 24, 1991.

Related Functions

Function	Description
DATEVALUE	Converts a date in the form of text to a serial number
DAY, MONTH, and YEAR	Convert serial numbers to days, months, and years
NOW	Returns the serial number of the current date and time
TIMEVALUE	Converts a time in the form of text to a serial number
TODAY	Returns the serial number of today's date

DATEVALUE

Returns the serial number of the date represented by *date_text*. Use DATEVALUE to convert a date represented by text to a serial number.

Syntax

DATEVALUE(*date_text*)

Date_text is text that returns a date in a Microsoft Excel date format. Using the default date system in Microsoft Excel for Windows, *date_text* must represent a date from January 1, 1900 to December 31, 2078. Using the default date system in Microsoft Excel for the Macintosh, *date_text* must represent a date from January 1, 1904 to December 31, 2078. DATEVALUE returns the #VALUE! error value if *date_text* is out of this range.

If the year portion of *date_text* is omitted, DATEVALUE uses the current year from your computer's built-in clock. Time information in *date_text* is ignored.

Remarks

Most functions automatically convert date values to serial numbers.

Note Microsoft Excel for Windows and Microsoft Excel for the Macintosh use different date systems as their default. For more information, see NOW.

Examples

The following examples use the 1900 Date System:

DATEVALUE("8/22/55") equals 20323

DATEVALUE("22-AUG-55") equals 20323

Assuming your computer's built-in clock is set to 1992 and you are using the 1900 Date System:

DATEVALUE("5-JUL") equals 33790

Related Functions

Function	Description
NOW	Returns the serial number of the current date and time
TIMEVALUE	Converts a time in the form of text to a serial number
TODAY	Returns the serial number of today's date

DAVERAGE

Averages the values in the *field* column of records in the *database* which match the *criteria*. For more information about Microsoft Excel database functions, see Database Functions.

Syntax

DAVERAGE(*database,field,criteria*)

DAY

Returns the day of the month corresponding to *serial_number*. The day is given as an integer ranging from 1 to 31.

Syntax

DAY(*serial_number*)

Serial_number is the date-time code used by Microsoft Excel for date and time calculations. You can give *serial_number* as text, such as "4-15-91" or "15-Apr-1991", instead of as a number. The text is automatically converted to a serial number. For more information about *serial_number*, see NOW.

Note Microsoft Excel for Windows and Microsoft Excel for the Macintosh use different date systems as their default. For more information, see NOW.

Examples

DAY("4-Jan") equals 4

DAY("15-Apr-1991") equals 15

DAY("8/11/91") equals 11

Related Functions

Function	Description
NOW	Returns the serial number of the current date and time
TODAY	Returns the serial number of today's date
YEAR, MONTH, WEEKDAY, HOUR, MINUTE, and SECOND	Convert serial numbers into years, months, days of the week, hours, minutes, and seconds

DAYS360

Returns the number of days between two dates based on a 360-day year (twelve 30-day months). Use this function to help compute payments if your accounting system is based on twelve 30-day months.

Syntax

DAYS360(*start_date,end_date*)

Start_date and *end_date* are the two dates between which you want to know the number of days.

- The arguments can be either text strings using numbers to represent the month, day, and year (for example, "1/30/91" or "1-30-91"), or they can be serial numbers representing the dates.

- If *start_date* occurs after *end_date*, DAYS360 returns a negative number.

Tip To determine the number of days between two dates in a normal year, you can use normal subtraction—for example, "12/31/91"–"1/1/91" equals 364.

Example

DAYS360("1/30/91","2/1/91") equals 1

Related Function

Function	Description
DAY	Converts a serial number to a day of the month

DB

Returns the real depreciation of an asset for a specific period using the fixed-declining balance method.

Syntax

DB(*cost,salvage,life,period,month*)

Cost is the initial cost of the asset.

Salvage is the value at the end of the depreciation (sometimes called the salvage value of the asset).

Life is the number of periods over which the asset is being depreciated (sometimes called the useful life of the asset).

Period is the period for which you want to calculate the depreciation. *Period* must use the same units as *life*.

Month is the number of months in the first year. If *month* is omitted, it is assumed to be 12.

Remarks

The fixed-declining balance method computes depreciation at a fixed rate. DB uses the following formulas to calculate depreciation for a period:

(*cost* – total depreciation from prior periods) * *rate*

where

rate = 1 – ((*salvage* / *cost*) ^ (1 / *life*)), rounded to three decimal places

Depreciation for the first and last periods are special cases. For the first period, DB uses this formula:

cost * *rate* * *month* / 12

For the last period, DB uses this formula:

((*cost* – total depreciation from prior periods) * *rate* * (12 – *month*)) / 12

Examples

Suppose a factory purchases a new machine. The machine costs $1,000,000 and has a lifetime of six years. The salvage value of the machine is $100,000. The following examples show depreciation over the life of the machine. The results are rounded to whole numbers.

DB(1000000,100000,6,1,7) equals $186,083
DB(1000000,100000,6,2,7) equals $259,639
DB(1000000,100000,6,3,7) equals $176,814
DB(1000000,100000,6,4,7) equals $120,411
DB(1000000,100000,6,5,7) equals $82,000
DB(1000000,100000,6,6,7) equals $55,842
DB(1000000,100000,6,7,7) equals $15,845

Related Functions

Function	Description
DDB	Returns the depreciation of an asset for a specified period using the double-declining balance method
SLN	Returns the straight-line depreciation of an asset for one period

Related Functions

Function	Description
SYD	Returns the sum-of-years' digits depreciation of an asset for a specified period
VDB	Returns the depreciation of an asset for a specified or partial period using a declining balance method

DCOUNT

Counts the cells that contain numbers that match the *criteria* in the *field* column of records in the *database*.

The *field* argument is optional. If *field* is omitted, DCOUNT counts all records in the database which match the criteria. For more information about Microsoft Excel database functions, see Database Functions.

Syntax

DCOUNT(*database*,*field*,*criteria*)

DCOUNTA

Counts the cells that are not blank and that satisfy the *criteria* in the *field* column of records in the *database*. For more information, see Database Functions.

Syntax

DCOUNTA(*database*,*field*,*criteria*)

DDB

Returns the depreciation of an asset for a specific period using the double-declining balance method or some other method you specify.

Syntax

DDB(*cost*,*salvage*,*life*,*period*,*factor*)

Cost is the initial cost of the asset.

Salvage is the value at the end of the depreciation (sometimes called the salvage value of the asset).

Life is the number of periods over which the asset is being depreciated (sometimes called the useful life of the asset).

Period is the period for which you want to calculate the depreciation. *Period* must use the same units as *life*.

Factor is the rate at which the balance declines. If *factor* is omitted, it is assumed to be 2 (the double-declining balance method).

All five arguments must be positive numbers.

Remarks

The double-declining balance method computes depreciation at an accelerated rate. Depreciation is highest in the first period and decreases in successive periods. DDB uses the following formula to calculate depreciation for a period:

cost − *salvage*(total depreciation from prior periods) ∗ *factor* / *life*

Change *factor* if you do not want to use the double-declining balance method.

Examples

Suppose a factory purchases a new machine. The machine costs $2400 and has a lifetime of 10 years. The salvage value of the machine is $300. The following examples show depreciation over several periods. The results are rounded to two decimal places.

DDB(2400,300,3650,1) equals $1.32, the first day's depreciation. Microsoft Excel automatically assumes that *factor* is 2.

DDB(2400,300,120,1,2) equals $40.00, the first month's depreciation.

`DDB(2400,300,10,1,2)` equals $480.00, the first year's depreciation.

`DDB(2400,300,10,2,1.5)` equals $306.00, the second year's depreciation using a *factor* of 1.5 instead of the double-declining balance method.

`DDB(2400,300,10,10)` equals $22.12, the 10th year's depreciation. Microsoft Excel automatically assumes that *factor* is 2.

Related Functions

Function	Description
SLN	Returns the straight-line depreciation of an asset for one period
SYD	Returns the sum-of-years' digits depreciation of an asset for a specified period
VDB	Returns the depreciation of an asset for a specified or partial period using a declining balance method

DEC2BIN

Converts a decimal integer to binary.

If this function is not available, you must install the Analysis ToolPak add-in macro. For more information, see "Managing Add-in Commands and Functions" in Chapter 4 in Book 2 of the *Microsoft Excel User's Guide*.

Syntax

DEC2BIN(*number,places*)

Number is the decimal integer you want to convert. If *number* is negative, *places* is ignored and DEC2BIN returns a 10-character (10-bit) binary number in which the most significant bit is the sign bit. The remaining 9 bits are magnitude bits. Negative numbers are represented using two's-complement notation.

Places is the number of characters to use. If *places* is omitted, DEC2BIN uses the minimum number of characters necessary. *Places* is useful for padding the return value with leading 0s (zeros).

Remarks

- If *number* < –512 or if *number* > 511, DEC2BIN returns the #NUM! error value.

- If *number* is non-numeric, DEC2BIN returns the #VALUE! error value.

- If DEC2BIN requires more than *places* characters, it returns the #NUM! error value.

- If *places* is not an integer, it is truncated.

- If *places* is non-numeric, DEC2BIN returns the #VALUE! error value.

- If *places* is negative, DEC2BIN returns the #NUM! error value.

Examples

`DEC2BIN(9,4)` equals 1001

`DEC2BIN(-100)` equals 1110011100

Related Functions

Function	Description
BIN2DEC	Converts a binary number to decimal
HEX2DEC	Converts a hexadecimal number to decimal
OCT2DEC	Converts an octal number to decimal

DEC2HEX

Converts a decimal integer to hexadecimal.

If this function is not available, you must install the Analysis ToolPak add-in macro. For more information, see "Managing Add-in Commands and Functions" in Chapter 4 in Book 2 of the *Microsoft Excel User's Guide*.

Syntax

DEC2HEX(*number,places*)

Number is the decimal integer you want to convert. If *number* is negative, *places* is ignored and DEC2HEX returns a 10-character (40-bit) hexadecimal number in which the most significant bit is the sign bit. The remaining 39 bits are magnitude bits. Negative numbers are represented using two's-complement notation.

Places is the number of characters to use. If *places* is omitted, DEC2HEX uses the minimum number of characters necessary. *Places* is useful for padding the return value with leading 0s (zeros).

Remarks

- If *number* < –549,755,813,888 or if *number* > 549,755,813,887, DEC2HEX returns the #NUM! error value.

- If *number* is non-numeric, DEC2HEX returns the #VALUE! error value.

- If DEC2HEX requires more than *places* characters, it returns the #NUM! error value.

- If *places* is not an integer, it is truncated.

- If *places* is non-numeric, DEC2HEX returns the #VALUE! error value.

- If *places* is negative, DEC2HEX returns the #NUM! error value.

Examples

DEC2HEX(100,4) equals 0064

DEC2HEX(-54) equals FFFFFFFFCA

Related Functions

Function	Description
BIN2DEC	Converts a binary number to decimal
HEX2DEC	Converts a hexadecimal number to decimal
OCT2DEC	Converts an octal number to decimal

DEC2OCT

Converts a decimal integer to octal.

If this function is not available, you must install the Analysis ToolPak add-in macro. For more information, see "Managing Add-in Commands and Functions" in Chapter 4 in Book 2 of the *Microsoft Excel User's Guide*.

Syntax

DEC2OCT(*number,places*)

Number is the decimal integer you want to convert. If *number* is negative, *places* is ignored and DEC2OCT returns a 10-character (30-bit) octal number in which the most significant bit is the sign bit. The remaining 29 bits are magnitude bits. Negative numbers are represented using two's-complement notation.

Places is the number of characters to use. If *places* is omitted, DEC2OCT uses the minimum number of characters necessary. *Places* is useful for padding the return value with leading 0s (zeros).

Remarks

- If *number* < –536,870,912 or if *number* > 536,870,911, DEC2OCT returns the #NUM! error value.

- If *number* is non-numeric, DEC2OCT returns the #VALUE! error value.

- If DEC2OCT requires more than *places* characters, it returns the #NUM! error value.

- If *places* is not an integer, it is truncated.

- If *places* is non-numeric, DEC2OCT returns the #VALUE! error value.

- If *places* is negative, DEC2OCT returns the #NUM! error value.

Examples

DEC2OCT(58,3) equals 072

DEC2OCT(-100) equals 7777777634

Related Functions

Function	Description
BIN2DEC	Converts a binary number to decimal
HEX2DEC	Converts a hexadecimal number to decimal
OCT2DEC	Converts an octal number to decimal

DEFINE.NAME

Macro Sheets Only

Equivalent to choosing the Define Name command from the Formula menu. Defines a name on the active worksheet or macro sheet. Use DEFINE.NAME instead of SET.NAME when you want to define a name on the active document. For detailed information about the Define Name command, see online Help.

Syntax

DEFINE.NAME*(name_text,refers_to,macro_type, shortcut_text,hidden,category)*
DEFINE.NAME?*(name_text,refers_to,macro_type, shortcut_text,hidden,category)*

Name_text   is the text you want to use as the name. Names must start with a letter, cannot include spaces or symbols, and cannot look like cell references.

Refers_to   describes what *name_text* should refer to, and can be any of the following values.

If *refers_*to is	Then *name_text* is
A number, text, or logical value	Defined to refer to that value
An external reference, such as !$A\$1 or SALES!$A$1:$C$3	Defined to refer to those cells

If *refers_*to is	Then *name_text* is
A formula in the form of text, such as "=2*PI()/360" (if the formula contains references, they must be R1C1-style references, such as "=R2C2*(1+ RC[−1])")	Defined to refer to that formula
Omitted	Defined to refer to the current selection

The next two arguments, *macro_type* and *shortcut_text,* apply only if the document in the active window is a macro sheet.

Macro_type   is a number from 1 to 3 that indicates the type of macro.

Macro_type	Type of macro
1	Custom function (also known as a function macro)
2	Command macro
3 or omitted	None (that is, *name_text* does not refer to a macro)

Shortcut_text   is a text value that specifies the macro shortcut key. *Shortcut_text* must be a single letter, such as "z" or "Z".

Hidden   is a logical value specifying whether to define the name as a hidden name. If *hidden* is TRUE, Microsoft Excel defines the name as a hidden name; if FALSE or omitted, Microsoft Excel defines the name normally.

Category   is a number or text identifying the category of a custom function and corresponds to categories in the Function Category list box.

- Categories are numbered starting with 1, the first category in the list.

- If *category* is text but is not one of the existing function types, Microsoft Excel creates a new category and assigns your custom function to it.

Remarks

- You can use hidden names to define values that you want to prevent the user from seeing or changing; they do not appear in the Define Name, Paste Name, or Goto dialog boxes. Hidden names can only be created with the DEFINE.NAME macro function.

- If you are recording a macro and you define a name to refer to a formula, Microsoft Excel converts A1-style references to R1C1-style references. For example, if the active cell is C2, and you define the name Previous to refer to =B2, Microsoft Excel records that command as DEFINE.NAME("Previous","=RC[–1]").

- In DEFINE.NAME?, the dialog-box form of the function, if *refers_to* is not specified, the current selection is proposed in the Refers To box. Also, if a name is not specified, text in the active cell is proposed as the name.

- For information about using text, number, and logical arguments, see "Converting Data Types" in the first section, "About Functions."

Examples

The following macro formula defines the name Inflation on the active worksheet to refer to the value 0.12:

```
DEFINE.NAME("Inflation",0.12)
```

If the range A1:C3 is selected, each of the following macro formulas defines the name Sales on the active worksheet to refer to that selection:

```
DEFINE.NAME("Sales")
DEFINE.NAME("Sales",SELECTION())
DEFINE.NAME("Sales","=R1C1:R3C3")
DEFINE.NAME("Sales",!$A$1:$C$3)
```

The following macro formula defines the name Previous to refer to the relative reference RC[–1]:

```
DEFINE.NAME("Previous","=RC[-1]")
```

If the range A1:C3 is selected, the following macro formula defines the name Sales on the active worksheet to refer to A1:C1, the first row of the selection:

```
DEFINE.NAME("Sales",INDEX(SELECTION(),1,0))
```

Using R1C1-style references, the following macro formula defines the name SalesAverage to refer to the formula AVERAGE(R1C1:R1C5):

```
DEFINE.NAME("SalesAverage",
"=AVERAGE(R1C1:R1C5)")
```

The following macro formula defines the custom function COUNTPARTS in the custom category Data Entry to refer to cell C3 on the active macro sheet:

```
DEFINE.NAME("COUNTPARTS",!$C$3,1,,,"Data
Entry")
```

Related Functions

Function	Description
DELETE.NAME	Deletes a name
GET.DEF	Returns a name matching a definition
GET.NAME	Returns the definition of a name
NAMES	Returns the names defined in a document
SET.NAME	Defines a name as a value

DEFINE.STYLE

Macro Sheets Only

Equivalent to choosing the Define button in the Style dialog box, which appears when you choose the Style command from the Format menu. Creates and changes cell styles. There are seven syntax forms of this function. Use syntax 1 of DEFINE.STYLE to define styles based on the format of the active cell. To create a style by specifying number, font, and other formats, use syntaxes 2 through 7 of DEFINE.STYLE. For detailed information about the Style command, see online Help.

Syntax 1

By example

DEFINE.STYLE(*style_text,number,font, alignment,border,pattern,protection*)
DEFINE.STYLE?(*style_text,number,font, alignment,border,pattern,protection*)

Style_text   is the name, as text, that you want to assign to the style.

The following arguments are logical values corresponding to check boxes in the expanded Style dialog box. If an argument is TRUE, Microsoft Excel selects the check box and uses the corresponding format of the active cell in the style; if FALSE, Microsoft Excel clears the check box and omits formatting descriptions for that attribute. If *style_text* is omitted and all selected cells have identical formatting, the default is TRUE; if cells have different formatting, the default is FALSE.

Number   corresponds to the Number check box.

Font   corresponds to the Font check box.

Alignment   corresponds to the Alignment check box.

Border   corresponds to the Border check box.

Pattern   corresponds to the Pattern check box.

Protection   corresponds to the Protection check box.

Examples

The following macro formula defines a new style named Headings, which has all the formatting attributes of the active cell.

```
DEFINE.STYLE("Headings")
```

If a Headings style is already defined, the above formula replaces the current definition of the style with the formatting attributes of the active cell.

The following macro formula uses the number, font, and border attributes of the active cell to create a new style called Titles:

```
DEFINE.STYLE("Titles",TRUE,TRUE,FALSE,TRUE,
FALSE,FALSE)
```

Related Functions

Function	Description
APPLY.STYLE	Applies a style to the selection
DELETE.STYLE	Deletes a cell style
MERGE.STYLES	Imports styles from another document into the active document

DEFINE.STYLE

Macro Sheets Only

Equivalent to choosing the Define button in the Style dialog box, which appears when you choose the Style command from the Format menu. Creates and changes cell styles. Use one of the following syntax forms of DEFINE.STYLE to select cell formats for a new style or to alter the formats of an existing style. Use syntax 1 of DEFINE.STYLE to define styles based on the format of the active cell. For detailed information about the Style command, see online Help.

Syntax 2

Number format, using the arguments from the FORMAT.NUMBER function

DEFINE.STYLE(*style_text,attribute_num, format_text*)

Syntax 3

Font format, using the arguments from the FORMAT.FONT function

DEFINE.STYLE(*style_text,attribute_num, name_text,size_num,bold,italic,underline,strike, color, outline,shadow*)

Syntax 4

Alignment, using the arguments from the ALIGNMENT function

DEFINE.STYLE(*style_text,attribute_num, horiz_align,wrap,vert_align,orientation*)

Syntax 5

Border, using the arguments from the BORDER function

DEFINE.STYLE(*style_text,attribute_num, left,right,top,bottom,left_color,right_color, top_color, bottom_color)*

Syntax 6

Pattern, using the arguments from the cell form of the PATTERNS function

DEFINE.STYLE(*style_text,attribute_num, apattern,afore,aback)*

Syntax 7

Cell protection, using the arguments from the CELL.PROTECTION function

DEFINE.STYLE(*style_text,attribute_num,locked, hidden)*

Style_text   is the name, as text, that you want to assign to the style.

Attribute_num   is a number from 2 to 7 that specifies which attribute of the style, such as its font, alignment, or number format, you want to designate with this function.

Attribute_num	Specifies
2	Number format
3	Font format
4	Alignment
5	Border
6	Pattern
7	Cell protection

Remarks

- The remaining arguments are different for each form and are identical to arguments in the corresponding function. For example, form 2 of DEFINE.STYLE defines the number format of a style and corresponds to the FORMAT.NUMBER function. The exception is form 5, which does not include every argument for BORDER. For details on the values you can use for these arguments, see the description under the corresponding function.

- If you define a style using one of these forms, then any attributes you don't explicitly define are not changed.

Example

The following portion of a macro creates a new style named Totals, sets alignment to centered, sets a number format, and sets the font to Courier, 14-point bold.

	B	C
10	=DEFINE.STYLE("Totals",4,3)	Sets alignment to centered
11	=DEFINE.STYLE("Totals",2,"$#,##0_);[Red]($#,##0)")	Sets number format
12	=DEFINE.STYLE("Totals",3,"Courier",14,TRUE)	Sets font format

Related Functions

Function	Description
APPLY.STYLE	Applies a style to the selection
DELETE.STYLE	Deletes a cell style
MERGE.STYLES	Imports styles from another document into the active document

DEGREES

Converts radians into degrees.

If this function is not available, you must install the Add-in Functions add-in macro. For more information, see "Managing Add-in Commands and Functions" in Chapter 4 in Book 2 of the *Microsoft Excel User's Guide*.

Syntax

DEGREES(*angle in_radians*)

Angle_in_radians is the angle in radians that you want to convert.

Example

DEGREES(PI()) equals 180

Related Function

Function	Description
RADIANS	Converts degrees to radians

DELETE.ARROW

Macro Sheets Only

Equivalent to choosing the Delete Arrow command from the Chart menu. Deletes the selected arrow. For detailed information about the Delete Arrow command, see online Help.

Syntax

DELETE.ARROW( )

If the selection is not an arrow or if the active document is not a chart, DELETE.ARROW returns the #VALUE! error value and interrupts the macro.

Tip Use the SELECT function (chart syntax), with the number of the arrow you want to delete—for example, SELECT ("Arrow 1")—to select the arrow before using the DELETE.ARROW function. You can also use the CLEAR function to delete the arrow.

Related Functions

Function	Description
CLEAR	Clears specified information from the selected cells or chart
DELETE.OVERLAY	Deletes the overlay on a chart

DELETE.BAR

Macro Sheets Only

Deletes a custom menu bar.

Syntax

DELETE.BAR(*bar_num*)

Bar_num is the ID number of the custom menu bar you want to delete.

Tip Rather than trying to discover the ID number of the menu bar you want to delete, use a reference to the ADD.BAR function that created the bar. For example, the following macro formula deletes the menu bar created by the ADD.BAR function in the cell named ReportsBar:

DELETE.BAR(ReportsBar)

For information about custom menus, see Chapter 8 in Book 2 of the *Microsoft Excel User's Guide*.

Related Functions

Function	Description
ADD.BAR	Adds a menu bar
SHOW.BAR	Displays a menu bar

DELETE.COMMAND

Macro Sheets Only

Deletes a command from a custom or built-in menu. Use DELETE.COMMAND to remove commands you don't want the user to have access to.

Syntax

DELETE.COMMAND(*bar_num,menu, command*)

Bar_num is the menu bar from which you want to delete the command. *Bar_num* can be the ID number of a built-in or custom menu bar. See ADD.COMMAND for a list of ID numbers for built-in menu bars.

Menu is the menu from which you want to delete the command. *Menu* can be the name of a menu as text or the number of a menu. Menus are numbered starting with 1 from the left of the screen.

Command is the command you want to delete. *Command* can be the name of the command as text or the number of the command; the first command on a menu is in position 1.

- If the specified command does not exist, DELETE.COMMAND returns the #VALUE! error value and interrupts the macro.

- After a command is deleted, the *command* number for all commands below that command is decreased by one.

- When you delete a built-in command, DELETE.COMMAND returns a unique ID number for that command. You can use this ID number with ADD.COMMAND to restore the built-in command to the original menu.

For more information about custom menus, see Chapter 8 in Book 2 of the *Microsoft Excel User's Guide.*

Example

The following macro formula removes the Compile Reports command from the Reports menu on a custom menu bar created by the ADD.BAR function in a cell named Financials.

```
DELETE.COMMAND(Financials,"Reports",
"Compile Reports")
```

Related Functions

Function	Description
ADD.COMMAND	Adds a command to a menu
CHECK.COMMAND	Adds or deletes a check mark to or from a command
ENABLE.COMMAND	Enables or disables a menu or custom command
RENAME.COMMAND	Changes the name of a command or menu

DELETE.DIRECTORY

Macro Sheets Only

Deletes an empty directory or folder. If the specified directory or folder is not empty, DELETE.DIRECTORY returns FALSE.

If this function is not available, you must load FILEFNS.XLA from the Library directory (in Microsoft Excel for Windows) or File Functions from the Macro Library folder (in Microsoft Excel for the Macintosh) in the directory or folder where you installed Microsoft Excel. For more information, see "Managing Add-in Commands and Functions" in Chapter 4 in Book 2 of the *Microsoft Excel User's Guide.*

Syntax

DELETE.DIRECTORY(*path_text*)

Path_text is the name of the directory or folder in the current directory or folder, or the path of the directory or folder you want to delete.

Examples

In Microsoft Excel for Windows, the following macro formula deletes the empty SALEWEST directory from the current directory:

```
DELETE.DIRECTORY("SALEWEST")
```

The following macro formula deletes the empty SALEWEST directory from the directory C:\WORD\REPORTS:

```
DELETE.DIRECTORY("C:\WORD\REPORTS\
SALEWEST")
```

In Microsoft Excel for the Macintosh, the following macro formula deletes the empty AUGUST SALES folder from the current folder:

```
DELETE.DIRECTORY("AUGUST SALES")
```

The following macro formula deletes the empty AUGUST SALES folder from the folder HARD DISK:WORD:REPORTS:

```
DELETE.DIRECTORY("HARD DISK:WORD:
REPORTS:AUGUST SALES")
```

Related Functions

Function	Description
CREATE.DIRECTORY	Creates a directory or folder
FILE.DELETE	Deletes a file
FILE.EXISTS	Tests for the existence of a file, directory, or folder

DELETE.FORMAT

Macro Sheets Only

Equivalent to deleting the specified format with the Number command from the Format menu. Deletes a specified custom number format.

Syntax

DELETE.FORMAT(*format_text*)

Format_text is the custom format given as a text string, for example, "000-00-0000". If you specify a built-in Microsoft Excel format, DELETE.FORMAT returns the #VALUE! error value.

Remarks

When you delete a custom number format, all numbers formatted with that number format are formatted with the General format.

Example

The following macro gets the custom number format of the active cell and deletes it.

	A	B	C
1	Names	Formulas	Comments
2			
3		RemoveFormat	Removes format of active cell
4	DelFormat	=GET.CELL(7,ACTIVE.CELL())	Gets format of active cell
5		=DELETE.FORMAT(DelFormat)	Deletes the format
6		=RETURN()	

Related Functions

Function	Description
FORMAT.NUMBER	Applies a number format to the selection
GET.CELL	Returns information about the specified cell

DELETE.MENU

Macro Sheets Only

Deletes a menu from a menu bar. Use DELETE.MENU to delete menus you have added to menu bars when the supporting macro sheet is closed (using an Auto Close macro), or any time you want to remove a menu.

Syntax

DELETE.MENU(*bar_num,menu*)

Bar_num is the menu bar from which you want to delete the menu. *Bar_num* can be the number of a Microsoft Excel built-in menu bar or the number returned by a previously run ADD.BAR function. For a list of ID numbers for built-in menu bars, see ADD.COMMAND.

Menu is the menu you want to delete. *Menu* can be either the name of a menu as text or the number of a menu. Menus are numbered starting with 1 from the left of the screen. If the specified menu does not exist, DELETE.MENU returns the #VALUE! error value and interrupts the macro. After a menu is deleted, the *menu* number for each menu to the right of that menu is decreased by 1.

For more information about custom menus, see Chapter 8 in Book 2 of the *Microsoft Excel User's Guide*.

Remarks

You cannot delete a shortcut menu. Instead, use ENABLE.COMMAND to prevent the user from accessing a shortcut menu.

Example

The following macro formula deletes the Reports menu from the custom menu bar created by the ADD.BAR function in a cell named Financials:

```
DELETE.MENU(Financials,"Reports")
```

Related Functions

Function	Description
ADD.MENU	Adds a menu to a menu bar
DELETE.BAR	Deletes a menu bar
DELETE.COMMAND	Deletes a command from a menu
ENABLE.COMMAND	Enables or disables a menu or custom command

DELETE.NAME

Macro Sheets Only

Equivalent to deleting a name on the active document with the Define Name command from the Formula menu. Deletes the specified name. For detailed information about the Define Name command, see online Help.

Syntax

DELETE.NAME(*name_text*)

Name_text is a text value specifying the name that you want to delete. For information about using text arguments, see "Converting Data Types" in the first section, "About Functions."

Important Formulas that use names in their arguments may return incorrect or error values when a name used in the formula is deleted.

Example

The following macro formula deletes the name Inflation from the active document:

```
DELETE.NAME("Inflation")
```

Related Functions

Function	Description
DEFINE.NAME	Defines a name on the active workheet or macro sheet
GET.NAME	Returns the definition of a name
SET.NAME	Defines a name as a value

DELETE.OVERLAY

Macro Sheets Only

Equivalent to choosing the Delete Overlay command from the Chart menu (full menus). Deletes an overlay from a chart. If the chart has no overlay, DELETE.OVERLAY takes no action and returns TRUE. For detailed information about the Delete Overlay command, see online Help.

Syntax

DELETE.OVERLAY( )

Related Functions

All the 2-D GALLERY functions, which create the seven 2-D chart types, include a *delete_overlay* argument. If *delete_overlay* is set to TRUE, the existing overlay is deleted and the new format is applied to the main chart.

DELETE.STYLE

Macro Sheets Only

Equivalent to choosing the Delete button from the expanded Style dialog box, which appears when you choose the Style command from the Format menu. Deletes a style from a document. Cells formatted with the deleted style revert to the Normal style.

For detailed information about the Style command, see online Help.

Syntax

DELETE.STYLE*(style_text)*

Style_text   is the name of a style to be deleted. If *style_text* does not exist, DELETE.STYLE returns the #VALUE! error value and interrupts the macro.

For more information about using text arguments, see "Converting Data Types" in the first section, "About Functions."

Remarks

You can only delete styles from the active document. External references are not permitted as part of the *style_text* argument.

Examples

The following macro formula deletes the custom style named Titles on the active document:

```
DELETE.STYLE("Titles")
```

The following macro formula deletes the style of the active cell:

```
DELETE.STYLE(GET.CELL(40))
```

Related Functions

Function	Description
APPLY.STYLE	Applies a style to the selection
DEFINE.STYLE	Creates or changes a cell style
MERGE.STYLES	Merges styles from another document into the active document

DELETE.TOOL

Macro Sheets Only

Equivalent to selecting a tool and dragging it to an area other than a toolbar. Deletes a tool from a toolbar.

Syntax

DELETE.TOOL*(bar_id,position)*

Bar_id   specifies the name or number of a toolbar from which you want to delete a tool. For detailed information about *bar_id*, see ADD.TOOL.

Position   specifies the position of the tool within the toolbar. *Position* starts with 1 at the left side (if horizontal) or at the top (if vertical).

Example

The following macro formula deletes the third tool from the left (if horizontal or floating) or from the top (if vertical) in Toolbar11:

```
DELETE.TOOL("Toolbar11",3)
```

Related Functions

Function	Description
ADD.TOOL	Adds one or more tools to a toolbar
ADD.TOOLBAR	Creates a new toolbar with the specified tools
DELETE.TOOLBAR	Deletes custom toolbars

DELETE.TOOLBAR

Macro Sheets Only

Equivalent to choosing the Delete button from the Show Toolbars dialog box, which appears when you choose the Toolbars command from the Options menu. Deletes a custom toolbar.

Syntax

DELETE.TOOLBAR(*bar_name*)

Bar_name specifies the name of the toolbar that you want to delete. For detailed information about *bar_name,* see ADD.TOOL.

Remarks

- You cannot delete built-in toolbars.

- If DELETE.TOOLBAR successfully deletes the toolbar, it returns TRUE. If you try to delete a built-in toolbar, DELETE.TOOLBAR returns the #VALUE! error value and takes no other action.

Example

The following macro formula deletes Toolbar12:

```
DELETE.TOOLBAR("Toolbar12")
```

Related Functions

Function	Description
ADD.TOOLBAR	Creates a new toolbar with the specified tools
RESET.TOOLBAR	Resets a built-in toolbar to its initial default setting

DELTA

Tests whether two values are equal. Returns 1 if *number1* = *number2*; returns 0 otherwise. Use this function to filter a set of values. For example, by summing several DELTA functions you calculate the count of equal pairs. This function is also known as the Kronecker Delta function.

If this function is not available, you must install the Analysis ToolPak add-in macro. For more information, see "Managing Add-in Commands and Functions" in Chapter 4 in Book 2 of the *Microsoft Excel User's Guide.*

Syntax

DELTA(*number1,number2*)

Number1 is the first number.

Number2 is the second number. If omitted, *number2* is assumed to be zero.

Remarks

- If *number1* is non-numeric, DELTA returns the #VALUE! error value.

- If *number2* is non-numeric, DELTA returns the #VALUE! error value.

Examples

DELTA(5,4) equals 0

DELTA(5,5) equals 1

DELTA(0.5,0) equals 0

Related Function

Function	Description
GESTEP	Tests whether a number is greater than a threshold value

DEMOTE

Macro Sheets Only

Equivalent to clicking the Demote tool. Demotes the selected rows or columns in an outline. Use DEMOTE to change the configuration of an outline by demoting rows or columns of information.

Syntax

DEMOTE(*row_col*)
DEMOTE?(*row_col*)

Row_col   specifies whether to demote rows or columns.

Row_col	Demotes
1 or omitted	Rows
2	Columns

Remarks

- If the selection consists of an entire row or rows, then rows are demoted even if *row_col* is 2. Similarly, selection of an entire column overrides *row_col* 1.

- If the selection is unambiguous (an entire row or column), then DEMOTE? will not display the dialog box.

Related Functions

Function	Description
PROMOTE	Promotes the selection in an outline
SHOW.DETAIL	Expands or collapses a portion of an outline
SHOW.LEVELS	Displays a specific number of levels of an outline

DEREF

Macro Sheets Only

Returns the value of the cells in a reference.

Syntax

DEREF*(reference)*

Reference   is the cell or cells from which you want to obtain a value. If *reference* is the reference of a single cell, DEREF returns the value of that cell. If *reference* is the reference of a range of cells, DEREF returns the array of values in those cells. If *reference* refers to the active sheet, it must be an absolute reference. Relative references are converted to absolute references.

Remarks

In most formulas, there is no difference between using a value and using the reference of a cell containing that value. The reference is automatically converted to the value, as necessary. For example, if cell A1 contains the value 2, then the formula =A1+1, like the formula =2+1, returns the result 3, because the reference A1 is converted to the value 2. However, in a few functions, such as the SET.NAME function, references are not automatically converted to values. Instead, those functions behave differently depending on whether an argument is a reference or a value.

Example

See the sixth example for SET.NAME.

DESCR

Macro Sheets Only

Generates descriptive statistics for data in the input range. For more information, see "Analyzing Statistical or Engineering Data" in Chapter 1 in Book 2 of the *Microsoft Excel User's Guide*.

If this function is not available, you must install the Analysis ToolPak add-in macro. For more information, see "Managing Add-in Commands and Functions" in Chapter 4 in Book 2 of the *Microsoft Excel User's Guide*.

Syntax

DESCR*(**inprng,outrng,**grouped,labels,summary, ds_large,ds_small,confid)*

Inprng   is the input range.

Outrng   is the first cell (the upper-left cell) in the output table.

Grouped   is a text character that indicates whether the data in the input range is organized by row or column.

- If *grouped* is "C" or omitted, then the data is organized by column.

- If *grouped* is "R" then the data is organized by row.

Labels is a logical value that describes where the labels are located in the input range, as shown in the following table:

Labels	Grouped	Labels are in
TRUE	"C"	First row of the input range.
TRUE	"R"	First column of the input range.
FALSE or omitted	(ignored)	No labels. All cells in the input range are data.

Summary is a logical value. If TRUE, DESCR reports the summary statistics. If FALSE or omitted, no summary statistics are reported.

Ds_large is an integer k. If *ds_large* is present, DESCR reports the k-th largest data point. If *ds_large* is omitted, the value is not reported.

Ds_small is an integer k. If *ds_small* is present, DESCR reports the k-th smallest data point. If *ds_small* is omitted, the value is not reported.

Confid is the confidence level of the mean. If *confid* is given, DESCR reports the confidence interval for the input range. If *confid* is omitted, the confidence interval is 95%. For more information about the confidence interval calculation, see CONFIDENCE.

Related Functions

Function	Description
AVERAGE	Returns the average of its arguments
CONFIDENCE	Returns a confidence interval for a population
KURT	Returns the kurtosis of a data set
LARGE	Returns the k-th largest value in a data set
MAX	Returns the maximum value in a list of arguments
MEDIAN	Returns the median of the given numbers
MIN	Returns the minimum value in a list of arguments

Function	Description
MODE	Returns the most common value in a data set
SKEW	Returns the skewness of a distribution
SMALL	Returns the k-th smallest value in a data set
STDEV	Estimates standard deviation based on a sample
VAR	Estimates variance based on a sample

DEVSQ

Returns the sum of squares of deviations of data points from their sample mean.

Syntax

DEVSQ(*number1*,*number2*,...)

Number1,number2,... are 1 to 30 arguments for which you want to calculate the sum of squared deviations. You can also use a single array or a reference to an array instead of arguments separated by commas.

Remarks

- The arguments should be numbers, or names, arrays, or references that contain numbers.

- If an array or reference argument contains text, logical values, or empty cells, those values are ignored; however, cells with the value zero are included.

- The equation for the sum of squared deviations is:

$$DEVSQ = \sum (x - \bar{x})^2$$

Example

DEVSQ(4,5,8,7,11,4,3) equals 48

Related Functions

Function	Description
AVEDEV	Returns the average of absolute deviations of data points from their mean
STDEV	Estimates standard deviation based on a sample
STDEVP	Calculates standard deviation based on the entire population
VAR	Estimates variance based on a sample
VARP	Calculates variance based on the entire population

DGET

Extracts single values from a database. Use DGET to extract a single field that matches the criteria from a database. If no record matches the criteria, DGET returns the #VALUE! error value. If more than one record matches the criteria, DGET returns the #NUM! error value. For more information about Microsoft Excel database functions, see "Database Functions."

Syntax

DGET(*database,field,criteria*)

DIALOG.BOX

Macro Sheets Only

Displays the dialog box described in a dialog box definition table.

Syntax

DIALOG.BOX(*dialog_ref*)

Dialog_ref is a reference to a dialog box definition table on a worksheet or macro document, or an array containing the definition table.

- The dialog box definition table is described in more detail in Chapter 8 in Book 2 of the *Microsoft Excel User's Guide.*

- If an OK button in the dialog box is chosen, DIALOG.BOX enters values in fields as specified in the *dialog_ref* area and returns the position number of the button chosen. The position numbers start with 1 in the second row of the dialog box definition table.

- If the Cancel button in the dialog box is chosen, DIALOG.BOX returns FALSE.

The dialog box definition table must be at least seven columns wide and two rows high. The definitions of each column in a dialog box definition table are listed in the following table.

Column type	Column number
Item number	1
Horizontal position	2
Vertical position	3
Item width	4
Item height	5
Text	6
Initial value or result	7

The first row of *dialog_ref* defines the position, size, and name of the dialog box. It can also specify the default selected item and the reference for the Help button. The position is specified in columns 2 and 3, the size in columns 4 and 5, and the name in column 6. To specify a default item, place the item's position number in column 7. You can place the reference for the Help button in row 1, column 1 of the table, but the preferred location is column 7 in the row where the Help button is defined. Row 1, column 1 is usually left blank.

The following table lists the numbers for the items you can display in a dialog box.

Dialog-box item	Item number
Default OK button	1
Cancel button	2
OK button	3
Default Cancel button	4
Static text	5

Dialog-box item	Item number
Text edit box	6
Integer edit box	7
Number edit box	8
Formula edit box	9
Reference edit box	10
Option button group	11
Option button	12
Check box	13
Group box	14
List box	15
Linked list box	16
Icons	17
Linked file list box (in Microsoft Excel for Windows only)	18
Linked drive and directory box (in Microsoft Excel for Windows only)	19
Directory text box	20
Drop-down list box	21
Drop-down combination edit/list box	22
Picture button	23
Help button	24

Remarks

- Add 100 to an item number in the above table to define the item as a *trigger*. A trigger is a dialog box item that, when chosen, returns to your macro (as choosing OK would) but continues to display the dialog box, allowing your macro to change the dialog box definition or display an alert message or another dialog box. The Help button, edit boxes, group boxes, static text, and icons cannot be triggers.

- Add 200 to an item number to define it as *dimmed*. A dimmed (gray) item cannot be chosen or selected. For example, 203 is a dimmed OK button. You can use item 223 to include a picture in your dialog box that does not behave like a button.

- If a trigger has been chosen and you still want to clear a dynamic dialog box from the screen, use DIALOG.BOX(FALSE). This is useful if you want to confirm that the dialog box has been filled out correctly before dismissing it.

- For more information about dynamic dialog boxes, see "Creating Dynamic Dialog Boxes" in Chapter 8 in Book 2 of the *Microsoft Excel User's Guide*.

- The dialog box definition table can be an array. If *dialog_ref* is an array instead of a reference, DIALOG.BOX returns a modified copy of that array, along with the results of the dialog box in the seventh column. (The first item in the seventh column is the position number of the chosen button or of a triggered item.) This is useful if you want to preserve the original dialog box definition table since DIALOG.BOX does not modify the original array argument. If you cancel the dialog box, or if a dialog box error occurs, DIALOG.BOX returns FALSE instead of an array.

Example

For complete examples of dialog box definition tables and the resulting dialog boxes, see Chapter 8 in Book 1 of the *Microsoft Excel User's Guide*.

Related Functions

Function	Description
ALERT	Displays a dialog box and a message
INPUT	Displays a dialog box for user input

DIRECTORIES

Macro Sheets Only

Returns a horizontal array of all of the subdirectories or subfolders in the specified path or in the current directory or folder.

If this function is not available, you must load FILEFNS.XLA from the Library directory (in Microsoft Excel for Windows) or File Functions from the Macro Library folder (in Microsoft Excel for the Macintosh) in the directory or folder where you installed Microsoft Excel. For more information, see "Managing Add-in Commands and Functions" in Chapter 4 in Book 2 of the *Microsoft Excel User's Guide.*

Syntax

DIRECTORIES(*path_text*)

Path_text   is the directory or folder from which you want to return a list of subdirectories or subfolders. If *path_text* is omitted, DIRECTORIES returns a list of the subdirectories or subfolders inside the current directory or folder.

Examples

The following macro formula returns an array of the subdirectories or subfolders in the current directory or folder:

DIRECTORIES("")

In Microsoft Excel for Windows, the following macro formula returns an array of the subdirectories in the directory C:\WORD\SALES:

DIRECTORIES("C:\WORD\SALES")

The following macro formula defines the name Paths to refer to the subdirectories in C:\WORD\SALES:

SET.NAME("Paths",DIRECTORIES("C:\WORD\SALES")

In Microsoft Excel for the Macintosh, the following macro formula returns an array of the folders in the folder HARD DISK:WORD:SALES:

DIRECTORIES("HARD DISK:WORD:SALES")

The following macro formula defines the name Paths to refer to the subfolders in HARD DISK:WORD:SALES:

SET.NAME("Paths",DIRECTORIES("HARD DISK:WORD:SALES"))

Related Functions

Function	Description
CREATE.DIRECTORY	Creates a directory or folder
DELETE.DIRECTORY	Deletes an empty directory
DIRECTORY	Sets the current drive and directory to a specified path
FILE.EXISTS	Tests for the existence of a file, directory, or folder
FILES	Returns the filenames in the specified directory or folder

DIRECTORY

Macro Sheets Only

Sets the current drive and directory or folder to the specified path and returns the name of the new directory or folder as text. Use DIRECTORY to get the name of the current directory or folder for use with the OPEN and SAVE.AS functions or to specify a directory or folder from which to return a list of files with the FILES function.

Syntax

DIRECTORY(*path_text*)

Path_text   is the drive and directory or folder you want to change to.

- If *path_text* is not specified, DIRECTORY returns the name of the current directory or folder as text.

- If *path_text* does not include a drive specifier, the current drive is assumed.

Examples

In Microsoft Excel for Windows, the following macro formula sets the directory to \EXCEL\MODELS on the current drive and returns the value "*drive*:\EXCEL\MODELS":

```
DIRECTORY("\EXCEL\MODELS")
```

The following macro formula sets the current drive to E and sets the directory to \EXCEL\MODELS on E. It returns the value "E:\EXCEL\MODELS":

```
DIRECTORY("E:\EXCEL\MODELS")
```

In Microsoft Excel for the Macintosh, the following macro formula sets the folder to HARD DISK: APPS:EXCEL:FINANCIALS and returns the value "HARD DISK:APPS:EXCEL:FINANCIALS":

```
DIRECTORY("HARD DISK:APPS:EXCEL:
FINANCIALS")
```

Related Functions

Function	Description
CREATE.DIRECTORY	Creates a directory or folder
DELETE.DIRECTORY	Deletes an empty directory
DIRECTORIES	Returns an array of subdirectories or subfolders in the specified path
FILES	Returns the filenames in the specified directory or folder

DISABLE.INPUT

Macro Sheets Only

Blocks all input from the keyboard and mouse to Microsoft Excel (except input to displayed dialog boxes). Use DISABLE.INPUT to prevent input from the user or from other applications.

Syntax

DISABLE.INPUT(*logical*)

Logical   is a logical value specifying whether input is currently disabled. If *logical* is TRUE, input is disabled; if FALSE, input is reenabled.

Remarks

Disabling input can be useful if you are using dynamic data exchange (DDE) to communicate with Microsoft Excel from another application. For information about dynamic data exchange, see Chapter 8 in Book 2 of the *Microsoft Excel User's Guide*.

Important   Be sure to end any macro that uses DISABLE.INPUT(TRUE) with a DISABLE.INPUT(FALSE) function. If you do not include DISABLE.INPUT(FALSE) to allow non-dialog-box input, you will not be able to take any actions on your computer after the macro has finished.

Related Functions

Function	Description
CANCEL.KEY	Disables macro interruption
WORKSPACE	Changes workspace settings

DISC

Returns the discount rate for a security.

If this function is not available, you must install the Analysis ToolPak add-in macro. For more information, see "Managing Add-in Commands and Functions" in Chapter 4 in Book 2 of the *Microsoft Excel User's Guide*.

Syntax

DISC(*settlement,maturity,pr,redemption,basis*)

Settlement   is the security's settlement date, expressed as a serial date number.

Maturity   is the security's maturity date, expressed as a serial date number.

Pr   is the security's price per $100 face value.

Redemption   is the security's redemption value per $100 face value.

Basis   is the type of day count basis to use.

Basis	Day count basis
0 or omitted	30/360
1	Actual/actual
2	Actual/360
3	Actual/365

Remarks

- *Settlement, maturity,* and *basis* are truncated to integers.

- If any argument is non-numeric, DISC returns the #VALUE! error value.

- If *settlement* or *maturity* is not a valid serial date number, DISC returns the #NUM! error value.

- If *pr* ≤ 0 or if *redemption* ≤ 0, DISC returns the #NUM! error value.

- If *basis* < 0 or if *basis* > 3, DISC returns the #NUM! error value.

- If *settlement* ≥ *maturity,* DISC returns the #NUM! error value.

Example

A bond has the following terms:

February 15, 1991 settlement date
June 10, 1991 maturity date
97.975 price
$100 redemption value
Actual/360 basis

The bond discount rate (in the 1900 Date System) is:

DISC(33284,33399,97.975,100,2) equals 0.063391 or 6.3391%

Related Functions

Function	Description
DATE	Returns the serial number of a particular date
PRICEDISC	Returns the price per $100 face value of a discounted security
YIELDDISC	Returns the annual yield for a discounted security

DISPLAY

Macro Sheets Only

Equivalent to choosing the Display command from the Options menu. Controls whether the screen displays formulas, gridlines, row and column headings, and other screen attributes. There are two syntax forms of this function. Use syntax 1 to control screen display. For detailed information about the Display command, see online Help.

Arguments for this syntax form correspond to options and check boxes in the Display dialog box. Arguments that correspond to check boxes are logical values. If an argument is TRUE, Microsoft Excel selects the check box; if FALSE, Microsoft Excel clears the check box.

Syntax 1

For controlling screen display

DISPLAY(*formulas,gridlines,headings,zeros, color_num,reserved,outline,page_breaks, object_num*)
DISPLAY?(*formulas,gridlines,headings,zeros, color_num,reserved,outline,page_breaks, object_num*)

Formulas   corresponds to the Formulas check box. The default is FALSE on worksheets and TRUE on macro sheets.

Gridlines   corresponds to the Gridlines check box. The default is TRUE.

Headings   corresponds to the Row & Column Headings check box. The default is TRUE.

Zeros   corresponds to the Zero Values check box. The default is TRUE.

Color_num   is a number from 0 to 16 corresponding to the gridline and heading colors in the Display dialog box; 0 corresponds to automatic color and is the default value.

Reserved   is reserved for certain international versions of Microsoft Excel.

Outline corresponds to the Outline Symbols check box. The default is TRUE.

Page_breaks corresponds to the Automatic Page Breaks check box. The default is FALSE.

Object_num is a number from 1 to 3 corresponding to the display options in the Object box.

Object_num	Corresponds to
1 or omitted	Show All
2	Show Placeholders
3	Hide

Example

The following macro formula turns off gridlines and row and column headings, and leaves all other settings at the default values:

```
DISPLAY(,FALSE,FALSE)
```

Related Functions

Function	Description
WORKSPACE	Changes workspace settings
ZOOM	Enlarges or reduces a document in the active window

DISPLAY

Macro Sheets Only

Equivalent to choosing the commands from the Info menu. Controls which commands on the Info window are in effect. There are two syntax forms of this function. Use syntax 2 to control the display of the Info window. The Info window must be active to use this form of DISPLAY. For detailed information about the Info menu commands, see online Help.

Arguments in this sytax form correspond to commands on the Info menu with the same names. For example, *cell* corresponds to the Cell command on the Info menu. All the arguments except *precedents* and *dependents* are logical values.

For these arguments:

- If the argument is TRUE, Microsoft Excel displays the corresponding Info item.
- If the argument is FALSE, Microsoft Excel does not display the corresponding Info item.
- If the argument is omitted, the status of the item is unchanged.

Syntax 2

For controlling Info window display

DISPLAY(*cell,formula,value,format,protection, names,precedents,dependents,note*)

Precedents is a number from 1 to 3 that specifies which precedents to list, according to the following table.

Dependents is a number from 1 to 3 that specifies which dependents to list, according to the following table.

Precedents or dependents	List
0	None
1	Direct only
2	All levels

Related Functions

Function	Description
SHOW.INFO	Controls the display of the Info window
ZOOM	Enlarges or reduces a document in the active window

DMAX

Returns the largest number in the *field* column of records in the *database* that match the *criteria*. For more information about Microsoft Excel database functions, see "Database Functions."

Syntax

DMAX(*database,field,criteria*)

DMIN

Returns the smallest number in the *field* column of records in the *database* that match the *criteria*. For more information about Microsoft Excel database functions, see "Database Functions."

Syntax

DMIN(*database,field,criteria*)

DOCUMENTS

Macro Sheets Only

Returns, as a horizontal array in text form, the names of the specified open documents in alphabetic order. DOCUMENTS lists workbooks and unbound sheets, but does not list bound sheets. Use DOCUMENTS to retrieve the names of open documents to use in other functions that manipulate open documents.

Syntax

DOCUMENTS(*type_num,match_text*)

Type_num is a number specifying whether to include add-in documents in the array of documents, according to the following table.

Type_num	Returns
1 or omitted	Names of all open documents except add-in documents
2	Names of add-in documents only
3	Names of all open documents

Match_text specifies the documents whose names you want returned and can include wildcard characters. If *match_text* is omitted, DOCUMENTS returns the names of all open documents.

Remarks

- Use the INDEX function to select individual document names from the array to use in other functions that take document names as arguments.

- Use COLUMNS to count the number of entries in the array.

- Use TRANSPOSE to change a horizontal array to a vertical one.

- Since the DOCUMENTS function only returns actual document names, it ignores any changes made by the WINDOW.TITLE function.

Examples

In Microsoft Excel for Windows, if your workspace contains windows named BUDGET.XLS, CHART1, ACTUAL.XLS:1, ACTUAL.XLS:2, and BOOK.XLW, then:

DOCUMENTS(1) equals the four-cell array {"ACTUAL.XLS","BOOK.XLW", "BUDGET.XLS","CHART1"}

In Microsoft Excel for the Macintosh, if your workspace contains windows named BUDGET CHART1, ACTUALS, ACTUALS:2, and BOOK then:

DOCUMENTS(1) equals the four-cell array {"ACTUALS","BOOK","BUDGET","CHART1"}

The following macro hides all displayed documents:

	A	B	C
1	Names	Formulas	Comments
2			
3		HideAllDocuments	
4		=SET.NAME("Docs",DOCUMENTS())	Names document array
5		=FOR("Counter",1,COLUMNS(Docs))	Begins FOR loop
6	Name	=INDEX(Docs,Counter)	Gets name of document
7		=ACTIVATE(Name)	Switches to the document
8		=HIDE()	Hides the document
9		=NEXT()	Ends the loop
10		=RETURN()	

Related Functions

Function	Description
FILES	Returns the filenames in the specified directory or folder
GET.DOCUMENT	Returns information about a document
GET.WINDOW	Returns information about a window
WINDOWS	Returns the names of all open windows

DOLLAR

Converts a number to text using currency format, with the decimals rounded to the specified place. The format used is $#,##0.00_);($#,##0.00).

Syntax

DOLLAR(*number,decimals*)

Number   is a number, a reference to a cell containing a number, or a formula that evaluates to a number.

Decimals   is the number of digits to the right of the decimal point. If *decimals* is negative, *number* is rounded to the left of the decimal point. If you omit *decimals*, it is assumed to be 2.

Remarks

The major difference between formatting a cell containing a number with the Number command from the Format menu and formatting a number directly with the DOLLAR function is that DOLLAR converts its result to text. A number formatted with the Number command is still a number. You can continue to use numbers formatted with DOLLAR in formulas, because Microsoft Excel converts numbers entered as text values to numbers when it calculates.

Examples

DOLLAR(1234.567,2) equals "$1234.57"

DOLLAR(1234.567,-2) equals "$1200"

DOLLAR(-1234.567,-2) equals "($1200)"

DOLLAR(-0.123,4) equals "($0.1230)"

DOLLAR(99.888) equals "$99.89"

Related Functions

Function	Description
FIXED	Formats a number as text with a fixed numbr of decimals
TEXT	Formats a number and converts it to text
VALUE	Converts a text argument to a number

DOLLARDE

Converts a dollar price expressed as a fraction into a dollar price expressed as a decimal number. Use DOLLARDE to convert fractional dollar numbers, such as securities prices, to decimal numbers.

If this function is not available, you must install the Analysis ToolPak add-in macro. For more information, see "Managing Add-in Commands and Functions" in Chapter 4 in Book 2 of the *Microsoft Excel User's Guide*.

Syntax

DOLLARDE(*fractional_dollar,fraction*)

Fractional_dollar   is a number expressed as a fraction.

Fraction   is the integer to use in the denominator of the fraction.

Remarks

- If either argument is non-numeric, DOLLARDE returns the #VALUE! error value.

- If *fraction* is not an integer, it is truncated.

- If *fraction* ≤ 0, DOLLARDE returns the #NUM! error value.

Examples

DOLLARDE(1.02,16) equals 1.125

DOLLARDE(1.1,8) equals 1.125

Related Functions

Function	Description
DOLLAR	Converts a number to text, using currency format
DOLLARFR	Converts a dollar price, expressed as a decimal number, into a dollar price, expressed as a fraction

DOLLARFR

Converts a dollar price expressed as a decimal number into a dollar price expressed as a fraction. Use DOLLARFR to convert decimal numbers to fractional dollar numbers, such as securities prices.

If this function is not available, you must install the Analysis ToolPak add-in macro. For more information, see "Managing Add-in Commands and Functions" in Chapter 4 in Book 2 of the *Microsoft Excel User's Guide.*

Syntax

DOLLARFR(*decimal_dollar,fraction*)

Decimal_dollar   is a decimal number.

Fraction   is the integer to use in the denominator of a fraction.

Remarks

- If either argument is non-numeric, DOLLARFR returns the #VALUE! error value.
- If *fraction* is not an integer, it is truncated.
- If *fraction* ≤ 0, DOLLARFR returns the #NUM! error value.

Examples

DOLLARFR(1.125,16) equals 1.02

DOLLARFR(1.125,8) equals 1.1

Related Functions

Function	Description
DOLLAR	Converts a number to text, using currency format
DOLLARDE	Converts a dollar price, expressed as a fraction, into a dollar price, expressed as a decimal number

DPRODUCT

Multiplies the values in the *field* column of records in the *database* that match the *criteria*. For more information about Microsoft Excel database functions, see "Database Functions."

Syntax

DPRODUCT(*database,field,criteria*)

DSTDEV

Estimates the standard deviation of a population based on a sample, using the numbers in the *field* column of records in the *database* that match the *criteria*. For more information about Microsoft Excel database functions, see "Database Functions."

Syntax

DSTDEV(*database,field,criteria*)

DSTDEVP

Calculates the standard deviation of a population based on the entire population, using the numbers in the *field* column of records in the *database* that match the *criteria*. For more information about Microsoft Excel database functions, see "Database Functions."

Syntax

DSTDEVP(*database,field,criteria*)

DSUM

Adds the numbers in the *field* column of records in the *database* that match the *criteria*. For more information about Microsoft Excel database functions, see "Database Functions."

Syntax

DSUM(*database,field,criteria*)

DUPLICATE

Macro Sheets Only

Duplicates the selected object. If an object is not selected, returns the #VALUE! error value and interrupts the macro.

Syntax

DUPLICATE( )

Related Functions

Function	Description
COPY	Copies and pastes data or objects
PASTE	Pastes cut or copied data

DURATION

Returns the Macaulcy duration for an assumed par value of $100. Duration is defined as the weighted average of the present value of the cash flows, and is used as a measure of a bond price's response to changes in yield.

If this function is not available, you must install the Analysis ToolPak add-in macro. For more information, see "Managing Add-in Commands and Functions" in Chapter 4 in Book 2 of the *Microsoft Excel User's Guide.*

Syntax

DURATION(*settlement,maturity,coupon,yld, frequency,basis*)

Settlement is the security's settlement date, expressed as a serial date number.

Maturity is the security's maturity date, expressed as a serial date number.

Coupon is the security's annual coupon rate.

Yld is the security's annual yield.

Frequency is the number of coupon payments per year. For annual payments, *frequency* = 1; for semi-annual, *frequency* = 2; for quarterly, *frequency* = 4.

Basis is the type of day count basis to use.

Basis	Day count basis
0 or omitted	30/360
1	Actual/actual
2	Actual/360
3	Actual/365

Remarks

- *Settlement*, *maturity*, *frequency*, and *basis* are truncated to integers.

- If any argument is non-numeric, DURATION returns the #VALUE! error value.

- If *settlement* or *maturity* is not a valid serial date number, DURATION returns the #NUM! error value.

- If *coupon* < 0 or if *yld* < 0, DURATION returns the #NUM! error value.

- If *frequency* is any number other than 1, 2, or 4, DURATION returns the #NUM! error value.

- If *basis* < 0 or if *basis* > 3, DURATION returns the #NUM! error value.

- If *settlement* ≥ *maturity*, DURATION returns the #NUM! error value.

Example

A bond has the following terms:

January 1, 1986 settlement date
January 1, 1994 maturity date
8% semiannual coupon
9.0% yield
Actual/actual basis

The duration (in the 1900 Date System) is:

DURATION(31413,34335,0.08,0.09,2,1)
equals 5.993775

Related Functions

Function	Description
DATE	Returns the serial number of a particular date
MDURATION	Returns the Macauley modified duration for a security with an assumed par value of $100

DVAR

Estimates the variance of a population based on a sample, using the numbers in the *field* column of records in the *database* that match the *criteria*. For more information about Microsoft Excel database functions, see "Database Functions."

Syntax

DVAR(*database,field,criteria*)

DVARP

Calculates the variance of a population based on the entire population, using the numbers in the *field* column of records in the *database* that match the *criteria*. For more information about Microsoft Excel database functions, see "Database Functions."

Syntax

DVARP(*database,field,criteria*)

ECHO

Macro Sheets Only

Controls screen updating while a macro is running. If a large macro uses many commands that update the screen, use ECHO to make the macro run faster.

Syntax

ECHO(*logical*)

Logical   is a logical value specifying whether screen updating is on or off.

- If *logical* is TRUE, Microsoft Excel selects screen updating.
- If *logical* is FALSE, Microsoft Excel clears screen updating.
- If *logical* is omitted, Microsoft Excel changes the current screen update condition.

Remarks

- Screen updating is always turned back on when a macro ends.
- You can use GET.WORKSPACE to determine whether screen updating is on or off.

EDATE

Returns the serial number date that is the indicated number of months before or after *start_date*. Use EDATE to calculate maturity dates or due dates that fall on the same day of the month as the date of issue.

If this function is not available, you must install the Analysis ToolPak add-in macro. For more information, see "Managing Add-in Commands and Functions" in Chapter 4 in Book 2 of the *Microsoft Excel User's Guide*.

Syntax

EDATE(*start_date,months*)

Start_date is a serial date number that represents the start date.

Months is the number of months before or after *start_date*. A positive value for *months* yields a future date; a negative value yields a past date.

Remarks

- If either argument is non-numeric, EDATE returns the #VALUE! error value.

- If *start_date* is not a valid serial date number, EDATE returns the #NUM! error value.

- If *months* is not an integer, it is truncated.

Examples

EDATE(DATEVALUE("01/15/91"),1) equals 33284 or 02/15/91

EDATE(DATEVALUE("03/31/91"),-1) equals 33297 or 02/28/91

Related Functions

Function	Description
DATE	Returns the serial number of a particular date
EOMONTH	Returns the serial number date for the last day of the month before or after a specified number of months
NETWORKDAYS	Returns the number of whole workdays between two dates
WORKDAY	Returns the serial number of the date before or after a specified number of workdays

EDIT.COLOR

Macro Sheets Only

Equivalent to choosing the Edit button from the Color Palette dialog box, which appears when you choose the Color Palette command from the Options menu. Defines the color for one of the 16 color palette boxes.

Use EDIT.COLOR if you want to use a color that is not currently on the palette and if your system hardware has more than 16 colors available. After you set the color for the color box, any items previously formatted with that color are displayed in the new color. For detailed information about the Color Palette command, see online Help.

Syntax

EDIT.COLOR(*color_num,red_value,green_value, blue_value*)
EDIT.COLOR?(*color_num*)

Color_num is a number from 1 to 16 specifying one of the 16 color palette boxes for which you want to set the color.

Red_value, green_value, and *blue_value* are numbers that specify how much red, green, and blue are in each color.

- In Microsoft Excel for Windows, *red_value, green_value,* and *blue_value* are numbers from 0 to 255.

- In Microsoft Excel for the Macintosh, *red_value, green_value,* and *blue_value* are also numbers from 0 to 255. However, the color editing dialog box displays numbers from 0 to 65,535. Microsoft Excel automatically converts the numbers between the two ranges. This allows you to display similar colors in all operating environments without modifying your macros.

- If *red_value, green_value,* and *blue_value* are all set to 255, the resulting color is white. If they are all set to zero, the resulting color is black.

- If *red_value, green_value,* or *blue_value* is omitted, Microsoft Excel assumes it to be the appropriate value for that *color_num*.

Remarks

- The number of unique colors that you can choose from and the number of colors that can be displayed on the screen at the same time are determined by your system hardware.

- EDIT.COLOR does not use hue, saturation, or brightness values. If you are using the macro recorder and set the color of a color palette box using hue, saturation, and luminance, Microsoft Excel records the corresponding red, green, and blue values instead.

- The dialog-box form of this function, EDIT.COLOR?(*color_num*), displays your system's color editing dialog box. The default *red_value, green_value,* and *blue_value* are determined by the current settings for the *color_num* you specify. *Color_num* is a required argument.

Example

The following macro formula sets the first color box on the color palette to black:

```
EDIT.COLOR(1,0,0,0)
```

Related Function

Function	Description
COLOR.PALETTE	Copies a color palette from one document to another

EDIT.DELETE

Macro Sheets Only

Equivalent to choosing the Delete command from the Edit menu. Removes the selected cells from the worksheet and shifts other cells to close up the space. For detailed information about the Delete command, see online Help.

Syntax

EDIT.DELETE(*shift_num*)
EDIT.DELETE?(*shift_num*)

Shift_num is a number from 1 to 4 specifying whether to shift cells left or up after deleting the current selection or else to delete the entire row or column.

Shift_num	Result
1	Shifts cells left
2	Shifts cells up
3	Deletes entire row
4	Deletes entire column

- If *shift_num* is omitted and if one cell or a horizontal range is selected, EDIT.DELETE shifts cells up.

- If *shift_num* is omitted and a vertical range is selected, EDIT.DELETE shifts cells left.

Related Function

Function	Description
CLEAR	Clears specified information from the selected cells or chart

EDIT.OBJECT

Macro Sheets Only

Equivalent to choosing the Edit Object command from the object shortcut menu. Starts the application associated with the selected object and makes the object available for editing or other actions. For detailed information about the Edit Object command, see online Help.

Syntax

EDIT.OBJECT(*verb_num*)

Verb_num is a number specifying which verb to use while working with the object—that is, what you want to do with the object.

- The available verbs are determined by the object's source application. 1 often specifies "edit," and 2 often specifies "play" (for sound, animation, and so on). For more information, consult the documentation for the object's application to see how it supports object linking and embedding (OLE).

- If the object does not support multiple verbs, *verb_num* is ignored.

- If *verb_num* is omitted, it is assumed to be 1.

Remarks

Your macro pauses while you're editing the object and resumes when you return to Microsoft Excel.

Related Function

Function	Description
INSERT.OBJECT	Creates an object of a specified type

EDIT.REPEAT

Macro Sheets Only

Equivalent to choosing the Repeat command from the Edit menu. Repeats certain actions and commands. EDIT.REPEAT is available in the same situations as the Repeat command. For detailed information about the Repeat command, see online Help.

Syntax

EDIT.REPEAT( )

EDIT.SERIES

Macro Sheets Only

Equivalent to choosing the Edit Series command from the Chart menu. Creates or changes chart series by adding a new SERIES formula or modifying an existing SERIES formula in a chart. Use EDIT.SERIES when you want to change the data that is plotted in a chart.

Syntax

EDIT.SERIES(*series_num,name_ref,x_ref,y_ref, z_ref,plot_order*)
EDIT.SERIES?(*series_num,name_ref,x_ref,y_ref, z_ref,plot_order*)

Series_num   is the number of the series you want to change. If *series_num* is 0 or omitted, Microsoft Excel creates a new data series.

Name_ref   is the name of the data series. It can be an external reference to a single cell, a name defined as a single cell, or a name defined as a sequence of characters. *Name_ref* can also be text (for example, "Projected Sales").

X_ref   is an external reference to the name of the worksheet and the cells that contain one of the following sets of data:

- Category labels for all charts except xy (scatter) charts

- X-coordinate data for xy (scatter) charts

Y_ref   is an external reference to the name of the worksheet and the cells that contain values (or *y*-coordinate data in xy (scatter) charts) for all 2-D charts. *Y_ref* is required in 2-D charts but does not apply to 3-D charts.

Z_ref   is an external reference to the name of the worksheet and the cells that contain values for all 3-D charts. *Z_ref* is required in 3-D charts but does not apply to 2-D charts.

Plot_order   is a number specifying whether the data series is plotted first, second, and so on, in the chart.

- No two series can have the same *plot_order*.

- If you assign a *plot_order* to a series, Microsoft Excel plots that series in the order you specify, and the series that previously had that plot order (and any series following it) has its plot order increased by one.

- If you add a series to a chart with an overlay, the number of series in the main chart does not change, so if the series is added to the main chart, then the series that was plotted last in the main chart will be plotted first in the overlay chart. To change which series is plotted first in the overlay chart, use the Overlay command from the Format menu or the FORMAT.OVERLAY function.

- If you omit *plot_order* when you add a new series, then Microsoft Excel plots that series last and assigns it the correct *plot_order* value.

- The maximum value for *plot_order* is 255.

Remarks

X_ref, y_ref, and *z_ref* can be arrays or references to a nonadjacent selection, although they cannot be names that refer to a nonadjacent selection. If you specify a nonadjacent selection for any of these arguments, make sure you include the necessary sets of parentheses so that Microsoft Excel does not treat the components of the references as separate arguments. See the following second example.

Tip To delete a data series, use the SELECT and FORMULA macro functions as shown in the following portion of a macro, where *n* is the series number.

	A	B	C
5		=SELECT ("S*n*")	
6		=FORMULA("")	

You can also use the CLEAR function.

Examples

In Microsoft Excel for Windows, the following macro formula changes the second data series on the active chart so that its category labels are in cells A2:A5, its *y*-values are in cells C2:C5, and its plot order is 3. The series name is February Sales, and the data for the chart comes from a worksheet named SALES.XLS.

```
EDIT.SERIES(2,"February
Sales",SALES.XLS!$A$2:$A$5,
SALES.XLS!$C$2:$C$5,,3)
```

The following macro formula defines the second data series as the previous example does, except that the *y*-values are in the nonadjacent selection A8:A9, A13:A14, and A20:A21.

```
EDIT.SERIES(2,"February
Sales",SALES.XLS!$A$2:$A$5,
(SALES.XLS!$A$8:$A$9,SALES.XLS!$A$13:$A$14,
SALES.XLS!$A$20:$A$21),,3)
```

In Microsoft Excel for the Macintosh, the following macro formula changes the second data series on the active chart so that its category labels are in cells A2:A5, its *y*-values are in cells C2:C5, and its plot order is 3. The series name is February Sales, and the data for the chart comes from a worksheet named SALES.

```
EDIT.SERIES(2,"February
Sales",SALES!$A$2:$A$5,
SALES!$C$2:$C$5,,3)
```

The following macro formula defines the second data series as the previous example does, except that the *y*-values are in the nonadjacent selection A8:A9, A13:A14, and A20:A21.

```
EDIT.SERIES(2,"February
Sales",SALES!$A$2:$A$5,
(SALES!$A$8:$A$9,SALES!$A$13:$A$14,
SALES!$A$20:$A$21),,3)
```

EDITION.OPTIONS

Macro Sheets Only

Sets options in, or performs actions on, the specified publisher or subscriber. In Microsoft Excel for Windows, EDITION.OPTIONS also allows you to cancel a publisher or subscriber created in Microsoft Excel for the Macintosh.

Syntax

EDITION.OPTIONS(*edition_type,edition_name, reference,option,appearance,size,formats*)

Edition_type is the number 1 or 2 specifying the type of edition.

Edition_type	Type of edition
1	Publisher
2	Subscriber

Edition_name is the name of the edition you want to change the edition options for or to perform actions on. If *edition_name* is omitted, *reference* is required.

Reference specifies the range (given in text form as a name or an R1C1-style reference) occupied by the publisher or subscriber.

- *Reference* is required if you have more than one publisher or subscriber of *edition_name* on the active document. Use *reference* to specify the location of the publisher or subscriber for which you want to set options.

- If *edition_type* is 1 and the publisher is an embedded chart, or if *edition_type* is 2 and the subscriber is a picture, *reference* is the object identifier as displayed in the reference area.

- If *reference* is omitted, *edition_name* is required.

Option is a number from 1 to 6 specifying the edition option you want to set or the action you want to take, according to the following two tables. *Options* 2 to 6 are only available if you are using Microsoft Excel for the Macintosh with system software version 7.0 or later.

If a publisher is specified, then *option* applies as follows.

Option	Action
1	Cancels the publisher
2	Sends the edition now
3	Selects the range or object published to the specified edition
4	Automatically updates the edition when the file is saved
5	Updates the edition on request only
6	Changes the edition file as specified by *appearance, size,* and *formats*

If a subscriber is specified, then *option* applies as follows.

Option	Action
1	Cancels the subscriber
2	Gets the latest edition
3	Opens the publisher document
4	Automatically updates when new data is available
5	Update on request only

The following three arguments are available only when *option* is 6.

Appearance specifies whether the selection is published as shown on screen or as shown when printed. The default value for *appearance* is 1 if the selection is a worksheet or macro sheet and 2 if the selection is a chart.

Appearance	Selection is published
1	As shown on screen
2	As shown when printed

Size specifies the size of a published chart. *Size* is only available if a chart is to be published.

Size	Chart size is published
1 or omitted	As shown on screen
2	As shown when printed

Formats is a number specifying the format of the file.

Formats	File format
1 or omitted	PICT
2	BIFF
4	RTF
8	VALU

You can also use the sum of the allowable file formats. For example, a value of 6 specifies BIFF and RTF.

Examples

The following macro formula opens the document (and application) that published the edition named Monthly Totals:

```
EDITION.OPTIONS(2,"Monthly Totals",,3)
```

The following macro checks the most recent edition date for a subscriber and, if that date is more than three days ago, updates the edition.

	A	B	C
1	Names	Formulas	Comments
2			
3		UpdateSubscriber	
4	Date	=GET.LINK.INFO("Subscriber 1",1,6)	Gets last update date
5	Date2	=DATEVALUE(DATE)	Converts it to a value
6		=IF(Date2<NOW()–2,,HALT())	If more than 2 days ago...
7		=EDITION.OPTIONS(2,"Subscriber 1",,2)	Updates the edition
8		=RETURN()	

Related Functions

Function	Description
CREATE.PUBLISHER	Creates a publisher from the selection
GET.LINK.INFO	Returns information about a link
SUBSCRIBE.TO	Inserts contents of an edition into the active document

EFFECT

Returns the effective annual interest rate, given the nominal annual interest rate and the number of compounding periods per year.

If this function is not available, you must install the Analysis ToolPak add-in macro. For more information, see "Managing Add-in Commands and Functions" in Chapter 4 in Book 2 of the *Microsoft Excel User's Guide.*

Syntax

EFFECT(*nominal_rate,npery*)

Nominal_rate is the nominal interest rate.

Npery is the number of compounding periods per year.

Remarks

- *Npery* is truncated to an integer.
- If either argument is non-numeric, EFFECT returns the #VALUE! error value.
- If *nominal_rate* ≤ 0 or if *npery* < 1, EFFECT returns the #NUM! error value.

Example

EFFECT(5.25%,4) equals 0.053543 or 5.3543%

Related Function

Function	Description
NOMINAL	Returns the annual nominal interest rate

ELSE

Macro Sheets Only

Used with IF, ELSE.IF, and END.IF to control which functions are carried out in a macro. ELSE signals the beginning of a group of formulas in a macro sheet that will be carried out if the results of all preceding ELSE.IF statements and the preceding IF statement are FALSE. Use ELSE with IF, ELSE.IF, and END.IF when you want to perform multiple actions based on a condition. This method is preferable to using GOTO because it makes your macros more structured.

Syntax

ELSE( )

Remarks

ELSE must be entered in a cell by itself. In other words, the cell can contain only "=ELSE()".

For more information about ELSE, ELSE.IF, END.IF, and IF, and for examples of these functions, see form 2 of the IF function.

Related Functions

Function	Description
ELSE.IF	Specifies an action to take if an IF or another ELSE.IF function returns FALSE
END.IF	Ends a group of macro functions started with an IF statement
IF	Specifies an action to take if a logical test is TRUE

ELSE.IF

Macro Sheets Only

Used with IF, ELSE, and END.IF to control which functions are carried out in a macro. ELSE.IF signals the beginning of a group of formulas in a macro sheet that will be carried out if the preceding IF or ELSE.IF function returns FALSE and if logical_test is TRUE. Use ELSE.IF with IF, ELSE, and END.IF when you want to perform multiple actions based on a condition. This method is preferable to using GOTO because it makes your macros more structured.

Syntax

ELSE.IF(*logical_test*)

Logical_test is a logical value that ELSE.IF uses to determine what functions to carry out next—that is, where to branch.

- If *logical_test* is TRUE, Microsoft Excel carries out the functions between the ELSE.IF function and the next ELSE.IF, ELSE, or END.IF function.

- If *logical_test* is FALSE, Microsoft Excel immediately branches to the next ELSE.IF, ELSE, or END.IF function.

Remarks

- ELSE.IF must be entered in a cell by itself.

- *Logical_test* will always be evaluated, even if the ELSE.IF section is not reached (due to a previous IF or ELSE.IF *logical_test* evaluating to TRUE). For this reason, you should not use formulas that carry out actions for *logical_test*. If you need to base the ELSE.IF condition on the return value of a formula that carries out an action, use the form "ELSE, IF(*logical_test*), and END.IF" in place of "ELSE.IF(*logical_test*)."

For more information about ELSE, ELSE.IF, END.IF, and IF, and for examples of these functions, see form 2 of the IF function.

Related Functions

Function	Description
CHOOSE	Chooses a value from a list of values
ELSE	Specifies an action to take if an IF function returns FALSE
END.IF	Ends a group of macro functions started with an IF statement
IF	Specifies an action to take if a logical test is TRUE

EMBED

Displayed in the formula bar when an embedded object is selected. EMBED cannot be entered on a worksheet or used in a macro.

Syntax

EMBED(*object_type*,*item*)

Object_type is the name of the application and document type that created the embedded object. For example, the *object_type* arguments used when Microsoft Excel documents are embedded in other applications are "ExcelWorksheet" and "ExcelChart".

Item is the area selected to copy, and determines the view on the embedded document. When *item* is empty text (""), EMBED creates a view on the entire document.

Remarks

If you delete the EMBED formula, the embedded object remains on the document as a graphic, and the link to the creating application is deleted. Double-clicking the object no longer starts the creating application.

ENABLE.COMMAND

Macro Sheets Only

Enables or disables a custom command or menu. Disabled commands appear dimmed and can't be chosen. Use ENABLE.COMMAND to control which commands the user can choose in a menu bar.

Syntax

ENABLE.COMMAND(*bar_num,menu, command,enable*)

Bar_num is the menu bar in which a command resides. *Bar_num* can be the number of a built-in menu bar or the number returned by a previously run ADD.BAR function. See ADD.COMMAND for a list of the built-in menu bar numbers.

Menu is the menu on which the command resides. *Menu* can be either the name of a menu as text or the number of a menu. Menus are numbered starting with 1 from the left of the screen.

Command is the command you want to enable or disable. *Command* can be either the name of the command as text or the number of the command. The top command on a menu is command 1. If *command* is 0, ENABLE.COMMAND enables or disables the entire menu.

Enable is a logical value specifying whether the command should be enabled or disabled. If *enable* is TRUE, Microsoft Excel enables the command; if FALSE, it disables the command.

Remarks

- You cannot disable built-in commands. If the specified command is a built-in command or does not exist, ENABLE.COMMAND returns the #VALUE! error value and interrupts the macro.

- For information about custom menus, see Chapter 8 in Book 2 of the *Microsoft Excel User's Guide*.

- You can hide any shortcut menu from users by using ENABLE.COMMAND with *command* set to 0.

Example

The following macro formula disables a custom command that had been added previously to the Formula menu on the worksheet and macro sheet menu bar:

```
ENABLE.COMMAND(1,"Formula","Audit...",
FALSE)
```

Related Functions

Function	Description
ADD.COMMAND	Adds a command to a menu
CHECK.COMMAND	Adds or deletes a check mark to or from a command
DELETE.COMMAND	Deletes a command from a menu
RENAME.COMMAND	Changes the name of a command or menu

ENABLE.TOOL

Macro Sheets Only

Enables or disables a tool on a toolbar. An enabled tool can be accessed by the user. Disabled tools may still be visible but cannot be accessed. Use ENABLE.TOOL to control which tools the user can choose in a particular situation.

Syntax

ENABLE.TOOL(*bar_id,position,enable*)

Bar_id is the number or name of a toolbar on which the tool resides. For detailed information about *bar_id*, see ADD.TOOL.

Position specifies the position of the tool on the toolbar. *Position* starts with 1 at the left side (if horizontal) or from the top (if vertical).

Enable specifies whether the tool can be accessed. If *enable* is TRUE or omitted, the user can access the tool; if FALSE, the user cannot access it.

Remarks

Microsoft Excel sounds a tone if you click a disabled tool.

Example

The following macro formula enables the fourth tool in Toolbar1:

```
ENABLE.TOOL("Toolbar1",4,TRUE)
```

Related Function

Function	Description
GET.TOOL	Returns information about a tool or tools on a toolbar

END.IF

Macro Sheets Only

Ends a block of functions associated with the preceding IF function. You must include one and only one END.IF function for each macro-sheets-only syntax form (syntax 2) of the IF function in a macro. Syntax 1 of the IF function, which can be used on both worksheets and macro sheets, does not require an END.IF function. Use END.IF with IF, ELSE, and ELSE.IF when you want to perform multiple actions based on a condition. This method is preferable to using GOTO because it makes your macros more structured.

Syntax

END.IF( )

Remarks

- If you accidentally omit an END.IF function, your macro will end with an error at the cell containing the first IF function that does not have a corresponding END.IF function.

- END.IF must be entered in a cell by itself.

- For more information about ELSE, ELSE.IF, END.IF, and IF, and for examples of these functions, see form 2 of the IF function.

Related Functions

Function	Description
ELSE	Specifies an action to take if an IF function returns FALSE
ELSE.IF	Specifies an action to take if an IF or another ELSE.IF function returns FALSE
IF	Specifies an action to take if a logical test is TRUE

ENTER.DATA

Macro Sheets Only

Turns on Data Entry mode and allows you to select only and to enter data into the unlocked cells in the current selection (the data entry area). Use ENTER.DATA when you want to enter data only in a specific part of your worksheet. You can then use that part of the worksheet as a simple data form.

Syntax

ENTER.DATA*(logical)*

Logical   is a logical value that turns Data Entry mode on or off.

- If *logical* is TRUE, Data Entry mode is turned on; if FALSE, Data Entry mode is turned off and data entry, cell movement, and cell selection return to normal. If *logical* is omitted, ENTER.DATA toggles Data Entry mode.

- *Logical* can also be the number 2. This setting turns on Data Entry mode and prevents the ESC key from turning it off.

Remarks

- In Data Entry mode, you can move the active cell and select cell ranges only in the data entry area. The arrow keys and the TAB and SHIFT+TAB keys move from one unlocked cell to the next, wrapping to the first or last unlocked cell in the next or previous column when the end of a column is reached. The HOME and END keys move to the first and last cell in the data entry area, respectively. You cannot select entire rows or columns, and clicking a cell outside the data entry area does not select it.

- The only commands available in Data Entry mode are commands normally available to protected worksheets.

- To turn off Data Entry mode, press ESC (unless *logical* is 2), activate another window, or use another ENTER.DATA function. If you use another ENTER.DATA function, you will usually design your macros in one of two ways:

  - The macro turns on Data Entry mode, pauses while you enter data, resumes, and then turns off Data Entry mode.

  - The macro turns on Data Entry mode and ends. After entering data, another macro turns off Data Entry mode; this latter macro could be assigned to a "Finished" button, for example.

With either method, you can use Microsoft Excel's ON functions to resume or run other macros based on an event, such as pressing the CONTROL+D keys. See the examples below.

Tips

- Normally you use Data Entry mode to enter data, but you can also prevent someone from entering data or moving the active cell by locking all the cells in the current selection before turning on Data Entry mode. This is useful if you want a user to view a range of cells but not change it or move the active cell. Similarly, if you unlock certain cells, you can restrict the user's movement to the Data Entry area only.

- To prevent someone from activating another document, which would turn off Data Entry mode, use the ON.WINDOW function or an Auto_Deactivate macro.

Examples

The following macro turns on Data Entry mode and ends. To turn off Data Entry mode, press ESC.

	A	B	C
1	Names	Formulas	Comments
2			
3		EnterDataMode	
4		=ENTER.DATA(TRUE)	
13		=RETURN()	

The following macro turns on Data Entry mode, pauses the macro so you can enter data, and defines an event (pressing CTRL+D) to resume the macro. When the main macro resumes, it turns off Data Entry mode. Pressing ESC will not turn off Data Entry mode as it normally would.

	A	B	C
1	*Names*	*Formulas*	*Comments*
2			
3		EnterDataMode	
4		=ON.KEY("^d","ResumeOnD")	Defines event to resume
5		=ENTER.DATA(2)	Turns on Data Entry mode
6		=PAUSE()	Allows user to enter data
7		=ENTER.DATA(FALSE)	Turns off Data Entry mode
8		=RETURN()	
9			
10			
11		ResumeOnD	Resumes macro
12		=RESUME()	
13			

The following macro turns on Data Entry mode and ends. A second macro turns Data Entry mode off; it runs when CTRL+D is pressed.

	A	B	C
1	*Names*	*Formulas*	*Comments*
2			
3		EnterDataMode	
4		=ON.KEY("^d","DataEntryOff")	Defines event to turn off
5		=ENTER.DATA(2)	Data Entry mode
6		=RETURN()	
7			
8			
9		DataEntryOff	
10		=ENTER.DATA(FALSE)	
11		=RETURN()	

Related Function

Function	Description
FORMULA	Enters values into a cell or range or onto a chart

EOMONTH

Returns the serial number date for the last day of the month that is the indicated number of months before or after *start_date*. Use EOMONTH to calculate maturity dates or due dates that fall on the last day of the month.

If this function is not available, you must install the Analysis ToolPak add-in macro. For more information, see "Managing Add-in Commands and Functions" in Chapter 4 in Book 2 of the *Microsoft Excel User's Guide*.

Syntax

EOMONTH(*start_date,months*)

Start_date   is a serial date number that represents the start date.

Months   is the number of months before or after *start_date*. A positive value for *months* yields a future date; a negative value yields a past date.

Remarks

- If either argument is non-numeric, EOMONTH returns the #VALUE! error value.

- If *start_date* is not a valid serial date number, EOMONTH returns the #NUM! error value.

- If *months* is not an integer, it is truncated.

- If *start_date* plus *months* yields an invalid serial date number, EOMONTH returns the #NUM! error value.

Examples

EOMONTH(DATEVALUE("01/01/91"),1) equals 33297 or 2/28/91

EOMONTH(DATEVALUE("01/01/91"),-1) equals 33238 or 12/31/90

Related Functions

Function	Description
DATE	Returns the serial number of a particular date
EDATE	Returns the serial number of the date before or after a specified number of months
NETWORKDAYS	Returns the number of whole workdays between two dates
WORKDAY	Returns the serial number of the date before or after a specified number of workdays

ERF

Returns the error function integrated between *lower_limit* and *upper_limit*.

If this function is not available, you must install the Analysis ToolPak add-in macro. For more information, see "Managing Add-in Commands and Functions" in Chapter 4 in Book 2 of the *Microsoft Excel User's Guide*.

Syntax

ERF(*lower_limit,upper_limit*)

Lower_limit   is the lower bound for integrating ERF.

Upper_limit   is the upper bound for integrating ERF. If omitted, ERF integrates between zero and *lower_limit*.

Remarks

- If *lower_limit* is non-numeric, ERF returns the #VALUE! error value.

- If *lower_limit* is negative, ERF returns the #NUM! error value.

- If *upper_limit* is non-numeric, ERF returns the #VALUE! error value.

- If *upper_limit* is negative, ERF returns the #NUM! error value.

$$\mathrm{ERF}(z) = \frac{2}{\sqrt{\pi}} \int_0^z e^{-t^2} \, dt$$

$$\mathrm{ERF}(a,b) = \frac{2}{\sqrt{\pi}} \int_a^b e^{-t^2} \, dt = \mathrm{ERF}(b) - \mathrm{ERF}(a)$$

Examples

ERF(0.74500) equals 0.70793

ERF(1) equals 0.84270

Related Function

Function	Description
ERFC	Returns the complementary error function

ERFC

Returns the complementary error function integrated between x and ∞.

If this function is not available, you must install the Analysis ToolPak add-in macro. For more information, see "Managing Add-in Commands and Functions" in Chapter 4 in Book 2 of the *Microsoft Excel User's Guide*.

Syntax

ERFC(*x*)

X   is the lower bound for integrating ERF.

Remarks

- If x is non-numeric, ERFC returns the #VALUE! error value.

- If x is negative, ERFC returns the #NUM! error value.

$$\mathrm{ERFC}(x) = \frac{2}{\sqrt{\pi}} \int_x^\infty e^{-t^2} \, dt = 1 - \mathrm{ERF}(x)$$

Example

ERFC(1) equals 0.1573

Related Function

Function	Description
ERF	Returns the error function

ERROR

Macro Sheets Only

Specifies what action to take if an error is encountered while a macro is running. Use ERROR to control whether Microsoft Excel error messages are displayed, or to run your own macro when an error is encountered.

Syntax

ERROR(*enable_logical,macro_ref*)

Enable_logical is a logical value or number that selects or clears error-checking.

- If *enable_logical* is FALSE or 0, all error-checking is cleared. If error-checking is cleared and an error is encountered while a macro is running, Microsoft Excel ignores it and continues. Error-checking is selected again by an ERROR(TRUE) statement, or when the macro stops running.

- If *enable_logical* is TRUE or 1, you can either select normal error-checking (by omitting the other argument) or specify a macro to run when an error is encountered by using the *macro_ref* argument. When normal error-checking is active, the Macro Error dialog box is displayed when an error is encountered. You can choose to halt the macro, start single-stepping through the macro, continue running the macro normally, or go to the macro cell where the error occurred.

- If *enable_logical* is 2 and *macro_ref* is omitted, error-checking is normal except that if the user chooses the Cancel button in an alert message, ERROR returns FALSE and the macro is not interrupted.

- If *enable_logical* is 2 and *macro_ref* is given, the macro goes to that *macro_ref* when an error is encountered. If the user chooses the Cancel button in an alert message, FALSE is returned and the macro is not interrupted.

Macro_ref specifies a macro to run if *enable_logical* is TRUE, 1, or 2 and an error is encountered. It can be either the name of the macro or a cell reference. If *enable_logical* is FALSE or 0, *macro_ref* is ignored.

Important Both ERROR(FALSE) and ERROR(TRUE,*macro_ref*) keep Microsoft Excel from displaying any messages at all, including the message asking whether to save changes when you close an unsaved document. If you want alert messages but not error messages to be displayed, use ERROR(2,*macro_ref*).

Remarks

You can use GET.WORKSPACE to determine whether error-checking is on or off.

Examples

ERROR(FALSE) clears error-checking.

ERROR(TRUE,Recover) selects error-checking and runs the macro named Recover when an error is encountered.

In the following macro, ERROR(TRUE, ForceMenus) runs the macro ForceMenus if an error occurs in the current macro.

	B	C
1	*Formulas*	*Comments*
2		
3	**AddEditCommand**	
4	=ERROR(TRUE,ForceMenus)	Sets macro to run if error
5	=ADD.COMMAND(2,"Edit",EditCommand)	Tries to add a command
6	=RETURN()	

Also see the example for FREAD and the second example for ARGUMENT.

Related Functions

Function	Description
CANCEL.KEY	Disables macro interruption
LAST.ERROR	Returns the reference of the cell where the last error occurred
ON.KEY	Runs a macro when a specified key is pressed

ERROR.TYPE

Returns a number corresponding to one of Microsoft Excel's error values. Use ERROR.TYPE to determine what type of error occurred so that your macro can run an appropriate error-handling subroutine. ERROR.TYPE can also be used on a worksheet.

Syntax

ERROR.TYPE(*error_val*)

Error_val   is the error value whose identifying number you want to find. Although *error_val* can be the actual error value, it will usually be a reference to a cell containing a formula that you want to test.

If *error_val* is	ERROR.TYPE returns
#NULL!	1
#DIV/0!	2
#VALUE!	3
#REF!	4
#NAME?	5
#NUM!	6
#N/A	7
Anything else	#N/A

Example

The following macro formula checks the cell named Ratio to see if it contains a #DIV/0! error value. If it does, a subroutine named DivisionByZero is run.

```
IF(ERROR.TYPE(Ratio)=2,DivisionByZero())
```

Related Functions

Function	Description
ISERR	Returns TRUE if the value is any error except #N/A
ISERROR	Returns TRUE if the value is any error value

EVALUATE

Macro Sheets Only

Evaluates a formula or expression that is in the form of text and returns the result.

Syntax

EVALUATE(*formula_text*)

Formula_text   is the expression in the form of text that you want to evaluate.

Remarks

Using EVALUATE is similar to selecting an expression within a formula in the formula bar and pressing the Recalculate key (F9 in Microsoft Excel for Windows and COMMAND+= in Microsoft Excel for the Macintosh). EVALUATE replaces an expression with a value.

Example

Suppose you want to know the value of a cell named LabResult1, LabResult2, or LabResult3, where the 1, 2, or 3 is specified by the name TrialNum whose value may change as the macro runs. You can use the following formula to calculate the value:

```
EVALUATE("LabResult"&TrialNum)
```

EVEN

Returns *number* rounded up to the nearest even integer. You can use this function for processing items that come in twos. For example, a packing crate accepts rows of one or two items. The crate is full when the number of items, rounded up to the nearest two, matches the crate's capacity.

Syntax

EVEN*(number)*

Number   is the value to round.

Remarks

- If *number* is non-numeric, EVEN returns the #VALUE! error value.

- Regardless of the sign of *number,* a value is rounded up when adjusted away from zero. If *number* is an even integer, no rounding occurs.

Examples

EVEN(1.5) equals 2

EVEN(3) equals 4

EVEN(2) equals 2

EVEN(−1) equals −2

Related Functions

Function	Description
CEILING	Rounds a number up to the nearest integer
FLOOR	Rounds a number down, towards zero
INT	Rounds a number down to the nearest integer
ODD	Rounds a number up to the nearest odd integer
ROUND	Rounds a number to a specified number of digits
TRUNC	Truncates a number to an integer

EXACT

Compares two text strings and returns TRUE if they are exactly the same, FALSE otherwise. EXACT is case-sensitive but ignores formatting differences. Use EXACT to test text being entered onto a document.

Syntax

EXACT*(text1,text2)*

Text1   is the first text string.

Text2   is the second text string.

Examples

EXACT("word","word") equals TRUE

EXACT("Word","word") equals FALSE

EXACT("w ord","word") equals FALSE

To make sure that a user-entered value matches a value in a range, enter the following formula as an array in a cell. To enter a formula as an array in a single cell, press CTRL+SHIFT+ENTER (in Microsoft Excel for Windows) or COMMAND+ENTER (in Microsoft Excel for the Macintosh). The name TestValue refers to a cell containing a user-entered value; the name CompareRange refers to a list of text values to be checked.

{=OR(EXACT(TestValue,CompareRange))}

Related Functions

Function	Description
LEN	Returns the number of characters in a text string
SEARCH	Finds one text value within another (not case-sensitive)

EXEC

Macro Sheets Only

Starts a separate program. Use EXEC to start other programs with which you want to communicate. Use EXEC with Microsoft Excel's other DDE functions (INITIATE, EXECUTE, and SEND.KEYS) to create a channel to another program and to send keystrokes and commands to the program. (SEND.KEYS is available only in Microsoft Excel for Windows.)

Syntax 1 is for Microsoft Excel for Windows. Syntax 2 is for Microsoft Excel for the Macintosh.

Syntax 1

For Microsoft Excel for Windows

EXEC(**program_text**,*window_num*)

Syntax 2

For Microsoft Excel for the Macintosh

EXEC(**program_text**,,*background, preferred_size_only*)

Important Microsoft Excel for the Macintosh requires system software version 7.0 or later for the last two arguments of this function.

Program_text is the name, as a text string, of any executable file or, in Microsoft Excel for Windows, any data file that is associated with an executable file.

- Use paths when the file or program to be started is not in the current directory or folder.

- In Microsoft Excel for Windows, *program_text* can include any arguments and switches that are accepted by the program to be started. Also, if *program_text* is the name of a file associated with a specific installed program, EXEC starts the program and loads the specified file.

Window_num is a number from 1 to 3 that specifies how the window containing the program should appear. *Window_num* is only available for use with Microsoft Excel for Windows. The *window_num* argument is allowed on the Macintosh, but it is ignored.

Window_num	Window appears
1	Normal size
2 or omitted	Minimized size
3	Maximized size

Background is a logical value that determines whether the program specified by *program_text* is opened as the active program or in the background, leaving Microsoft Excel as the active program. If *background* is TRUE, the program is started in the background; if FALSE or omitted, the program is started in the foreground. *Background* is only available for use with Microsoft Excel for the Macintosh and system software version 7.0 or later.

Preferred_size_only is a logical value that determines the amount of memory allocated to the program. If *preferred_size_only* is TRUE, the program is opened with its preferred memory allocation; if FALSE or omitted, it opens with the available memory if greater than its minimum requirement. *Preferred_size_only* is only available for use with Microsoft Excel for the Macintosh and system software version 7.0 or later. For information about changing the preferred memory size, see your Macintosh documentation.

Remarks

In Microsoft Excel for Windows and in Microsoft Excel for the Macintosh with system software version 7.0, if the EXEC function is successful, it returns the task ID number of the started program. The task ID number is a unique number that identifies a program. Use the task ID number in other macro functions, such as APP.ACTIVATE, to refer to the program. In Microsoft Excel for the Macintosh with system software version 6.0, if EXEC is successful, it returns TRUE. If EXEC is unsuccessful, it returns the #VALUE! error value.

Examples

In Microsoft Excel for Windows, the following macro formula starts Microsoft Word and loads the document SALES.DOC:

```
EXEC("SALES.DOC")
```

The following macro formula starts the program SEARCH.EXE. Use paths when the file or program to be started is not in the current directory:

```
EXEC("C:\WINDOWS\SEARCH.EXE")
```

The following macro formula starts Microsoft Word for Windows and loads the document SALES.DOC:

```
EXEC("WINWORD.EXE SALES.DOC")
```

The following portion of a macro opens the file MEMO1.DOC in Microsoft Word for Windows, opens a communications channel to the document, and sends commands and keystrokes to Word for Windows.

	A	B	C
5		=EXEC("C:\WINWORD.EXE C:MEMO1.DOC")	Starts Word; opens MEMO1
6	Num	=INITIATE("WINWORD","C:MEMO1.DOC")	Opens a channel to same
7		=EXECUTE(Num,"%t~")	Chooses Format Character
8		=SEND.KEYS("%b",FALSE)	Sends ALT+b to Word

In Microsoft Excel for the Macintosh, the following macro formula starts Microsoft Word:

```
EXEC("HARD DISK:APPS:WORD")
```

Related Functions

Function	Description
APP.ACTIVATE	Switches to another application
EXECUTE	Carries out a command in another application
INITIATE	Opens a channel to another application
SEND.KEYS	Sends a key sequence to an application
TERMINATE	Closes a channel to another application

EXECUTE

Macro Sheets Only

Carries out commands in another program. Use with EXEC, INITIATE, and SEND.KEYS to run another program through Microsoft Excel. (SEND.KEYS is available only in Microsoft Excel for Windows.)

Important Microsoft Excel for the Macintosh requires system software version 7.0 or later for this function.

Syntax

EXECUTE(*channel_num,execute_text*)

Channel_num is a number returned by a previously run INITIATE function. *Channel_num* refers to a channel through which Microsoft Excel communicates with another program.

Execute_text is a text string representing commands you want to carry out in the program specified by *channel_num.* The form of *execute_text* depends on the program you are referring to. To include specific key sequences in *execute_text,* use the format described under *key_text* in the ON.KEY function.

For information about accessing other programs, see Chapter 3 in Book 2 of the *Microsoft Excel User's Guide.*

If EXECUTE is not successful, it returns one of the following error values:

Value returned	Situation
#VALUE!	*Channel_num* is not a valid channel number.
#N/A	The program you are accessing is busy.
#DIV/0!	The program you are accessing does not respond after a certain length of time and you have pressed ESC to cancel.
#REF!	The EXECUTE request is refused.

Remarks

Commands sent to another program with EXECUTE will not work when a dialog box is displayed in the program. In Microsoft Excel for Windows, you can use SEND.KEYS to send commands that make selections in a dialog box.

Examples

The following macro formula sends the number 25 and a carriage return to the application identified by *channel_num* 14:

```
EXECUTE(14,"25~")
```

Also see the fourth example for EXEC.

Related Functions

Function	Description
EXEC	Starts another application
INITIATE	Opens a channel to another application
POKE	Sends data to another application
REQUEST	Returns data from another application
SEND.KEYS	Sends a key sequence to an application
TERMINATE	Closes a channel to another application

EXP

Returns *e* raised to the power of *number*. The constant *e* equals 2.71828182845904, the base of the natural logarithm.

Syntax

EXP(*number*)

Number   is the exponent applied to the base *e*.

Remarks

- To calculate powers of other bases, use the exponentiation operator (^).
- EXP is the inverse of LN, the natural logarithm of *number*.

Examples

EXP(1)   equals 2.718282 (the approximate value of *e*)

EXP(2)   equals e^2, or 7.389056

EXP(LN(3))   equals 3

Related Functions

Function	Description
IMEXP	Returns the exponential of a complex number
LN	Returns the natural logarithm of a number
LOG	Returns the logarithm of a number to a specified base

EXPON

Macro Sheets Only

Predicts a value based on the forecast for the prior period, adjusted for the error in that prior forecast. For more information, see "Analyzing Statistical or Engineering Data" in Chapter 1 in Book 2 of the *Microsoft Excel User's Guide*.

If this function is not available, you must install the Analysis ToolPak add-in macro. For more information, see "Managing Add-in Commands and Functions" in Chapter 4 in Book 2 of the *Microsoft Excel User's Guide*.

Syntax

EXPON(*inprng,outrng,damp,stderrs,chart*)

Inprng   is the input range.

Outrng   indicates the starting location of the output range.

Damp is the damping factor. If omitted, *damp* is 0.3.

Stderrs is a logical value. If TRUE, standard error values are included in the output table. If FALSE, standard errors are not included.

Chart is a logical value. If TRUE, EXPON generates a chart for the actual and forecast values. If FALSE, the chart is not generated.

Related Functions

Function	Description
FORECAST	Returns a value along a linear trend
GROWTH	Returns values along an exponential trend
MOVEAVG	Returns values along a moving average trend
TREND	Returns values along a linear trend

EXPONDIST

Returns the exponential distribution function. Use EXPONDIST to model the time between events, such as how long an automated bank teller takes to deliver cash. For example, you can use EXPONDIST to determine the probability that the process takes at most one minute.

Syntax

EXPONDIST(*x,lambda,cumulative*)

X is the value of the function.

Lambda is the parameter value.

Cumulative is a logical value that indicates which form of the exponential function to provide. If *cumulative* is TRUE, EXPONDIST returns the cumulative distribution function; if FALSE, it returns the probability density function.

Remarks

- If *x* or *lambda* is non-numeric, EXPONDIST returns the #VALUE! error value.

- If $x < 0$, EXPONDIST returns the #NUM! error value.

- If $lambda \leq 0$, EXPONDIST returns the #NUM! error value.

- The equation for the probability density function is:

$$f(x;\lambda) = \lambda e^{-\lambda x}$$

- The equation for the cumulative distribution function is:

$$F(x;\lambda) = 1 - e^{-\lambda x}$$

Examples

EXPONDIST(0.2,10,TRUE) equals 0.864665

EXPONDIST(0.2,10,FALSE) equals 1.353353

Related Functions

Function	Description
GAMMADIST	Returns the gamma distribution
POISSON	Returns the Poisson probability distribution

EXTEND.POLYGON

Macro Sheets Only

Adds vertices to a polygon. This function must immediately follow a CREATE.OBJECT function or another EXTEND.POLYGON function. Use multiple EXTEND.POLYGON functions to create arbitrarily complex polygons. It is generally easier to use the macro recorder to enter this function on your macro sheet.

Syntax

EXTEND.POLYGON(*array*)

Array is an array of values, or a reference to a range of cells containing values, that indicate the position of vertices in the polygon. The position is measured in points and is relative to the upper-left corner of the polygon's bounding rectangle.

- A vertex is a point. Each vertex is defined by a pair of coordinates in one row of *array*.

- The polygon is defined by the *array* argument to the CREATE.OBJECT function and to all the immediately following EXTEND.POLYGON functions.

- If the polygon contains many vertices, one array may not be sufficient to define it. If the number of elements in the formula exceeds 1024, you must include additional EXTEND.POLYGON functions. If you're recording a macro, Microsoft Excel automatically records additional EXTEND.POLYGON functions as needed.

Related Functions

Function	Description
CREATE.OBJECT	Creates an object
FORMAT.SHAPE	Inserts, moves, or deletes vertices of the selected polygon

EXTRACT

Macro Sheets Only

Equivalent to choosing the Extract command from the Data menu. Finds database records that match the criteria defined in the criteria range and copies them into a separate extract range. For detailed information about the Extract command, see online Help.

Syntax

EXTRACT(*unique*)
EXTRACT?(*unique*)

Unique is a logical value corresponding to the Unique Records Only check box in the Extract dialog box.

- If *unique* is TRUE, Microsoft Excel selects the check box and excludes duplicate records from the extract list.

- If *unique* is FALSE or omitted, Microsoft Excel clears the check box and extracts all records matching the criteria.

Example

The following macro extracts unique records into two extract ranges based on two sets of criteria. The text strings ("Criteria1", "ExtractRange1", and so on) indicate names on the external worksheet.

	A	B	C
1	Names	Formulas	Comments
2			
3		**ExtractMultipleRanges**	
4		=DEFINE.NAME("Criteria","=Criteria1")	Defines first criteria
5		=FORMULA.GOTO("ExtractRange1")	Selects first extract range
6		=EXTRACT(TRUE)	Extracts unique records
7		=DEFINE.NAME("Criteria","=Criteria2")	Defines second criteria
8		=FORMULA.GOTO("ExtractRange2")	Selects second extract range
9		=EXTRACT(TRUE)	
10		=RETURN()	

Related Functions

Function	Description
DATA.FIND	Finds records in a database
SET.CRITERIA	Defines the name Criteria for the selected range on the active sheet
SET.DATABASE	Defines the name Database for the selected range on the active sheet
SET.EXTRACT	Defines the name Extract for the selected range on the active sheet

FACT

Returns the factorial of a number. The factorial of a number is equal to 1*2*3*...* *number*.

Syntax

FACT(*number*)

Number   is the nonnegative number you want the factorial of. If *number* is not an integer, it is truncated.

Examples

FACT(1) equals 1

FACT(1.9) equals FACT(1) equals 1

FACT(0) equals 1

FACT(-1) equals #NUM!

FACT(5) equals 1*2*3*4*5 equals 120

Related Functions

Function	Description
DPRODUCT	Multiplies the values in a particular field of records that match the criteria in a database
FACTDOUBLE	Returns the double factorial of a number
PRODUCT	Multiplies its arguments

FACTDOUBLE

Returns the double factorial of a number.

If this function is not available, you must install the Analysis ToolPak add-in macro. For more information, see "Managing Add-in Commands and Functions" in Chapter 4 in Book 2 of the *Microsoft Excel User's Guide*.

Syntax

FACTDOUBLE(*number*)

Number   is the value for which to return the double factorial. If *number* is not an integer, it is truncated.

Remarks

- If *number* is non-numeric, FACTDOUBLE returns the #VALUE! error value

- If *number* is negative, FACTDOUBLE returns the #NUM! error value.

- If *number* is even:
  $$n!! = n(n-2)(n-4)\ldots(4)(2)$$

- If *number* is odd:
  $$n!! = n(n-2)(n-4)\ldots(3)(1)$$

Examples

FACTDOUBLE(6) equals 48

FACTDOUBLE(7) equals 105

Related Functions

Function	Description
FACT	Returns the factorial of a number
MULTINOMIAL	Returns the multinomial of a set of numbers

FALSE

Returns the logical value FALSE.

Syntax

FALSE( )

Remarks

You can also type the word FALSE directly into the worksheet or formula, and Microsoft Excel interprets it as the logical value FALSE.

FASTMATCH

Returns the relative position of an element in an array that matches the specified value. Use FASTMATCH instead of MATCH when you need to search large sorted arrays.

If this function is not available, you must install the Add-in Functions add-in macro. For more information, see "Managing Add-in Commands and Functions" in Chapter 4 in Book 2 of the *Microsoft Excel User's Guide*.

Syntax

FASTMATCH(*lookup_value,lookup_array, type_of_match*)

Lookup_value is the value you're searching for within *lookup_array*.

Lookup_array is an array or a range of cells within which you are searching for a match.

Type_of_match is the number –1, 0, or 1. *Type_of_match* specifies how Microsoft Excel matches *lookup_value* with values in *lookup_array*.

- If *type_of_match* is 1, FASTMATCH finds the largest value that is less than or equal to *lookup_value. Lookup_array* must be placed in ascending order: …–2, –1, 0, 1, 2,…A–Z, FALSE, TRUE, and so on.

- If *type_of_match* is –1, FASTMATCH finds the smallest value that is greater than or equal to *lookup_value. Lookup_array* must be placed in descending order: TRUE, FALSE, Z–A,…2, 1, 0, –1, –2,…, and so on.

- If *type_of_match* is omitted, it is assumed to be 1.

- If *type_of_match* is not –1, 0, or 1, FASTMATCH returns the #VALUE! error value.

Remarks

- Like MATCH, FASTMATCH does not distinguish between uppercase and lowercase letters.

- Unlike MATCH, FASTMATCH requires the values in *lookup_array* to be in sorted order. This is because FASTMATCH uses a binary search algorithm instead of the slower sequential algorithm used by MATCH.

Examples

See the examples for MATCH.

FCLOSE

Macro Sheets Only

Closes the specified file.

Syntax

FCLOSE(*file_num*)

File_num is the number of the file you want to close. *File_num* is returned by the FOPEN function that originally opened the file. If *file_num* is not a valid file number, FCLOSE halts the macro and returns the #VALUE! error value.

Examples

See the examples for FOPEN and RESULT.

Related Functions

Function	Description
CLOSE	Closes the active window
FILE.CLOSE	Closes the active document
FOPEN	Opens a file with the type of permission specified

FDIST

Returns the *F* probability distribution. You can use this function to determine whether two data sets have different degrees of diversity. For example, you can examine test scores given to men and women entering high school and determine if the variability in the females is different from that found in the males.

Syntax

FDIST(*x,degrees_freedom1,degrees_freedom2*)

X is the value at which to evaluate the function.

Degrees_freedom1 is the numerator degrees of freedom.

Degrees_freedom2 is the denominator degrees of freedom.

Remarks

- If any argument is non-numeric, FDIST returns the #VALUE! error value.

- If *x* is negative, FDIST returns the #NUM! error value.

- If *degrees_freedom1* or *degrees_freedom2* is not an integer, it is truncated.

- If *degrees_freedom1* < 1 or *degrees_freedom1* $\geq$ 10^{10}, FDIST returns the #NUM! error value.

- If *degrees_freedom2* < 1 or *degrees_freedom2* $\geq$ 10^{10}, FDIST returns the #NUM! error value.

Example

FDIST(15.20704,6,4) equals 0.01

Related Functions

Function	Description
FINV	Returns the inverse of the *F* probability distribution
FTEST	Returns the results of an *F*-test

FILE.CLOSE

Macro Sheets Only

Equivalent to choosing the Close command from the File menu. Closes the active document. For a workbook, FILE.CLOSE closes all documents in the workbook. Use FILE.CLOSE instead of CLOSE when you want to close an entire document instead of just one window in a document. For detailed information about the Close command, see online Help.

Syntax

FILE.CLOSE(*save_logical*)

Save_logical is a logical value specifying whether to save the file before closing it.

For a file:

Save_logical	Result
TRUE	Saves the file
FALSE	Does not save the file
Omitted	If you've made changes to the file, displays a dialog box asking if you want to save the file

For a workbook:

Save_logical	Result
TRUE	Saves changes to all of the documents in the workbook
FALSE	Does not save any changes to documents in the workbook
Omitted	For the workbook and for each unbound document in the workbook that you have made changes to, displays a dialog box asking if you want to save the changes made to that document

Remarks

If you make any changes to the contents of a workbook, such as which documents are included, their order, whether or not they are bound, and so on, then a message will be displayed reminding you that there are unsaved changes, regardless of the *save_logical* value.

Note When you use the CLOSE function, Microsoft Excel does not run any Auto_Close macros before closing the document.

Related Functions

Function	Description
CLOSE	Closes the active window
CLOSE.ALL	Closes all unprotected windows
FCLOSE	Closes a text file

FILE.DELETE

Macro Sheets Only

Equivalent to choosing the Delete command from the File menu. Deletes a file from the disk. Although you will normally delete files manually, you can, for example, use FILE.DELETE in a macro to delete temporary files created by the macro. For detailed information about the Delete command, see online Help.

Syntax

FILE.DELETE(*file_text*)
FILE.DELETE?(*file_text*)

File_text   is the name of the file to delete.

Remarks

- If Microsoft Excel can't find *file_text,* it displays a message saying that it cannot delete the file. To avoid this, include the entire path in *file_text.* See the following second and fifth examples. You can also use FILES to generate an array of filenames and then check if the file you want to delete is in the array. For an example of how to see if an entry is in an array, see OR.

- If a file is open when you delete it, the file is removed from the disk but remains open in Microsoft Excel.

- In the dialog-box form, FILE.DELETE?, you can use an asterisk (*) to represent any series of characters and a question mark (?) to represent any single character. See the following third and sixth examples.

Examples

In Microsoft Excel for Windows, the following macro formula deletes a file called CHART1.XLC from the current directory:

```
FILE.DELETE("CHART1.XLC")
```

The following macro formula deletes a file called 89INFO.XLS kept in the EXCEL\SALES subdirectory:

```
FILE.DELETE("C:\EXCEL\SALES\89INFO.XLS")
```

The following macro formula displays the Delete dialog box listing all documents whose extensions begin with the letters "XL":

```
FILE.DELETE?("*.XL?")
```

In Microsoft Excel for the Macintosh, the following macro formula deletes a file called CHART1 from the current folder:

```
FILE.DELETE("CHART1")
```

The following macro formula deletes a file called 1989 INFO kept in a series of nested folders:

```
FILE.DELETE("HARD DISK:EXCEL 3:SALES
WORKSHEETS:1989 INFO")
```

The following macro formula displays the Delete dialog box listing all documents beginning with the word "Clients":

```
FILE.DELETE?("Clients*")
```

Related Functions

Function	Description
FILE.CLOSE	Closes the active document
FILE.EXISTS	Tests for the existence of a file, directory, or folder
FILES	Returns the filenames in the specified directory or folder

FILE.EXISTS

Macro Sheets Only

Checks for the existence of a file or a directory or folder. Returns TRUE if it exists; otherwise, returns FALSE.

If this function is not available, you must load FILEFNS.XLA from the Library directory (in Microsoft Excel for Windows) or File Functions from the Macro Library folder (in Microsoft Excel for the Macintosh) in the directory or folder where you installed Microsoft Excel. For more information, see "Managing Add-in Commands and Functions" in Chapter 4 in Book 2 of the *Microsoft Excel User's Guide.*

Syntax

FILE.EXISTS*(path_text)*

Path_text is the name of the file or the directory or folder you wish to find. If the file or the directory or folder is not in the current directory or folder, you must give the full path of the file.

Examples

In Microsoft Excel for Windows, the following macro formula checks for the existence of the file named SALES.XLT in the current directory:

`FILE.EXISTS("SALES.XLT")`

The following macro formula checks for the existence of the file named SALES.XLT in the directory C:\WORD\SALES:

`FILE.EXISTS("C:\WORD\SALES\SALES.XLT")`

The following macro formula checks for the existence of the directory named C:\WORD\SALES:

`FILE.EXISTS("C:\WORD\SALES")`

In Microsoft Excel for the Macintosh, the following macro formula checks for the existence of a file named SALES TEMPLATE in the current folder:

`FILE.EXISTS("SALES TEMPLATE")`

The following macro formula checks for the existence of a file named SALES TEMPLATE in the folder HARD DISK:WORD:REPORTS:

`FILE.EXISTS("HARD DISK:WORD:REPORTS:SALES TEMPLATE")`

The following macro formula checks for the existence of the folder named HARD DISK:WORD:REPORTS:

`FILE.EXISTS("HARD DISK:WORD:REPORTS")`

Related Functions

Function	Description
CREATE.DIRECTORY	Creates a directory or folder
DELETE.DIRECTORY	Deletes an empty directory

FILES

Macro Sheets Only

Returns a horizontal text array of the names of all files in the specified directory or folder. Use FILES to build a list of filenames upon which you want your macro to operate.

Syntax

FILES*(directory_text)*

Directory_text specifies which directories or folders to return filenames from.

- *Directory_text* accepts an asterisk (*) to represent a series of characters and a question mark (?) to represent a single character in filenames.

- If *directory_text* is not specified, FILES returns filenames from the current directory.

Remarks

If you enter FILES in a single cell, only one filename is returned. You will normally use FILES with SET.NAME to assign the returned array to a name. See the last example below.

Tips You can use COLUMNS to count the number of entries in the returned array. You can use TRANSPOSE to change a horizontal array to a vertical one.

Examples

In Microsoft Excel for Windows, the following macro formula returns the names of all files starting with the letter F in the current directory or folder:

```
FILES("F*.*")
```

When entered as an array formula in several cells, the following macro formula returns the filenames in the current directory to those cells. If the directory contains fewer files than can fit in the selected cells, the #N/A error value appears in the extra cells.

```
FILES()
```

In Microsoft Excel for Windows, the following macro formula returns all files starting with "SALE" and ending with the .XLC extension in the \EXCEL\CHARTS subdirectory:

```
FILES("C:\EXCEL\CHARTS\SALE*.XLC")
```

In Microsoft Excel for the Macintosh, the following macro formula returns all files starting with "SALE" in the nested CHART folder:

```
FILES("DISK:EXCEL:CHART:SALE*")
```

The following macro opens all files matching DirText.

	A	B	C
1	Names	Formulas	Comments
2			
3		OpenFiles	
4	DirText	=INPUT("Enter the files to open",2)	Text can include wildcards
5		=SET.NAME("FileArray",FILES(DirText))	Stores array in a name
6		=IF(ISERROR(COLUMNS(FileArray)))	If empty, no columns
7		= ALERT("No files match directory text",2)	
8		=ELSE()	Otherwise, matching files
9		= FOR("Index",1,COLUMNS(FileArray))	Loops once for each
10	NextFile	= INDEX(FileArray,1,Index)	Retrieves the next filename
11		= OPEN(NextFile)	And opens the file
12		= NEXT()	
13		=END.IF()	
14		=RETURN()	

Related Functions

Function	Description
DOCUMENTS	Returns the names of the specified open documents
FILE.DELETE	Deletes a file
OPEN	Opens a document

FILL.AUTO

Macro Sheets Only

Equivalent to copying cells or automatically filling a selection by dragging the fill selection handle with the mouse (the AutoFill feature). For more information, see "Filling a Range of Adjacent Cells" in Chapter 6 in Book 1 of the *Microsoft Excel User's Guide*.

Syntax

FILL.AUTO(*destination_ref,copy_only*)

Destination_ref is the range of cells into which you want to fill data. The top, bottom, left, or right end of *destination_ref* must include all of the cells in the source reference (the current selection).

Copy_only is a logical value specifying whether to copy cells or perform an AutoFill operation. If *copy_only* is TRUE, Microsoft Excel copies the current selection into *destination_ref;* if FALSE or omitted, Microsoft Excel automatically fills the cells in *destination_ref* based on the size and contents of the current selection.

Examples

The following macro formulas both perform an AutoFill operation. The destination includes the source cells and the five rows beneath the source cells:

```
FILL.AUTO("RC:R[5]C",FALSE)

FILL.AUTO(ACTIVE.CELL():
OFFSET(ACTIVE.CELL(),5,0),FALSE)
```

Related Functions

Function	Description
COPY	Copies and pastes data or objects
DATA.SERIES	Fills a range of cells with a series of numbers or dates

FILL.DOWN
FILL.LEFT
FILL.RIGHT
FILL.UP

Macro Sheets Only

Equivalent to choosing the Fill Down, Fill Left, Fill Right, and Fill Up commands, respectively, from the Edit menu. For detailed information about the Fill commands, see online Help.

Syntax

FILL.DOWN( )
FILL.LEFT( )
FILL.RIGHT( )
FILL.UP( )

FILL.DOWN copies the contents and formats of the cells in the top row of a selection into the rest of the rows in the selection.

FILL.LEFT copies the contents and formats of the cells in the right column of a selection into the rest of the columns in the selection.

FILL.RIGHT copies the contents and formats of the cells in the left column of a selection into the rest of the columns in the selection.

FILL.UP copies the contents and formats of the cells in the bottom row of a selection into the rest of the rows in the selection.

Remarks

- If you have a multiple selection, each range in the selection is filled separately with the contents of the source range.

- To choose the Fill Left and Fill Up commands, press SHIFT while selecting the Edit menu.

Related Functions

Function	Description
COPY	Copies and pastes data or objects
DATA.SERIES	Fills a range of cells with a series of numbers or dates
FILL.AUTO	Copies cells or automatically fills a selection
FORMULA.FILL	Enters a formula in the specified range

FILL.GROUP

Macro Sheets Only

Equivalent to choosing the Fill Group command from the Edit menu. Copies the contents of the active worksheet's selection to the same area on all other worksheets in the group. Use FILL.GROUP to fill a range of cells on all worksheets in a group at once. For detailed information about the Fill Group command, see online Help.

Syntax

FILL.GROUP(*type_num*)
FILL.GROUP?(*type_num*)

Type_num   is a number from 1 to 3 that corresponds to the choices in the Fill Group dialog box.

Type_num	Type of information filled
1	All
2	Formulas
3	Formats

Related Functions

Function	Description
NEW	Creates a new document
WORKGROUP	Creates a group from an array of worksheet names

FIND

Finds one string of text within another string of text and returns the number of the character at which *find_text* first occurs. You can also use SEARCH to find one string of text within another, but unlike SEARCH, FIND is case-sensitive and doesn't allow wildcard characters.

Syntax

FIND(*find_text*,*within_text*,*start_at_num***)**

Find_text   is the text you want to find.

- If *find_text* is "" (empty text), FIND matches the first character in the search string (that is, the character numbered *start_at_num* or 1).

- *Find_text* cannot contain any wildcard characters.

Within_text   is the text containing the text you want to find.

Start_at_num   specifies the character at which to start the search. The first character in *within_text* is character number 1. If you omit *start_at_num*, it is assumed to be 1.

Remarks

- If *find_text* does not appear in *within_text*, FIND returns the #VALUE! error value.

- If *start_at_num* is not greater than zero, FIND returns the #VALUE! error value.

- If *start_at_num* is greater than the length of *within_text*, FIND returns the #VALUE! error value.

Examples

FIND("M","Miriam McGovern") equals 1

FIND("m","Miriam McGovern") equals 6

FIND("M","Miriam McGovern",3) equals 8

Suppose you have a list of parts and serial numbers in a worksheet, and you want to extract the names of the parts, but not the serial numbers, from each cell. You can use the FIND function to find the # symbol, and the MID function to omit the serial number. In the following worksheet, starting from row 2, each cell in column B contains these formulas using relative A1-style references:

MID(A2,1,FIND(" #",A2,1)-1) in cell B2

MID(A3,1,FIND(" #",A3,1)-1) in cell B3

and so on for the other cells in column B.

	A	B
1	**With serial number**	**Without serial number**
2	Ceramic Insulators #124-TD45-87	Ceramic Insulators
3	Copper Coils #12-671-6772	Copper Coils
4	Variable Resistors #116010	Variable Resistors
5	Blank Circuit Boards #44XT-56889-3	Blank Circuit Boards
6	AND Gate Arrays #8TRE995-4455-X1	AND Gate Arrays
7	7-Segment LED Displays #33-67-81524-2	7-Segment LED Displays
8	2-Input Toggle Switches #2-1-555-GFR44	2-Input Toggle Switches

Related Functions

Function	Description
EXACT	Checks to see if two text values are identical
LEN	Returns the number of characters in a text string
MID	Returns a specific number of characters from a text string starting at the position you specify
SEARCH	Finds one text value within another (not case-sensitive)

FINV

Returns the inverse of the F probability distribution. If $p = \text{FDIST}(x,\ldots)$, then $\text{FINV}(p,\ldots) = x$.

The F distribution can be used in an F-test that compares the degree of variability in two data sets. For example, you can analyze income distributions in the United States and Canada to determine whether the two countries have a similar degree of diversity.

Syntax

FINV(*probability,degrees_freedom1, degrees_freedom2*)

Probability   is a probability associated with the *F* cumulative distribution.

Degrees_freedom1   is the numerator degrees of freedom.

Degrees_freedom2   is the denominator degrees of freedom.

Remarks

- If any argument is non-numeric, FINV returns the #VALUE! error value.

- If *probability* < 0 or probability > 1, FINV returns the #NUM! error value.

- If *degrees_freedom1* or *degrees_freedom2* is not an integer, it is truncated.

- If *degrees_freedom1* < 1 or *degrees_freedom1* $\geq$ 10^{10}, FINV returns the #NUM! error value.

- If *degrees_freedom2* < 1 or *degrees_freedom2* $\geq$ 10^{10}, FINV returns the #NUM! error value.

FINV can be used to return critical values from the *F* distribution. For example, the output of an ANOVA calculation often includes data for the *F* statistic, *F* probability, and *F* critical value at the 0.05 significance level. To return the critical value of *F*, use the significance level as the *probability* argument to FINV.

FINV uses an iterative technique for calculating the function. Given a probability value, FINV iterates until the result is accurate to within $\pm 3 \times 10^{-7}$. If FINV does not converge after 100 iterations, the function returns the #N/A error value.

Example

FINV(0.01,6,4) equals 15.20675

Related Functions

Function	Description
FDIST	Returns the *F* probability distribution
FTEST	Returns the result of an *F*-test

FISHER

Returns the Fisher transformation at *x*. This transformation produces a function that is approximately normally distributed rather than skewed. Use this function to perform hypothesis testing on the correlation coefficient.

Syntax

FISHER(*x*)

X   is a numeric value for which you want the transformation.

- If *x* is non-numeric, FISHER returns the #VALUE! error value.

- If *x* ≤ -1 or if *x* ≥ 1, FISHER returns the #NUM! error value.

Remarks

The equation for the Fisher transformation is:

$$z' = \frac{1}{2} \ln\left(\frac{1 + x}{1 - x}\right)$$

Example

FISHER(0.75) equals 0.972955

Related Functions

Function	Description
CORREL	Returns the correlation coefficient between two data sets
COVAR	Returns covariance, the average of the products of paired deviations
FISHERINV	Returns the inverse of the Fisher transformation

Function	Description
MCORREL	Returns the correlation coefficient of two or more data sets
MCOVAR	Returns the covariance between two or more data sets

FISHERINV

Returns the inverse of the Fisher transformation. Use this transformation when analyzing correlations between ranges or arrays of data. If y = FISHER(x), then FISHERINV(y) = x.

Syntax

FISHERINV(*y*)

Y is the value for which you want to perform the inverse of the transformation.

Remarks

If y is non-numeric, FISHERINV returns the #VALUE! error value.

The equation for the inverse of the Fisher transformation is:

$$x = \frac{e^{2y} - 1}{e^{2y} + 1}$$

Example

FISHERINV(0.972955) equals 0.75

Related Functions

Function	Description
CORREL	Returns the correlation coefficient between two data sets
COVAR	Returns covariance, the average of the products of paired deviations
FISHER	Returns the Fisher transformation
MCORREL	Returns the correlation coefficient of two or more data sets
MCOVAR	Returns the covariance between two or more data sets

FIXED

Rounds a number to the specified number of decimals, formats the number in decimal format using a period and commas, and returns the result as text.

Syntax

FIXED(*number,decimals,no_commas*)

Number is the number you want to round and convert to text.

Decimals is the number of digits to the right of the decimal point.

No_commas is a logical value that, if TRUE, prevents FIXED from including commas in the returned text. If *no_commas* is FALSE or omitted, then the returned text includes commas as usual.

- Numbers in Microsoft Excel can never have more than 15 significant digits, but *decimals* can be as large as 127.

- If *decimals* is negative, *number* is rounded to the left of the decimal point.

- If you omit *decimals*, it is assumed to be 2.

Remarks

The major difference between formatting a cell containing a number with the Number command from the Format menu and formatting a number directly with the FIXED function is that FIXED converts its result to text. A number formatted with the Number command is still a number.

Examples

FIXED(1234.567,1) equals "1234.6"

FIXED(1234.567,-1) equals "1230"

FIXED(-1234.567,-1) equals "–1230"

FIXED(44.332) equals "44.33"

Related Functions

Function	Description
DOLLAR	Converts a number to text, using currency format
ROUND	Rounds a number to a specified number of digits
TEXT	Formats a number and converts it to text
VALUE	Converts a text argument to a number

FLOOR

Rounds *number* down to the nearest multiple of *significance*.

Syntax

FLOOR(*number,significance*)

Number   is the numeric value you want to round.

Significance   is the multiple to which you want to round.

Remarks

- If either argument is non-numeric, FLOOR returns the #VALUE! error value.

- If *number* and *significance* have different signs, FLOOR returns the #NUM! error value.

- Regardless of the sign of *number,* a value is rounded up when adjusted away from zero. If *number* is an exact multiple of *significance,* no rounding occurs.

Examples

FLOOR(2.5,1) equals 2

FLOOR(-2.5,-2) equals -2

FLOOR(-2.5,2) equals #NUM!

FLOOR(1.5,0.1) equals 1.5

FLOOR(0.234,0.01) equals 0.23

Related Functions

Function	Description
CEILING	Rounds a number up to the nearest integer
EVEN	Rounds a number up to the nearest even integer
INT	Rounds a number down to the nearest integer
ODD	Rounds a number up to the nearest odd integer
ROUND	Rounds a number to a specified number of digits
TRUNC	Truncates a number to an integer

FONT

Macro Sheets Only

Equivalent to choosing the Font command from the Options menu in Microsoft Excel for the Macintosh version 1.5 or earlier. This function is included only for macro compatibility. Sets the font for the Normal style. Microsoft Excel now uses the FORMAT.FONT and DEFINE.STYLE functions. For more information, see FORMAT.FONT and DEFINE.STYLE.

Syntax

FONT(*name_text,size_num*)
FONT?(*name_text,size_num*)

Related Functions

Function	Description
DEFINE.STYLE	Creates or changes a cell style
FORMAT.FONT	Applies a font to the selection

FOPEN

Macro Sheets Only

Opens a file with the type of permission specified. Unlike OPEN, FOPEN does not load the file into memory and display it; instead, FOPEN establishes a channel with the file so that you can exchange information with it. If the file is opened successfully, FOPEN returns a file ID number. If it can't open the file, FOPEN returns the #N/A error value. Use the file ID number with other file functions (such as FREAD, FWRITE, and FSIZE) when you want to get information from or send information to the file.

Syntax

FOPEN(*file_text,access_num*)

File_text is the name of the file you want to open.

Access_num is a number from 1 to 3 specifying what type of permission to allow to the file:

Access_num	Type of permission
1 or omitted	Can read and write to the file (read/write permission)
2	Can read the file, but can't write to the file (read-only permission)
3	Creates a new file with read/write permission

- If the file doesn't exist and *access_num* is 3, FOPEN creates a new file.

- If the file does exist and *access_num* is 3, FOPEN replaces the contents of the file with any information you supply using the FWRITE or FWRITELN functions.

- If the file doesn't exist and *access_num* is 1 or 2, FOPEN returns the #N/A error value.

Remarks

Use FCLOSE to close a file after you finish using it.

Example

The following macro opens a file, writes the contents of the selected nonblank cells on the active worksheet to the file, and then closes the file.

	A	B	C
1	Names	Formulas	Comments
2			
3		WriteSelection	Writes cells to text file
4	FileName	=INPUT("Name of file to write:",2)	Asks for a text filename
5	FileNumber	=FOPEN(FileName,3)	Creates read/write file
6		=FOR.CELL("CurrentCell",,TRUE)	Loops for nonblank cells
7		=FWRITE(FileNumber,CurrentCell)	Writes contents to the file
8		=NEXT()	
9		=FCLOSE(FileNumber)	
10		=RETURN()	

Notice that FCLOSE and FWRITE depend on the value that FOPEN returns in cell B5.

Also see examples for FPOS, FREAD, and RESULT.

Related Functions

Function	Description
FCLOSE	Closes a text file
FREAD	Reads characters from a text file
FWRITE	Writes characters to a text file
OPEN	Opens a document

FOR

Macro Sheets Only

Starts a FOR–NEXT loop. The instructions between FOR and NEXT are repeated until the loop counter reaches a specified value. Use FOR when you need to repeat instructions a specified number of times. Use FOR.CELL when you need to repeat instructions over a range of cells.

Syntax

FOR(*counter_text,start_num,end_num, step_num*)

Counter_text is the name of the loop counter in the form of text.

Start_num is the value initially assigned to *counter_text*.

End_num is the last value assigned to *counter_text*.

Step_num is a value added to the loop counter after each iteration. If *step_num* is omitted, it is assumed to be 1.

Remarks

- Microsoft Excel follows these steps as it executes a FOR–NEXT loop:

Step	Action
1	Sets *counter_text* to the value *start_num*.
2	If *counter_text* is greater than *end_num* (or less than *end_num* if *step_num* is negative), the loop ends, and the macro continues with the function after the NEXT function.
	If *counter_text* is less than or equal to *end_num* (or greater than or equal to *end_num* if *step_num* is negative), the macro continues in the loop.
3	Carries out functions up to the following NEXT function. The NEXT function must be below the FOR function and in the same column.
4	Adds *step_num* to the loop counter.
5	Returns to the FOR function and proceeds as described in step 2.

- You can interrupt a FOR–NEXT loop by using the BREAK function.

- For more information about looping in macros, see Chapter 7 in Book 2 of the *Microsoft Excel User's Guide*.

Example

The following macro uses a FOR–NEXT loop to unhide all hidden windows.

	A	B	C
1	Names	Formulas	Comments
2			
3		**UnhideAllWindows**	
4		=SET.NAME("WinArray",WINDOWS())	Names of open windows
5		=FOR("Counter",1,COLUMNS(WinArray))	Begins a FOR–NEXT loop
6	WinName	=INDEX(WinArray,1,Counter)	Name of one window
7	Hidden	=GET.WINDOW(7,WinName)	Hidden sheets?
8		=IF(Hidden,UNHIDE(WinName))	Unhides hidden sheets
9		=NEXT()	Continues the loop
10		=RETURN()	

Also see examples for FILES and FREAD.

Related Functions

Function	Description
BREAK	Interrupts a FOR–NEXT, FOR.CELL–NEXT, or WHILE–NEXT loop
FOR.CELL	Starts a FOR.CELL–NEXT loop
NEXT	Ends a FOR–NEXT, FOR.CELL–NEXT, or WHILE–NEXT loop
WHILE	Starts a WHILE–NEXT loop

FOR.CELL

Macro Sheets Only

Starts a FOR.CELL–NEXT loop. This function is similar to FOR, except that the instructions between FOR.CELL and NEXT are repeated over a range of cells, one cell at a time, and there is no loop counter.

Syntax

FOR.CELL(*ref_name,area_ref,skip blanks*)

Ref_name is the name in the form of text that Microsoft Excel gives to the one cell in the range that is currently being operated on; *ref_name* refers to a new cell during each loop.

Area_ref is the range of cells on which you want the FOR.CELL–NEXT loop to operate and can be a multiple selection. If *area_ref* is omitted, it is assumed to be the current selection.

Skip_blanks is a logical value specifying whether Microsoft Excel skips blank cells as it operates on the cells in *area_ref.*

Skip_blanks	Result
TRUE	Skips blank cells in *area_ref*
FALSE or omitted	Operates on all cells in *area_ref*

Remarks

FOR.CELL operates on each cell in a row from left to right one area at a time before moving to the next row in the selection.

Example

The following macro replaces the contents of each nonblank cell in the current selection with its cube root. This macro assumes that the appropriate worksheet is active and that each cell in the current selection contains a number.

	A	B	C
1	Names	Formulas	Comments
2			
3		CubeRoot	Calculates the cube root
4		=FOR.CELL("CurrentCell",,TRUE)	Loops for each nonblank cell
5		=FORMULA(CurrentCell^(1/3),CurrentCell)	Cube root of CurrentCell
6		=NEXT()	
7		=RETURN()	

Also see examples for FOPEN and FPOS.

Related Functions

Function	Description
BREAK	Interrupts a FOR–NEXT, FOR.CELL–NEXT, or WHILE–NEXT loop
FOR	Starts a FOR–NEXT loop
NEXT	Ends a FOR–NEXT, FOR.CELL–NEXT, or WHILE–NEXT loop
WHILE	Starts a WHILE–NEXT loop

FORECAST

Returns a predicted value for x based on a linear regression of known x- and y-arrays or ranges of data. You can use this function to predict future sales, inventory requirements, or consumer trends.

Syntax

FORECAST(*x,known_y's,known_x's*)

X is the data point for which you want to predict a value.

Known_y's is the dependent array or range of data.

Known_x's is the independent array or range of data.

Remarks

- If x is non-numeric, FORECAST returns the #VALUE! error value.

- If *known_y's* and *known_x's* are empty or contain a different number of data points, FORECAST returns the #N/A error value.

- If the variance of *known_x's* equals zero, then FORECAST returns the #DIV/0! error value.

Example

FORECAST(30,{6,7,9,15,21}, {20,28,31,38,40}) equals 10.60725

Related Functions

Function	Description
EXPON	Predicts a value based on the forecast for the prior period
GROWTH	Returns values along an exponential trend
LINEST	Returns parameters of a linear trend
LOGEST	Returns parameters of an exponential trend
MOVEAVG	Returns values along a moving average trend
TREND	Returns values along a linear trend

FORMAT.AUTO

Macro Sheets Only

Equivalent to choosing the AutoFormat command from the Format menu or clicking the AutoFormat tool. Formats the selected range of cells from a built-in gallery of formats. For detailed information about the AutoFormat command, see online Help.

Syntax

FORMAT.AUTO(*format_num,number,font, alignment,border,pattern,width*)
FORMAT.AUTO?(*format_num,number,font, alignment,border,pattern,width*)

Format_num is a number corresponding to the formats in the Table Format list box in the AutoFormat dialog box. If omitted, it is assumed to be 1.

The following arguments are logical values corresponding to the Formats To Apply check boxes in the AutoFormat dialog box. If an argument is TRUE or omitted, Microsoft Excel selects the check box; if FALSE, Microsoft Excel clears the check box.

Number corresponds to the Number check box.

Font corresponds to the Font check box.

Alignment corresponds to the Alignment check box.

Border corresponds to the Border check box.

Pattern corresponds to the Pattern check box.

Width corresponds to the Column Width/Row Height check box.

Related Functions

Function	Description
ALIGNMENT	Aligns or wraps text in cells
BORDER	Adds a border to the selected cell or object
FORMAT.FONT	Applies a font to the selection
FORMAT.NUMBER	Applies a number format to the selection

Function	Description
FORMAT.TEXT	Formats a worksheet text box or a chart text item
PATTERNS	Changes the appearance of the selected object

FORMAT.FONT

Macro Sheets Only

Equivalent to choosing the Font command from the Format menu. Applies a font to the selection. FORMAT.FONT has three syntax forms. Syntax 1 is for cells; syntax 2 is for text boxes and buttons; syntax 3 is used with all chart items (axes, labels, text, and so on). For detailed information about the Font command, see online Help.

Syntax 1

Cells

FORMAT.FONT(*name_text,size_num,bold,italic, underline,strike,color,outline,shadow*)
FORMAT.FONT?(*name_text,size_num,bold,italic, underline,strike,color,outline,shadow*)

Syntax 2

Text boxes and buttons on worksheets and macro sheets

FORMAT.FONT(*name_text,size_num,bold,italic, underline,strike,color,outline,shadow, object_id_text,start_num,char_num*)
FORMAT.FONT?(*name_text,size_num,bold,italic, underline,strike,color,outline,shadow, object_id_text,start_num,char_num*)

Syntax 3

Chart items including unattached chart text

FORMAT.FONT(*color,backgd,apply,name_text, size_num,bold,italic,underline,strike,outline, shadow*)
FORMAT.FONT?(*color,backgd,apply,name_text, size_num,bold,italic,underline,strike,outline, shadow*)

Arguments correspond to check boxes or options in the Font dialog box. Arguments that correspond to check boxes are logical values. If an argument is TRUE, Microsoft Excel selects the check box; if FALSE, Microsoft Excel clears the check box. If an argument is omitted, the format is not changed.

Name_text is the name of the font as it appears in the Font dialog box. For example, Courier is a font name.

Size_num is the font size, in points.

Bold corresponds to the Bold check box in previous versions of Microsoft Excel. Makes the selection bold, if applicable.

Italic corresponds to the Italic check box in previous versions of Microsoft Excel. Makes the selection italic, if applicable.

Underline corresponds to the Underline check box.

Strike corresponds to the Strikeout check box.

Color is a number from 0 to 16 corresponding to the colors in the Font dialog box; 0 corresponds to automatic color.

Outline corresponds to the Outline check box. Outline fonts are available in Microsoft Excel for the Macintosh. For macro compatibility, this argument is ignored by Microsoft Excel for Windows.

Shadow corresponds to the Shadow check box. Shadow fonts are available in Microsoft Excel for the Macintosh. For macro compatibility, this argument is ignored by Microsoft Excel for Windows.

Object_id_text identifies the text box you want to format (for example, "Text 1", "Text 2", and so on). You can also use the object number alone without the text identifier. If this argument is omitted, Microsoft Excel formats text in the currently selected text box.

Start_num specifies the first character to be formatted. If *start_num* is omitted, it is assumed to be 1 (the first character in the text box).

Char_num specifies how many characters to format. If *char_num* is omitted, Microsoft Excel formats all characters in the text box starting at *start_num*.

Backgd is a number from 1 to 3 specifying which type of background to apply to text in a chart.

Backgd	Type of background applied
1	Automatic
2	Transparent
3	Opaque

Apply corresponds to the Apply To All check box. This argument applies to data labels only.

Remarks

Some extended TrueType styles do not have corresponding arguments to FORMAT.FONT. To access an extended TrueType font style, append the style name to the font name in *name_text*. For example, the font Taipei can be formatted in an upside-down style by specifying "Taipei Upside-down" as the *name_text* argument. For more information about TrueType, see your Microsoft Windows documentation.

Examples

In Microsoft Excel for Windows, the following macro formula formats the selected range of cells with the 10-point Courier bold italic font:

```
FORMAT.FONT("Courier",10,TRUE,TRUE,FALSE,
FALSE,0)
```

In Microsoft Excel for the Macintosh, the following macro formula formats the selected range of cells with the 10-point Courier bold italic font:

```
FORMAT.FONT("Courier",10,TRUE,TRUE,FALSE,
FALSE,0,FALSE,FALSE)
```

Note For macro compatibility with Microsoft Excel for the Macintosh, the presence of the *outline* and *shadow* arguments in the preceding formula would not prevent the macro from working on Microsoft Excel for Windows, nor would their absence prevent it from working on the Macintosh.

Related Functions

Function	Description
ALIGNMENT	Aligns or wraps text in cells
FORMAT.NUMBER	Applies a number format to the selection
FORMAT.TEXT	Formats a worksheet text box or a chart text item

FORMAT.LEGEND

Macro Sheets Only

Equivalent to choosing the Legend command from the Format menu. Determines the position and orientation of the legend on a chart and returns TRUE; returns an error message if the legend is not already selected. For detailed information about the Legend command, see online Help.

Syntax

FORMAT.LEGEND(*position_num*)
FORMAT.LEGEND?(*position_num*)

Position_num is a number from 1 to 5 specifying the position of the legend.

Position_num	Position of legend
1	Bottom
2	Corner
3	Top
4	Right
5	Left

Example

The following macro formula moves the selected legend to the bottom of the chart:

```
FORMAT.LEGEND(1)
```

Related Functions

Function	Description
FORMAT.MOVE	Moves the selected object
LEGEND	Adds or deletes a chart legend

FORMAT.MAIN

Macro Sheets Only

Equivalent to choosing the Main Chart command from the Format menu. Formats a chart according to the arguments you specify. For detailed information about the Main Chart command, see online Help.

Syntax

FORMAT.MAIN(*type_num,view,overlap, gap_width,vary,drop,hilo,angle,gap_depth, chart_depth,up_down,series_line,labels*)
FORMAT.MAIN?(*type_num,view,overlap, gap_width,vary,drop,hilo,angle,gap_depth, chart_depth,up_down,series_line,labels*)

Type_num is a number from 1 to 13 specifying the type of chart.

Type_num	Chart
1	Area
2	Bar
3	Column
4	Line
5	Pie
6	XY (Scatter)
7	3-D Area
8	3-D Column
9	3-D Line
10	3-D Pie
11	Radar
12	3-D Bar
13	3-D Surface

View is a number specifying one of the views in the Data View box in the Main Chart dialog box. The view varies depending on the type of chart.

Overlap is a number from −100 to 100 specifying how you want bars or columns to be positioned. It corresponds to the Overlap box in the Main Chart dialog box. *Overlap* is ignored if *type_num* is not 2 or 3 (bar or column chart).

- If *overlap* is positive, it specifies the percentage of overlap you want for bars or columns. For example, 50 would cause one half of a bar or column to be covered by an adjacent bar or column. A value of zero prevents bars or columns from overlapping.

- If *overlap* is negative, then bars or columns are separated by the specified percentage of the maximum available distance between any two bars or columns.

- If *overlap* is omitted, it is assumed to be 0 (bars or columns do not overlap), or it is unchanged if a value was previously set.

Gap_width   is a number from 0 to 500 specifying the space between bar or column clusters as a percentage of the width of a bar or column. It corresponds to the Gap Width box in the Main Chart dialog box.

- *Gap_width* is ignored if *type_num* is not 2, 3, 8, or 12 (bar or column chart).

- If *gap_width* is omitted, it is assumed to be 50, or it is unchanged if a value was previously set.

Several of the following arguments are logical values corresponding to check boxes in the Main Chart dialog box. If an argument is TRUE, Microsoft Excel selects the corresponding check box; if FALSE, Microsoft Excel clears the check box. If an argument is omitted, the setting is unchanged.

Vary   corresponds to the Vary By Categories check box. *Vary* applies only to charts with one data series and is not available for area charts.

Drop   corresponds to the Drop Lines check box. *Drop* is available only for area and line charts.

Hilo   corresponds to the Hi-Lo Lines check box. *Hilo* is available only for line charts.

Angle   is a number from 0 to 360 specifying the angle of the first pie slice (in degrees) if the chart is a pie chart. If *angle* is omitted, it is assumed to be 0, or it is unchanged if a value was previously set.

The next two arguments are for 3-D charts only.

Gap_depth   is a number from 0 to 500 specifying the depth of the gap in front of and behind a bar, column, area, or line as a percentage of the depth of the bar, column, area, or line. *Gap_depth* corresponds to the Gap Depth box in the Main Chart dialog box.

- *Gap_depth* is ignored if the chart is a pie chart or if it is not a 3-D chart.

- If *gap_depth* is omitted and the chart is a 3-D chart, *gap_depth* is assumed to be 50, or it is unchanged if a value was previously set. If *gap_depth* is omitted and the view is side-by-side, stacked, or stacked 100%, *gap_depth* is assumed to be 0, or it is unchanged if a value was previously set.

Chart_depth   is a number from 20 to 2000 specifying the visual depth of the chart as a percentage of the width of the chart. *Chart_depth* corresponds to the Chart Depth box in the Main Chart dialog box.

- *Chart_depth* is ignored if the chart is not a 3-D chart.

- If *chart_depth* is omitted, it is assumed to be 100, or it is unchanged if a value was previously set.

The next three arguments are logical values corresponding to check boxes in the Main Chart dialog box. If an argument is TRUE, Microsoft Excel selects the corresponding check box; if FALSE, Microsoft Excel clears the check box. If an argument is omitted, the setting is unchanged.

Up_down   corresponds to the Up/Down Bars check box. *Up_down* is available only for line charts.

Series_line   corresponds to the Series Lines check box. *Series_line* is available only for stacked bar and column charts.

Labels   corresponds to the Radar Axis Labels check box. *Labels* is available only for radar charts.

Example

The following macro formula formats the main chart as a 3-D column chart with a side-by-side view, no overlap between the columns, 100% gap depth, and 150% chart depth. All other arguments are default values.

```
FORMAT.MAIN(8,1,0, , , , , ,100,150)
```

Related Function

Function	Description
FORMAT.OVERLAY	Formats an overlay chart

FORMAT.MOVE

Macro Sheets Only

Equivalent to moving an object with the mouse. Moves the selected object to the specified position and, if successful, returns TRUE. If the selected object cannot be moved, FORMAT.MOVE returns FALSE. There are two syntax forms of this function. Use syntax 1 to move worksheet objects. Use syntax 2 to move chart items. It is generally easier to use the macro recorder to enter this function on your macro sheet.

Syntax 1

Worksheet objects

FORMAT.MOVE(*x_offset,y_offset,reference*)
FORMAT.MOVE?(*x_offset,y_offset,reference*)

X_offset   specifies the horizontal position to which you want to move the object and is measured in points from the upper-left corner of the object to the upper-left corner of the cell specified by *reference*. A point is 1/72nd of an inch.

Y_offset   specifies the vertical position to which you want to move the object and is measured in points from the upper-left corner of the object to the upper-left corner of the cell specified by *reference*.

Reference   specifies which cell or range of cells to place the object in relation to.

- If *reference* is a range of cells, only the upper-left cell is used.
- If *reference* is omitted, it is assumed to be cell A1.

Remarks

The position of an object is based on its upper-left corner. For ovals and arcs, the position is based on the upper-left corner of the bounding rectangle of the object.

Example

The following macro formula moves an object on the active worksheet so that it is 10 points horizontally offset and 15 points vertically offset from cell D4:

```
FORMAT.MOVE(10,15,!$D$4)
```

Related Functions

Function	Description
CREATE.OBJECT	Creates an object
FORMAT.SIZE	Sizes an object
WINDOW.MOVE	Moves a window

FORMAT.MOVE

Macro Sheets Only

Equivalent to moving an object with the mouse. Moves the base of the selected object to the specified position and, if successful, returns TRUE. If the selected object cannot be moved, FORMAT.MOVE returns FALSE. There are two syntax forms of this function. Use syntax 2 to move chart items. Use syntax 1 to move worksheet objects. It is generally easier to use the macro recorder to enter this function on your macro sheet.

Syntax 2

Chart items

FORMAT.MOVE*(x_pos,y_pos)*
FORMAT.MOVE?*(x_pos,y_pos)*

X_pos specifies the horizontal position to which you want to move the object and is measured in points from the base of the object to the lower-left corner of the window. A point is 1/72nd of an inch.

Y_pos specifies the vertical position to which you want to move the object and is measured in points from the base of the object to the lower-left corner of the window.

Remarks

- The base of a text label on a chart is the lower-left corner of the text rectangle.

- The base of an arrow is the end without the arrowhead.

- The base of a pie slice is the point.

Example

On a chart, the following macro formula moves the base of the selected chart object 10 points to the right of and 20 points above the lower-left corner of the window:

```
FORMAT.MOVE(10,20)
```

Related Functions

Function	Description
FORMAT.SIZE	Sizes an object
WINDOW.MOVE	Moves a window

FORMAT.NUMBER

Macro Sheets Only

Equivalent to choosing the Number command from the Format menu. Formats numbers, dates, and times in the selected cells. Use FORMAT.NUMBER to apply built-in formats or to create and apply custom formats.

Syntax

FORMAT.NUMBER*(format_text)*
FORMAT.NUMBER?*(format_text)*

Format_text is a format string, such as "#,##0.00", specifying which format to apply to the selection.

For information about number and text formats, see Chapter 7 in Book 1 of the *Microsoft Excel User's Guide*.

Example

The following macro formula applies a custom time format to the selected cells:

```
FORMAT.NUMBER("h"" hours ""m"" minutes
""s"" seconds""")
```

The preceding format would display 3:45:30 as "3 hours 45 minutes 30 seconds".

Related Functions

Function	Description
DELETE.FORMAT	Deletes the specified custom number format
FORMAT.FONT	Applies a font to the selection
FORMAT.TEXT	Formats a worksheet text box or a chart text item

FORMAT.OVERLAY

Macro Sheets Only

Equivalent to choosing the Overlay command from the Format menu. Formats the overlay chart according to the arguments you specify. For detailed information about the Overlay command, see online Help.

Syntax

FORMAT.OVERLAY*(type_num,view,overlap, gap_width,vary,drop,hilo,angle,series_dist, series_num,up_down,series_line,labels)*
FORMAT.OVERLAY?*(type_num,view,overlap, gap_width,vary,drop,hilo,angle,series_dist, series_num,up_down,series_line,labels)*

Type_num   is a number specifying the type of chart.

Type_num	Chart
1	Area
2	Bar
3	Column
4	Line
5	Pie
6	XY (Scatter)
11	Radar

View   is a number specifying one of the views in the Data View box in the Overlay dialog box. The view varies depending on the type of chart.

Overlap   is a number from –100 to 100 specifying how you want bars or columns to be positioned. It corresponds to the Overlap box in the Overlay dialog box. *Overlap* is ignored if *type_num* is not 2 or 3 (bar or column chart).

- If *overlap* is positive, it specifies the percentage of overlap you want for bars or columns. For example, 50 would cause one-half of a bar or column to be covered by an adjacent bar or column.

- If *overlap* is negative, then bars or columns are separated by the specified percentage of the maximum available distance between any two bars or columns.

- If *overlap* is omitted, it is assumed to be 0 (bars or columns do not overlap), or it is unchanged if a value was previously set.

Gap_width   is a number from 0 to 500 specifying the space between bar or column clusters as a percentage of the width of a bar or column. *Gap_width* corresponds to the Gap Width box in the Overlay dialog box.

- *Gap_width* is ignored if *type_num* is not 2 or 3 (bar or column chart).

- If *gap_width* is omitted, it is assumed to be 50, or it is unchanged if a value was previously set.

Several of the following arguments are logical values corresponding to check boxes in the Overlay dialog box. If an argument is TRUE, Microsoft Excel selects the corresponding check box; if FALSE, Microsoft Excel clears the check box. If an argument is omitted, the setting is unchanged.

Vary   corresponds to the Vary By Categories check box. *Vary* is not available for area charts.

Drop   corresponds to the Drop Lines check box. *Drop* is available only for area and line charts.

Hilo   corresponds to the Hi-Lo Lines check box. *Hilo* is available only for line charts.

Angle   is a number from 0 to 360 specifying the angle of the first pie slice (in degrees) if the chart is a pie chart. If *angle* is omitted, it is assumed to be 0, or it is unchanged if a value was previously set.

Series_dist   is the number 1 or 2 and specifies automatic or manual series distribution.

- If *series_dist* is 1 or omitted, Microsoft Excel uses automatic series distribution.

- If *series_dist* is 2, Microsoft Excel uses manual series distribution, and you must specify which series is first in the distribution by using the *series_num* argument.

Series_num   is the number of the first series in the overlay chart and corresponds to the First Overlay Series box in the Overlay dialog box. If *series_dist* is 1 (automatic series distribution), this argument is ignored.

Up_down   corresponds to the Up/Down Bars check box. *Up_down* is available only for line charts.

Series_line   corresponds to the Series Lines check box. *Series_line* is available only for stacked bar and column charts.

Labels   corresponds to the Radar Axis Labels check box. *Labels* is available only for radar charts.

Example

The following macro formula formats the overlay chart as a line chart with a normal view (*view* 1), hi-lo lines, and manual series distribution with series number 3 specified as the first series in the overlay. All other arguments are default values.

```
FORMAT.OVERLAY(4,1, , , , ,TRUE,,2,3)
```

Related Functions

Function	Description
DELETE.OVERLAY	Deletes the overlay on a chart
FORMAT.MAIN	Formats a main chart

FORMAT.SHAPE

Macro Sheets Only

Equivalent to clicking the reshape tool on the Drawing toolbar and then inserting, moving, or deleting vertices of the selected polygon. A vertex is a point defined by a pair of coordinates in one row of the array that defines the polygon. The array is created by CREATE.OBJECT and EXTEND.POLYGON functions.

Syntax

FORMAT.SHAPE(*vertex_num,insert,reference, x_offset,y_offset*)

Vertex_num   is a number corresponding to the vertex you want to insert, move, or delete.

Insert   is a logical value specifying whether to insert a vertex, or move or delete a vertex.

- If *insert* is TRUE, Microsoft Excel inserts a vertex between the vertices *vertex_num* and *vertex_num*–1. The number of the new vertex then becomes *vertex_num*. The number of the vertex previously identified by *vertex_num* becomes *vertex_num*+1, and so on.

- If *insert* is FALSE, Microsoft Excel deletes the vertex (if the remaining arguments are omitted) or moves the vertex to the position specified by the remaining arguments.

Reference   is the reference from which the vertex you are inserting or moving is measured—the cell or range of cells to use as the basis for the *x* and *y* offsets.

- If *reference* is a range of cells, only the upper-left cell is used.

- If *reference* is omitted, the vertex is measured from the upper-left corner of the polygon's bounding rectangle.

X_offset   is the horizontal distance from the upper-left corner of *reference* to the vertex. *X_offset* is measured in points. A point is 1/72nd of an inch.

Y_offset   is the vertical distance from the upper-left corner of *reference* to the vertex. *Y_offset* is measured in points.

Remarks

You cannot delete a vertex if only two vertices remain.

Examples

The following macro formula deletes the second vertex of the selected polygon:

```
FORMAT.SHAPE(2,FALSE)
```

The following macro formula moves the thirteenth vertex 6 points to the right and 4 points below the upper-left corner of cell B5 on the active worksheet:

```
FORMAT.SHAPE(13,FALSE,!$B$5,6,4)
```

The following macro formula inserts a new vertex between vertices 2 and 3. The new vertex is 60 points to the right and 75 points below the upper-left corner of the polygon's bounding rectangle:

```
FORMAT.SHAPE(3,TRUE,,60,75)
```

Related Functions

Function	Description
CREATE.OBJECT	Creates an object
EXTEND.POLYGON	Adds vertices to a polygon

FORMAT.SIZE

Macro Sheets Only

Equivalent to sizing an object with the mouse. Sizes the selected object and returns TRUE. If the selected chart object cannot be sized, FORMAT.SIZE returns FALSE. There are two syntax forms of this function. Use syntax 1 to size worksheet objects and chart items absolutely. Use syntax 2 relative to a cell or range of cells to size only worksheet objects. It is generally easier to use the macro recorder to enter this function on your macro sheet.

Syntax 1

Worksheet objects and chart items, absolute

FORMAT.SIZE(*width,height*)
FORMAT.SIZE?(*width,height*)

Width specifies the width of the selected object, measured in points. A point is 1/72nd of an inch.

Height specifies the height of the selected object, measured in points.

You do not always have to use both arguments. For example, if you specify height and not width, the height changes but the width does not.

Remarks

- The base of a text label on a chart is the lower-left corner of the text rectangle.

- The base of an arrow is the end without the arrowhead.

Example

The following macro formula sizes the selected object to 175 by 111 points:

```
FORMAT.SIZE(175,111)
```

Related Functions

Function	Description
FORMAT.MOVE	Moves the selected object
SIZE	Changes the size of a window

FORMAT.SIZE

Macro Sheets Only

Equivalent to sizing an object with the mouse. Sizes the selected worksheet object and returns TRUE. If the selected object cannot be sized, FORMAT.SIZE returns FALSE. There are two syntax forms of this function. Use syntax 2 to size worksheet objects relative to a cell or range of cells. Use syntax 1 to size worksheet objects and chart items. It is generally easier to use the macro recorder to enter this function on your macro sheet.

Syntax 2

Worksheet objects, relative

FORMAT.SIZE(*x_off,y_off,reference*)
FORMAT.SIZE?(*x_off,y_off,reference*)

X_off specifies the width of the selected object and is measured in points from the lower-right corner of the object to the upper-left corner of *reference*. A point is 1/72nd of an inch. If omitted, *x_off* is assumed to be 0.

Y_off specifies the height of the selected object and is measured in points from the lower-right corner of the object to the upper-left corner of *reference*. If omitted, *y_off* is assumed to be 0.

Reference specifies the cell or range of cells to use as the basis for the offset and for sizing. If *reference* is a range of cells, only the upper-left cell in the range is used.

Examples

Suppose you want to change the size of an object from this size:

to this size:

In the second illustration, the right edge of the object is about 34 points offset from the left edge of cell D7 (if it were 0 points offset, the right edge of the object would be directly over the left edge of column D). The bottom edge of the object is offset about 6 points from the upper edge of cell D7.

The following macro formula sizes the object approximately as shown:

```
FORMAT.SIZE(34,6,D7)
```

Related Functions

Function	Description
FORMAT.MOVE	Moves the selected object
SIZE	Changes the size of a window

FORMAT.TEXT

Macro Sheets Only

Equivalent to choosing the Text command from the Format menu. Formats the selected worksheet text box or button or any text item on a chart. For detailed information about the Text command, see online Help.

Syntax

FORMAT.TEXT(*x_align,y_align,orient_num, auto_text,auto_size,show_key,show_value*)
FORMAT.TEXT?(*x_align,y_align,orient_num, auto_text,auto_size,show_key,show_value*)

Arguments correspond to check boxes or options in the Text dialog box. Arguments that correspond to check boxes are logical values. If an argument is TRUE, Microsoft Excel selects the check box; if FALSE, Microsoft Excel clears the check box; if omitted, the current setting is used.

X_align is a number from 1 to 4 specifying the horizontal alignment of the text.

X_align	Horizontal alignment
1	Left
2	Center
3	Right
4	Justify

Y_align is a number from 1 to 4 specifying the vertical alignment of the text.

Y_align	Vertical alignment
1	Top
2	Center
3	Bottom
4	Justify

Orient_num is a number from 0 to 3 specifying the orientation of the text.

Orient_num	Text orientation
0	Horizontal
1	Vertical
2	Upward
3	Downward

Auto_text corresponds to the Automatic Text check box. If the selected text was created with the Attach Text command from the Chart menu and later edited, this option restores the original text. *Auto_text* is ignored for text boxes on worksheets and macro sheets.

Auto_size corresponds to the Automatic Size check box. If you have changed the size of the border around the selected text, this option restores the border to automatic size. Automatic size makes the border fit exactly around the text no matter how you change the text.

Show_key corresponds to the Show Key check box. This argument applies only if the selected text is an attached data label on a chart.

Show_value corresponds to the Show Value check box. This argument applies only if the selected text is an attached data label on a chart.

The following list summarizes which arguments apply to each type of text item.

Text item	Arguments that apply
Worksheet text box or button	*X_align, y_align, orient_num, auto_size*
Attached data label	All arguments
Unattached text label	*X_align, y_align, orient_num, auto_size*
Tickmark label	*Orient_num*

Example

The following macro formula formats the selected text so that its horizontal alignment is to the right, its vertical alignment is to the bottom, its orientation is downward, the Automatic Text option is off, and the Automatic Size option is on. Assume that the text is not an attached data label.

```
FORMAT.TEXT(3,3,3,FALSE,TRUE,,)
```

Related Functions

Function	Description
CREATE.OBJECT	Creates an object
FORMAT.FONT	Applies a font to the selection
FORMULA	Enters values into a cell or range or onto a chart

FORMULA

Macro Sheets Only

Enters a formula in the active cell or in a reference. There are two syntax forms of this function. Use syntax 1 to enter numbers, text, references, and formulas in a worksheet Although syntax 1 can also be used to enter values on a macro sheet, you will not generally use FORMULA for this purpose. Use syntax 2 to enter a formula in a chart. For information about setting values on a macro sheet, see "Remarks" later in this topic.

Syntax 1

Worksheets and macro sheets

FORMULA(*formula_text,reference*)

Formula_text can be text, a number, a reference, or a formula in the form of text, or a reference to a cell containing any of the above.

Reference specifies where *formula_text* is to be entered. It can be a reference to a cell in the active worksheet or an external reference to a worksheet. If *reference* is omitted, *formula_text* is entered in the active cell.

If the active document is a worksheet, using FORMULA is equivalent to entering *formula_text* in the cell specified by *reference*. *Formula_text* is entered just as if you typed it in the formula bar.

- If *formula_text* is a formula, the formula is entered. Text arguments must be surrounded by double sets of quotation marks. For example, to enter the formula =IF($A$1="Hello World",1,0) in the active cell with the FORMULA function, you would use the formula
  ```
  FORMULA("=IF(R1C1=""Hello World""",1,
  0)")
  ```

  If *formula_text* is a number, text, or logical value, the value is entered as a constant.

- If *formula_text* contains references, they must be R1C1-style references, such as "=RC[1]*(1+R1C1)". If you are recording a macro when you enter a formula, Microsoft Excel converts A1-style references to R1C1-style references. For example, if you enter the formula =B2*(1+$A$1) in cell C2 while recording, Microsoft Excel records that action as =FORMULA("=RC[-1]*(1+R1C1)").

Remarks

Consider the following guidelines as you choose a function to set values on a worksheet or macro sheet:

- Use FORMULA to enter formulas and change values in a worksheet cell.

- SET.VALUE changes values on the macro sheet. Use SET.VALUE to assign initial values to a reference and to store values during the calculation of the macro.

- SET.NAME creates names on the macro sheet. Use SET.NAME to create a name and immediately assign a value to the name.

Examples

If the active document is a worksheet, the following macro formula enters the number constant 523 in the active cell:

```
FORMULA(523)
```

If the active document is a worksheet, the following macro formula enters the result of the INPUT function in cell A5:

```
FORMULA(INPUT("Enter a formula:",0),!$A$5)
```

If you're using R1C1-style references and the active document is a worksheet, the following macro formula enters the formula =RC[-1]*(1+R1C1) in the active cell:

```
FORMULA("=RC[-1]*(1+R1C1)")
```

If the active document is a worksheet, the following macro formulas enter the number 1000 in the cell two rows down and three columns right from the active cell. The R1C1-style formula is shorter, but the OFFSET method may provide faster performance in larger macro sheets.

```
FORMULA(1000,OFFSET(ACTIVE.CELL(),2,3))
FORMULA(1000,"R[2]C[3]")
```

The following macro formula enters the phrase "Year to Date" in cell B4 on the sheet named SALES.XLS:

```
FORMULA("Year to Date",SALES.XLS!B4)
```

Related Functions

Function	Description
FORMULA.ARRAY	Enters an array
FORMULA.FILL	Enters a formula in the specified range
SET.VALUE	Sets the value of a cell on a macro sheet

FORMULA

Macro Sheets Only

Enters a text label or SERIES formula in a chart. To enter formulas on a worksheet or macro sheet, use syntax 1 of this function.

Syntax 2

Charts

FORMULA(*formula_text*)

Formula_text is the text label or SERIES formula you want to enter into the chart.

It	Then
Formula_text can be treated as a text label and the current selection is a text label	The selected text label is replaced with *formula_text*.
Formula_text can be treated as a text label and there is no current selection or the current selection is not a text label	*Formula_text* creates a new text label.
Formula_text can be treated as a SERIES formula and the current selection is a SERIES formula	The selected SERIES formula is replaced with *formula_text*.
Formula_text can be treated as a SERIES formula and the current selection is not a SERIES formula	*Formula_text* creates a new SERIES formula.

Remarks

You would normally use the EDIT.SERIES function to create or edit a chart series. For more information, see EDIT.SERIES.

Example

The following macro formula enters a SERIES formula on the chart. If the current selection is a SERIES formula, it is replaced:

```
FORMULA("=SERIES(""Title"",,{1,2,3},1)")
```

Related Function

Function	Description
EDIT.SERIES	Creates or changes a chart series

FORMULA.ARRAY

Macro Sheets Only

Enters a formula as an array formula in the range specified or in the current selection. Equivalent to entering an array formula while pressing CTRL+SHIFT+ENTER in Microsoft Excel for Windows or COMMAND+ENTER in Microsoft Excel for the Macintosh.

Syntax

FORMULA.ARRAY(*formula_text,reference*)

Formula_text is the text you want to enter in the array. For more information on *formula_text,* see the first form of FORMULA.

Reference specifies where *formula_text* is entered. It can be a reference to a cell on the active worksheet or an external reference to a named document. *Reference* must be a R1C1-style reference in text form. If *reference* is omitted, *formula_text* is entered in the active cell.

Examples

If the selection is D25:E25, the following macro formula enters the array formula {=D22:E22+D23:E23} in the range D25:E25:

```
FORMULA.ARRAY("=R[-3]C:R[-3]C[1]+
R[-2]C:R[-2]C[1]")
```

Regardless of the selection, the following macro formula enters the array formula {=D22:E22+D23:E23} in the range D25:E25:

```
FORMULA.ARRAY("=R[-3]C:R[-3]C[1]
+R[-2]C:R[-2]C[1]","R25C4:R25C5")
```

To use FORMULA.ARRAY to put an array in a specific document, specify the name of the document as an external reference in the *reference* argument. In Microsoft Excel for Windows, using "SALES.XLS!R25C3:R25C4" as the *reference* argument in the preceding example would enter the array in cells C25:D25 on the worksheet named SALES.XLS. In Microsoft Excel for the Macintosh, using "SALES!R25C3:R25C4" as the *reference* argument would enter the array in the same cells in the worksheet named SALES.

Related Functions

Function	Description
FORMULA	Enters values into a cell or range or onto a chart
FORMULA.FILL	Enters a formula in the specified range

FORMULA.CONVERT

Macro Sheets Only

Changes the style and type of references in a formula between A1 and R1C1 and between relative and absolute. Use FORMULA.CONVERT to convert references of one style or type to another style or type.

Syntax

FORMULA.CONVERT(*formula_text,from_a1, to_a1,to_ref_type,rel_to_ref*)

Formula_text is the formula, given as text, containing the references you want to change. *Formula_text* must be a valid formula, and an equal sign must be included.

From_a1 is a logical value specifying whether the references in *formula_text* are in A1 or R1C1 style. If *from_a1* is TRUE, references are in A1 style; if FALSE, references are in R1C1 style.

To_a1 is a logical value specifying the form for the references FORMULA.CONVERT returns. If *to_a1* is TRUE, references are returned in A1 style; if FALSE, references are returned in R1C1 style. If *to_a1* is omitted, the reference style is not changed.

To_ref_type is a number from 1 to 4 specifying the reference type of the returned formula. If *to_ref_type* is omitted, the reference type is not changed.

To_ref_type	Reference type returned
1	Absolute
2	Absolute row, relative column
3	Relative row, absolute column
4	Relative

Rel_to_ref is an absolute reference that specifies what cell the relative references are or should be relative to.

Examples

Use FORMULA.CONVERT to convert relative references entered by the user in an INPUT function or custom dialog box into absolute references. The following macro formula converts the given formula to an absolute, R1C1-style reference:

`FORMULA.CONVERT("=A1:A10",TRUE,FALSE, 1)` equals "=R1C1:R10C1"

The following macro formula converts the references in the given formula to relative, A1-style references:

`FORMULA.CONVERT("=SUM(R10C2:R15C2)", FALSE,TRUE,4)` equals "=SUM(B10:B15)"

Tip To put the converted formula into a cell or range of cells, use the FORMULA.CONVERT function as the *formula_text* argument to the FORMULA function.

Related Functions

Function	Description
ABSREF	Returns the absolute reference of a range of cells to another range
RELREF	Returns a relative reference

FORMULA.FILL

Macro Sheets Only

Enters a formula in the range specified or in the current selection. Equivalent to entering a formula in a range of cells while pressing CTRL in Microsoft Excel for Windows or OPTION in Microsoft Excel for the Macintosh.

Syntax

FORMULA.FILL(*formula_text,reference*)

Formula_text is the text with which you want to fill the range. For more information on *formula_text*, see FORMULA.

Reference specifies where *formula_text* is entered. It can be a reference to a range in the active worksheet or an external reference to a named document. If omitted, *formula_text* is entered in the current selection.

Examples

If the active range is D25:E25, the following macro formula puts the formula SUM(D15:D24) in cell D25 and SUM(E15:E24) in cell E25:

```
FORMULA.FILL("=SUM(R[-1]C:R[-10]C)")
```

The following macro formula puts the formula SUM(D15:D24) in cell D25 and SUM(E15:E24) in cell E25, no matter what the active cell or range is:

```
FORMULA.FILL("=SUM(R[-1]C:R[-10]C)",
"R25C4:R25C5")
```

In Microsoft Excel for Windows, the following macro formula also puts the formula SUM(D15:D24) in cell D25 and SUM(E15:E24) in cell E25, on the worksheet named SALES.XLS:

```
FORMULA.FILL("=SUM(R[-1]C:R[-10]C)",
"SALES.XLS!R25C4:R25C5")
```

In Microsoft Excel for the Macintosh, the following macro formula also puts the formula SUM(D15:D24) in cell D25 and SUM(E15:E24) in cell E25, on the worksheet named SALES:

```
FORMULA.FILL("=SUM(R[-1]C:R[-10]C)",
"SALES!R25C4:R25C5")
```

Also see the last example for REFTEXT.

Related Functions

Function	Description
DATA.SERIES	Fills a range of cells with a series of numbers or dates
FORMULA	Enters values into a cell or range or onto a chart
FORMULA.ARRAY	Enters an array

FORMULA.FIND

Macro Sheets Only

Equivalent to choosing the Find command from the Formula menu. Selects the next or previous cell containing the specified text and returns TRUE. If a matching cell is not found, FORMULA.FIND returns FALSE and displays a message. For detailed information about the Find command, see online Help.

Syntax

FORMULA.FIND(*text,in_num,at_num,by_num, dir_num,match_case*)
FORMULA.FIND?(*text,in_num,at_num,by_num, dir_num,match_case*)

Text is the text you want to find. *Text* corresponds to the Find What box in the Find dialog box.

In_num is a number from 1 to 3 specifying where to search.

In_num	Searches
1	Formulas
2	Values
3	Notes

At_num is the number 1 or 2 and specifies whether to find cells containing only *text* or also cells containing *text* within a longer string of characters.

At_num	Searches for *text* as
1	A whole string (the only value in the cell)
2	Either a whole string or part of a longer string

By_num is the number 1 or 2 and specifies whether to search by rows or by columns.

By_num	Searches by
1	Rows
2	Columns

Dir_num is the number 1 or 2 and specifies whether to search for the next or previous occurrence of *text*.

Dir_num	Searches for
1 or omitted	The next occurrence of *text*
2	The previous occurrence of *text*

Match_case is a logical value corresponding to the Match Case check box in the Find dialog box. If *match_case* is TRUE, Microsoft Excel matches characters exactly, including uppercase and lowercase; if FALSE or omitted, matching is not case-sensitive.

Remarks

- In Microsoft Excel for Windows, the dialog-box form of FORMULA.FIND is equivalent to pressing SHIFT+F5.
- If more than one cell is selected when you use FORMULA.FIND, Microsoft Excel searches only that selection.

Example

The following macro formula searches by columns for the next occurrence of "units per month":

```
FORMULA.FIND("units per month",2,2,2,1)
```

Also see the third example for MAX.

FORMULA.FIND.NEXT
FORMULA.FIND.PREV

Macro Sheets Only

Equivalent to pressing F7 and SHIFT+F7 in Microsoft Excel for Windows, or COMMAND+H and COMMAND+SHIFT+H in Microsoft Excel for the Macintosh. These functions find the next and previous cells on the worksheet, as specified in the Find dialog box, and return TRUE. (To see the Find dialog box, choose Find from the Formula menu.) If a matching cell is not found, the functions return FALSE. For more information see FORMULA.FIND.

Syntax

FORMULA.FIND.NEXT( )
FORMULA.FIND.PREV( )

Related Function

Function	Description
DATA.FIND	Selects records in a database that match the specified criteria
FORMULA.FIND	Finds text in a document

FORMULA.GOTO

Macro Sheets Only

Equivalent to choosing the Goto command from the Formula menu or to pressing F5. Scrolls through the worksheet and selects a named area or reference. Use FORMULA.GOTO to select a range on any open document; use SELECT to select a range on the active document. For detailed information about the Goto command, see online Help.

Syntax

FORMULA.GOTO*(reference,corner)*
FORMULA.GOTO?*(reference,corner)*

Reference   specifies where to scroll and what to select.

- *Reference* should be either an external reference to a document, an R1C1-style reference in the form of text (see the second example following), or a name.

- If the Goto command has already been carried out, *reference* is optional. If *reference* is omitted, it is assumed to be the reference of the cells you selected before the previous Goto command or FORMULA.GOTO macro function was carried out. This feature distinguishes FORMULA.GOTO from SELECT.

Corner   is a logical value that specifies whether to scroll through the window so that the upper-left cell in *reference* is in the upper-left corner of the active window. If *corner* is TRUE, Microsoft Excel places *reference* in the upper-left corner of the window; if FALSE or omitted, Microsoft Excel scrolls through normally.

Tip   Microsoft Excel keeps a list of the cells you've selected with previous FORMULA.GOTO functions or Goto commands. When you use FORMULA.GOTO with GET.WORKSPACE(41), which returns a horizontal array of previous Goto selections, you can backtrack through multiple previous selections. See the last example below.

Remarks

- If you are recording a macro when you choose the Goto command, the reference you enter in the Reference box of the Goto dialog box is recorded as text in the R1C1 reference style.

- If you are recording a macro when you double-click a cell that has precedents on another worksheet, Microsoft Excel records a FORMULA.GOTO function.

Examples

Each of the following macro formulas goes to cell A1 on the active worksheet:

```
FORMULA.GOTO(!$A$1)
FORMULA.GOTO("R1C1")
```

Each of the following macro formulas goes to the cells named Sales on the active worksheet and scrolls through the worksheet so that the upper-left corner of Sales is in the upper-left corner of the window:

```
FORMULA.GOTO(!Sales,TRUE)
FORMULA.GOTO("Sales",TRUE)
```

In Microsoft Excel for Windows, each of the following macro formulas goes to cells B2:C3 on a worksheet named BUDGET.XLS:

```
FORMULA.GOTO(BUDGET.XLS!$B$2:$C$3)
FORMULA.GOTO("BUDGET.XLS!R2C2:R3C3")
```

In Microsoft Excel for the Macintosh, each of the following macro formulas goes to cells B2:C3 on a worksheet named BUDGET:

```
FORMULA.GOTO(BUDGET!$B$2:$C$3)
FORMULA.GOTO("BUDGET!R2C2:R3C3")
```

The following macro formula goes to the cells that were selected by the third most recent FORMULA.GOTO function or Goto command:

```
FORMULA.GOTO(INDEX(GET.WORKSPACE(41),1,3))
```

Related Functions

Function	Description
HSCROLL or VSCROLL	Horizontally or vertically scrolls through a document by percentage or by column or row number
SELECT	Selects a cell, worksheet object, or chart item

FORMULA.REPLACE

Macro Sheets Only

Equivalent to choosing the Replace command from the Formula menu. Finds and replaces characters in cells on your worksheet. For detailed information about the Replace command, see online Help.

Syntax

FORMULA.REPLACE(*find_text,replace_text, look_at,look_by,active_cell,match_case*)
FORMULA.REPLACE?(*find_text, replace_text,look_at,look_by,active_cell, match_case*)

Find_text is the text you want to find. You can use the wildcard characters, question mark (?) and asterisk (*), in *find_text*. A question mark matches any single character; an asterisk matches any sequence of characters. If you want to find an actual question mark or asterisk, type a tilde (~) before the character.

Replace_text is the text you want to replace *find_text* with.

Look_at is a number specifying whether you want *find_text* to match the entire contents of a cell or any string of matching characters.

Look_at	Looks for *find_text*
1	As the entire contents of a cell
2 or omitted	As part of the contents of a cell

Look_by is a number specifying whether to search horizontally (through rows) or vertically (through columns).

Look_by	Looks for *find_text*
1 or omitted	By rows
2	By columns

Active_cell is a logical value specifying the cells in which *find_text* is to be replaced.

- If *active_cell* is TRUE, *find_text* is replaced in the active cell only.

- If *active_cell* is FALSE, *find_text* is replaced in the entire selection, or, if the selection is a single cell, in the entire document.

Match_case is a logical value corresponding to the Match Case check box in the Replace dialog box. If *match_case* is TRUE, Microsoft Excel selects the check box; if FALSE, Microsoft Excel clears the check box. If *match_case* is omitted, the status of the check box is unchanged.

Remarks

- In FORMULA.REPLACE?, the dialog-box form of the function, omitted arguments are assumed to be the same arguments used in the previous replace operation. If there was no previous replace operation, omitted text arguments are assumed to be "" (empty text).

- The result of FORMULA.REPLACE must be a valid cell entry. For example, you cannot replace "=" with "==" at the beginning of a formula.

- If more than a single cell is selected before you use FORMULA.REPLACE, only the selected cells are searched.

Examples

The following macro formula replaces 7 with 8 in the entire selection, or in the entire document if the selection is a single cell:

FORMULA.REPLACE("7","8")

The following macro formula searches the selection and replaces any instances of "y" followed by any two characters, with "y" alone:

FORMULA.REPLACE("y??","y")

The following macro formula searches the selection and replaces any instances of "y" followed by any characters, with "y" alone:

FORMULA.REPLACE("y*","y")

The following macro formula searches the active cell and replaces any instances of "y" followed by two question marks, with "y" alone:

```
FORMULA.REPLACE("y~?~?","y",,,TRUE,)
```

Related Functions

Function	Description
FORMULA.FIND	Finds text in a document
REPLACE	Replaces characters within text

FOURIER

Macro Sheets Only

Performs a Fourier transform. For more information, see "Engineering Analysis Tools" in Chapter 1 in Book 2 of the *Microsoft Excel User's Guide*.

If this function is not available, you must install the Analysis ToolPak add-in macro. For more information, see "Managing Add-in Commands and Functions" in Chapter 4 in Book 2 of the *Microsoft Excel User's Guide*.

Syntax

FOURIER(*inprng,outrng,inverse*)

Inprng is the input range. The number of cells in the input range must be equal to a power of two (2, 4, 8, 16, …).

Outrng is the first cell in the output range.

Inverse is a logical value. If TRUE, an inverse Fourier transform is performed. If FALSE or omitted, a forward Fourier transform is performed.

Related Function

Function	Description
SAMPLE	Samples data

FPOS

Macro Sheets Only

Sets the position of a file. The position of a file is where a character is read from or written to by an FREAD, FREADLN, FWRITE, or FWRITELN function. Use FPOS when you want to write characters to or read characters from specific locations. For example, to append text to the end of a file, you must set the position to the end of the file; otherwise, you might accidentally overwrite existing characters in the file.

Syntax

FPOS(*file_num,position_num*)

File_num is the unique ID number of the file for which you want to set the position. *File_num* is returned by a previously executed FOPEN function. If *file_num* is not valid, FPOS returns the #VALUE! error value.

Position_num is the location in the file that a character will be read from or written to.

- The first position in a file is 1—the location of the first character.

- The last position in the file is the same as the value returned by FSIZE. For example, the last position in a file with 280 characters is 280.

- If *position_num* is omitted, FPOS returns the current position of the file—that is, the number corresponding to where the next character will be read from or written to.

Whenever you read a character from or write a character to a file, the file's position is automatically incremented.

Examples

The following macro appends to a text file the contents of the current selection on the active worksheet. FSIZE returns the number of characters in the file, which is the same as the position of the last character, and the macro writes cell contents, followed by a carriage return, to that location.

	A	B	C
11	*Names*	*Formulas*	*Comments*
12			
13		**AppendTextToFile**	Adds current selection to file
14	FileName	=INPUT("Name of file to append:",2)	
15	FileNumber	=FOPEN(FileName,1)	Opens the file as read/write
16	LastChar	=FSIZE(FileNumber)	Gets last char number
17		=FPOS(FileNumber,(LastChar+1))	Positions file after last char
18		=FOR.CELL("CurrentCell")	
19		=FWRITELN(FileNumber,CurrentCell)	Writes cell contents to file
20		=NEXT()	
21		=FCLOSE(FileNumber)	
22		=RETURN()	

Suppose you have a file created by another application, where the first five characters in that file are special codes that have no meaning in Microsoft Excel. With the FPOS function, you can skip the first five characters and then read the rest of the file using the FREADLN function.

	A	B	C
25	*Names*	*Formulas*	*Comments*
26			
27		**SkipFiveChars**	Skips characters; reads file
28	FileName	=INPUT("Name of file to read:",2)	
29	FileNumber	=FOPEN(FileName,2)	Opens file as read-only
30		=FPOS(FileNumber,6)	Skips first five characters
31		=WHILE(FPOS(FileNumber)<=FSIZE(FileNu	Reads until end of file
32	ReadLine	=FREADLN(FileNumber)	
33		=FORMULA(ReadLine)	Places line in active cell
34		=SELECT(OFFSET(ACTIVE.CELL(),1,0))	Moves active cell to next row
35		=NEXT()	
36		=FCLOSE(FileNumber)	
37		=RETURN()	

The complete formula in cell B31 is:

=WHILE(FPOS(FileNumber)<=FSIZE(FileNumber))

Also see the example for RESULT.

Related Functions

Function	Description
FCLOSE	Closes a text file
FOPEN	Opens a file with the type of permission specified
FREAD	Reads characters from a text file
FREADLN	Reads a line from a text file
FWRITE	Writes characters to a text file
FWRITELN	Writes a line to a text file

FREAD

Macro Sheets Only

Reads characters from a file, starting at the current position in the file. (For more information about a file's position, see FPOS.) If FREAD is successful, it returns the text to the cell containing FREAD. If the end of the file is reached or if FREAD can't read the file, it returns the #N/A error value. Use FREAD instead of FREADLN when you need to read a specific number of characters from a text file.

Syntax

FREAD(*file_num,num_chars*)

File_num   is the unique ID number of the file you want to read data from. *File_num* is returned by a previously executed FOPEN function. If *file_num* is not valid, FREAD returns the #VALUE! error value.

Num_chars   specifies how many characters to read from the file. FREAD can read up to 255 characters at a time.

Example

The following macro reads a file and displays its characters along with their code numbers. In each row of the active worksheet, the macro places 16 decimal codes in the first 16 cells; it places the corresponding 16 characters in the 17th cell.

This is similar to some debugging or memory "dump" programs that show in rows the hexadecimal codes for 16 bytes and the 16 ASCII characters corresponding to those codes (some codes cannot be displayed because they do not correspond to printable characters). This macro assumes that the correct external worksheet is active when you run it.

	A	B	C
1	*Names*	*Formulas*	*Comments*
2			
3		**Main Program**	Characters to codes
4		**DisplayCharacterCodes**	
5		=OpenFile()	Opens the file
6		=SetUpScreen()	Sets up the screen
7		=ReadCharacters()	Reads chars and codes
8		=FCLOSE(File Number)	
9		=RETURN()	
10			
11		**OpenFile**	Subroutine to open the file
12		=ERROR(FALSE)	Disables error messages
13	FileName	=INPUT("Name of file to read",2)	Asks for the filename
14	FileNumber	=FOPEN(FileName,2)	Tries to open the file
15		=IF(ISERROR(FileNumber))	If file not there, displays
16		=ALERT("File not available",2)	error message
17		=HALT()	and halts the macro
18		=END.IF()	
19		=ERROR(TRUE)	Enables error messages
20		=RETURN()	
21			
22			
23		**SetUpScreen**	Sets up the screen
24		=SELECT(!$A:$P)	Selects the first 16 columns
25		=COLUMN.WIDTH(3)	Narrows the columns
26		=SELECT(!$A$1)	Selects the upper-left cell
27		=RETURN()	
28			
29			
30		**ReadCharacters**	Reads and displays chars
31		=ECHO(FALSE)	Turns off screen updating
32	LastChar	=FSIZE(FileNumber)	Position of last character
33		=SET.NAME("TextString","")	Initializes text variable
34		=FOR("Counter",1,LastChar)	Loops for each character
35		=IF(AND(Counter<>1,MOD(Counter−1,16)=0	Have 16 chars been read?
36		=FORMULA(TextString)	Places 16 chars in col 17
37		=SET.NAME("TextString","")	Re-initializes text variable
38		=SELECT(OFFSET(ACTIVE.CELL(),1,−16))	Moves to next cell
39		=END.IF()	
40	NextChar	=FREAD(FileNumber,1)	Reads the next character
41		=FORMULA(CODE(NextChar))	Puts char in the active cell
42		=SET.NAME("TextString",TextString&NextCh	Adds char to variable
43		=SELECT(OFFSET(ACTIVE.CELL(),0,1))	Selects the next cell
44		=NEXT()	
45		=IF(MOD(Counter,16)<>0,FORMULA(TextStr	Puts text variable in col 17
46		=FCLOSE(File Number)	Closes the file
47		=RETURN()	

The complete formulas in cells B35, B42, and B45 are:

```
=IF(AND(Counter<>1,MOD(Counter-1,16)=0))
=SET.NAME("TextString",TextString&NextChar)
=IF(MOD(Counter,16)<>0,FORMULA(TextString,
"RC17"))
```

Related Functions

Function	Description
FOPEN	Opens a file with the type of permission specified
FREADLN	Reads a line from a text file
FWRITE	Writes characters to a text file

FREADLN

Macro Sheets Only

Reads characters from a file, starting at the current position in the file and continuing to the end of the line, placing the characters in the cell containing FREADLN. (For more information about a file's position, see FPOS.) If FREADLN is successful, it returns the text it read, up to but not including the carriage-return and linefeed characters at the end of the line (in Microsoft Excel for Windows) or the carriage-return character at the end of the line (in Microsoft Excel for the Macintosh). If the current file position is the end of the file or if FREADLN can't read the file, it returns the #N/A error value.

Syntax

FREADLN(*file_num*)

File_num is the unique ID number of the file you want to read data from. *File_num* is returned by a previously executed FOPEN function. If *file_num* is not valid, FREADLN returns the #VALUE! error value.

Example

See the second example for FPOS.

Related Functions

Function	Description
FREAD	Reads characters from a text file
FWRITE	Writes characters to a text file
FWRITELN	Writes a line to a text file

FREEZE.PANES

Macro Sheets Only

Equivalent to choosing the Freeze Panes or Unfreeze Panes commands from the Window menu or clicking the Freeze Panes or Unfreeze Panes tool. Splits the active window into panes, creates frozen panes, or freezes or unfreezes existing panes. Use FREEZE.PANES to keep row or column titles on the screen while scrolling to other parts of the worksheet. For detailed information about the Freeze Panes and Unfreeze Panes commands, see online Help.

Syntax

FREEZE.PANES(*logical,col_split,row_split*)

Logical is a logical value specifying which command FREEZE.PANES is equivalent to.

- If *logical* is TRUE, the function is equivalent to the Freeze Panes command. It freezes panes if they exist, or creates them, splits them at the specified position, and freezes them if they do not exist. If the panes are already frozen, FREEZE.PANES takes no action.

- If *logical* is FALSE, the function is equivalent to the Unfreeze Panes command. If no panes exist, FREEZE.PANES takes no action.

- If *logical* is omitted, FREEZE.PANES creates and then freezes panes if no panes exist, freezes existing panes if they're not currently frozen, or unfreezes existing panes if they're currently frozen.

Col_split specifies where to split the window vertically and is measured in columns from the left of the window.

Row_split specifies where to split the window horizontally and is measured in rows from the top of the window.

Col_split and *row_split* are ignored unless *logical* is TRUE and split panes do not exist.

Remarks

To create panes without freezing or unfreezing them, use the SPLIT function. You can freeze the panes later using the FREEZE.PANES function.

Example

If no panes exist, the following macro formula splits the active window into panes above and to the left of the active cell and then freezes them.

```
FREEZE.PANES()
```

Related Functions

Function	Description
ACTIVATE	Switches to a window
SPLIT	Splits a window

FREQUENCY

Returns a frequency distribution as a vertical array. For a given set of values and a given set of bins (or intervals), a frequency distribution counts how many of the values occur in each interval.

Syntax

FREQUENCY(*data_array,bins_array*)

Data_array is an array of or reference to a set of values for which you want to count frequencies. If *data_array* contains no values, FREQUENCY returns an array of zeros.

Bins_array is an array of or reference to intervals into which you want to group the values in *data_array*. If *bins_array* contains no values, FREQUENCY returns the number of elements in *data_array*.

Remarks

- The number of elements in the returned array is one more than the number of elements in *bins_array*.

- FREQUENCY ignores blank cells and text.

- If any cell in *data_array* or *bins_array* contains an error value, FREQUENCY returns an array of #N/A error values.

Example

	A	B	C	D
1	79			
2	85			
3	78			
4	85		70	0
5	83		79	2
6	81		89	5
7	95			2
8	88			
9	97			

Suppose a worksheet lists scores for a test. When entered as an array, you could use FREQUENCY to count the number of scores corresponding to the letter grade ranges 0–70, 71–79, 80–89, and 90–100. This example assumes all test scores are integers.

FREQUENCY(A1:A9,C4:C6) equals {0;2;5;2}

Related Functions

Function	Description
COUNT	Counts how many numbers are in the list of arguments
DCOUNT	Counts the cells containing numbers from a specified database and criteria
TABLE	Creates a table based on input values and formulas

FSIZE

Macro Sheets Only

Returns the number of characters in a file. Use FSIZE to determine the size of the file, which is the same as the position of the last character in the file.

Syntax

FSIZE(*file_num*)

File_num   is the unique ID number of the file whose size you want to know. *File_num* is returned by a previously executed FOPEN function. If *file_num* is not valid, FSIZE returns the #VALUE! error value.

Example

See the examples for FPOS and FREAD.

Related Functions

Function	Description
FOPEN	Opens a file with the type of permission specified
FPOS	Sets the position in a text file

FTEST

Returns the results of an *F*-test. An *F*-test returns the one-tailed probability that the variances in *array1* and *array2* are not significantly different. Use this function to determine if two samples have different variances. For example, given test scores from public and private schools, you can test if these schools have different levels of diversity.

Syntax

FTEST(*array1,array2*)

Array1   is the first array or range of data.

Array2   is the second array or range of data.

Remarks

- The arguments should be numbers, or names, arrays, or references that contain numbers.

- If an array or reference argument contains text, logical values, or empty cells, those values are ignored; however, cells with the value zero are included.

- If the number of data points in *array1* or *array2* is less than 2, or if the variance of *array1* or *array2* is zero, FTEST returns the #DIV/0! error value.

Example

FTEST({6,7,9,15,21},{20,28,31,38,40}) equals 0.648318

Related Functions

Function	Description
FDIST	Returns the *F* probability distribution
FINV	Returns the inverse of the *F* probability distribution

FTESTV

Macro Sheets Only

Performs a two-sample *F*-test. For more information, see "Analyzing Statistical or Engineering Data" in Chapter 1 in Book 2 of the *Microsoft Excel User's Guide*.

If this function is not available, you must install the Analysis ToolPak add-in macro. For more information, see "Managing Add-in Commands and Functions" in Chapter 4 in Book 2 of the *Microsoft Excel User's Guide*.

Syntax

FTESTV*(inprng1,inprng2,outrng,labels)*

Inprng1   is the input range for the first data set.

Inprng2   is the input range for the second data set.

Outrng   is the first cell (the upper-left cell) in the output table.

Labels   is a logical value.

- If *labels* is TRUE, then the first row or column of *inprng1* and *inprng2* contain labels.

- If *labels* is FALSE or omitted, all cells in *inprng* are considered data. Microsoft Excel generates appropriate data labels for the output table.

Related Functions

Function	Description
FDIST	Returns the *F* probability distribution
FINV	Returns the inverse of the *F* probability distribution
FTEST	Returns the result of an *F*-test

FULL

Macro Sheets Only

Equivalent to pressing CTRL+F10 (full size) and CTRL+F5 (previous size) or double-clicking the title bar in Microsoft Excel for Windows version 3.0 or earlier. Equivalent to double-clicking the title bar or clicking the zoom box in Microsoft Excel for the Macintosh version 3.0 or earlier. This function is included only for macro compatibility. To perform the equivalent of a FULL(TRUE) function in Microsoft Excel version 4.0, use the WINDOW.MAXIMIZE function. To perform the equivalent of a FULL(FALSE) function in Microsoft Excel version 4.0, use the WINDOW.RESTORE function.

Syntax

FULL*(logical)*

FV

Returns the future value of an investment based on periodic, constant payments and a constant interest rate.

Syntax

FV*(rate,nper,pmt,pv,type)*

For a more complete description of the arguments in FV and for more information on annuity functions, see PV.

Rate   is the interest rate per period.

Nper   is the total number of payment periods in an annuity.

Pmt is the payment made each period; it cannot change over the life of the annuity. Typically, *pmt* contains principal and interest but no other fees or taxes.

Pv is the present value, or the lump-sum amount that a series of future payments is worth right now. If *pv* is omitted, it is assumed to be 0.

Type is the number 0 or 1 and indicates when payments are due. If *type* is omitted, it is assumed to be 0.

Set *type* equal to	If payments are due
0	At the end of the period
1	At the beginning of the period

Remarks

- Make sure that you are consistent about the units you use for specifying *rate* and *nper*. If you make monthly payments on a four-year loan at 12 percent annual interest, use 12%/12 for *rate* and 4*12 for *nper*. If you make annual payments on the same loan, use 12% for *rate* and 4 for *nper*.

- For all the arguments, cash you pay out, such as deposits to savings, is represented by negative numbers; cash you receive, such as dividend checks, is represented by positive numbers.

Examples

FV(0.5%,10,-200,-500,1) equals $2581.40

FV(1%,12,-1000) equals $12,682.50

FV(11%/12,35,-2000,,1) equals $82,846.25

Suppose you want to save money for a special project occurring a year from now. You deposit $1000 into a savings account that earns 6 percent annual interest compounded monthly (monthly interest of 6%/12, or 0.5%). You plan to deposit $100 at the beginning of every month for the next 12 months. How much money will be in the account at the end of 12 months?

FV(0.5%,12,-100,-1000,1) equals $2301.40

Related Functions

Function	Description
FVSCHEDULE	Returns the future value of an initial principal after applying a series of compound interest rates
IPMT	Returns the interest payment for an investment for a given period
NPER	Returns the number of periods for an investment
PMT	Returns the periodic payment for an annuity
PPMT	Returns the payment on the principal for an investment for a given period
PV	Returns the present value of an investment
RATE	Returns the interest rate per period of an annuity

FVSCHEDULE

Returns the future value of an initial principal after applying a series of compound interest rates. Use FVSCHEDULE to calculate future value of an investment with a variable or adjustable rate.

If this function is not available, you must install the Analysis ToolPak add-in macro. For more information, see "Managing Add-in Commands and Functions" in Chapter 4 in Book 2 of the *Microsoft Excel User's Guide*.

Syntax

FVSCHEDULE(*principal,schedule*)

Principal is the present value.

Schedule is an array of interest rates to apply.

Remarks

- If *principal* is non-numeric, FVSCHEDULE returns the #VALUE! error value.

- The values in *schedule* can be numbers or blank cells; any other value produces the #VALUE! error value for FVSCHEDULE. Blank cells are taken as zeros (no interest).

Example

FVSCHEDULE(1,{0.09,0.11,0.1}) equals 1.33089

Related Function

Function	Description
FV	Returns the future value of an investment

FWRITE

Macro Sheets Only

Writes text to a file, starting at the current position in that file. (For more information about a file's position, see FPOS.) If FWRITE can't write to the file, it returns the #N/A error value.

Syntax

FWRITE(*file_num,text*)

File_num   is the unique ID number of the file you want to write data to. *File_num* is returned by a previously executed FOPEN function. If *file_num* is not valid, FWRITE returns the #VALUE! error value.

Text   is the text you want to write to the file.

Example

See the example for FOPEN.

Related Functions

Function	Description
FOPEN	Opens a file with the type of permission specified
FREAD	Reads characters from a text file
FWRITELN	Writes a line to a text file

FWRITELN

Macro Sheets Only

Writes text, followed by a carriage return and linefeed, to a file, starting at the current position in that file. (For more information about a file's position, see FPOS.) If FWRITELN can't write to the file, it returns the #N/A error value. Use FWRITELN instead of FWRITE when you want to append a carriage return and linefeed to each group of characters that you write to a text file.

Remarks

In Microsoft Excel for the Macintosh, FWRITELN writes text followed by a carriage return only.

Syntax

FWRITELN(*file_num,text*)

File_num   is the unique ID number of the file you want to write data to. *File_num* is returned by a previously executed FOPEN function. If *file_num* is not valid, FWRITELN returns the #VALUE! error value.

Text   is the text you want to write to the file.

Example

See the first example in FPOS.

Related Functions

Function	Description
FOPEN	Opens a file with the type of permission specified
FREAD	Reads characters from a text file
FWRITE	Writes characters to a text file

GALLERY.3D.AREA

Macro Sheets Only

Equivalent to choosing the 3-D Area command from the Gallery menu that is available when a chart is the active document. Changes the format of the active chart to a 3-D area chart. For detailed information about the 3-D Area command, see online Help.

Syntax

GALLERY.3D.AREA*(type_num)*
GALLERY.3D.AREA?*(type_num)*

Type_num   is the number of a format in the 3-D Area dialog box that you want to apply to the 3-D area chart.

Example

The following macro formula applies the first format in the 3-D Area dialog box to the main chart:

```
GALLERY.3D.AREA(1)
```

GALLERY.3D.BAR

Macro Sheets Only

Equivalent to choosing the 3-D Bar command from the Gallery menu that is available when a chart is the active document. Changes the active chart to a 3-D bar chart. For detailed information about the 3-D Bar command, see online Help.

Syntax

GALLERY.3D.BAR*(type_num)*
GALLERY.3D.BAR?*(type_num)*

Type_num   is the number of a format in the 3-D Bar dialog box that you want to apply to the 3-D bar chart.

Example

The following macro formula applies the first format in the 3-D Bar dialog box to the main chart:

```
GALLERY.3D.BAR(1)
```

GALLERY.3D.COLUMN

Macro Sheets Only

Equivalent to choosing the 3-D Column command from the Gallery menu that is available when a chart is the active document. Changes the format of the active chart to a 3-D column chart. For detailed information about the 3-D Column command, see online Help.

Syntax

GALLERY.3D.COLUMN*(type_num)*
GALLERY.3D.COLUMN?*(type_num)*

Type_num   is the number of a format in the 3-D Column dialog box that you want to apply to the 3-D column chart.

Example

The following macro formula applies the first format in the 3-D Column dialog box to the main chart:

```
GALLERY.3D.COLUMN(1)
```

GALLERY.3D.LINE

Macro Sheets Only

Equivalent to choosing the 3-D Line command from the Gallery menu that is available when a chart is the active document. Changes the format of the active chart to a 3-D line chart. For detailed information about the 3-D Line command, see online Help.

Syntax

GALLERY.3D.LINE*(type_num)*
GALLERY.3D.LINE?*(type_num)*

Type_num   is the number of a format in the 3-D Line dialog box that you want to apply to the 3-D line chart.

Example

The following macro formula applies the first format in the 3-D Line dialog box to the main chart:

```
GALLERY.3D.LINE(1)
```

GALLERY.3D.PIE

Macro Sheets Only

Equivalent to choosing the 3-D Pie command from the Gallery menu that is available when a chart is the active document. Changes the format of the active chart to a 3-D pie chart. For detailed information about the 3-D Pie command, see online Help.

Syntax

GALLERY.3D.PIE*(type_num)*
GALLERY.3D.PIE?*(type_num)*

Type_num   is the number of a format in the 3-D Pie dialog box that you want to apply to the 3-D pie chart.

Example

The following macro formula applies the first format in the 3-D Pie dialog box to the main chart:

```
GALLERY.3D.PIE(1)
```

GALLERY.3D.SURFACE

Macro Sheets Only

Equivalent to choosing the 3-D Surface command from the Gallery menu that is available when a chart is the active document. Changes the active chart to a 3-D surface chart. For detailed information about the 3-D Surface command, see online Help.

Syntax

GALLERY.3D.SURFACE*(type_num)*
GALLERY.3D.SURFACE?*(type_num)*

Type_num   is the number of a format in the 3-D Surface dialog box that you want to apply to the 3-D surface chart.

Example

The following macro formula applies the first format in the 3-D Surface dialog box to the main chart:

```
GALLERY.3D.SURFACE(1)
```

GALLERY.AREA

Macro Sheets Only

Equivalent to choosing the Area command from the Gallery menu that is available when a chart is the active document. Changes the format of the active chart to an area chart. For detailed information about the Area command, see online Help.

Syntax

GALLERY.AREA*(type_num,delete_overlay)*
GALLERY.AREA?*(type_num,delete_overlay)*

Type_num   is the number of a format in the Area dialog box that you want to apply to the area chart.

Delete_overlay   is a logical value specifying whether to delete an overlay chart.

- If *delete_overlay* is TRUE, Microsoft Excel deletes the overlay chart, if present, and applies the new format to the main chart.

- If *delete_overlay* is FALSE or omitted, Microsoft Excel applies the new format to either the main chart or the overlay chart, depending on the location of the selected series.

Example

The following macro formula deletes the overlay chart, if it is present, and applies the first format in the gallery to the main chart:

```
GALLERY.AREA(1,TRUE)
```

GALLERY.BAR

Macro Sheets Only

Equivalent to choosing the Bar command from the Gallery menu that is available when a chart is the active document. Changes the format of the active chart to a bar chart. For detailed information about the Bar command, see online Help.

Syntax

GALLERY.BAR(*type_num,delete_overlay*)
GALLERY.BAR?(*type_num,delete_overlay*)

Type_num is the number of a format in the Bar dialog box that you want to apply to the bar chart.

Delete_overlay is a logical value specifying whether to delete an overlay chart.

- If *delete_overlay* is TRUE, Microsoft Excel deletes the overlay chart, if present, and applies the new format to the main chart.

- If *delete_overlay* is FALSE or omitted, Microsoft Excel applies the new format to either the main chart or the overlay chart, depending on the location of the selected series.

GALLERY.COLUMN

Macro Sheets Only

Equivalent to choosing the Column command from the Gallery menu that is available when a chart is the active document. Changes the format of the active chart to a column chart. For detailed information about the Column command, see online Help.

Syntax

GALLERY.COLUMN(*type_num,delete_overlay*)
GALLERY.COLUMN?(*type_num, delete_overlay*)

Type_num is the number of a format in the Column dialog box that you want to apply to the column chart.

Delete_overlay is a logical value specifying whether to delete an overlay chart.

- If *delete_overlay* is TRUE, Microsoft Excel deletes the overlay chart, if present, and applies the new format to the main chart.

- If *delete_overlay* is FALSE or omitted, Microsoft Excel applies the new format to either the main chart or the overlay chart, depending on the location of the selected series.

Example

The following macro formula deletes the overlay chart, if it is present, and applies the first format in the gallery to the main chart:

```
GALLERY.COLUMN(1,TRUE)
```

GALLERY.LINE

Macro Sheets Only

Equivalent to choosing the Line command from the Gallery menu that is available when a chart is the active document. Changes the format of the active chart to a line chart. For detailed information about the Line command, see online Help.

Syntax

GALLERY.LINE(*type_num,delete_overlay*)
GALLERY.LINE?(*type_num,delete_overlay*)

Type_num is the number of a format in the Line dialog box that you want to apply to the line chart.

Delete_overlay   is a logical value specifying whether to delete an overlay chart.

- If *delete_overlay* is TRUE, Microsoft Excel deletes the overlay chart, if present, and applies the new format to the main chart.

- If *delete_overlay* is FALSE or omitted, Microsoft Excel applies the new format to either the main chart or the overlay chart, depending on the location of the selected series.

Example

The following macro formula deletes the overlay chart, if it is present, and applies the first format in the gallery to the main chart:

```
GALLERY.LINE(1,TRUE)
```

GALLERY.PIE

Macro Sheets Only

Equivalent to choosing the Pie command from the Gallery menu that is available when a chart is the active document. Changes the format of the active chart to a pie chart. For detailed information about the Pie command, see online Help.

Syntax

GALLERY.PIE*(type_num,delete_overlay)*
GALLERY.PIE?*(type_num,delete_overlay)*

Type_num   is the number of a format in the Pie dialog box that you want to apply to the pie chart.

Delete_overlay   is a logical value specifying whether to delete an overlay chart.

- If *delete_overlay* is TRUE, Microsoft Excel deletes the overlay chart, if present, and applies the new format to the main chart.

- If *delete_overlay* is FALSE or omitted, Microsoft Excel applies the new format to either the main chart or the overlay chart, depending on the location of the selected series.

Example

The following macro formula deletes the overlay chart, if it is present, and applies the first format in the gallery to the main chart:

```
GALLERY.PIE(1,TRUE)
```

GALLERY.RADAR

Macro Sheets Only

Equivalent to choosing the Radar command from the Gallery menu that is available when a chart is the active document. Changes the format of the active chart to a radar chart. For detailed information about the Radar command, see online Help.

Syntax

GALLERY.RADAR*(type_num,delete_overlay)*
GALLERY.RADAR?*(type_num,delete_overlay)*

Type_num   is the number of a format in the Radar dialog box that you want to apply to the radar chart.

Delete_overlay   is a logical value specifying whether to delete an overlay chart.

- If *delete_overlay* is TRUE, Microsoft Excel deletes the overlay chart, if present, and applies the new format to the main chart.

- If *delete_overlay* is FALSE or omitted, Microsoft Excel applies the new format to either the main chart or the overlay chart, depending on the location of the selected series.

GALLERY.SCATTER

Macro Sheets Only

Equivalent to choosing the XY (Scatter) command from the Gallery menu that is available when a chart is the active document. Changes the format of the active chart to an xy (scatter) chart. For detailed information about the XY (Scatter) command, see online Help.

Syntax

GALLERY.SCATTER*(type_num,delete_overlay)*
GALLERY.SCATTER?*(type_num,delete_overlay)*

Type_num is the number of a format in the XY (Scatter) dialog box that you want to apply to the xy (scatter) chart.

Delete_overlay is a logical value specifying whether to delete an overlay chart.

- If *delete_overlay* is TRUE, Microsoft Excel deletes the overlay chart, if present, and applies the new format to the main chart.

- If *delete_overlay* is FALSE or omitted, Microsoft Excel applies the new format to either the main chart or the overlay chart, depending on the location of the selected series.

Example

The following macro formula deletes the overlay chart, if it is present, and applies the first format in the gallery to the main chart:

```
GALLERY.SCATTER(1,TRUE)
```

GAMMADIST

Returns the gamma distribution function. You can use this function to study variables that may have a skewed distribution. The gamma distribution is commonly used in queuing analysis.

Syntax

GAMMADIST*(x,alpha,beta,cumulative)*

X is the value at which you want to evaluate the distribution.

Alpha is a parameter to the distribution.

Beta is a parameter to the distribution. If *beta* = 1, GAMMADIST returns the standard gamma distribution.

Cumulative is a logical value that determines the form of the function. If *cumulative* is TRUE, GAMMADIST returns the cumulative distribution function; if FALSE, it returns the probability mass function.

Remarks

- If *x, alpha,* or *beta* is non-numeric, GAMMADIST returns the #VALUE! error value.

- If *x* < 0, GAMMADIST returns the #NUM! error value.

- If *alpha* ≤ 0 or if *beta* ≤ 0, GAMMADIST returns the #NUM! error value.

- The equation for the gamma distribution is:

$$f(x;\alpha,\beta) = \frac{1}{\beta^{\alpha}\Gamma(\alpha)} x^{\alpha-1}e^{-\frac{x}{\beta}}$$

The standard gamma distribution is:

$$f(x;\alpha) = \frac{x^{\alpha-1}e^{-x}}{\Gamma(\alpha)}$$

- When *alpha* = 1, GAMMADIST returns the exponential distribution with:

$$\lambda = \frac{1}{\beta}$$

- For a positive integer *n*, when *alpha* = n/2, *beta* = 2, and *cumulative* = TRUE, GAMMADIST returns (1 – CHIDIST(*x*)) with *n* degrees of freedom.

- When *alpha* is a positive integer, GAMMADIST is also known as the Erlang distribution.

Examples

```
GAMMADIST(10,9,2,FALSE)
```
equals 0.032639

```
GAMMADIST(10,9,2,TRUE)
```
equals 0.068094

Related Functions

Function	Description
CHIDIST	Returns one-tailed probability of the chi-squared distribution
EXPONDIST	Returns the exponential distribution
GAMMAINV	Returns the inverse of the gamma cumulative distribution

GAMMAINV

Returns the inverse of the gamma cumulative distribution function. If p = GAMMADIST(x,…), then GAMMAINV(p,…) = x

You can use this function to study a variable whose distribution may be skewed.

Syntax

GAMMAINV(*probability,alpha,beta*)

Probability   is the probability associated with the gamma distribution.

Alpha   is a parameter to the distribution.

Beta   is a parameter to the distribution. If *beta* = 1, GAMMAINV returns the standard gamma distribution.

Remarks

- If any argument is non-numeric, GAMMAINV returns the #VALUE! error value.

- If *probability* < 0 or *probability* > 1, GAMMAINV returns the #NUM! error value.

- If *alpha* ≤ 0 or if *beta* ≤ 0, GAMMAINV returns the #NUM! error value.

- If *beta* ≤ 0, GAMMAINV returns the #NUM! error value.

- GAMMAINV uses an iterative technique for calculating the function. Given a probability value, GAMMAINV iterates until the result is accurate to within $\pm\ 3 \times 10^{-7}$. If GAMMAINV does not converge after 100 iterations, the function returns the #N/A error value.

Example

GAMMAINV(0.068094,9,2) equals 10

Related Function

Function	Description
GAMMADIST	Returns the gamma distribution

GAMMALN

Returns the natural logarithm of the gamma function, $\Gamma(x)$.

Syntax

GAMMALN(*x*)

X   is the value for which you want to calculate GAMMALN.

Remarks

- If x is non-numeric, GAMMALN returns the #VALUE! error value.

- If $x \le 0$, GAMMALN returns the #NUM! error value.

- The number e raised to the GAMMALN(i) power, where i is an integer, returns the same result as $(i - 1)!$.

Examples

GAMMALN(4) equals 1.791759

EXP(GAMMALN(4)) equals 6 or $(4 - 1)!$

Related Function

Function	Description
FACT	Returns the factorial of a number

GCD

Returns the greatest common divisor of two or more integers. The greatest common divisor is the largest integer that divides both *number1* and *number2* without a remainder.

If this function is not available, you must install the Analysis ToolPak add-in macro. For more information, see "Managing Add-in Commands and Functions" in Chapter 4 in Book 2 of the *Microsoft Excel User's Guide*.

Syntax

GCD(*number1*,*number2*,...)

Number1,number2,... are 1 to 29 values. If any value is not an integer, it is truncated.

Remarks

- If any argument is non-numeric, GCD returns the #VALUE! error value.

- If any argument is less than zero, GCD returns the #NUM! error value.

- One divides any value evenly.

- A prime number has only itself and one as even divisors.

Examples

GCD(5,2) equals 1

GCD(24,36) equals 12

GCD(7,1) equals 1

GCD(5,0) equals 5

Related Function

Function	Description
LCM	Returns the least common multiple

GEOMEAN

Returns the geometric mean of an array or range of positive data. For example, you can use GEOMEAN to calculate average growth rate given compound interest with variable rates.

Syntax

GEOMEAN(*number1*,*number2*,...)

Number1,number2,... are 1 to 30 arguments for which you want to calculate the mean. You can also use a single array or a reference to an array instead of arguments separated by commas.

Remarks

- The arguments should be numbers, or names, arrays, or references that contain numbers.

- If an array or reference argument contains text, logical values, or empty cells, those values are ignored; however, cells with the value zero are included.

- If any data point ≤ 0, GEOMEAN returns the #NUM! error value.

- The equation for the geometric mean is:

$$GM_{\bar{y}} = \sqrt[n]{y_1 y_2 y_3 \ldots y_n}$$

Example

GEOMEAN(4,5,8,7,11,4,3) equals 5.476987

Related Functions

Function	Description
AVERAGE	Returns the average of its arguments
HARMEAN	Returns the harmonic mean
MEDIAN	Returns the median of the given numbers
MODE	Returns the most common value in a data set
TRIMMEAN	Returns the mean of the interior of a data set

GESTEP

Returns 1 if *number* ≥ *step*; returns 0 otherwise. Use this function to filter a set of values. For example, by summing several GESTEP functions you calculate the count of values that exceed a threshold.

If this function is not available, you must install the Analysis ToolPak add-in macro. For more information, see "Managing Add-in Commands and Functions" in Chapter 4 in Book 2 of the *Microsoft Excel User's Guide.*

Syntax

GESTEP(*number,step*)

Number   is the value to test against *step*.

Step   is the threshold value. If you omit a value for *step,* GESTEP uses zero.

Remarks

If any argument is non-numeric, GESTEP returns the #VALUE! error value.

Examples

GESTEP(5,4) equals 1

GESTEP(5,5) equals 1

GESTEP(-4,-5) equals 1

GESTEP(-1,0) equals 0

Related Function

Function	Description
DELTA	Test whether two numbers are equal

GET.BAR

Macro Sheets Only

Returns the number of the active menu bar. There are two syntax forms of GET.BAR. Use syntax 1 to return information that you can use with other functions that manipulate menu bars. For a list of the ID numbers for Microsoft Excel's built-in menu bars, see ADD.COMMAND.

For information about menu bars, see "Creating a Custom Menu Bar" in Chapter 8 in Book 2 of the *Microsoft Excel User's Guide.*

Syntax 1

Menu bar numbers

GET.BAR( )

Example

The following macro formula assigns the name OldBar to the number of the active menu bar. This is useful if you will need to restore the current menu bar after displaying another custom menu bar.

```
SET.NAME("OldBar",GET.BAR())
```

Related Functions

Function	Description
ADD.BAR	Adds a menu bar
SHOW.BAR	Displays a menu bar

GET.BAR

Macro Sheets Only

Returns the name or position number of a specified command on a menu or of a specified menu on a menu bar. There are two syntax forms of GET.BAR. Use syntax 2 to return information that you can use with functions that add, delete, or alter menu commands.

Syntax 2

Command or menu names or numbers

GET.BAR(*bar_num,menu,command*)

Bar_num is the number of a menu bar containing the menu or command about which you want information. *Bar_num* can be the number of a built-in menu bar or the number returned by a previously run ADD.BAR function. For a list of the ID numbers for Microsoft Excel's built-in menu bars, see ADD.COMMAND.

Menu is the menu on which the command resides or the menu whose name or position you want. *Menu* can be the name of the menu as text or the number of the menu. Menus are numbered starting with 1 from the left of the menu bar.

Command is the command whose name or number you want returned. *Command* can be the name of the command from the menu as text, in which case the number is returned, or the number of the command from the menu, in which case the name is returned. Commands are numbered starting with 1 from the top of the menu. If *command* is 0, the name or position number of the menu is returned. If an ellipsis (...) follows a command name, such as the New... command on the File menu, then you must include the ellipsis when referring to that command. See the following examples.

Remarks

- If an ampersand is used to indicate the access key in the name of a custom command, the ampersand is included in the name returned by GET.BAR. All built-in commands have an ampersand before the letter used as the access key.

- If the command name or position specified does not exist, GET.BAR returns the #N/A error value.

Examples

In the default worksheet and macro sheet menu bar:

GET.BAR(1,"File","Print...") equals 13

GET.BAR(1,"File",13) equals "&Print...^tCTRL+SHIFT+F12" (where ^t is a tab character)

GET.BAR(1,1,"New") equals #N/A

GET.BAR(1,1,"New...") equals 1

Related Functions

Function	Description
ADD.COMMAND	Adds a command to a menu
DELETE.COMMAND	Deletes a command from a menu
GET.TOOLBAR	Retrieves information about a toolbar
RENAME.COMMAND	Changes the name of a command or menu

GET.CELL

Macro Sheets Only

Returns information about the formatting, location, or contents of a cell. Use GET.CELL in a macro whose behavior is determined by the status of a particular cell.

Syntax

GET.CELL(*type_num,reference*)

Type_num is a number that specifies what type of cell information you want. The following list shows the possible values of *type_num* and the corresponding results.

Type_num	Returns
1	Absolute reference of the upper-left cell in *reference,* as text in the current workspace reference style.
2	Row number of the top cell in *reference*.
3	Column number of the leftmost cell in *reference*.

Type_num	Returns
4	Same as TYPE(*reference*).
5	Contents of *reference*.
6	Formula in *reference,* as text, in either A1 or R1C1 style depending on the workspace setting.
7	Number format of the cell, as text (for example, "m/d/yy" or "General").
8	Number indicating the cell's horizontal alignment: 1 = General 2 = Left 3 = Center 4 = Right 5 = Fill 6 = Justify 7 = Center across cells
9	Number indicating the left-border style assigned to the cell: 0 = No border 1 = Thin line 2 = Medium line 3 = Dashed line 4 = Dotted line 5 = Thick line 6 = Double line 7 = Hairline
10	Number indicating the right-border style assigned to the cell. See *type_num* 9 for descriptions of the numbers returned.
11	Number indicating the top-border style assigned to the cell. See *type_num* 9 for descriptions of the numbers returned.
12	Number indicating the bottom-border style assigned to the cell. See *type_num* 9 for descriptions of the numbers returned.
13	Number from 0 to 18, indicating the pattern of the selected cell as displayed in the Patterns dialog box, which appears when you choose the Patterns command from the Format menu. If no pattern is selected, returns 0.
14	If the cell is locked, returns TRUE; otherwise FALSE.
15	If the cell is hidden, returns TRUE; otherwise FALSE.

Type_num	Returns
16	A two-item horizontal array containing the width of the active cell and a logical value indicating whether the cell's width is set to change as the standard width changes (TRUE) or is a custom width (FALSE).
17	Row height of cell, in points.
18	Name of font, as text.
19	Size of font, in points.
20	If the cell is bold, returns TRUE; otherwise FALSE.
21	If the cell is italic, returns TRUE; otherwise FALSE.
22	If the cell is underlined, returns TRUE; otherwise FALSE.
23	If the cell is struck through, returns TRUE; otherwise FALSE.
24	Font color as a number in the range 1 to 16. If font color is automatic, returns 0.
25	If the cell's font is outlined, returns TRUE; otherwise FALSE. Outline font format is not supported by Microsoft Excel for Windows.
26	If the cell is shadowed, returns TRUE; otherwise FALSE. Shadow font format is not supported by Microsoft Excel for Windows.
27	Number indicating whether a manual page break occurs at the cell: 0 = No break 1 = Row 2 = Column 3 = Both row and column
28	Row level (outline).
29	Column level (outline).
30	If the row containing the active cell is a summary row, returns TRUE; otherwise FALSE.
31	If the column containing the active cell is a summary column, returns TRUE; otherwise FALSE.
32	Name of the document containing the cell.
33	If the cell is formatted to wrap, returns TRUE; otherwise FALSE.

Type_num	Returns
34	Left-border color as a number in the range 1 to 16. If color is automatic, returns 0.
35	Right-border color as a number in the range 1 to 16. If color is automatic, returns 0.
36	Top-border color as a number in the range 1 to 16. If color is automatic, returns 0.
37	Bottom-border color as a number in the range 1 to 16. If color is automatic, returns 0.
38	Shade foreground color as a number in the range 1 to 16. If color is automatic, returns 0.
39	Shade background color as a number in the range 1 to 16. If color is automatic, returns 0.
40	Style of the cell, as text.
41	Returns the formula in the active cell without translating it (useful for international macro sheets).
42	The horizontal distance, measured in points, from the left edge of the active window to the left edge of the cell. May be a negative number if the window is scrolled beyond the cell.
43	The vertical distance, measured in points, from the top edge of the active window to the top edge of the cell. May be a negative number if the window is scrolled beyond the cell.
44	The horizontal distance, measured in points, from the left edge of the active window to the right edge of the cell. May be a negative number if the window is scrolled beyond the cell.
45	The vertical distance, measured in points, from the top edge of the active window to the bottom edge of the cell. May be a negative number if the window is scrolled beyond the cell.
46	If the cell contains a text note, returns TRUE; otherwise FALSE.
47	If the cell contains a sound note, returns TRUE; otherwise FALSE.
48	If the cells contains a formula, returns TRUE; if a constant, returns FALSE.

Type_num	Returns
49	If the cell is part of an array, returns TRUE; otherwise FALSE.
50	Number indicating the cell's vertical alignment: 1 = Top 2 = Center 3 = Bottom
51	Number indicating the cell's vertical orientation: 0 = Horizontal 1 = Vertical 2 = Upward 3 = Downward
52	The cell prefix (or text alignment) character, or empty text ("") if the cell does not contain one.
53	Contents of the cell as it is currently displayed, as text, including any additional numbers or symbols resulting from the cell's formatting.

Reference is a cell or a range of cells from which you want information.

- If *reference* is a range of cells, the cell in the upper-left corner of the first range in *reference* is used.

- If *reference* is omitted, the active cell is assumed.

Tip Use GET.CELL(17) to determine the height of a cell and GET.CELL(44) – GET.CELL(42) to determine the width.

Examples

The following macro formula returns TRUE if cell B4 on worksheet Sheet1 is bold:

```
GET.CELL(20,Sheet1!$B$4)
```

You can use the information returned by GET.CELL to initiate an action. The following macro formula runs a custom function named BoldCell if the GET.CELL formula returns FALSE:

```
IF(GET.CELL(20,Sheet1!$B$4),,BoldCell())
```

Related Functions

Function	Description
ABSREF	Returns the absolute reference of a range of cells to another range
ACTIVE.CELL	Returns the reference of the active cell
GET.FORMULA	Returns the contents of a cell
GET.NAME	Returns the definition of a name
GET.NOTE	Returns characters from a note
RELREF	Returns a relative reference

GET.CHART.ITEM

Macro Sheets Only

Returns the vertical or horizontal position of a point on a chart item. Use these position numbers with FORMAT.MOVE and FORMAT.SIZE to change the position and size of chart items.

Syntax

GET.CHART.ITEM(*x_y_index,point_index, item_text*)

X_y_index is a number specifying which of the coordinates you want returned.

X_y_index	Coordinate returned
1	Horizontal coordinate
2	Vertical coordinate

Point_index is a number specifying the point on the chart item. These indexes are described later. If *point_index* is omitted, it is assumed to be 1.

If the specified item is a point, *point_index* must be 1.

If the specified item is any line other than a data line, use the following values for *point_index*.

Point_index	Chart item position
1	Lower or left
2	Upper or right

If the selected item is a rectangle or an area in an area chart, use the following values for *point_index*.

Point_index	Chart item position
1	Upper left
2	Upper middle
3	Upper right
4	Right middle
5	Lower right
6	Lower middle
7	Lower left
8	Left middle

If the selected item is an arrow, use the following values for *point_index*.

Point_index	Chart item position
1	Arrow shaft
2	Arrowhead

If the selected item is a pie slice, use the following values for *point_index*.

Point_index	Chart item position
1	Outermost counterclockwise point
2	Outer center point
3	Outermost clockwise point
4	Midpoint of the most clockwise radius
5	Center point
6	Midpoint of the most counterclockwise radius

Item_text is a selection code that specifies which item of a chart to select. See the chart form of SELECT for the *item_text* codes to use for each item of a chart.

- If *item_text* is omitted, it is assumed to be the currently selected item.

- If *item_text* is omitted and no item is selected, GET.CHART.ITEM returns the #VALUE! error value.

Remarks

If the specified item does not exist, or if a chart is not active when the function is carried out, the #VALUE! error value is returned.

Examples

The following macro formulas return the horizontal and vertical locations, respectively, of the top of the main-chart value axis:

```
GET.CHART.ITEM(1,2,"Axis 1")
GET.CHART.ITEM(2,2,"Axis 1")
```

You could then use FORMAT.MOVE to move a floating text item to the position returned by these two formulas.

Related Functions

Function	Description
GET.DOCUMENT	Returns information about a document
GET.FORMULA	Returns the contents of a cell

GET.DEF

Macro Sheets Only

Returns the name, as text, that is defined for a particular area, value, or formula in a document. Use GET.DEF to get the name corresponding to a definition. To get the definition of a name, use GET.NAME.

Syntax

GET.DEF(*def_text,document_text,type_num*)

Def_text can be anything you can define a name to refer to, including a reference, a value, or a formula.

- References must be given in R1C1 style, such as "R3C5".

- If *def_text* is a value or formula, it is not necessary to include the equal sign that is displayed in the Refers To box in the Name dialog box, which appears when you choose the Name command from the Define menu.

- If there is more than one name for *def_text*, GET.DEF returns the first name. If no name matches *def_text*, GET.DEF returns the #NAME? error value.

Document_text specifies the worksheet or macro sheet that *def_text* is on. If *document_text* is omitted, it is assumed to be the active macro sheet.

Type_num is a number from 1 to 3 specifying which types of names are returned.

Type_num	Returns
1 or omitted	Normal names only
2	Hidden names only
3	All names

Examples

If the specified range in Sheet4 is named Sales, the following macro formula returns "Sales":

```
GET.DEF("R2C2:R9C6","Sheet4")
```

If the value 100 in Sheet4 is defined as Constant, the following macro formula returns "Constant":

```
GET.DEF("100","Sheet4")
```

If the specified formula in Sheet4 is named SumTotal, the following macro formula returns "SumTotal":

```
GET.DEF("SUM(R1C1:R10C1)","Sheet4")
```

If 3 is defined as the hidden name Counter on the active macro sheet, the following macro formula returns "Counter":

```
GET.DEF("3",,2)
```

Related Functions

Function	Description
GET.CELL	Returns information about the specified cell
GET.NAME	Returns the definition of a name
GET.NOTE	Returns characters from a note
NAMES	Returns the names defined on a document

GET.DOCUMENT

Macro Sheets Only

Returns information about a document.

Syntax

GET.DOCUMENT(*type_num,*name_text)

Type_num   is a number that specifies what type of document information you want. The following lists show the possible values of *type_num* and the corresponding results.

Type_num	Returns
1	Name of the document *name_text,* as text. The document name does not include the drive, directory or folder, or window number.
2	Path of the directory or folder containing *name_text,* as text. If the document *name_text* hasn't been saved yet, returns the #N/A error value.
3	Number indicating the type of document: 1 = Worksheet 2 = Chart 3 = Macro sheet 4 = Info window if active 5 = Workbook

Type_num	Returns
4	If changes have been made to the document since it was last saved, returns TRUE; otherwise FALSE.
5	If the document is read-only, returns TRUE; otherwise FALSE.
6	If the document is password protected, returns TRUE; otherwise FALSE.
7	If cells in a document, the contents of a workbook, or the series in a chart are protected, returns TRUE; otherwise FALSE.
8	If document windows are protected, returns TRUE; otherwise FALSE.

The next four values of *type_num* apply only to charts.

Type_num	Returns
9	Number indicating the type of the main chart: 1 = Area 2 = Bar 3 = Column 4 = Line 5 = Pie 6 = XY (scatter) 7 = 3-D area 8 = 3-D column 9 = 3-D line 10 = 3-D pie 11 = Radar 12 = 3-D bar 13 = 3-D surface
10	Number indicating the type of the overlay chart. Same as 1, 2, 3, 4, 5, 6, and 11 for main chart above. If there is no overlay chart, returns the #N/A error value.
11	Number of series in the main chart.
12	Number of series in the overlay chart.

The next values of *type_num* apply to worksheets and macro sheets and to charts when appropriate.

Type_num	Returns
9	Number of the first used row. If the document is empty, returns 0.
10	Number of the last used row. If the document is empty, returns 0.
11	Number of the first used column. If the document is empty, returns 0.
12	Number of the last used column. If the document is empty, returns 0.
13	Number of windows. If the document is a workbook, always returns 1.
14	Number indicating calculation mode: 1 = Automatic 2 = Automatic except tables 3 = Manual
15	If the Iteration check box is selected in the Calculation dialog box, returns TRUE; otherwise FALSE.
16	Maximum number of iterations.
17	Maximum change between iterations.
18	If the Update Remote References check box is selected in the Calculation dialog box, returns TRUE; otherwise FALSE.
19	If the Precision As Displayed check box is selected in the Calculation Options dialog box, returns TRUE; otherwise FALSE.
20	If the 1904 Date System check box is selected in the Calculation Options dialog box, returns TRUE; otherwise FALSE.

Type_num values of 21 through 29 correspond to the four default fonts in previous versions of Microsoft Excel. These values are provided only for macro compatibility.

The next values of *type_num* apply to worksheets and macro sheets, and to charts if indicated.

Type_num	Returns
30	Horizontal array of consolidation references for the current document, in the form of text. If the list is empty, returns the #N/A error value.

Type_num	Returns
31	Number from 1 to 11, indicating the function used in the current consolidation. The function that corresponds to each number is listed under the CONSOLIDATE function earlier in this manual. The default function is SUM.
32	Three-item horizontal array indicating the status of the check boxes in the Data Consolidate dialog box. An item is TRUE if the check box is selected or FALSE if the check box is cleared. The first item indicates the Top Row check box, the second the Left Column check box, and the third the Create Links To Source Data check box.
33	If the Recalculate Before Saving check box is selected in the Calculation dialog box, returns TRUE; otherwise FALSE.
34	If the document is read-only recommended, returns TRUE; otherwise FALSE.
35	If the document is write-reserved, returns TRUE; otherwise FALSE.
36	Name of the user with current write permission for the document.
37	Number corresponding to the file type of the document as displayed in the Save As dialog box.
38	If the Summary Rows Below Detail check box is selected in the Outline dialog box, returns TRUE; otherwise FALSE.
39	If the Summary Columns To Right Of Detail check box is selected in the Outline dialog box, returns TRUE; otherwise FALSE.
40	If the Create Backup File check box is selected in the Save As dialog box, returns TRUE; otherwise FALSE.
41	Number from 1 to 3 indicating whether objects are displayed: 1 = All objects are displayed 2 = Placeholders for pictures and charts 3 = All objects are hidden
42	Horizontal array of all objects in the document. If there are no objects, returns the #N/A error value.

Type_num	Returns
43	If the Save External Link Values check box is selected in the Calculation dialog box, returns TRUE; otherwise FALSE.
44	If objects in a document are protected, returns TRUE; otherwise FALSE.
45	A number from 0 to 3 indicating how windows are synchronized: 0 = Not synchronized 1 = Synchronized horizontally 2 = Synchronized vertically 3 = Synchronized horizontally and vertically
46	A seven-item horizontal array of print settings that can be set by the LINE.PRINT macro function: – Setup text – Left margin – Right margin – Top margin – Bottom margin – Page length – A logical value indicating whether output will be formatted (TRUE) or unformatted (FALSE) when printed
47	If the Alternate Expression Evaluation check box is selected in the Calculation dialog box, returns TRUE; otherwise FALSE.
48	The standard column width setting.

The next values of *type_num* correspond to printing and page settings.

Type_num	Returns
49	The starting page number, or 1 if none is specified.
50	The total number of pages that would be printed based on current settings, excluding notes, or 1 if the document is a chart.
51	The total number of pages that would be printed if you print only notes, or the #N/A error value if the document is a chart.
52	Four-item horizontal array indicating the margin settings (left, right, top, bottom) in the currently specified units.

Type_num	Returns
53	A number indicating the orientation: 1 = Portrait 2 = Landscape
54	The header as a text string, including formatting codes.
55	The footer as a text string, including formatting codes.
56	Horizontal array of two logical values corresponding to horizontal and vertical centering.
57	If row or column headings are to be printed, returns TRUE; otherwise FALSE.
58	If gridlines are to be printed, returns TRUE; otherwise FALSE.
59	If cell colors are to be printed, returns TRUE; otherwise FALSE.
60	A number from 1 to 3 indicating how the chart will be sized when it's printed: 1 = Size on screen 2 = Scale to fit page 3 = Use full page
61	A number indicating the pagination order: 1 = Down, then Over 2 = Over, then Down Returns the #N/A error value if the document is a chart.
62	Percentage of reduction or enlargement, or 100% if none is specified. Returns the #N/A error value if not supported by the current printer or if the document is a chart.
63	A two-item horizontal array indicating the number of pages to which the printout should be scaled to fit, with the first item equal to the width (or #N/A if no width scaling is specified) and the second item equal to the height (or #N/A if no height scaling is specified). #N/A is also returned if the document is a chart.
64	An array of row numbers corresponding to rows that are immediately below a manual or automatic page break.
65	An array of column numbers corresponding to columns that are immediately to the right of a manual or automatic page break.

Note GET.DOCUMENT(62) and
GET.DOCUMENT(63) are mutually exclusive.
If one returns a value, then the other returns the
#N/A error value.

The next values of *type_num* correspond to various
document settings.

Type_num	Returns
66	In Microsoft Excel for Windows, if the Alternate Formula Entry check box is selected in the Calculation dialog box, returns TRUE; otherwise FALSE.
67	If the workbook document is bound, returns TRUE; otherwise FALSE. If the document is not part of a workbook, returns the #N/A error value.
68	If the document is part of a workbook, returns the name of the workbook; if not part of a workbook returns the #N/A error value. If the document is part of multiple workbooks and is not bound, returns an array of the workbooks' names.

Name_text is the name of an open document. If
name_text is omitted, it is assumed to be the active
document.

Examples

The following macro formula returns TRUE if the
contents of the active document are protected:

```
GET.DOCUMENT(7)
```

In Microsoft Excel for Windows, the following
macro formula returns the number of windows in
SALES.XLS:

```
GET.DOCUMENT(13,"SALES.XLS")
```

In Microsoft Excel for the Macintosh, the following
macro formula returns 3 if the overlay chart on
SALES CHART is a column chart:

```
GET.DOCUMENT(10,"SALES CHART")
```

To find out if SHEET1 is password-protected and if
its contents and windows are protected, enter the
following formula in a three-cell horizontal array:

```
GET.DOCUMENT({6,7,8},"SHEET1")
```

Related Functions

Function	Description
GET.CELL	Returns information about the specified cell
GET.WINDOW	Returns information about a window
GET.WORKSPACE	Returns information about the workspace

GET.FORMULA

Macro Sheets Only

Returns the contents of a cell as they would appear
in the formula bar. The contents are given as text,
for example, "=2*PI()/360". If the formula contains
references, they are returned as R1C1-style
references, such as "-RC[1]*(1+R1C1)". Use
GET.FORMULA to get a formula from a cell in
order to edit its arguments. Use GET.CELL(6) to
get a formula in either A1 or R1C1 format,
depending on the workspace setting.

Syntax

GET.FORMULA *(reference)*

Reference is a cell or range of cells on a
worksheet or macro sheet.

- If a range of cells is selected, GET.FORMULA
returns the contents of the upper-left cell in
reference.

- *Reference* can be an external reference.

- *Reference* can be the object identifier of a
picture created by the camera tool.

- *Reference* can also be a reference to a chart
series in the form "S*n*" where *n* is the number of
the series. When a chart series is specified,
GET.FORMULA returns the series formula
using R1C1-style references.

Tip If you want to get the formula in the active cell, use the ACTIVE.CELL function as the *reference* argument.

Examples

If cell A3 on the active worksheet contains the number 523, then:

GET.FORMULA(!$A$3) equals "523"

If cell C2 on the active worksheet contains the formula =B2*(1+$A$1), then:

GET.FORMULA(!$C$2) equals "=RC[-1]*(1+R1C1)"

The following macro formula returns the contents of the active cell on the active document:

GET.FORMULA(ACTIVE.CELL())

Related Functions

Function	Description
GET.CELL	Returns information about the specified cell
GET.DEF	Returns a name matching a definition
GET.NAME	Returns the definition of a name
GET.NOTE	Returns characters from a note

GET.LINK.INFO

Macro Sheets Only

Returns information about the specified link. Use GET.LINK.INFO to get information about the update settings of a link.

Syntax

GET.LINK.INFO(*link_text,type_num,type_of_link, reference*)

Link_text is the path of the link as displayed in the Links dialog box, which appears when you choose the Links command from the File menu.

Type_num is a number that specifies what type of information about the currently selected link to return. *Type_num* 2 applies only to publishers and subscribers in Microsoft Excel for the Macintosh.

Type_num	Returns
1	If the link is set to automatic update, returns 1; otherwise 2.
2	Date of the latest edition as a serial number. Returns #N/A if *link_text* is not a publisher or a subscriber.

Type_of_link is a number from 1 to 6 that specifies what type of link you want to get information about.

Type_of_link	Link document type
1	Not applicable
2	DDE link
3	Not applicable
4	Not applicable
5	Publisher
6	Subscriber

Reference specifies the cell range in R1C1 format of the publisher or subscriber that you want information about. *Reference* is required if you have more than one publisher or subscriber of a single edition name on the active document. Use *reference* to specify the location of the subscriber you want to return information about. If the subscriber is a picture, or if the publisher is an embedded chart, *reference* is the number of the object as displayed in the reference area.

Remarks

- If Microsoft Excel cannot find *link_text,* or if *type_of_link* does not match the link specified by *link_text,* GET.LINK.INFO returns the #VALUE! error value.

- If you have more than one subscriber to the edition *link_text* or if the same area is published more than once, you must specify *reference*.

Example

In Microsoft Excel for Windows, the following macro formula returns information about a DDE link to a Microsoft Word for Windows document. The document is named NEWPROD.DOC.

```
GET.LINK.INFO("WordDocument|C:\WINWORD\
NEWPROD.DOC!DDE_LINK1",1,2)
```

In Microsoft Excel for the Macintosh, the following macro formula returns information about a link to a publisher defined in cells A1:C3 on a document named New Products.

```
GET.LINK.INFO("A1:C3 New Products Edition
#1",2,5,"'New Products'!R1C1:R3C3")
```

Related Functions

Function	Description
CREATE.PUBLISHER	Creates a publisher from the selection
SUBSCRIBE.TO	Inserts contents of an edition into the active document
UPDATE.LINK	Updates a link to another document

GET.NAME

Macro Sheets Only

Returns the definition of a name as it appears in the Refers To box of the Define Name dialog box, which appears when you choose the Define Name command from the Formula menu. If the definition contains references, they are given as R1C1-style references. Use GET.NAME to check the value defined by a name. To get the name corresponding to a definition, use GET.DEF.

Syntax

GET.NAME(*name_text*)

Name_text can be a name defined on the macro sheet; an external reference to a name defined on the active document, for example, "!Sales"; or an external reference to a name defined on a particular open worksheet, for example, "SHEET1!Sales". *Name_text* can also be a hidden name.

Remarks

If the Cells check box has been selected in the Protect Document dialog box to protect the document containing the name, GET.NAME returns the #N/A error value. To see the Protect Document dialog box, choose Protect Document from the Options menu.

Examples

If the name Sales on a macro sheet is defined as the number 523, then:

`GET.NAME("Sales")` equals "=523"

If the name Profit on the active worksheet is defined as the formula =Sales–Costs, then:

`GET.NAME("!Profit")` equals "=Sales–Costs"

If the name Database on the active worksheet is defined as the range A1:F500, then:

`GET.NAME("!Database")` equals "=R1C1:R500C6"

Related Functions

Function	Description
DEFINE.NAME	Defines a name on the active worksheet or macro sheet
GET.CELL	Returns information about the specified cell
GET.DEF	Returns a name matching a definition
NAMES	Returns the names defined in a document
SET.NAME	Defines a name as a value

GET.NOTE

Macro Sheets Only

Returns characters from a note. Use GET.NOTE to move the contents of a note to a cell or text box or to another cell note.

Syntax

GET.NOTE(*cell_ref,start_char,num_chars*)

Cell_ref is the cell to which the note is attached. If *cell_ref* is omitted, the note attached to the active cell is returned.

Start_char is the number of the first character in the note to return. If *start_char* is omitted, it is assumed to be 1, the first character in the note.

Num_chars is the number of characters to return. *Num_chars* must be less than or equal to 255. If *num_chars* is omitted, it is assumed to be the length of the note attached to *cell_ref*.

Examples

The following macro formula returns the first 200 characters in the note attached to cell A3 on the active sheet:

```
GET.NOTE(!$A$3,1,200)
```

In Microsoft Excel for Windows, the following macro formula returns the 10th through the 39th characters of the note attached to cell C2 on SALES.XLS:

```
GET.NOTE("SALES.XLS!R2C3",10,30)
```

In Microsoft Excel for the Macintosh, the following macro formula returns the 10th through the 39th characters of the note attached to cell C2 on SALES:

```
GET.NOTE("SALES!R2C3",10,30)
```

Related Functions

Function	Description
GET.CELL	Returns information about the specified cell
NOTE	Creates or changes a cell note
SOUND.NOTE	Records or imports sound into or erases sound from cell notes

GET.OBJECT

Macro Sheets Only

Returns information about the specified object. Use GET.OBJECT to return information you can use in other macro formulas that manipulate objects.

Syntax

GET.OBJECT(*type_num,object_id_text,start_num, count_num*)

Type_num is a number specifying the type of information you want returned about an object. GET.OBJECT returns the #VALUE! error value if an object isn't specified or if more than one object is selected.

Type_num	Returns
1	Number specifying the type of the selected object: 1 = Line 2 = Rectangle 3 = Oval 4 = Arc 5 = Embedded chart 6 = Text box 7 = Button 8 = Picture 9 = Closed polygon 10 = Open polygon (freehand drawing)
2	If the object is locked, returns TRUE; otherwise FALSE.
3	Z-order position (layering) of the object.
4	Reference of the cell under the upper-left corner of the object as text in R1C1 reference style; for a line or arc, returns the start point.

Type_num	Returns
5	*X* offset from the upper-left corner of the cell under the upper-left corner of the object, measured in points.
6	*Y* offset from the upper-left corner of the cell under the upper-left corner of the object, measured in points.
7	Reference of the cell under the lower-right corner of the object as text in R1C1 reference style; for a line or arc, returns the end point.
8	*X* offset from the upper-left corner of the cell under the lower-right corner of the object, measured in points.
9	*Y* offset from the upper-left corner of the cell under the lower-right corner of the object, measured in points.
10	Name, including the filename, of the macro assigned to the object. If no macro is assigned, returns FALSE.
11	Number indicating how the object moves and sizes: 1 = Object moves and sizes with cells 2 = Object moves with cells 3 = Object is fixed

Values 12 to 21 for *type_num* apply only to text boxes and buttons. If another type of object is selected, GET.OBJECT returns the #VALUE! error value.

Type_num	Returns
12	Text starting at *start_num* for *count_num* characters.
13	Font name of all text starting at *start_num* for *count_num* characters. If the text contains more than one font name, returns the #N/A error value.
14	Font size of all text starting at *start_num* for *count_num* characters. If the text contains more than one font size, returns the #N/A error value.
15	If all text starting at *start_num* for *count_num* characters is bold, returns TRUE. If text contains only partial bold formatting, returns the #N/A error value.

Type_num	Returns
16	If all text starting at *start_num* for *count_num* characters is italic, returns TRUE. If text contains only partial italic formatting, returns the #N/A error value.
17	If all text starting at *start_num* for *count_num* characters is underlined, returns TRUE. If text contains only partial underline formatting, returns the #N/A error value.
18	If all text starting at *start_num* for *count_num* characters is struck through, returns TRUE. If text contains only partial struck-through formatting, returns the #N/A error value.
19	In Microsoft Excel for the Macintosh, if all text starting at *start_num* for *count_num* characters is outlined, returns TRUE. If text contains only partial outline formatting, returns the #N/A error value. Always returns FALSE in Microsoft Excel for Windows.
20	In Microsoft Excel for the Macintosh, if all text starting at *start_num* for *count_num* characters is shadowed, returns TRUE. If text contains only partial shadow formatting, returns the #N/A error value. Always returns FALSE in Microsoft Excel for Windows.
21	Number from 0 to 16 indicating the color of all text starting at *start_num* for *count_num* characters; if color is automatic, returns 0. If more than one color is used, returns the #N/A error value.

Values 22 to 25 for *type_num* also apply only to text boxes and buttons. If another type of object is selected, GET.OBJECT returns the #N/A error value.

Type_num	Returns
22	Number indicating the horizontal alignment of text: 1 = Left 2 = Center 3 = Right 4 = Justified

Type_num	Returns
23	Number indicating the vertical alignment of text: 1 = Top 2 = Center 3 = Bottom 4 = Justified
24	Number indicating the orientation of text: 0 = Horizontal 1 = Vertical 2 = Upward 3 = Downward
25	If button or text box is set to automatic sizing, returns TRUE; otherwise FALSE.

The following values for *type_num* apply to all objects, except where indicated.

Type_num	Returns
26	If the object is visible, returns TRUE; if the object has been hidden by the HIDE.OBJECT function, returns FALSE.
27	Number indicating the type of the border or line: 0 = Custom 1 = Automatic 2 = None
28	Number indicating the style of the border or line as shown in the Style box in the Patterns dialog box: 0 = None 1 = Solid line 2 = Dashed line 3 = Dotted line 4 = Dashed dotted line 5 = Dashed double-dotted line 6 = 50% gray line 7 = 75% gray line 8 = 25% gray line
29	Number from 0 to 16 indicating the color of the border or line; if the border is automatic, returns 0.
30	Number indicating the weight of the border or line: 1 = Hairline 2 = Thin 3 = Medium 4 = Thick

Type_num	Returns
31	Number indicating the type of fill: 0 = Custom 1 = Automatic 2 = None
32	Number from 1 to 18 indicating the fill pattern as shown in the Patterns dialog box.
33	Number from 0 to 16 indicating the foreground color of the fill pattern; if the fill is automatic, returns 0. If the object is a line, returns the #N/A error value.
34	Number from 0 to 16 indicating the background color of the fill pattern; if the fill is automatic, returns 0. If the object is a line, returns the #N/A error value.
35	Number indicating the width of the arrowhead: 1 = Narrow 2 = Medium 3 = Wide If the object is not a line, returns the #N/A error value.
36	Number indicating the length of the arrowhead: 1 = Short 2 = Medium 3 = Long If the object is not a line, returns the #N/A error value.
37	Number indicating the style of the arrowhead: 1 = No head 2 = Open head 3 = Closed head If the object is not a line, returns the #N/A error value.
38	If the border has round corners, returns TRUE; if the corners are square, returns FALSE. If the object is a line, returns the #N/A error value.
39	If the border has a shadow, returns TRUE; if the border has no shadow, returns FALSE. If the object is a line, returns the #N/A error value.
40	If the Lock Text check box in the Object Protection dialog box is selected, returns TRUE; otherwise FALSE.

Type_num	Returns
41	If objects are set to be printed, returns TRUE; otherwise FALSE.
42	The horizontal distance, measured in points, from the left edge of the active window to the left edge of the object. May be a negative number if the window is scrolled beyond the object.
43	The vertical distance, measured in points, from the top edge of the active window to the top edge of the object. May be a negative number if the window is scrolled beyond the object.
44	The horizontal distance, measured in points, from the left edge of the active window to the right edge of the object. May be a negative number if the window is scrolled beyond the object.
45	The vertical distance, measured in points, from the top edge of the active window to the bottom edge of the object. May be a negative number if the window is scrolled beyond the object.
46	The number of vertices in a polygon, or the #N/A error value if the object is not a polygon.
47	A *count_num* by 2 array of vertex coordinates starting at *start_num* in a polygon's array of vertices.

Object_id_text   is the name and number, or number alone, of the object you want information about. *Object_id_text* is the text displayed in the reference area when the object is selected. If *object_id_text* is omitted, it is assumed to be the selected object. If *object_id_text* is omitted and no object is selected, GET.OBJECT returns the #REF! error value and interrupts the macro.

Start_num   is the number of the first character in the text box or button or the first vertex in a polygon you want information about. *Start_num* is ignored unless a text box, button, or polygon is specified by *type_num* and *object_id_text*. If *start_num* is omitted, it is assumed to be 1.

Count_num   is the number of characters in a text box or button, or the number of vertices in a polygon, starting at *start_num*, that you want information about. *Count_num* is ignored unless a text box, button, or polygon is specified by *type_num* and *object_id_text*. If *count_num* is omitted, it is assumed to be 255.

Tip   Use GET.OBJECT(45) – GET.OBJECT(43) to determine the height of an object and GET.OBJECT(44) – GET.OBJECT(42) to determine the width.

Examples

The following macro formula returns the reference of the cell under the upper-left corner of the object Oval 3 (assume the cell is E2):

```
GET.OBJECT(4,"Oval 3") returns "R2C5"
```

The following macro formula changes the protection status of the object Rectangle 2 if it is locked:

```
IF(GET.OBJECT(2,"Rectangle 2"),
OBJECT.PROTECTION(FALSE))
```

The following macro formula returns characters 25 through 185 from the object Text 5:

```
GET.OBJECT(12,"Text 5",25,160)
```

Related Functions

Function	Description
CREATE.OBJECT	Creates an object
FORMAT.FONT	Applies a font to the selection
OBJECT.PROTECTION	Controls how an object is protected
PLACEMENT	Determines an object's relationship to underlying cells

GET.TOOL

Macro Sheets Only

Returns information about a tool or tools on a toolbar. Use GET.TOOL to get information about a tool to use with functions that add, delete, or alter tools.

Syntax

GET.TOOL(*type_num,bar_id,position*)

Type_num   specifies what type of information you want GET.TOOL to return.

Type_num	Returns
1	The tool's ID number. Gaps are represented by zeros.
2	The reference of the macro assigned to the tool. If no macro is assigned, GET.TOOL returns the #N/A error value.
3	If the tool button is down, returns TRUE. If the tool button is up, returns FALSE.
4	If the tool is enabled, returns TRUE. If the tool is disabled, returns FALSE.
5	A logical value indicating the type of the face on the tool: TRUE = bitmap FALSE = a default tool face
6	The *help_text* reference associated with the custom tool. If the tool is built-in, returns #N/A.
7	The *balloon_text* reference associated with the custom tool. If the tool is built-in, returns the #N/A error value.

Bar_id   specifies the number or name of the toolbar for which you want information. For detailed information about *bar_id,* see ADD.TOOL.

Position   specifies the position of the tool on the toolbar. *Position* starts with 1 at the left side (if horizontal) or at the top (if vertical). A position can be occupied by a tool or a gap.

Example

The following macro formula requests the help text associated with the third tool in Toolbar2:

```
GET.TOOL(6,"Toolbar2",3)
```

Related Functions

Function	Description
ADD.TOOL	Adds one or more tools to a toolbar
DELETE.TOOL	Deletes a tool from a toolbar
ENABLE.TOOL	Enables or disables a tool on a toolbar
GET.TOOLBAR	Retrieves information about a toolbar

GET.TOOLBAR

Macro Sheets Only

Returns information about one toolbar or all toolbars. Use GET.TOOLBAR to get information about a toolbar to use with functions that add, delete, or alter toolbars.

Syntax

GET.TOOLBAR(*type_num,bar_id*)

Type_num   specifies what type of information to return. If *type_num* is 8 or 9, GET.TOOLBAR returns an array of names or numbers of all visible or hidden toolbars. Otherwise, *bar_id* is required, and GET.TOOLBAR returns the requested information about the specified toolbar.

Type_num	Returns
1	A horizontal array of all tool IDs on the toolbar, ordered by position. Gaps are represented by zeros.
2	Number indicating the horizontal position (x-coordinate) of the toolbar in the docked or floating region. For more information, see SHOW.TOOLBAR.
3	Number indicating the vertical position (y-coordinate) of the toolbar in the docked or floating region.

Type_num	Returns
4	Number indicating the width of the toolbar in points.
5	Number indicating the height of the toolbar in points.
6	Number indicating the toolbar location: 1 = Top dock in the workspace 2 = Left dock in the workspace 3 = Right dock in the workspace 4 = Bottom dock in the workspace 5 = Floating
7	If the toolbar is visible, returns TRUE. If the toolbar is hidden, returns FALSE.
8	An array of toolbar IDs (names or numbers in the *bar_id* array) for all toolbars, visible and hidden.
9	An array of toolbar IDs (names or numbers in the *bar_id* array) for all visible toolbars.

Bar_id specifies the number or name of a toolbar for which you want information. If *type_num* is 8 or 9, Microsoft Excel ignores *bar_id*. For detailed information about *bar_id,* see ADD.TOOL.

Remarks

If you request position information for a hidden toolbar, Microsoft Excel returns the position where the toolbar would appear if shown.

Examples

The following macro formula returns information about the width of Toolbar1:

```
GET.TOOLBAR(4,"Toolbar1")
```

The following macro formula returns the IDs of all visible toolbars and names the array All_Bar_Ids:

```
SET.NAME("All_Bar_Ids",GET.TOOLBAR(9))
```

Related Functions

Function	Description
ADD.TOOLBAR	Creates a new toolbar with the specified tools
DELETE.TOOLBAR	Deletes custom toolbars
GET.TOOL	Returns information about a tool or tools on a toolbar

GET.WINDOW

Macro Sheets Only

Returns information about a window. Use GET.WINDOW in a macro that requires the status of a window, such as its name, size, position, and display options.

Syntax

GET.WINDOW(*type_num,window_text*)

Type_num is a number that specifies what type of window information you want. The following list shows the possible values of *type_num* and the corresponding results:

Type_num	Returns
1	Name of the document in the window as text
2	Number of the window
3	X position, measured in points from the left edge of the workspace (in Microsoft Excel for Windows) or screen (in Microsoft Excel for the Macintosh) to the left edge of the window
4	Y position, measured in points from the bottom edge of the formula bar to the top edge of the window
5	Width, measured in points
6	Height, measured in points
7	If window is hidden, returns TRUE; otherwise FALSE

The rest of the values for *type_num* apply only to worksheets and macro sheets, except where indicated:

Type_num	Returns
8	If formulas are displayed, returns TRUE; otherwise FALSE
9	If gridlines are displayed, returns TRUE; otherwise FALSE
10	If row and column headings are displayed, returns TRUE; otherwise FALSE
11	If zeros are displayed, returns TRUE; otherwise FALSE
12	Gridline and heading color as a number in the range 1 to 16, corresponding to the colors in the Display Options dialog box; if color is automatic, returns 0

Values 13 to 16 for *type_num* return arrays that specify which rows or columns are at the top and left edges of the panes in the window and the widths and heights of those panes.

- The first number in the array corresponds to the first pane, the second number to the second pane, and so on.

- If the edge of the pane occurs at the boundary between rows or columns, the number returned is an integer.

- If the edge of the pane occurs within a row or column, the number returned has a fractional part that represents the fraction of the row or column visible within the pane.

- The numbers can be used as arguments to the SPLIT function to split a window at specific locations.

Type_num	Returns
13	Leftmost column number of each pane, in a horizontal numeric array
14	Top row number of each pane, in a horizontal numeric array
15	Number of columns in each pane, in a horizontal numeric array

Type_num	Returns
16	Number of rows in each pane, in a horizontal numeric array
17	Number indicating the active pane: 1 = Upper, left, or upper-left 2 = Right or upper-right 3 = Lower or lower-left 4 = Lower-right
18	If window has a vertical split, returns TRUE; otherwise FALSE
19	If window has a horizontal split, returns TRUE; otherwise FALSE
20	If window is maximized, returns TRUE; otherwise FALSE
21	Reserved
22	If the Outline Symbols check box is selected in the Display Options dialog box, returns TRUE; otherwise FALSE
23	Number indicating the size of the document window (including charts): 1 = Restored 2 = Minimized (displayed as an icon) 3 = Maximized
24	If panes are frozen on the active window, returns TRUE; otherwise FALSE
25	The numeric magnification of the active window (as a percentage of normal size) as set in the Window Zoom dialog box, or 100 if none is specified

Window_text   is the name that appears in the title bar of the window that you want information about. If *window_text* is omitted, it is assumed to be the active window.

Examples

If the active window contains the document Macro1, then:

```
GET.WINDOW(1) equals "Macro1"
```

If the title of the active window is Macro1:3, then:

`GET.WINDOW(2)` equals 3

In Microsoft Excel for Windows, the following macro formula returns the gridline and heading color of REPORT.XLS:

`GET.WINDOW(12,"REPORT.XLS")`

In Microsoft Excel for the Macintosh, the following macro formula returns the gridline and heading color of REPORT MASTER:

`GET.WINDOW(12,"REPORT MASTER")`

Related Functions

Function	Description
GET.DOCUMENT	Returns information about a document
GET.WORKSPACE	Returns information about the workspace

GET.WORKBOOK

Macro Sheets Only

Returns information about a workbook document.

Syntax

GET.WORKBOOK(*type_num,name_text*)

Type_num is a number that specifies what type of workbook information you want.

Type_num	Returns
1	The names of all documents in the workbook, as a horizontal array of text values
2	The name of the active document in the workbook
3	The names of the currently selected documents in the workbook, as a horizontal array of ext values
4	The number of documents in the workbook

Name_text is the name of an open workbook. If *name_text* is omitted, it is assumed to be the active workbook.

Example

The following macro formula returns the name of the active document in the workbook named SALES.XLW:

`GET.WORKBOOK(2,"SALES.XLW")`

Related Functions

Function	Description
GET.DOCUMENT	Returns information about a document
WORKBOOK.SELECT	Selects the specified documents in a workbook

GET.WORKSPACE

Macro Sheets Only

Returns information about the workspace. Use GET.WORKSPACE in a macro that depends on the status of the workspace, such as the environment, version number, and available memory.

Syntax

GET.WORKSPACE(*type_num*)

Type_num is a number specifying the type of workspace information you want. The following list shows the *type_num* values and their corresponding results.

Type_num	Returns
1	Name of the environment in which Microsoft Excel is running, as text, followed by the environment's version number.
2	The version number of Microsoft Excel, as text (for example, "4.0").
3	If fixed decimals are set, returns the number of decimals; otherwise, returns 0.
4	If in R1C1 mode, returns TRUE; if in A1 mode, returns FALSE.

Type_num	Returns
5	If scroll bars are displayed, returns TRUE; otherwise FALSE.
6	If the status bar is displayed, returns TRUE; otherwise FALSE.
7	If the formula bar is displayed, returns TRUE; otherwise FALSE.
8	If remote DDE requests are enabled, returns TRUE; otherwise FALSE.
9	Returns the alternate menu key as text; if no alternate menu key is set, returns the #N/A error value.
10	Number indicating special modes: 1 = Data Find 2 = Copy 3 = Cut 4 = Data Entry 5 = Unused 6 = Copy and Data Entry 7 = Cut and Data Entry If no special mode is set, returns 0.
11	X position of the Microsoft Excel workspace window, measured in points from the left edge of the screen to the left edge of the window. In Microsoft Excel for the Macintosh, always returns 0.
12	Y position of the Microsoft Excel workspace window, measured in points from the top edge of the screen to the top edge of the window. In Microsoft Excel for the Macintosh, always returns 0.
13	Usable workspace width, in points.
14	Usable workspace height, in points.
15	Number indicating maximized or minimized status of Microsoft Excel: 1 = Neither 2 = Minimized 3 = Maximized Microsoft Excel for the Macintosh always returns 3.
16	Amount of memory free (in kilobytes).
17	Total memory available to Microsoft Excel (in kilobytes).
18	If a math coprocessor is present, returns TRUE; otherwise FALSE.

Type_num	Returns
19	If a mouse is present, returns TRUE; otherwise FALSE. In Microsoft Excel for the Macintosh, always returns TRUE.
20	If a group is present in the workspace, returns a horizontal array of documents in the group; otherwise returns the #N/A error value.
21	If the Microsoft Excel version 3.0 toolbar is displayed, returns TRUE; otherwise FALSE.
22	DDE-application-specific error code.
23	Full path of the default startup directory or folder.
24	Full path of the alternate startup directory or folder; returns the #N/A error value if no alternate path has been specified.
25	If Microsoft Excel is set for relative recording, returns TRUE; if set for absolute recording, returns FALSE.
26	Name of user.
27	Name of organization.
28	If Microsoft Excel menus are switched to by the alternate menu or help key, returns 1; if Lotus 1-2-3 Help is switched to, returns 2.
29	If alternate navigation keys are enabled, returns TRUE.
30	A nine-item horizontal array of global (default) print settings that can be set by the LINE.PRINT function: – Setup text – Left margin – Right margin – Top margin – Bottom margin – Page length – Logical value indicating whether to wait after printing each page (TRUE) or use continuous form feeding (FALSE) – Logical value indicating whether the printer has automatic line feeding (TRUE) or requires line feed characters (FALSE) – The number of the printer port

Type_num	Returns
31	If a currently running macro is in single step mode, returns TRUE; otherwise FALSE.
32	The current location of Microsoft Excel as a complete path.
33	A horizontal array of the names in the File New list, in the order they appear.
34	A horizontal array of template files (with complete paths) in the File New list, in the order they appear (returns the names of custom template files and the #N/A error value for built-in document types).
35	If a macro is paused, returns TRUE; FALSE otherwise.
36	If the Cell Drag And Drop check box is selected in the Options Workspace dialog box, returns TRUE; otherwise FALSE.
37	A 45-item horizontal array of the items related to country versions and settings. Use the following macro formula to return a specific item, where *number* is a number in the list below:

INDEX(GET.WORKSPACE(37),*number*)

These values apply to country codes:
1 Number corresponding to the country version of Microsoft Excel.
2 Number corresponding to the current country setting in the Microsoft Windows Control Panel or the country number as determined by your Apple system software

These values apply to number separators:
3 Decimal separator
4 Zero (or 1000) separator
5 List separator

These values apply to R1C1-style references:
6 Row character
7 Column character
8 Lowercase row character
9 Lowercase column character
10 Character used instead of the left bracket ([)
11 Character used instead of the right bracket (])

Type_num	Returns

These values apply to array characters:
12 Character used instead of the left bracket ({)
13 Character used instead of the right bracket (})
14 Column separator
15 Row separator
16 Alternate array item separator to use if the current array separator is the same as the decimal separator

These values apply to format code symbols:
17 Date separator
18 Time separator
19 Year symbol
20 Month symbol
21 Day symbol
22 Hour symbol
23 Minute symbol
24 Second symbol
25 Currency symbol
26 "General" symbol

These values apply to format codes:
27 Number of decimal digits to use in currency formats
28 Number indicating the current format for negative currencies
0 = ($currency) or (currency$)
1 = –$currency or –currency$
2 = $–currency or currency–$
3 = $currency– or currency$–
where *currency* is any number and the $ represents the current currency symbol.
29 Number of decimal digits to use in noncurrency number formats
30 Number of characters to use in month names
31 Number of characters to use in weekday names
32 Number indicating the date order
0 = Month-Day-Year
1 = Day-Month-Year
2 = Year-Month-Day

Type_num	Returns
	These values apply to logical format values:
	33 TRUE if using 24-hour time; FALSE if using 12-hour time.
	34 TRUE if not displaying functions in English; otherwise FALSE.
	35 TRUE if using the metric system; FALSE if using the English measurement system.
	36 TRUE if a space is added before the currency symbol; otherwise FALSE.
	37 TRUE if currency symbol precedes currency values; FALSE if it follows currency values.
	38 TRUE if using minus sign for negative numbers; FALSE if using parentheses.
	39 TRUE if trailing zeros are displayed for zero currency values; otherwise FALSE.
	40 TRUE if leading zeros are displayed for zero currency values; otherwise FALSE.
	41 TRUE if leading zero is displayed in months (when months are displayed as numbers); otherwise FALSE.
	42 TRUE if leading zero is shown in days (when days are displayed as numbers); otherwise FALSE.
	43 TRUE if using four-digit years; FALSE if using two-digit years.
	44 TRUE if date order is month-day-year when displaying dates in long form; FALSE if date order is day-month-year.
	45 TRUE if leading zero is shown in the time; otherwise FALSE.
38	The number 0, 1, or 2 indicating the type of error-checking as set by the ERROR function. For more information, see ERROR.
39	A reference to the currently defined error-handling macro (set by the ERROR function), or the #N/A error value if none is specified.
40	If screen updating is turned on (set by the ECHO function), returns TRUE; otherwise FALSE.

Type_num	Returns
41	A horizontal array of cell ranges, as R1C1-style text, that were previously selected with the Goto command from the Formula menu or the FORMULA.GOTO macro function.
42	If your computer is capable of playing sounds, returns TRUE; otherwise FALSE.
43	If your computer is capable of recording sounds, returns TRUE; otherwise FALSE.
44	A three-column array of all currently registered procedures in dynamic link libraries (DLLs). The first column contains the names of the DLLs that contain the procedures (in Microsoft Excel for Windows) or the names of the files that contain the code resources (in Microsoft Excel for the Macintosh). The second column contains the names of the procedures in the DLLs (in Microsoft Excel for Windows) or code resources (in Microsoft Excel for the Macintosh). The third column contains text strings specifying the data types of the return values, and the number and data types of the arguments. For more information, see the Appendix.
45	If Microsoft Windows for Pen Computing is running, returns TRUE; otherwise FALSE.
46	If the Move After Enter check box is selected in the Options Workspace dialog box, returns TRUE; otherwise FALSE.

Related Functions

Function	Description
GET.DOCUMENT	Returns information about a document
GET.WINDOW	Returns information about a window

GOAL.SEEK

Macro Sheets Only

Equivalent to choosing the Goal Seek command from the Formula menu. Calculates the values necessary to achieve a specific goal. If the goal is an amount returned by a formula, the GOAL.SEEK function calculates values that, when supplied to your formula, cause your formula to return the amount you want. For detailed information about the Goal Seek command, see online Help.

Syntax

GOAL.SEEK(*target_cell,target_value, variable_cell*)
GOAL.SEEK?(*target_cell,target_value, variable_cell*)

Target_cell　corresponds to the Set Cell box in the Goal Seek dialog box and is a reference to the cell containing the formula. If *target_cell* does not contain a formula, Microsoft Excel displays an error message.

Target_value　corresponds to the To Value box in the Goal Seek dialog box and is the value you want the formula in *target_cell* to return. This value is called a goal.

Variable_cell　corresponds to the By Changing Cell box in the Goal Seek dialog box and is the single cell that you want Microsoft Excel to change so that the formula in *target_cell* returns *target_value*. *Target_cell* must depend on *variable_cell*; if it does not, Microsoft Excel will not be able to find a solution.

Tip　You can also use Microsoft Excel Solver to help solve your math equations for optimal values. For more information, see Chapter 2 in Book 2 of the *Microsoft Excel User's Guide*.

Example

Suppose a worksheet has a cell named Polynomial containing the formula $-(X^3)+(3*X^2)+6$ and another cell named X that is empty. The X in Polynomial refers to the cell named X. The following macro formulas solve the equation on the active worksheet so that it equals 15:

```
GOAL.SEEK("Polynomial",15,"X")
GOAL.SEEK(!Polynomial,15,!X)
```

The result is 1.426 and is stored in cell X on the active worksheet. The formula in Polynomial evaluates to 15.000.

Related Functions

Related functions include the SOLVER functions, such as SOLVER.OPTIONS, SOLVER.SOLVE, and so on.

GOTO

Macro Sheets Only

Directs a macro to continue running at the upper-left cell of *reference*. Use GOTO to direct macro execution to another cell or a named range.

Syntax

GOTO(*reference*)

Reference　is a cell reference or a name that is defined as a reference. *Reference* can be an external reference to another macro sheet. If that macro sheet is not open, GOTO displays a message.

Tip　It's often preferable to use IF, ELSE, ELSE.IF, and END.IF instead of GOTO when you want to perform multiple actions based on a condition because the IF method makes your macros more structured.

Examples

If A1 contains the #N/A error value, then when the following formula is calculated, the macro branches to C3:

```
IF(ISERROR($A$1),GOTO($C$3),)
```

You can also use macro names with GOTO statements. The following macro formula branches macro execution to a macro named Compile:

```
GOTO(Compile)
```

Because Compile is a named range, it should not be enclosed in quotation marks.

Related Function

Function	Description
FORMULA.GOTO	Selects a named area or reference on any open document

GRIDLINES

Macro Sheets Only

Equivalent to choosing the Gridlines command from the Chart menu. Allows you to turn chart gridlines on and off. For detailed information about the Gridlines command, see online Help.

Arguments are logical values corresponding to the check boxes in the Gridlines dialog box. If an argument is TRUE, Microsoft Excel selects the check box; if FALSE, Microsoft Excel clears the check box. If omitted, the setting is not changed

Syntax

GRIDLINES(*x_major,x_minor,y_major,y_minor, z_major,z_minor*)
GRIDLINES?(*x_major,x_minor,y_major,y_minor, z_major,z_minor*)

X_major corresponds to the Category (X) Axis: Major Gridlines check box.

X_minor corresponds to the Category (X) Axis: Minor Gridlines check box.

Y_major corresponds to the Value (Y) Axis: Major Gridlines check box. On 3-D charts, *y_major* corresponds to the Series (Y) Axis: Major Gridlines check box.

Y_minor corresponds to the Value (Y) Axis: Minor Gridlines check box. On 3-D charts, *y_minor* corresponds to the Series (Y) Axis: Minor Gridlines check box.

Z_major corresponds to the Value (Z) Axis: Major Gridlines check box (3-D only).

Z_minor corresponds to the Value (Z) Axis: Minor Gridlines check box (3-D only).

GROUP

Macro Sheets Only

Equivalent to choosing the Group command from the Format menu. Creates a single object from several selected objects and returns the object identifier of the group (for example, "Group 5"). Use GROUP to combine a number of objects so that you can move or resize them together. For detailed information about the Group command, see online Help.

If no object is selected, only one object is selected, or a group is already selected, GROUP returns the #VALUE! error value and interrupts the macro.

Syntax

GROUP( )

Related Function

Function	Description
UNGROUP	Separates a grouped object

GROWTH

Fits an exponential curve to the data *known_y's* and *known_x's*, and returns the *y*-values along that curve for the array of *new_x's* that you specify. For more information about exponential curves, see LOGEST.

Syntax

GROWTH(***known_y's***,*known_x's*,*new_x's*,*const*)

Known_y's   is the set of *y*-values you already know in the relationship $y = b*m^x$.

- If the array *known_y's* is in a single column, then each column of *known_x's* is interpreted as a separate variable.

- If the array *known_y's* is in a single row, then each row of *known_x's* is interpreted as a separate variable.

- If any of the numbers in *known_y's* is 0 or negative, GROWTH returns the #NUM! error value.

Known_x's   is an optional set of *x*-values that you may already know in the relationship $y = b*m^x$.

- The array *known_x's* can include one or more sets of variables. If only one variable is used, *known_y's* and *known_x's* can be ranges of any shape, as long as they have equal dimensions. If more than one variable is used, *known_y's* must be a vector (that is, a range with a height of one row or a width of one column).

- If *known_x's* is omitted, it is assumed to be the array {1,2,3,...} that is the same size as *known_y's*.

New_x's   are new *x*-values for which you want GROWTH to return corresponding *y*-values.

- *New_x's* must include a column (or row) for each independent variable, just as *known_x's* does. So, if *known_y's* is in a single column, *known_x's* and *new_x's* should have the same number of columns. If *known_y's* is in a single row, *known_x's* and *new_x's* should have the same number of rows.

- If *new_x's* is omitted, it is assumed to be the same as *known_x's*.

- If both *known_x's* and *new_x's* are omitted, they are assumed to be the array {1,2,3,...} that is the same size as *known_y's*.

Const   is a logical value specifying whether to force the constant *b* to equal 1.

- If *const* is TRUE or omitted, *b* is calculated normally.

- If *const* is FALSE, *b* is set equal to 1 and the *m*-values are adjusted so that $y = m^x$.

Remarks

- Formulas that return arrays must be entered as array formulas.

- When entering an array constant for an argument such as *known_x's,* use commas to separate values in the same row and semicolons to separate rows.

Examples

This example uses the same data as the LOGEST example. The sales for the 11th through the 16th months are 33,100, 47,300, 69,000, 102,000, 150,000, and 220,000 units. Assume that these values are entered into six cells named UnitsSold.

When entered as an array formula, the following macro formula predicts sales for months 17 and 18 based on sales for the previous six months:

GROWTH(UnitsSold,{11;12;13;14;15;16}, {17;18}) equals {320,197;468,536}

If the exponential trend continues, sales for months 17 and 18 will be 320197 and 468536 units, respectively.

You could use other sequential numbers for the *x*-value arguments, and the predicted sales would be the same. For example, you could use the default value for *known_x's,* {1;2;3;4;5;6}:

GROWTH(UnitsSold,,{7;8},) equals {320197;468536}

Related Functions

Function	Description
DATA.SERIES	Fills a range of cells with a series of numbers or dates
FILL.AUTO	Copies cells or automatically fills a selection
LOGEST	Also calculates a regression curve, but returns the parameters of that curve instead of an array of *y*-values along the curve
TREND and LINEST	Similar to GROWTH and LOGEST, but fit your data to a straight line

HALT

Macro Sheets Only

Stops all macros from running. Use HALT instead of RETURN to prevent a macro from returning to the macro that called it.

Syntax

HALT(*cancel_close*)

Cancel_close   is a logical value that specifies whether a macro sheet, when encountering the HALT function in an Auto_Close macro, is closed.

- If *cancel_close* is TRUE, Microsoft Excel halts the macro and prevents the document from being closed.

- If *cancel_close* is FALSE or omitted, Microsoft Excel halts the macro and allows the document to be closed.

- If *cancel_close* is specified in a macro that is not an Auto_Close macro, it is ignored and the HALT function simply stops the current macro.

Remarks

You can prevent an Auto_Close or Auto_Open macro from running by holding down the SHIFT key while opening or closing the document.

Examples

If A1 contains the #N/A error value, then when the following macro formula is calculated, the macro halts:

```
IF(ISERROR(A1),HALT(),GOTO(D4))
```

The following macro formula at the end of an Auto_Close macro ends the macro and prevents the document from being closed:

```
HALT(TRUE)
```

Related Functions

Function	Description
BREAK	Interrupts a FOR–NEXT, FOR.CELL–NEXT, or WHILE–NEXT loop
RETURN	Ends the currently running macro

HARMEAN

Returns the harmonic mean of a data set. The harmonic mean is the reciprocal of the arithmetic mean of reciprocals.

Syntax

HARMEAN(***number1,number2,...***)

Number1,number2,...   are 1 to 30 arguments for which you want to calculate the mean. You can also use a single array or a reference to an array instead of arguments separated by commas.

Remarks

- The arguments should be numbers, or names, arrays, or references that contain numbers.

- If an array or reference argument contains text, logical values, or empty cells, those values are ignored; however, cells with the value zero are included.

- If any data point ≤ 0, HARMEAN returns the #NUM! error value.

- The harmonic mean is always less than the geometric mean, which is always less than the arithmetic mean.

- The equation for the harmonic mean is:

$$\frac{1}{H_y} = \frac{1}{n} \sum \frac{1}{Y_i}$$

Example

HARMEAN(4,5,8,7,11,4,3) equals 5.028376

Related Functions

Function	Description
AVERAGE	Returns the average of its arguments
GEOMEAN	Returns the geometric mean
MEDIAN	Returns the median of numbers
MODE	Returns the most common value in a data set
TRIMMEAN	Returns the mean of the interior of a data set

HELP

Macro Sheets Only

Starts or switches to Help and displays the specified custom Help topic. Use HELP with custom Help files to create your own Help system, which can be used just like the built-in Microsoft Excel Help.

Syntax

HELP(*help_ref*)

Help_ref is a reference to a topic in a Help file, in the form "filename!topic_number".

- *Help_ref* must be given as text.

- If *help_ref* is omitted, HELP displays the Contents topic for Microsoft Excel Help.

Remarks

- Microsoft Excel for Windows does not support the use of Help files in the text file format for custom Help. If you need to convert text Help files to the standard Help file format, you can obtain a conversion kit by contacting your software vendor or Microsoft Corporation.

- If you want to create custom Help with advanced features in Microsoft Excel for Windows, you need the Microsoft Windows Help compiler version 3.1 or later. To obtain the compiler, you can purchase the Microsoft® Windows Software Development Kit from your software vendor or Microsoft Corporation.

- In Microsoft Excel for the Macintosh, custom Help files are plain text files or text files with line breaks.

- For more information about custom Help topics, see "Creating a Custom Help Topic" in Chapter 8 in Book 2 of the *Microsoft Excel User's Guide*.

Tip In Microsoft Excel for Windows, the following macro formula switches back to Microsoft Excel when Help is active:

APP.ACTIVATE()

The following macro formula closes Help when Help is active:

SEND.KEYS("%{F4}")

Examples

In Microsoft Excel for Windows, the following macro formula displays the Help topic numbered 101 in the file CUSTHELP.DOC. The Help window remains open if the user switches to another window or application.

HELP("CUSTHELP.DOC!101")

If the custom Help file is not in the current directory, specify the full path along with the name of the file. For example:

HELP("C:\EXCEL\CUSTHELP.DOC!101")

In Microsoft Excel for the Macintosh, the following macro formula displays the Help topic numbered 101 in the file CUSTOM HELP:

```
HELP("CUSTOM HELP!101")
```

If the custom Help file is not in the current folder, specify the full path along with the name of the file. For example:

```
HELP("HARD DISK:EXCEL:HELP:
CUSTOM HELP!101")
```

HEX2BIN

Converts a hexadecimal number to binary.

If this function is not available, you must install the Analysis ToolPak add-in macro. For more information, see "Managing Add-in Commands and Functions" in Chapter 4 in Book 2 of the *Microsoft Excel User's Guide*.

Syntax

HEX2BIN(*number,places*)

Number   is the hexadecimal number you want to convert. *Number* may not contain more than 10 characters. The most significant bit of *number* is the sign bit. The remaining 9 bits are magnitude bits. Negative numbers are represented using two's-complement notation.

Places   is the number of characters to use. If *places* is omitted, HEX2BIN uses the minimum number of characters necessary. *Places* is useful for padding the return value with leading 0s (zeros).

Remarks

- If *number* is negative, HEX2BIN ignores *places* and returns a 10-character binary number.

- If *number* is negative, it cannot be less than FFFFFFFE00, and if *number* is positive, it cannot be greater than 1FF.

- If *number* is not a valid hexadecimal number, HEX2BIN returns the #NUM! error value.

- If HEX2BIN requires more than *places* characters, it returns the #NUM! error value.

- If *places* is not an integer, it is truncated.

- If *places* is non-numeric, HEX2BIN returns the #VALUE! error value.

- If *places* is negative, HEX2BIN returns the #NUM! error value.

Examples

HEX2BIN("F",8) equals 00001111

HEX2BIN("B7") equals 10110111

HEX2BIN("FFFFFFFFFF") equals 1111111111

Related Functions

Function	Description
BIN2HEX	Converts a binary number to hexadecimal
DEC2HEX	Converts a decimal number to hexadecimal
OCT2HEX	Converts an octal number to hexadecimal

HEX2DEC

Converts a hexadecimal number to decimal.

If this function is not available, you must install the Analysis ToolPak add-in macro. For more information, see "Managing Add-in Commands and Functions" in Chapter 4 in Book 2 of the *Microsoft Excel User's Guide*.

Syntax

HEX2DEC(*number*)

Number   is the hexadecimal number you want to convert. *Number* may not contain more than 10 characters (40 bits). The most significant bit of *number* is the sign bit. The remaining 39 bits are magnitude bits. Negative numbers are represented using two's-complement notation.

Remarks

If *number* is not a valid hexadecimal number, HEX2DEC returns the #NUM! error value.

Examples

HEX2DEC("A5") equals 165

HEX2DEC("FFFFFFFF5B") equals –165

HEX2DEC("3DA408B9") equals 1034160313

Related Functions

Function	Description
BIN2HEX	Converts a binary number to hexadecimal
DEC2HEX	Converts a decimal number to hexadecimal
OCT2HEX	Converts an octal number to hexadecimal

HEX2OCT

Converts a hexadecimal number to octal.

If this function is not available, you must install the Analysis ToolPak add-in macro. For more information, see "Managing Add-in Commands and Functions" in Chapter 4 in Book 2 of the *Microsoft Excel User's Guide*.

Syntax

HEX2OCT(*number,places*)

Number   is the hexadecimal number you want to convert. *Number* may not contain more than 10 characters. The most significant bit of *number* is the sign bit. The remaining 39 bits are magnitude bits. Negative numbers are represented using two's-complement notation.

Places   is the number of characters to use. If *places* is omitted, HEX2OCT uses the minimum number of characters necessary. *Places* is useful for padding the return value with leading 0s (zeros).

Remarks

- If *number* is negative, HEX2OCT ignores *places* and returns a 10-character octal number.

- If *number* is negative, it cannot be less than FFE0000000, and if *number* is positive, it cannot be greater than 1FFFFFFF.

- If *number* is not a valid hexadecimal number, HEX2OCT returns the #NUM! error value.

- If HEX2OCT requires more than *places* characters, it returns the #NUM! error value.

- If *places* is not an integer, it is truncated.

- If *places* is non-numeric, HEX2OCT returns the #VALUE! error value.

- If *places* is negative, HEX2OCT returns the #NUM! error value.

Examples

HEX2OCT("F",3) equals 017

HEX2OCT("3B4E") equals 35516

HEX2OCT("FFFFFFFF00") equals 7777777400

Related Functions

Function	Description
BIN2HEX	Converts a binary number to hexadecimal
DEC2HEX	Converts a decimal number to hexadecimal
OCT2HEX	Converts an octal number to hexadecimal

HIDE

Macro Sheets Only

Equivalent to choosing the Hide command from the Window menu. Hides the active window. For detailed information about the Hide command, see online Help.

Syntax

HIDE( )

Tip Hiding windows can speed up your macros. You can switch to hidden windows with the ACTIVATE function. You can continue to use functions that refer to specific sheets, such as FORMULA and the GET functions, even when those sheets are hidden.

Related Function

Function	Description
UNHIDE	Displays a hidden window

HIDE.OBJECT

Macro Sheets Only

Hides or displays the specified object.

Syntax

HIDE.OBJECT(*object_id_text,hide*)

Object_id_text is the name and number, or number alone, of the object, as text, as it appears in the reference area when the object is selected. The name of the object is also the text returned by the CREATE.OBJECT function, so *object_id_text* can be a reference to a cell containing CREATE.OBJECT. To give the name of more than one object, use the following format for *object_id_text*:

`"oval 3,text 2,arc 5"`

If *object_id_text* is omitted, the function operates on all selected objects. If no object is selected or if the object specified by *object_id_text* does not exist, HIDE.OBJECT returns the #VALUE! error value.

Hide is a logical value that specifies whether to hide or display the specified object. If *hide* is TRUE or omitted, Microsoft Excel hides the object; if FALSE, Microsoft Excel displays the object.

Remarks

Objects are not automatically selected after they are unhidden.

Examples

The following macro formula hides the selected object:

`HIDE.OBJECT(,TRUE)`

The following macro formula displays the object named Oval 3:

`HIDE.OBJECT("Oval 3",FALSE)`

The following macro formula displays the three specified objects:

`HIDE.OBJECT("oval 3,text 2,arc 5",FALSE)`

Related Functions

Function	Description
CREATE.OBJECT	Creates an object
DISPLAY	Controls how an object is displayed

HISTOGRAM

Macro Sheets Only

Calculates individual and cumulative percentages for a range of data and a corresponding range of data bins. For more information, see "Analyzing Statistical or Engineering Data" in Chapter 1 in Book 2 of the *Microsoft Excel User's Guide*.

If this function is not available, you must install the Analysis ToolPak add-in macro. For more information, see "Managing Add-in Commands and Functions" in Chapter 4 in Book 2 of the *Microsoft Excel User's Guide*.

Syntax

HISTOGRAM(*inprng,outrng,binrng,pareto,chartc, chart*)

Inprng is the input range.

Outrng is the first cell (the upper-left cell) in the output table.

Binrng is an optional set of numbers that define the bin ranges. The values must be in ascending order.

Pareto is a logical value.

- If *pareto* is TRUE, data in the output table is presented in both ascending-bin order and descending-frequency order.

- If *pareto* is FALSE or omitted, data in the output table is presented in ascending-bin order only.

Chartc is a logical value. If *chartc* is TRUE, HISTOGRAM generates a cumulative percentages column in the output table. If both *chartc* and *chart* are TRUE, HISTOGRAM also includes a cumulative percentage line in the histogram chart. If omitted, *chartc* is FALSE.

Chart is a logical value. If *chart* is TRUE, HISTOGRAM generates a histogram chart in addition to the output table. If omitted, *chart* is FALSE.

Related Function

Function	Description
MODE	Returns the most common value in a data set

HLINE

Macro Sheets Only

Scrolls through the active window by a specific number of columns. Returns the #VALUE! error value if the active document is a chart.

Syntax

HLINE(*num_columns*)

Num_columns is the number of columns in the active worksheet or macro sheet you want to scroll through horizontally.

- If *num_columns* is positive, HLINE scrolls to the right.

- If *num_columns* is negative, HLINE scrolls to the left.

- *Num_columns* must be between −256 and 256, inclusive.

Related Functions

Function	Description
HPAGE	Horizontally scrolls through the active window one window at a time
HSCROLL	Horizontally scrolls through a document by percentage or by column number
VLINE	Vertically scrolls through the active window by rows
VPAGE	Vertically scrolls through the active window one window at a time
VSCROLL	Vertically scrolls through a document by percentage or by row number

HLOOKUP

Searches the top row of an array for a particular value, and returns the value in the indicated cell. Use HLOOKUP when your comparison values are located in a row across the top of a table of data and you want to look down a specified number of rows. Use VLOOKUP when your comparison values are located in a column to the left or right of the data you want to find.

Syntax

HLOOKUP(*lookup_value,table_array, row_index_num*)

Lookup_value is the value to be found in the first row of the table. *Lookup_value* can be a value, a reference, or a ext string.

Table_array is a table of information in which data is looked up. Use a reference to a range or a range name, such as Database.

- The values in the first row of *table_array* can be text, numbers, or logical values.

- The values in the first row of *table_array* must be placed in ascending order: …–2, –1, 0, 1, 2,… , A–Z, FALSE, TRUE; otherwise HLOOKUP may not give the correct value.

- Uppercase and lowercase text are equivalent.

- You can put values in ascending order by selecting the values, choosing the Sort command from the Data menu, and selecting Sort By Columns and Ascending.

Row_index_num is the row number in *table_array* from which the matching value should be returned. A *row_index_num* of 1 returns the first row value in *table_array*, a *row_index_num* of 2 returns the second row value in *table_array,* and so on. If *row_index_num* is less than 1, HLOOKUP returns the #VALUE! error value; if *row_index_num* is greater than the number of rows on *table_array*, HLOOKUP returns the #REF! error value.

Remarks

- If HLOOKUP can't find *lookup_value*, it uses the largest value that is less than *lookup_value*.

- If *lookup_value* is smaller than the smallest value in the first row of *table_array*, HLOOKUP returns the #N/A error value.

Examples

	A	B	C	D	E	F	G
1		Axles	Bearings	Bolts	Gears	Tires	Wheels
2		4	3	6	2	5	1
3		5	4	7	3	6	2
4		6	5	8	4	7	3
5		7	6	9	5	8	4
6		8	7	10	6	9	5
7		9	8	11	7	10	6
8		10	9	12	8	11	7
9		11	10	13	9	12	8
10		12	11	14	10	13	9

In the preceding worksheet:

HLOOKUP("Tires",B1:G10,3) equals 6

HLOOKUP("Bolts",B1:G10,5) equals 9

HLOOKUP("Bearings",B1:G10,7) equals 8

Table_array can also be an array constant:

HLOOKUP(3,{1,2,3;"a","b","c";"d","e", "f"},2) equals "c"

Related Functions

Function	Description
INDEX	Uses an index to choose a value from a reference or array
LOOKUP and MATCH	Look up values in a reference or array
VLOOKUP	Looks in the first column of an array and moves across the row to return the value of a cell

HOUR

Returns the hour corresponding to *serial_number*. The hour is given as an integer, ranging from 0 (12:00 A.M.) to 23 (11:00 P.M.).

Syntax

HOUR(*serial_number*)

Serial_number is the date-time code used by Microsoft Excel for date and time calculations. You can give *serial_number* as text, such as "16:48:00" or "4:48:00 PM", instead of as a number. The text is automatically converted to a serial number. For more information about serial numbers, see NOW.

Note Microsoft Excel for Windows and Microsoft Excel for the Macintosh use different date systems as their default. For more information, see NOW.

Examples

HOUR(0.7) equals 16

HOUR(29747.7) equals 16

HOUR("3:30:30 PM") equals 15

Related Functions

Function	Description
NOW	Returns the serial number of the current date and time
YEAR, MONTH, DAY, WEEKDAY, MINUTE, and SECOND	Converts serial numbers into years, months, days, days of the week, minutes, and seconds respectively

HPAGE

Macro Sheets Only

Horizontally scrolls through the active window one window at a time. Use HPAGE to change the displayed area of a worksheet or macro sheet.

Syntax

HPAGE(*num_windows*)

Num_windows   specifies the number of windows to scroll through the active window horizontally. A window is defined as the number of visible columns. If three columns are visible in the window, HPAGE scrolls through in increments of three columns.

- If *num_windows* is positive, HPAGE scrolls to the right.

- If *num_windows* is negative, HPAGE scrolls to the left.

Example

The following macro formula scrolls through the active window 14 windows to the right:

```
HPAGE(14)
```

Related Functions

Function	Description
HLINE	Horizontally scrolls through the active window by columns
HSCROLL	Horizontally scrolls through a document by percentage or by column number

Function	Description
VLINE	Vertically scrolls through the active window by rows
VPAGE	Vertically scrolls through the active window one window at a time
VSCROLL	Vertically scrolls through a document by percentage or by row number

HSCROLL

Macro Sheets Only

Horizontally scrolls through the active document by percentage or by column number.

Syntax

HSCROLL(*position*,*col_logical*)

Position   specifies the column you want to scroll to. *Position* can be an integer representing the column number or a fraction or percentage representing the horizontal position of the column in the document. If *position* is 0, HSCROLL scrolls through your document to its leftmost edge. If *position* is 1, HSCROLL scrolls through your document to its rightmost edge.

Col_logical   is a logical value specifying how the function scrolls.

- If *col_logical* is TRUE, HSCROLL scrolls through the document to column *position*.

- If *col_logical* is FALSE or omitted, then HSCROLL scrolls through the document to the horizontal position represented by the fraction *position*.

Remarks

- To scroll to a specific column n, either use HSCROLL(n,TRUE) or use HSCROLL(n/256). To scroll to column 38, for example, use HSCROLL(38,TRUE) or HSCROLL(38/256).

- If you are recording a macro and move the scroll box several times in a row, the recorder only records the final location of the scroll box, omitting any intermediate steps. Remember that scrolling does not change the active cell or the selection.

Examples

The following macro formulas all scroll through the document to column 128 (column DX in A1 format), 50% of the way across the document:

```
HSCROLL(128,TRUE)
HSCROLL(50%)
HSCROLL(0.5,FALSE)
HSCROLL(128/256)
```

Also see the last example for VSCROLL.

Related Functions

Function	Description
HLINE	Horizontally scrolls through the active window by columns
HPAGE	Horizontally scrolls through the active window one window at a time
VLINE	Vertically scrolls through the active window by rows
VPAGE	Vertically scrolls through the active window one window at a time
VSCROLL	Vertically scrolls through a document by percentage or row number

HYPGEOMDIST

Returns the hypergeometric distribution. HYPGEOMDIST returns the probability of a given number of sample successes, given the sample size, population successes, and population size. Use HYPGEOMDIST for problems with a finite population, where each observation is either a success or a failure, and where each subset of a given size is chosen with equal likelihood.

Syntax

HYPGEOMDIST(*sample_s,number_sample, population_s,number_population*)

Sample_s   is the number of successes in the sample.

Number_sample   is the size of the sample.

Population_s   is the number of successes in the population.

Number_population   is the population size.

Remarks

- All arguments are truncated to integers.

- If any argument is non-numeric, HYPGEOMDIST returns the #VALUE! error value.

- If *sample_s* < 0 or *sample_s* is greater than the lesser of *number_sample* or *population_s,* HYPGEOMDIST returns the #NUM! error value.

- If *sample_s* is less than the larger of 0 or (*number_sample – number_population + population_s*), HYPGEOMDIST returns the #NUM! error value.

- If *number_sample* < 0 or *number_sample* > *number_population,* HYPGEOMDIST returns the #NUM! error value.

- If *population_s* < 0 or *population_s* > *number_population,* HYPGEOMDIST returns the #NUM! error value.

- If *number_population* < 0, HYPGEOMDIST returns the #NUM! error value.

- The equation for the hypergeometric distribution is:

$$P(X = x) = h(x;n, M, N) = \frac{\binom{M}{x}\binom{N - M}{n - x}}{\binom{N}{n}}$$

where:

x = sample_s

n = number_sample

M = population_s

N = number_population

HYPGEOMDIST is used in sampling without replacement from a finite population.

Example

A sampler of chocolates contains 20 pieces. Eight pieces are caramels, and the remaining 12 are nuts. If a person selects 4 pieces at random, the following function returns the probability that exactly 1 piece is a caramel.

HYPGEOMDIST(1,4,8,20) equals 0.363261

Related Functions

Function	Description
BINOMDIST	Returns the individual term binomial distribution
COMBIN	Returns the number of combinations for a given number of objects
FACT	Returns the factorial of a number
NEGBINOMDIST	Returns the negative binomial distribution
PERMUT	Returns the number of permutations for a given number of objects

IF

Returns one value if *logical_test* evaluates to TRUE and another value if it evaluates to FALSE.

There are two syntax forms of the IF function. Syntax 1 can be used on worksheets and macro sheets. Syntax 2 can only be used on macro sheets in conjunction with the ELSE, ELSE.IF, and END.IF functions.

Use IF to conduct conditional tests on values and formulas and to branch based on the result of that test. The outcome of the test determines the value returned by the IF function.

Syntax 1

Worksheets and macro sheets

IF(*logical_test,value_if_true,value_if_false*)

Logical_test   is any value or expression that can be evaluated to TRUE or FALSE.

Value_if_true   is the value that is returned if *logical_test* is TRUE. If *logical_test* is TRUE and *value_if_true* is omitted, TRUE is returned.

Value_if_false   is the value that is returned if *logical_test* is FALSE. If *logical_test* is FALSE and *value_if_false* is omitted, FALSE is returned.

Remarks

- Up to seven IF functions can be nested as *value_if_true* and *value_if_false* arguments to construct more elaborate tests. See the following last example.

- If you are using IF in a macro, *value_if_true* and *value_if_false* can also be GOTO functions, other macros, or action-taking functions.

For example, the following formula is allowed in a macro:

```
IF(Number>10,GOTO(Large),GOTO(Small))
```

In the preceding example, if Number is greater than 10, then *logical_test* is TRUE, the *value_if_true* statement is evaluated, and the macro function GOTO(Large) is run. If Number is less than or equal to 10, then *logical_test* is FALSE, *value_if_false* is evaluated, and the macro function GOTO(Small) is run.

- When the *value_if_true* and *value_if_false* arguments are evaluated, IF returns the value returned by those statements. In the preceding example, if the number is not greater than 10, TRUE is still returned if the second GOTO statement is successful.

- If any of the arguments to IF are arrays, every element of the array is evaluated when the IF statement is carried out. If some of the *value_if_true* and *value_if_false* arguments are action-taking functions, all of the actions are taken. For example, the following macro formula runs both ALERT functions:

```
IF({TRUE,FALSE},ALERT("One",2),
ALERT("Two",2))
```

Examples

In the following example, if the value referred to by the name File is equal to "Chart", *logical_test* is TRUE and the macro function NEW(2) is carried out, otherwise, *logical_test* is FALSE and NEW(1) is carried out:

```
IF(File="Chart",NEW(2),NEW(1))
```

The following worksheet shows actual and predicted expense for January through April.

	A	B	C
1		Actual Expenses	Predicted Expenses
2	January	1500	900
3	February	500	900
4	March	500	925
5	April	600	925

You could write a macro to check whether you are over budget for a particular month, generating text for a message with the following formulas:

```
IF(B2>C2,"Over Budget","OK")
```
equals "Over Budget"

```
IF(B3>C3,"Over Budget","OK")
```
equals "OK"

Suppose you want to assign letter grades to numbers referenced by the name Average. See the following table.

If Average is	Then return
Greater than 89	A
From 80 to 89	B
From 70 to 79	C
From 60 to 69	D
Less than 60	F

You could use the following nested IF function:

```
IF(Average>89,"A",IF(Average>79,"B",
IF(Average>69,"C",IF(Average>59,"D","F"))))
```

In the preceding example, the second IF statement is also the *value_if_false* argument to the first IF statement. Similarly, the third IF statement is the *value_if_false* argument to the second IF statement. For example, if the first *logical_test* (Average>89) is TRUE, "A" is returned. If the first *logical_test* is FALSE, the second IF statement is evaluated, and so on.

Related Functions

Function	Description
AND	Returns TRUE if all its arguments are TRUE
FALSE	Returns the logical value FALSE
NOT	Reverses the logic of its argument
OR	Returns TRUE if any argument is TRUE
TRUE	Returns the logical value TRUE

IF

Macro Sheets Only

Used with ELSE, ELSE.IF, and END.IF to control which formulas in a macro are executed. There are two syntax forms of the IF function. Syntax 2 can be used only on macro sheets; use it when you want your macro to branch to a particular set of functions based on the outcome of a logical test. Syntax 1 can be used on worksheets and macro sheets.

Syntax 2

Macro sheets only

IF(*logical_test*)

Logical_test   is a logical value that IF uses to determine which functions to carry out next—that is, where to branch.

- If *logical_test* is TRUE, Microsoft Excel carries out the functions between the IF function and the next ELSE, ELSE.IF, or END.IF function. Instructions between ELSE.IF or ELSE and END.IF are not carried out.

- If *logical_test* is FALSE, Microsoft Excel immediately branches to the next ELSE.IF, ELSE, or END.IF function.

Tips

- Use IF with ELSE, ELSE.IF, and END.IF when you want to perform multiple actions based on a condition. This method is preferable to using GOTO because it makes your macros more structured.

- If your macro ends with an error at a cell containing this form of the IF function, make sure there is a corresponding END.IF function.

Example

The following macro asks for the age of someone applying for an insurance policy. Three things can happen: If the person is under 18, the insurance agent must attach a rider for children to the policy. If the person is between 18 and 34 (younger than 35), the macro calls a subroutine macro to display a new menu. If the person is over 34, the insurance agent must use another form. This macro assumes that the subroutines AttachChildRider and InsuranceMenu are defined on other parts of the macro sheet.

	A	B	C
1	Names	Formulas	Comments
2			
3		**ApplyForInsurancePolicy**	
4	Age	=INPUT("Enter applicant's age:",1)	
5		=IF(Age<18)	
6	ChildRider	=ALERT("This policy is for adults. Do you wa	
7		=IF(ChildRider)	
8		=AttachChildRider(Age)	Runs subroutine
9		=END.IF()	
10		=ELSE.IF(Age<35)	
11		=InsuranceMenu(Age)	Runs subroutine
12		=ELSE()	
13		=ALERT("Use application form 2.",2)	
14		=END.IF()	
15		=RETURN()	

Following is the complete formula in cell B6:

```
=ALERT("This policy is for adults. Do you
want to attach a rider for children?",1)
```

Tip You can indent formulas in a macro. To indent a formula, type as many spaces as you want between the equal sign and the first letter of the formula. The following macro shows how the preceding macro looks when you indent formulas in it.

	A	B	C
1	Names	Formulas	Comments
2			
3		ApplyForInsurancePolicy	
4	Age	=INPUT("Enter applicant's age:",1)	
5		=IF(Age<18)	
6	ChildRider	= ALERT("This policy is for adults. Do you	
7		= IF(ChildRider)	
8		= AttachChildRider(Age)	Runs subroutine
9		= END.IF()	
10		=ELSE.IF(Age<35)	
11		= InsuranceMenu(Age)	Runs subroutine
12		= ELSE()	
13		= ALERT("Use application form 2.",2)	
14		=END.IF()	
15		=RETURN()	

For more information about indenting formulas in macros, see Chapter 7 in Book 2 of the *Microsoft Excel User's Guide*.

Also see examples for ARGUMENT, FILES, UNHIDE, and WHILE.

Related Functions

Function	Description
CHOOSE	Chooses a value from a list of values
ELSE	Specifies an action to take if an IF function returns FALSE
ELSE.IF	Specifies an action to take if an IF or another ELSE.IF function returns FALSE
END.IF	Ends a group of macro functions started with an IF statement

IMABS

Returns the absolute value (modulus) of a complex number in $x + y$i or $x + y$j text format.

If this function is not available, you must install the Analysis ToolPak add-in macro. For more information, see "Managing Add-in Commands and Functions" in Chapter 4 in *Book 2 of the Microsoft Excel User's Guide*.

Syntax

IMABS(*inumber*)

Inumber   is a complex number for which you want the absolute value.

Remarks

- Use COMPLEX to convert real and imaginary coefficients into a complex number.

- If *inumber* is not text, IMABS returns the #VALUE! error value.

- If *inumber* is not in the form $x + y$i or $x + y$j, IMABS returns the #NUM! error value.

- The absolute value of a complex number is:

$$IMABS(z) = |z| = \sqrt{x^2 + y^2}$$

where:

$z = x + y$i

Example

IMABS("5+12i") equals 13

Related Functions

Related functions include other complex number functions such as IMSUM, IMAGINARY, IMREAL, and so on.

IMAGINARY

Returns the imaginary coefficient of a complex number in $x + yi$ or $x + yj$ text format.

If this function is not available, you must install the Analysis ToolPak add-in macro. For more information, see "Managing Add-in Commands and Functions" in Chapter 4 in Book 2 of the *Microsoft Excel User's Guide*.

Syntax

IMAGINARY*(inumber)*

Inumber is a complex number for which you want the imaginary coefficient.

Remarks

- Use COMPLEX to convert real and imaginary coefficients into a complex number.

- If *inumber* is not text, IMAGINARY returns the #VALUE! error value.

- If *inumber* is not in the form $x + yi$ or $x + yj$, IMAGINARY returns the #NUM! error value.

Examples

IMAGINARY("3+4i") equals 4

IMAGINARY("0-j") equals -1

IMAGINARY(4) equals 0

Related Functions

Related functions include other complex number functions such as IMABS, IMSUM, IMREAL, and so on.

IMARGUMENT

Returns the argument θ, an angle expressed in radians, such that:

$$x + yi = |x + yi| \times e^{i\theta} = |x + yi|(\cos \theta + i \sin \theta)$$

If this function is not available, you must install the Analysis ToolPak add-in macro. For more information, see "Managing Add-in Commands and Functions" in Chapter 4 in Book 2 of the *Microsoft Excel User's Guide*.

Syntax

IMARGUMENT*(inumber)*

Inumber is a complex number for which you want the argument θ.

Remarks

- Use COMPLEX to convert real and imaginary coefficients into a complex number.

- If *inumber* is not text, IMARGUMENT returns the #VALUE! error value.

- If *inumber* is not in the form $x + yi$ or $x + yj$, IMARGUMENT returns the #NUM! error value.

- IMARGUMENT is calculated as follows:

$$\text{IMARGUMENT}(z) = \tan^{-1}\left(\frac{y}{x}\right) = \theta$$

where:

$$z = x + yi$$

Example

IMARGUMENT("3+4i") equals 0.927295

Related Functions

Related functions include other complex number functions such as IMABS, IMAGINARY, IMREAL, and so on.

IMCONJUGATE

Returns the complex conjugate of a complex number in $x + yi$ or $x + yj$ text format.

If this function is not available, you must install the Analysis ToolPak add-in macro. For more information, see "Managing Add-in Commands and Functions" in Chapter 4 in Book 2 of the *Microsoft Excel User's Guide.*

Syntax

IMCONJUGATE(*inumber*)

Inumber is a complex number for which you want the conjugate.

Remarks

- Use COMPLEX to convert real and imaginary coefficients into a complex number.

- If *inumber* is not text, IMCONJUGATE returns the #VALUE! error value.

- If *inumber* is not in the form $x + yi$ or $x + yj$, IMCONJUGATE returns the #NUM! error value.

- The conjugate of a complex number is:
  $$\text{IMCONJUGATE}(x + yi) = \bar{z} = (x - yi)$$

Example

IMCONJUGATE("3+4i") equals 3 – 4i

Related Functions

Related functions include other complex number functions such as IMABS, IMAGINARY, IMREAL, and so on.

IMCOS

Returns the cosine of a complex number in $x + yi$ or $x + yj$ text format.

If this function is not available, you must install the Analysis ToolPak add-in macro. For more information, see "Managing Add-in Commands and Functions" in Chapter 4 in Book 2 of the *Microsoft Excel User's Guide.*

Syntax

IMCOS(*inumber*)

Inumber is a complex number for which you want the cosine.

Remarks

- Use COMPLEX to convert real and imaginary coefficients into a complex number.

- If *inumber* is not text, IMCOS returns the #VALUE! error value.

- If *inumber* is not in the form $x + yi$ or $x + yj$, IMCOS returns the #NUM! error value.

- The cosine of a complex number is:
  $$\cos(x + yi) = \cos x \cos yi - \sin x \sin yi$$

Example

IMCOS("1+i") equals 0.83373 – 0.988898i

Related Functions

Related functions include other complex number functions such as IMABS, IMAGINARY, IMREAL, and so on.

IMDIV

Returns the quotient of two complex numbers in $x + yi$ or $x + yj$ text format.

If this function is not available, you must install the Analysis ToolPak add-in macro. For more information, see "Managing Add-in Commands and Functions" in Chapter 4 in Book 2 of the *Microsoft Excel User's Guide.*

Syntax

IMDIV(*inumber1,inumber2*)

Inumber1 is the complex numerator or dividend.

Inumber2 is the complex denominator or divisor.

Remarks

- Use COMPLEX to convert real and imaginary coefficients into a complex number.

- If *inumber1* or *inumber2* is not text, IMDIV returns the #VALUE! error value.

- If *inumber1* or *inumber2* is not in the form $x + yi$ or $x + yj$, IMDIV returns the #NUM! error value.

- The quotient of two complex numbers is:

$$\text{IMDIV}(z_1, z_2) = \frac{(a + bi)}{(c + di)} = \frac{(ac + bd) + (bc - ad)i}{c^2 + d^2}$$

Example

IMDIV("-238+240i","10+24i") equals 5 + 12i

Related Functions

Related functions include other complex number functions such as IMABS, IMAGINARY, IMREAL, and so on.

IMEXP

Returns the exponential of a complex number in $x + yi$ or $x + yj$ text format.

If this function is not available, you must install the Analysis ToolPak add-in macro. For more information, see "Managing Add-in Commands and Functions" in Chapter 4 in Book 2 of the *Microsoft Excel User's Guide.*

Syntax

IMEXP(*inumber*)

Inumber is a complex number for which you want the exponential.

Remarks

- Use COMPLEX to convert real and imaginary coefficients into a complex number.

- If *inumber* is not text, IMEXP returns the #VALUE! error value.

- If *inumber* is not in the form $x + yi$ or $x + yj$, IMEXP returns the #NUM! error value.

- The exponential of a complex number is:

$$\text{IMEXP}(z) = e^{(x+yi)} = e^x e^{yi} = e^x (\cos y + i \sin y)$$

Example

IMEXP("1+i") equals 1.468694 + 2.287355i

Related Functions

Related functions include other complex number functions such as IMABS, IMAGINARY, IMREAL, and so on.

IMLN

Returns the natural logarithm of a complex number in $x + yi$ or $x + yj$ text format.

If this function is not available, you must install the Analysis ToolPak add-in macro. For more information, see "Managing Add-in Commands and Functions" in Chapter 4 in Book 2 of the *Microsoft Excel User's Guide.*

Syntax

IMLN(*inumber*)

Inumber is a complex number for which you want the natural logarithm.

Remarks

- Use COMPLEX to convert real and imaginary coefficients into a complex number.

- If *inumber* is not text, IMLN returns the #VALUE! error value.

- If *inumber* is not in the form $x + y$i or $x + y$j, IMLN returns the #NUM! error value.

- The natural logarithm of a complex number is:

$$\ln(x + yi) = \ln \sqrt{x^2 + y^2} + i \tan^{-1}\left(\frac{y}{x}\right)$$

Example

IMLN("3+4i") equals 1.609438 + 0.927295i

Related Functions

Related functions include other complex number functions such as IMABS, IMAGINARY, IMREAL, and so on.

IMLOG10

Returns the common logarithm (base 10) of a complex number in $x + y$i or $x + y$j text format.

If this function is not available, you must install the Analysis ToolPak add-in macro. For more information, see "Managing Add-in Commands and Functions" in Chapter 4 in Book 2 of the *Microsoft Excel User's Guide.*

Syntax

IMLOG10(*inumber*)

Inumber is a complex number for which you want the common logarithm.

Remarks

- Use COMPLEX to convert real and imaginary coefficients into a complex number.

- If *inumber* is not text, IMLOG10 returns the #VALUE! error value.

- If *inumber* is not in the form $x + y$i or $x + y$j, IMLOG10 returns the #NUM! error value.

- The common logarithm of a complex number can be calculated from the natural logarithm as follows:

$$\log_{10}(x + yi) = (\log_{10} e)\ln(x + yi)$$

Example

IMLOG10("3+4i") equals 0.69897 + 0.402719i

Related Functions

Related functions include other complex number functions such as IMABS, IMAGINARY, IMREAL, and so on.

IMLOG2

Returns the base-2 logarithm of a complex number in $x + y$i or $x + y$j text format.

If this function is not available, you must install the Analysis ToolPak add-in macro. For more information, see "Managing Add-in Commands and Functions" in Chapter 4 in Book 2 of the *Microsoft Excel User's Guide.*

Syntax

IMLOG2(*inumber*)

Inumber is a complex number for which you want the base-2 logarithm.

Remarks

- Use COMPLEX to convert real and imaginary coefficients into a complex number.

- If *inumber* is not text, IMLOG2 returns the #VALUE! error value.

- If *inumber* is not in the form $x + y$i or $x + y$j, IMLOG2 returns the #NUM! error value.

- The base-2 logarithm of a complex number can be calculated from the natural logarithm as follows:

$$\log_2(x + yi) = (\log_2 e)\ln(x + yi)$$

Example

`IMLOG2("3+4i")` equals 2.321928 + 1.337804i

Related Functions

Related functions include other complex number functions such as IMABS, IMAGINARY, IMREAL, and so on.

IMPOWER

Returns a complex number in $x + yi$ or $x + yj$ text format raised to an integer power.

If this function is not available, you must install the Analysis ToolPak add-in macro. For more information, see "Managing Add-in Commands and Functions" in Chapter 4 in Book 2 of the *Microsoft Excel User's Guide.*

Syntax

IMPOWER*(inumber,number)*

Inumber is a complex number you want to raise to a power.

Number is the power to which you want to raise the complex number.

Remarks

- Use COMPLEX to convert real and imaginary coefficients into a complex number.

- If *inumber* is not text, IMPOWER returns the #VALUE! error value.

- If *inumber* is not in the form $x + yi$ or $x + yj$, IMPOWER returns the #NUM! error value.

- If *number* is non-numeric, IMPOWER returns the #VALUE! error value.

- If *number* is not an integer, it is truncated.

- A complex number raised to a power is calculated as follows:

$$(x + yi)^n = r^n e^{in\theta} = r^n \cos n\theta + ir^n \sin n\theta$$

where:

$$r = \sqrt{x^2 + y^2}$$

and:

$$\theta = \tan^{-1}\left(\frac{y}{x}\right)$$

Example

`IMPOWER("2+3i",3)` equals −46 + 9i

Related Functions

Related functions include other complex number functions such as IMABS, IMAGINARY, IMREAL, and so on.

IMPRODUCT

Returns the product of two complex numbers in $x + yi$ or $x + yj$ text format.

If this function is not available, you must install the Analysis ToolPak add-in macro. For more information, see "Managing Add-in Commands and Functions" in Chapter 4 in Book 2 of the *Microsoft Excel User's Guide.*

Syntax

IMPRODUCT*(inumber1,inumber2)*

Inumber1 is the complex number multiplicand.

Inumber2 is the complex number multiplier.

Remarks

- Use COMPLEX to convert real and imaginary coefficients into a complex number.

- If *inumber1* or *inumber2* is not text, IMPRODUCT returns the #VALUE! error value.

- If *inumber1* or *inumber2* is not in the form $x + y$i or $x + y$j, IMPRODUCT returns the #NUM! error value.

  The product of two complex numbers is:

  $(a + bi)(c + di) = (ac - bd) + (ad + bc)i$

Examples

IMPRODUCT("3+4i","5-3i") equals 27 + 11i

IMPRODUCT("1+2i",30) equals 30 + 60i

Related Functions

Related functions include other complex number functions such as IMABS, IMAGINARY, IMREAL, and so on.

IMREAL

Returns the real coefficient of a complex number in $x + y$i or $x + y$j text format.

If this function is not available, you must install the Analysis ToolPak add-in macro. For more information, see "Managing Add-in Commands and Functions" in Chapter 4 in Book 2 of the *Microsoft Excel User's Guide.*

Syntax

IMREAL(*inumber*)

Inumber   is a complex number for which you want the real coefficient.

Remarks

- Use COMPLEX to convert real and imaginary coefficients into a complex number.

- If *inumber* is not text, IMREAL returns the #VALUE! error value.

- If *inumber* is not in the form $x + y$i or $x + y$j, IMREAL returns the #NUM! error value.

Example

IMREAL("6-9i") equals 6

Related Functions

Related functions include other complex number functions such as IMABS, IMSIN, IMAGINARY, and so on.

IMSIN

Returns the sine of a complex number in $x + y$i or $x + y$j text format.

If this function is not available, you must install the Analysis ToolPak add-in macro. For more information, see "Managing Add-in Commands and Functions" in Chapter 4 in Book 2 of the *Microsoft Excel User's Guide.*

Syntax

IMSIN(*inumber*)

Inumber   is a complex number for which you want the sine.

Remarks

- Use COMPLEX to convert real and imaginary coefficients into a complex number.

- If *inumber* is not text, IMSIN returns the #VALUE! error value.

- If *inumber* is not in the form $x + y$i or $x + y$j, IMSIN returns the #NUM! error value.

- The sine of a complex number is:

$$\sin(x + yi) = \sin x \cos yi + \cos x \sin yi$$

Example

IMSIN("3+4i") equals $3.853738 - 27.016813$i

Related Functions

Related functions include other complex number functions such as IMABS, IMAGINARY, IMREAL, and so on.

IMSQRT

Returns the square root of a complex number in $x + y$i or $x + y$j text format.

If this function is not available, you must install the Analysis ToolPak add-in macro. For more information, see "Managing Add-in Commands and Functions" in Chapter 4 in Book 2 of the *Microsoft Excel User's Guide.*

Syntax

IMSQRT(*inumber*)

Inumber is a complex number for which you want the square root.

Remarks

- Use COMPLEX to convert real and imaginary coefficients into a complex number.

- If *inumber* is not text, IMSQRT returns the #VALUE! error value.

- If *inumber* is not in the form $x + y$i or $x + y$j, IMSQRT returns the #NUM! error value.

- The square root of a complex number is:

$$\sqrt{x + yi} = \sqrt{r}\cos\left(\frac{\theta}{2}\right) + i\sqrt{r}\sin\left(\frac{\theta}{2}\right)$$

where:

$$r = \sqrt{x^2 + y^2}$$

and:

$$\theta = \tan^{-1}\left(\frac{y}{x}\right)$$

Example

IMSQRT("1+i") equals $1.098684 + 0.45509$i

Related Functions

Related functions include other complex number functions such as IMABS, IMAGINARY, IMREAL, and so on.

IMSUB

Returns the difference of two complex numbers in $x + y$i or $x + y$j text format.

If this function is not available, you must install the Analysis ToolPak add-in macro. For more information, see "Managing Add-in Commands and Functions" in Chapter 4 in Book 2 of the *Microsoft Excel User's Guide.*

Syntax

IMSUB(*inumber1,inumber2*)

Inumber1 is the complex number from which to subtract *inumber2*.

Inumber2 is the complex number to subtract from *inumber1*.

Remarks

- Use COMPLEX to convert real and imaginary coefficients into a complex number.

- If *inumber* is not text, IMSUB returns the #VALUE! error value.

- If *inumber* is not in the form $x + y$i or $x + y$j, IMSUB returns the #NUM! error value.

- The difference of two complex numbers is:

$$(a + bi) - (c + di) = (a - c) + (b - d)i$$

Example

```
IMSUB("13+4i","5+3i")  equals 8 + i
```

Related Functions

Related functions include other complex number functions such as IMABS, IMAGINARY, IMREAL, and so on.

IMSUM

Returns the sum of two or more complex numbers in $x + y$i or $x + y$j text format.

If this function is not available, you must install the Analysis ToolPak add-in macro. For more information, see "Managing Add-in Commands and Functions" in Chapter 4 in Book 2 of the *Microsoft Excel User's Guide.*

Syntax

IMSUM(*inumber1,inumber2,inumber3,...*)

Inumber1,inumber2,inumber3,...   are from 1 to 12 complex numbers to add.

Remarks

- Use COMPLEX to convert real and imaginary coefficients into a complex number.

- If any argument is not text, IMSUM returns the #VALUE! error value.

- If any argument is not in the form $x + y$i or $x + y$j, IMSUM returns the #NUM! error value.

- The sum of two complex numbers is:

$$(a + bi) + (c + di) = (a + c) + (b + d)i$$

Example

```
IMSUM("3+4i","5-3i")  equals 8 + i
```

Related Functions

Related functions include other complex number functions such as IMABS, IMAGINARY, IMREAL, and so on.

INDEX

Returns the reference of the cell at the intersection of a particular row and column. If the reference is made up of nonadjacent selections, you can pick the selection to look in.

The INDEX function has two syntax forms: reference and array. The reference form always returns a reference; the array form always returns a value or an array of values.

Syntax 1

Reference form

INDEX(*reference,row_num,column_num, area_num)*

Reference   is a reference to one or more cell ranges.

- If you are entering a nonadjacent selection for *reference,* enclose *reference* in parentheses. For an example of using INDEX with a nonadjacent selection, see the fifth example following.

- If each area in *reference* contains only one row or column, the *row_num* or *column_num* argument, respectively, is optional. For example, for a single row *reference,* use INDEX(*reference,,column_num*).

Row_num is the number of the row in *reference* from which to return a reference.

Column_num is the number of the column in *reference* from which to return a reference.

Area_num selects a range in *reference* from which to return the intersection of *row_num* and *column_num*. The first area selected or entered is numbered 1, the second is 2, and so on. If *area_num* is omitted, INDEX uses area 1.

For example, if *reference* describes the cells (A1:B4,D1:E4,G1:H4), then *area_num* 1 is the range A1:B4, *area_num* 2 is the range D1:E4, and *area_num* 3 is the range G1:H4.

After *reference* and *area_num* have selected a particular range, *row_num* and *column_num* select a particular cell: *row_num* 1 is the first row in the range, *column_num* 1 is the first column, and so on. The reference returned by INDEX is the intersection of *row_num* and *column_num*.

If you set *row_num* or *column_num* to 0, INDEX returns the reference for the entire column or row, respectively.

Remarks

- *Row_num*, *column_num*, and *area_num* must point to a cell within *reference;* otherwise, INDEX returns the #REF! error value. If *row_num* and *column_num* are omitted, INDEX returns the area in *reference* specified by *area_num*.

- The result of the INDEX function is a reference and is interpreted as such by other formulas. Depending on the formula, the return value of INDEX may be used as a reference or as a value. For example, the macro formula CELL("width",INDEX(A1:B2,1,2)) is equivalent to CELL("width",B1). The CELL function uses the return value of INDEX as a cell reference. On the other hand, a formula such as 2*INDEX(A1:B2,1,2) translates the return value of INDEX into the number in cell B1.

Examples

In the following worksheet, the range A2:C6 is named Fruit, the range A8:C11 is named Nuts, and the range A1:C11 is named Stock.

	A	B	C
1		Price	Count (lbs.)
2	Apples	$0.69	40
3	Bananas	$0.34	38
4	Lemons	$0.55	15
5	Oranges	$0.25	25
6	Pears	$0.59	40
7			
8	Almonds	$2.80	10
9	Cashews	$3.55	16
10	Peanuts	$1.25	20
11	Walnuts	$1.75	12

INDEX(Fruit,2,3) equals the reference C3, containing 38

INDEX(Nuts,1,1) equals the reference A8, containing "Almonds"

INDEX(Fruit,2,4) equals the #REF! error value, because the *column_num* argument (4) is out of range

INDEX(Stock,1,2) equals the reference B2, containing "Price"

INDEX((A1:C6,A8:C11),2,2,2) equals the reference B9, containing $3.55

SUM(INDEX(Stock,0,3,1)) equals SUM(C1:C11) equals 216

SUM(B2:INDEX(Fruit,5,2)) equals SUM(B2:B6) equals 2.42

Related Functions

Function	Description
CHOOSE	Chooses a value from a list of values
HLOOKUP	Looks in the top row of an array and returns the value of the indicated cell

Related Functions

Function	Description
LOOKUP and MATCH	Look up values in a reference or array
VLOOKUP	Looks in the first column of an array and moves across the row to return the value of a cell

INDEX

Returns the value of an element in an array, selected by the row and column number indexes.

The INDEX function has two syntax forms: reference and array. The reference form always returns a reference; the array form always returns a value or array of values. Use the array form when the first argument to INDEX is an array constant.

Syntax 2

Array form

INDEX(*array,row_num,column_num*)

Array   is a range of cells entered as an array.

Row_num   selects the row in *array* from which to return a value. If *row_num* is omitted, *column_num* is required.

Column_num   selects the column in *array* from which to return a value. If *column_num* is omitted, *row_num* is required.

- If both the *row_num* and *column_num* arguments are used, INDEX returns the value in the cell at the intersection of *row_num* and *column_num*.

- If *array* contains only one row or column, the corresponding *row_num* or *column_num* argument is optional.

- If *array* has more than one row and more than one column, and only *row_num* or *column_num* is used, INDEX returns an array of the entire row or column in *array*.

- If you set *row_num* or *column_num* to 0, INDEX returns the array of values for the entire column or row, respectively. To use values returned as an array, enter the INDEX function as an array in a horizontal array of cells. Arrays are entered by pressing CTRL+SHIFT+ENTER (in Microsoft Excel for Windows) or COMMAND+RETURN (in Microsoft Excel for the Macintosh).

Remarks

Row_num and *column_num* must point to a cell within *array*; otherwise, INDEX returns the #REF! error value.

Examples

INDEX({1,2;3,4},2,2) equals 4

If entered as an array formula, then:

INDEX({1,2;3,4},0,2) equals {2;4}

Related Functions

Function	Description
CHOOSE	Chooses a value from a list of values
HLOOKUP	Looks in the top row of an array and returns the value of the indicated cell
LOOKUP and MATCH	Look up values in a reference or array
VLOOKUP	Looks in the first column of an array and moves across the row to return the value of a cell

INDIRECT

Returns the reference specified by *ref_text*. References are immediately evaluated to display their contents. Use INDIRECT to get the value stored in a cell indicated by a reference in another cell.

Syntax

INDIRECT(*ref_text,a1*)

Ref_text is a reference to a cell that contains an A1-style reference, an R1C1-style reference, or a name defined as a reference. If *ref_text* is not a valid cell reference, INDIRECT returns the #REF! error value.

A1 is a logical value that specifies what type of reference is contained in the cell *ref_text*.

- If *a1* is TRUE or omitted, *ref_text* is interpreted as an A1-style reference.

- If *a1* is FALSE, *ref_text* is interpreted as an R1C1-style reference.

Examples

If cell A1 contains the text "B2", and cell B2 contains the value 1.333, then:

INDIRECT($A$1) equals 1.333

If the workspace is set to display R1C1-style references, cell R1C1 contains R2C2, and cell R2C2 contains the value 1.333, then:

INT(INDIRECT(R1C1,FALSE)) equals 1

If B3 contains the text "George", and a cell defined as George contains the value 10, then:

INDIRECT($B$3) equals 10

Related Functions

Function	Description
OFFSET	Returns a reference offset from a given reference
TEXTREF	Converts text to a reference

INFO

Returns information about the current operating environment.

Syntax

INFO(*type_text*)

Type_text is text specifying what type of information you want returned.

Type_text	Returns
"directory"	Path of the current directory or folder
"memavail"	Amount of memory available, in bytes
"memused"	Amount of memory being used for data
"numfile"	Number of active worksheets
"origin"	Absolute A1-style reference, as text, prepended with "$A:" for Lotus 1-2-3 release 3.x compatibility
"osversion"	Current operating system version, as text
"recalc"	Current recalculation mode; returns "Automatic" or "Manual"
"release"	Version of Microsoft Excel, as text
"system"	Name of the operating environment: Macintosh = "mac" Windows = "pcdos"
"totmem"	Total memory available, including memory already in use, in bytes

Examples

The following macro formula returns 2 if two worksheets are currently open:

INFO("numfile")

Related Functions

Function	Description
CELL	Returns information about the formatting, location, or contents of a cell
DIRECTORY	Sets the current drive and directory to a specified path
GET.DOCUMENT	Returns information about a document
GET.WORKSPACE	Returns information about the workspace

INITIATE

Macro Sheets Only

Opens a dynamic data exchange (DDE) channel to an application and returns the number of the open channel. Once you have opened a channel to another application with INITIATE, you can use EXECUTE and SEND.KEYS to control the other application from a Microsoft Excel macro. (SEND.KEYS is available only with Microsoft Excel for Windows.) If INITIATE is successful, it returns the number of the open channel. All the subsequent DDE macro functions use this number to specify the channel. If INITIATE is unsuccessful, it returns the #N/A error value.

Important   Microsoft Excel for the Macintosh requires system software version 7.0 or later for this function.

Syntax

INITIATE(*app_text,topic_text*)

App_text   is the DDE name of the application with which you want to begin a DDE session, in text form. The form of *app_text* depends on the application you are accessing. The DDE name of Microsoft Excel, for example, is "Excel".

Topic_text   describes something, such as a document or a record in a database, in the application that you are accessing; the form of *topic_text* depends on the application you are accessing. Microsoft Excel accepts the names of the current documents as *topic_text*, as well as the name "System".

For more information about DDE, see Chapter 8 in Book 2 of the *Microsoft Excel User's Guide*.

Remarks

- You can specify an instance of an application by appending the application's task ID number to the *app_text* argument. If you start an application by using the EXEC function, EXEC returns the task ID number for that instance of the application.

- If more than one instance of an application is running and you do not specify which instance you would like to open a channel to, INITIATE displays a dialog box from which you can choose the instance you want. You can prevent this dialog box from appearing by disabling or redirecting errors with the ERROR function.

Examples

The following macro formula opens a channel to the document named MEMO in the application named WORD:

```
INITIATE("WORD","MEMO")
```

In Microsoft Excel for Windows, the following macro starts Word for Windows, opens a document, executes some formatting commands, and terminates the link between the two documents.

	A	B	C
1	*Names*	*Formulas*	*Comments*
2			
3		**FromWord**	
4		=EXEC("WINWORD C:\SALES.DOC",3)	Starts Word, loads file
5	Channel	=INITIATE("WINWORD","C:\SALES.DOC")	Initiates channel to Word
6		=EXECUTE(Channel,"+{(DOWN 3)}")	Selects 3 lines down
7		=EXECUTE(Channel,"%ec")	Copies the selection
8		=APP.ACTIVATE(,FALSE)	Activates Microsoft Excel
9		=SELECT("R2C3")	Selects C2
10		=PASTE()	Pastes text
11		=TERMINATE(Channel)	Terminates Word channel
12		=RETURN()	

In Microsoft Excel for the Macintosh, the following macro starts Word, executes some commands, and terminates the link between the two documents.

	A	B	C
1	*Names*	*Formulas*	*Comments*
2			
3		**FromWord**	
4		=EXEC("HardDisk:Microsoft Word")	Starts Word
5	Channel	=INITIATE("Microsoft Word","Untitled")	Initiates channel to Word
6		=EXECUTE(Channel,"^V")	Pastes Clipboard
7		=EXECUTE(Channel,"^P~")	Sends the print command
8		=APP.ACTIVATE(,FALSE)	Activates Microsoft Excel
9		=CREATE.OBJECT(6,"R9C2",,,"R15C4",,)	Creates a text box
10		=PASTE()	Pastes text into box
11		=TERMINATE(Channel)	Terminates Word channel
12		=RETURN()	

Related Functions

Function	Description
POKE	Sends data to another application
REQUEST	Returns data from another application
TERMINATE	Closes a channel to another application

INPUT

Macro Sheets Only

Displays a dialog box for user input. Returns the information entered in the dialog box. Use INPUT to display a simple dialog box for the user to enter information to be used in a macro.

The dialog box has an OK and a Cancel button. If you choose the OK button, INPUT returns the default value specified or the value typed in the edit box. If you choose the Cancel button, INPUT returns FALSE.

Syntax

INPUT(*message_text,type_num,title_text,default, x_pos,y_pos,help_ref*)

Message_text is the text to be displayed in the dialog box. *Message_text* must be enclosed in quotation marks.

Type_num is a number specifying the type of data to be entered.

Type_num	Data type
0	Formula
1	Number
2	Text
4	Logical
8	Reference
16	Error
64	Array

You can also use the sum of the allowable data types for *type_num*. For example, for an input box that can accept formulas, text, or numbers, set *type_num* equal to 3 (the sum of 0, 1, and 2, which are the type specifiers for formula, number, and text). If *type_num* is omitted, it is assumed to be 2.

- If *type_num* is 0, INPUT returns the formula in the form of text, for example, "=2*PI()/360".

- To enter a formula, include an equal sign at the beginning of the formula; otherwise the formula is returned as text.

- If the formula contains references, they are returned as R1C1-style references, for example, "=RC[-1]*(1+R1C1)".

- If *type_num* is 8, INPUT returns an absolute reference to the specified cells.

- If you enter a single-cell reference in the dialog box, the value in that cell is returned by the INPUT function.

- If the information entered in the dialog box is not of the correct data type, Microsoft Excel attempts to convert it to the specified type. If the information can't be converted, Microsoft Excel displays an error message. For information about data types, see "Converting Data Types" in the first section, "About Functions."

Title_text is text specifying a title to be displayed in the title bar of the dialog box. If *title_text* is omitted, it is assumed to be "Input".

Default   specifies a value to be shown in the edit box when the dialog box is initially displayed. If *default* is omitted, the edit box is left empty.

X_pos, y_pos   specify the horizontal and vertical position, in points, of the dialog box. A point is 1/72nd of an inch. If either or both arguments are omitted, the dialog box is centered in the corresponding direction.

Help_ref   is a reference to a custom online Help topic in a text file, in the form "filename!topic_number".

- If *help_ref* is present, a Help button appears in the lower-right corner of the dialog box. Choosing the Help button starts Help and displays the specified topic.

- If *help_ref* is omitted, no Help button appears.

- *Help_ref* must be given as text.

For more information about custom Help topics, see HELP and "Creating a Custom Help Topic" in Chapter 8 in Book 2 of the *Microsoft Excel User's Guide*.

Remarks

Relative references entered in formulas in the INPUT dialog box are relative to the active cell at the time the INPUT function is calculated. If you are using the reference entered into the dialog box in a cell other than the active cell, it may not refer to the cells you intend it to. For example, if the active cell is A3 and you enter the formula "=A1+A2" in an INPUT dialog box, intending to add the values in those cells, and then use the FORMULA function to enter the formula in cell B3, the formula in cell B3 will read "=B1+B2" because you gave a relative reference. You can use FORMULA.CONVERT to solve this problem.

Examples

In Microsoft Excel for Windows, the following macro formula displays the following dialog box:

```
INPUT("Enter the inflation rate:",1,
"Inflation Rate",,,,"CUSTHELP.DOC!101")
```

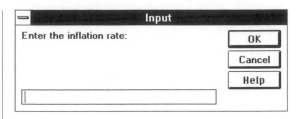

If you then enter 12%, INPUT returns the value 0.12.

In Microsoft Excel for the Macintosh, the following macro formula displays the following dialog box:

```
INPUT("Enter the inflation rate:",1,
"Inflation Rate",,,,"CUSTOM HELP!101")
```

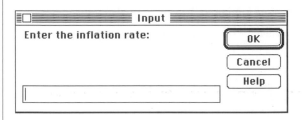

If you then enter 12%, INPUT returns the value 0.12.

If the active cell is C2 and you enter the formula =B2*(1+$A$1) in response to the following macro formula:

```
INPUT("Enter your monthly increase
formula:",0)
```

INPUT returns "=RC[-1]*(1+R1C1)"

If you select the range $A$2:$A$8 in the INPUT dialog box:

```
REFTEXT(INPUT("Please make your
selection.",8))  returns R2C1:R8C1
```

Related Functions

Function	Description
ALERT	Displays a dialog box and a message
DIALOG.BOX	Displays a custom dialog box

INSERT

Macro Sheets Only

Equivalent to choosing the Insert command from the Edit menu. Inserts a blank cell or range of cells or pastes cells from the Clipboard into a worksheet. Shifts the selected cells to accommodate the new ones. The size and shape of the inserted range are the same as those of the current selection. For detailed information about the Insert command, see online Help.

Syntax

INSERT(*shift_num*)
INSERT?(*shift_num*)

Shift_num is a number from 1 to 4 specifying which way to shift the cells. If an entire row or column is selected, *shift_num* is optional (and is ignored if specified). If *shift_num* is omitted, Microsoft Excel shifts cells in the logical direction based on the selection.

Shift_num	Direction
1	Shift cells right
2	Shift cells down
3	Shift entire row
4	Shift entire column

Remarks

If you have just cut or copied information to the Clipboard, INSERT performs both an insert and a paste operation. First, Microsoft Excel inserts new blank cells into the worksheet; then, Microsoft Excel pastes information from the Clipboard into the newly inserted cells. If you have used the INSERT function in macros written for Microsoft Excel version 2.2 or earlier, make sure you consider this feature when you use your old macros with later versions of Microsoft Excel.

Related Functions

Function	Description
COPY	Copies and pastes data or objects
CUT	Cuts or moves data or objects
EDIT.DELETE	Removes cells from a sheet
PASTE	Pastes cut or copied data

INSERT.OBJECT

Macro Sheets Only

Equivalent to choosing the Insert Object command from the Edit menu, and then selecting an object type and choosing the OK button. Creates an embedded object whose source data is supplied by another application, and places it on Microsoft Excel's object layer. Also starts an application of the appropriate class for the specified object type. For detailed information about the Insert Object command, see online Help.

Syntax

INSERT.OBJECT(*object_class*)
INSERT.OBJECT?(*object_class*)

Object_class is a text string containing the classname for the object you want to create.

- *Object_class* is the classname corresponding to the Object Type selection in the Insert Object dialog box.

- For more information about object classnames, consult the documentation for your source application to see how it supports object linking and embedding (OLE).

Remarks

- If INSERT.OBJECT starts another application, your macro pauses. Your macro resumes when you return to Microsoft Excel.

- Although you will not normally use Microsoft Excel classnames in a Microsoft Excel macro, you may need them in macros written for other applications. Microsoft Excel's classnames include "ExcelWorksheet", "ExcelChart", and "ExcelMacrosheet".

Example

The following macro formula embeds a new Microsoft Word object.

```
INSERT.OBJECT("WordDocument")
```

Related Function

Function	Description
EDIT.OBJECT	Edits an object

INT

Rounds a number down to the nearest integer.

Syntax

INT(*number*)

Number is the real number you want to round down to an integer.

Examples

INT(8.9) equals 8

INT(-8.9) equals –9

The following formula returns the decimal part of a positive real number in cell A1:

```
A1-INT(A1)
```

Related Functions

Function	Description
CEILING	Rounds a number up to the nearest integer
FLOOR	Rounds a number down, toward zero
MOD	Gives the remainder from division

Function	Description
MROUND	Returns a number rounded to the nearest multiple
ROUND	Rounds a number to a specified number of digits
TRUNC	Truncates a number to an integer

INTERCEPT

Returns the intercept of the linear regression line through data points in *known_x's* and *known_y's*. The intercept is the point at which the regression line through the values in *known_x's* and *known_y's* intersects the y-axis. Use the intercept when you want to determine the value of the dependent variable when the independent variable is zero. For example, you can use INTERCEPT to predict a metal's electrical resistance at 0°C when your data points were taken at room temperature and higher.

Syntax

INTERCEPT(*known_y's,known_x's*)

Known_y's is the dependent set of observations or data.

Known_x's is the independent set of observations or data.

Remarks

- The arguments should be numbers, or names, arrays, or references that contain numbers.

- If an array or reference argument contains text, logical values, or empty cells, those values are ignored; however, cells with the value zero are included.

- If *known_y's* and *known_x's* contain a different number of data points, or contain no data points, INTERCEPT returns the #N/A error value.

- The equation for the intercept of the regression line is:

$$a = \overline{Y} - b\overline{X}$$

where the slope is calculated as:

$$b = \frac{n\Sigma xy - (\Sigma x)(\Sigma y)}{n\Sigma x^2 - (\Sigma x)^2}$$

Example

INTERCEPT({2,3,9,1,8},{6,5,11,7,5}) equals 0.0483871

Related Functions

Function	Description
FORECAST	Returns a value along a linear trend
GROWTH	Returns values along an exponential trend
LINEST	Returns the parameters of a linear trend
LOGEST	Returns the parameters of an exponential trend
PEARSON	Returns the Pearson product moment correlation coefficient
RSQ	Returns the r^2 value of the linear regression line
SLOPE	Returns the slope of the linear regression line
STEYX	Returns the standard error of the predicted y value for each x in the regression
TREND	Returns values along a linear trend

INTRATE

Returns the interest rate for a fully invested security.

If this function is not available, you must install the Analysis ToolPak add-in macro. For more information, see "Managing Add-in Commands and Functions" in Chapter 4 in Book 2 of the *Microsoft Excel User's Guide.*

Syntax

INTRATE(*settlement,maturity,investment, redemption,basis*)

Settlement is the security's settlement date, expressed as a serial date number.

Maturity is the security's maturity date, expressed as a serial date number.

Investment is the amount invested in the security.

Redemption is the amount to be received at maturity.

Basis is the type of day count basis to use.

Basis	Day count basis
0 or omitted	30/360
1	Actual/actual
2	Actual/360
3	Actual/365

Remarks

- *Settlement, maturity,* and *basis* are truncated to integers.

- If any argument is non-numeric, INTRATE returns the #VALUE! error value.

- If *settlement* or *maturity* is not a valid serial date number, INTRATE returns the #NUM! error value.

- If *investment* ≤ 0 or if *redemption* ≤ 0, INTRATE returns the #NUM! error value.

- If *basis* < 0 or if *basis* > 3, INTRATE returns the #NUM! error value.

- If *settlement* > *maturity*, INTRATE returns the #NUM! error value.

Example

A bond has the following terms:

February 15, 1991 settlement (issue) date
May 15, 1991 maturity date
1,000,000 investment
1,014,420 redemption value
Actual/360 basis

The bond discount rate (in the 1900 Date System) is:

`INTRATE(33284,33373,1000000,1014420,2)` equals 0.058328 or 5.8328%

Related Functions

Function	Description
DATE	Returns the serial number of a particular date
RECEIVED	Returns the amount received at maturity for a fully invested security

IPMT

Returns the interest payment for a given period for an investment based on periodic, constant payments and a constant interest rate. For a more complete description of the arguments in IPMT and for more information on annuity functions, see PV.

Syntax

IPMT(*rate,per,nper,pv,fv,type*)

Rate   is the interest rate per period.

Per   is the period for which you want to find the interest, and must be in the range 1 to *nper*.

Nper   is the total number of payment periods in an annuity.

Pv   is the present value, or the lump-sum amount that a series of future payments is worth right now.

Fv   is the future value, or a cash balance you want to attain after the last payment is made. If *fv* is omitted, it is assumed to be 0 (the future value of a loan, for example, is 0).

Type   is the number 0 or 1 and indicates when payments are due. If *type* is omitted, it is assumed to be 0.

Set *type* equal to	If payments are due
0	At the end of the period
1	At the beginning of the period

Remarks

- Make sure that you are consistent about the units you use for specifying *rate* and *nper*. If you make monthly payments on a four-year loan at 12 percent annual interest, use 12%/12 for *rate* and 4*12 for *nper*. If you make annual payments on the same loan, use 12% for *rate* and 4 for *nper*.

- For all the arguments, cash you pay out, such as deposits to savings, is represented by negative numbers; cash you receive, such as dividend checks, is represented by positive numbers.

Examples

The following formula calculates the interest due in the first month of a three-year $8000 loan at 10 percent annual interest:

`IPMT(0.1/12,1,36,8000)` equals –$66.67

The following formula calculates the interest due in the last year of a three-year $8000 loan at 10 percent annual interest, where payments are made yearly:

`IPMT(0.1,3,3,8000)` equals –$292.45

Related Functions

Function	Description
ACCRINT	Returns the accrued interest for a security that pays periodic interest
ACCRINTM	Returns the accrued interest for a security that pays interest at maturity
CUMIPMT	Returns the cumulative interest paid between two periods
INTRATE	Returns the interest rate for a fully invested security
PMT	Returns the periodic payment for an annuity
PPMT	Returns the payment on the principal for an investment for a given period
RATE	Returns the interest rate per period of an annuity

IRR

Returns the internal rate of return for a series of periodic cash flows represented by the numbers in *values*. These cash flows do not have to be even, as they would be for an annuity. The internal rate of return is the interest rate received for an investment consisting of payments (negative values) and income (positive values) that occur at regular periods.

Syntax

IRR(*values,guess*)

Values is an array or a reference to cells that contain numbers for which you want to calculate the internal rate of return.

- *Values* must contain at least one positive value and one negative value to calculate the internal rate of return.

- IRR uses the order of *values* to interpret the order of cash flows. Be sure to enter your payment and income values in the sequence you want.

- If an array or reference argument contains text, logical values, or empty cells, those values are ignored.

Guess is a number that you guess is close to the result of IRR.

- Microsoft Excel uses an iterative technique for calculating IRR. Starting with *guess,* IRR cycles through the calculation until the result is accurate within 0.00001 percent. If IRR can't find a result that works after 20 tries, the #NUM! error value is returned.

- In most cases you do not need to provide *guess* for the IRR calculation. If *guess* is omitted, it is assumed to be 0.1 (10 percent).

- If IRR gives the #NUM! error value, or if the result is not close to what you expected, try again with a different value for *guess.*

Examples

Suppose you want to start a restaurant business. You estimate it will cost $70,000 to start the business and expect to net the following income in the first five years: $12,000, $15,000, $18,000, $21,000, and $26,000.

	A	B	C
1	Initial Investment	($70,000)	
2	Year 1 Income	$12,000	
3	Year 2 Income	$15,000	
4	Year 3 Income	$18,000	
5	Year 4 Income	$21,000	
6	Year 5 Income	$26,000	

To calculate the investment's internal rate of return after four years:

IRR(B1:B5) equals –2.12%

To calculate the internal rate of return after five years:

IRR(B1:B6) equals 8.66%

To calculate the internal rate of return after two years, you need to include a *guess:*

IRR(B1:B3,-10%) equals –44.35%

Remarks

IRR is closely related to NPV, the net present value function. The rate of return calculated by IRR is the interest rate corresponding to a zero net present value. The following macro formula demonstrates how NPV and IRR are related:

NPV(IRR(B1:B6),B1:B6) equals 3.60E–08 (Within the accuracy of the IRR calculation, the value 3.60E–08 is effectively 0.)

Related Functions

Function	Description
MIRR	Returns the internal rate of return where positive and negative cash flows are financed at different rates
NPV	Returns the net present value of an investment based on a series of periodic cash flows and a discount rate

Function	Description
RATE	Returns the interest rate per period of an annuity
XIRR	Returns the internal rate of return for a schedule of cash flows
XNPV	Returns the net present value for a schedule of cash flows

IS Functions

This section describes the nine worksheet functions used for testing the type of a value or reference.

Each of these functions, referred to collectively as the IS functions, checks the type of *value* and returns TRUE or FALSE depending on the outcome. For example, the ISBLANK function returns the logical value TRUE if *value* is a reference to an empty cell; otherwise it returns FALSE.

Syntax

ISBLANK(*value*)
ISERR(*value*)
ISERROR(*value*)
ISLOGICAL(*value*)
ISNA(*value*)
ISNONTEXT(*value*)
ISNUMBER(*value*)
ISREF(*value*)
ISTEXT(*value*)

Value   is the blank (empty cell), error, logical, text, number, or reference value, or name referring to any of these, that you want to test.

Function	Returns TRUE if
ISBLANK	*Value* refers to an empty cell.
ISERR	*Value* refers to any error value except #N/A.
ISERROR	*Value* refers to any error value (#N/A, #VALUE!, #REF!, #DIV/0!, #NUM!, #NAME?, or #NULL!).

Function	Returns TRUE if
ISLOGICAL	*Value* refers to a logical value.
ISNA	*Value* refers to the #N/A (value not available) error value.
ISNONTEXT	*Value* refers to any item that is not text. (Note that this function returns TRUE if *value* refers to a blank cell.)
ISNUMBER	*Value* refers to a number.
ISREF	*Value* refers to a reference.
ISTEXT	*Value* refers to text.

Remarks

- The *value* arguments to the IS functions are not converted. For example, in most other functions where a number is required, the text value "19" is converted to the number 19. However, in the formula ISNUMBER("19"), "19" is not converted from a text value, and the ISNUMBER function returns FALSE.

- If *value* is an array, the IS functions test only the first element in the array. This is true even if the formulas containing the IS functions are array formulas.

- The IS functions are useful in formulas and macros for testing the outcome of a calculation. When combined with the IF function, they provide a method for locating errors in formulas (see the following examples).

Examples

ISLOGICAL(TRUE) equals TRUE

ISLOGICAL("TRUE") equals FALSE

ISNUMBER(4) equals TRUE

	A	B	C	D
1		Gold	Silver	Oil
2	Region1	$350.89	$5.99	$20.22
3	Region2	$330.92	#REF!	$21.00
4	Region3	#N/A	$6.71	$20.50

In the preceding worksheet:

ISBLANK(C1) equals FALSE

ISERROR(C3) equals TRUE

ISNA(C3) equals FALSE

ISNA(B4) equals TRUE

ISERR(B4) equals FALSE

ISNUMBER(B3) equals TRUE (if the $330.92 was entered as a number and not as text)

ISREF(Region1) equals TRUE (if Region1 is defined as a range name)

ISTEXT(A2) equals TRUE (if Region1 is formatted as text)

On another worksheet, suppose you want to calculate the average of the range A1:A4, but you can't be sure that the cells contain numbers. The formula AVERAGE(A1:A4) returns the #DIV/0! error value if A1:A4 does not contain any numbers. To allow for this case, you could use the following formula to locate potential errors:

```
IF(ISERROR(AVERAGE(A1:A4)),"No Numbers",
AVERAGE(A1:A4))
```

Related Functions

Function	Description
GET.CELL	Returns information about the specified cell
ISEVEN	Returns TRUE if the number is even
ISODD	Returns TRUE if the number is odd
TYPE	Returns a number indicating the data type of a value

ISEVEN

Returns TRUE if *number* is even, or FALSE if *number* is odd.

If this function is not available, you must install the Analysis ToolPak add-in macro. For more information, see "Managing Add-in Commands and Functions" in Chapter 4 in Book 2 of the *Microsoft Excel User's Guide*.

Syntax

ISEVEN(*number*)

Number is the value to test. If *number* is not an integer, it is truncated.

Remarks

If *number* is non-numeric, ISEVEN returns the #VALUE! error value.

Examples

ISEVEN(-1) equals FALSE

ISEVEN(2.5) equals TRUE

ISEVEN(5) equals FALSE

Related Function

Function	Description
ISODD	Returns TRUE if the number is odd

ISODD

Returns TRUE if *number* is odd, or FALSE if *number* is even.

If this function is not available, you must install the Analysis ToolPak add-in macro. For more information, see "Managing Add-in Commands and Functions" in Chapter 4 in Book 2 of the *Microsoft Excel User's Guide*.

Syntax

ISODD(*number*)

Number is the value to test. If *number* is not an integer, it is truncated.

Remarks

If *number* is non-numeric, ISODD returns the #VALUE! error value.

Examples

ISODD(-1) equals TRUE

ISODD(2.5) equals FALSE

ISODD(5) equals TRUE

Related Function

Function	Description
ISEVEN	Returns TRUE if the number is even

JUSTIFY

Macro Sheets Only

Equivalent to choosing the Justify command from the Format menu (full menus). Rearranges the text in a range so that it fills the range evenly. For detailed information about the Justify command, see online Help.

Syntax

JUSTIFY( )

Related Function

Function	Description
ALIGNMENT	Aligns or wraps text in cells

KURT

Returns the kurtosis of a data set. Kurtosis characterizes the relative peakedness or flatness of a distribution compared to the normal distribution. Positive kurtosis indicates a relatively peaked distribution. Negative kurtosis indicates a relatively flat distribution.

Syntax

KURT(*number1,number2,…*)

Number1,number2,… are 1 to 30 arguments for which you want to calculate kurtosis.

Remarks

- The arguments should be numbers, or names, arrays, or references that contain numbers.

- If an array or reference argument contains text, logical values, or empty cells, those values are ignored; however, cells with the value zero are included.

- If there are less than four data points, or if the standard deviation of the sample equals zero, KURT returns the #DIV/0! error value.

- Kurtosis is defined as:

$$\left\{ \frac{n(n+1)}{(n-1)(n-2)(n-3)} \sum \left(\frac{x_i - \bar{x}}{s} \right)^4 \right\} - \frac{3(n-1)^2}{(n-2)(n-3)}$$

where *s* is the sample standard deviation.

Example

KURT(3,4,5,2,3,4,5,6,4,7) returns –0.1518

Related Functions

Function	Description
SKEW	Returns the skewness of a distribution
STDEV	Estimates standard deviation based on a sample
STDEVP	Calculates standard deviation based on the entire population
VAR	Estimates variance based on a sample
VARP	Calculates variance based on the entire population

LARGE

Returns the *k*-th largest value in a data set. You can use this function to select a value based on its relative standing. For example, you can use LARGE to return the highest, runner-up, or third-place score.

Syntax

LARGE(*array,k*)

Array   is the array or range of data for which you want to determine the *k*-th largest value.

K   is the position (from the largest) in the array or cell range of data to return.

Remarks

- If *array* is empty, LARGE returns the #NUM! error value.

- If $k \leq 0$ or if *k* is greater than the number of data points, LARGE returns the #NUM! error value.

If *n* is the number of data points in a range, then LARGE(*array,*1) returns the largest value and LARGE(*array,n*) returns the smallest value.

Examples

LARGE({3,4,5,2,3,4,5,6,4,7},3) equals 5

LARGE({3,4,5,2,3,4,5,6,4,7},7) equals 4

Related Functions

Function	Description
PERCENTILE	Returns the *k*-th percentile of values in a range
PERCENTRANK	Returns the percentage rank of a value in a data set
QUARTILE	Returns the quartile of a data set
SMALL	Returns the *k*-th smallest value in a data set

LAST.ERROR

Macro Sheets Only

Returns the reference of the cell where the last macro sheet error occurred. If no error has occurred, LAST.ERROR returns the #N/A error value. Use LAST.ERROR in conjunction with the ERROR function to quickly locate errors.

Syntax

LAST.ERROR( )

Related Function

Function	Description
ERROR	Specifies what action to take if an error is encountered while a macro is running

LCM

Returns the least common multiple of integers. The least common multiple is the smallest positive integer that is a multiple of all integer arguments *number1, number2,* and so on. Use LCM to add fractions with different denominators.

If this function is not available, you must install the Analysis ToolPak add-in macro. For more information, see "Managing Add-in Commands and Functions" in Chapter 4 in Book 2 of the *Microsoft Excel User's Guide.*

Syntax

LCM(*number1,number2,...*)

Number1,number2,...   are 1 to 29 values for which you want the least common multiple. If value is not an integer, it is truncated.

Remarks

- If any argument is non-numeric, LCM returns the #VALUE! error value.

- If any argument is less than one, LCM returns the #NUM! error value.

Examples

LCM(5,2) equals 10

LCM(24,36) equals 72

Related Function

Function	Description
GCD	Returns the greatest common divisor

LEFT

Returns the first (or leftmost) character or characters in a text string.

Syntax

LEFT(*text,num_chars*)

Text   is the text string containing the characters you want to extract.

Num_chars   specifies how many characters you want LEFT to return.

- *Num_chars* must be greater than or equal to zero.

- If *num_chars* is greater than the length of *text*, LEFT returns all of *text*.

- If *num_chars* is omitted, it is assumed to be 1.

Examples

LEFT("Sale Price",4) equals "Sale"

If A1 contains "Sweden", then:

LEFT(A1) equals "S"

Suppose a hardware store assigns stock numbers to its products. The first three characters of the stock number identify the product vendor. On a worksheet, assume that Stock refers to a cell containing a stock number and that VendorTable is a sorted two-column table containing all the vendor numbers in the first column and the corresponding vendor names in the second.

You can use the LEFT function to obtain the first three characters of the stock number (a vendor number) and the VLOOKUP function to return the vendor's name as shown in the following formula:

VLOOKUP(LEFT(Stock,3),VendorTable,2)

Related Functions

Function	Description
MID	Returns a specific string starting at the position you specify
RIGHT	Extracts the rightmost characters from a text value

LEGEND

Macro Sheets Only

Equivalent to choosing the Add Legend and Delete Legend commands from the Chart menu. Adds a legend to or removes a legend from a chart. For detailed information about the Add Legend and Delete Legend commands, see online Help.

Syntax

LEGEND(*logical*)

Logical   is a logical value specifying which command LEGEND is equivalent to.

- If *logical* is TRUE or omitted, LEGEND is equivalent to the Add Legend command.

- If *logical* is FALSE, LEGEND is equivalent to the Delete Legend command.

- If *logical* is FALSE and the active chart has no legend, LEGEND takes no action.

Related Function

Function	Description
FORMAT.LEGEND	Determines the position and orientation of the legend on a chart

LEN

Returns the number of characters in a text string.

Syntax

LEN(*text*)

Text is the text whose length you want to find. Spaces count as characters.

Examples

`LEN("Phoenix, AZ")` equals 11

`LEN("")` equals 0

The following macro formula starts a FOR–NEXT loop on a macro sheet. The number of iterations is equal to the length of a string named CheckText:

`FOR("Counter",1,LEN(CheckText))`

Also see the third example for CODE.

Related Functions

Function	Description
EXACT	Checks to see if two text values are identical
SEARCH	Finds one text value within another (not case-sensitive)

LINE.PRINT

Macro Sheets Only

Prints the active document using methods compatible with those of Lotus 1-2-3. LINE.PRINT does not use the Microsoft Windows printer drivers. Unless you have a specific need for the LINE.PRINT function, use the PRINT function instead.

Note This function is only available in Microsoft Excel for Windows.

Syntax 1

Go, Line, Page, Align, and Clear

LINE.PRINT(*command,file,append*)

Syntax 2

Document settings

LINE.PRINT(*command,setup_text,leftmarg, rightmarg,topmarg,botmarg,pglen,formatted*)

Syntax 3

Global settings

LINE.PRINT(*command,setup_text,leftmarg, rightmarg,topmarg,botmarg,pglen,wait,autolf,port, update*)

Command is a number corresponding to the command you want LINE.PRINT to carry out. For syntax 2, *command* must be 5. For syntax 3, *command* must be 6.

Command	Command that is carried out
1	Go
2	Line
3	Page
4	Align
5	Document settings
6	Global settings (saved in EXCEL4.INI)
7	Clear (change to current global settings)

File is the name of a file to which you want to print. If omitted, Microsoft Excel prints to the printer port determined by the current global settings.

Append is a logical value specifying whether to append text to *file*. If TRUE, the file you are printing is appended to *file*; if FALSE or omitted, the file you are printing overwrites the contents of *file*.

Setup_text is text that includes a printer initialization sequence or other control codes to prepare your printer for printing. If omitted, no setup text is used.

Leftmarg is the size of the left margin measured in characters from the left side of the page. If omitted, it is assumed to be 4.

Rightmarg is the size of the right margin measured in characters from the left side of the page. If omitted, it is assumed to be 76.

Topmarg is the size of the top margin measured in lines from the top of the page. If omitted, it is assumed to be 2.

Botmarg is the size of the bottom margin measured in lines from the bottom of the page. If omitted, it is assumed to be 2.

Pglen is the number of lines on one page. If omitted, it is assumed to be 66 (11 inches with 6 lines per inch). If you're using an HP LaserJet or compatible printer, set *pglen* to 60 (the printer reserves six lines).

Formatted is a logical value specifying whether to format the output. If TRUE or omitted, the output is formatted; if FALSE, it is not formatted.

Wait is a logical value specifying whether to wait after printing a page. If TRUE, Microsoft Excel waits; if FALSE or omitted, Microsoft Excel continues printing.

Autolf is a logical value specifying whether your printer has automatic line feeding. If TRUE, Microsoft Excel prints lines normally; if FALSE or omitted, Microsoft Excel sends an additional line feed character after printing each line.

Port is a number from 1 to 8 specifying which port to use when printing.

Port	Port used when printing
1 or omitted	LPT1
2	COM1
3	LPT2
4	COM2
5	LPT1
6	LPT2
7	LPT3
8	LPT4

Update is a logical value specifying whether to update and save global settings. If TRUE, the settings are saved in the EXCEL.INI file; if FALSE or omitted, the global settings are not saved.

Remarks

The default values for print settings on your document are determined by the current global settings.

Example

The following macro formula prints the currently defined print area to the currently defined printer port:

```
LINE.PRINT(1)
```

LINEST

Uses the "least squares" method to calculate a straight line that best fits your data and returns an array that describes the line. The equation for the line is:

$$y = m_1x_1 + m_2x_2 + \cdots + b \text{ or } y = mx + b$$

where the dependent y-value is a function of the independent x-values. The m-values are coefficients corresponding to each x-value, and b is a constant value. Note that y, x, and m can be vectors. The array that LINEST returns is $\{m_n, m_{n-1}, \ldots, m_1, b\}$. LINEST can also return additional regression statistics.

Syntax

LINEST(*known_y's,known_x's,const,stats***)**

Known_y's is the set of y-values you already know in the relationship $y = mx + b$.

- If the array *known_y's* is in a single column, then each column of *known_x's* is interpreted as a separate variable.

- If the array *known_y's* is in a single row, then each row of *known_x's* is interpreted as a separate variable.

Known_x's is an optional set of x-values that you may already know in the relationship $y = mx + b$.

- The array *known_x's* can include one or more sets of variables. If only one variable is used, *known_y's* and *known_x's* can be ranges of any shape, as long as they have equal dimensions. If more than one variable is used, *known_y's* must be a vector (that is, a range with a height of one row or a width of one column).

- If *known_x's* is omitted, it is assumed to be the array $\{1,2,3,\ldots\}$ that is the same size as *known_y's*.

Const is a logical value specifying whether to force the constant b to equal 0.

- If *const* is TRUE or omitted, b is calculated normally.

- If *const* is FALSE, b is set equal to 0 and the m-values are adjusted to fit $y = mx$.

Stats is a logical value specifying whether to return additional regression statistics.

- If *stats* is TRUE, LINEST returns the additional regression statistics, so the returned array is $\{m_n,m_{n-1},\ldots,m_1,b;se_n,se_{n-1},\ldots,se_1,se_b;r^2,se_y; F,df;ss_{reg},ss_{resid}\}$.

- If *stats* is FALSE or omitted, LINEST returns only the m-coefficients and the constant b.

The additional regression statistics are:

Statistic	Description
$se_1,se_2,$ $\ldots,se_n$	The standard error values for the coefficients $m_1,m_2,\ldots,m_n$.
se_b	The standard error value for the constant b (se_b = #N/A when *const* is FALSE).
r^2	The coefficient of determination. Compares estimated and actual y-values and ranges in value from 0 to 1. If it is 1, there is a perfect correlation in the sample—there is no difference between the estimated y-value and the actual y-value. At the other extreme, if the coefficient of determination is 0, the regression equation is not helpful in predicting a y-value. For information about how r^2 is calculated, see "Remarks" later in this topic.
se_y	The standard error for the y estimate.
F	The F statistic, or the F-observed value. Use the F statistic to determine whether the observed relationship between the dependent and independent variables occurs by chance.

Statistic	Description
df	The degrees of freedom. Use the degrees of freedom to help you find F-critical values in a statistical table. Compare the values you find in the table to the F statistic returned by LINEST to determine a confidence level for the model.
ss_{reg}	The regression sum of squares.
ss_{resid}	The residual sum of squares.

The following illustration shows the order in which the additional regression statistics are returned.

m_n	m_{n-1}	. . .	m_2	m_1	b
se_n	se_{n-1}	. . .	se_2	se_1	se_b
r^2	se_y				
F	df				
ss_{reg}	ss_{resid}				

Remarks

- You can describe any straight line with the slope and the y-intercept:

  Slope (m):
  To find the slope of a line, often written as m, take two points on the line, (x_1,y_1) and (x_2,y_2); the slope is equal to $(y_2 - y_1)/(x_2 - x_1)$.

  Y-intercept (b):
  The y-intercept of a line, often written as b, is the value of y at the point where the line crosses the y-axis.

  The equation of a straight line is $y = mx + b$. Once you know the values of m and b, you can calculate any point on the line by plugging the y- or x-value into that equation. You can also use the TREND function. For more information, see TREND.

- When you have only one independent x-variable, you can obtain the slope and y-intercept values directly by using the following formulas:

  Slope:
  INDEX(LINEST(*known_y's,known_x's*),1)

  Y-intercept:
  INDEX(LINEST(*known_y's,known_x's*),2)

- The accuracy of the line calculated by LINEST depends on the degree of scatter in your data. The more linear the data, the more accurate the LINEST model. LINEST uses the method of least squares for determining the best fit for the data. When you have only one independent x-variable, the calculations for m and b are based on the following formulas:

$$m = \frac{n\left(\sum xy\right) - \left(\sum x\right)\left(\sum y\right)}{n\left(\sum\left(x^2\right)\right) - \left(\sum x\right)^2}$$

$$b = \frac{\left(\sum y\right)\left(\sum\left(x^2\right)\right) - \left(\sum x\right)\left(\sum xy\right)}{n\left(\sum\left(x^2\right)\right) - \left(\sum x\right)^2}$$

- The line- and curve-fitting functions LINEST and LOGEST can calculate the best straight line or exponential curve that fits your data. However, you have to decide which of the two results best fits your data. You can calculate TREND(*known_y's,known_x's*) for a straight line, or GROWTH(*known_y's, known_x's*) for an exponential curve. These functions, without the *new_x's* argument, return an array of y-values predicted along that line or curve at your actual data points. You can then compare the predicted values with the actual values. You may want to chart them both for a visual comparison.

- In regression analysis, Microsoft Excel calculates for each point the squared difference between the y-value estimated for that point and its actual y-value. The sum of these squared differences is called the residual sum of squares. Microsoft Excel then calculates the sum of the squared differences between the actual y-values and the average of the y-values, which is called the total sum of squares (regression sum of squares + residual sum of squares). The smaller the residual sum of squares is compared with the total sum of squares, the larger the value of the coefficient of determination, r^2, which is an indicator of how well the equation resulting from the regression analysis explains the relationship among the variables.

- Formulas that return arrays must be entered as array formulas.

- When entering an array constant such as *known_x's* as an argument, use commas to separate values in the same row and semicolons to separate rows. Separator characters may be different depending on your country settings.

- You should note that the y-values predicted by the regression equation may not be valid if they are outside the range of the y-values you used to determine the equation.

Example 1   Slope and Y-intercept

LINEST({1,9,5,7},{0,4,2,3}) equals {2,1}, the slope = 2 and y-intercept = 1.

Example 2   Simple Linear Regression

Suppose a small business has sales of $3100, $4500, $4400, $5400, $7500, and $8100 during the first six months of the fiscal year. Assuming that the values are entered in the range B2:B7, you can use the following simple linear regression model to estimate sales for the ninth month.

SUM(LINEST(B2:B7)*{9,1}) equals SUM({1000,2000}*{9,1}) equals $11,000

In general, SUM({*m,b*}*{*x*,1}) equals $mx + b$, the estimated y-value for a given x-value. You can also use the TREND function.

Example 3   Multiple Linear Regression

Suppose a commercial developer is considering purchasing a group of small office buildings in an established business district.

The developer can use multiple linear regression analysis to estimate the value of an office building in a given area based on the following variables.

Variable	Refers to the
y	Assessed value of the office building
x_1	Floor space in square feet
x_2	Number of offices

Variable	Refers to the
x_3	Number of entrances
x_4	Age of the office building in years

This example assumes that a straight-line relationship exists between each of the independent variables (x_1, x_2, x_3, and x_4) and the dependent variable (y), the value of office buildings in the area.

The developer randomly chooses a sample of 11 office buildings from a possible 1500 office buildings and obtains the following data.

	A	B	C	D	E
1	x1	x2	x3	x4	y
	Floor Space	Offices	Entrances	Age	Value
2	2,310	2	2	20	$142,000
3	2,333	2	2	12	$144,000
4	2,356	3	1.5	33	$151,000
5	2,379	3	2	43	$150,000
6	2,402	2	3	53	$139,000
7	2,425	4	2	23	$169,000
8	2,448	2	1.5	99	$126,000
9	2,471	2	2	34	$142,900
10	2,494	3	3	23	$163,000
11	2,517	4	4	55	$169,000
12	2,540	2	3	22	$149,000

"Half an entrance" means an entrance for deliveries only. When entered as an array, the following formula:

```
LINEST(E2:E12,A2:D12,TRUE,TRUE)
```

returns the following output.

	A	B	C	D	E
14	-234.23716	2553.21066	12529.7682	27.6413874	52317.8305
15	13.2680115	530.669152	400.066838	5.42937404	12237.3616
16	0.99674799	970.578463	#N/A	#N/A	#N/A
17	459.753674	0	#N/A	#N/A	#N/A
18	1732393319	5652135.32	#N/A	#N/A	#N/A

The multiple regression equation, $y = m_1*x_1 + m_2*x_2 + m_3*x_3 - m_4*x_4 + b$, can now be obtained using the values from row 14:

$$y = 27.64*x_1 + 12,530*x_2 + 2,553*x_3 - 234.24*x_4 + 52,318$$

The developer can now estimate the assessed value of an office building in the same area which has 2500 square feet, three offices, and two entrances, and which is 25 years old, by using the following equation:

$$y = 27.64*2500 + 12530*3 + 2553*2 - 234.24*25 + 52318 = \$158,261$$

You can also use the TREND function to calculate this value. For more information, see TREND.

Example 4   Using the F and R^2 Statistics

In the previous example, the coefficient of determination, or r^2, is 0.99675 (see cell A16 in the output for LINEST), which would indicate a strong relationship between the independent variables and the sale price. You can use the F statistic to determine whether these results, with such a high r^2 value, occurred by chance.

Assume for the moment that in fact there is no relationship among the variables, but that you have drawn a rare sample of 11 office buildings which causes the statistical analysis to demonstrate a strong relationship. The term "Alpha" is used for the probability of erroneously concluding that there is a relationship.

There is a relationship among the variables if the F-observed statistic is greater than the F-critical value. The F-critical value can be obtained by referring to a table of F-critical values in many statistics textbooks. To read the table, assume a single-tailed test, use an Alpha value of 0.05, and for the degrees of freedom (abbreviated in most tables as $v1$ and $v2$), use $v1 = k = 4$ and $v2 = n - (k + 1) = 11 - (4 + 1) = 6$, where k is the number of variables in the regression analysis and n is the number of data points. The F-critical value is 4.53.

The F-observed value is 459.753674 (cell A17), which is substantially greater than the F-critical value of 4.53. Therefore, the regression equation is useful in predicting the assessed value of office buildings in this area.

Example 5   Calculating the *t*-Statistics

Another hypothesis test will determine whether each slope coefficient is useful in estimating the assessed value of an office building in example 3. For example, to test the age coefficient for statistical significance, divide –234.24 (age slope coefficient) by 13.268 (the estimated standard error of age coefficients in cell A15). The following is the *t*-observed value:

$$t = m_4 \div se_4 = -234.24 \div 13.268 = -17.7$$

If you consult a table in a statistics manual, you will find that *t*-critical, single tail, with 6 degrees of freedom and Alpha = 0.05 is 1.94 . Since the absolute value of *t*, 17.7, is greater than 1.94, age is an important variable when estimating the assessed value of an office building. Each of the other independent variables can be tested for statistical significance in a similar manner. The following are the *t*-observed values for each of the independent variables:

Variable	*t*-observed value
Floor space	5.1
Number of offices	31.3
Number of entrances	4.8
Age	–17.7

These values all have an absolute value greater than 1.94; therefore, all the variables used in the regression equation are useful in predicting the assessed value of office buildings in this area.

Related Functions

Function	Description
DATA.SERIES	Fills a range of cells with a series of numbers or dates
FILL.AUTO	Copies and automatically fills a selection

Function	Description
GROWTH and LOGEST	Similar to TREND and LINEST, but fit an exponential curve to your data instead of a straight line
TREND	Calculates a straight line, but returns an array of predicted *y*-values instead of the parameters of the line

LINKS

Macro Sheets Only

Returns, as a horizontal array of text values, the names of all worksheets referred to by external references in the document specified. Use LINKS with OPEN.LINKS to open supporting documents.

Syntax

LINKS(*document_text,type_num*)

Document_text   is the name of a document, including its path. If *document_text* is omitted, LINKS operates on the active document. If the document specified by *document_text* is not open, LINKS returns the #N/A error value.

Type_num   is a number from 1 to 6 specifying the type of linked documents to return.

Type_num	Returns
1 or omitted	Microsoft Excel link
2	DDE link
3	Reserved
4	Not applicable
5	Publisher
6	Subscriber

Remarks

- If the active document contains no external references, LINKS returns the #N/A error value.

- With the INDEX function, you can select individual worksheet names from the array for use in other functions that take document names as arguments.

- The names of the documents are always returned in alphabetic order. If supporting sheets are open, LINKS returns the names of the documents; if supporting sheets are closed, LINKS includes the full path of each document.

- If *type_num* is 5 or 6, LINKS returns a two-row array in which the first row contains the edition name and the second row contains the reference.

Examples

If a chart named Chart1 is open and contains links to worksheets Data1 and Data2, and the LINKS function shown below is entered as an array into a two-cell horizontal range:

LINKS("Chart1") equals "Data1" in the first cell of the range and "Data2" in the second cell.

In Microsoft Excel for Windows, if the chart named VARIANCE.XLC is open and contains data series that refer to worksheets named BUDGET.XLS and ACTUAL.XLS, then:

OPEN.LINKS(LINKS("VARIANCE.XLS")) opens BUDGET.XLS and ACTUAL.XLS.

In Microsoft Excel for the Macintosh, if the worksheet named SALES 1991 is open and contains references to the worksheets WEST SALES, SOUTH SALES, and EAST SALES, then:

OPEN.LINKS(LINKS("SALES 1991")) opens WEST SALES, SOUTH SALES, and EAST SALES.

Related Functions

Function	Description
CHANGE.LINK	Changes supporting worksheet links
GET.LINK.INFO	Returns information about a link
OPEN.LINKS	Opens specified supporting documents
UPDATE.LINK	Updates a link to another document

LIST.NAMES

Macro Sheets Only

Equivalent to choosing the Paste Name command on the Formula menu and selecting the Paste List option button. Lists all names (except hidden names) defined on your worksheet. LIST.NAMES also lists the cells to which the names refer; whether a macro corresponding to a particular name is a command macro or a custom function; the shortcut key for each command macro; and the category of the custom functions. For detailed information about the Paste Name command, see online Help.

Syntax

LIST.NAMES( )

Remarks

- If the current selection is a single cell or five or more columns wide, LIST.NAMES pastes all five types of information about worksheet names into five columns. The first column contains cell names. The second column contains the corresponding cell references. The third column contains the number 1 if the name refers to a custom function, the number 2 if it refers to a command macro, or 0 if it refers to anything else. The fourth column lists the shortcut keys for command macros. The fifth column contains a category name for custom functions or the number of the built-in category.

- If the selection includes fewer than five columns, LIST.NAMES omits the information that would have been pasted into the other columns.

- When you use LIST.NAMES, Microsoft Excel completely replaces the contents of the cells it pastes into.

Example

The following macro scrolls to the first unused column of the active worksheet, pastes a list of names and information about the names defined on that worksheet, and prints the list.

	A	B	C
1	Names	Formulas	Comments
2			
3		PrintNames	
4		=SELECT.SPECIAL(11)	Selects last cell with data
5		=SELECT("R1C"&COLUMN(ACTIVE.CELL(	Selects cell below and right
6		=LIST.NAMES()	Lists name information
7		=SET.PRINT.AREA()	Sets the print area
8		=PRINT(1,,,1,FALSE,FALSE,1,FALSE,1)	
9		=RETURN()	

The complete formula in cell B5 is:

```
SELECT("R1C"&COLUMN(ACTIVE.CELL())+1)
```

Related Functions

Function	Description
GET.DEF	Returns a name matching a definition
GET.NAME	Returns the definition of a name
NAMES	Returns the names defined in a document

LN

Returns the natural logarithm of a number. Natural logarithms are based on the constant e (2.71828182845904).

Syntax

LN(*number*)

Number is the positive real number for which you want the natural logarithm.

LN is the inverse of the EXP function.

Examples

LN(86) equals 4.454347

LN(2.7182818) equals 1

LN(EXP(3)) equals 3

EXP(LN(4)) equals 4

Related Functions

Function	Description
EXP	Returns e raised to the power of a given number
IMLN	Returns the natural logarithm of a complex number
IMLOG10	Returns the base-10 logarithm of a complex number
IMLOG2	Returns the base-2 logarithm of a complex number
LOG	Returns the logarithm of a number to a specified base
LOG10	Returns the base-10 logarithm of a number

LOG

Returns the logarithm of a number to the base you specify.

Syntax

LOG(*number,base*)

Number is the positive real number for which you want the logarithm.

Base is the base of the logarithm. If *base* is omitted, it is assumed to be 10.

Examples

LOG(10) equals 1

LOG(8,2) equals 3

LOG(86,2.7182818) equals 4.454347

Related Functions

Function	Description
EXP	Returns e raised to the power of a given number
IMLN	Returns the natural logarithm of a complex number
IMLOG10	Returns the base-10 logarithm of a complex number
IMLOG2	Returns the base-2 logarithm of a complex number
LN	Returns the natural logarithm of a number
LOG10	Returns the base-10 logarithm of a number

LOG10

Returns the base-10 logarithm of a number.

Syntax

LOG10(*number*)

Number is the positive real number for which you want the base-10 logarithm.

Examples

LOG10(86) equals 1.934498451

LOG10(10) equals 1

LOG10(1E5) equals 5.00E+00

LOG10(10^5) equals 5

Related Functions

Function	Description
EXP	Returns e raised to the power of a given number
IMLN	Returns the natural logarithm of a complex number
IMLOG10	Returns the base-10 logarithm of a complex number
IMLOG2	Returns the base-2 logarithm of a complex number
LN	Returns the natural logarithm of a number
LOG	Returns the logarithm of a number to a specified base

LOGEST

Calculates an exponential curve that fits your data and returns an array that describes the curve. The equation for the curve is

$$y = (b*(m_1{}^\wedge x_1)*(m_2{}^\wedge x_2)*\cdots) \text{ or } y = b*m^\wedge x$$

where the dependent y-value is a function of the independent x-values. The m-values are bases corresponding to each exponent x-value, and b is a constant value. Note that y, x, and m can be vectors. The array that LOGEST returns is $\{m_n, m_{n-1}, \ldots, m_1, b\}$.

Syntax

LOGEST(*known_y's,known_x's,const,stats*)

Known_y's is the set of y-values you already know in the relationship $y = b*m^\wedge x$.

- If the array *known_y's* is in a single column, then each column of *known_x's* is interpreted as a separate variable.

- If the array *known_y's* is in a single row, then each row of *known_x's* is interpreted as a separate variable.

Known_x's is an optional set of *x*-values that you may already know in the relationship $y = b*m^x$.

- The array *known_x's* can include one or more sets of variables. If only one variable is used, *known_y's* and *known_x's* can be ranges of any shape, as long as they have equal dimensions. If more than one variable is used, *known_y's* must be a vector (that is, a range with a height of one row or width of one column).

- If *known_x's* is omitted, it is assumed to be the array {1,2,3,…} that is the same size as *known_y's*.

Const is a logical value specifying whether to force the constant *b* to equal 1.

- If *const* is TRUE or omitted, *b* is calculated normally.

- If *const* is FALSE, *b* is set equal to 1, and the *m*-values are fitted to $y = m^x$.

Stats is a logical value specifying whether to return additional regression statistics.

- If *stats* is TRUE, LOGEST returns the additional regression statistics, so the returned array is $\{m_n,m_{n-1},…,m_1,b;se_n,se_{n-1},…,se_1,se_b;r^2,se_y; F,df;ss_{reg},ss_{resid}\}$.

- If *stats* is FALSE or omitted, LOGEST returns only the *m*-coefficients and the constant *b*.

For more information about the additional regression statistics, see LINEST.

Remarks

- The more a plot of your data resembles an exponential curve, the better the calculated line will fit your data. Like LINEST, LOGEST returns an array of values that describes a relationship among the values, but LINEST fits a straight line to your data; LOGEST fits an exponential curve. For more information, see LINEST.

- When you have only one independent *x*-variable, you can obtain the *m* and *b* values directly by using the following formulas:

  m:
  INDEX(LOGEST(*known_y's,known_x's*),1)

  b:
  INDEX(LOGEST(*known_y's,known_x's*),2)

  You can use the $y = b*m^x$ equation to predict future values of *y,* but Microsoft Excel provides the GROWTH function to do this for you. For more information, see GROWTH.

- Formulas that return arrays must be entered as array formulas.

- When entering an array constant such as *known_x's* as an argument, use commas to separate values in the same row and semicolons to separate rows. Separator characters may be different depending on your country setting.

- You should note that the *y*-values predicted by the regression equation may not be valid if they are outside the range of *y*-values you used to determine the equation.

Example

After 10 months of sluggish sales, a company experiences exponential growth in sales after putting a new product on the market. In the subsequent 6 months, sales increased to 33,100, 47,300, 69,000, 102,000, 150,000, and 220,000 units per month. Assume that these values are entered into six cells named UnitsSold. When entered as an array formula:

```
LOGEST(UnitsSold,{11;12;13;14;15;16},TRUE,
TRUE)
```

generates the following output.

	D	E	F
1	1.46327563	495.30477	
2	0.0026334	0.03583428	
3	0.99980862	0.01101631	
4	20896.8011	4	
5	2.53601883	0.00048544	

$y = b*m_1{}^\wedge x_1$ or using the values from cells D1:E1:

$y = 495.3 * 1.4633^x$

You can estimate sales for future months by substituting the month number for x in this equation, or you can use the GROWTH function. For more information, see GROWTH.

You can use the additional regression statistics (cells D2:E5) to determine how useful the equation is for predicting future values.

Important   The methods you use to test an equation using LOGEST are similar to the methods for LINEST. However, the additional statistics LOGEST returns are based on the following linear model:

$$\ln y = x_1 \ln m_1 + \cdots + x_n \ln m_n + \ln b$$

You should keep this in mind when you evaluate the additional statistics, especially the se_i and se_b values, which should be compared to $\ln m_i$ and $\ln b$, not to m_i and b. For more information, consult an advanced statistics manual.

Related Functions

Function	Description
DATA.SERIES	Fills a range of cells with a series of numbers or dates
FILL.AUTO	Copies cells or automatically fills a selection
GROWTH	Also calculates an exponential curve, but returns an array of predicted y-values instead of the parameters of the curve
LINEST and TREND	Similar to LOGEST and GROWTH but fit a straight line instead of an exponential curve to your data

LOGINV

Returns the inverse of the lognormal cumulative distribution function of x, where $\ln(x)$ is normally distributed with parameters *mean* and *standard_dev*. If $p = \text{LOGNORMDIST}(x,\ldots)$ then $\text{LOGINV}(p,\ldots) = x$.

Use the lognormal distribution to analyze logarithmically transformed data.

Syntax

LOGINV(*probability,mean,standard_dev*)

Probability   is a probability associated with the lognormal distribution.

Mean   is the mean of $\ln(x)$.

Standard_dev   is the standard deviation of $\ln(x)$.

The inverse of the lognormal distribution function is:

$$\text{LOGINV}(p, \mu, \sigma) = e^{[\mu + \sigma \times (NORMSINV(p))]}$$

Remarks

- If any argument is non-numeric, LOGINV returns the #VALUE! error value.

- If *probability* < 0 or *probability* > 1, LOGINV returns the #NUM! error value.

- If *standard_dev* ≤ 0, LOGINV returns the #NUM! error value.

Example

`LOGINV(0.039084,3.5,1.2)` equals 4.000014

Related Functions

Function	Description
EXP	Returns e raised to the power of a given number
LN	Returns the natural logarithm of a number

Function	Description
LOG	Returns the logarithm of a number to a specified base
LOG10	Returns the base-10 logarithm of a number
LOGNORMDIST	Returns the lognormal distribution

LOGNORMDIST

Returns the lognormal cumulative distribution function of x, where $\ln(x)$ is normally distributed with parameters *mean* and *standard_dev*. Use this function to analyze data that has been logarithmically transformed.

Syntax

LOGNORMDIST(*x,mean,standard_dev*)

X is the value at which to evaluate the function.

Mean   is the mean of $\ln(x)$.

Standard_dev   is the standard deviation of $\ln(x)$.

Remarks

- If any argument is non-numeric, LOGNORMDIST returns the #VALUE! error value.

- If $x \leq 0$ or if *standard_dev* ≤ 0, LOGNORMDIST returns the #NUM! error value.

- The equation for the lognormal cumulative distribution function is:

$$LOGNORMDIST(x, \mu, \sigma) =$$
$$NORMSDIST\left(\frac{\ln(x) - \mu}{\sigma}\right)$$

Example

LOGNORMDIST(4,3.5,1.2) equals 0.039084

Related Functions

Function	Description
EXP	Returns *e* raised to the power of a given number
LN	Returns the natural logarithm of a number
LOG	Returns the logarithm of a number to a specified base
LOG10	Returns the base-10 logarithm of a number
LOGINV	Returns the inverse of the lognormal distribution

LOOKUP

The LOOKUP function has two syntax forms, vector and array. This section discusses the vector form; the next section discusses the array form.

A vector is an array that contains only one row or one column. The vector form of LOOKUP looks in a vector for a value, moves to the corresponding position in a second vector, and returns this value. Use this form of the LOOKUP function when you want to be able to specify the range that contains the values you want to match. The other form of LOOKUP automatically looks in the first column or row.

Syntax 1

Vector form

LOOKUP(*lookup_value,lookup_vector, result_vector*)

Lookup_value   is a value that LOOKUP searches for in the first vector. *Lookup_value* can be a number, text, a logical value, or a name or reference that refers to a value.

Lookup_vector   is a range that contains only one row or one column. The values in *lookup_vector* can be text, numbers, or logical values.

Important The values must be placed in ascending order: ,–2, –1, 0, 1, 2, ...,, A–Z, FALSE, TRUE; otherwise, LOOKUP may not give the correct value. Uppercase and lowercase text are equivalent.

Result_vector is a range that contains only one row or column. It should be the same size as *lookup_vector*.

- If LOOKUP can't find the *lookup_value*, it matches the largest value in *lookup_vector* that is less than or equal to *lookup_value*.

- If *lookup_value* is smaller than the smallest value in *lookup_vector*, LOOKUP gives the #N/A error value.

Examples

	A	B	C
1	Frequency	Color	
2	4.14234	red	
3	4.19342	orange	
4	5.17234	yellow	
5	5.77343	green	
6	6.38987	blue	
7	7.31342	violet	

In the preceding worksheet:

LOOKUP(4.91,A2:A7,B2:B7) equals "orange"

LOOKUP(5.00,A2:A7,B2:B7) equals "orange"

LOOKUP(7.66,A2:A7,B2:B7) equals "violet"

LOOKUP(7.66E-14,A2:A7,B2:B7) equals #N/A, because 7.66E–14 is less than the smallest value in the *lookup_vector* A2:A7

Related Functions

Function	Description
HLOOKUP	Looks in the top row of an array and returns the value of the indicated cell
INDEX	Uses an index to choose a value from a reference or array
VLOOKUP	Looks in the first column of an array and moves across the row to return the value of a cell

LOOKUP

The LOOKUP function has two syntax forms, vector and array. This section discusses the array form; the previous section discusses the vector form.

The array form of LOOKUP looks in the first row or column of an array for the specified value, moves down or across to the last cell, and returns the value of the cell. Use this form of LOOKUP when the values you want to match are in the first row or column of the array. Use the other form of LOOKUP when you want to be able to specify the location of the column or row.

Tip In general, it's best to use the HLOOKUP or VLOOKUP function instead of the array form of LOOKUP. This form of LOOKUP is provided for compatibility with other spreadsheet programs.

Syntax 2

Array form

LOOKUP(*lookup_value,array*)

Lookup_value is a value that LOOKUP searches for in an array. *Lookup_value* can be a number, text, a logical value, or a name or reference that refers to a value.

- If LOOKUP can't find the *lookup_value*, it uses the largest value in the array that is less than or equal to *lookup_value*.

- If *lookup_value* is smaller than the smallest value in the first row or column (depending on the array dimensions), LOOKUP returns the #N/A error value.

Array   is a range of cells that contains text, numbers, or logical values that you want to compare with *lookup_value*.

The array form of LOOKUP is very similar to the HLOOKUP and VLOOKUP functions. The difference is that HLOOKUP searches for *lookup_value* in the first row, VLOOKUP searches in the first column, and LOOKUP searches according to the dimensions of *array*.

- If *array* is square, or covers an area that is wider than it is tall (more columns than rows), LOOKUP searches for *lookup_value* in the first row.

- If *array* is taller than it is wide (more rows than columns), LOOKUP searches in the first column.

- HLOOKUP and VLOOKUP allow you to index down or across, but LOOKUP always selects the last value in the row or column.

Important   The values must be placed in ascending order: ...,–2, –1, 0, 1, 2, ..., A–Z, FALSE, TRUE; otherwise, LOOKUP may not give the correct value. Uppercase and lowercase text are equivalent.

Examples

LOOKUP("C",{"a","b","c","d";1,2,3,4}) equals 3

LOOKUP("bump",{"a",1;"b",2;"c",3}) equals 2

Related Functions

Function	Description
HLOOKUP	Looks in the top row of an array and returns the value of the indicated cell
INDEX	Uses an index to choose a value from a reference or array
MATCH	Looks up values in a vector or array
VLOOKUP	Looks in the first column of an array and moves across the row to return the value of a cell

LOWER

Converts all uppercase letters in a text string to lowercase.

Syntax

LOWER(*text*)

Text   is the text you want to convert to lowercase. LOWER does not change characters in *text* that are not letters.

Examples

LOWER("E. E. Cummings") equals "e. e. cummings"

LOWER("Apt. 2B") equals "apt. 2b"

Lower is similar to PROPER and UPPER. Also see examples for PROPER.

Related Functions

Function	Description
PROPER	Capitalizes the first letter in each word of a text value
UPPER	Converts text to uppercase

MAIN.CHART

Macro Sheets Only

Equivalent to choosing the Main Chart command from the Format menu when a chart document is active in Microsoft Excel version 2.2 or earlier. This function is included only for macro compatibility. To format main charts in Microsoft Excel version 3.0 or later, use the FORMAT.MAIN function.

Syntax

MAIN.CHART(*type_num,stack,100,vary,overlap, drop,hilo,overlap%,cluster,angle*)
MAIN.CHART?(*type_num,stack,100,vary,overlap, drop,hilo,overlap%,cluster,angle*)

MAIN.CHART.TYPE

Macro Sheets Only

Equivalent to choosing the Main Chart Type command from the Chart menu in Microsoft Excel for the Macintosh version 1.5 or earlier. This function is included only for macro compatibility. To format a main chart or to specify a main chart type in Microsoft Excel version 3.0 or later, use the FORMAT.MAIN function, which is equivalent to the Main Chart command on the Format menu.

Syntax

MAIN.CHART.TYPE(*type_num*)

MATCH

Returns the relative position of an element in an array that matches a specified value in a specified way. Use MATCH instead of one of the LOOKUP functions when you need the position of a matched item instead of the item itself.

Syntax

MATCH(*lookup_value,lookup_array, match_type*)

Lookup_value   is the value you use to find the value you want in a table.

- *Lookup_value* is the value you want to match in *lookup_array*. For example, when you look up someone's number in a telephone book, you are using the person's name as the lookup value, but the telephone number is the value you want.

- *Lookup_value* can be a value (number, text, or logical value) or a cell reference to a number, text, or logical value.

Lookup_array   is a contiguous range of cells containing possible lookup values. *Lookup_array* can be an array or an array reference.

Match_type   is the number –1, 0, or 1. *Match_type* specifies how Microsoft Excel matches *lookup_value* with values in *lookup_array*.

- If *match_type* is 1, MATCH finds the largest value that is less than or equal to *lookup_value*. *Lookup_array* must be placed in ascending order: …–2, –1, 0, 1, 2,…A–Z, FALSE, TRUE.

- If *match_type* is 0, MATCH finds the first value that is exactly equal to *lookup_value*. *Lookup_array* can be in any order.

- If *match_type* is –1, MATCH finds the smallest value that is greater than or equal to *lookup_value*. *Lookup_array* must be placed in descending order: TRUE, FALSE, Z–A,…2, 1, 0, –1, –2,…, and so on.

- If *match_type* is omitted, it is assumed to be 1.

Remarks

- MATCH returns the position of the matched value within *lookup_array*, not the value itself. For example: MATCH("b",{"a","b","c"},0) returns 2, the relative position of "b" within the array {"a","b","c"}.

- MATCH does not distinguish between uppercase and lowercase letters when matching text values.

- If MATCH is unsuccessful in finding a match, it returns the #N/A error value.

- If *match_type* is 0 and *lookup_value* is text, *lookup_value* can contain the wildcard characters, asterisk (*) and question mark (?). An asterisk matches any sequence of characters; a question mark matches any single character.

Examples

	A	B	C
1	Income (in Yen)	U.S. Dollars	U.S. Tax Rate
2	¥5,365,000.00	$37,000.00	21.50%
3	¥5,510,000.00	$38,000.00	21.67%
4	¥5,655,000.00	$39,000.00	21.84%
5	¥5,800,000.00	$40,000.00	21.99%
6	¥5,945,000.00	$41,000.00	22.14%
7	¥6,090,000.00	$42,000.00	22.28%
8	¥6,235,000.00	$43,000.00	22.41%
9	¥6,380,000.00	$44,000.00	22.54%
10	¥6,525,000.00	$45,000.00	22.67%
11	¥6,670,000.00	$46,000.00	22.90%
12	¥6,815,000.00	$47,000.00	23.11%
13	¥6,960,000.00	$48,000.00	23.32%
14	¥7,105,000.00	$49,000.00	23.51%
15	¥7,249,998.55	$49,999.99	23.69%

Note that C2:C15 contains text formatted as percent numbers.

In the preceding worksheet:

MATCH(39000,B2:B15,1) equals 3

MATCH(49800,B2:B15) equals 13

MATCH(38000,B2:B15,0) equals 2

MATCH(39000,B2:B15,-1) equals the #N/A error value because the range B2:B15 is ordered incorrectly for *match_type* –1 matching (the order must be descending to be correct).

MATCH("22*",C2:C15,0) equals 5 because MATCH looks for the first text beginning with 22.

MATCH("2?.32%",C2:C15,0) equals 12

Suppose Yen refers to A2:A15, YenDollar to A2:C15, and MyIncome to a cell containing the number ¥6,301,126.33. This formula:

"Your tax rate is "&LOOKUP(MyIncome, YenDollar)&", which places you in tax bracket number "&MATCH(MyIncome,Yen)&"."

produces this result:

"Your tax rate is 22.41%, which places you in tax bracket number 7."

Related Functions

Function	Description
HLOOKUP, VLOOKUP, and LOOKUP	Look up values in a reference or array
INDEX	Uses an index to choose a value from a reference or array

MAX

Returns the largest number in the list of arguments.

Syntax

MAX(*number1,number2,...*)

Number1, number2,... are 1 to 30 numbers for which you want to find the maximum value.

- You can specify arguments that are numbers, empty cells, logical values, or text representations of numbers. Arguments that are error values or text that cannot be translated into numbers cause errors.

- If an argument is an array or reference, only numbers in that array or reference are used. Empty cells, logical values, text, or error values in the array or reference are ignored.

- If the arguments contain no numbers, MAX returns 0.

Examples

If A1:A5 contains the numbers 10, 7, 9, 27, and 2, then:

MAX(A1:A5) equals 27

MAX(A1:A5,30) equals 30

Suppose you have a worksheet containing columns of text and one column of numbers (each row contains several text cells and one number cell). The following macro finds the row on the active worksheet containing the largest number and selects this row so that it will be easier to find among the other rows.

	A	B	C
1	Names	Formulas	Comments
2			
3		FindMaximumValue	
4		=SELECT(!$A$1)	Searches from first cell
5	MaxValue	=MAX(!$1:$16384)	Searches entire worksheet
6		=FORMULA.FIND(MaxValue,2,1,1,1)	Moves to cell with max value
7		=SELECT("R")	Selects that row
8		=RETURN()	

Related Functions

Function	Description
DMAX	Returns the maximum value from selected database entries
MIN	Returns the minimum value in a list of arguments

MCORREL

Macro Sheets Only

Returns a correlation matrix that measures the correlation between two or more data sets that are scaled to be independent of the unit of measurement. For more information, see "Analyzing Statistical or Engineering Data" in Chapter 1 in Book 2 of the *Microsoft Excel User's Guide*.

If this function is not available, you must install the Analysis ToolPak add-in macro. For more information, see "Managing Add-in Commands and Functions" in Chapter 4 in Book 2 of the *Microsoft Excel User's Guide*.

Syntax

MCORREL(*inprng,outrng,grouped,labels*)

Inprng is the input range.

Outrng is the first cell (the upper-left cell) in the output table.

Grouped is a text character that indicates whether the data in the input range is organized by row or column.

- If *grouped* is "C" or omitted, then the data is organized by column.

- If *grouped* is "R", then the data is organized by row.

Labels is a logical value that describes where the labels are located in the input range, as shown in the following table:

Labels	Grouped	Labels are in
TRUE	"C"	First row of the input range.
TRUE	"R"	First column of the input range.
FALSE or omitted	(ignored)	No labels. All cells in the input range are data.

Related Functions

Function	Description
CORREL	Returns the correlation coefficient between two data sets
COVAR	Returns covariance, the average of products of paired deviations
MCOVAR	Returns the covariance between two or more data sets

MCOVAR

Macro Sheets Only

Returns a covariance matrix that measures the covariance between two or more data sets. For more information, see "Analyzing Statistical or Engineering Data" in Chapter 1 in Book 2 of the *Microsoft Excel User's Guide*.

If this function is not available, you must install the Analysis ToolPak add-in macro. For more information, see "Managing Add-in Commands and Functions" in Chapter 4 in Book 2 of the *Microsoft Excel User's Guide*.

Syntax

MCOVAR*(inprng,outrng,grouped,labels)*

Inprng   is the input range.

Outrng   is the first cell (the upper-left cell) in the output table.

Grouped   is a text character that indicates whether the data in the input range is organized by row or column.

■ If *grouped* is "C" or omitted, then the data is organized by column.

■ If *grouped* is "R", then the data is organized by row.

Labels   is a logical value that describes where the labels are located in the input range, as shown in the following table:

Labels	Grouped	Labels are in
TRUE	"C"	First row of the input range
TRUE	"R"	First column of the input range
FALSE or omitted	(ignored)	No labels. All cells in the input range are data.

Related Functions

Function	Description
CORREL	Returns the correlation coefficient between two data sets
COVAR	Returns covariance, the average of products of paired deviations
MCORREL	Returns the correlation coefficient of two or more data sets that are scaled to be independent of the unit of measurement

MDETERM

Returns the matrix determinant of an array.

Syntax

MDETERM*(array)*

Array   is a numeric array with an equal number of rows and columns.

■ *Array* can be given as a cell range, for example, A1:C3; as an array constant, such as {1,2,3;4,5,6;7,8,9}; or as a name to either of these.

■ If any cells in *array* are empty or contain text, MDETERM returns the #VALUE! error value.

■ MDETERM also returns #VALUE! if *array* does not have an equal number of rows and columns.

Remarks

- The matrix determinant is a number derived from the values in *array*. For a three-row, three-column array, A1:C3, the determinant is defined as:

  MDETERM(A1:C3) equals
  A1*(B2*C3–B3*C2) + A2*(B3*C1–B1*C3) + A3*(B1*C2–B2*C1)

- Matrix determinants are generally used for solving systems of mathematical equations that involve several variables.

- MDETERM is calculated with an accuracy of approximately 16 digits, which may lead to a small numeric error when the cancellation is not complete. For example, the determinant of a singular matrix may differ from zero by 1E–16.

Examples

	A	B	C	D	E
1	1	3	8	5	
2	1	3	6	1	
3	1	1	1	0	
4	7	9	10	2	

In the preceding worksheet:

MDETERM(A1:D4) equals –20

MDETERM(B2:D4) equals –5

MDETERM(B2:C3) equals –3

MDETERM(A1:D2) equals #VALUE! because the range A1:D2 does not have an equal number of rows and columns.

MDETERM(A1:E5) equals #VALUE! because A1:E5 contains empty cells.

Related Functions

Function	Description
MINVERSE	Returns the matrix inverse of an array
MMULT	Returns the matrix product of two arrays
TRANSPOSE	Returns the transpose of an array

MDURATION

Returns the modified Macauley duration for a security with an assumed par value of $100.

If this function is not available, you must install the Analysis ToolPak add-in macro. For more information, see "Managing Add-in Commands and Functions" in Chapter 4 in Book 2 of the *Microsoft Excel User's Guide*.

Syntax

MDURATION(*settlement,maturity,coupon,yld, frequency,basis*)

Settlement is the security's settlement date, expressed as a serial date number.

Maturity is the security's maturity date, expressed as a serial date number.

Coupon is the security's annual coupon rate.

Yld is the security's annual yield.

Frequency is the number of coupon payments per year. For annual payments, *frequency* = 1; for semi-annual, *frequency* = 2; for quarterly, *frequency* = 4.

Basis is the type of day count basis to use.

Basis	Day count basis
0 or omitted	30/360
1	Actual/actual
2	Actual/360
3	Actual/365

Remarks

- *Settlement, maturity, frequency,* and *basis* are truncated to integers.

- If any argument is non-numeric, MDURATION returns the #VALUE! error value.

- If *settlement* or *maturity* is not a valid serial date number, MDURATION returns the #NUM! error value.

- If *yld* < 0 or if *coupon* < 0, MDURATION returns the #NUM! error value.

- If *frequency* is any number other than 1, 2, or 4, MDURATION returns the #NUM! error value.

- If *basis* < 0 or if *basis* > 3, MDURATION returns the #NUM! error value.

- If *settlement* ≥ *maturity,* MDURATION returns the #NUM! error value.

- Modified duration is defined as follows:

$$\text{MDURATION} = \frac{\text{DURATION}}{1 + \left(\dfrac{\text{Market yield}}{\text{Coupon payments per year}} \right)}$$

Example

A bond has the following terms:

January 1, 1986 settlement date
January 1, 1994 maturity date
8.0% semiannual coupon
9.0% yield
Actual/actual basis

The modified duration (in the 1900 Date System) is:

MDURATION(33239,36631,0.8,0.9,2,1) equals 5.73567

Related Functions

Function	Description
DATE	Returns the serial number of a particular date
DURATION	Returns the annual duration of a security with periodic interest payments

MEDIAN

Returns the median of the given numbers. The median is the number in the middle of a set of numbers; that is, half the numbers have values that are greater than the median and half have values that are less.

Syntax

MEDIAN(*number1,number2,...*)

Number1, number2,... are 1 to 30 numbers for which you want the median.

- The arguments should be numbers or names, arrays, or references that contain numbers. Microsoft Excel examines all the numbers in each reference or array argument.

- If an array or reference argument contains text, logical values, or empty cells, those values are ignored; however, cells with the value zero are included.

Remarks

If there is an even number of numbers in the set, then MEDIAN calculates the average of the two numbers in the middle. See the second example following.

Examples

MEDIAN(1,2,3,4,5) equals 3

MEDIAN(1,2,3,4,5,6) equals 3.5, the average of 3 and 4

Related Functions

Function	Description
AVERAGE	Returns the average of its arguments
COUNT	Counts how many numbers are in the list of arguments
COUNTA	Counts how many values are in the list of arguments
DAVERAGE	Returns the average of selected database entries
MODE	Returns the most common value in a data set
SUM	Adds its arguments

MERGE.STYLES

Macro Sheets Only

Equivalent to choosing the Merge button from the Style dialog box, which appears when you choose the Style command from the Format menu. Merges all the styles from another document into the active document. Use MERGE.STYLES when you want to import styles from another document. For detailed information about the Style command, see online Help.

Syntax

MERGE.STYLES(*document_text*)

Document_text is the name of a document from which you want to merge styles into the active document.

Remarks

If any styles from the document being merged have the same name as styles in the active document, a dialog box appears asking if you want to replace the existing definitions of the styles with the "merged" definitions of the styles. If you choose the Yes button, all the definitions are replaced; if you choose the No button, all the original definitions in the active document are retained.

Examples

In Microsoft Excel for Windows, the following macro formula merges the styles from the document REPORT.XLS into the active document:

```
MERGE.STYLES("REPORT.XLS")
```

In Microsoft Excel for the Macintosh, the following macro formula merges the styles from the document REPORT into the active document:

```
MERGE.STYLES("REPORT")
```

Related Functions

Function	Description
DEFINE.STYLE	Creates or changes a cell style
DELETE.STYLE	Deletes a cell style

MESSAGE

Macro Sheets Only

Displays and removes messages in the message area of the status bar. MESSAGE is useful for displaying text that doesn't need a response, such as commands in user-defined menus.

Syntax

MESSAGE(*logical,text*)

Logical is a logical value specifying whether to display or remove a message.

- If *logical* is TRUE, Microsoft Excel displays *text* in the message area of the status bar.

- If *logical* is FALSE, Microsoft Excel removes any messages, and the status bar is returned to normal (that is, command help messages are displayed).

Text is the message you want to display in the status bar. If *text* is "" (empty text), Microsoft Excel removes any messages currently displayed in the status bar.

Remarks

- Only one message can be displayed in the status bar at a time. Messages are always displayed in the same place.

- MESSAGE works the same way whether the status bar is displayed or not. You can, for example, use MESSAGE while the status bar isn't displayed. As soon as you display the status bar, you see your message.

- If you display any message (even empty text) and don't remove it with MESSAGE(FALSE), that message is displayed until you quit Microsoft Excel.

Example

The following lines in a macro display a message warning that you must wait for a moment while the macro calls a subroutine. Only the last few lines of the calling macro are shown. Assume that the subroutine FindRoot is defined on another part of the worksheet.

	A	B	C
33		=BEEP()	Signals the message
34		=MESSAGE(TRUE,"One moment please...")	Displays the message
35		=FindRoot(Polynomial)	Calls the subroutine
36		=MESSAGE(FALSE)	
37		=RETURN()	

You could also use the ALERT function to get the user's attention; however, this would interrupt the macro and would require the user's intervention before the macro could continue.

Related Functions

Function	Description
ALERT	Displays a dialog box and a message
BEEP	Sounds a tone

MID

Returns a specific number of characters from a text string, starting at the position you specify.

Syntax

MID(*text,start_num,num_chars*)

Text is the text string containing the characters you want to extract.

Start_num is the position of the first character you want to extract in *text*. The first character in *text* has *start_num* 1, and so on.

- If *start_num* is greater than the length of *text*, MID returns "" (empty text).

- If *start_num* is less than the length of *text*, but *start_num* plus *num_chars* exceeds the length of *text*, MID returns the characters up to the end of *text*.

- If *start_num* is less than 1, MID returns the #VALUE! error value.

Num_chars specifies how many characters to return from text. If *num_chars* is negative, MID returns the #VALUE! error value.

Examples

MID("Fluid Flow",1,5) equals "Fluid"

MID("Fluid Flow",7,20) equals "Flow"

MID("1234",5,5) equals "" (empty text)

Also see the examples for CODE and FIND.

Related Functions

Function	Description
FIND	Finds one text value within another (case-sensitive)
LEFT	Returns the leftmost characters from a text value
RIGHT	Returns the rightmost characters from a text value
SEARCH	Finds one text value within another (not case-sensitive)

MIN

Returns the smallest number in the list of arguments.

Syntax

MIN(*number1,number2,...*)

Number1, number2,... are 1 to 30 numbers for which you want to find the minimum value.

- You can specify arguments that are numbers, empty cells, logical values, or text representations of numbers. Arguments that are error values or text that cannot be translated into numbers cause errors.

- If an argument is an array or reference, only numbers in that array or reference are used. Empty cells, logical values, text, or error values in the array or reference are ignored.

- If the arguments contain no numbers, MIN returns 0.

Examples

If A1:A5 contains the numbers 10, 7, 9, 27, and 2, then:

MIN(A1:A5) equals 2

MIN(A1:A5,0) equals 0

MIN is similar to MAX. Also see the examples for MAX.

Related Functions

Function	Description
DMIN	Returns the minimum value from selected database entries
MAX	Returns the maximum value in a list of arguments

MINUTE

Returns the minute corresponding to *serial_number*. The minute is given as an integer, ranging from 0 to 59.

Syntax

MINUTE(*serial_number*)

Serial_number is the date-time code used by Microsoft Excel for date and time calculations. You can give *serial_number* as text, such as "16:48:00" or "4:48:00 P.M.", instead of as a number. The text is automatically converted to a serial number. For more information about *serial_number,* see NOW.

Remarks

Microsoft Excel for Windows and Microsoft Excel for the Macintosh use different date systems as their default. For more information, see NOW.

Examples

MINUTE("4:48:00 PM") equals 48

MINUTE(0.01) equals 14

MINUTE(4.02) equals 28

Related Functions

Function	Description
NOW	Returns the serial number of the current date and time
YEAR, MONTH, DAY, WEEKDAY, HOUR, and SECOND	Convert serial numbers into years, months, days, days of the week, hours, and seconds, respectively

MINVERSE

Returns the inverse matrix for the matrix stored in an array.

Syntax

MINVERSE(*array*)

Array is a numeric array with an equal number of rows and columns.

- *Array* can be given as a cell range, such as A1:C3; as an array constant, such as {1,2,3;4,5,6;7,8,9}; or as a name for either of these.

- If any cells in *array* are empty or contain text, MINVERSE returns the #VALUE! error value.

- MINVERSE also returns the #VALUE! error value if *array* does not have an equal number of rows and columns.

Remarks

- Formulas that return arrays must be entered as array formulas. For information about arrays, see "Creating and Using an Array Formula" in Chapter 5 in Book 1 of the *Microsoft Excel User's Guide.*

- Inverse matrices, like determinants, are generally used for solving systems of mathematical equations involving several variables. The product of a matrix and its inverse is the identity matrix—the square array in which the diagonal values equal 1 and all other values equal 0. For example, the following illustration shows the two-row, two-column identity matrix in cells A1:B2, and the four-row, four-column identity matrix in cells D1:G4.

	A	B	C	D	E	F	G
1	1	0		1	0	0	0
2	0	1		0	1	0	0
3				0	0	1	0
4				0	0	0	1
5							

- The following worksheet shows how the inverse of a two-row, two-column matrix is calculated. The letters a, b, c, and d represent any four numbers. The matrix D1:E2 is the inverse of the matrix A1:B2 on this worksheet.

	A	B	C	D	E
1	a	b		d/(a*d–b*c)	b/(b*c–a*d)
2	c	d		c/(b*c–a*d)	a/(a*d–b*c)
3					

- MINVERSE is calculated with an accuracy of approximately 16 digits, which may lead to a small numeric error when the cancellation is not complete.

- Some square matrices cannot be inverted, and will return the #NUM! error value with MINVERSE. The determinant for a noninvertable matrix is 0.

Examples

	A	B	C	D
1	1	2	1	
2	3	4	–1	
3	0	2	0	
4				

In the preceding worksheet:

MINVERSE(B2:C3) equals {0,0.5;–1,2}

MINVERSE(A1:C3) equals {0.25,0.25,–0.75; 0,0,0.5;0.75,–0.25,–0.25}

MINVERSE(A1:D4) equals #VALUE!, because A1:D4 contains empty cells.

Tip Use the INDEX function to access individual elements from the inverse matrix. For example, in the preceding worksheet:

INDEX(MINVERSE(A1:C3),1,1) equals 0.25

INDEX(MINVERSE(B2:C3),2,2) equals 2

Related Functions

Function	Description
MDETERM	Returns the matrix determinant of an array
MMULT	Returns the matrix product of two arrays
TRANSPOSE	Returns the transpose of an array

MIRR

Returns the modified internal rate of return for a series of periodic cash flows. MIRR considers both the cost of the investment and the interest received on reinvestment of cash.

Syntax

MIRR(*values,finance_rate,reinvest_rate*)

Values   is an array or a reference to cells that contain numbers. These numbers represent a series of payments (negative values) and income (positive values) occurring at regular periods.

- *Values* must contain at least one positive value and one negative value to calculate the modified internal rate of return. Otherwise, MIRR returns the #DIV/0! error value.

- If an array or reference argument contains text, logical values, or empty cells, those values are ignored, however, cells with the value zero are included.

Finance_rate is the interest rate you pay on the money used in the cash flows.

Reinvest_rate is the interest rate you receive on the cash flows as you reinvest them.

Remarks

- MIRR uses the order of *values* to interpret the order of cash flows. Be sure to enter your payment and income values in the sequence you want and with the correct signs (positive values for cash received, negative values for cash paid).

- If *n* is the number of cash flows in *values,* frate is the *finance_rate,* and rrate is the *reinvest_rate,* then the formula for MIRR is:

$$\left(\frac{-\text{NPV}(rrate, values[positive]) * (1 + rrate)^n}{\text{NPV}(frate, values[negative]) * (1 + frate)} \right)^{\frac{1}{n-1}} - 1$$

Examples

Suppose you're a commercial fisherman just completing your fifth year of operation. Five years ago, you borrowed $120,000 at 10 percent annual interest to purchase a boat. Your catches have yielded $39,000, $30,000, $21,000, $37,000, and $46,000. During these years you reinvested your profits, earning 12% annually.

	A	B	C	D
1	Initial Cost	($120,000)		
2	Year 1 Income	$39,000		
3	Year 2 Income	$30,000		
4	Year 3 Income	$21,000		
5	Year 4 Income	$37,000		
6	Year 5 Income	$46,000		

To calculate the investment's modified rate of return after five years:

MIRR(B1:B6,10%,12%) equals 12.61%

To calculate the modified rate of return after three years:

MIRR(B1:B4,10%,12%) equals −4.80%

To calculate the five-year modified rate of return based on a *reinvest_rate* of 14%

MIRR(B1:B6,10%,14%) equals 13.48%

Related Functions

Function	Description
IRR	Returns the internal rate of return for a series of cash flows
RATE	Returns the interest rate per period of an annuity
XIRR	Returns the internal rate of return for a schedule of cash flows
XNPV	Returns the net present value for a schedule of cash flows

MMULT

Returns the matrix product of two arrays. The result is an array with the same number of rows as *array1* and the same number of columns as *array2*.

Syntax

MMULT*(array1,array2)*

Array1,array2 are the arrays you want to multiply.

- The number of columns in *array1* must be the same as the number of rows in *array2,* and both arrays must contain only numbers.

- *Array1* and *array2* can be given as cell ranges, array constants, or references.

- If any cells are empty or contain text, or if the number of columns in *array1* is different from the number of rows in *array2*, MMULT returns the #VALUE! error value.

Remarks

- The matrix product array a of two arrays b and c is:

$$a_{ij} = \sum_{k=1}^{n} b_{ik} c_{kj}$$

where i is the row number and j is the column number.

- Formulas that return arrays must be entered as array formulas. For information about arrays, see "Creating and Using an Array Formula" in Chapter 5 in Book 1 of the *Microsoft Excel User's Guide*.

Examples

	A	B	C	D	E
1	1	3	0	2	0
2	7	2	0	0	2
3	1	0	0		
4					

In the preceding worksheet:

MMULT(A1:B2,D1:E2) equals {2,6;14,4}

MMULT(B1:C2,D1:E2) equals {6,0;4,0}

MMULT(A1:C3,D1:E2) equals #VALUE!, because A1:C3 has three columns and D1:E2 has only two rows.

Related Functions

Function	Description
MDETERM	Returns the matrix determinant of an array
MINVERSE	Returns the matrix inverse of an array
TRANSPOSE	Returns the transpose of an array

MOD

Returns the remainder (modulus) after *number* is divided by *divisor*. The result has the same sign as *divisor*.

Syntax

MOD(*number,divisor*)

Number is the number for which you want to find the remainder.

Divisor is the number by which you want to divide *number*. If *divisor* is 0, MOD returns the #DIV/0! error value.

Remarks

The MOD function can be expressed in terms of the INT function:

MOD(n,d) = n - d*INT(n/d)

Examples

MOD(3,2) equals 1

MOD(-3,2) equals 1

MOD(3,-2) equals –1

MOD(-3,-2) equals –1

Related Functions

Function	Description
INT	Rounds a number down to the nearest integer
ROUND	Rounds a number to a specified number of digits
TRUNC	Truncates a number to an integer

MODE

Returns the most frequently occurring value in an array or range of data. Like MEAN and MEDIAN, MODE is a location measure

Syntax

MODE(*number1,number2,...*)

Number1,number2,... are 1 to 30 arguments for which you want to calculate the mode. You can also use a single array or a reference to an array instead of arguments separated by commas.

Remarks

- The arguments should be numbers, or names, arrays, or references that contain numbers.

- If an array or reference argument contains text, logical values, or empty cells, those values are ignored; however, cells with the value zero are included.

- If the data set contains no duplicate data points, MODE returns the #N/A error value.

The mode is the most frequently occurring value; the median is the middle value; and the mean is the average value. No single measure of central tendency provides a complete picture of the data. Suppose data is clustered in three areas, half around a single low value, and half around two large values. Both AVERAGE and MEDIAN may return a value in the relatively empty middle, while MODE may return the dominant low value.

Example

MODE({5.6,4,4,3,2,4}) equals 4

Related Functions

Function	Description
AVERAGE	Returns the average of its arguments
GEOMEAN	Returns the geometric mean
HARMEAN	Returns the harmonic mean
MEDIAN	Returns the median of the given numbers
TRIMMEAN	Returns the mean of the interior of a data set

MONTH

Returns the month corresponding to *serial_number*. The month is given as an integer, ranging from 1 (January) to 12 (December).

Syntax

MONTH(*serial_number*)

Serial_number is the date-time code used by Microsoft Excel for date and time calculations. You can give *serial_number* as text, such as "4-15-1991" or "15-Apr-1991", instead of as a number. The text is automatically converted to a serial number. For more information about *serial_number*, see NOW.

Remarks

Microsoft Excel for Windows and Microsoft Excel for the Macintosh use different date systems as their default. For more information, see NOW.

Examples

MONTH("6-May") equals 5

MONTH(366) equals 12

MONTH(367) equals 1

Related Functions

Function	Description
YEAR, DAY, WEEKDAY, HOUR, MINUTE, and SECOND	Convert serial numbers into years, days, days of the week, hours, minutes, and seconds, respectively

MOVE

Macro Sheets Only

Equivalent to moving a window by dragging its title bar in Microsoft Excel version 3.0 or earlier. MOVE is also equivalent to choosing the Move command from the Control menu in Microsoft Windows. This function is included only for macro compatibility and will be converted to WINDOW.MOVE when you open older macro sheets. For more information, see WINDOW.MOVE.

Syntax

MOVE(*x_pos,y_pos,window_text*)
MOVE?(*x_pos,y_pos,window_text*)

MOVE.TOOL

Macro Sheets Only

Moves or copies a tool from one toolbar to another.

Syntax

MOVE.TOOL(*from_bar_id,from_bar_position,*
to_bar_id,to_bar_position,copy,width)

From_bar_id specifies the number or name of a toolbar from which you want to move or copy the tool. For detailed information, see the description of *bar_id* in ADD.TOOL.

From_bar_position specifies the current position of the tool within the toolbar. *From_bar_position* starts with 1 at the left side (if horizontal) or at the top (if vertical).

To_bar_id specifies the number or name of a toolbar to which you want to move or paste the tool. For detailed information, see the description of *bar_id* in ADD.TOOL. *To_bar_id* is optional if you are moving a tool within the same toolbar.

To_bar_position specifies where you want to move or paste the tool within the toolbar. *To_bar_position* starts with 1 at the left side (if horizontal) or at the top (if vertical). If the position is already occupied by another tool, Microsoft Excel removes that tool. *To_bar_position* is optional if you are only adjusting the width of a drop-down list.

Copy is a logical value specifying whether to copy the tool. If *copy* is TRUE, the tool is copied; if FALSE or omitted, the tool is moved.

Width is the width, measured in points, of a drop-down list. If the tool you are moving is not a drop-down list, *width* is ignored.

Example

The following macro formula moves the first tool on the standard toolbar to the third position on the formatting toolbar. Assume the tool is not a drop-down list.

```
MOVE.TOOL(1,1,2,3)
```

Related Functions

Function	Description
ADD.TOOL	Adds one or more tools to a toolbar
COPY.TOOL	Copies a tool face to the Clipboard
GET.TOOL	Returns information about a tool or tools on a toolbar

MOVEAVG

Macro Sheets Only

Projects values in a forecast period, based on the average value of the variable over a specific number of preceding periods. For more information, see "Analyzing Statistical or Engineering Data" in Chapter 1 in Book 2 of the *Microsoft Excel User's Guide*.

If this function is not available, you must install the Analysis ToolPak add-in macro. For more information, see "Managing Add-in Commands and Functions" in Chapter 4 in Book 2 of the *Microsoft Excel User's Guide*.

Syntax

MOVEAVG(*inprng,outrng,interval,stderrs,chart*)

Inprng is the input range.

Outrng is the first cell (the upper-left cell) in the output table.

Interval is the number of values to include in the moving average. If omitted, *interval* is 3.

Stderrs is a logical value.

- If *stderrs* is TRUE, standard error values are included in the output table.
- If *stderrs* is FALSE or omitted, standard errors are not included in the output table.

Chart is a logical value.

- If *chart* is TRUE, then MOVEAVG generates a chart for the actual and forecast values.
- If *chart* is FALSE or omitted, the chart is not generated.

Related Functions

Function	Description
EXPON	Predicts a value based on the forecast for the prior period
FORECAST	Returns a value along a linear trend
GROWTH	Returns values along an exponential trend
TREND	Returns values along a linear trend

MROUND

Returns a number rounded to the desired multiple.

If this function is not available, you must install the Analysis ToolPak add-in macro. For more information, see "Managing Add-in Commands and Functions" in Chapter 4 in Book 2 of the *Microsoft Excel User's Guide*.

Syntax

MROUND(*number,multiple*)

Number is the value to round.

Multiple is the multiple to which you want to round *number*.

Remarks

MROUND rounds up, away from zero, if the remainder of dividing *number* by *multiple* is greater than or equal to half the value of *multiple*.

Examples

MROUND(10,3) equals 9

MROUND(-10,-3) equals –9

MROUND(1.3,0.2) equals 1.4

MROUND(5,-2) equals #NUM!

Related Functions

Function	Description
CEILING	Rounds a number up to the nearest integer
EVEN	Rounds a number up to the nearest even integer
FLOOR	Rounds a number down, toward zero
ODD	Rounds a number up to the nearest odd integer
ROUND	Rounds a number to a specified number of digits
TRUNC	Truncates a number to an integer

MULTINOMIAL

Returns the ratio of the factorial of a sum of values to the product of factorials.

If this function is not available, you must install the Analysis ToolPak add-in macro. For more information, see "Managing Add-in Commands and Functions" in Chapter 4 in Book 2 of the *Microsoft Excel User's Guide*.

Syntax

MULTINOMIAL(*number1,number2,...*)

Number1,number2,... are 1 to 29 values for which you want the multinomial.

Remarks

- If any argument is non-numeric, MULTINOMIAL returns the #VALUE! error value.

- If any argument is less than one, MULTINOMIAL returns the #NUM! error value.

- The multinomial is:

$$\text{MULTINOMIAL}(a, b, c) = \frac{(a + b + c)!}{a!\,b!\,c!}$$

Example

```
MULTINOMIAL(2,3,4) equals 1260
```

Related Functions

Function	Description
FACT	Returns the factorial of a number
FACTDOUBLE	Returns the double factorial of a number

N

Returns a value converted to a number.

Syntax

N(*value*)

Value is the value you want converted. N converts values listed in the following table.

If *value* is or refers to	N returns
A number	That number
A date, in one of Microsoft Excel's built-in date formats	The serial number of that date
TRUE	1
Anything else	0

Remarks

It is not generally necessary to use the N function in a formula, since Microsoft Excel automatically converts values as necessary. This function is provided for compatibility with other spreadsheet programs. For information about how Microsoft Excel converts values, see "Converting Data Types" in the first section, "About Functions." Also see Chapter 7 in Book 2 of the *Microsoft Excel User's Guide*.

Examples

	A	B	C	D
1	7	odd	TRUE	
2	8	even	TRUE	
3	13	odd	FALSE	
4	14	even	FALSE	

In the preceding worksheet:

`N(A1)` equals 7

`N(B2)` equals 0, because B2 contains text

`N(C2)` equals 1, because C2 contains TRUE

`N("7")` equals 0, because "7" is text

`N("4/17/91")` equals 0, because "4/17/91" is text

Related Functions

Function	Description
GET.CELL	Returns information about the specified cell
T	Converts its arguments to text

NA

Returns the error value #N/A. #N/A is the error value that means "no value is available." Use NA to mark empty cells. By entering #N/A in cells where you are missing information, you can avoid the problem of unintentionally including empty cells in your calculations. (When a formula refers to a cell containing #N/A, the formula returns the #N/A error value.)

Syntax

NA( )

Remarks

- You must include the empty parentheses with the function name. Otherwise, Microsoft Excel will not recognize it as a function.

- You can also type the value #N/A directly into a cell. The NA function is provided for compatibility with other spreadsheet programs.

Related Function

Function	Description
ISNA	Returns TRUE if a value is the #N/A error value

NAMES

Macro Sheets Only

Returns, as a horizontal array of text, the specified names defined in the specified document. The returned array lists the names in alphabetic order. Use NAMES instead of LIST.NAMES when you want to return the names to the macro sheet instead of to the active worksheet.

Syntax

NAMES(*document_text,type_num,match_text*)

Document_text is text that specifies the document whose names you want returned. If *document_text* is omitted, it is assumed to be the active document.

Type_num is a number from 1 to 3 that specifies whether to include hidden names in the returned array.

If *type_num* is	NAMES returns
1 or omitted	Normal names only
2	Hidden names only
3	All names

Match_text is text that specifies the names you want returned and can include wildcard characters. If *match_text* is omitted, all names are returned.

Remarks

- Hidden names are defined using the DEFINE.NAME macro function and do not appear in the Paste Name, Define Name, or Goto dialog boxes.

- NAMES returns a horizontal array, so you will normally enter this function as an array in several horizontal cells or define a name to refer to the array that NAMES returns. If you want the names in a vertical array instead, use the TRANSPOSE function.

- You can use the COLUMNS function to count the number of entries in the array.

Example

The following macro formula returns all names on the active document starting with the letter P.

```
NAMES(,3,"P*")
```

Related Functions

Function	Description
DEFINE.NAME	Defines a name on the active worksheet or macro sheet
DELETE.NAME	Deletes a name
GET.DEF	Returns a name matching a definition
GET.NAME	Returns the definition of a name
LIST.NAMES	Lists names and their associated information
SET.NAME	Defines a name as a value

NEGBINOMDIST

Returns the negative binomial distribution. NEGBINOMDIST returns the probability that there will be *number_f* failures before the *number_s*-th success, when the constant probability of a success is *probability_s*. This function is similar to the binomial distribution, except that the number of successes is fixed and the number of trials is variable. Like the binomial, trials are assumed to be independent.

For example, you need to find 10 people with excellent reflexes, and you know the probability that a candidate has these qualifications is 0.3. NEGBINOMDIST calculates the probability that you will interview a certain number of unqualified candidates before finding all 10 qualified candidates.

Syntax

NEGBINOMDIST(*number_f,number_s, probability_s*)

Number_f   is the number of failures.

Number_s   is the threshold number of successes.

Probability_s   is the probability of a success.

Remarks

- *Number_f* and *number_s* are truncated to integers.

- If any argument is non-numeric, NEGBINOMDIST returns the #VALUE! error value.

- If *probability_s* < 0 or if *probability* > 1, NEGBINOMDIST returns the #NUM! error value.

- If (*number_f* + *number_s* – 1) ≤ 0, NEGBINOMDIST returns the #NUM! error value.

- The equation for the negative binomial distribution is:

$$nb(x;r,p) = \binom{x+r-1}{r-1} p^r (1-p)^x$$

where *x* is *number_f*, *r* is *number_s*, and *p* is *probability_s*.

Example

NEGBINOMDIST(10,5,0.25) equals 0.055049

Related Functions

Function	Description
BINOMDIST	Returns the individual term binomial distribution
COMBIN	Returns the number of combinations for a given number of objects
FACT	Returns the factorial of a number
HYPGEOMDIST	Returns the hypergeometric distribution
PERMUT	Returns the number of permutations for a given number of objects

NETWORKDAYS

Returns the number of whole working days between *start_date* and *end_date*. Working days exclude weekends and any dates identified in *holidays*. Use NETWORKDAYS to calculate employee benefits that accrue based on the number of days worked during a specific term.

If this function is not available, you must install the Analysis ToolPak add-in macro. For more information, see "Managing Add-in Commands and Functions" in Chapter 4 in Book 2 of the *Microsoft Excel User's Guide*.

Syntax

NETWORKDAYS(*start_date,end_date,holidays*)

Start_date is a serial date number that represents the start date.

End_date is a serial date number that represents the end date.

Holidays is an optional set of one or more serial date numbers to exclude from the working calendar, such as state and federal holidays and floating holidays.

Remarks

- If any argument is non-numeric, NETWORKDAYS returns the #VALUE! error value.

- If any argument is not a valid serial date number, NETWORKDAYS returns the #NUM! error value.

Example

```
NETWORKDAYS(DATEVALUE("10/01/91"),
DATEVALUE("12/01/91"),
DATEVALUE("11/28/91")) equals 43
```

Related Functions

Function	Description
EDATE	Returns the serial number of the date that is the indicated number of months before or after the start date
EOMONTH	Returns the serial number of the date for the last day of the month before or after a specified number of months
NOW	Returns the serial number of the current date and time
WORKDAY	Returns the serial number of the date before or after a specified number of workdays

NEW

Macro Sheets Only

Equivalent to choosing the New command from the File menu. Creates a new Microsoft Excel document or opens a template. For detailed information about the New command, see online Help.

Syntax

NEW(*type_num, xy_series, add_logical*)
NEW?(*type_num,xy_series, add_logical*)

Type_num specifies the type of file to create, as shown in the following table. If *type_num* is omitted, the new document will be the same type as that of the active document.

Type_num	Document
1	Worksheet
2	Chart
3	Macro sheet
4	International macro sheet
5	Workbook
Quoted text	Template

Xy_series is a number from 0 to 3 that specifies how data is arranged in a chart.

Xy_series	Result
0	Displays a dialog box if the selection is ambiguous.
1 or omitted	The first row/column is the first data series.
2	The first row/column contains the category (*x*) axis labels.
3	The first row/column contains the *x*-values; the created chart is an xy (scatter) chart.

Add_logical specifies whether or not to add the active document to the open workbook. If *add_logical* is TRUE, the document is added; if FALSE or omitted, it is not added.

Add_logical is ignored if *type_num* is 5.

Remarks

You can also use NEW to create new sheets from templates that exist in the startup directory or folder, using for *type_num* the text that appears in the File New list box. To create new sheets from any template that is not in the start-up directory, use the OPEN function. For more information about templates, see "Creating and Using a Document Template" in Chapter 4 in Book 1 of the *Microsoft Excel User's Guide*.

Examples

The following macro formula creates a new chart with the data in the first row/column as the category (*x*) axis labels:

NEW(2,2)

Related Functions

Function	Description
NEW.WINDOW	Creates a new window for an existing worksheet or macro sheet
OPEN	Opens a document

NEW.WINDOW

Macro Sheets Only

Equivalent to choosing the New Window command from the Window menu. Creates a new window for the active worksheet or macro sheet. For detailed information about the New Window command, see online Help.

Syntax

NEW.WINDOW( )

After you use NEW.WINDOW, use the WINDOW.MOVE, WINDOW.SIZE, and ARRANGE.ALL functions to size and position the new window.

Related Functions

Function	Description
ARRANGE.ALL	Arranges all displayed windows to fill the workspace and synchronizes windows for scrolling
WINDOW.MOVE	Moves a window
WINDOW.SIZE	Changes the size of a window

NEXT

Macro Sheets Only

Ends a FOR–NEXT, FOR.CELL–NEXT, or WHILE–NEXT loop and continues carrying out the current macro with the formula that follows the NEXT function. For information about loops, see FOR, WHILE, or FOR.CELL, or Chapter 7 in Book 2 of the *Microsoft Excel User's Guide*.

Syntax

NEXT( )

NOMINAL

Returns the nominal annual interest rate given the effective rate and the number of compounding periods per year.

If this function is not available, you must install the Analysis ToolPak add-in macro. For more information, see "Managing Add-in Commands and Functions" in Chapter 4 in Book 2 of the *Microsoft Excel User's Guide*.

Syntax

NOMINAL(*effect_rate,npery*)

Effect_rate   is the effective interest rate.

Npery   is the number of compounding periods per year.

Remarks

- *Npery* is truncated to an integer.

- If either argument is non-numeric, NOMINAL returns the #VALUE! error value.

- If *effective_rate* ≤ 0 or if *npery* < 1, NOMINAL returns the #NUM! error value.

Example

NOMINAL(5.3543%,4) equals 0.0525 or 5.25%

Related Function

Function	Description
EFFECT	Returns the effective annual interest rate

NORMDIST

Returns the normal distribution function for the specified mean and standard deviation. This function has a very wide range of applications in statistics, including hypothesis testing.

Syntax

NORMDIST(*x,mean,standard_dev,cumulative*)

X   is the value for which you want the distribution.

Mean   is the arithmetic mean of the distribution.

Standard_dev   is the standard deviation of the distribution.

Cumulative   is a logical value that determines the form of the function. If *cumulative* is TRUE, NORMDIST returns the cumulative distribution function; if FALSE, it returns the probability mass function.

Remarks

- If any argument is non-numeric, NORMDIST returns the #VALUE! error value.

- If *standard_dev* ≤ 0, NORMDIST returns the #NUM! error value.

- If *mean* = 0 and *standard_dev* = 1, NORMDIST returns the standard normal distribution, NORMSDIST.

- The equation for the normal density function is:

$$f\left(x;\mu,\sigma\right) = \frac{1}{\sqrt{2\pi}\sigma}\, e^{-\left(\frac{(x-\mu)^2}{2\sigma^2}\right)}$$

Example

NORMDIST(42,40,1.5,TRUE) equals 0.908789

Related Functions

Function	Description
NORMINV	Returns the inverse of the standard normal cumulative distribution
NORMSDIST	Returns the standard normal cumulative distribution
NORMSINV	Returns the inverse of the standard normal cumulative distribution
STANDARDIZE	Returns a normalized value
ZTEST	Returns the two-tailed *P*-value of a z-test

NORMINV

Returns the inverse of the normal cumulative distribution for the specified mean and standard deviation.

Syntax

NORMINV(*probability,mean,standard_dev*)

Probability   is a probability corresponding to the normal distribution.

Mean   is the arithmetic mean of the distribution.

Standard_dev   is the standard deviation of the distribution.

Remarks

- If any argument is non-numeric, NORMINV returns the #VALUE! error value.

- If *probability* < 0 or if *probability* > 1, NORMINV returns the #NUM! error value.

- If *standard_dev* ≤ 0, NORMINV returns the #NUM! error value.

NORMINV uses the standard normal distribution if *mean* = 0 and *standard_dev* = 1 (see NORMSINV).

NORMINV uses an iterative technique for calculating the function. Given a probability value, NORMINV iterates until the result is accurate to within $\pm 3 \times 10^{-7}$. If NORMINV does not converge after 100 iterations, the function returns the #N/A error value.

Example

NORMINV(0.908789,40,1.5) equals 42

Related Functions

Function	Description
NORMDIST	Returns the normal cumulative distribution
NORMSDIST	Returns the standard normal cumulative distribution
NORMSINV	Returns the inverse of the standard normal cumulative distribution
STANDARDIZE	Returns a normalized value
ZTEST	Returns the two-tailed *P*-value of a *z*-test

NORMSDIST

Returns the standard normal cumulative distribution function. The distribution has a mean of zero and a standard deviation of one. Use this function in place of a table of standard normal curve areas.

Syntax

NORMSDIST(*z*)

Z is the value for which you want the distribution.

Remarks

- If *z* is non-numeric, NORMSDIST returns the #VALUE! error value.

- The equation for the standard normal density function is:

$$f(z;0,1) = \frac{1}{\sqrt{2\pi}} e^{-\frac{z^2}{2}}$$

Example

NORMSDIST(1.333333) equals 0.908789

Related Functions

Function	Description
NORMDIST	Returns the normal cumulative distribution
NORMINV	Returns the inverse of the standard normal cumulative distribution
NORMSINV	Returns the inverse of the standard normal cumulative distribution
STANDARDIZE	Returns a normalized value
ZTEST	Returns the two-tailed *P*-value of a *z*-test

NORMSINV

Returns the inverse of the standard normal cumulative distribution. The distribution has a mean of zero and a standard deviation of one.

Syntax

NORMSINV(*probability*)

Probability is a probability corresponding to the normal distribution.

Remarks

- If *probability* is non-numeric, NORMSINV returns the #VALUE! error value.

- If *probability* < 0 or if *probability* > 1, NORMINV returns the #NUM! error value.

NORMSINV uses an iterative technique for calculating the function. Given a probability value, NORMSINV iterates until the result is accurate to within $\pm 3 \times 10^{-7}$. If NORMSINV does not converge after 100 iterations, the function returns the #N/A error value.

Example

NORMSINV(0.908789) equals 1.3333

Related Functions

Function	Description
NORMDIST	Returns the normal cumulative distribution
NORMSDIST	Returns the standard normal cumulative distribution
NORMINV	Returns the inverse of the standard normal cumulative distribution
STANDARDIZE	Returns a normalized value
ZTEST	Returns the two-tailed *P*-value of a *z*-test

NOT

Reverses the value of its argument. Use NOT when you want to make sure a value is not equal to one particular value.

Syntax

NOT(*logical*)

Logical is a value or expression that can be evaluated to TRUE or FALSE. If *logical* is FALSE, NOT returns TRUE; if *logical* is TRUE, NOT returns FALSE.

Examples

NOT(FALSE) equals TRUE

NOT(1+1=2) equals FALSE

Related Functions

Function	Description
AND	Returns TRUE if all its arguments are TRUE
OR	Returns TRUE if any argument is TRUE

NOTE

Macro Sheets Only

Equivalent to choosing the Note command from the Formula menu. Creates a note or replaces characters in a note. Use NOTE to create a cell note or to replace a specified number of characters with other text. For detailed information about the Note command, see online Help.

Syntax

NOTE(*add_text,cell_ref,start_char,num_chars*)
NOTE?( )

Add_text is text of up to 255 characters you want to add to a note. *Add_text* must be enclosed in quotation marks.

- If *add_text* is omitted, it is assumed to be "" (empty text) unless the note includes sound.

- If a note contains sound and you omit *add_text*, Microsoft Excel deletes the entire note, but if you explicitly specify empty text, Microsoft Excel deletes only the text, not the sound (see the second example following). To erase only the sound, use the SOUND.NOTE function.

Cell_ref is the cell to which you want to add the note text. If *cell_ref* is omitted, *add_text* is added to the active cell's note.

Start_char is the number of the character at which you want *add_text* to be added. If *start_char* is omitted, it is assumed to be 1. If there is no existing note, *start_char* is ignored.

Num_chars   is the number of characters that you want to replace in the note. If *num_chars* is omitted, it is assumed to be equal to the length of the note.

Remarks

- NOTE returns the number of the last character entered in the cell note. This is useful if you want to know how many characters are in the text string so it can be manipulated with other functions such as RIGHT, LEFT, and MID.

- The dialog-box form of this function, NOTE?, takes no arguments.

To find out if a cell has a note attached to it, use GET.CELL.

Examples

NOTE( ) deletes the note attached to the active cell.

NOTE("") deletes the text, but not sound, in the note attached to the active cell.

The following macro formula attaches a new note, "Attached are the first fiscal quarter sales figures", to cell A1 on the active document:

NOTE("Attached are the first fiscal quarter sales figures",!$A$1)

The following macro formula inserts the text, "Assumptions begin with this row", at position 1000 in the note attached to cell A1, or at the end of the note if the note has fewer than 1000 characters:

NOTE("Assumptions begin with this row",!$A$1,1000)

Related Functions

Function	Description
GET.NOTE	Returns characters from a note
SOUND.NOTE	Records or imports sounds into or erases sound from cell notes

NOW

Returns the serial number of the current date and time.

Syntax

NOW( )

Remarks

- Microsoft Excel for Windows and Microsoft Excel for the Macintosh use different default date systems. Microsoft Excel for Windows uses the 1900 Date System, in which serial numbers range from 1 to 65,380, corresponding to the dates January 1, 1900, through December 31, 2078. Microsoft Excel for the Macintosh uses the 1904 Date System, in which serial numbers range from 0 to 63,918, corresponding to the dates January 1, 1904, through December 31, 2078.

- Numbers to the right of the decimal point in the serial number represent the time; numbers to the left represent the date. For example, in the 1900 Date System, the serial number 367.5 represents the date-time combination 12:00 P.M., January 1, 1901.

- You can change the date system by selecting or clearing the 1904 Date System check box in the Calculation dialog box, which appears when you choose the Calculation command from the Options menu.

- The date system is changed automatically when you open a document from another platform. For example, if you are working in Microsoft Excel for Windows and you open a document created in Microsoft Excel for the Macintosh, the 1904 Date System check box is selected automatically.

- The NOW function changes only when the worksheet is calculated or when the macro containing the function is run. It is not updated continuously.

Examples

If you are using the 1900 Date System and your computer's built-in clock is set to 12:30:00 P.M., 1-Jan-1987, then:

NOW( ) equals 31778.52083

Ten minutes later:

NOW( ) equals 31778.52778

Related Functions

Function	Description
DATE	Returns the serial number of a particular date
TODAY	Returns the serial number of today's date
YEAR, MONTH, DAY, WEEKDAY, HOUR, MINUTE, and SECOND	Convert serial numbers to years, months, days, days of the week, hours, minutes, and seconds, respectively

NPER

Returns the number of periods for an investment based on periodic, constant payments and a constant interest rate.

Syntax

NPER(*rate,pmt,pv,fv,type*)

For a more complete description of the arguments in NPER and for more information about annuity functions, see PV.

Rate   is the interest rate per period.

Pmt   is the payment made each period; it cannot change over the life of the annuity. Typically, *pmt* contains principal and interest but no other fees or taxes.

Pv   is the present value, or the lump-sum amount that a series of future payments is worth right now.

Fv   is the future value, or a cash balance you want to attain after the last payment is made. If *fv* is omitted, it is assumed to be 0 (the future value of a loan, for example, is 0).

Type   is the number 0 or 1 and indicates when payments are due.

Set *type* equal to	If payments are due
0 or omitted	At the end of the period
1	At the beginning of the period

Examples

NPER(12%/12,-100,-1000,10000,1) equals 60

NPER(1%,-100,-1000,10000) equals 60

NPER(1%,-100,1000) equals 11

Related Functions

Function	Description
FV	Returns the future value of an investment
IPMT	Returns the interest payment for an investment for a given period
PMT	Returns the periodic payment for an annuity
PPMT	Returns the payment on the principal for an investment for a given period
PV	Returns the present value of an investment
RATE	Returns the interest rate per period of an annuity

NPV

Returns the net present value of an investment based on a series of periodic cash flows and a discount rate. The net present value of an investment is today's value of a series of future payments (negative values) and income (positive values).

Syntax

NPV(*rate,value1,value2,...*)

Rate   is the rate of discount over the length of one period.

Value1, value2,... are 1 to 29 arguments representing the payments and income.

- *Value1, value2,...* must be equally spaced in time and occur at the end of each period.

- NPV uses the order of *value1, value2,...* to interpret the order of cash flows. Be sure to enter your payment and income values in the correct sequence.

- Arguments that are numbers, empty cells, logical values, or text representations of numbers are counted; arguments that are error values or text that cannot be translated into numbers are ignored.

- If an argument is an array or reference, only numbers in that array or reference are counted. Empty cells, logical values, text, or error values in the array or reference are ignored.

Remarks

- The NPV investment begins one period before the date of the *value1* cash flow and ends with the last cash flow in the list. The NPV calculation is based on future cash flows. If your first cash flow occurs at the beginning of the first period, the first value must be added to the NPV result, not included in the *values* arguments. For more information, see the examples below.

- If *n* is the number of cash flows in the list of *values*, the formula for NPV is:

$$NPV = \sum_{i=1}^{n} \frac{values_i}{(1 + rate)^i}$$

- NPV is similar to the PV function (present value). The primary difference between PV and NPV is that PV allows cash flows to begin either at the end or at the beginning of the period. Unlike the variable NPV cash flow values, PV cash flows must be constant throughout the investment. For information about annuities and financial functions, see PV.

- NPV is also related to the IRR function (internal rate of return). IRR is the *rate* for which NPV equals zero: NPV(IRR(…),…)=0.

Examples

Suppose you're considering an investment in which you pay $10,000 one year from today and receive an annual income of $3000, $4200, and $6800 in the three years that follow. Assuming an annual discount rate of 10 percent, the net present value of this investment is:

`NPV(10%,-10000,3000,4200,6800)` equals $1188.44

In the preceding example, you include the initial $10,000 cost as one of the *values,* because the payment occurs at the end of the first period.

Consider an investment that starts at the beginning of the first period. Suppose you're interested in buying a shoe store. The cost of the business is $40,000, and you expect to receive the following income for the first five years of operation: $8000, $9200, $10,000, $12,000, and $14,500. The annual discount rate is 8% this might represent the rate of inflation, or the interest rate of a competing investment.

	A	B	C	D
1	Investment	($40,000)		
2	Year 1 Income	$8,000		
3	Year 2 Income	$9,200		
4	Year 3 Income	$10,000		
5	Year 4 Income	$12,000		
6	Year 5 Income	$14,500		

The net present value of the shoe store investment is given by:

`NPV(8%,B2:B6)+B1` equals $1922.06

In the preceding example, you don't include the initial $40,000 cost as one of the *values,* because the payment occurs at the beginning of the first period.

Suppose your shoe store's roof collapses during the sixth year and you assume a loss of $9000 for that year. The net present value of the shoe store investment after six years is given by:

`NPV(8%,B2:B6,-9000)+B1` equals –$3749.47

Related Functions

Function	Description
FV	Returns the future value of an investment
IRR	Returns the internal rate of return for a series of cash flows
PV	Returns the present value of an investment
XNPV	Returns the net present value for a schedule of cash flows

OBJECT.PROPERTIES

Macro Sheets Only

Equivalent to choosing the Object Properties command from the Format menu. Determines how the selected object or objects are attached to the cells beneath them and whether they are printed. The way an object is attached to the cells beneath it affects how the object is moved or sized whenever you move or size the cells. For detailed information about the Object Properties command, see online Help.

OBJECT.PROPERTIES(*placement_type, print_object*)
OBJECT.PROPERTIES?(*placement_type, print_object*)

Placement_type is a number from 1 to 3 specifying how to attach the selected object or objects. If *placement_type* is omitted, the current status is unchanged.

If *placement_type* is	The selected object is
1	Moved and sized with cells.
2	Moved but not sized with cells.
3	Free-floating—it is not affected by moving and sizing cells.

Print_object is a logical value specifying whether to print the selected object or objects. If TRUE or omitted, the objects are printed; if FALSE, they are not printed.

Remarks

If an object is not selected, OBJECT.PROPERTIES interrupts the macro and returns the #VALUE! error value.

Related Functions

Function	Description
CREATE.OBJECT	Creates an object
FORMAT.MOVE	Moves the selected object
FORMAT.SIZE	Changes the size of the selected object

OBJECT.PROTECTION

Macro Sheets Only

Equivalent to choosing the Object Protection command from the Format menu. Changes the protection status of the selected object. For detailed information about the Object Protection command, see online Help.

Syntax

OBJECT.PROTECTION(*locked,lock_text*)
OBJECT.PROTECTION?(*locked,lock_text*)

Locked is a logical value that determines whether the selected object is locked or unlocked. If *locked* is TRUE, Microsoft Excel locks the object; if FALSE, Microsoft Excel unlocks the object.

Lock_text is a logical value that determines whether text in a text box or button can be changed. *Lock_text* applies only if the object is a text box or button. If *lock_text* is TRUE or omitted, text cannot be changed; if FALSE, text can be changed.

Remarks

- You cannot lock or unlock an individual object with OBJECT.PROTECTION when document protection is selected for objects in the Protect Document dialog box.

- If an object is not selected, the function returns the #VALUE! error value and halts the macro.

- In order for an object to be protected, you must use the PROTECT.DOCUMENT(,,,TRUE) function after changing the object's status with OBJECT.PROTECTION.

Related Function

Function	Description
PROTECT.DOCUMENT	Controls protection for the active document

OCT2BIN

Converts an octal number to binary.

If this function is not available, you must install the Analysis ToolPak add-in macro. For more information, see "Managing Add-in Commands and Functions" in Chapter 4 in Book 2 of the *Microsoft Excel User's Guide*.

Syntax

OCT2BIN(*number,places*)

Number is the octal number you want to convert. *Number* may not contain more than 10 characters. The most significant bit of *number* is the sign bit. The remaining 29 bits are magnitude bits. Negative numbers are represented using two's-complement notation.

Places is the number of characters to use. If *places* is omitted, OCT2BIN uses the minimum number of characters necessary. *Places* is useful for padding the return value with leading 0s (zeros).

Remarks

- If *number* is negative, OCT2BIN ignores *places* and returns a 10-character binary number.

- If *number* is negative, it cannot be less than 7777777000, and if *number* is positive, it cannot be greater than 777.

- If *number* is not a valid octal number, OCT2BIN returns the #NUM! error value.

- If OCT2BIN requires more than *places* characters, it returns the #NUM! error value.

- If *places* is not an integer, it is truncated.

- If *places* is non-numeric, OCT2BIN returns the #VALUE! error value.

- If *places* is negative, OCT2BIN returns the #NUM! error value.

Examples

OCT2BIN(3,3) equals 011

OCT2BIN(7777777000) equals 1000000000

Related Functions

Function	Description
BIN2OCT	Converts a binary number to octal
DEC2OCT	Converts a decimal number to octal
HEX2OCT	Converts a hexadecimal number to octal

OCT2DEC

Converts an octal number to decimal.

If this function is not available, you must install the Analysis ToolPak add-in macro. For more information, see "Managing Add-in Commands and Functions" in Chapter 4 in Book 2 of the *Microsoft Excel User's Guide*.

Syntax

OCT2DEC(*number*)

Number is the octal number you want to convert. *Number* may not contain more than 10 octal characters (30 bits). The most significant bit of *number* is the sign bit. The remaining 29 bits are magnitude bits. Negative numbers are represented using two's-complement notation.

Remarks

If *number* is not a valid octal number, OCT2DEC returns the #NUM! error value.

Examples

OCT2DEC(54) equals 44

OCT2DEC(7777777533) equals –165

Related Functions

Function	Description
BIN2OCT	Converts a binary number to octal
DEC2OCT	Converts a decimal number to octal
HEX2OCT	Converts a hexadecimal number to octal

OCT2HEX

Converts an octal number to hexadecimal.

If this function is not available, you must install the Analysis ToolPak add-in macro. For more information, see "Managing Add-in Commands and Functions" in Chapter 4 in Book 2 of the *Microsoft Excel User's Guide*.

Syntax

OCT2HEX(*number,places*)

Number is the octal number you want to convert. *Number* may not contain more than 10 octal characters (30 bits). The most significant bit of *number* is the sign bit. The remaining 29 bits are magnitude bits. Negative numbers are represented using two's-complement notation.

Places is the number of characters to use. If *places* is omitted, OCT2HEX uses the minimum number of characters necessary. *Places* is useful for padding the return value with leading 0s (zeros).

Remarks

- If *number* is negative, OCT2HEX ignores *places* and returns a 10-character hexadecimal number.

- If *number* is not a valid octal number, OCT2HEX returns the #NUM! error value.

- If OCT2HEX requires more than *places* characters, it returns the #NUM! error value.

- If *places* is not an integer, it is truncated.

- If *places* is non-numeric, OCT2HEX returns the #VALUE! error value.

- If *places* is negative, OCT2HEX returns the #NUM! error value.

Examples

OCT2HEX(100,4) equals 0040

OCT2HEX(7777777533) equals FFFFFFFF5B

Related Functions

Function	Description
BIN2OCT	Converts a binary number to octal
DEC2OCT	Converts a decimal number to octal
HEX2OCT	Converts a hexadecimal number to octal

ODD

Returns *number* rounded up to the nearest odd integer.

Syntax

ODD(*number*)

Number is the value to round.

Remarks

- If *number* is non-numeric, ODD returns the #VALUE! error value.

- Regardless of the sign of *number,* a value is rounded up when adjusted away from zero. If *number* is an odd integer, no rounding occurs.

Examples

ODD(1.5) equals 3

ODD(3) equals 3

ODD(2) equals 3

ODD(-1) equals -1

ODD(-2) equals -3

Related Functions

Function	Description
CEILING	Rounds a number up to the nearest integer
EVEN	Rounds a number up to the nearest even integer
FLOOR	Rounds a number down, toward zero
INT	Rounds a number down to the nearest integer
ROUND	Rounds a number to a specified number of digits
TRUNC	Truncates a number to an integer

ODDFPRICE

Returns the price per $100 face value of a security having an odd (short or long) first period.

If this function is not available, you must install the Analysis ToolPak add-in macro. For more information, see "Managing Add-in Commands and Functions" in Chapter 4 in Book 2 of the *Microsoft Excel User's Guide*.

Syntax

ODDFPRICE(*settlement,maturity,issue, first_coupon,rate,yld,redemption,frequency,basis*)

Settlement   is the security's settlement date, expressed as a serial date number.

Maturity   is the security's maturity date, expressed as a serial date number.

Issue   is the security's issue date, expressed as a serial date number.

First_coupon   is the security's first coupon date, expressed as a serial date number.

Rate   is the security's interest rate.

Yld   is the security's annual yield.

Redemption   is the security's redemption value per $100 face value.

Frequency   is the number of coupon payments per year. For annual payments, *frequency* = 1; for semi-annual, *frequency* = 2; for quarterly, *frequency* = 4.

Basis   is the type of day count basis to use.

Basis	Day count basis
0 or omitted	30/360
1	Actual/actual
2	Actual/360
3	Actual/365

Remarks

- *Settlement, maturity, issue, first_coupon,* and *basis* are truncated to integers.

- If any argument is non-numeric, ODDFPRICE returns the #VALUE! error value.

- If *settlement, maturity, issue,* or *first_coupon* is not a valid serial date number, ODDFPRICE returns the #NUM! error value.

- If *rate* < 0 or if *yld* < 0, ODDFPRICE returns the #NUM! error value.

- If *basis* < 0 or if *basis* > 3, ODDFPRICE returns the #NUM! error value.

- The following date condition must be satisfied; otherwise, ODDFPRICE returns the #NUM! error value:

  maturity > *first_coupon* > *settlement* > *issue*

Related Functions

Function	Description
DATE	Returns the serial number of a particular date
ODDFYIELD	Returns the yield of a security with an odd first period
ODDLPRICE	Returns the price per $100 face value of a security with an odd last period
ODDLYIELD	Returns the yield of a security with an odd last period

ODDFYIELD

Returns the yield of a security that has an odd (short or long) first period.

If this function is not available, you must install the Analysis ToolPak add-in macro. For more information, see "Managing Add-in Commands and Functions" in Chapter 4 in Book 2 of the *Microsoft Excel User's Guide.*

Syntax

ODDFYIELD(*settlement,maturity,issue, first_coupon,rate,pr,redemption,frequency,basis*)

Settlement is the security's settlement date, expressed as a serial date number.

Maturity is the security's maturity date expressed as a serial date number.

Issue is the security's issue date, expressed as a serial date number.

First_coupon is the security's first coupon date, expressed as a serial date number.

Rate is the security's interest rate.

Pr is the security's price.

Redemption is the security's redemption value per $100 face value.

Frequency is the number of coupon payments per year. For annual payments, *frequency* = 1; for semi-annual, *frequency* = 2; for quarterly, *frequency* = 4.

Basis is the type of day count basis to use.

Basis	Day count basis
0 or omitted	30/360
1	Actual/actual
2	Actual/360
3	Actual/365

Remarks

- *Settlement, maturity, issue, first_coupon,* and *basis* are truncated to integers.

- If any argument is non-numeric, ODDFYIELD returns the #VALUE! error value.

- If *settlement, maturity, issue,* or *first_coupon* is not a valid serial date number, ODDFYIELD returns the #NUM! error value.

- If *rate* < 0 or if *pr* ≤ 0, ODDFYIELD returns the #NUM! error value.

- If *basis* < 0 or if *basis* > 3, ODDFYIELD returns the #NUM! error value.

- The following date condition must be satisfied; otherwise, ODDFYIELD returns the #NUM! error value:

  maturity > first_coupon > settlement > issue

Related Functions

Function	Description
DATE	Returns the serial number of a particular date
ODDFPRICE	Returns the price per $100 face value of a security with an odd first period
ODDLPRICE	Returns the price per $100 face value of a security with an odd last period
ODDLYIELD	Returns the yield of a security with an odd last period

ODDLPRICE

Returns the price per $100 face value of a security having an odd (short or long) last coupon period.

If this function is not available, you must install the Analysis ToolPak add-in macro. For more information, see "Managing Add-in Commands and Functions" in Chapter 4 in Book 2 of the *Microsoft Excel User's Guide.*

Syntax

ODDLPRICE(*settlement,maturity,last_coupon,rate, yld,redemption,frequency,basis*)

Settlement is the security's settlement date, expressed as a serial date number.

Maturity is the security's maturity date, expressed as a serial date number.

Last_coupon is the security's last coupon date, expressed as a serial date number.

Rate is the security's interest rate.

Yld is the security's annual yield.

Redemption is the security's redemption value per $100 face value.

Frequency is the number of coupon payments per year. For annual payments, *frequency* = 1; for semi-annual, *frequency* = 2; for quarterly, *frequency* = 4.

Basis is the type of day count basis to use.

Basis	Day count basis
0 or omitted	30/360
1	Actual/actual
2	Actual/360
3	Actual/365

Remarks

- *Settlement, maturity, last_coupon,* and *basis* are truncated to integers.

- If any argument is non-numeric, ODDLPRICE returns the #VALUE! error value.

- If *settlement, maturity, or last_coupon* is not a valid serial date number, ODDLPRICE returns the #NUM! error value.

- If *rate* < 0 or if *yld* < 0, ODDLPRICE returns the #NUM! error value.

- If *basis* < 0 or if *basis* > 3, ODDLPRICE returns the #NUM! error value.

- The following date condition must be satisfied; otherwise, ODDLPRICE returns the #NUM! error value:

    maturity > *last_coupon* > *settlement*

Related Functions

Function	Description
DATE	Returns the serial number of a particular date
ODDFPRICE	Returns the price per $100 face value of a security with an odd first period
ODDFYIELD	Returns the yield of a security with an odd first period
ODDLYIELD	Returns the yield of a security with an odd last period

ODDLYIELD

Returns the yield of a security that has an odd (short or long) last period.

If this function is not available, you must install the Analysis ToolPak add-in macro. For more information, see "Managing Add-in Commands and Functions" in Chapter 4 in Book 2 of the *Microsoft Excel User's Guide.*

Syntax

ODDLYIELD(*settlement,maturity,last_coupon,rate, pr,redemption,frequency,basis*)

Settlement is the security's settlement date, expressed as a serial date number.

Maturity is the security's maturity date, expressed as a serial date number.

Last_coupon is the security's last coupon date, expressed as a serial date number.

Rate is the security's interest rate.

Pr is the security's price.

Redemption is the security's redemption value per $100 face value.

Frequency is the number of coupon payments per year. For annual payments, *frequency* = 1; for semi-annual, *frequency* = 2; for quarterly, *frequency* = 4.

Basis is the type of day count basis to use.

Basis	Day count basis
0 or omitted	30/360
1	Actual/actual
2	Actual/360
3	Actual/365

Remarks

- *Settlement, maturity, last_coupon,* and *basis* are truncated to integers.

- If any argument is non-numeric, ODDLYIELD returns the #VALUE! error value.

- If *settlement, maturity,* or *last_coupon* is not a valid serial date number, ODDLYIELD returns the #NUM! error value.

- If *rate* < 0 or if *pr* ≤ 0, ODDLYIELD returns the #NUM! error value.

- If *basis* < 0 or if *basis* > 3, ODDLYIELD returns the #NUM! error value.

- The following date condition must be satisfied; otherwise, ODDLYIELD returns the #NUM! error value:

  maturity > last_coupon > settlement

Related Functions

Function	Description
DATE	Returns the serial number of a particular date
ODDFPRICE	Returns the price per $100 face value of a security with an odd first period
ODDLPRICE	Returns the price per $100 face value of a security with an odd last period
ODDFYIELD	Returns the yield of a security with an odd first period

OFFSET

Returns a reference of a specified height and width, offset from another reference by a specified number of rows and columns.

Syntax

OFFSET(*reference,rows,cols,height,width*)

Reference is the reference from which you want to base the offset. If *reference* is a multiple selection, OFFSET returns the #VALUE! error value.

Rows is the number of rows, up or down, that you want the upper-left cell to refer to. Using 5 as the *rows* argument specifies that the upper-left cell in the reference is five rows below *reference*. *Rows* can be positive or negative.

Cols is the number of columns, to the left or right, that you want the upper-left cell of the result to refer to. Using 5 as the *cols* argument specifies that the upper-left cell in the reference is five columns to the right of *reference*. *Cols* can be positive or negative.

If *rows* and *cols* offset *reference* over the edge of the worksheet, OFFSET returns the #REF! error value.

Height is the height, in number of rows, that you want the returned reference to be. *Height* must be a positive number.

Width is the width, in number of columns, that you want the returned reference to be. *Width* must be a positive number.

If *height* or *width* is omitted, it is assumed to be the same height or width as *reference*.

Remarks

OFFSET doesn't actually move any cells or change the selection; it just returns a reference. OFFSET can be used with any function expecting a reference argument. For example, to select a range offset from the current selection, use OFFSET with the SELECT and SELECTION functions. You can also select a cell offset from the current selection by using a relative reference with the SELECT function, for example, SELECT("R[1]C").

Examples

OFFSET(C3,2,3,1,1) equals F5. If you enter this formula on a worksheet, Microsoft Excel displays the value contained in cell F5.

OFFSET(C3:E5,-1,0,3,3) equals C2:E4

OFFSET(C3:E5,0,-3,3,3) equals #REF!

The following macro formula selects a range of the same size as the current selection one row down:

SELECT(OFFSET(SELECTION(),1,0))

The following macro formula puts the result of the DOCUMENTS function into a range with a height of one row and a width corresponding to the number of columns returned by the COLUMNS function, and offset from the active cell by one row and one column:

FORMULA.ARRAY(DOCUMENTS(),
OFFSET(ACTIVE.CELL(),1,1,1,
COLUMNS(DOCUMENTS())))

Related Functions

Function	Description
ABSREF	Returns the absolute reference of a range of cells to another range
RELREF	Returns a relative reference

ON Functions

Macro Sheets Only

ON functions allow you to specify a macro to be run when a certain event occurs. The ON functions turn on and off this special event handling.

ON functions are turned on by specifying the type of event to wait for, such as recalculation, a specific time, or a key to be pressed, and the macro to be run when the event occurs. ON functions are turned off by using the same formula but omitting the argument specifying the macro to be run.

For more information about specific ON functions, see the following descriptions.

ON.DATA

Macro Sheets Only

Runs a specified macro when another application sends data to a particular document via dynamic data exchange (DDE) or via Publish and Subscribe on the Macintosh. Links to documents in other applications are called remote references. For more information about creating and using remote references, see Chapter 3 in Book 2 of the *Microsoft Excel User's Guide*.

Syntax

ON.DATA(*document_text,macro_text*)

Important Microsoft Excel for the Macintosh requires system software version 7.0 or later for this function.

Document_text is the name of the document to which remote data will be sent or the name of the source of the remote data.

- If *document_text* is the name of the remote data source, it must be in the form *appltopic!item*. You can use the form *appltopic* to include all items for a particular topic, or *appl* to specify an app alone, but you must include the | to indicate that you are specifying the name of a data source.

- If *document_text* is omitted, the macro specified by *macro_text* is run whenever remote data is sent to any document not already assigned to another ON.DATA function.

- In Microsoft Excel for the Macintosh, *document_text* can also be the name of a published edition file. Unless the file is in the current folder, *document_text* must include the complete path.

Macro_text is the nameof, or an R1C1-style reference to, a macro that you want to run when data comes into the document or from the source specified by *document_text*. The mame or reference must be in text form.

- If *macro_text* is omitted, the ON.DATA function is turned off for the specified document or source.

Remarks

- ON.DATA remains in effect until you either clear it or quit Microsoft Excel. You can clear ON.DATA by specifying *document_text* and omitting the *macro_text* argument.

- If the macro sheet containing *macro_text* is closed when data is sent to *document_text,* an error is returned.

- If the incoming data causes recalculation, Microsoft Excel first runs the macro *macro_text* and then performs the recalculation.

Examples

In Microsoft Excel for Windows, the following macro formula runs the macro AddOrders when data is sent to the worksheet ORDERSDB.XLS:

```
ON.DATA("ORDERSDB.XLS","AddOrders")
```

In Microsoft Excel for the Macintosh, the following macro formula runs the macro beginning at cell R2C3 when data is sent to the worksheet SALES DATABASE:

```
ON.DATA("SALES DATABASE","R2C3")
```

The following macro formula runs the macro SentAll when Q+E sends all its Query1 data to Microsoft Excel:

```
ON.DATA("QE|Query1!ALL","SentAll")
```

Related Functions

Function	Description
ERROR	Specifies what action to take if an error is encountered while a macro is running
INITIATE	Opens a channel to another application
ON.ENTRY	Runs a macro when data is entered
ON.RECALC	Runs a macro when a document is recalculated

ON.DOUBLECLICK

Macro Sheets Only

Runs a macro when you double-click any cell or object on the specified worksheet or macro sheet or double-click any item on the specified chart.

Syntax

ON.DOUBLECLICK(*sheet_text,macro_text*)

Sheet_text is a text value specifying the name of a document. If *sheet_text* is omitted, the macro is run whenever you double-click any document not specified by a previous ON.DOUBLECLICK formula.

Macro_text is the name of, or an R1C1-style reference to, a macro you want to run when you double-click the document specified by *sheet_text*. The name or refrence must be in text form. If *macro_text* is omitted, double-clicking reverts to its normal behavior, and any macros assigned by previous ON.DOUBLECLICK functions are turned off.

Remarks

- ON.DOUBLECLICK overrides Microsoft Excel's normal double-click behavior, such as displaying cell notes or displaying the Patterns dialog box.

- To determine what cell, object, or chart item has been double-clicked, use a CALLER function in the macro specified by *macro_text*.

- ON.DOUBLECLICK does not affect objects to which ASSIGN.TO.OBJECT macros have already been assigned. Use ON.DOUBLECLICK (TRUE) to make Microsoft Excel carry out the normal double-click behavior on the current selection.

Related Functions

Function	Description
ASSIGN.TO.OBJECT	Assigns a macro to an object
ON.WINDOW	Runs a macro when you switch to a window

ON.ENTRY

Macro Sheets Only

Runs a macro when you enter data into any cell on the specified document.

Syntax

ON.ENTRY(*sheet_text,macro_text*)

Sheet_text   is a text value specifying the name of a document. If *sheet_text* is omitted, the macro is run whenever you enter data into any worksheet or macro sheet.

Macro_text   is the name of, or an R1C1-style reference to, a macro you want to run when you enter data into the document specified by *sheet_text*. The name or reference must be in text form. If *macro_text* is omitted, entering data reverts to its normal behavior, and any macros assigned by previous ON.ENTRY functions are turned off.

Remarks

- The macro is run only when you enter data using the formula bar, not when you use edit commands or macro functions.

- To determine what cell had data entered into it, use a CALLER function in the macro specified by *macro_text*.

Related Functions

Function	Description
ENTER.DATA	Turns Data Entry mode on or off
ON.RECALC	Runs a macro when a document is recalculated

ON.KEY

Macro Sheets Only

Runs a specified macro when a particular key or key combination is pressed.

Syntax

ON.KEY(*key_text,macro_text*)

Key_text   can specify any single key, or any key combined with ALT, CTRL, or SHIFT, or any combination of those keys (in Microsoft Excel for Windows) or COMMAND, CTRL, OPTION, or SHIFT or any combination of those keys (in Microsoft Excel for the Macintosh). Each key is represented by one or more characters, such as "a" for the character a, or "{ENTER}" for the ENTER key.

To specify characters that aren't displayed when you press the key, such as ENTER or TAB, use the codes shown in the following table. Each code in the table represents one key on the keyboard.

Key	Code
BACKSPACE	"{BACKSPACE}" or "{BS}"
BREAK	"{BREAK}"
CAPS LOCK	"{CAPSLOCK}"
CLEAR	"{CLEAR}"
DELETE or DEL	"{DELETE}" or "{DEL}"

Key	Code
DOWN	"{DOWN}"
END	"{END}"
ENTER (numeric keypad)	"{ENTER}"
ENTER	"~" (tilde)
ESC	"{ESCAPE} or {ESC}"
HELP	"{HELP}"
HOME	"{HOME}"
INS	"{INSERT}"
LEFT	"{LEFT}"
NUM LOCK	"{NUMLOCK}"
PAGE DOWN	"{PGDN}"
PAGE UP	"{PGUP}"
RETURN	"{RETURN}"
RIGHT	"{RIGHT}"
SCROLL LOCK	"{SCROLLLOCK}"
TAB	"{TAB}"
UP	"{UP}"
F1 through F15	"{F1}" through "{F15}"

In Microsoft Excel for Windows, you can also specify keys combined with SHIFT and/or CTRL and/or ALT. In Microsoft Excel for the Macintosh, you can also specify keys combined with SHIFT and/or CTRL and/or OPTION and/or COMMAND. To specify a key combined with another key or keys, use the following table.

To combine with	Precede the key code by
SHIFT	"+" (plus sign)
CTRL	"^" (caret)
ALT or OPTION	"%" (percent sign)
COMMAND	"*" (asterisk)

To assign a macro to one of the special characters (+, ^, %, and so on), enclose the character in brackets. For example, ON.KEY("^{+}", "InsertItem") assigns a macro named InsertItem to the key sequence CTRL+PLUS SIGN.

Macro_text is the name of a macro that you want to run when *key_text* is pressed. The reference must be in text form.

- If *macro_text* is "" (empty text), nothing happens when *key_text* is pressed. This form of ON.KEY disables the normal meaning of keystrokes in Microsoft Excel.

- If *macro_text* is omitted, *key_text* reverts to its normal meaning in Microsoft Excel, and any special key assignments made with previous ON.KEY functions are cleared.

Remarks

- ON.KEY remains in effect until you clear it or quit Microsoft Excel. You can clear ON.KEY by specifying *key_text* and omitting the *macro_text* argument.

- If the macro sheet containing *macro_text* is closed when you press *key_text,* an error is returned.

Examples

Suppose you wanted the key combination SHIFT+CTRL+RIGHT to run the macro Print. You use the following macro formula:

```
ON.KEY("+^{RIGHT}","Print")
```

To return SHIFT+CTRL+RIGHT to its normal meaning, you would use the following macro formula:

```
ON.KEY("^{RIGHT}")
```

To disable SHIFT+CTRL+RIGHT altogether, you would use the following macro formula:

```
ON.KEY("+^{RIGHT}","")
```

The following macro runs the UNLOCKED.NEXT function whenever ENTER is pressed. The ON.KEY function assigns a macro to run when ENTER is pressed. The ResetEnterKey macro returns ENTER to its normal function. Use this macro when you want ENTER to automatically move to the next cell on a protected sheet.

	A	B	C
1	Names	Formulas	Comments
2			
3		SetEnterKey	
4		=ON.KEY("~","EnterNext")	Runs EnterNext on ENTER
5		=ON.KEY("^~","EnterPrev")	Runs EnterPrev on CTRL+ENTER
6		=RETURN()	
7			
8			
9	EnterNext	=UNLOCKED.NEXT()	Goes to next unlocked cell
10		=RETURN()	
11			
12			
13	EnterPrev	=UNLOCKED.PREV()	Goes to previous unlocked cell
14		=RETURN()	
15			
16			
17	ResetEnter	=ON.KEY("~")	Returns ENTER to normal
18		=ON.KEY("^~")	Returns CTRL+ENTER to normal
19		=RETURN()	

Related Functions

Function	Description
CANCEL.KEY	Disables macro interruption
ERROR	Specifies what action to take if an error is encountered while a macro is running
SEND.KEYS	Sends a key sequence to an application

ON.RECALC

Macro Sheets Only

Runs a macro when a specific document is recalculated. Use ON.RECALC to perform an operation on a document each time the document is recalculated, such as checking that a certain condition is still being met.

Syntax

ON.RECALC(*sheet_text,macro_text*)

Sheet_text   is the name of a document, given as text. If *sheet_text* is omitted, the macro is run whenever any open document not specified by a previous ON.RECALC formula is recalculated. Only one ON.RECALC formula can be run for each recalculation.

Macro_text   is the name of, or an R1C1-style reference to, a macro you want to run when the worksheet specified by *sheet_text* is recalculated. The name or reference must be in text form. The macro will be run each time the document is recalculated until ON.RECALC is cleared. If *macro_text* is omitted, recalculating reverts to its normal behavior, and any macros assigned by previous ON.RECALC functions are turned off.

Remarks

A macro specified to be run by ON.RECALC is not run by actions taken by other macros. For example, a macro specified by ON.RECALC will not be run after the CALCULATE.NOW function is carried out, but will be run if you change data in a sheet set to calculate automatically or choose the Calc Now button in the Calculation Options dialog box. This dialog box appears when you choose the Calculation command from the Options menu.

Examples

In Microsoft Excel for Windows, the following macro formula specifies that the macro Printer on the macro sheet AUTOREPT.XLM be run when the document named REPORT.XLS is recalculated:

```
ON.RECALC("REPORT.XLS",
"AUTOREPT.XLM!Printer")
```

In Microsoft Excel for the Macintosh, the following macro formula turns off ON.RECALC for the document named SALES:

```
ON.RECALC("SALES")
```

The following macro checks a particular value every time the worksheet is recalculated, and alerts the user if the value exceeds a certain amount.

	B	C
1	Formulas	Comments
2		
3	RecalcCheck	
4	=ON.RECALC("BUDGET.XLS","CheckTotal")	Checks the total
5	=RETURN()	
6		
7		
8	CheckTotal	
9	=IF(BUDGET.XLS!TotalMisc>10000,,ALERT("You are ove	Alert user if value is too high
10	=RETURN()	

Following is the complete formula in cell B9.

```
=IF(BUDGET.XLS!TotalMisc>10000,ALERT("You
are over budget for miscellaneous
expenses.",3))
```

Related Functions

Function	Description
CALCULATE.DOCUMENT	Calculates the active document only
CALCULATE.NOW	Calculates all open documents immediately
CALCULATION	Controls calculation settings
ON.ENTRY	Runs a macro when data is entered

ON.TIME

Macro Sheets Only

Runs a macro at a specified time. Use ON.TIME to run a macro at a specific time of day or after a specified period has passed.

Syntax

ON.TIME(*time,macro_text,tolerance,insert_logical*)

Time is the time and date, given as a serial number, at which the macro is to be run. If *time* does not include a date (that is, if *time* is a serial number less than 1), the macro is run the next time *time* occurs.

Macro_text is the name of, or an R1C1-style reference to, a macro to run at the specified time.

Tolerance is the time and date, given as a serial number, that you are willing to wait until and still have the macro run. For example, if Microsoft Excel is not in Ready, Copy, Cut, or Find mode at *time,* because another macro is running, but is in Ready mode 15 seconds later, and *tolerance* is set to *time* plus 30 seconds, the macro specified by *macro_text* will run. If Microsoft Excel was not in Ready mode within 30 seconds, the macro would not run. If *tolerance* is omitted, it is assumed to be infinite.

Insert_logical is a logical value specifying whether you want *macro_text* to run at *time.* Use *insert_logical* when you want to clear a previously set ON.TIME formula. If *insert_logical* is TRUE or omitted, the macro specified by *macro_text* is carried out at *time.* If *insert_logical* is FALSE and *macro_text* is not set to run at *time,* ON.TIME returns the #VALUE error value.

Examples

The following macro formula runs a macro called Test once at 5:00:00 P.M. when Microsoft Excel is in Ready mode:

```
ON.TIME("5:00:00 PM","Test")
```

The following macro formula runs a macro called Test 5 seconds after the formula is evaluated:

```
ON.TIME(NOW()+"00:00:05","Test")
```

The following macro formula runs a macro called Test 10 seconds after the formula is evaluated. If Microsoft Excel is not in Ready mode at that time (because it is in Edit mode, for example), the *tolerance* argument specifies 5 seconds of additional time to wait to run the macro. If Microsoft Excel is still not in Ready mode at that time, *macro_text* is not run.

```
ON.TIME(NOW()+"00:00:10","Test",NOW()
+"00:00:15")
```

Related Function

Function	Description
NOW	Returns the serial number of the current date and time

ON.WINDOW

Macro Sheets Only

Runs a specified macro when you switch to a particular window.

Syntax

ON.WINDOW(*window_text,macro_text*)

Window_text   is the name of a window in the form of text. If *window_text* is omitted, ON.WINDOW starts the macro whenever you switch to any window, except for windows that are named in other ON.WINDOW statements.

Macro_text   is the name of, or an R1C1-style reference to, a macro to run when you switch to *window_text*. If *macro_text* is omitted, switching to *window_text* no longer runs the previously specified macro.

Remarks

- A macro specified to be run by ON.WINDOW is not run when other macros switch to the window or when a command to switch to a window is received through a DDE channel. Instead, ON.WINDOW responds to a user's actions, such as clicking a window with the mouse, choosing the Goto command from the Formula menu, and so on.

- If a worksheet or macro sheet has an Auto_Activate or Auto_Deactivate macro defined for it, those macros will be run after the macro specified by ON.WINDOW. For more information, see "Running a Command Macro" in Chapter 6 in Book 2 of the *Microsoft Excel User's Guide*.

Examples

In Microsoft Excel for Windows, the following macro formula runs the macro beginning at cell R1C2 when you switch to the window MAIN.XLM:

```
ON.WINDOW("MAIN.XLM","R1C2")
```

The following macro formula stops the macro from running when you switch to MAIN.XLM:

```
ON.WINDOW("MAIN.XLM")
```

In Microsoft Excel for the Macintosh, the following macro formula runs the macro named ShowAlert when you switch to the window MAIN WINDOW:

```
ON.WINDOW("MAIN WINDOW","ShowAlert")
```

The following macro formula stops the macro from running when you switch to MAIN WINDOW:

```
ON.WINDOW("MAIN WINDOW")
```

Related Functions

Function	Description
GET.WINDOW	Returns information about a window
ON.KEY	Runs a macro when a specified key is pressed
WINDOWS	Returns the names of all open windows

OPEN

Macro Sheets Only

Equivalent to choosing the Open command from the File menu. Opens an existing document. For detailed information about the Open command, see online Help.

Syntax

OPEN(*file_text,*update_links,read_only, format,prot_pwd,write_res_pwd, ignore_rorec,file_origin,custom_delimit, add_logical)

OPEN?(*file_text,update_links,read_only, format,prot_pwd,write_res_pwd, ignore_rorec,file_origin,custom_delimit, add_logical)

File_text   is the name, as text, of the document you want to open. *File_text* can include a drive and path. In the dialog-box form in Microsoft Excel for Windows, *file_text* can include an asterisk (*) to represent any sequence of characters and a question mark (?) to represent any single character.

Update_links   specifies whether and how to update external and remote references. If *update_links* is omitted, Microsoft Excel displays a message asking if you want to update links.

If *update_links* is	Then Microsoft Excel
0	Updates neither external nor remote references
1	Updates external references only
2	Updates remote references only
3	Updates external and remote references

Note   When you are opening a file in WKS, WK1, or WK3 format, the *update_links* argument specifies whether Microsoft Excel generates charts from any graphs attached to the WKS, WK1, or WK3 file.

If *update_links* is	Charts are
0	Not created
2	Created

Read_only   corresponds to the Read Only check box in the Open dialog box. If *read_only* is TRUE, the document can be modified but changes cannot be saved; if FALSE or omitted, changes to the document can be saved.

Format   specifies what character to use as a delimiter when opening text files. If *format* is omitted, Microsoft Excel uses the current delimiter setting.

If *format* is	Values are separated by
1	Tabs
2	Commas
3	Spaces
4	Semicolons
5	Nothing
6	Custom characters

Prot_pwd   is the password, as text, required to unprotect a protected file. If *prot_pwd* is omitted and *file_text* requires a password, the Password dialog box is displayed. Passwords are case-sensitive. Passwords are not recorded when you open a document and supply the password with the macro recorder on.

Write_res_pwd   is the password, as text, required to open a read-only file with full write privileges. If *write_res_pwd* is omitted and *file_text* requires a password, the Password dialog box is displayed.

Ignore_rorec   is a logical value that controls whether the read-only recommended message is displayed. If *ignore_rorec* is TRUE, Microsoft Excel prevents display of the message; if FALSE or omitted, and if *read_only* is also FALSE or omitted, Microsoft Excel displays the alert when opening a read-only recommended document.

File_origin   is a number specifying whether a text file originated on the Macintosh or in Windows.

File_origin	Original operating environment
1	Macintosh
2	Windows (ANSI)
3	MS-DOS (PC-8)
Omitted	Current operating environment

Custom_delimit   is the character you want to use as a custom delimiter when opening text files.

- *Custom_delimit* is text or a reference or formula that returns text, such as CHAR(124).

- *Custom_delimit* is required if *delimiter_num* is 6; it is ignored if *delimiter_num* is not 6.

- Only the first character in *custom_delimit* is used.

Add_logical   is a logical value that specifies whether or not to add *file_text* to the open workbook. If *add_logical* is TRUE, the document is added; if FALSE or omitted, it is not added.

Examples

In Microsoft Excel for Windows, the following macro formula opens the file SALES.XLS as read only, updates both external and remote references, and supplies the password "Frankly":

```
OPEN("SALES.XLS",3,TRUE,,"Frankly")
```

The following formula opens the file SALES.XLS in the specified path:

```
OPEN("C:\SYSTEM\EXCEL\SALES.XLS")
```

In Microsoft Excel for the Macintosh, the following formula opens the file LIST DATA with edit privileges, updates no references, and specifies the data as comma separated.

```
OPEN("LIST DATA",0,FALSE,2)
```

The following formula opens the file LIST DATA in the specified path:

```
OPEN("Hard Disk:Excel:LIST DATA")
```

Related Functions

Function	Description
CLOSE	Closes the active window
FCLOSE	Closes a text file
FOPEN	Opens a file with the type of permission specified
OPEN.LINKS	Opens specified supporting documents

OPEN.LINKS

Macro Sheets Only

Equivalent to choosing the Links command from the File menu. Use OPEN.LINKS with the LINKS function to open documents linked to a particular document. For detailed information about the Links command, see online Help.

Syntax

OPEN.LINKS(*document_text1,document_text2,..., read_only,type_of_link*)
OPEN.LINKS?(*document_text1, document_text2,...,read_only,type_of_link*)

Document_text1,document_text2,...   are 1 to 12 arguments that are the names of supporting documents in the form of text, or arrays or references that contain text.

Read_only   corresponds to the Read Only check box in the File Links dialog box. If *read_only* is TRUE, the document can be modified but changes cannot be saved; if FALSE or omitted, changes to the document can be saved. *Read_only* applies only to Microsoft Excel, WKS, and SYLK documents.

Type_of_link   is a number from 1 to 6 that specifies what type of link you want to get information about.

Type_of_link	Link document type
1	Microsoft Excel link
2	DDE link
3	Reserved
4	Not applicable
5	Subscriber
6	Publisher

Remarks

You can generate an array of the names of linked documents with the LINKS function.

Examples

In Microsoft Excel for Windows, if a chart named PERFORM.XLC is open and contains data series that refer to worksheets named BUDGET.XLS and ACTUAL.XLS, these worksheets are opened when this macro formula is calculated:

```
OPEN.LINKS(LINKS())
```

In Microsoft Excel for the Macintosh, if a chart named PERFORMANCE CHART is open and contains data series that refer to worksheets named BUDGET and ACTUAL, these worksheets are opened when this formula is calculated:

```
OPEN.LINKS(LINKS())
```

Related Functions

Function	Description
CHANGE.LINK	Changes supporting worksheet links
GET.LINK.INFO	Returns information about a link
LINKS	Returns the name of all linked documents
UPDATE.LINK	Updates a link to another document

OPEN.MAIL

Macro Sheets Only

Equivalent to choosing the Open Mail command from the File menu. Opens files sent via Microsoft® Mail that Microsoft Excel can open. For detailed information about the Open Mail command, see online Help.

Note This function is only available if you are using Microsoft Excel for the Macintosh and Microsoft Mail version 2.0 or later.

Syntax

OPEN.MAIL(*subject,comments*)
OPEN.MAIL?(*subject,comments*)

Subject is the subject of the message containing a file that Microsoft Excel can open.

- For each message whose subject matches the *subject* argument and contains a file that Microsoft Excel can open, the file is opened in Microsoft Excel; if the message has no unread enclosures, it is deleted from the list of pending mail.

- If *subject* is omitted, then for all messages containing files that Microsoft Excel can open, the files are opened; each message that has no unread enclosures is deleted from the list of pending mail.

Comments is a logical value that specifies whether comments associated with the Microsoft Excel files are displayed. If *comments* is TRUE, Microsoft Excel displays the comments; if FALSE, comments are not displayed. If omitted, the current setting is not changed.

Tips

- If you use consistent subjects in your Microsoft Mail messages, you can easily create a macro that always opens mail messages with certain files attached. For example, an OPEN.MAIL formula with *subject* specified as "Weekly Report" would open the Microsoft Excel file attached to the message containing that subject each week.

- In OPEN.MAIL?, the dialog-box form of the function, the currently running macro pauses while the Microsoft Mail documents window is displayed. The macro resumes after you close the Microsoft Mail documents window.

Examples

The following macro formula opens the Microsoft Excel file attached to the Microsoft Mail message with the subject heading "Payroll Data" without displaying comments:

```
OPEN.MAIL("Payroll Data",FALSE)
```

The following macro formula displays the Microsoft Mail documents window and all messages readable by Microsoft Excel:

```
OPEN.MAIL?()
```

Related Function

Function	Description
SEND.MAIL	Sends the active document

OR

Returns TRUE if one or more of the arguments is TRUE; returns FALSE if all arguments are FALSE.

Syntax

OR(*logical1,logical2,...*)

Logical1, logical2,... are 1 to 30 conditions you want to test that can be either TRUE or FALSE.

- The arguments should be logical values or arrays or references that contain logical values.

- If an array or reference argument contains text, numbers, or empty cells, those values are ignored.

- If the specified range contains no logical values, OR returns the #VALUE! error value.

Examples

OR(TRUE) equals TRUE

OR(1+1=1,2+2=5) equals FALSE

If A1:A3 contains the values TRUE, FALSE, and TRUE, then:

OR(A1:A3) equals TRUE

The following macro formula checks the contents of the active cell. If the cell contains the single character "c" or "s", the OR formula returns TRUE and the macro branches to an area named FinishRefresh:

```
IF(OR(ACTIVE.CELL()="c",ACTIVE.CELL()="s"),
GOTO(FinishRefresh))
```

The preceding example shows how to use the worksheet form of the IF function on a macro sheet. You could also use the macro sheet form. For more information, see IF.

Also see the example for EXACT.

Tip You can use an OR array formula to see if a value occurs in an array. For example, the following macro uses Microsoft Excel's type conversion feature to compare a given account number to a list of account numbers. The OR formula in cell B5 is entered as an array formula; this causes Microsoft Excel to expand the account number into an array of the same size as the list of account numbers. This is useful if you want to see if a value occurs anywhere in an array. If the account number is in the list, the macro calls a subroutine to check the account activity; otherwise, an error message is displayed.

	A	B	C
1	Names	Formulas	Comments
2			
3		CheckAccount	
4	AccountNum	=INPUT("Enter the account number",2)	Asks for the account number
5	InTheList	=OR(AccountNum=List)	Checks the account list
6		=IF(InTheList)	If it's in the list, then...
7		=CheckAccountActivity(AccountNum)	Calls subroutine
8		=ELSE()	
9		=ALERT("The account number is not in the li	Otherwise displays message
10		=END.IF()	and ends
11		=RETURN()	

To enter the OR formula as an array, press CTRL+SHIFT (in Microsoft Excel for Windows) or COMMAND+SHIFT (in Microsoft Excel for the Macintosh).

The complete formula in cell B9 is:

```
=ALERT("The account number is not in the
list",2)
```

Related Functions

Function	Description
AND	Returns TRUE if all its arguments are TRUE
NOT	Reverses the logic of its argument

OUTLINE

Macro Sheets Only

Equivalent to choosing the Outline command from the Formula menu. Creates an outline and defines settings for automatically creating outlines. For detailed information about the Outline command, see online Help.

The first three arguments are logical values corresponding to check boxes in the Outline dialog box. If an argument is TRUE, Microsoft Excel selects the check box; if FALSE, Microsoft Excel clears the check box. If an argument is omitted, the check box is left in its current state.

Syntax

OUTLINE(*auto_styles,row_dir,col_dir, create_apply*)
OUTLINE?(*auto_styles,row_dir,col_dir, create_apply*)

Auto_styles corresponds to the Automatic Styles check box.

Row_dir corresponds to the Summary Rows Below Detail check box.

Col_dir corresponds to the Summary Columns To Right Of Detail check box.

Create_apply is the number 1 or 2 and corresponds to the Create button and the Apply Styles button.

Create_apply	Result
1	Creates an outline with the current settings
2	Applies outlining styles to the selection based on outline levels
Omitted	Corresponds to choosing the OK button to set the other outline settings

Example

The following macro formula creates an outline, turns on automatic outlining styles, and specifies that the summary columns and rows are to the right and below the detail, respectively:

```
OUTLINE(TRUE,TRUE,TRUE,1)
```

Related Functions

Function	Description
DEMOTE	Demotes the selection in an outline
PROMOTE	Promotes the selection in an outline

OVERLAY

Macro Sheets Only

Equivalent to choosing the Overlay command from the Format menu in Microsoft Excel version 2.2 or earlier. This function is included only for macro compatibility. To format an overlay chart in Microsoft Excel version 3.0 or later, use the FORMAT.OVERLAY function, which is equivalent to choosing the Overlay command from the Format menu.

Syntax

OVERLAY*(type_num,stack,100,vary,overlap,drop, hilo,overlap%,cluster,angle,series_num,auto)*
OVERLAY?*(type_num,stack,100,vary,overlap, drop,hilo,overlap%,cluster,angle,series_num,auto)*

OVERLAY.CHART.TYPE

Macro Sheets Only

Equivalent to choosing the Overlay Chart Type command from the Chart menu in Microsoft Excel for the Macintosh version 1.5 or earlier. This function is included only for macro compatibility. To format an overlay chart or to specify an overlay chart type in Microsoft Excel version 3.0 or later, use the FORMAT.OVERLAY function, which is equivalent to choosing the Overlay command from the Format menu.

Syntax

OVERLAY.CHART.TYPE*(type_num)*

PAGE.SETUP

Macro Sheets Only

Equivalent to choosing the Page Setup command from the File menu. Use PAGE.SETUP to control the printed appearance of your documents. For detailed information about the Page Setup command, see online Help.

There are two syntax forms of PAGE.SETUP. Syntax 1 applies if the active document is a worksheet or macro sheet; syntax 2 applies if the active document is a chart.

Arguments correspond to check boxes and text boxes in the Page Setup dialog box. Arguments that correspond to check boxes are logical values. If an argument is TRUE, Microsoft Excel selects the check box; if FALSE, Microsoft Excel clears the check box. Arguments for margins are always in inches, regrdless of your cuntry setting.

Syntax 1

Worksheets and macro sheets

PAGE.SETUP*(head,foot,left,right,top,bot,hdng, grid,h_cntr,v_cntr,orient,paper_size,scale,pg_num, pg_order,bw_cells)*

PAGE.SETUP?*(head,foot,left,right,top,bot,hdng, grid,h_cntr,v_cntr,orient,paper_size,scale,pg_num, pg_order,bw_cells)*

Syntax 2

Charts

PAGE.SETUP*(head,foot,left,right,top,bot,size, h_cntr,v_cntr,orient,paper_size,scale,pg_num)*

PAGE.SETUP?*(head,foot,left,right,top,bot,size, h_cntr,v_cntr,orient,paper_size,scale,pg_num)*

Head   specifies the text and formatting codes for the document header. For information about formatting codes, see "Remarks" later in this topic.

Foot   specifies the text and formatting codes for the document footer.

Left   corresponds to the Left box and is a number specifying the left margin.

Right   corresponds to the Right box and is a number specifying the right margin.

Top   corresponds to the Top box and is a number specifying the top margin.

Bot   corresponds to the Bottom box and is a number specifying the bottom margin.

Hdng corresponds to the Row & Column Headings check box. *Hdng* is available only in the worksheet and macro sheet form of the function.

Grid corresponds to the Cell Gridlines check box. *Grid* is available only in the worksheet and macro sheet form of the function.

H_cntr corresponds to the Center Horizontally check box in the Page Setup dialog box.

V_cntr corresponds to the Center Vertically check box in the Page Setup dialog box.

Orient determines the direction in which your document is printed.

Orient	Print format
1	Portrait
2	Landscape

Paper_size is a number from 1 to 26 that specifies the size of the paper.

Paper_size	Paper type
1	Letter
2	Letter (small)
3	Tabloid
4	Ledger
5	Legal
6	Statement
7	Executive
8	A3
9	A4
10	A4 (small)
11	A5
12	B4
13	B5
14	Folio
15	Quarto
16	10x14
17	11x17
18	Note

Paper_size	Paper type
19	ENV9
20	ENV10
21	ENV11
22	ENV12
23	ENV14
24	C Sheet
25	D Sheet
26	E Sheet

Scale is a number representing the percentage to increase or decrease the size of the document. All scaling retains the aspect ratio of the original. *Scale* is ignored when using printers that do not provide scaling.

- To specify a percentage of reduction or enlargement, set *scale* to the percentage.

- For worksheets and macros, you can specify the number of pages that the printout should be scaled to fit. Set *scale* to a two-item horizontal array, with the first item equal to the width and the second item equal to the height. If no constraint is necessary in one direction, you can set the corresponding value to #N/A.

- *Scale* can also be a logical value. To fit the print area on a single page, set *scale* to TRUE.

Pg_num specifies the number of the first page. *Pg_num* must be greater than or equal to 1. If omitted, PAGE.SETUP retains the existing *pg_num*.

Pg_order specifies whether pagination is left-to-right and then down, or top-to-bottom and then right.

Pg_order	Pagination
1	Top-to-bottom, then right
2	Left-to-right, then down

Bw-cells   is a logical value that specifies whether to print cells and text boxes in color.

- If *bw_cells* is TRUE, Microsoft Excel prints cell text and borders in black and cell backgrounds in white.

- If *bw_cells* is FALSE , Microsoft Excel prints cell text, borders, and background patterns in color.

Size   is a number corresponding to the options in the Chart Size box, and determines how you want the chart printed on the page within the margins. *Size* is available only in the chart form of the function.

Size	Size to print the chart
1	Screen size
2	Fit to page
3	Full page

Remarks

Microsoft Excel version 4.0 no longer requires you to enter formatting codes to format headers and footers, but the codes are still supported and recorded by the macro recorder. You can include these codes as part of the *head* and *foot* text strings to align portions of the header or footer to the left, right, or center; to include the page number, date, time, or document name; and to print the header or footer in bold or italic.

Formatting code	Result
&L	Left-aligns the characters that follow.
&C	Centers the characters that follow.
&R	Right-aligns the characters that follow.
&B	Turns bold printing on or off.
&I	Turns italic printing on or off.
&U	Turns underline printing on or off.
&S	Turns strikethrough printing on or off.
&O	Turns outline printing on or off (Macintosh only).

Formatting code	Result
&H	Turns shadow printing on or off (Macintosh only).
&D	Prints the current date.
&T	Prints the current time.
&F	Prints the name of the document.
&P	Prints the page number.
&P+*number*	Prints the page number plus *number.*
&P–*number*	Prints the page number minus *number.*
&&	Prints a single ampersand.
& "*fontname*"	Prints the characters that follow in the specified font. Be sure to include the double quotation marks.
&*nn*	Prints the characters that follow in the specified font size. Use a two-digit number to specify a size in points.
&N	Prints the total number of pages in the document.

Related Functions

Function	Description
DISPLAY	Controls screen and Info Window display
GET.DOCUMENT	Returns information about a document
PRINT	Prints the active document
WORKSPACE	Changes workspace settings

PARSE

Macro Sheets Only

Equivalent to choosing the Parse command from the Data menu. Distributes the contents of the current selection to fill several adjacent columns; the selection can be no more than one column wide. Use PARSE to reorganize data, especially data that you've read from files created by another application, such as a database. For detailed information about the Parse command, see online Help.

Syntax

PARSE(*parse_text,destination_ref*)
PARSE?(*parse_text,destination_ref*)

Parse_text is the parse line in the form of text. It is a copy of the first nonblank cell in the selected column, with square brackets indicating where to distribute (or parse) text. If *parse_text* is omitted, Microsoft Excel guesses where to place the brackets based on the spacing and formatting of data.

Destination_ref is a reference to the upper-left corner of the range of cells where you want to place the parsed data. If *destination_ref* is omitted, it is assumed to be the the the current selection, so the parsed data will replace the original data.

Remarks

- In most cases, it's easier to record the Parse command than to enter the PARSE function manually.

- When you use the PARSE function or choose the Parse command from the Data menu, Microsoft Excel splits the first column into as many columns as you specify with *parse_text* and replaces any information in those columns.

- If the delimiter (separator) character occurs at regularly spaced intervals, the parse fields you specify with *parse_text* will have a fixed length, and you can select the column and use the PARSE function as described above. However, if the delimiter character occurs randomly, the parse fields will have a variable length, so you should use the Smart Parse command contained in FLATFILE.XLA (in Microsoft Excel for Windows) or Flat File (in Microsoft Excel for the Macintosh) in the Microsoft Excel LIBRARY directory.

When installed, the Smart Parse command appears on the Data menu. In Microsoft Excel for Windows, use the following macro formula to start Smart Parse from your macro:

```
RUN("FLATFILE.XLA!mcp05.SmartParse",
TRUE)
```

In Microsoft Excel for the Macintosh, use the following macro formula:

```
RUN("'Flat File'!mcp05.SmartParse",
TRUE)
```

Example

The following macro formula parses the current selection and places the parsed data starting in cell A1 on the active worksheet. Microsoft Excel guesses how to parse the data based on the spacing and formatting of the original data.

```
PARSE(,!$A$1)
```

Related Functions

Function	Description
MID	Returns a specific string starting at the position you specify
SEARCH	Finds one text value within another (not case-sensitive)

PASTE

Macro Sheets Only

Equivalent to choosing the Paste command from the Edit menu. Pastes a selection or object that you copied or cut using the COPY or CUT function. Use PASTE when you want to paste all components of the selection. To paste only specific components of the selection, use PASTE.SPECIAL. For detailed information about the Paste command, see online Help.

Syntax

PASTE(*to_reference*)

To_reference is a reference to the cell or range of cells where you want to paste what you have copied. If *to_ref*erence is omitted, Microsoft Excel pastes to the current selection.

Example

See the example for SHOW.CLIPBOARD.

Related Functions

Function	Description
COPY	Copies and pastes data or objects
CUT	Cuts or moves data or objects
FORMULA	Enters values into a cell or range or onto a chart
INSERT	Inserts cells
PASTE.LINK	Pastes copied data and establishes a link to its source
PASTE.SPECIAL	Pastes specific components of copied data

PASTE.LINK

Macro Sheets Only

Equivalent to choosing the Paste Link command from the Edit menu. Pastes copied data or objects and establishes a link to the source of the data or object. The source can be either another Microsoft Excel worksheet or another application. Use PASTE.LINK when you want Microsoft Excel to automatically update the paste area with any changes that occur in the source. For detailed information about the Paste Link command, see online Help.

Syntax

PASTE.LINK( )

Note To work properly, the application you are linking to must support dynamic data exchange (DDE) or object linking and embedding (OLE). For more information, see "Using Dynamic Data Exchange (DDE) in Command Macros" in Chapter 8 in Book 2 of the *Microsoft Excel User's Guide.*

Related Functions

Function	Description
COPY	Copies and pastes data or objects
CUT	Cuts or moves data or objects
PASTE	Pastes cut or copied data
PASTE.SPECIAL	Pastes specific components of copied data

PASTE.PICTURE

Macro Sheets Only

Equivalent to choosing the Paste Picture command from the Edit menu. Pastes a picture of the Clipboard contents onto the worksheet. This picture is not linked, so changes to the source data will not be reflected in the picture. For detailed information about the Paste Picture command, see online Help.

Syntax

PASTE.PICTURE( )

Related Functions

Function	Description
COPY.PICTURE	Creates a picture of the current selection for use in another program
PASTE.PICTURE.LINK	Pastes a linked picture of the currently copied area

PASTE.PICTURE.LINK

Macro Sheets Only

Equivalent to choosing the Paste Picture Link command from the Edit menu or to using the camera tool on the utility toolbar. Pastes a linked picture of the Clipboard contents. This picture is linked, so changes to the source data will be reflected in the picture. For detailed information about the Paste Picture Link command, see online Help.

Syntax

PASTE.PICTURE.LINK( )

Related Functions

Function	Description
COPY.PICTURE	Creates a picture of the current selection for use in another program
CREATE.OBJECT	Creates an object
PASTE.PICTURE	Pastes a picture of the currently copied area

PASTE.SPECIAL

Macro Sheets Only

Equivalent to choosing the Paste Special command from the Edit menu. Pastes the specified components from the copy area into the current selection. The PASTE.SPECIAL function has four syntax forms. Use syntax 1 if you are pasting into a worksheet or macro sheet. For detailed information about the Paste Special command, see online Help.

Syntax 1

From a worksheet to a worksheet

PASTE.SPECIAL(*paste_num,operation_num, skip_blanks,transpose*)
PASTE.SPECIAL?(*paste_num,operation_num, skip_blanks,transpose*)

Paste_num is a number from 1 to 5 specifying what to paste.

Paste_num	Pastes
1	All
2	Formulas
3	Values
4	Formats
5	Notes

Operation_num is a number from 1 to 5 specifying which operation to perform when pasting.

Operation_num	Action
1	None
2	Add
3	Subtract
4	Multiply
5	Divide

Skip_blanks is a logical value corresponding to the Skip Blanks check box in the Paste Special dialog box.

- If *skip_blanks* is TRUE, Microsoft Excel skips blanks in the copy area when pasting.
- If *skip_blanks* is FALSE, Microsoft Excel pastes normally.

Transpose is a logical value corresponding to the Transpose check box in the Paste Special dialog box.

- If *transpose* is TRUE, Microsoft Excel transposes rows and columns when pasting.
- If *transpose* is FALSE, Microsoft Excel pastes normally.

Example

The following macro formula pastes all formulas, values, formats, and notes, and subtracts the numeric contents of the Clipboard from the numbers in the current selection. It also skips blank cells.

```
PASTE.SPECIAL(1,3,TRUE,FALSE)
```

Related Functions

Function	Description
FORMULA	Enters values into a cell or range or onto a chart
PASTE	Pastes cut or copied data
PASTE.LINK	Pastes copied data and establishes a link to its source

PASTE.SPECIAL

Macro Sheets Only

Equivalent to choosing the Paste Special command from the Edit menu on the Chart menu bar. Pastes the specified components from the copy area into a chart. The PASTE.SPECIAL function has four syntax forms. Use syntax 2 if you have copied from a worksheet and are pasting into a chart.

Syntax 2

From a worksheet to a chart

PASTE.SPECIAL(*rowcol,series,categories,replace*)
PASTE.SPECIAL?(*rowcol,series,categories, replace*)

Rowcol   is the number 1 or 2 and specifies whether the values corresponding to a particular data series are in rows or columns. Enter 1 for rows or 2 for columns.

Series   is a logical value corresponding to the Series Names In First Column (or First Row, depending on the value of *rowcol*) check box in the Paste Special dialog box.

- If *series* is TRUE, Microsoft Excel selects the check box and uses the contents of the cell in the first column of each row (or first row of each column) as the name of the data series in that row (or column).

- If *series* is FALSE, Microsoft Excel clears the check box and uses the contents of the cell in the first column of each row (or first row of each column) as the first data point of the data series.

Categories   is a logical value corresponding to the Categories (X Labels) In First Row (or First Column, depending on the value of *rowcol*) check box in the Paste Special dialog box.

- If *categories* is TRUE, Microsoft Excel selects the check box and uses the contents of the first row (or column) of the selection as the categories for the chart.

- If *categories* is FALSE, Microsoft Excel clears the check box and uses the contents of the first row (or column) as the first data series in the chart.

Replace   is a logical value corresponding to the Replace Existing Categories check box in the Paste Special dialog box.

- If *replace* is TRUE, Microsoft Excel selects the check box and applies categories while replacing existing categories with information from the copied cell range.

- If *replace* is FALSE, Microsoft Excel clears the check box and applies new categories without replacing any old ones.

Example

The following macro formula pastes to a chart. Values are in rows, with series names in the first column.

```
PASTE.SPECIAL(1,TRUE,FALSE,FALSE)
```

For information on adding data to a chart or changing the orientation of chart data, see CHART.WIZARD.

PASTE.SPECIAL

Macro Sheets Only

Equivalent to choosing the Paste Special command from the Edit menu on the Chart menu bar. Pastes the specified components from the copy area into a chart. The PASTE.SPECIAL function has four syntax forms. Use syntax 3 if you have copied from a chart and are pasting into a chart.

Syntax 3

From a chart to a chart

PASTE.SPECIAL(*paste_num*)
PASTE.SPECIAL?(*paste_num*)

Paste_num is a number from 1 to 3 specifying what to paste.

Paste_num	Pastes
1	All (formats and data series)
2	Formats only
3	Formulas (data series) only

PASTE.SPECIAL

Macro Sheets Only

Equivalent to choosing the Paste Special command from the Edit menu when pasting data from another application into Microsoft Excel.

Syntax 4

From another application

PASTE.SPECIAL(*format_text,pastelink_logical*)
PASTE.SPECIAL?(*format_text,pastelink_logical*)

Format_text is text specifying the type of data you want to paste from the Clipboard.

- The valid data types vary depending on the application from which the data was copied. For example, if you're copying data from Microsoft Word, some of the data types are "Microsoft Document Object", "Picture", and "Text".

- For more information about object classes, see your Microsoft Windows or Apple system software documentation.

Pastelink_logical is a logical value specifying whether to link the pasted data to its source application.

- If *pastelink_logical* is TRUE, Microsoft Excel updates the pasted information whenever it changes in the source application.

- If *pastelink_logical* is FALSE or omitted, the information is pasted without a link.

- If Microsoft Excel or the source application does not support linking for the specified *format_text*, then *pastelink logical* is ignored.

Example

If a text object was copied to the Clipboard in Microsoft Word for Windows, the following macro formula pastes it into Microsoft Excel :

```
PASTE.SPECIAL("Text",TRUE)
```

If an object was copied to the Clipboard in Microsoft Word for Windows, the following macro formula embeds a copy of the object into Microsoft Excel:

```
PASTE.SPECIAL("Word Document Object")
```

PASTE.TOOL

Macro Sheets Only

Equivalent to selecting a tool and choosing the Paste Tool Face command from the Edit menu. Pastes a tool face from the Clipboard to a specified position on a toolbar. For more information about the Paste Tool Face command, see online Help.

Syntax

PASTE.TOOL(*bar_id,position*)

Bar_id specifies the number or name of the toolbar into which you want to paste the tool face. For detailed information about *bar_id,* see ADD.TOOL.

Position specifies the position within the toolbar of the tool on which you want to paste the tool face. *Position* starts with 1 at the left side (if horizontal) or at the top (if vertical).

Example

The following macro formula pastes a tool face into position 4 of Toolbar1.

```
PASTE.TOOL("Toolbar1",4)
```

Related Function

Function	Description
COPY.TOOL	Copies a tool face

PATTERNS

Macro Sheets Only

Equivalent to choosing the Patterns command from the Format menu. Changes the appearance of the selected cells or objects or the selected chart item (you can select only one chart item at a time). The PATTERNS function has eight syntax forms: syntax 1 is for cells on a worksheet or macro sheet. Syntax 2 is for lines or arrows on a worksheet, macro sheet, or chart. Syntax 3 is for objects on a worksheet or macro sheet. Syntax 4 through syntax 8 are for chart items.

Syntax 1

Cells

PATTERNS(*apattern,afore,aback*)
PATTERNS?(*apattern,afore,aback*)

Syntax 2

Lines (arrows) on worksheets or charts

PATTERNS(*lauto,lstyle,lcolor,lwt,hwidth, hlength,htype*)
PATTERNS?(*lauto,lstyle,lcolor,lwt,hwidth, hlength,htype*)

Syntax 3

Text boxes, rectangles, ovals, arcs, and pictures on worksheets or macro sheets

PATTERNS(*bauto,bstyle,bcolor,bwt,shadow, aauto,apattern,afore,aback,rounded*)
PATTERNS?(*bauto,bstyle,bcolor,bwt,shadow, aauto,apattern,afore,aback,rounded*)

Syntax 4

Chart plot areas, bars, columns, pie slices, and text labels

PATTERNS(*bauto,bstyle,bcolor,bwt,shadow, aauto,apattern,afore,aback,invert,apply*)
PATTERNS?(*bauto,bstyle,bcolor,bwt,shadow, aauto,apattern,afore,aback,invert,apply*)

Syntax 5

Chart axes

PATTERNS(*lauto,lstyle,lcolor,lwt,tmajor,tminor, tlabel*)
PATTERNS?(*lauto,lstyle,lcolor,lwt,tmajor,tminor, tlabel*)

Syntax 6

Chart gridlines, hi-lo lines, drop lines, lines on a picture line chart, and picture charts of bar, and column charts

PATTERNS(*lauto,lstyle,lcolor,lwt,apply*)
PATTERNS?(*lauto,lstyle,lcolor,lwt,apply*)

Syntax 7

Chart data lines

PATTERNS(*lauto,lstyle,lcolor,lwt,mauto,mstyle, mfore,mback,apply*)
PATTERNS?(*lauto,lstyle,lcolor,lwt,mauto,mstyle, mfore,mback,apply*)

Syntax 8

Picture chart markers

PATTERNS(*type,picture_units,apply*)
PATTERNS?(*type,picture_units,apply*)

The following argument descriptions are in alphabetic order. Arguments correspond to check boxes, list boxes, and options in the Patterns dialog box for the selected item. The default for each argument reflects the setting in the dialog box.

Aauto is a number from 0 to 2 specifying area settings (that is, the object's "surface area").

If *aauto* is	Area settings are
0	Set by the user (custom)
1	Automatic (set by Microsoft Excel)
2	None

Aback is a number from 1 to 16 corresponding to the 16 area background colors in the Patterns dialog box.

Afore is a number from 1 to 16 corresponding to the 16 area foreground colors in the Patterns dialog box.

Apattern is a number corresponding to the area patterns in the Patterns dialog box. If an object is selected, *apattern* can be from 1 to 18; if a cell is selected, *apattern* can be from 0 to 18. If *apattern* is 0 and a cell is selected, Microsoft Excel applies no pattern.

Apply is a logical value corresponding to the Apply To All check box. This argument applies only when a chart data point or a data series is selected.

- If *apply* is TRUE, Microsoft Excel applies any formatting changes to all items that are similar to the selected item on the chart.

- If *apply* is FALSE, Microsoft Excel applies formatting changes only to the selected item on the chart.

Bauto is a number from 0 to 2 specifying border settings.

If *bauto* is	Border settings are
0	Set by the user (custom)
1	Automatic (set by Microsoft Excel)
2	None

Bcolor is a number from 1 to 16 corresponding to the 16 border colors in the Patterns dialog box.

Bstyle is a number from 1 to 8 corresponding to the eight border styles in the Patterns dialog box.

Bwt is a number from 1 to 4 corresponding to the four border weights in the Patterns dialog box.

If *bwt* is	Border is
1	Hairline
2	Thin
3	Medium
4	Thick

Hlength is a number from 1 to 3 specifying the length of the arrowhead.

If *hlength* is	Arrowhead is
1	Short
2	Medium
3	Long

Htype is a number from 1 to 3 specifying the style of the arrowhead.

If *htype* is	Style of arrowhead is
1	No head
2	Open head
3	Closed head

Hwidth is a number from 1 to 3 specifying the width of the arrowhead.

If *hwidth* is	Arrowhead is
1	Narrow
2	Medium
3	Wide

Invert is a logical value corresponding to the Invert If Negative check box in the Patterns dialog box. This argument applies only to data markers.

- If *invert* is TRUE, Microsoft Excel inverts the pattern in the selected item if it corresponds to a negative number.

- If *invert* is FALSE, Microsoft Excel removes the inverted pattern, if present, from the selected item corresponding to a negative value.

Lauto is a number from 0 to 2 specifying line settings.

If *lauto* is	Line settings are
0	Set by the user (custom)
1	Automatic (set by Microsoft Excel)
2	None

Lcolor is a number from 1 to 16 corresponding to the 16 line colors in the Patterns dialog box.

Lstyle is a number from 1 to 8 corresponding to the eight line styles in the Patterns dialog box.

Lwt is a number from 1 to 4 corresponding to the four line weights in the Patterns dialog box.

If *lwt* is	Line is
1	Hairline
2	Thin
3	Medium
4	Thick

Mauto is a number from 0 to 2 specifying marker settings.

If *mauto* is	Marker settings are
0	Set by the user
1	Automatic (set by Microsoft Excel)
2	None

Mback is a number from 1 to 16 corresponding to the 16 marker background colors in the Patterns dialog box.

Mfore is a number from 1 to 16 corresponding to the 16 marker foreground colors in the Patterns dialog box.

Mstyle is a number from 1 to 9 corresponding to the nine marker styles in the Patterns dialog box.

Picture_units is the number of units you want each picture to represent in a scaled, stacked picture chart. This argument applies only to picture charts and only if *type* is 3.

Rounded is a logical value corresponding to the Round Corners check box and specifying whether to make the corners on text boxes and rectangles rounded. If *rounded* is TRUE, the corners are rounded; if FALSE, the corners are square. If the selection is an arc or an oval, *rounded* is ignored.

Shadow is a logical value corresponding to the Shadow check box. *Shadow* does not apply to area charts or bars in bar charts. If *shadow* is TRUE, Microsoft Excel adds a shadow to the selected item; if FALSE, Microsoft Excel removes the shadow, if one is present, from the selected item. If the selection is an arc, *shadow* is ignored.

Tlabel is a number from 1 to 4 specifying the position of tick labels.

If *tlabel* is	Tick label position is
1	None
2	Low
3	High
4	Next to axis

Tmajor is a number from 1 to 4 specifying the type of major tick marks.

If *tmajor* is	Type of major tick marks is
1	None
2	Inside
3	Outside
4	Cross

Tminor is a number from 1 to 4 specifying the type of minor tick marks.

If *tminor* is	Type of minor tick marks is
1	None
2	Inside
3	Outside
4	Cross

Type is a number from 1 to 3 specifying the type of pictures to use in a picture chart.

If *type* is	Pictures should be
1	Stretched to reach a particular value
2	Stacked on top of each other to reach a particular value
3	Stacked on top of each other, but you specify the number of units each picture represents

Remarks

- You can select many graphic objects on a worksheet or macro sheet and apply formatting to them at the same time, but you can select only one chart item at a time.

- If you select multiple objects and if one or more of the objects requires a different form of the PATTERNS function, then choose the syntax corresponding to the object with the most formatting attributes—that is, the syntax with the most arguments. If you specify an argument that does not apply to an item, the argument has no effect on that item.

- To apply formatting to similar items on a chart, use the *apply* argument described above.

Example

The following macro formula formats the selected text box with custom borders in border style 1 and border color 5, a shadow, and rounded corners. All other arguments are left in the default settings.

```
PATTERNS(0,1,5,,TRUE,,,,,TRUE)
```

Related Functions

Function	Description
FORMAT.FONT	Applies a font to the selection
FORMAT.TEXT	Formats a worksheet text box or a chart text item

PAUSE

Macro Sheets Only

Pauses a macro. Use the PAUSE function, instead of choosing the Pause button in the Single Step dialog box, as a debugging tool when you do not wish to step through a macro. You can also use PAUSE to enter and edit data, to work directly with Microsoft Excel commands, or to perform other actions that are not normally available when a macro is running.

Syntax

PAUSE(*no_tool*)

No_tool is a logical value specifying whether to display the Resume toolbar when the macro is paused. If *no_tool* is TRUE, the toolbar is not displayed; if FALSE, the toolbar is displayed; if omitted, the toolbar is displayed unless you previously clicked the close box on the toolbar.

Remarks

- All commands and tools that are available when no macro is running are still available when a macro is paused.

- You can run other macros while a macro is paused, but you can pause only one macro at a time. If a macro is paused when you run a second macro containing a PAUSE function, choosing Macro Resume resumes only the second macro; you cannot resume or return to the first macro automatically.

- PAUSE is ignored in custom functions, unless you manually run them by choosing the Run command from the Macro menu. PAUSE is also ignored if it's placed in a formula for which the resume behavior would be unclear, such as:

```
IF(Cost<10,AND(PAUSE(),SUM(!$A$1:$A$4)))
```

- If one macro runs a second macro that pauses, Microsoft Excel locks the calling cell in the first macro. If you try to edit this cell, Microsoft Excel displays an error message.

- To resume a paused macro, choose the Resume Macro tool on the toolbar, choose the Resume command from the Macro menu, or run a macro containing a RESUME function.

- If one macro runs a second macro that pauses and you need to halt only the paused macro, use RESUME(2) instead of HALT. HALT halts all macros and prevents resuming or returning to any macro. For more information, see RESUME.

For more information about pausing and resuming macros and using other debugging tools, see "Testing a Command Macro" in Chapter 7 in Book 2 of the *Microsoft Excel User's Guide*.

Tip   Since the automatic Resume toolbar can be customized, you can create a custom toolbar that will appear whenever a macro pauses.

Example

The following macro formula checks to see if a variable named TestValue is greater than 9. If it is, the macro pauses; otherwise, the macro continues normally.

```
IF(TestValue>9,PAUSE())
```

Also see the example for ENTER.DATA.

Related Functions

Function	Description
HALT	Stops all macros from running
RESUME	Resumes a paused macro
STEP	Turns on macro single-stepping

PEARSON

Returns the Pearson product moment correlation coefficient, *r,* a dimensionless index that ranges from −1.0 to 1.0 inclusive, and reflects the extent of a linear relationship between two data sets.

Syntax

PEARSON(*array1,array2*)

Array1   is a set of independent values.

Array2   is a set of dependent values.

Remarks

- The arguments should be numbers, or names, arrays, or references that contain numbers.

- If an array or reference argument contains text, logical values, or empty cells, those values are ignored; however, cells with the value zero are included.

- If *array1* and *array2* are empty or have a different number of data points, PEARSON returns the #N/A error value.

- The *r* value of the regression line is:

$$r = \frac{n(\Sigma XY) - (\Sigma X)(\Sigma Y)}{\sqrt{\left[n\Sigma X^2 - (\Sigma X)^2\right]\left[n\Sigma Y^2 - (\Sigma Y)^2\right]}}$$

Example

PEARSON({9,7,5,3,1},{10,6,1,5,3}) equals 0.699379

Related Functions

Function	Description
INTERCEPT	Returns the intercept of the linear regression line
LINEST	Returns parameters of a linear trend
RSQ	Returns the r^2 value of the linear regression line
SLOPE	Returns the slope of the linear regression line
STEYX	Returns the standard error of the predicted y-value for each x in the regression

PERCENTILE

Returns the value from *array* at the k-th percentile. You can use this function to establish a threshold of acceptance. For example, you can decide to examine candidates that score above the 90th percentile.

Syntax

PERCENTILE*(array,k)*

Array   is the array or range of data that defines relative standing.

K   is the percentile value in the range 0..1, inclusive.

Remarks

- If *array* is empty or contains more than 8191 data points, PERCENTILE returns the #NUM! error value.

- If k is non-numeric, PERCENTILE returns the #VALUE! error value.

- If k is < 0 or if k > 1, PERCENTILE returns the #NUM! error value.

- If k is not a multiple of $1/(n-1)$, PERCENTILE interpolates to determine the value at the kth percentile.

Example

`PERCENTILE({1,2,3,4},0.3)` equals 1.9

Related Functions

Function	Description
LARGE	Returns the k-th largest value in a data set
MAX	Returns the maximum value in a list of arguments
MEDIAN	Returns the median of the given numbers
MIN	Returns the minimum value in a list of arguments
PERCENTRANK	Returns the percentage rank of a value in a data set
QUARTILE	Returns the quartile of a data set
SMALL	Returns the k-th smallest value in a data set

PERCENTRANK

Returns the percentage rank of x among the values in *array*. This function can be used to evaluate the relative standing of an observation in a data set. For example, you can use PERCENTRANK to evaluate the standing of an aptitude test score among the population of scores for the test.

Syntax

PERCENTRANK*(array,x,significance)*

Array   is the array or range of data with numeric values that defines relative standing.

X   is the value for which you want to know the rank.

Significance   is an optional value that identifies the number of significant digits for the returned percentage value. If omitted, PERCENTRANK uses three digits (0.xxx%).

Remarks

- If *array* is empty, PERCENTRANK returns the #NUM! error value.

- If *significance* < 1, PERCENTRANK returns the #NUM! error value.

- If *x* does not match one of the values in *array,* PERCENTRANK interpolates to return the correct percentage rank.

Example

PERCENTRANK({1,2,3,4,5,6,7,8,9,10},4) equals 0.33

Related Functions

Function	Description
LARGE	Returns the *k*-th largest value in a data set
MAX	Returns the maximum value in a list of arguments
MEDIAN	Returns the median of the given numbers
MIN	Returns the minimum value in a list of arguments
PERCENTILE	Returns the *k*-th percentile of values in a range
QUARTILE	Returns the quartile of a data set
SMALL	Returns the *k*-th smallest value in a data set

PERMUT

Returns the number of permutations of groups of *number_chosen* objects that can be selected from *number* objects. A permutation is any sct or subset of objects or events where internal order is significant. Permutations are different than combinations, for which the internal order is not significant. Use this function for lottery-style probability calculations.

Syntax

PERMUT(*number,number_chosen*)

Number   is an integer that describes the number of objects.

Number_chosen   is an integer that describes the number of objects in each permutation.

Remarks

- Both arguments are truncated to integers.

- If *number* or *number_chosen* is non-numeric, PERMUT returns the #VALUE! error value.

- If *number* ≤ 0 or if *number_chosen* < 0, PERMUT returns the #NUM! error value.

- If *number* < *number_chosen,* PERMUT returns the #NUM! error value.

- The equation for the number of permutations is:

$$P_{k,n} = \frac{n!}{(n-k)!}$$

Example

Suppose you want to calculate the odds of selecting a winning lottery number. Each lottery number contains three numbers, each of which can be between 0 and 99, inclusive. The following function calculates the number of possible permutations.

PERMUT(100,3) equals 970,200

Related Functions

Function	Description
BINOMDIST	Returns the individual term binomial distribution
COMBIN	Returns the number of combinations for a given number of objects

Function	Description
CRITBINOM	Returns the smallest value for which the cumulative binomial distribution is less than or equal to a criterion value
FACT	Returns the factorial of a number
HYPGEOMDIST	Returns the hypergeometric distribution
NEGBINOMDIST	Returns the negative binomial distribution

PI

Returns the number 3.14159265358979, the mathematical constant π, accurate to 15 digits.

Syntax

PI( )

Examples

PI()/2 equals 1.57079...

SIN(PI()/2) equals 1

If the radius of a circle is stored in a cell named Radius, the following macro formula calculates the area of the circle:

PI()*(Radius^2)

Related Functions

Function	Description
COS	Returns the cosine of a number
SIN	Returns the sine of the given angle
TAN	Returns the tangent of a number

PLACEMENT

Maoro Shoots Only

Equivalent to choosing the Object Placement command from the Format menu in Microsoft Excel version 3.0. Determines how the selected object or objects are attached to the cells beneath them. This function is included only for macro compatibility and will be converted to OBJECT.PROPERTIES when you load older macro sheets. For more information, see OBJECT.PROPERTIES.

Syntax

PLACEMENT(*placement_type*)
PLACEMENT?(*placement_type*)

PMT

Returns the periodic payment for an annuity based on constant payments and a constant interest rate.

Syntax

PMT(*rate,nper,pv,fv,type*)

For a more complete description of the arguments in PMT, see PV.

Rate is the interest rate per period.

Nper is the total number of payment periods in an annuity.

Pv is the present value—the total amount that a series of future payments is worth now.

Fv is the future value, or a cash balance you want to attain after the last payment is made. If *fv* is omitted, it is assumed to be 0 (the future value of a loan, for example, is 0).

Type is the number 0 or 1 and indicates when payments are due.

Set *type* equal to	If payments are due
0 or omitted	At the end of the period
1	At the beginning of the period

Remarks

- The payment returned by PMT includes principal and interest but no taxes, reserve payments, or fees sometimes associated with annuities.

- Make sure that you are consistent about the units you use for specifying *rate* and *nper*. If you make monthly payments on a four-year loan at 12 percent annual interest, use 12%/12 for *rate* and 4*12 for *nper*. If you make annual payments on the same loan, use 12% for *rate* and 4 for *nper*.

Tip To find the total amount paid over the duration of the annuity, multiply the returned PMT value by *nper*.

Examples

The following macro formula returns the monthly payment on a $10,000 loan at an annual rate of 8% that you must pay off in 10 months:

PMT(8%/12,10,10000) equals −$1037.03

For the same loan, if payments are due at the beginning of the period, the payment is:

PMT(8%/12,10,10000,0,1) equals −$1030.16

The following macro formula returns the amount someone must pay to you each month if you loan that person $5000 at 12% and want to be paid back in five months:

PMT(12%/12,5,-5000) equals $1030.20

Suppose you want to save $50,000 in 18 years by saving a constant amount each month. If you assume you'll be able to earn 6% interest on your savings, you can use PMT to determine how much to save each month:

PMT(6%/12,18*12,0,50000) equals −$129.08

If you pay $129.08 into a 6% savings account every month for 18 years, you will have $50,000.

Related Functions

Function	Description
FV	Returns the future value of an investment
IPMT	Returns the interest payment for an investment for a given period
NPER	Returns the number of periods for an investment
PPMT	Returns the payment on the principal for an investment for a given period
PV	Returns the present value of an investment
RATE	Returns the interest rate per period of an annuity

POISSON

Returns the Poisson probability distribution. A common application of the Poisson distribution is predicting the number of events over a specific time, such as the number of cars arriving at a toll plaza in one minute.

Syntax

POISSON(*x,mean,cumulative*)

X   is the number of events.

Mean   is the expected numeric value.

Cumulative   is a logical value that determines the form of the probability distribution returned. If *cumulative* is TRUE, POISSON returns the cumulative Poisson probability that the number of random events occurring will be between zero and *x* inclusive; if FALSE, it returns the Poisson probability mass function that the number of events occurring will be exactly *x*.

Remarks

- If *x* is not an integer, it is truncated.

- If *x* or *mean* is non-numeric, POISSON returns the #VALUE! error value.

- If $x \leq 0$, POISSON returns the #NUM! error value.

- If $mean \leq 0$, POISSON returns the #NUM! error value.

Examples

POISSON(2,5,FALSE) equals 0.084224

POISSON(2,5,TRUE) equals 0.124652

Related Function

Function	Description
EXPONDIST	Returns the exponential distribution

POKE

Macro Sheets Only

Sends data to another application. Use POKE to send data to documents in other applications you are communicating with through dynamic data exchange (DDE).

Syntax

POKE(*channel_num*,*item_text*,*data_ref*)

Important Microsoft Excel for the Macintosh requires system software version 7.0 or later for this function.

Channel_num is the channel number returned by a previously run INITIATE function.

Item_text is text that identifies the item you want to send data to in the application you are accessing through *channel_num*. The form of *item_text* depends on the application connected to *channel_num*.

Data_ref is a reference to the document containing the data to send.

If POKE is not successful, it returns the following values.

Value returned	Meaning
#VALUE!	*Channel_num* is not a valid channel number.
#DIV/0!	The application you are accessing does not respond after a certain length of time, and you press ESC to cancel.
#REF!	POKE is refused.

For information about accessing other applications, see Chapter 3 in Book 2 of the *Microsoft Excel User's Guide*.

Examples

In Microsoft Excel for Windows, the following macro inserts the text from cell C3 into the Microsoft Word for Windows document SALES.DOC at the start of the document.

	A	B	C
1	*Names*	*Formulas*	*Comments*
2			
3		**SendData**	
4	SendChanl	=INITIATE("WINWORD","C:\SALES.DOC")	
5		=POKE(SendChanl,"StartOfDoc",C3)	Send comments to doc
6		=TERMINATE(SendChanl)	
7		=RETURN()	

In Microsoft Excel for the Macintosh, the following macro inserts the text from cell C3 into the Microsoft Word document named Report.

	A	B	C
1	*Names*	*Formulas*	*Comments*
2			
3		**SendData**	
4	SendChanl	=INITIATE("Word","HardDisk.Apps:Word:Report")	
5		=POKE(SendChanl,"TopicName",C3)	Send comments to doc
6		=TERMINATE(SendChanl)	
7		=RETURN()	

Related Functions

Function	Description
INITIATE	Opens a channel to another application
REQUEST	Returns data from another application
TERMINATE	Closes a channel to another application

PPMT

Returns the payment on the principal for a given period for an investment based on periodic, constant payments and a constant interest rate.

Syntax

PPMT(*rate,per,nper,pv,fv,type*)

For a more complete description of the arguments in PPMT, see PV.

Rate   is the interest rate per period.

Per   specifies the period and must be in the range 1 to *nper*.

Nper   is the total number of payment periods in an annuity.

Pv   is the present value—the total amount that a series of future payments is worth now.

Fv   is the future value, or a cash balance you want to attain after the last payment is made. If *fv* is omitted, it is assumed to be 0 (the future value of a loan, for example, is 0).

Type   is the number 0 or 1 and indicates when payments are due.

Set *type* equal to	If payments are due
0 or omitted	At the end of the period
1	At the beginning of the period

Remarks

Make sure that you are consistent about the units you use for specifying *rate* and *nper*. If you make monthly payments on a four-year loan at 12 percent annual interest, use 12%/12 for *rate* and 4*12 for *nper*. If you make annual payments on the same loan, use 12% for *rate* and 4 for *nper*.

Examples

The following formula returns the principal payment for the first month of a two-year $2000 loan at 10% annual interest:

PPMT(10%/12,1,24,2000) equals −$75.62

The following function returns the principal payment for the last year of a 10-year $200,000 loan at 8% annual interest:

PPMT(8%,10,10,200000) equals −$27,598.05

Related Functions

Function	Description
FV	Returns the future value of an investment
IPMT	Returns the interest payment for an investment for a given period
NPER	Returns the number of periods for an investment
PMT	Returns the periodic payment for an annuity
PV	Returns the present value of an investment
RATE	Returns the interest rate per period of an annuity

PRECISION

Macro Sheets Only

Equivalent to selecting or clearing the Precision As Displayed check box in the Calculation Options dialog box, which appears when you choose the Calculation command from the Options menu. Controls how values are stored in cells. Use PRECISION when the results of formulas do not seem to match the values used to calculate the formulas.

Syntax

PRECISION(*logical*)

Logical   is a logical value corresponding to the Precision As Displayed check box in the Calculation dialog box.

- If *logical* is TRUE, Microsoft Excel stores future entries at full precision (15 digits).

- If *logical* is FALSE or omitted, Microsoft Excel stores values exactly as they are displayed.

Caution   The PRECISION function may permanently alter your data. PRECISION(FALSE) causes Microsoft Excel to change values on your worksheet or macro sheet to match displayed values. PRECISION(TRUE) causes Microsoft Excel to store future values at full precision, but it does not restore previously entered numbers to their original values.

Remarks

- Precision As Displayed does not affect numbers in General format. Numbers in General format are always calculated to full precision.

- Microsoft Excel calculates slightly faster when using full precision because with Precision As Displayed selected, Microsoft Excel has to round off numbers as it calculates.

Related Functions

Function	Description
FORMAT.NUMBER	Applies a number format to the selection
WORKSPACE	Changes workspace settings

PREFERRED

Macro Sheets Only

Equivalent to choosing the Preferred command from the Gallery menu, which is available when a chart is the active document.

Changes the format of the active chart to the format currently defined by the Set Preferred command or the SET.PREFERRED macro function. For detailed information about the Preferred command, see online Help.

Syntax

PREFERRED( )

Related Function

Function	Description
SET.PREFERRED	Changes the default chart format

PRESS.TOOL

Macro Sheets Only

Formats a tool so that it appears either normal or depressed into the screen.

Syntax

PRESS.TOOL(*bar_id,position,down*)

Bar_id   specifies the number or name of the toolbar in which you want to change the tool appearance. For detailed information about *bar_id*, see ADD.TOOL.

Position   specifies the position of the tool within the toolbar. *Position* starts with 1 at the left side (if horizontal) or at the top (if vertical).

Down   is a logical value specifying the appearance of the tool. If *down* is TRUE, the tool appears depressed into the screen; if FALSE or omitted, it appears normal (up).

Remarks

This function applies only to custom tools to which macros have already been assigned. An error occurs if you try to process any other type of tool.

Example

The following macro formula sets the tool image to normal (up).

```
PRESS.TOOL("Toolbar4",3,FALSE)
```

Related Functions

Function	Description
ADD.TOOL	Adds one or more tools to a toolbar
DELETE.TOOL	Deletes a tool from a toolbar

PRICE

Returns the price per $100 face value of a security that pays periodic interest.

If this function is not available, you must install the Analysis ToolPak add-in macro. For more information, see "Managing Add-in Commands and Functions" in Chapter 4 in Book 2 of the *Microsoft Excel User's Guide.*

Syntax

PRICE(*settlement,maturity,rate,yld,redemption, frequency,basis*)

Settlement is the security's settlement date, expressed as a serial date number.

Maturity is the security's maturity date, expressed as a serial date number.

Rate is the security's annual coupon rate.

Yld is the security's annual yield.

Redemption is the security's redemption value per $100 face value.

Frequency is the number of coupon payments per year. For annual payments, *frequency* = 1; for semi-annual, *frequency* = 2; for quarterly, *frequency* = 4.

Basis is the type of day count basis to use.

Basis	Day count basis
0 or omitted	30/360
1	Actual/actual
2	Actual/360
3	Actual/365

Remarks

- *Settlement, maturity, frequency,* and *basis* are truncated to integers.

- If any argument is non-numeric, PRICE returns the #VALUE! error value.

- If *settlement* or *maturity* is not a valid serial date number, PRICE returns the #NUM! error value.

- If *yld* < 0 or if *rate* < 0, PRICE returns the #NUM! error value.

- If *redemption* $\leq$ 0, PRICE returns the #NUM! error value.

- If *frequency* is any number other than 1, 2, or 4, PRICE returns the #NUM! error value.

- If *basis* < 0 or if *basis* > 3, PRICE returns the #NUM! error value.

- If *settlement* $\geq$ *maturity,* PRICE returns the #NUM! error value.

Example

A bond has the following terms:

February 15, 1991 settlement date
November 15, 1999 maturity date
5.75% semiannual coupon
6.50% yield
$100 redemption value
30/360 basis

The bond price (in the 1900 Date System) is:

```
PRICE(33284,36479,0.0575,0.065,100,
2,0) equals 95.04287
```

Related Functions

Function	Description
DATE	Returns the serial number of a particular date
YIELD	Returns the yield on a security that pays periodic interest

PRICEDISC

Returns the price per $100 face value of a discounted security.

If this function is not available, you must install the Analysis ToolPak add-in macro. For more information, see "Managing Add-in Commands and Functions" in Chapter 4 in Book 2 of the *Microsoft Excel User's Guide.*

Syntax

PRICEDISC(*settlement,maturity,discount, redemption,basis*)

Settlement is the security's settlement date, expressed as a serial date number.

Maturity is the security's maturity date, expressed as a serial date number.

Discount is the security's discount rate.

Redemption is the security's redemption value per $100 face value.

Basis is the type of day count basis to use.

Basis	Day count basis
0 or omitted	30/360
1	Actual/actual
2	Actual/360
3	Actual/365

Remarks

- *Settlement, maturity,* and *basis* are truncated to integers.

- If any argument is non-numeric, PRICEDISC returns the #VALUE! error value.

- If *settlement* or *maturity* is not a valid serial date number, PRICEDISC returns the #NUM! error value.

- If *discount* ≤ 0 or if *redemption* ≤ 0, PRICEDISC returns the #NUM! error value.

- If *basis* < 0 or if *basis* > 3, PRICEDISC returns the #NUM! error value.

- If *settlement* ≥ *maturity,* PRICEDISC returns the #NUM! error value.

Example

A bond has the following terms:

February 15, 1991 settlement date
March 1, 1991 maturity date
5.25% discount rate
$100 redemption value
Actual/360 basis

The bond price (in the 1900 Date System) is:

```
PRICEDISC(33284,33298,0.0525,100,2)
```
equals 99.79583

Related Functions

Function	Description
DATE	Returns the serial number of a particular date
DISC	Returns the discount rate for a security
YIELDDISC	Returns the annual yield for a discounted security

PRICEMAT

Returns the price per $100 face value of a security that pays interest at maturity.

If this function is not available, you must install the Analysis ToolPak add-in macro. For more information, see "Managing Add-in Commands and Functions" in Chapter 4 in Book 2 of the *Microsoft Excel User's Guide.*

Syntax

PRICEMAT(*settlement,maturity,issue,rate,yld, basis*)

Settlement   is the security's settlement date, expressed as a serial date number.

Maturity   is the security's maturity date, expressed as a serial date number.

Issue   is the security's issue date, expressed as a serial date number.

Rate   is the security's interest rate at date of issue.

Yld   is the security's annual yield.

Basis   is the type of day count basis to use.

Basis	Day count basis
0 or omitted	30/360
1	Actual/actual
2	Actual/360
3	Actual/365

Remarks

- *Settlement, maturity, issue,* and *basis* are truncated to integers.

- If any argument is non-numeric, PRICEMAT returns the #VALUE! error value.

- If *settlement, maturity,* or *issue* is not a valid serial date number, PRICEMAT returns the #NUM! error value.

- If *rate* < 0 or if *yld* < 0, PRICEMAT returns the #NUM! error value.

- If *basis* < 0 or if *basis* > 3, PRICEMAT returns the #NUM! error value.

- If *settlement* ≥ *maturity*, PRICEMAT returns the #NUM! error value.

Example

A bond has the following terms:

February 15, 1991 settlement date
April 13, 1991 maturity date
November 11, 1990 issue date
6.1% semiannual coupon
6.1% yield
30/360 basis

The price (in the 1900 Date System) is:

PRICEMAT(33284,33341,33188,0.061, 0.061,0) equals 99.98449888

Related Functions

Function	Description
DATE	Returns the serial number of a particular date
YIELDMAT	Returns the annual yield of a security that pays interest at maturity

PRINT

Macro Sheets Only

Equivalent to choosing the Print command from the File menu. Prints the active document. For detailed information about the Print command, see online Help.

Arguments correspond to options, check boxes, and edit boxes in the Print dialog box. Arguments corresponding to check boxes are logical values. If an argument is TRUE, Microsoft Excel selects the check box; if FALSE, Microsoft Excel clears the check box.

Syntax

PRINT(*range_num,from,to,copies,draft,preview, print_what,color,feed,quality,v_quality*)

PRINT?(*range_num,from,to,copies,draft,preview, print_what,color,feed,quality,v_quality*)

Range_num is a number specifying which pages to print.

Range num	Prints the following pages
1	All the pages
2	Prints a specified range. If *range_num* is 2, then *from* and *to* are required arguments.

From specifies the first page to print. This argument is ignored unless *range_num* equals 2.

To specifies the last page to print. This argument is ignored unless *range_num* equals 2.

Copies specifies the number of copies to print. If omitted, the default is 1.

Draft corresponds to the Fast, but no graphics check box. If omitted, the Fast, but no graphics check box is not changed.

Preview corresponds to the Preview check box. If omitted, the Preview check box is not changed.

Print_what is a number from 1 to 3 that specifies what parts of the worksheet or macro sheet to print. If a chart is the active document, *print_what* is ignored. If omitted, the setting is not changed.

Print_what	Prints
1	Sheet only
2	Notes only
3	Sheet and then notes

Color corresponds to the Print Using Color check box. *Color* is available only in Microsoft Excel for the Macintosh. If omitted, the setting is not changed.

Feed is a number specifying the type of paper feed. *Feed* is available only in Microsoft Excel for the Macintosh.

Feed	Type of paper feed
1 or omitted	Continuous (paper cassette)
2	Cut sheet or manual (manual feed)

Quality corresponds to the Print Quality box and specifies the DPI output quality you want If omitted, print quality is not changed. This argument is only available in Microsoft Excel for Windows.

V_quality corresponds to the Print Quality box if you have specified a printer where the horizontal and vertical resolution is not equal, such as a dot-matrix printer. If omitted, print quality is not changed. This argument is only available in Microsoft Excel for Windows.

Examples

The following macro formula prints two copies of pages 5 through 7, including notes, in color.

```
PRINT(2,5,7,2,FALSE,FALSE,3,TRUE,)
```

Related Functions

Function	Description
PAGE.SETUP	Sets page printing specifications
PRINT.PREVIEW	Previews pages and page breaks before printing
PRINTER.SETUP	Identifies the printer
SET.PRINT.AREA	Defines the print area
SET.PRINT.TITLES	Defines text to print as titles

PRINT.PREVIEW

Macro Sheets Only

Equivalent to choosing the Print Preview command from the File menu. Previews the pages and page breaks of the active document on the screen before printing. For detailed information about the Print Preview command, see online Help.

Syntax

PRINT.PREVIEW( )

Related Function

Function	Description
PRINT	Prints the active document

PRINTER.SETUP

Macro Sheets Only

Equivalent to choosing the Page Setup command from the File menu and then choosing the Printer Setup button in Microsoft Excel for Windows. Use PRINTER.SETUP to change the printer you are using.

Syntax

PRINTER.SETUP(*printer_text*)
PRINTER.SETUP?(*printer_text*)

Printer_text is the name of the printer you want to switch to. Enter *printer_text* exactly as it appears in the Setup dialog box.

Note This function is only available in Microsoft Excel for Windows.

Example

The following macro formula changes the printer to an HP LaserJet Plus attached to COM1:

```
PRINTER.SETUP("HP LaserJet+ on COM1:")
```

Related Functions

Function	Description
PAGE.SETUP	Sets page printing specifications
PRINT	Prints the active document

PROB

Returns the probability that values in *x_range* are between the *lower_limit* and *upper_limit*. If *upper_limit* is not supplied, returns the probability that values in *x_range* are equal to *lower_limit*.

Syntax

PROB(*x_range,prob_range,lower_limit, upper_limit*)

X_range is the range of numeric values of *x* with which there are associated probabilities.

Prob_range is a set of probabilities associated with values in *x_range*.

Lower_limit is the lower bound on the value for which you want a probability.

Upper_limit is the optional upper bound on the value for which you want a probability.

Remarks

- If any value in *prob_range* ≤ 0 or if any value in *prob_range* > 1, PROB returns the #NUM! error value.

- If the sum of the values in *prob_range* $\neq 1$, PROB returns the #NUM! error value.

- If *upper_limit* is omitted, PROB returns the probability of being equal to *lower_limit*.

- If *x_range* and *prob_range* contain a different number of data points, PROB returns the #N/A error value.

Examples

PROB({0,1,2,3},{0.2,0.3,0.1,0.4},2) equals 0.1

PROB({0,1,2,3},{0.2,0.3,0.1,0.4},1,3) equals 0.8

Related Functions

Function	Description
BINOMDIST	Returns the individual term binomial distribution
CRITBINOM	Returns the smallest value for which the cumulative binomial distribution is less than or equal to a criterion value

PRODUCT

Multiplies all the numbers given as arguments and returns the product.

Syntax

PRODUCT(*number1*,*number2*,...)

Number1, number2,...   are 1 to 30 numbers that you want to multiply.

- Arguments that are numbers, logical values, or text representations of numbers are counted; arguments that are error values or text that cannot be translated into numbers cause errors.

- If an argument is an array or reference, only numbers in the array or reference are counted. Empty cells, logical values, text, or error values in the array or reference are ignored.

Examples

If cells A2:C2 contain 5, 15, and 30:

PRODUCT(A2:C2) equals 2250

PRODUCT(A2:C2,2) equals 4500

Related Functions

Function	Description
FACT	Returns the factorial of a number
SUM	Adds its arguments
SUMPRODUCT	Returns the sum of the products of corresponding array components

PROMOTE

Macro Sheets Only

Equivalent to clicking the promote button. Promotes the currently selected rows or columns in an outline. Use PROMOTE to change the configuration of an outline by promoting rows or columns of information.

Syntax

PROMOTE(*rowcol*)
PROMOTE?(*rowcol*)

Rowcol   specifies whether to promote rows or columns.

Rowcol	Demotes
1 or omitted	Rows
2	Columns

Remarks

- If the selection consists of an entire row or rows, then rows are promoted even if *rowcol* is 2. Similarly, selection of an entire column overrides *rowcol* 1.

- Also, if the selection is unambiguous (an entire row or column), then PROMOTE? will not display the dialog box.

Related Functions

Function	Description
DEMOTE	Demotes the selection in an outline
SHOW.DETAIL	Expands or collapses a portion of an outline
SHOW.LEVELS	Displays a specific number of levels of an outline

PROPER

Capitalizes the first letter in *text* and any other letters in *text* that follow any character other than a letter. Converts all other letters to lowercase.

Syntax

PROPER(*text*)

Text   is text enclosed in quotation marks, a formula that returns text, or a reference to a cell containing the text you want to partially capitalize.

Examples

PROPER("this is a TITLE") equals "This Is A Title"

PROPER("2-cent's worth") equals "2-Cent'S Worth"

PROPER("76BudGet") equals "76Budget"

Suppose you keep information about vendors and parts in several similar worksheets. The following lines in a macro subroutine use the PROPER and UPPER functions to correct errors in capitalization that might occur when someone updates one of these worksheets using a custom dialog box. Assume that the custom dialog box is defined on another part of the macro sheet.

	A	B	C
20	*Names*	*Formulas*	*Comments*
21			
22		**CorrectDialogBox**	Corrects case
23		=FORMULA(PROPER(DialogVendor),"Vendor")	These lines copy the
24		=FORMULA(PROPER(DialogStreet),"Street")	corrected values from
25		=FORMULA(PROPER(DialogCity),"City")	a dialog-box area on
26		=FORMULA(UPPER(DialogState),"State")	the macro sheet to six
27		=FORMULA(DialogZip,"Zip")	named cells on the
28		=FORMULA(DialogPart,"Part")	active worksheet.
29		=RETURN()	

The names Vendor, Street, City, State, Zip, and Part refer to specific cells on the external, active worksheet.

Related Functions

Function	Description
LOWER	Converts text to lowercase
UPPER	Converts text to uppercase

PROTECT.DOCUMENT

Macro Sheets Only

Equivalent to choosing the Protect Document and Unprotect Document commands from the Options menu if a worksheet, macro sheet, or workbook is the active document. Equivalent to choosing the Protect Document and Unprotect Document commands from the Chart menu if a chart is the active document. Adds protection to or removes protection from the active worksheet, macro sheet, workbook, or chart. Use PROTECT.DOCUMENT to prevent yourself or others from changing cell contents, objects, or window configurations in a document. For detailed information about the Protect and Unprotect Document commands, see online Help.

Syntax

PROTECT.DOCUMENT(*contents,windows, password,objects*)

PROTECT.DOCUMENT?(*contents,windows, password,objects*)

Contents is a logical value corresponding to a check box in the Protect Document dialog box. For worksheets or macro sheets, *contents* corresponds to the Cells check box. For charts, *contents* corresponds to the Chart check box. For workbooks, *contents* corresponds to the Contents check box.

- If *contents* is TRUE or omitted, Microsoft Excel selects the check box and protects cells on the worksheet or macro sheet. For a workbook, Microsoft Excel protects the list of documents in the workbook. For a chart, Microsoft Excel protects the entire chart (including objects).

- If *contents* is FALSE, Microsoft Excel clears the check box (and removes protection if the correct password is supplied).

Windows is a logical value corresponding to the Windows check box in the Protect Document dialog box for all document types.

- If *windows* is TRUE, Microsoft Excel selects the check box and prevents a document's windows from being moved or sized.

- If *windows* is FALSE or omitted, Microsoft Excel clears the check box (and removes protection if the correct password is supplied).

Password is the password you specify in the form of text to protect or unprotect the file.

- If *password* is omitted when you protect a document, then you will be able to remove protection without a password. This is useful if you want only to protect the document from accidental changes.

- If *password* is omitted when you try to remove protection from a document that was protected with a password, the normal password dialog box is displayed.

- Passwords are not recorded into the PROTECT.DOCUMENT function when you use the macro recorder.

Objects is a logical value. This argument applies only to worksheets and macro sheets. *Objects* corresponds to the Objects check box in the Protect Document dialog box.

- If *objects* is TRUE or omitted, Microsoft Excel selects the check box and protects all locked objects on the worksheet or macro sheet.

- If *objects* is FALSE, Microsoft Excel clears the check box.

Remarks

- If *contents, windows,* and *objects* are FALSE, PROTECT.DOCUMENT carries out the Unprotect Document command. If *contents, windows,* or *objects* is TRUE, it carries out the Protect Document command.

- Make sure you protect macro sheets that protect or unprotect worksheets. If you type a password directly into the macro function either to protect or unprotect a worksheet —for example, PROTECT.DOCUMENT(TRUE,TRUE, "XD1411C",TRUE)—then someone could open the macro sheet and see the password needed to unprotect the document.

- You can use the following commands, or their corresponding macro functions, on unprotected cells in a protected document: Copy, Paste, Fill Right, and Fill Down, all on the Edit menu; and Paste Name and Paste Function, both on the Formula menu.

Warning If you forget the password of a document that was previously protected with a password, you cannot unprotect the document.

Example

The following macro formula protects the active document's contents, windows, and objects without a password:

```
PROTECT.DOCUMENT(TRUE,TRUE,,TRUE)
```

Related Functions

Function	Description
CELL.PROTECTION	Controls protection for the selected cells
ENTER.DATA	Turns Data Entry mode on and off

Function	Description
OBJECT.PROTECTION	Controls how an object is protected
SAVE.AS	Saves a document and allows you to specify the name, file type, password, backup file, and location of the document

PTTESTM

Macro Sheets Only

Performs a paired two-sample Student's *t*-Test for means. For more information, see "Analyzing Statistical or Engineering Data" in Chapter 1 in Book 2 of the *Microsoft Excel User's Guide*.

If this function is not available, you must install the Analysis ToolPak add-in macro. For more information, see "Managing Add-in Commands and Functions" in Chapter 4 in Book 2 of the *Microsoft Excel User's Guide*.

Syntax

PTTESTM(*inprng1,inprng2,outrng,*labels,alpha, difference)

Inprng1   is the input range for the first data set.

Inprng2   is the input range for the second data set.

Outrng   is the first cell (the upper-left cell) in the output table.

Labels   is a logical value.

- If *labels* is TRUE, then labels are in the first row or column of the input ranges.

- If *labels* is FALSE or omitted, all cells in *inprng1* and *inprng2* are considered data. The output table will include default row or column headings.

Alpha   is the confidence level for the test. If omitted, *alpha* is 0.05.

Difference   is the hypothesized mean difference. If omitted, *difference* is 0.

Related Functions

Function	Description
PTTESTV	Performs a two-sample Student's *t*-Test, assuming unequal variances
TDIST	Returns the Student's *t*-distribution
TTEST	Returns the probability associated with a Student's *t*-Test
TTESTM	Performs a two-sample Student's *t*-Test for means, assuming equal variances

PTTESTV

Macro Sheets Only

Performs a two-sample Student's *t*-Test, assuming unequal variances. For more information, see "Analyzing Statistical or Engineering Data" in Chapter 1 in Book 2 of the *Microsoft Excel User's Guide*.

If this function is not available, you must install the Analysis ToolPak add-in macro. For more information, see "Managing Add-in Commands and Functions" in Chapter 4 in Book 2 of the *Microsoft Excel User's Guide*.

Syntax

PTTESTV(*inprng1,inprng2,outrng,*labels,alpha)

Inprng1   is the input range for the first data set.

Inprng2   is the input range for the second data set.

Outrng   is the first cell (the upper-left cell) in the output table.

Labels   is a logical value.

- If *labels* is TRUE, then labels are in the first row or column of the input ranges.

- If *labels* is FALSE or omitted, all cells in *inprng1* and *inprng2* are considered data. The output table will include default row or column headings.

Alpha   is the confidence level for the test. If omitted, *alpha* is 0.05.

Related Functions

Function	Description
PTTESTM	Performs a paired two-sample Student's *t*-Test for means
TDIST	Returns the Student's *t*-distribution
TTEST	Returns the probability associated with a Student's *t*-Test
TTESTM	Performs a two-sample Student's *t*-Test for means, assuming equal variances

PV

Returns the present value of an investment. The present value is the total amount that a series of future payments is worth now. For example, when you borrow money, the loan amount is the present value to the lender.

Syntax

PV(*rate,nper,pmt,fv,type*)

Rate is the interest rate per period. For example, if you obtain an automobile loan at a 10% annual interest rate and make monthly payments, your interest rate per month is 10%/12, or 0.83%. You would enter 10%/12, or 0.83%, or 0.0083, into the formula as the *rate*.

Nper is the total number of payment periods in an annuity. For example, if you get a four-year car loan and make monthly payments, your loan has 4*12 (or 48) periods. You would enter 48 into the formula for *nper*.

Pmt is the payment made each period and cannot change over the life of the annuity. Typically, *pmt* includes principal and interest but no other fees or taxes. For example, the monthly payments on a $10,000, four-year car loan at 12% are $263.33. You would enter –263.33 into the formula as the *pmt*.

Fv is the future value, or a cash balance you want to attain after the last payment is made. If *fv* is omitted, it is assumed to be 0 (the future value of a loan, for example, is 0). For example, if you want to save $50,000 to pay for a special project in 18 years, then $50,000 is the future value. You could then make a conservative guess at an interest rate and determine how much you must save each month.

Type is the number 0 or 1 and indicates when payments are due.

Set *type* equal to	If payments are due
0 or omitted	At the end of the period
1	At the beginning of the period

Remarks

- Make sure that you are consistent about the units you use for specifying *rate* and *nper*. If you make monthly payments on a four-year loan at 12% annual interest, use 12%/12 for *rate* and 4*12 for *nper*. If you make annual payments on the same loan, use 12% for *rate* and 4 for *nper*.

- The following functions apply to annuities:

CUMIPMT	PPMT
CUMPRINC	PV
FV	RATE
FVSCHEDULE	XIRR
IPMT	XNPV
PMT	

An annuity is a series of constant cash payments made over a continuous period. For example, a car loan or a mortgage is an annuity. For more information, see the description for each annuity function.

- In annuity functions, cash you pay out, such as a deposit to savings, is represented by a negative number; cash you receive, such as a dividend check, is represented by a positive number. For example, a $1000 deposit to the bank would be represented by the argument –1000 if you are the depositor and by the argument 1000 if you are the bank.

- Microsoft Excel solves for one financial argument in terms of the others. If *rate* is not 0, then:

$$pv*(1+rate)^{nper}+pmt(1+rate*type)*$$

$$\left(\frac{(1+rate)^{nper}-1}{rate}\right)+fv=0$$

If *rate* is 0, then:

$$(pmt*nper)+pv+fv=0$$

Example

Suppose you're thinking of buying an insurance annuity that pays $500 at the end of every month for the next 20 years. The cost of the annuity is $60,000 and the money paid out will earn 8%. You want to determine whether this would be a good investment. Using the PV function you find that the present value of the annuity is:

`PV(0.08/12,12*20,500,,0)` equals −$59,777.15

The result is negative because it represents money that you would pay—an outgoing cash flow. The present value of the annuity ($59,777.15) is less than what you are asked to pay ($60,000). Therefore, you determine this would not be a good investment.

Related Functions

Function	Description
FV	Returns the future value of an investment
IPMT	Returns the interest payment for an investment for a given period
NPER	Returns the number of periods for an investment
PMT	Returns the periodic payment for an annuity
PPMT	Returns the payment on the principal for an investment for a given period
RATE	Returns the interest rate per period of an annuity

QUARTILE

Returns a quartile from the data points in *array*. Quartiles often are used in sales and survey data to divide populations into groups. For example, you can use QUARTILE to find the top 25% of incomes in a population.

Syntax

QUARTILE *(array,quart)*

Array   is the array or cell range of numeric values for which you want the quartile value.

Quart   indicates which value to return.

If *quart* equals	QUARTILE returns
0	Minimum value
1	First quartile (25th percentile)
2	Median value (50th percentile)
3	Third quartile (75th percentile)
4	Maximum value

Remarks

- If *array* is empty or contains more than 8191 data points, QUARTILE returns the #NUM! error value.

- If any data point in *array* is non-numeric, or if *quart* is non-numeric, QUARTILE returns the #VALUE! error value.

- If *quart* is not an integer, it is truncated.

- If *quart* < 0 or if *quart* > 4, QUARTILE returns the #NUM! error value.

- MIN, MEDIAN, and MAX return the same value as QUARTILE when *quart* is equal to 0, 2, and 4, respectively.

Example

`QUARTILE({1,2,4,7,8,9,10,12},1)` equals 3.5

Related Functions

Function	Description
LARGE	Returns the *k*-th largest value in a data set
MAX	Returns the maximum value in a list of arguments
MEDIAN	Returns the median of the given numbers
MIN	Returns the minimum value in a list of arguments
PERCENTILE	Returns the *k*-th percentile of values in a range
PERCENTRANK	Returns the percentage rank of a value in a data set
SMALL	Returns the *k*-th smallest value in a data set

QUIT

Macro Sheets Only

Equivalent to choosing the Exit command from the File menu in Microsoft Excel for Windows. Equivalent to choosing the Quit command from the File menu in Microsoft Excel for the Macintosh. Quits Microsoft Excel and closes any open documents. If open documents have unsaved changes, Microsoft Excel displays a message asking if you want to save them. You can use QUIT in an Auto_Close macro to force Microsoft Excel to quit when a particular worksheet or macro sheet is closed.

Syntax

QUIT( )

Caution   QUIT will not ask whether you want to save changes if you have cleared error-checking with an ERROR(FALSE) function.

Remarks

When you use the QUIT function, Microsoft Excel does not run any Auto_Close macros before closing the document.

Related Function

Function	Description
FILE.CLOSE	Closes the active document

QUOTIENT

Returns the integer portion of a division. Use this function when you want to discard the remainder of a division.

If this function is not available, you must install the Analysis ToolPak add-in macro. For more information, see "Managing Add-in Commands and Functions" in Chapter 4 in Book 2 of the *Microsoft Excel User's Guide*.

Syntax

QUOTIENT*(numerator,denominator)*

Numerator   is the dividend.

Denominator   is the divisor.

Remarks

If either argument is non-numeric, QUOTIENT returns the #VALUE! error value.

Examples

QUOTIENT(5,2) equals 2

QUOTIENT(4.5,3.1) equals 1

QUOTIENT(-10,3) equals –3

Related Function

Function	Description
MOD	Returns the remainder from division

RADIANS

Converts degrees into radians.

If this function is not available, you must install the Add-in Functions add-in macro. For more information, see "Managing Add-in Commands and Functions" in Chapter 4 in Book 2 of the *Microsoft Excel User's Guide.*

Syntax

RADIANS(*angle_in_degrees*)

Angle_in_degrees is an angle in degrees that you want to convert.

Example

RADIANS(270) equals 4.712389 ($3\pi/2$ radians)

Related Function

Function	Description
DEGREES	Converts radians to degrees

RAND

Returns an evenly distributed random number greater than or equal to 0 and less than 1. A new random number is returned every time the worksheet is calculated.

Syntax

RAND( )

Tips

- To generate a random real number between *a* and *b*, use:

  RAND()*(*b–a*)+*a*

- To generate a random integer, use the RANDBETWEEN function.

- If you want to use RAND to generate a random number but don't want the numbers to change every time the cell is calculated, you can enter =RAND( ) in the formula bar and choose the Calc Now button in the Options Calculation dialog box to change the formula to a random number.

Examples

To generate a random number greater than or equal to 0 but less than 100:

RAND( )*100

Related Functions

Function	Description
RANDBETWEEN	Returns a random number between the numbers you specify
RANDOM	Fills a range with independent random or patterned numbers drawn from one of several distributions

RANDBETWEEN

Returns an evenly distributed random integer within a given range. A new random number is returned every time the worksheet is calculated.

If this function is not available, you must install the Add-in Functions add-in macro. For more information, see "Managing Add-in Commands and Functions" in Chapter 4 in Book 2 of the *Microsoft Excel User's Guide.*

Syntax

RANDBETWEEN(*bottom,top*)

Bottom is the smallest integer RANDBETWEEN will return.

Top is the largest integer RANDBETWEEN will return.

Related Functions

Function	Description
RAND	Returns a random number between 0 and 1
RANDOM	Fills a range with independent random or patterned numbers drawn from one of several distributions

RANDOM

Macro Sheets Only

Fills a range with independent random or patterned numbers drawn from one of several distributions. For more information, see "Analyzing Statistical or Engineering Data" in Chapter 1 in Book 2 of the *Microsoft Excel User's Guide*.

If this function is not available, you must install the Analysis ToolPak add-in macro. For more information, see "Managing Add-in Commands and Functions" in Chapter 4 in Book 2 of the *Microsoft Excel User's Guide*.

RANDOM provides six different random distributions and one patterned data option. Because the distributions require different argument lists, there are seven syntax forms for RANDOM.

Syntax 1

Uniform distribution

RANDOM(*outrng, variables, points, **distribution**, seed, from, to*)

Syntax 2

Normal distribution

RANDOM(*outrng, variables, points, **distribution**, seed, mean, standard_dev*)

Syntax 3

Bernoulli distribution

RANDOM(*outrng, variables, points, **distribution**, seed, probability*)

Syntax 4

Binomial distribution

RANDOM(*outrng, variables, points, **distribution**, seed, probability, trials*)

Syntax 5

Poisson distribution

RANDOM(*outrng, variables, points, **distribution**, seed, lambda*)

Syntax 6

Patterned distribution

RANDOM(*outrng, variables, points, **distribution**, seed, from, to, step, repeat_num, repeat_seq*)

Syntax 7

Discrete distribution

RANDOM(*outrng, variables, points, **distribution**, seed, inprng*)

Outrng is the first cell (the upper-left cell) in the output table.

Variables is the number of random number sets to generate. RANDOM will generate *variables* columns of random numbers. If omitted, *variables* is equal to the number of columns in the output range.

Points is the number of data points per random number set. RANDOM will generate *points* rows of random numbers for each random number set. If omitted, *points* is equal to the number of rows in the output range. *Points* is ignored when *distribution* is 6 (Patterned).

Distribution indicates the type of number distribution.

Distribution	Distribution type
1	Uniform
2	Normal
3	Bernoulli
4	Binomial
5	Poisson
6	Patterned
7	Discrete

Seed is an optional value with which to begin random number generation. *Seed* is ignored when *distribution* is 6 (Patterned) or 7 (Discrete).

From is the lower bound.

To is the upper bound.

Mean is the mean.

Standard_dev is the standard deviation.

Probability is the probability of success on each trial.

Trials is the number of trials.

Lambda is the Poisson distribution parameter.

Step is the increment between *from* and *to*.

Repeat_num is the number of times to repeat each value.

Repeat_seq is the number of times to repeat each sequence of values.

Inprng is a two-column range of values and their probabilities.

Related Function

Function	Description
RAND	Returns a random number between 0 and 1

RANK

Returns the rank of a number in a list of numbers. The rank of a number is its size relative to other values in a list. (If you were to sort the list, the rank of the number would be its position.)

Syntax

RANK(*number,ref,order*)

Number is the number whose rank you want to find.

Ref is an array of, or a reference to, a list of numbers. Non-numeric values in *ref* are ignored.

Order is a number specifying how to rank *number*.

- If *order* is 0 or omitted, Microsoft Excel ranks *number* as if *ref* were a list sorted in descending order.

- If *order* is any non-zero value, Microsoft Excel ranks *number* as if *ref* were a list sorted in ascending order.

Remarks

RANK gives duplicate numbers the same rank. However, the presence of duplicate numbers affects the ranks of subsequent numbers. For example, in a list of integers, if the number 10 appears twice and has a rank of 5, then 11 would have a rank of 7 (no number would have a rank of 6).

Examples

If A1:A5 contain the numbers 7, 3.5, 3.5, 1, and 2, respectively, then:

```
RANK(A2,A1:A5,1) equals 3
RANK(A1,A1:A5,1) equals 5
```

RANKPERC

Macro Sheets Only

Returns a table that contains the ordinal and percent rank of each value in a data set. For more information, see "Analyzing Statistical or Engineering Data" in Chapter 1 in Book 2 of the *Microsoft Excel User's Guide*.

If this function is not available, you must install the Analysis ToolPak add-in macro. For more information, see "Managing Add-in Commands and Functions" in Chapter 4 in Book 2 of the *Microsoft Excel User's Guide*.

Syntax

RANKPERC*(inprng,outrng,grouped,labels)*

Inprng is the input range.

Outrng is the first cell (the upper-left cell) in the output table.

Grouped is a text character that indicates whether the data in the input range is organized by row or column.

- If *grouped* is "C" or omitted, then the data is organized by column.

- If *grouped* is "R", then the data is organized by row.

Labels is a logical value that describes where the labels are located in the input range, as shown in the following table:

Labels	Grouped	Labels are in
TRUE	"C"	First row of the input range.
TRUE	"R"	First column of the input range.
FALSE or omitted	(ignored)	No labels. All cells in the input range are data.

Related Functions

Function	Description
PERCENTILE	Returns the *k*-th percentile of values in a range
PERCENTRANK	Returns the percentage rank of a value in a data set
QUARTILE	Returns the quartile of a data set
SMALL	Returns the *k*-th smallest value in a data set

RATE

Returns the interest rate per period for an annuity. RATE is calculated by iteration and can have zero or more solutions. If the successive results of RATE do not converge to within 0.0000001 after 20 iterations, RATE returns the #NUM! error value.

Syntax

RATE*(nper,pmt,pv,fv,type,guess)*

See PV for a complete description of the arguments *nper, pmt, pv, fv,* and *type*.

Nper is the total number of payment periods in an annuity.

Pmt is the payment made each period and cannot change over the life of the annuity. Typically, *pmt* includes principal and interest but no other fees or taxes.

Pv is the present value—the total amount that a series of future payments is worth now.

Fv is the future value, or a cash balance you want to attain after the last payment is made. If *fv* is omitted, it is assumed to be 0 (the future value of a loan, for example, is 0).

Type is the number 0 or 1 and indicates when payments are due.

Set *type* equal to	If payments are due
0 or omitted	At the end of the period
1	At the beginning of the period

Guess   is your guess for what the rate will be.

- If you omit *guess,* it is assumed to be 10%.

- If RATE does not converge, try different values for *guess*. RATE usually converges if *guess* is between 0 and 1.

Remarks

Make sure that you are consistent about the units you use for specifying *rate* and *nper*. If you make monthly payments on a four-year loan at 12% annual interest, use 12%/12 for *rate* and 4*12 for *nper*. If you make annual payments on the same loan, use 12% for *rate* and 4 for *nper*.

Example

To calculate the rate of a four-year $8000 loan with monthly payments of $200:

RATE(48,-200,8000)   equals 0.77%

This is the monthly rate, because the period is monthly. The annual rate is 0.77%*12, which equals 9.24%.

Related Functions

Function	Description
FV	Returns the future value of an investment
IPMT	Returns the interest payment for an investment for a given period
NPER	Returns the number of periods for an investment
PMT	Returns the periodic payment for an annuity
PPMT	Returns the payment on the principal for an investment for a given period
PV	Returns the present value of an investment

RECEIVED

Returns the amount received at maturity for a fully invested security.

If this function is not available, you must install the Analysis ToolPak add-in macro. For more information, see "Managing Add-in Commands and Functions" in Chapter 4 in Book 2 of the *Microsoft Excel User's Guide.*

Syntax

RECEIVED*(settlement,maturity,investment, discount,basis)*

Settlement   is the security's settlement date, expressed as a serial date number.

Maturity   is the security's maturity date, expressed as a serial date number.

Investment   is the amount invested in the security.

Discount   is the security's discount rate.

Basis   is the type of day count basis to use.

Basis	Day count basis
0 or omitted	30/360
1	Actual/actual
2	Actual/360
3	Actual/365

Remarks

- *Settlement, maturity,* and *basis* are truncated to integers.

- If any argument is non-numeric, RECEIVED returns the #VALUE! error value.

- If *settlement* or *maturity* is not a valid serial date number, RECEIVED returns the #NUM! error value.

- If *investment* ≤ 0 or if *discount* ≤ 0, RECEIVED returns the #NUM! error value.

- If *basis* < 0 or if *basis* > 3, RECEIVED returns the #NUM! error value.

- If *settlement* $\geq$ *maturity,* RECEIVED returns the #NUM! error value.

Example

A bond has the following terms:

February 15, 1991 settlement (issue) date
May 15, 1991 maturity date
1,000,000 investment
5.75% discount rate
Actual/360 basis

The bond discount rate (in the 1900 Date System) is:

`RECEIVED(33284,33373,1000000,0.0575,2)` equals 1,014,420.266

Related Functions

Function	Description
DATE	Returns the serial number of a particular date
INTRATE	Returns the interest rate for a fully invested security

REFTEXT

Macro Sheets Only

Converts a reference to an absolute reference in the form of text. Use REFTEXT when you need to manipulate references with text functions. After manipulating the reference text, you can convert it back into a normal reference by using TEXTREF.

Syntax

REFTEXT(*reference,a1*)

Reference   is the reference you want to convert.

A1   is a logical value specifying A1-style or R1C1-style references.

- If *a1* is TRUE, REFTEXT returns an A1-style reference.

- If *a1* is FALSE or omitted, REFTEXT returns an R1C1-style reference.

Examples

`REFTEXT(C3,TRUE)` equals "$C$3"

`REFTEXT(D2:F2)` equals "R2C2:R2C6"

If the active cell is B9 on the active worksheet named SHEET1, then:

`REFTEXT(ACTIVE.CELL())` equals "SHEET1!R9C2"

`REFTEXT(ACTIVE.CELL(),TRUE)` equals "SHEET1!$B$9"

Suppose that you have two worksheets named SHEET1 and SHEET2, and you want to be able to quickly move from a specified range on SHEET1 to the same range on SHEET2. For example, if cell B5 is active on SHEET1, then the following subroutine selects cell B5 on SHEET2.

	A	B	C
31	Names	Formulas	Comments
32			
33		SelectCorrespondingCell	
34	TempSheet	=REFTEXT(ACTIVE.CELL(),)	Gets active cell's reference
35	PermText	=SUBSTITUTE(TempSheet,"SHEET1","Shee	Changes the text
36		=FORMULA.GOTO(TEXTREF(PermText),)	Converts PermText to ref
37		=RETURN()	

Following is the complete formula in cell B35.

`=SUBSTITUTE(TempSheet,"SHEET1","SHEET2",1)`

FORMULA.GOTO is used instead of SELECT because it works with any open worksheet; SELECT works only with the active worksheet.

The following macro automatically inserts a series of formulas in the current horizontal selection on the active worksheet. The formulas calculate the average of the cells above the selection. This is similar to the AutoSum button on the standard toolbar except that the macro calculates averages, not sums. For example, if cells A3:E10 contained a block of numbers and if the current selection was A15:E15, the macro would place five AVERAGE formulas in A15:E15 (AVERAGE(A3:A10), AVERAGE(B3:B10), and so on).

	A	B	C
1	*Names*	*Formulas*	*Comments*
2			
3		**AnyAutoAverage**	
4	StartCell	=REFTEXT(SELECTION())	Gets reference of range
5		=SELECT.END(3)	Selects bottom cell
6	Cell1	=RELREF(ACTIVE.CELL(),TEXTREF(StartCell))	Gets reference of first cell
7		=SELECT.END(3)	Selects top cell of range
8	Cell2	=RELREF(ACTIVE.CELL(),TEXTREF(StartCell))	Gets reference of last cell
9		=FORMULA.FILL("=AVERAGE("&Cell1&":"&Cell2	Inserts formula
10		=SELECT(TEXTREF(StartCell))	
11		=RETURN()	

Following is the complete formula in cell B9.

```
=FORMULA.FILL("=AVERAGE("&Cell1&":
"&Cell2&")",TEXTREF(StartCell))
```

Also see the last example for TEXTREF.

Related Functions

Function	Description
ABSREF	Returns the absolute reference of a range of cells to another range
DEREF	Returns the values of cells in the reference
OFFSET	Returns a reference offset from a given reference
RELREF	Returns a relative reference
TEXTREF	Converts text to a reference

REGISTER

Macro Sheets Only

Registers the specified dynamic link library (DLL) or code resource and returns the register ID. You can also specify a custom function name and argument names that will appear in the Paste Function dialog box. If you register a command (*macro_type* = 2), you can also specify a shortcut key.

For more information about DLLs and code resources, see the Appendix, "Using the CALL and REGISTER Functions."

Note   Because Microsoft Excel for Windows and Microsoft Excel for the Macintosh use different types of code resources, REGISTER has a slightly different syntax form when used in each operating environment.

Syntax 1

For Microsoft Excel for Windows

REGISTER(*module_text,procedure,type_text, function_text,argument_text,macro_type,category, shortcut_text*)

Syntax 2

For Microsoft Excel for the Macintosh

REGISTER(*file_text,resource,type_text, function_text,argument_text,macro_type,category, shortcut_text*)

Module_text or *file_text*   is text specifying the name of the DLL that contains the function (in Microsoft Excel for Windows) or the name of the file that contains the code resource (in Microsoft Excel for the Macintosh).

Procedure or *resource*   is text specifying the name of the function in the DLL (in Microsoft Excel for Windows) or the name of the code resource (in Microsoft Excel for the Macintosh). In Microsoft Excel for Windows, you can also use the ordinal value of the function from the EXPORTS statement in the module-definition file (.DEF). In Microsoft Excel for the Macintosh, you can also use the resource ID number. The ordinal value or resource ID number should not be in text form.

This argument may be omitted for stand-alone DLLs or code resources. In this case, REGISTER will register all functions or code resources and then return *module_text* or *file_text*.

Type_text is text specifying the data type of the return value and the data types of all arguments to the DLL or code resource. The first letter of type_text specifies the return value. The codes you use for type_text are described in detail in the Appendix, "Using the CALL and REGISTER Functions." For stand-alone DLLs or code resources (XLLs), you can omit this argument.

Function_text is text specifying the name of the function as you want it to appear in the Paste Function dialog box. If you omit this argument, the function will not appear in the Paste Function dialog box.

Argument_text is text specifying the names of the arguments you want to appear in the Paste Function dialog box. Argument names should be separated by commas.

Macro_type specifies the macro type: 1 for a function or 2 for a command. If macro_type is omitted, it is assumed to be 1 (function).

Category specifies the function category in the Paste Function dialog box in which you want the registered function to appear. You can use the category number or the category name for category. If you use the category name, be sure to enclose it in double quotation marks. If category is omitted, it is assumed to be 14 (User Defined).

Category number	Category name
1	Financial
2	Date & Time
3	Math & Trig
4	Text
5	Logical
6	Lookup & Matrix
7	Database
8	Statistical
9	Information
10	Commands (macro sheets only)

Category number	Category name
11	Actions (macro sheets only)
12	Customizing (macro sheets only)
13	Macro Control (macro sheets only)
14	User Defined

Shortcut_text is a character specifying the shortcut key for the registered command. The shortcut key is case-sensitive. This argument is used only if macro_type = 2 (command). If shortcut_text is omitted, the command will not have a shortcut key.

Example   Syntax 1

In Microsoft Excel for Windows, the following macro formula registers the GetTickCount function from Microsoft Windows. This function returns the number of milliseconds that have elapsed since Microsoft Windows was started.

```
REGISTER("User","GetTickCount","J")
```

Assuming that the REGISTER function is in cell A5, after your macro registers GetTickCount, you can use the CALL function to return the number of milliseconds that have elapsed:

```
CALL(A5)
```

Example   Syntax 1 with optional *function_text*

You can use the following macro formula to register the GetTickCount function from Microsoft Windows and assign the custom name GetTicks to it. To do this, include "GetTicks" as the optional *function_text* argument to the REGISTER function.

```
REGISTER("User","GetTickCount","J",
"GetTicks",,1,9)
```

After the function is registered, the custom name GetTicks will appear in the Information function category (category = 9) in the Paste Function dialog box.

Microsoft Excel Function Reference

You can call the function from the same macro sheet on which it was registered using the following formula:

```
GetTicks()
```

You can call the function from another document (worksheet or macro sheet) by including the name of the original macro sheet in the formula. For example, assuming the macro sheet on which GetTicks was registered is named MACRO1.XLM, the following formula calls the function from another sheet:

```
MACRO1.XLM!GetTicks()
```

Tip You can use functions in a DLL or code resource directly on a worksheet without first registering them from a macro sheet. Use syntax 2a or 2b of the CALL function. For more information, see CALL.

Related Functions

Function	Description
CALL	Calls a procedure in a dynamic link library or code resource
REGISTER.ID	Returns the register ID of the resource
UNREGISTER	Removes a registered code resource from memory

REGISTER.ID

Returns the register ID of the specified dynamic link library (DLL) or code resource that has been previously registered. If the DLL or code resource has not been registered, this function registers the DLL or code resource, and then returns the register ID.

REGISTER.ID can be used on worksheets (unlike REGISTER), but you cannot specify a function name and argument names with REGISTER.ID.

For more information about DLLs and code resources, see the Appendix, "Using the CALL and REGISTER Functions."

Note Because Microsoft Excel for Windows and Microsoft Excel for the Macintosh use different types of code resources, REGISTER.ID has a slightly different syntax form when used in each operating environment.

Syntax 1

For Microsoft Excel for Windows

REGISTER.ID(*module_text,procedure, type_text*)

Syntax 2

For Microsoft Excel for the Macintosh

REGISTER.ID (*file_text,resource, type_text*)

Module_text or *file_text*   is text specifying the name of the DLL that contains the function (in Microsoft Excel for Windows) or the name of the file that contains the code resource (in Microsoft Excel for the Macintosh).

Procedure or *resource*   is text specifying the name of the function in the DLL (in Microsoft Excel for Windows) or the name of the code resource (in Microsoft Excel for the Macintosh). In Microsoft Excel for Windows, you can also use the ordinal value of the function from the EXPORTS statement in the module-definition file (.DEF). In Microsoft Excel for the Macintosh, you can also use the resource ID number. The ordinal value or resource ID number should not be in text form.

Type_text   is text specifying the data type of the return value and the data types of all arguments to the DLL or code resource. The first letter of *type_text* specifies the return value. The codes you use for *type_text* are described in detail in the Appendix, "Using the CALL and REGISTER Functions." If the function or code resource is already registered, you can omit this argument.

Examples

The following formula registers the GetTickCount function from Microsoft Windows, and returns the register ID:

```
REGISTER.ID("User","GetTickCount","J!")
```

Assuming that GetTickCount was already registered on another worksheet using the preceding formula, the following formula returns the register ID for GetTickCount:

```
REGISTER.ID("User","GetTickCount")
```

Related Functions

Function	Description
CALL	Calls a procedure in a dynamic link library or code resource
REGISTER	Registers a code resource
UNREGISTER	Removes a registered code resource from memory

REGRESS

Macro Sheets Only

Performs multiple linear regression analysis. For more information, see "Analyzing Statistical or Engineering Data" in Chapter 1 in Book 2 of the *Microsoft Excel User's Guide*.

If this function is not available, you must install the Analysis ToolPak add-in macro. For more information, see "Managing Add-in Commands and Functions" in Chapter 4 in Book 2 of the *Microsoft Excel User's Guide*.

Syntax

REGRESS(*inpyrng,inpxrng,*constant,labels,confid, *soutrng,*residuals,sresiduals,rplots,lplots,*routrng,* nplots,*poutrng*)

Inpyrng is the input range for the *y*-values (dependent variable).

Inpxrng is the input range for the *x*-values (independent variable).

Constant is a logical value. If constant is TRUE, the *y*-intercept is assumed to be zero (the regression line passes through the origin). If *constant* is FALSE or omitted, the *y*-intercept is assumed to be a non-zero number.

Labels is a logical value.

- If *labels* is TRUE, then the first row or column of the input ranges contain labels.

- If *labels* is FALSE or omitted, all cells in *inpyrng* and *inpxrng* are considered data. Microsoft Excel will then generate the appropriate data labels for the output table.

Confid is an additional confidence level to apply to the regression. If omitted, *confid* is 95%.

Soutrng is the first cell (the upper-left cell) in the summary output table.

Residuals is a logical value. If *residuals* is TRUE, REGRESS includes residuals in the output table. If *residuals* is FALSE or omitted, residuals are not included.

Sresiduals is a logical value. If *sresiduals* is TRUE, REGRESS includes standardized residuals in the output table. If *sresid* is FALSE or omitted, standardized residuals are not included.

Rplots is a logical value. If *rplots* is TRUE, REGRESS generates separate charts for each *x* versus the residual. If *rplots* is FALSE or omitted, separate charts are not generated.

Lplots is a logical value. If *lplots* is TRUE, REGRESS generates a chart showing the regression line fitted to the observed values. If *lplots* is FALSE or omitted, the chart is not generated.

Routrng is the first cell (the upper-left cell) in the residuals output table.

Nplots is a logical value. If *nplots* is TRUE, REGRESS generates a chart of normal probabilities. If *nplots* is FALSE or omitted, the chart is not generated.

Poutrng is the first cell (the upper-left cell) in the probability data output table.

Related Functions

Function	Description
FORECAST	Returns a value along a linear trend
GROWTH	Returns values along an exponential trend
LINEST	Returns the parameters of a linear trend
LOGEST	Returns the parameters of an exponential trend
TREND	Returns values along a linear trend

RELREF

Macro Sheets Only

Returns the reference of a cell or cells relative to the upper-left cell of *rel_to_ref*. The reference is given as an R1C1-style relative reference in the form of text, such as "R[1]C[1]".

Syntax

RELREF(*reference,rel_to_ref*)

Reference is the cell or cells to which you want to create a relative reference.

Rel_to_ref is the cell from which you want to create the relative reference.

Tip If you know the absolute reference of a cell that you want to include in a formula, but your formula requires a relative reference, use RELREF to generate the relative reference. This is especially useful with the FORMULA function, since its *formula_text* argument requires R1C1-style references, and RELREF returns relative R1C1-style references. You can also use the FORMULA.CONVERT function to convert absolute references to relative references.

Examples

RELREF($A$1,$C$3) equals "R[–2]C[–2]"

RELREF($A$1:$E$5,$C$3:$G$7) equals "R[–2]C[–2]:R[2]C[2]"

RELREF($A$1:$E$5,$C$3) equals "R[–2]C[–2]:R[2]C[2]"

The following macro enters a formula to sum a specified range into a specified cell using RELREF.

	A	B	C
1	Names	Formulas	Comments
2			
3		RangeSum	
4		=SET.NAME("WkCell",INPUT("Destination?",8))	Sets name for dest cell
5	DestRef	=RELREF(INPUT("Range?",8),WkCell)	Gets reference of sum range
6		=FORMULA("=SUM("&DestRef&")",WkCell)	Puts formula in dest cell
7		=RETURN()	

Related Functions

Function	Description
ABSREF	Returns the absolute reference of a range of cells to another range
DEREF	Returns the value of the cells in the reference
OFFSET	Returns a reference offset from a given reference

REMOVE.PAGE.BREAK

Macro Sheets Only

Equivalent to choosing the Remove Page Break command from the Options menu. Removes manual page breaks that you set with the SET.PAGE.BREAK function or the Set Page Break command on the Options menu. If the active cell is not below or to the right of a manual page break, REMOVE.PAGE.BREAK takes no action. If the entire document is selected, REMOVE.PAGE.BREAK removes all manual page breaks. REMOVE.PAGE.BREAK does not remove automatic page breaks.

Syntax

REMOVE.PAGE.BREAK( )

Related Function

Function	Description
SET.PAGE.BREAK	Sets manual page breaks

RENAME.COMMAND

Macro Sheets Only

Changes the name of a built-in or custom menu command or the name of a menu. Use RENAME.COMMAND to change the name of a command on a menu, for example, when you create two custom commands that toggle on the menu. Examples of two built-in commands that toggle are the Set Page Break and Remove Page Break commands.

Syntax

RENAME.COMMAND(*bar_num,menu, command,name_text*)

Bar_num can be either the number of one of the Microsoft Excel built-in menu bars or the number returned by a previously run ADD.BAR function. See ADD.COMMAND for a list of ID numbers for built-in menu bars.

Menu can be either the name of a menu as text or the number of a menu. Menus are numbered starting with 1 from the left of the screen.

Command can be either the name of the command as text or the number of the command to be renamed (the first command on a menu is command 1). If *command* is 0, RENAME.COMMAND renames the menu instead of the command. Because other macros can change the position of custom menu commands, you should use the name of the command rather than a number whenever possible.

If the specified menu bar, menu, or command does not exist, RENAME.COMMAND returns the #VALUE! error value and interrupts the macro.

Name_text is the new name for the command.

Tip To specify an access key for the new name, precede the character you want to use with an ampersand (&). The access key is indicated by an underline under one letter of a menu or command name. In Microsoft Excel for the Macintosh, you can use the Workspace Options dialog box to turn command underlining on or off. To see the Workspace Options dialog box, choose Workspace from the Options menu.

For information about custom menus, see Chapter 8 in Book 2 of the *Microsoft Excel User's Guide*.

Example

To rename the Show Totals command as Hide Totals, and to make the letter "H" in Hide Totals an access key, use the following macro formula:

```
RENAME.COMMAND(1,"File","Show Totals",
"&Hide Totals")
```

Related Functions

Function	Description
ADD.COMMAND	Adds a command to a menu
CHECK.COMMAND	Adds or deletes a check mark to or from a command
DELETE.COMMAND	Deletes a command from a menu
ENABLE.COMMAND	Enables or disables a menu or custom command

REPLACE

Replaces part of a text string with a different text string.

Syntax

REPLACE(*old_text,start_num,num_chars, new_text*)

Old_text   is text in which you want to replace some characters.

Start_num   is the position of the character in *old_text* that you want to replace with *new_text*.

Num_chars   is the number of characters in *old_text* that you want to replace with *new_text*.

New_text   is the text that will replace characters in *old_text*.

Examples

The following formula replaces five characters with *new_text,* starting with the sixth character in *old_text:*

```
REPLACE("abcdefghijk",6,5,"*") equals
"abcde*k"
```

The sixth through tenth characters are all replaced by "*".

The following formula replaces the last two digits of 1990 with 91:

```
REPLACE("1990",3,2,"91") equals "1991"
```

If cell A2 contains "123456", then:

```
REPLACE(A2,1,3,"@") equals "@456"
```

If the RIGHT function returns "ABCDEF", then:

```
REPLACE(RIGHT(A3,6),1,6,"*") equals "*"
```

Related Functions

Function	Description
FORMULA.REPLACE	Replaces text throughout a document
MID	Returns a specific string starting at the position you specify
SEARCH	Finds one text value within another (not case-sensitive)
SUBSTITUTE	Substitutes new text for old text in a text string
TRIM	Removes spaces from text

REPLACE.FONT

Macro Sheets Only

Replaces one of the four built-in fonts in Microsoft Excel for Windows version 2.1 or earlier with a new font and style. This function is included only for macro compatibility. To change the font of the selected cell or range as part of a macro, use the FORMAT.FONT function instead.

Syntax

REPLACE.FONT*(font_num,name_text,*
size_num,bold,italic,underline,strike,color,outline,
shadow)

Related Function

Function	Description
FORMAT.FONT	Applies a font to the selection

REPORT.DEFINE

Macro Sheets Only

Equivalent to choosing the Print Report command from the File menu and then choosing the Add option from the Print Report dialog box. Creates or replaces a report definition.

Note   If this function is not available, you must install the Reports add-in macro. For more information, see "Managing Add-in Commands and Functions" in Chapter 4 in Book 2 of the *Microsoft Excel User's Guide.*

Syntax

REPORT.DEFINE*(report_name,*
views_scenarios_array, pages_logical)

Report_name   specifies the name of the report.

Views_scenarios_array is an array that contains one or more rows of view and scenario pairs that define the report. Use the #N/A error value to indicate that there is no change to a position in the current view or scenario.

Pages_logical is a logical value that, if TRUE or omitted, specifies continuous page numbers for multiple sections or, if FALSE, resets page numbers to 1 for each new section.

Remarks

REPORT.DEFINE returns the #VALUE error value if *report_name* is invalid or if the document is protected.

Example

The following macro formula creates a report called R1 using continuous page numbers.

```
REPORT.DEFINE("R1",{"Detail","Best";
"Detail","Probable"},TRUE)
```

Related Functions

Function	Description
REPORT.DELETE	Removes a report from the active document
REPORT.PRINT	Prints a report

REPORT.DELETE

Macro Sheets Only

Equivalent to choosing the Print Report command from the File menu and then selecting a report in the Print Report dialog box and choosing the Delete button. Removes a report definition from the active document.

If this function is not available, you must install the Reports add-in macro. For more information, see "Managing Add-in Commands and Functions" in Chapter 4 in Book 2 of the *Microsoft Excel User's Guide*.

Syntax

REPORT.DELETE(*report_name*)

Report_name specifies the name of the report to be removed. *Report_name* can be any text that does not contain quotation marks.

Remarks

REPORT.DELETE returns the #VALUE error value if *report_name* is invalid or if the document is protected.

Example

The following macro formula removes the report R1 from the active document.

```
REPORT.DELETE("R1")
```

Related Functions

Function	Description
REPORT.DEFINE	Creates a report
REPORT.PRINT	Prints a report

REPORT.GET

Macro Sheets Only

Returns information about reports defined for the active document. Use REPORT.GET to return information you can use in other macro formulas that manipulate reports.

If this function is not available, you must install the Reports add-in macro. For more information, see "Managing Add-in Commands and Functions" in Chapter 4 in Book 2 of the *Microsoft Excel User's Guide*.

Syntax

REPORT.GET(*type_num,report_name*)

Type_num   is a number from 1 to 3 specifying the type of information to return, as shown in the following table.

Type_num	Returns
1	An array of reports from the active document or the #N/A error value if none are specified
2	An array of view and scenario pairs for the specified report in the active document. REPORT.GET returns the #N/A error value if you have chosen "[current]." Returns the #VALUE! error value if *name* is invalid or the document is protected.
3	If continuous page numbers are used, returns TRUE. If page numbers start at 1 for each section, returns FALSE. Returns the #VALUE! error value if *report_name* is invalid or the document is protected.

Report_name   specifies the name of a report in the active document.

Remarks

Report_name is required if *type_num* is 2 or 3.

Example

The following macro formula returns an array of reports from the active document.

```
REPORT.GET(1)
```

Related Functions

Function	Description
REPORT.DEFINE	Creates a report
REPORT.DELETE	Removes a report from the active document
REPORT.PRINT	Prints a report

REPORT.PRINT

Macro Sheets Only

Equivalent to choosing the Print button from the Print Reports dialog box. Prints a report.

If this function is not available, you must install the Reports add-in macro. For more information, see "Managing Add-in Commands and Functions" in Chapter 4 in Book 2 of the *Microsoft Excel User's Guide*.

Syntax

REPORT.PRINT(*report_name,copies_num, show_print_dlg_logical*)
REPORT.PRINT?(*report_name,copies_num*)

Report_name   specifies the name of a report in the active document.

Copies_num   is the number of copies you want to print. If omitted, the default is 1.

Show_print_dlg_logical   is a logical value that, if TRUE, displays a dialog box asking how many copies to print, or, if FALSE or omitted, prints the report immediately using existing print settings.

Remarks

REPORT.PRINT returns the #VALUE! error value if *report_name* is invalid or if the document is protected.

Example

The following macro formula prints report R1.

```
REPORT.PRINT("R1")
```

Related Functions

Function	Description
REPORT.DEFINE	Creates a report
REPORT.DELETE	Removes a report from the active document

REPT

Repeats text a given number of times. Use REPT to fill a cell with a number of instances of a text string.

Syntax

REPT(*text,number_times*)

Text   is the text you want to repeat.

Number_times   is a positive number specifying the number of times to repeat *text*. If *number_times* is 0, REPT returns "" (empty text). If *number_times* is not an integer, it is truncated. The result of the REPT function cannot be longer than 255 characters.

Tip   You can use this function to create a simple histogram on your worksheet.

Examples

REPT("*-",3) equals "*-*-*-"

If A3 contains "Sales", then:

REPT($A$3,2.9) equals "SalesSales"

Related Functions

Function	Description
ALIGNMENT	Aligns or wraps text in cells
FILL.DOWN, FILL.LEFT, FILL.RIGHT, and FILL.UP	Copy contents and formats of specified cells into the rest of the selection
FORMULA.FILL	Enters a formula in the specified range

REQUEST

Macro Sheets Only

Requests an array of a specific type of information from an application with which you have a dynamic data exchange (DDE) link. Use REQUEST with other Microsoft Excel DDE functions to move information from another application into Microsoft Excel.

Syntax

REQUEST(*channel_num,item_text*)

Important   Microsoft Excel for the Macintosh requires system software version 7.0 or later for this function.

Channel_num   is a number returned by a previously run INITIATE function. *Channel_num* refers to a channel through which Microsoft Excel communicates with another program.

Item_text   is a code indicating the type of information you want to request from another application. The form of *item_text* depends on the application connected to *channel_num*. For more information, see Chapter 3 in Book 2 of the *Microsoft Excel User's Guide*.

REQUEST returns the data as an array. For example, suppose the remote data to be returned came from a worksheet that looked like the following illustration.

	A	B	C	D	E	F
1	1	2	3			
2	4	5	6			

REQUEST would return that data as the following array:

{1,2,3;4,5,6}

If REQUEST is not successful, it returns the following error values.

Value returned	Situation
#VALUE!	*Channel_num* is not a valid channel number.
#N/A	The application you are accessing is busy doing something else.
#DIV/0!	The application you are accessing does not respond after a certain length of time, or you have pressed ESC or COMMAND+PERIOD to cancel.
#REF!	The request is refused.

Tip   Use the ERROR.TYPE function to distinguish between the different error values.

Example

In Microsoft Excel for Windows, the following macro opens a channel to Word for Windows and returns the text specified by the bookmark named BMK1.

	A	B	C
1	*Names*	*Formulas*	*Comments*
2			
3		GetParagraphs	
4	WChan	=INITIATE("WINWORD","C:\REPORT.DOC")	Initiates channel to Word
5		=REQUEST(WChan,"BMK1")	Returns text in bookmark
6		=TERMINATE(WChan)	Terminates channel to Word
7		=RETURN()	

Related Functions

Function	Description
EXECUTE	Carries out a command in another application
INITIATE	Opens a channel to another application
POKE	Sends data to another application
SEND.KEYS	Sends a key sequence to another application

RESET.TOOL

Macro Sheets Only

Equivalent to choosing the Reset Tool Face command from the Tool shortcut menu. Resets a tool to its original tool face. For detailed information about the Reset Tool Face command, see online Help.

Syntax

RESET.TOOL(*bar_id,position*)

Bar_id is the number or name of the toolbar containing the tool you want to reset. For detailed information about *bar_id,* see ADD.TOOL.

Position specifies the position of the tool within the toolbar. *Position* starts with 1 at the left side (if horizontal) or at the top (if vertical).

Example

The following macro formula resets the first tool on the Utility toolbar to its original tool face:

```
RESET.TOOL(3,1)
```

Related Functions

Function	Description
ADD.TOOL	Adds one or more tools to a toolbar
DELETE.TOOL	Deletes a tool from a toolbar
RESET.TOOLBAR	Resets a tool to its original tool face

RESET.TOOLBAR

Macro Sheets Only

Resets built-in toolbars to the default Microsoft Excel set.

Syntax

RESET.TOOLBAR(*bar_id*)

Bar_id specifies the number or name of the toolbar that you want to reset. For detailed information about *bar_id,* see ADD.TOOL.

Remarks

If RESET.TOOLBAR successfully resets the toolbar, it returns TRUE. If you try to reset a custom toolbar, RESET.TOOLBAR returns FALSE and takes no other action.

Example

The following macro formula resets the Formatting toolbar:

```
RESET.TOOLBAR(2)
```

Related Function

Function	Description
DELETE.TOOLBAR	Deletes custom toolbars

RESTART

Macro Sheets Only

Removes a number of RETURN statements from
the stack. When one macro calls another, the
RETURN statement at the end of the second macro
returns control to the calling macro. You can use the
RESTART function to determine which macro
regains control.

Syntax

RESTART(*level_num*)

Level_num is a number specifying the number
of previous RETURN statements you want to
be ignored. If *level_num* is omitted, the next
RETURN statement will halt macro execution.

For example, if the currently running macro has
two "ancestors," that is, was called by one macro
that, in turn, was called by another macro, using
RESTART(1) in the third macro returns control to
the first calling macro when the RETURN statement
is encountered. The RESTART(1) formula removes
one level of RETURN statements from Microsoft
Excel's memory so that the second macro is
skipped.

Remarks

RESTART is particularly useful if you frequently
use macros to call other macros that in turn call
other macros. Use RESTART in combination with
IF statements to prevent macro execution from
returning to macros that called, either directly or
indirectly, the currently running macro.

RESULT

Macro Sheets Only

Specifies the type of data a macro or custom
function returns. Use RESULT to make sure your
macros, custom dialog boxes, custom functions, or
subroutines return values of the correct data type.

Syntax

RESULT(*type_num*)

Type_num is a number specifying the data type.

Type_num	Type of returned data
1	Number
2	Text
4	Logical
8	Reference
16	Error
64	Array

- *Type_num* can be the sum of the numbers in
the preceding table to allow for more than one
possible result type. For example, if *type_num*
is 12, which equals 4 + 8, the result can be a
logical or a reference value.

- If you omit *type_num,* it is assumed to be 7.
Since 7 equals 1 + 2 + 4, the value returned can
be a number (1), text (2), or logical value (4).

For more information about using RESULT in
custom functions and subroutines, see Chapter 5 in
Book 2 of the *Microsoft Excel User's Guide.*

Examples

The following custom function returns profit as a
number (data type 1).

	A	B	C
1	Names	Formulas	Comments
2			
3		ProfitCalc	Calculates profit
4		=RESULT(1)	Result will be a number
5		=ARGUMENT("NumSold",1)	Defines the three arguments
6		=ARGUMENT("Cost",1)	
7		=ARGUMENT("SalePrice",1)	
8	Profit	=NumSold*(SalePrice–Cost)	Computes the profit
9		=RETURN(Profit)	Returns the profit

The following custom function returns an array (data type 64) of currency values. This macro assumes that the exchange rates (PoundsPerDollar, FrancsPerDollar, YenPerDollar, and MarksPerDollar) are defined and correctly named on the active worksheet.

	A	B	C
1	Names	Formulas	Comments
2			
3		**Currency**	Converts dollars
4		=RESULT(64)	Result will be an array
5		=ARGUMENT("Money")	
6	MoneyRange	=Money*!PoundsPerDollar	These four cells
7		=Money*!FrancsPerDollar	are named
8		=Money*!YenPerDollar	"MoneyRange"
9		=Money*!MarksPerDollar	
10		=RETURN(MoneyRange)	

The following subroutine macro returns the number of characters you want starting from any position in the specified file. This macro is analogous to the MID function, which returns a number of characters from a text string.

	A	B	C
31	Names	Formulas	Comments
32			
33		**ReadCharsFromPosition**	
34		=RESULT(2)	Result will be text
35		=ARGUMENT("FileName")	
36		=ARGUMENT("PositionNum")	
37		=ARGUMENT("NumChars")	
38	FileNumber	=FOPEN(FileName)	Obtains file number
39		=FPOS(FileNumber,PositionNum)	Positions file as specified
40	Characters	=FREAD(FileNumber,NumChars)	Reads specified characters
41		=FCLOSE(FileNumber)	Closes the file
42		=RETURN(Characters)	

In Microsoft Excel for Windows, the following macro formula would call the preceding subroutine and return 10 characters starting from the fifth character in a file named C:\BUDGETS\91PLAN.TXT:

```
ReadCharsFromPosition("C:\BUDGETS\91PLAN.
TXT",5,10)
```

In Microsoft Excel for the Macintosh, the following macro formula would call the preceding subroutine and return 10 characters starting from the fifth character in a file named HARD DISK:BUDGETS: PLAN FOR 91 (text):

```
ReadCharsFromPosition("HARD DISK:BUDGETS:
PLAN FOR 91 (text)",5,10)
```

Related Functions

Function	Description
ARGUMENT	Passes an argument to a macro
RETURN	Ends the currently running macro

RESUME

Macro Sheets Only

Equivalent to choosing the Resume command from the Macro menu. Resumes a paused macro. Returns TRUE if successful or the #VALUE! error value if no macro is paused. A macro can be paused by using the PAUSE function or choosing Pause from the Single Step dialog box, which appears when you choose the Step button from the Macro run dialog box. For detailed information about the Resume command, see online Help.

Syntax

RESUME(*type_num*)

Type_num is a number from 1 to 4 specifying how to resume.

Type_num	**How Microsoft Excel resumes**
1 or omitted	If paused by a PAUSE function, continues running the macro. If paused from the Single Step dialog box, returns to that dialog box.
2	Halts the paused macro
3	Continues running the macro
4	Opens the Single Step dialog box

For more information about pausing and resuming macros and using other debugging tools, see "Testing a Command Macro" in Chapter 7 in Book 2 of the *Microsoft Excel User's Guide*.

Tip You can use Microsoft Excel's ON functions to resume based on an event. For an example, see ENTER.DATA.

Remarks

- If one macro runs a second macro that pauses, and you need to halt only the paused macro, use RESUME(2) instead of HALT. HALT halts all macros and prevents resuming or returning to any macro.

- If the macro was paused from the Single Step dialog box, RESUME returns to the Single Step dialog box.

Related Functions

Function	Description
HALT	Stops all macros from running
PAUSE	Pauses a macro

RETURN

Macro Sheets Only

Ends the currently running macro. If the currently running macro is a subroutine macro that was called by another macro, control is returned to the calling macro. If the currently running macro is a custom function, control is returned to the formula that called the custom function. If the currently running macro is a command macro started by the user with the Run command on the Macro menu or a shortcut key or by clicking an object, control is returned to the user.

Syntax

RETURN(*value*)

Value   specifies what to return.

- If the macro is a custom function or a subroutine, *value* specifies what value to return. However, not all subroutines return values; the last line in macros that do not return values is =RETURN().

- If the macro is a command macro run by the user, *value* should be omitted.

For more information, see Chapter 7 in Book 2 of the *Microsoft Excel User's Guide*.

Remarks

RETURN signals the end of a macro. Every macro must end with a RETURN or HALT function, but not every macro returns values.

Example

For examples of custom functions and a subroutine macro that return values, see RESULT.

Related Functions

Function	Description
BREAK	Interrupts a FOR–NEXT, FOR.CELL–NEXT, or WHILE–NEXT loop
HALT	Stops all macros from running
RESULT	Specifies the data type a custom function returns

RIGHT

Returns the last (or rightmost) character or characters in a text string.

Syntax

RIGHT(*text*,*num_chars*)

Text   is the text string containing the characters you want to extract.

Num_chars   specifies how many characters you want to extract.

- *Num_chars* must be greater than or equal to zero.

- If *num_chars* is greater than the length of *text,* RIGHT returns all of *text.*

- If *num_chars* is omitted, it is assumed to be 1.

Examples

RIGHT("Sale Price",5) equals "Price"

RIGHT("Stock Number") equals "r"

RIGHT is similar to LEFT; for more examples, see LEFT.

Related Functions

Function	Description
LEFT	Returns the leftmost characters from a text value
MID	Returns a specific string starting at the position you specify

ROUND

Rounds a number to the specified number of digits.

Syntax

ROUND(*number,num_digits*)

Number   is the number you want to round.

Num_digits   specifies the number of digits to which you want to round *number.*

- If *num_digits* is greater than 0, then *number* is rounded to the specified number of decimal places.

- If *num_digits* is 0, then *number* is rounded to the nearest integer.

- If *num_digits* is less than 0, then *number* is rounded to the left of the decimal point.

Examples

ROUND(2.15,1) equals 2.2

ROUND(2.149,1) equals 2.1

ROUND(-1.475,2) equals −1.48

ROUND(21.5,-1) equals 20

Related Functions

Function	Description
CEILING	Rounds a number up to the nearest integer
FLOOR	Rounds a number down, toward zero
INT	Rounds a number down to the nearest integer
MOD	Returns the remainder from division
MROUND	Returns a number rounded to the nearest multiple
TRUNC	Truncates a number to an integer

ROW

Returns the row number of *reference.*

Syntax

ROW(*reference*)

Reference   is the cell or range of cells for which you want the row number.

- If *reference* is omitted, it is assumed to be the reference of the cell in which the ROW function appears.

- If *reference* is a range of cells and if ROW is entered as a vertical array, ROW returns the row numbers of *reference* as a vertical array.

- *Reference* cannot refer to multiple areas.

Examples

ROW(A3) equals 3

When entered as an array formula in three vertical cells:

ROW(A3:B5) equals {3;4;5}

If ROW is entered in C5, then:

ROW() equals ROW(C5) equals 5

The following macro formula tells you which row the active cell is in:

ROW(ACTIVE.CELL())

Related Functions

Function	Description
COLUMN	Returns the column number of a reference
ROWS	Returns the number of rows in a reference

ROW.HEIGHT

Macro Sheets Only

Equivalent to choosing the Row Height command from the Format menu. Changes the height of the rows in a reference. For detailed information about the Row Height command, see online Help.

Syntax

ROW.HEIGHT(*height_num,reference, standard_height,type_num*)
ROW.HEIGHT?(*height_num,reference, standard_height,type_num*)

Height_num specifies how high you want the rows to be in points. If *standard_height* is TRUE, *height_num* is ignored.

Reference specifies the rows for which you want to change the height.

- If *reference* is omitted, the reference is assumed to be the current selection.

- If *reference* is specified, it must be either an external reference to the active worksheet, such as !$2:$4 or !Database, or an R1C1-style reference in the form of text or a name, such as "R1:R3", "R[–4]:R[–2]", or Database.

- If *reference* is a relative R1C1-style reference in the form of text, it is assumed to be relative to the active cell.

Standard_height is a logical value that sets the row height as determined by the font in each row.

- If *standard_height* is TRUE, Microsoft Excel sets the row height to a standard height that may vary from row to row depending on the fonts used in each row, ignoring *height_num*.

- If *standard_height* is FALSE or omitted, Microsoft Excel sets the row height according to *height_num*.

Type_num is a number from 1 to 3 corresponding to selecting the Hide or Unhide button in the Row Height dialog box or setting the selection to a best-fit height.

Type_num	Action taken
1	Hides the row selection by setting the row height to 0
2	Unhides the row selection by setting the row height to the value set before the selection was hidden
3	Sets the row selection to a best-fit height, which varies from row to row depending on how large the font is in any cell in each row or on how many lines of text are wrapped

Remarks

- If any of the argument settings conflict, such as when *standard_height* is TRUE and *type_num* is 3, Microsoft Excel uses the *type_num* argument and ignores any arguments that conflict with *type_num*.

- If you are recording a macro while using a mouse, and you change row heights by dragging the row border, Microsoft Excel records the reference of the rows using R1C1-style references in the form of text. If Relative Record is on, Microsoft Excel uses R1C1-style relative references. If Absolute Record is on, Microsoft Excel uses R1C1-style absolute references.

Examples

The following macro formula makes the current selection the standard height:

```
ROW.HEIGHT(,,TRUE)
```

The following macro formula hides row 1:

```
ROW.HEIGHT(,"R1",,1) or ROW.HEIGHT(0,"R1")
```

The following macro formula restores row 1 to a best-fit height:

```
ROW.HEIGHT(,"R1",,3)
```

Related Function

Function	Description
COLUMN.WIDTH	Sets the widths of the specified columns

ROWS

Returns the number of rows in a reference or array.

Syntax

ROWS(*array*)

Array   is an array, an array formula, or a reference to a range of cells for which you want the number of rows.

Examples

```
ROWS(A1:C4)
```
equals 4

```
ROWS({1,2,3;4,5,6})
```
equals 2

The following macro formula calculates the number of rows in the current selection:

```
ROWS(SELECTION())
```

The following macro formula calculates the number of rows in the third area (specified by the *area_num* argument to INDEX) of the current multiple selection:

```
ROWS(INDEX(SELECTION(),,,3))
```

Related Functions

Function	Description
COLUMNS	Returns the number of columns in a reference
ROW	Returns the row number of a reference

RSQ

Returns the r^2 value of the linear regression line through data points in *known_y's* and *known_x's*. The r^2 value is the square of the Pearson product moment correlation coefficient. For more information, see PEARSON. The r^2 value can be interpreted as the proportion of the variance in *y* attributable to the variance in *x*.

Syntax

RSQ(*known_y's,known_x's*)

Known_y's   is an array or range of data points.

Known_x's   is an array or range of data points.

Remarks

- The arguments should be numbers, or names, arrays, or references that contain numbers.

- If an array or reference argument contains text, logical values, or empty cells, those values are ignored; however, cells with the value zero are included.

- If *known_y's* and *known_x's* are empty or have a different number of data points, RSQ returns the #N/A error value.

- The equation for the *r* value of the regression line is:

$$r = \frac{n(\Sigma XY) - (\Sigma X)(\Sigma Y)}{\sqrt{\left[n\Sigma X^2 - (\Sigma X)^2\right]\left[n\Sigma Y^2 - (\Sigma Y)^2\right]}}$$

Example

```
RSQ({2,3,9,1,8,7,5},{6,5,11,7,5,4,4})
```
equals 0.05795

Related Functions

Function	Description
CORREL	Returns the correlation coefficient between two data sets
COVAR	Returns covariance, the average of the products of paired deviations
INTERCEPT	Returns the intercept of the linear regression line
LINEST	Returns the parameters of a linear trend
LOGEST	Returns the parameters of an exponential trend
PEARSON	Returns the Pearson product moment correlation coefficient
SLOPE	Returns the slope of the linear regression line
STEYX	Returns the standard error of the predicted y value for each x in the regression
TREND	Returns values along a linear trend

RUN

Macro Sheets Only

Equivalent to choosing the Run command from the Macro menu. Runs a macro. For detailed information about the Run command, see online Help.

Syntax

RUN(*reference,step*)
RUN?(*reference,step*)

Reference is a reference to the macro you want to run or a number from 1 to 4 specifying an Auto macro to run.

If *reference* is	Specifies
1	All Auto_Open macros
2	All Auto_Close macros
3	All Auto_Activate macros
4	All Auto_Deactivate macros

- If *reference* is a range of cells, RUN begins with the macro function in the upper-left cell of *reference*.

- If the macro sheet containing the macro is not the active document, *reference* can be an external reference to the name of the macro, such as RUN(MACRO.XLM!Months) or an external R1C1-style reference to the location of the macro, such as RUN("MACRO.XLM!R2C3"). The reference must be in text form.

- If *reference* is omitted, the macro function in the active cell is carried out, and macro execution continues down that column.

Step is a logical value specifying that the macro is to be run in single-step mode. If *step* is TRUE, Microsoft Excel runs the macro in single-step mode; if FALSE or omitted, Microsoft Excel runs the macro normally.

Remarks

- RUN is recorded when you choose the Run command from the Macro menu while recording a macro. The reference you enter in the Run dialog box is recorded as text, with A1-style references converted to R1C1-style references.

- To run a macro from a macro sheet, you could alternatively enter the name of the macro as a formula, followed by a set of parentheses. For example, enter =MACRO.XLM!Months() instead of =RUN(MACRO.XLM!Months).

Examples

The following macro formula begins executing the macro commands at the active cell:

```
RUN()
```

In Microsoft Excel for Windows, each of the following macro formulas runs the macro beginning in the upper-left corner of the range named Months, which begins in cell B14, on the macro sheet MACROS.XLM:

```
RUN(MACROS.XLM!Months)
RUN("MACROS.XLM!R14C2")
```

In Microsoft Excel for the Macintosh, each of the following macro formulas runs the macro beginning in the upper-left corner of the range named Months, which begins in cell B14, on the macro sheet MACROS:

```
RUN(MACROS!Months)
RUN("MACROS!R14C2")
```

Related Functions

Function	Description
GOTO	Directs macro execution to another cell
ON functions	Run a macro when a specified condition is TRUE

SAMPLE

Macro Sheets Only

Samples data. For more information, see "Analyzing Statistical or Engineering Data" in Chapter 1 in Book 2 of the *Microsoft Excel User's Guide*.

If this function is not available, you must install the Analysis ToolPak add-in macro. For more information, see "Managing Add-in Commands and Functions" in Chapter 4 in Book 2 of the *Microsoft Excel User's Guide*.

Syntax

SAMPLE*(inprng,outrng,method,rate)*

Inprng   is the input range.

Outrng   is the first cell (the upper-left cell) in the output column.

Method   is a text character that indicates the type of sampling.

- If *method* is "P", then periodic sampling is used. The input range is sampled every *n*th cell, where *n = rate*.

- If *method* is "R", then random sampling is used. The output column will contain *rate* samples.

Rate   is the sampling rate, if *method* is "P" (periodic sampling). *Rate* is the number of samples to take if method is "R" (random sampling).

Related Function

Function	Description
FOURIER	Performs a Fourier transform

SAVE

Macro Sheets Only

Equivalent to choosing the Save command from the File menu. Saves the active document. For detailed information about the Save command, see online Help.

Syntax

SAVE( )

Remarks

Use the SAVE.AS function instead of SAVE when you want to change the filename or file type, specify a password, create a backup file, or save a file to a different directory or folder.

Related Functions

Function	Description
SAVE.AS	Saves a document and allows you to specify the name, file type, password, backup file, and location of the document
SAVE.WORKBOOK	Saves a workbook

SAVE.AS

Macro Sheets Only

Equivalent to choosing the Save As command from the File menu. Use SAVE.AS to specify a new filename, file type, protection password, or write-reservation password, or to create a backup file. You can also use SAVE.AS to save a file as an add-in document or a template. For detailed information about the Save As command, see online Help.

Syntax

SAVE.AS(*document_text,type_num,prot_pwd, backup,write_res_pwd,read_only_rec*)

SAVE.AS?(*document_text,type_num,prot_pwd, backup,write_res_pwd,read_only_rec*)

Document_text specifies the name of a document to save, such as SALES.XLS (in Microsoft Excel for Windows) or SALES (in Microsoft Excel for the Macintosh). You can include a full path in *document_text*, such as C:\EXCEL\ANALYZE.XLM (in Microsoft Excel for Windows) or HARDDISK:FINANCIALS: ANALYZE (in Microsoft Excel for the Macintosh).

Type_num is a number from 1 to 29 specifying the file format in which to save the document. For information about file formats, see "Saving a Document" in Chapter 4 in Book 1 of the *Microsoft Excel User's Guide*. The following table lists the file format corresponding to each *type_num*.

Type_num	File format
1 or omitted	Normal
2	SYLK
3	Text
4	WKS
5	WK1
6	CSV
7	DBF2
8	DBF3
9	DIF
10	Reserved

Type_num	File format
11	DBF4
12	Reserved
13	Reserved
14	Reserved
15	WK3
16	Microsoft Excel 2.x
17	Template
18	Add-in macro
19	Text (Macintosh)
20	Text (Windows)
21	Text (MS-DOS)
22	CSV (Macintosh)
23	CSV (Windows)
24	CSV (MS-DOS)
25	International macro
26	International add-in macro
27	Reserved
28	Reserved
29	Microsoft Excel 3.0

The following table shows which values of *type_num* apply to the four Microsoft Excel document types.

Document type	Type_num
Worksheet	All except 10, 12–14, 18, 25–28
Chart	1, 16, 17, 29
Macro sheet	1–3, 6, 9, 16–29
Workbook	1, 15

Prot_pwd corresponds to the Protection Password box in the Save Options dialog box.

- *Prot_pwd* is a password given as text or as a reference to a cell containing text. *Prot_pwd* should be no more than 15 characters.

- If a file is saved with a password, the password must be supplied for the file to be opened.

Backup is a logical value corresponding to the Create Backup File check box in the Save Options dialog box and specifies whether to make a backup document. If *backup* is TRUE, Microsoft Excel creates a backup file; if FALSE, no backup file is created; if omitted, the status is unchanged.

Write_res_pwd corresponds to the Write Reservation Password box in the Save Options dialog box and allows the user to write to a file. If a file is saved with a password and the password is not supplied when the file is opened, the file is opened read-only.

Read_only_rec is a logical value corresponding to the Read-Only Recommended check box in the Save Options dialog box.

- If *read_only_rec* is TRUE, Microsoft Excel saves the document as a read-only recommended document; if FALSE, Microsoft Excel saves the document normally; if omitted, Microsoft Excel uses the current settings.

- When you open a document that was saved as read-only recommended, Microsoft Excel displays a message recommending that you open the document as read-only.

Tip To mark the active file as saved without writing it to a disk, set *type_num* equal to 0 and omit all other arguments—that is, SAVE.AS(,0). This is useful for closing a document without saving changes and preventing Microsoft Excel from displaying a message asking to save changes.

Related Functions

Function	Description
CLOSE	Closes the active window
GET.DOCUMENT	Returns information about a document
SAVE	Saves the active document
SAVE.WORKBOOK	Saves a workbook

SAVE.TOOLBAR

Macro Sheets Only

Saves one or more toolbar definitions to a specified file.

Syntax

SAVE.TOOLBAR(*bar_id,filename*)

Bar_id is either the name or number of a toolbar whose definition you want to save or an array of toolbar names or numbers whose definitions you want to save. Use an array to save several toolbar definitions at the same time. For detailed information about *bar_id,* see ADD.TOOL. If *bar_id* is omitted, all toolbar definitions are saved.

Filename is text specifying the name of the destination file. If *filename* does not exist, Microsoft Excel creates a new file. If *filename* exists, Microsoft Excel overwrites the file. If *filename* is omitted, Microsoft Excel saves the toolbar or toolbars in EXCEL.XLB (in Microsoft Excel for Windows) or EXCEL TOOLBARS (in Microsoft Excel for the Macintosh).

Examples

In Microsoft Excel for Windows, the following macro formula saves Toolbar6 as \EXCDT\TOOLFILE.XLB.

```
SAVE.TOOLBAR("Toolbar6",
"\EXCDT\TOOLFILE.XLB")
```

In Microsoft Excel for the Macintosh, the following macro formula saves Toolbar6 as TOOLFILE.

```
SAVE.TOOLBAR("Toolbar6","TOOLFILE")
```

Related Functions

Function	Description
ADD.TOOLBAR	Creates a new toolbar with the specified tools
OPEN	Opens a document

SAVE.WORKBOOK

Macro Sheets Only

Equivalent to choosing the Save Workbook command from the File menu. Saves the workbook to which the active document belongs. For detailed information about the Save Workbook command, see online Help. For more information about workbooks, see "Managing Documents with Workbooks" in Chapter 4 in Book 1 of the *Microsoft Excel User's Guide.*

Syntax

SAVE.WORKBOOK(*document_text,type_num, prot_pwd,backup,write_res_pwd,read_only_rec*)

SAVE.WORKBOOK?(*document_text,type_num, prot_pwd,backup,write_res_pwd,read_only_rec*)

For a description of the arguments, see SAVE.AS.

Related Functions

Function	Description
CLOSE	Closes the active window
GET.DOCUMENT	Returns information about a document
SAVE	Saves the active document
SAVE.AS	Saves a document and allows you to specify the name, file type, password, backup file, and location of the document

SAVE.WORKSPACE

Macro Sheets Only

Equivalent to choosing the Workspace command from the Save menu in Microsoft Excel version 3.0 or earlier. This function is included only for macro compatibility and will be converted to SAVE.WORKBOOK when you open an older macro sheet. Although Microsoft Excel version 4.0 can open workspace files, you will normally use workbooks when you need to work with multiple documents at the same time. For more information, see "Managing Documents with Workbooks" in Chapter 4 in Book 1 of the *Microsoft Excel User's Guide.*

Syntax

SAVE.WORKSPACE(*name_text*)
SAVE.WORKSPACE?(*name_text*)

Related Function

Function	Description
SAVE.WORKBOOK	Saves a workbook

SCALE

Macro Sheets Only

Equivalent to choosing the Scale command from the Format menu, which is available when a chart is the active document. There are five syntax forms of this function. Syntax 1 of SCALE applies if the selected axis is a category (*x*) axis on a 2-D chart and the chart is not an xy (scatter) chart. Use this syntax of SCALE to change the position, formatting, and scaling of the category axis. For detailed information about the Scale command, see online Help.

Syntax 1

Category (*x*) axis, 2-D chart

SCALE(*cross,cat_labels,cat_marks,between,max, reverse*)
SCALE?(*cross,cat_labels,cat_marks,between,max, reverse*)

Arguments correspond to text boxes and check boxes in the Scale dialog box. Arguments corresponding to check boxes are logical values. If an argument is TRUE, Microsoft Excel selects the check box; if FALSE, Microsoft Excel clears the check box.

Cross is a number corresponding to the Value (Y) Axis Crosses At Category box. The default is 1. *Cross* is ignored if *max* is set to TRUE.

Cat_labels is a number corresponding to the Number Of Categories Between Tick Labels box. The default is 1.

Cat_marks is a number corresponding to the Number Of Categories Between Tick Marks box. The default is 1.

Between corresponds to the Value (Y) Axis Crosses Between Categories check box. This argument only applies if *cat_labels* is set to a number other than 1.

Max corresponds to the Value (Y) Axis Crosses At Maximum Category check box. If *max* is TRUE, it overrides any setting for *cross*.

Reverse corresponds to the Categories In Reverse Order check box.

Related Functions

Function	Description
AXES	Controls whether axes on a chart are visible
GRIDLINES	Controls whether chart gridlines are visible

SCALE

Macro Sheets Only

Equivalent to choosing the Scale command from the Format menu, which is available when the chart is the active document. There are five syntax forms of this function. Syntax 2 of SCALE applies if the selected axis is a value (*y*) axis on a 2-D chart, or either axis on an xy (scatter) chart. Use this syntax of SCALE to change the position, formatting, and scaling of the value axis. For detailed information about the Scale command, see online Help.

Syntax 2

Value (*y*) axis on a 2-D chart, or *x* or *y* (value) axis on an xy (scatter) chart

SCALE(*min_num,max_num,major,minor,cross, logarithmic,reverse,max*)
SCALE?(*min_num,max_num,major,minor,cross, logarithmic,reverse,max*)

The first five arguments correspond to the five range variables in the Scale dialog box. Each argument can be either the logical value TRUE or a number:

- If an argument is TRUE, Microsoft Excel selects the Auto check box.

- If an argument is a number, that number is used for the variable.

Min_num corresponds to thc Minimum box and is the minimum value for the value axis.

Max_num corresponds to the Maximum box and is the maximum value for the value axis.

Major corresponds to the Major Unit box and is the major unit of measure.

Minor corresponds to the Minor Unit box and is the minor unit of measure.

Cross corresponds to the Category (X) Axis Crosses At box for the value (*y*) axis of a 2-D chart or the Value (Y) Axis Crosses At box for the category (*x*) axis of an xy (scatter) chart.

The last three arguments are logical values corresponding to check boxes in the Scale dialog box. If an argument is TRUE, Microsoft Excel selects the check box; if FALSE, Microsoft Excel clears the check box.

Logarithmic corresponds to the Logarithmic Scale check box.

Reverse corresponds to the Values/Categories In Reverse Order check box.

Max corresponds to the Category/Value Axis Crosses At Maximum Value/Category check box.

SCALE

Macro Sheets Only

Equivalent to choosing the Scale command from the Format menu, which is available when a chart is the active document. There are five syntax forms of this function. Syntax 3 of SCALE applies if the selected axis is a category (*x*) axis on a 3-D chart. Use this syntax of SCALE to change the position, formatting, and scaling of the category axis. For detailed information about the Scale command, see online Help.

Syntax 3

Category (*x*) axis, 3-D chart

SCALE(*cat_labels,cat_marks,reverse,between*)
SCALE?(*cat_labels,cat_marks,reverse,between*)

Cat_labels is a number corresponding to the Number Of Categories Between Tick Labels box. The default is 1.

Cat_marks is a number corresponding to the Number Of Categories Between Tick Marks box. The default is 1.

Reverse corresponds to the Categories In Reverse Order check box in the Format Scale dialog box. If *reverse* is TRUE, Microsoft Excel selects the check box; if FALSE, Microsoft Excel clears the check box.

Between corresponds to the Value (Z) Axis Crosses Between Categories check box. If *between* is TRUE, Microsoft Excel selects the check box and the data points appear between categories. If *between* is FALSE or omitted, Microsoft Excel clears the check box.

SCALE

Macro Sheets Only

Equivalent to choosing the Scale command from the Format menu, which is available when the chart is the active document. There are five syntax forms of this function. Syntax 4 of SCALE applies if the selected axis is a series (*y*) axis on a 3-D chart. Use this syntax of SCALE to change the position, formatting, and scaling of the series axis. For detailed information about the Scale command, see online Help.

Syntax 4

Series (*y*) axis, 3-D chart

SCALE(*series_labels,series_marks,reverse*)
SCALE?(*series_labels,series_marks,reverse*)

Series_labels is a number corresponding to the Number Of Series Between Tick Labels box. The default is 1.

Series_marks is a number corresponding to the Number Of Series Between Tick Marks box. The default is 1.

Reverse is a logical value that corresponds to the Series In Reverse Order check box in the Scale dialog box. If *reverse* is TRUE, Microsoft Excel displays the series in reverse order; if FALSE or omitted, Microsoft Excel displays the series normally.

SCALE

Macro Sheets Only

Equivalent to choosing the Scale command from the Format menu, which is available when the chart is the active document. There are five syntax forms of this function. Syntax 5 of SCALE applies if the selected axis is a value (*z*) axis on a 3-D chart. Use this syntax of SCALE to change the position, formatting, and scaling of the value axis. For detailed information about the Scale command, see online Help.

Syntax 5

Value (*z*) axis, 3-D chart

SCALE(*min_num,max_num,major,minor,cross, logarithmic,reverse,min*)
SCALE?(*min_num,max_num,major,minor,cross, logarithmic,reverse,min*)

The first five arguments correspond to the five range variables in the Scale dialog box, as shown in the following list. Each argument can be either the logical value TRUE or a number.

- If TRUE or omitted, the Auto check box is selected.

- If a number, that number is used for the variable.

Min_num corresponds to the Minimum box and is the minimum value for the value axis.

Max_num corresponds to the Maximum box and is the maximum value for the value axis.

Major corresponds to the Major Unit box and is the major unit of measure.

Minor corresponds to the Minor Unit box and is the minor unit of measure.

Cross corresponds to the Floor (XY Plane) Crosses At: box.

The last three arguments are logical values corresponding to check boxes. If an argument is TRUE, Microsoft Excel selects the check box; if FALSE, Microsoft Excel clears the check box.

Logarithmic corresponds to the Logarithmic Scale check box.

Reverse corresponds to the Values In Reverse Order check box.

Min corresponds to the Floor (XY Plane) Crosses At Minimum Value check box.

SCENARIO.ADD

Macro Sheets Only

Equivalent to choosing the Scenario Manager command from the Formula menu and then choosing the Add button. Defines the specified values as a scenario. A scenario is a set of values to be used as input for a model on your worksheet. For more information about scenarios, see "Using Scenarios to Analyze Data" in Chapter 2 in Book 2 of the *Microsoft Excel User's Guide*.

If this function is not available, you must install the Scenario Manager add-in macro. For more information, see "Managing Add-in Commands and Functions" in Chapter 4 in Book 2 of the *Microsoft Excel User's Guide*.

Syntax

SCENARIO.ADD(*scen_name,value_array*)

Scen_name is the name of the scenario you want to define.

Value_array is a horizontal array of values you want to use as input for the model on your worksheet.

- Any entry that would be valid for a cell in your model can be a value in *value_array*.

- The values must be arranged in the same order as the model's input cells. The input cells are listed in the Changing Cells box in the Scenario Manager dialog box. Use SCENARIO.CELLS to define the list.

- If *value_array* is omitted, it is assumed to contain the current values of the input cells.

Related Function

Function	Description
REPORT.DEFINE	Creates a report

SCENARIO.CELLS

Macro Sheets Only

Equivalent to choosing the Scenario Manager command from the Formula menu and then editing the Changing Cells box. Defines the changing cells for a model on your worksheet. Changing cells are the cells into which values will be entered when you display a scenario. For more information about scenarios, see "Using Scenarios to Analyze Data" in Chapter 2 in Book 2 of the *Microsoft Excel User's Guide*.

If this function is not available, you must install the Scenario Manager add-in macro. For more information, see "Managing Add-in Commands and Functions" in Chapter 4 in Book 2 of the *Microsoft Excel User's Guide*.

Syntax

SCENARIO.CELLS(*changing_ref*)
SCENARIO.CELLS? *( )*

Changing_ref is a reference to the cells you want to define as input cells for the model. If *changing_ref* contains nonadjacent references, you must separate the reference areas by commas and enclose *changing_ref* in an extra set of parentheses. See the example below.

Example

The following macro formula defines a nonadjacent group of cells and a named reference as input cells for a model:

```
SCENARIO.CELLS((!$B$4,!$B$6,!$B$8,!Sales))
```

SCENARIO.DELETE

Macro Sheets Only

Equivalent to choosing the Scenario Manager command from the Formula menu and then selecting a scenario and choosing the Delete button. Deletes the specified scenario. For more information about scenarios, see "Using Scenarios to Analyze Data" in Chapter 2 in Book 2 of the *Microsoft Excel User's Guide*.

If this function is not available, you must install the Scenario Manager add-in macro. For more information, see "Managing Add-in Commands and Functions" in Chapter 4 in Book 2 of the *Microsoft Excel User's Guide*.

Syntax

SCENARIO.DELETE(*scen_name*)

Scen_name is the name of the scenario you want to delete.

Example

The following macro formula deletes the scenario named Best Case.

```
SCENARIO.DELETE("Best Case")
```

SCENARIO.GET

Macro Sheets Only

Returns the specified information about the scenarios defined on your worksheet. For more information about scenarios, see "Using Scenarios to Analyze Data" in Chapter 2 in Book 2 of the *Microsoft Excel User's Guide*.

If this function is not available, you must install the Scenario Manager add-in macro. For more information, see "Managing Add-in Commands and Functions" in Chapter 4 in Book 2 of the *Microsoft Excel User's Guide*.

Syntax

SCENARIO.GET*(type_num)*

Type_num   is a number from 1 to 6 specifying the type of information you want.

Type_num	Information returned
1	A horizontal array of all scenario names in the form of text
2	A reference to the changing cells (specified in the Changing Cells box of the Scenario Manager dialog box)
3	A reference to the result cells (specified in the Result Cells box in the Scenario Summary dialog box)
4	An array of scenario values. Each scenario is in a separate row.
5	A horizontal array of the creation date and time, expressed as a serial number, of each scenario.
6	A horizontal array containing the user name of the person to last change each scenario.

Remarks

In the returned array of scenario values, the number of rows is the number of scenarios, and the number of columns is the number of changing cells.

SCENARIO.SHOW

Macro Sheets Only

Equivalent to choosing the Scenario Manager command from the Formula menu and then selecting a scenario and choosing the Show button. Recalculates a model using the specified scenario and displays the result.

A scenario is a set of values to be used as input for a model on your worksheet. For more information about scenarios, see "Using Scenarios to Analyze Data" in Chapter 2 in Book 2 of the *Microsoft Excel User's Guide*.

If this function is not available, you must install the Scenario Manager add-in macro. For more information, see "Managing Add-in Commands and Functions" in Chapter 4 in Book 2 of the *Microsoft Excel User's Guide*.

Syntax

SCENARIO.SHOW*(scen_name)*

Scen_name   is the name of the previously defined scenario whose values you want to switch to.

SCENARIO.SHOW.NEXT

Macro Sheets Only

Equivalent to choosing the Scenario Manager command from the Formula menu, selecting the next scenario from the Scenarios list, and choosing the Show button. Recalculates a model using the next scenario and displays the result.

If this function is not available, you must install the Scenario Manager add-in macro. For more information, see "Managing Add-in Commands and Functions" in Chapter 4 in Book 2 of the *Microsoft Excel User's Guide*.

Syntax

SCENARIO.SHOW.NEXT*( )*

Remarks

After displaying the last scenario, running SCENARIO.SHOW.NEXT again displays the first scenario.

SCENARIO.SUMMARY

Macro Sheets Only

Equivalent to choosing the Scenario Manager command from the Formula menu and then choosing the Summary button. Generates a table summarizing the results of all the scenarios for the model on your worksheet. For more information about scenarios, see "Using Scenarios to Analyze Data" in Chapter 2 in Book 2 of the *Microsoft Excel User's Guide*.

If this function is not available, you must install the Scenario Manager add-in macro. For more information, see "Managing Add-in Commands and Functions" in Chapter 4 in Book 2 of the *Microsoft Excel User's Guide*.

Syntax

SCENARIO.SUMMARY*(result_ref)*
SCENARIO.SUMMARY?*(result_ref)*

Result_ref is a reference to the result cells you want to include in the summary report. Normally, *result_ref* refers to one or more cells containing the formulas that depend on the changing cell values for your model—that is, the cells that show the results of a particular scenario.

- If *result_ref* is omitted, no result cells are included in the report.

- If *result_ref* contains nonadjacent references, you must separate the reference areas by commas and enclose *result_ref* in an extra set of parentheses.

Remarks

- SCENARIO.SUMMARY generates a summary table of the changing cell and result cell values for each scenario.

- The table is generated on a new worksheet. The new worksheet becomes the active document after SCENARIO.SUMMARY runs.

SEARCH

Returns the number of the character at which a specific character or text string is first found, reading from left to right. Use SEARCH to discover the location of a character or text string within another text string, so that you can use the MID or REPLACE functions to change the text.

Syntax

SEARCH*(find_text,within_text,start_num)*

Find_text is the text you want to find. You can use the wildcard characters, question mark (?) and asterisk (*), in *find_text*. A question mark matches any single character; an asterisk matches any sequence of characters. If you want to find an actual question mark or asterisk, type a tilde (~) before the character. If *find_text* is not found, the #VALUE! error value is returned.

Within_text is the text in which you want to search for *find_text*.

Start_num is the character number in *within_text*, counting from the left, at which you want to start searching.

- If *start_num* is omitted, it is assumed to be 1.

- If *start_num* is not greater than 0 or is greater than the length of *within_text*, the #VALUE! error value is returned.

Tip Use *start_num* to skip a specified number of characters from the left of the text. For example, suppose you are working with a text string such as "AYF0093.YoungMensApparel". To find the number of the first "Y" in the descriptive part of the text string, set *start_num* equal to 8 so that the serial-number portion of the text is not searched. SEARCH begins with character 8, finds *find_text* at the next character, and returns the number 9. SEARCH always returns the number of characters from the left of the text string, not from *start_num*.

Remarks

- SEARCH does not distinguish between upper-case and lowercase letters when searching text.

- SEARCH is similar to FIND, except that FIND is case-sensitive.

Examples

SEARCH("e","Statements",1) equals 5

If cell B17 contains the word "margin" and cell A14 contains "Profit Margin", then:

SEARCH($B$17,$A$14) equals 8

Use SEARCH with the REPLACE function to provide REPLACE with the correct *start_num* at which to begin inserting new text. Using the same cell references as the previous example:

REPLACE($A$14,SEARCH($B$17,$A$14),6, "Amount") returns the text "Profit Amount".

Related Functions

Function	Description
FIND	Finds one text value within another (case-sensitive)
MID	Returns a specific string starting at the position you specify
REPLACE	Replaces characters within text
SUBSTITUTE	Substitutes new text for old text in a text string

SECOND

Returns the second corresponding to *serial_number*. The second is given as an integer in the range 0 to 59. Use SECOND to get the time in seconds indicated by a serial number.

Syntax

SECOND(*serial_number*)

Serial_number is the date-time code used by Microsoft Excel for date and time calculations. You can give *serial_number* as text, such as "16:48:23" or "4:48:47 PM", instead of as a number. The text is automatically converted to a serial number. For more information on *serial_number,* see NOW.

Remarks

Microsoft Excel for Windows and Microsoft Excel for the Macintosh use different date systems as their default. For more information, see NOW.

Examples

SECOND("4:48:18 PM") equals 18

SECOND(0.01) equals 24

SECOND(4.02) equals 48

Related Functions

Function	Description
DATE	Returns the serial number of a particular date
YEAR, MONTH, DAY, WEEKDAY, HOUR, and MINUTE	Convert serial numbers into years, months, days, days of the week, hours, and minutes

SELECT

Macro Sheets Only

Equivalent to selecting cells or changing the active cell. There are three syntax forms of SELECT. Use syntax 1 to select a cell on a worksheet or macro sheet; use one of the other syntax forms to select worksheet or macro sheet objects or chart items.

Syntax 1

Cells on a worksheet or macro sheet

SELECT(*selection,active_cell*)

Selection is the cell or range of cells you want to select. *Selection* can be a reference to the active worksheet, such as !$A$1:$A$3 or !Sales, or an R1C1-style reference to a cell or range relative to the active cell in the current selection, such as "R[–1]C[–1]:R[1]C[1]". The reference must be in text form. If *selection* is omitted, the current selection is used.

Active_cell is the cell in *selection* you want to make the active cell. *Active_cell* can be a reference to a single cell on the active worksheet, such as !$A$1, or an R1C1-style reference relative to the active cell, such as "R[–1]C[–1]". The reference must be in text form. If *active_cell* is omitted, SELECT makes the cell in the upper-left corner of *selection* the active cell.

Remarks

- *Active_cell* must be within *selection*. If it is not, an error message is displayed and SELECT returns the #VALUE! error value.

- If you are recording a macro using the Relative Record command from the Macro menu and you make a selection, Microsoft Excel records the action using R1C1-style relative references in the form of text.

- If you are recording using the Absolute Record command from the Macro menu, Microsoft Excel records the action using R1C1-style absolute references in the form of text.

- You cannot give an external reference to a specific document as the *selection* argument. The document on which you want to make a selection must be active when you use SELECT. Use FORMULA.GOTO to make a selection on an external worksheet or macro sheet.

Tip You can enter data in a cell without selecting the cell by using the reference arguments to the CUT, COPY, or FORMULA functions.

Examples

The following macro formula selects cells C3:E5 on the active worksheet and makes C5 the active cell:

```
SELECT(!$C$3:$E$5,!$C$5)
```

If the active cell is C3, the following macro formula selects cells E5:G7 and makes cell F6 the active cell in the selection:

```
SELECT("R[2]C[2]:R[4]C[4]","R[1]C[1]")
```

You can also make multiple nonadjacent selections with SELECT. The following macro formula selects a number of nonadjacent ranges:

```
SELECT("R1C1,R3C2:R4C3,R8C4:R10C5")
```

The following sequence of macro formulas moves the active cell right, left, down, and up within the selection, just as TAB, SHIFT+TAB, ENTER, and SHIFT+ENTER do:

```
SELECT(,"RC[1]")
SELECT(,"RC[-1]")
SELECT(,"R[1]C")
SELECT(,"R[-1]C")
```

Use SELECT with the OFFSET function to select a new range a specified distance away from the current range. For example, the following macro formula selects a range that is the same size as the current range, one column over:

```
SELECT(OFFSET(SELECTION(),0,1))
```

Related Functions

Function	Description
ACTIVE.CELL	Returns the reference of the active cell
SELECT.SPECIAL	Selects a group of cells belonging to a category
SELECTION	Returns the reference of the selection

SELECT

Macro Sheets Only

Equivalent to selecting objects on a worksheet or macro sheet. There are three syntax forms of SELECT. Use syntax 2 to select an object on which to perform an action; use one of the other syntax forms to select cells on a worksheet or macro sheet or items on a chart.

Syntax 2

Worksheet and macro sheet objects

SELECT(*object_id_text,replace*)

Object_id_text   is text that identifies the object to select. *Object_id_text* can be the name of more than one object. To give the name of more than one object, use the following format:

```
SELECT("Oval 3, Arc 2, Line 4")
```

The last item in the *object_id_text* list will be the active object. The active object is important when moving and sizing a group of objects. A multiple selection of objects is moved and sized relative to the upper-left corner of the active object.

Replace   is a logical value that specifies whether previously selected objects are included in the selection. If *replace* is TRUE or omitted, Microsoft Excel only selects the objects specified by *object_id_text;* if FALSE, it includes any objects that were previously selected. For example, if a button is selected and a SELECT formula selects an arc and an oval, TRUE leaves only the arc and oval selected, and FALSE includes the button with the arc and oval.

Remarks

Objects can be identified by their object type and number as described in CREATE.OBJECT, or by the unique number that specifies the order of their creation. For example, if the third object you create is an oval, you could use either "oval 3" or "3" as *object_id_text*.

Examples

The following macro formulas each select a number of objects and specify Arc 2 as the active object:

```
SELECT("Oval 3, Arc 1, Line 4, Arc 2")
SELECT("3, 1, 4, 2")
```

Related Functions

Function	Description
FORMAT.MOVE	Moves the selected object
FORMAT.SIZE	Changes the size of the selected objects
GET.OBJECT	Returns information about an object
SELECTION	Returns the reference of the selection

SELECT

Macro Sheets Only

Selects a chart object as specified by the selection code *item_text*. There are three syntax forms of SELECT. Use syntax 3 to select a chart item to which you want to apply formatting; use one of the other syntax forms to select cells or objects on a worksheet or macro sheet.

Syntax 3

Chart items

SELECT(*item_text,single_point*)

Item_text   is a selection code from the following table which specifies which chart object to select.

To select	Item_text
Entire chart	"Chart"
Plot area	"Plot"
Legend	"Legend"
Main chart value axis	"Axis 1"
Main chart category axis	"Axis 2"
Overlay chart value axis or 3-D series axis	"Axis 3"

To select	Item_text
Overlay chart category axis	"Axis 4"
Chart title	"Title"
Label for the main chart value axis	"Text Axis 1"
Label for the main chart category axis	"Text Axis 2"
Label for the main chart series axis	"Text Axis 3"
nth floating text item	"Text n"
nth arrow	"Arrow n"
Major gridlines of value axis	"Gridline 1"
Minor gridlines of value axis	"Gridline 2"
Major gridlines of category axis	"Gridline 3"
Minor gridlines of category axis	"Gridline 4"
Major gridlines of series axis	"Gridline 5"
Minor gridlines of series axis	"Gridline 6"
Main chart droplines	"Dropline 1"
Overlay chart droplines	"Dropline 2"
Main chart hi-lo lines	"Hiloline 1"
Overlay chart hi-lo lines	"Hiloline 2"
Main chart up bar	"UpBar1"
Overlay chart up bar	"UpBar2"
Main chart down bar	"DownBar1"
Overlay chart down bar	"DownBar2"
Main chart series line	"Seriesline1"
Overlay chart series line	"Seriesline2"
Entire series	"Sn"
Data associated with point m in series n if single_point is TRUE	"SnPm"
Text attached to point m of series n	"Text SnPm"
Series title text of series n of an area chart	"Text Sn"
Base of a 3-D chart	"Floor"
Back of a 3-D chart	"Walls"
Corners of a 3-D chart	"Corners"

Single_point is a logical value that determines whether to select a single point. *Single_point* is available only when *item_text* is "SnPm".

- If *single_point* is TRUE, Microsoft Excel selects a single point.

- If *single_point* is FALSE or omitted, Microsoft Excel selects a single point if there is only one series in the chart or selects the entire series if there is more than one series in the chart.

- If you specify *single_point* when *item_text* is any value other than "SnPm", SELECT returns an error value.

Examples

SELECT("Chart") selects the entire chart.

SELECT("Dropline 2") selects the droplines of an overlay chart.

SELECT("S1P3",TRUE) selects the third point in the first series.

SELECT("Text S1") selects the series title text of the first series in an area chart.

Related Function

Function	Description
SELECTION	Returns the reference of the selection

SELECT.CHART

Macro Sheets Only

Equivalent to the Select Chart command on the Chart menu. This function is equivalent to using the third form of SELECT with "Chart" as the *item_text* argument.

Syntax

SELECT.CHART( )

Remarks

This function is included for compatibility with macros written with Microsoft Excel for the Macintosh version 1.5 or earlier.

SELECT.END

Macro Sheets Only

Selects the cell at the edge of the range in the direction specified. Equivalent to pressing CTRL+ARROW in Microsoft Excel for Windows or COMMAND+ARROW in Microsoft Excel for the Macintosh.

Syntax

SELECT.END(*direction_num*)

Direction_num   is a number from 1 to 4 indicating the direction in which to move.

Direction_num	Direction
1	Left (equivalent to CTRL+LEFT ARROW or COMMAND+LEFT ARROW)
2	Right (equivalent to CTRL+RIGHT ARROW or COMMAND+RIGHT ARROW)
3	Up (equivalent to CTRL+UP ARROW or COMMAND+UP ARROW)
4	Down (equivalent to CTRL+DOWN ARROW or COMMAND+DOWN ARROW)

Related Function

Function	Description
SELECT.LAST.CELL	Selects the last cell on a worksheet or macro sheet that contains a formula, value, or format or that is referred to in a formula or name

SELECT.LAST.CELL

Macro Sheets Only

Equivalent to choosing the Select Special command from the Formula menu and selecting the Last Cell option. Selects the cell at the intersection of the last row and column that contains a formula, value, or format, or that is referred to in a formula or name. For detailed information about the Select Special command, see online Help.

Syntax

SELECT.LAST.CELL( )

Related Function

Function	Description
SELECT.END	Selects the last cell in a range

SELECT.PLOT.AREA

Macro Sheets Only

Equivalent to choosing the Select Plot Area command from the Chart menu. Selects the plot area of the active chart.

Syntax

SELECT.PLOT.AREA( )

Remarks

SELECT.PLOT.AREA is included only for compatibility with previous versions of Microsoft Excel for the Macintosh. SELECT.PLOT.AREA is the same as the SELECT("Plot") function.

Related Function

Function	Description
SELECT	Selects a cell, worksheet object, or chart

SELECT.SPECIAL

Macro Sheets Only

Equivalent to choosing the Select Special command from the Formula menu. Use SELECT.SPECIAL to select groups of similar cells in one of a variety of categories. For detailed information about the Select Special command, see online Help.

Syntax

SELECT.SPECIAL(*type_num,*value_type, levels)
SELECT.SPECIAL?(*type_num,*value_type, levels)

Type_num is a number from 1 to 13 corresponding to options in the Select Special dialog box and describes what to select.

Type_num	Description
1	Notes
2	Constants
3	Formulas
4	Blanks
5	Current region
6	Current array
7	Row differences
8	Column differences
9	Precedents
10	Dependents
11	Last cell
12	Visible cells only (outlining)
13	All objects

Value_type is a number specifying which types of constants or formulas you want to select. *Value_type* is available only when *type_num* is 2 or 3.

Value_type	Selects
1	Numbers
2	Text
4	Logical values
16	Error values

These values can be added to select more than one type. The default for *value_type* is 23, select all value types.

Levels is a number specifying how precedents and dependents are selected. *Levels* is available only when *type_num* is 9 or 10. The default is 1.

Levels	Selects
1	Direct only
2	All levels

SELECTION

Macro Sheets Only

Returns the reference or object identifier of the selection as an external reference. Use SELECTION to return information about the current selection for use in other macro formulas.

Syntax

SELECTION( )

If a cell or range of cells is selected, Microsoft Excel returns the corresponding external reference. If an object is selected, Microsoft Excel returns the object identifier listed in the following table.

Item selected	Identifier returned
Imported graphic	Picture *n*
Linked graphic	Picture *n*
Chart picture	Picture *n*
Linked chart	Chart *n*

Item selected	Identifier returned
Worksheet range	Picture *n*
Linked worksheet range	Picture *n*
Text box	Text *n*
Button	Button *n*
Rectangle	Rectangle *n*
Oval	Oval *n*
Line	Line *n*
Arc	Arc *n*
Group	Group *n*
Freehand drawing or polygon	Drawing *n*

SELECTION also returns the identifiers of chart items. The identifiers returned are the same as the identifiers you specify when you use the SELECT function. For a list of these identifiers, see the description of *item_text* in SELECT.

If you select cells and use the value returned by SELECTION in a function or operation, you usually get the value contained in the selection instead of its reference. References are automatically converted to the contents of the reference. If you want to work with the actual reference, use SET.NAME to assign a name to it, even if the reference refers to objects. See the last example following. You can also use the REFTEXT function to convert the reference to text, which you can then store or manipulate. See the example in TEXTREF.

Remarks

- If an object is selected, SELECTION returns the identifier of the object. If multiple objects are selected, it returns the identifiers of all the selected objects, as a string separated by commas.

- If more than 1024 characters would be returned, SELECTION returns the #VALUE! error value.

Examples

If the document in the active window is named SHEET1, and if A1:A3 is the selection, then:

SELECTION() equals SHEET1!A1:A3

The following macro formula moves the current selection one row down:

SELECT(OFFSET(SELECTION(),1,0))

The above formula is particularly useful for moving incrementally through a database to add or modify records.

The following macro formula defines the name "EntryRange" on the active worksheet to refer to one row below the current selection on the active worksheet:

DEFINE.NAME("EntryRange",
OFFSET(SELECTION(),1,0))

The following macro formula defines the name "Objects" on your macro sheet to refer to the object names in the current multiple selection:

SET.NAME("Objects",SELECTION())

Related Functions

Function	Description
ACTIVE.CELL	Returns the reference of the active cell
OFFSET	Returns a reference offset from a given reference
SELECT	Selects a cell, worksheet object, or chart

SEND.KEYS

Macro Sheets Only

Sends keystrokes to the active application just as if they were typed at the keyboard. Use SEND.KEYS to send keystrokes that perform actions and execute commands to applications you are running with Microsoft Excel's other dynamic data exchange (DDE) functions.

Syntax

SEND.KEYS(*key_text,wait_logical*)

Note   This function is available only in Microsoft Excel for Windows.

Key_text   is the key or key combination you want to send to another application. The format for *key_text* is described in the ON.KEY function.

Wait_logical   is a logical value that determines whether the macro continues before the actions caused by *key_text* are carried out.

- If *wait_logical* is TRUE, Microsoft Excel waits for the keys to be processed before returning control to the macro.

- If *wait_logical* is FALSE or omitted, the macro continues running without waiting for the keys to be processed.

Remarks

If Microsoft Excel is the active application, *wait_logical* is assumed to be FALSE, even if you enter *wait_logical* as TRUE. This is because if *wait_logical* is TRUE, Microsoft Excel waits for the keys to be processed in the other application before returning control to the macro. Microsoft Excel doesn't process keys while a macro is running.

Example

The following macro uses the Calculator application in Microsoft Excel for Windows to multiply some numbers, and then cuts the result and pastes it into Microsoft Excel.

	A	B	C
1	Names	Formulas	Comments
2			
3		CalcPaste	
4		=EXEC("CALC.EXE",1)	Starts the Calculator
5		=SEND.KEYS("10*30",TRUE)	Sends 10*30
6		=SEND.KEYS("~",TRUE)	Sends ENTER
7		=SEND.KEYS("%ec",TRUE)	Sends Edit Copy
8		=APP.ACTIVATE(,FALSE)	Switches to Microsoft Excel
9		=SELECT(!B1)	Selects cell B1
10		=PASTE()	Pastes result
11		=RETURN()	

Related Functions

Function	Description
APP.ACTIVATE	Switches to an application
EXECUTE	Carries out a command in another application
ON.KEY	Runs a macro when a specified key is pressed

SEND.MAIL

Macro Sheets Only

Equivalent to choosing the Send Mail command from the File menu. Sends the active document using Microsoft Mail. For detailed information about the Send Mail command, see online Help.

Syntax

SEND.MAIL(*recipients,subject,return_receipt*)
SEND.MAIL?(*recipients,subject,return_receipt*)

Important

- The arguments to the SEND.MAIL function are used only by Microsoft Excel for the Macintosh. In Microsoft Excel for Windows, both syntaxes (standard and dialog box) display a mail form into which you enter the message, address, and so on.

- To use SEND.MAIL in Microsoft Excel for Windows, you must be using a mail client that supports the Microsoft Windows Simple Mail Interface. For more information, see the documentation for your mail client.

Recipients is the name of the person to whom you want to send the mail. The name should be given as text.

- To specify more than one name, give the list of names as an array. For example, SEND.MAIL({"John","Paul","George", "Ringo"}) would send the active document to the four names in the array. You can also refer to a range on a worksheet or macro sheet that contains a list of names to whom you want the mail to be sent.

- To send mail to users on different Microsoft Mail servers, specify the server name along with the user name. The following text, as the *recipients* argument, sends mail to wandagr on server2, gregpr on the current server, and victorge on server7:

```
{"wandagr@server2","gregpr",
"victorge@server7"}
```

Subject is a text string that specifies the subject of the message. If *subject* is omitted, the name of the active document is used as the subject.

Return_receipt is a logical value that corresponds to the Return Receipt check box. If *return_receipt* is TRUE, Microsoft Excel selects the check box and sends a return receipt; if FALSE or omitted, Microsoft Excel clears the check box.

Examples

In Microsoft Excel for Windows, the following macro formula displays the Send Mail mail form:

```
SEND.MAIL?()
```

In Microsoft Excel for the Macintosh, the following macro formula sends the active document or group to John Peters, with the subject indicated and the Return Receipt check box selected:

```
SEND.MAIL("John Peters","Last Quarter's
Results",TRUE)
```

The following macro formula sends the active document or group to the four people indicated, with the subject indicated and the Return Receipt check box cleared:

```
SEND.MAIL({"John Peters","Mary Hopkins",
"Bill Perks","Stephanie Kurtz"},
"Weekly Report",FALSE)
```

Note that the list of names is surrounded by brackets and that commas separate the names.

The following macro formula sends the active document or group to the list of names found in the range named DistribList on the active macro sheet:

```
SEND.MAIL(DistribList,"Friday's Meeting",
FALSE)
```

Related Function

Function	Description
OPEN.MAIL	Opens files sent via Microsoft Mail that Microsoft Excel can open

SEND.TO.BACK

Macro Sheets Only

Equivalent to choosing the Send To Back command from the Format menu. Sends the selected object or objects to the back. Use SEND.TO.BACK to send selected objects behind other objects. For detailed information about the Send To Back command, see online Help.

If the selection is not an object or a group of objects, SEND.TO.BACK returns the #VALUE! error value and interrupts the macro.

Syntax

SEND.TO.BACK( )

Related Function

Function	Description
BRING.TO.FRONT	Brings selected objects to the front

SERIES

Charts Only

Represents a data series in the active chart. SERIES is used only in charts; you cannot enter it on a worksheet or macro sheet. You normally create or change data series by using the Chart Wizard or EDIT.SERIES macro function, which is equivalent to the Edit Series command on the Chart menu. However, you can edit a data series manually by selecting it, switching to the formula bar, and typing the changes.

Syntax

SERIES(*name_ref,categories,**values,plot_order**)*

Name_ref   is the name of the data series. It can be an external reference to a single cell or a name defined as a single cell. *Name_ref* can also be text enclosed in quotation marks (for example, "Projected Sales").

Categories   is an external reference to the name of the worksheet and to the cells that contain one of the following sets of data:

- Category labels for all charts except xy (scatter) charts
- X-coordinate data for xy (scatter) charts

Values   is an external reference to the name of the worksheet and to the cells that contain values (or *y*-coordinate data in scatter charts).

Plot_order   is an integer specifying whether the series is plotted first, second, or third, and so on, in the chart. No two series can have the same *plot_order*.

Remarks

- *Categories* and *values* can be arrays or references to a multiple selection, although they cannot be names that refer to a multiple selection. If you specify a multiple selection for any of these arguments, make sure you include the necessary sets of parentheses so that Microsoft Excel does not treat the components of the references as separate arguments.

- If either *categories* or *values* is a multiple selection, then all areas in that selection must be either vertical (more rows than columns) or horizontal (more columns than rows).

Related Functions

Function	Description
CHART.WIZARD	Creates and formats a chart
EDIT.SERIES	Creates or changes a chart series

SERIESSUM

Returns the sum of a power series based on the formula:

$$SERIES(x,n,m,a) = a_1 x^n + a_2 x^{(n+m)} + a_3 x^{(n+2m)} + \ldots + a_i x^{(n+(i-1)m)}$$

Many functions can be approximated by a power series expansion.

If this function is not available, you must install the Analysis ToolPak add-in macro. For more information, see "Managing Add-in Commands and Functions" in Chapter 4 in Book 2 of the *Microsoft Excel User's Guide*.

Syntax

SERIESSUM(*x,n,m,coefficients*)

X is the input value to the power series.

N is the initial power to which you want to raise *x*.

M is the step by which to increase *n* for each term in the series.

Coefficients is a set of coefficients by which each successive power of *x* is multiplied. The number of values in *coefficients* determines the number of terms in the power series. For example, if there are three values in *coefficients*, then there will be three terms in the power series.

Remarks

If any argument is non-numeric, SERIESSUM returns the #VALUE! error value.

Example

Given that cell A1 contains the formula =PI()/4, and cells E1:E4 contain the following set of values for *coefficients* (calculated using the FACT function):

$$\left[1, -\frac{1}{2!}, \frac{1}{4!}, -\frac{1}{6!} \right]$$

The following macro formula returns an approximation to the cosine of π/4 radians (45 degrees):

`SERIESSUM(A1,0,2,E1:E4)` equals .707103

SET.CRITERIA

Macro Sheets Only

Equivalent to choosing the Set Criteria command from the Data menu. Defines the name Criteria for the selected range on a worksheet or macro sheet. For detailed information about the Set Criteria command, see online Help.

Syntax

SET.CRITERIA( )

SET.DATABASE

Macro Sheets Only

Equivalent to choosing the Set Database command from the Data menu. Defines the name Database for the selected range on a worksheet or macro sheet. For detailed information about the Set Database command, see online Help.

Syntax

SET.DATABASE( )

SET.EXTRACT

Macro Sheets Only

Equivalent to choosing the Set Extract command from the Data menu. Defines the name Extract for the selected range on the active sheet. For detailed information about the Set Extract command, see online Help.

Syntax

SET.EXTRACT( )

SET.NAME

Macro Sheets Only

Defines a name on a macro sheet to refer to a value. The SET.NAME function is useful for storing values while the macro is calculating.

Syntax

SET.NAME(*name_text,*value)

Name_text is the name in the form of text that refers to *value.*

Value is the value you want to store in *name_text.*

- If *value* is omitted, the name *name_text* is deleted.

- If *value* is a reference, *name_text* is defined to refer to that reference.

Remarks

- If you want to define a name as a constant value, you can use the following syntax instead of SET.NAME:

  name_text=value

See the first two examples following.

- SET.NAME defines names as absolute references, even if a relative reference is specified. See the third and fourth examples following.

- If you want *name_text* to refer permanently to the value of a referenced cell rather than to the reference itself, you must use the DEREF function. Use of DEREF prevents *name_text* from referring to a new value every time the contents of the referenced cell changes. See the last example following.

Tips

- If you need to return an array to a macro sheet (for example, if the macro needs a list of all open windows), assign a name to the array instead of placing the array information in a range of cells. For example:

  ```
  SET.NAME("OpenDocuments",WINDOWS()) or
  SET.NAME("OpenDocuments",{"WORKSHEET1",
  "WORKSHEET2"})
  ```

- When you're debugging a macro and want to know the current value assigned to a name created by SET.NAME, you can halt the macro, choose Define Name from the Formula menu, and select the name from the Define Name dialog box.

Examples

Each of these formulas defines the name Counter to refer to the constant number 1 on the macro sheet:

```
SET.NAME("Counter",1)
Counter=1
```

Each of these formulas redefines Counter to refer to the current value of Counter plus 1:

```
SET.NAME("Counter",Counter+1)
Counter=Counter+1
```

The following macro formula defines the name Reference to refer to cell $A$1:

```
SET.NAME("Reference",A1)
```

The following macro formula defines the name Results to refer to the cells $A$1:$C$3:

```
SET.NAME("Results",A1:C3)
```

The following macro formula defines the name Range as the current selection:

```
SET.NAME("Range",SELECTION())
```

If $A$1 contains the value 2, the following macro formula defines the name Index to refer to the constant value 2:

```
SET.NAME("Index",DEREF(A1))
```

Also see examples for NAMES and FILES.

Related Functions

Function	Description
DEFINE.NAME	Defines a name on the active worksheet or macro sheet
SET.VALUE	Sets the value of a cell on a macro sheet

SET.PAGE.BREAK

Macro Sheets Only

Equivalent to choosing the Set Page Break command from the Options menu. Sets manual page breaks for a printed worksheet. Use SET.PAGE.BREAK to override the automatic page breaks. Setting a manual page break changes the automatic page breaks that follow it.

The page break occurs above and to the left of the active cell and appears as dotted lines if you have set up a printer. If the active cell is in column A, a manual page break is added only above the cell. If the active cell is in row 1, a manual page break is added only at the left edge of the cell. If the row or column next to the active cell already has a page break, SET.PAGE.BREAK takes no action.

Syntax

SET.PAGE.BREAK( )

Related Functions

Function	Description
PRINT.PREVIEW	Previews pages and page breaks before printing
REMOVE.PAGE.BREAK	Removes manual page breaks

SET.PREFERRED

Macro Sheets Only

Equivalent to choosing the Set Preferred command from the Gallery menu, which is available when a chart is the active document. Changes the default format that Microsoft Excel uses when you create a new chart or when you format a chart with the Preferred command from the Gallery menu or the PREFERRED macro function. When you use the SET.PREFERRED function, the format of the active chart becomes the preferred format. For detailed information about the Set Preferred command, see online Help.

Syntax

SET.PREFERRED( )

Related Function

Function	Description
PREFERRED	Changes the format of the active chart to the preferred format

SET.PRINT.AREA

Macro Sheets Only

Equivalent to choosing the Set Print Areas command from the Options menu. Defines the print area—the area that prints when you choose the File Print command. For detailed information about the Set Print Area command, see online Help.

Syntax

SET.PRINT.AREA( )

Remarks

- If you use SET.PRINT.AREA with a multiple selection and then use the PRINT function, the individual selections are printed one after the other in the order they were selected.

- To resume printing the entire worksheet, choose the Define Name command from the Formula menu, select the name Print_Area, and choose the Delete button.

Example

The following macro prints the database on the active external worksheet and then deletes the name Print_Area.

	A	B	C
1	Names	Formulas	Comments
2			
3		PrintDatabase	
4		=SELECT(!Database)	
5		=SET.PRINT.AREA()	
6		=PRINT()	
7		=DELETE.NAME("Print_Area")	
		=RETURN()	

Related Functions

Function	Description
PRINT	Prints the active document
SET.PRINT.TITLES	Identifies text to print as titles

SET.PRINT.TITLES

Macro Sheets Only

Equivalent to choosing the Set Print Titles command from the Options menu. Use SET.PRINT.TITLES if you want Microsoft Excel to print the titles whenever it prints any cells in a row or column that intersect the print titles area; a cell need only share the row or column with a print title for the title to be printed above or to the left of that cell.

Syntax

SET.PRINT.TITLES(*titles_for_columns_ref, titles_for_rows_ref*)
SET.PRINT.TITLES?(*titles_for_columns_ref, titles_for_rows_ref*)

Titles_for_columns_ref is a reference to the row to be used as a title for columns.

- If you specify part of a row, Microsoft Excel expands the title to a full row.

- If you omit *titles_for_columns_ref*, Microsoft Excel uses the existing row of column titles, if any.

- If you specify empty text (""), Microsoft Excel removes the row from the print titles definition.

Titles_for_rows_ref   is a reference to the column to be used as a title for rows.

- If you specify part of a column, Microsoft Excel expands the title to a full column.

- If you omit *titles_for_rows_ref,* Microsoft Excel uses the existing column of row titles, if any.

- If you specify empty text (""), Microsoft Excel removes the column from the print titles definition.

Remarks

- SET.PRINT.TITLES operates on the current document. If you specify a range that is invalid for the current document, Microsoft Excel returns the #VALUE error value.

- The print titles selection can be a multiple selection. Microsoft Excel names this selection Print_Titles when SET.PRINT.TITLES is run.

Example

The following macro formula specifies column B as the source for row titles and omits column titles.

```
SET.PRINT.TITLES("",$B$B)
```

Related Functions

Function	Description
DEFINE.NAME	Defines a name on the active worksheet or macro sheet
PRINT	Prints the active document
SET.PRINT.AREA	Definess the print area

SET.UPDATE.STATUS

Macro Sheets Only

Sets the update status of a link to automatic or manual. Use SET.UPDATE.STATUS to change the way a link is updated.

Syntax

SET.UPDATE.STATUS*(link_text,status, type_of_link)*

Link_text   is the path of the linked file for which you want to change the update status.

Status   is the number 1 or 2 and describes how you want the link to be updated.

Status	Update method
1	Automatic
2	Manual

Type_of_link   is a number from 1 to 4 that specifies what type of link you want to get information about.

Type_of_link	Link document type
1	Not available
2	DDE link
3	Not available
4	Not available

Example

In Microsoft Excel for Windows, the following macro formula sets the update status of the DDE link to Microsoft Word for Windows to manual:

```
SET.UPDATE.STATUS("WordDocument|'C:
\MEMO.DOC'!DDE.LINK1",2,2)
```

Related Functions

Function	Description
GET.LINK.INFO	Returns information about a link
UPDATE.LINK	Updates a link to another document

SET.VALUE

Macro Sheets Only

Changes the value of a cell or cells on the macro sheet—not the worksheet—without changing any formulas entered in those cells. Use SET.VALUE to assign initial values and to store values during the calculation of a macro. SET.VALUE is especially useful for initializing a dialog box and the conditional test in a WHILE loop. SET.VALUE assigns values to a specific reference or to the name of a reference that has already been defined. For information about creating a new name or entering data on a worksheet, see "Remarks" later in this topic.

Syntax

SET.VALUE(*reference,values*)

Reference   specifies the cell or cells on the macro sheet to which you want to assign a new value or values.

- If a cell in *reference* previously contained a formula, the formula is not changed, but the value of the cell might change. See the second example following.

- If *reference* is a reference to a range of cells, rather than to a single cell, then *values* should be an array of the same size. If not, Microsoft Excel expands it into multiple *values* using the normal rules for expanding arrays. See the third example following.

Values   is the value or set of values to which you want to assign the cell or cells in *reference*.

Remarks

Consider the following guidelines as you choose a function to set values on a worksheet or macro sheet:

- Use SET.VALUE to assign initial values to a reference (including names that have already been defined) on a macro sheet, and to store values during the calculation of a macro.

- Use FORMULA to enter values in a worksheet cell.

- Use SET.NAME to change the value of a name on a macro sheet (the name is created if it does not already exist). For more information, see SET.NAME.

- Use DEFINE.NAME to create or change the value of a name on a worksheet.

Examples

The following macro formula changes the value of cell A1 on the macro sheet to 1:

```
SET.VALUE($A$1,1)
```

Suppose the name TempAverage refers to a cell containing the formula AVERAGE(Temp1,Temp2, Temp3). The following formula assigns the value 99 to this cell, even if the average of the arguments is not 99, without changing the formula in TempAverage:

```
SET.VALUE(TempAverage,99)
```

The preceding formula is useful if a WHILE loop or some other conditional test depends on TempAverage and you want to force the conditional test to have a particular result. Of course, TempAverage is restored to its correct value as soon as it is recalculated. (Recall that unlike formulas in a worksheet, formulas in a macro sheet are not recalculated until the macro actually uses them.)

The following macro formula stores the values 1, 2, 3, and 4 in cells A1:B2:

```
SET.VALUE($A$1:$B$2,{1,2;3,4})
```

The following macro uses WHILE and FOR loops to generate prime numbers. As the macro generates more and more primes, it gradually slows down, and it ends when it can't find any more primes in the time you specify. SET.VALUE initializes variables when the macro starts.

	A	B	C
1	*Names*	*Formulas*	*Comments*
2			
3		**PrimeNumbers**	Returns prime numbers
4	StopSeconds	=INPUT("Stop after (seconds)?",1)	How long to look?
5		=SET.VALUE(Continue,TRUE)	
6		=SET.VALUE(NextNum,3)	Starts testing at 3
7		=SET.VALUE(CurrentTime,NOW())	Initializes time marker
8		=WHILE(Continue=TRUE)	Keeps testing more primes
9		=SET.NAME("TestFailed",FALSE)	Initialize TestFailed variable
10		=FOR("Divisor",3,INT(NextNum/2),2)	Odd number loop
11	Quotient	=NextNum/Divisor	
12		=IF((Quotient−TRUNC(Quotient))=0)	If no remainder, then
13		Divisor=NextNum−1	not prime; adjusts loop
14		TestFailed=TRUE	counter to cancel FOR
15		=END.IF()	loop; the test failed
16		=NEXT()	
17		=IF(TestFailed,GOTO(NextNum))	If failed, tests NextNum
18	Continue	=(SECOND(NOW()−CurrentTime))<StopSec	Time too long?
19	CurrentTime	=NOW()	
20		=FORMULA(NextNum)	Places prime in worksheet
21		=SELECT(OFFSET(ACTIVE.CELL(),1,0))	Moves to next row
22	NextNum	=NextNum+2	Tests next odd number
23		=NEXT()	
24		=RETURN()	

Following is the complete formula in cell B18:

```
=(SECOND(NOW()-CurrentTime))<StopSeconds
```

Related Functions

Function	Description
DEFINE.NAME	Defines a name on the active worksheet or macro sheet
FORMULA	Enters values into a cell or range or onto a chart
SET.NAME	Defines a name as a value

SHORT.MENUS

Macro Sheets Only

Equivalent to choosing the Short Menus command from the Options menu or the Chart menu in Microsoft Excel version 3.0 or earlier.

Syntax

SHORT.MENUS(*logical*)

SHOW.ACTIVE.CELL

Macro Sheets Only

Equivalent to choosing the Show Active Cell command from the Formula menu or to pressing CTRL+BACKSPACE in Microsoft Excel for Windows or COMMAND+DELETE in Microsoft Excel for the Macintosh. Scrolls the active window so the active cell becomes visible. If an object is selected, SHOW.ACTIVE.CELL returns the #VALUE! error value and halts the macro. For detailed information about the Show Active Cell command, see online Help.

Syntax

SHOW.ACTIVE.CELL( )

Related Functions

Function	Description
ACTIVE.CELL	Returns the reference of the active cell
FORMULA.GOTO	Selects a named area or reference on any open document

SHOW.BAR

Macro Sheets Only

Displays the specified menu bar. Use SHOW.BAR to display a menu bar you have created with the ADD.BAR function or to display a built-in Microsoft Excel menu bar.

Syntax

SHOW.BAR(*bar_num*)

Bar_num is the number of the menu bar you want to display. It can be the number of one of the Microsoft Excel built-in menu bars, the number returned by a previously executed ADD.BAR function, or a reference to a cell containing a previously executed ADD.BAR function.

If *bar_num* is omitted, Microsoft Excel displays the appropriate menu bar for the active document as shown in the following table.

If active window contains	Bar displayed
A worksheet or macro sheet	1
A chart	2
No active window	3
The Info window	4
A worksheet or macro sheet (short menus)	5
A chart (short menus)	6

Remarks

- When displaying a built-in menu bar, you can display only bars 1 or 5 if a worksheet or macro sheet is active, bars 2 or 6 if a chart is active, and so on. If you try to display a chart menu bar while a worksheet or macro sheet is active, SHOW.BAR returns an error and interrupts the current macro.

- Displaying a custom menu bar disables automatic menu-bar switching when different types of documents are selected. For example, if a custom menu bar is displayed and you switch to a chart, neither of the two chart menus is automatically displayed as it would be when you are using the built-in menu bars. Automatic menu-bar switching is reenabled when a built-in bar is displayed using SHOW.BAR.

For information about custom menus, see "Creating a Custom Menu" in Chapter 8 in Book 2 of the *Microsoft Excel User's Guide*.

Example

The following macro creates a new menu bar, adds menus to the new menu bar and a command to the built-in menu bar, and displays the new menu bar.

	A	B	C
1	*Names*	*Formulas*	*Comments*
2			
3		NewMenuBar	
4	NewBar	=ADD.BAR()	Creates a new menu bar
5		=ADD.MENU(NewBar,NewFile)	Adds NewFile menu
6		=ADD.MENU(NewBar,NewEdit)	Adds NewEdit menu
7		=ADD.MENU(NewBar,NewReport)	Adds NewReport menu
8		=ADD.MENU(NewBar,NewFormat)	Adds NewFormat menu
9		=ADD.MENU(NewBar,NewOptions)	Adds NewOptions menu
10		=ADD.COMMAND(1,"File",ShowNewBar)	Adds command to File menu
11		=SHOW.BAR(NewBar)	Displays NewBar
12		=RETURN()	

Related Functions

Function	Description
ADD.BAR	Adds a menu bar
DELETE.BAR	Deletes a menu bar
SHOW.TOOLBAR	Hides or displays a toolbar

SHOW.CLIPBOARD

Macro Sheets Only

Equivalent to choosing the Show Clipboard command from the Window menu in Microsoft Excel for the Macintosh or running the Clipboard application from the Control menu in Microsoft Excel for Windows. Displays the contents of the Clipboard in a new window. For detailed information about the Show Clipboard command, see online Help.

Syntax

SHOW.CLIPBOARD( )

Remarks

- In Microsoft Excel for Windows, the Clipboard must already bc available on the desktop if you want to display its contents in a new window. If it is not already available, you must run the SHOW.CLIPBOARD function twice—once to make the Clipboard application available and again to display it in a new window.

- If the Clipboard contains cells, the window shows the size of the Clipboard contents in rows and columns. If the Clipboard contains text cut from the formula bar, the window displays the text.

Example

The following macro asks if you want to see the Clipboard before you paste it in Microsoft Excel for the Macintosh.

	A	B	C
1	Names	Formulas	Comments
2			
3		**ShowBeforePasting**	
4	ViewBefore	=ALERT("View before pasting?",1)	
5		=IF(ViewBefore)	If OK, shows Clipboard
6		= SHOW.CLIPBOARD()	
7	Paste	= ALERT("Paste Clipboard?",1)	Asks if you want to paste
8		= IF(NOT(Paste))	If you don't paste, then
9		= CLOSE()	closes Clipboard
10		= RETURN()	and returns
11		= ELSE()	If you do paste, then
12		= CLOSE()	closes Clipboard first
13		= END.IF()	
14		=END.IF()	
15		=PASTE()	Pastes Clipboard contents
16		=RETURN()	

SHOW.DETAIL

Macro Sheets Only

Expands or collapses the detail under the specified expand or collapse button.

Syntax

SHOW.DETAIL(*rowcol,rowcol_num, expand*)

Rowcol   is a number that specifies whether to operate on rows or columns of data.

Rowcol	Operates on
1	Rows
2	Columns

Rowcol_num   is a number that specifies the row or column to expand or collapse. If you are in A1 mode, you must still give the column as a number. If *rowcol_num* is not a summary row or column, SHOW.DETAIL returns the #VALUE! error value and interrupts the macro.

Expand   is a logical value that specifies whether to expand or collapse the detail under the row or column. If *expand* is TRUE, Microsoft Excel expands the detail under the row or column; if FALSE, it collapses the detail under the row or column. If *expand* is omitted, the detail is expanded if it is currently collapsed and collapsed if it is currently expanded.

Examples

The following macro formula collapses the detail under column 4:

```
SHOW.DETAIL(2,4,FALSE)
```

The following macro formula either expands or collapses the detail under row 27, depending on its current state:

```
SHOW.DETAIL(1,27)
```

Related Function

Function	Description
SHOW.LEVELS	Displays a specific number of levels of an outline

SHOW.INFO

Macro Sheets Only

Equivalent to choosing the Workspace command from the Options menu and selecting the Info Window checkbox. Controls the display of the Info window. For detailed information about the Workspace command, see online Help.

Syntax

SHOW.INFO(*logical*)

Logical   controls the display of the Info window.

- If *logical* is TRUE, Microsoft Excel switches to the Info window.

- If the current window is the Info window and *logical* is FALSE, Microsoft Excel switches to the document linked to the Info window.

Tip   Before using SHOW.INFO, use ACTIVATE to switch to the document you want information about and SELECT or FORMULA.GOTO to select the cell or range you want information about.

Remarks

The Info window is not available when a chart is active. If SHOW.INFO is carried out when a chart is the active document, an Info window will be displayed for the worksheet or macro sheet that was most recently active.

Related Function

Function	Description
GET.CELL	Returns information about the specified cell

SHOW.LEVELS

Macro Sheets Only

Displays the specified number of row and column levels of an outline.

Syntax

SHOW.LEVELS(*row_level,col_level*)

Row_level   specifies the number of row levels of an outline to display. If the outline has fewer levels than specified by *row_level,* Microsoft Excel shows all levels. If *row_level* is omitted, no action is taken on rows.

Col_level   specifies the number of column levels of an outline to display. If the outline has fewer levels than specified by *col_level,* Microsoft Excel shows all levels. If *col_level* is omitted, no action is taken on columns.

Remarks

If you omit both arguments, SHOW.LEVELS returns the #VALUE! error value.

Example

The following macro formula displays row levels 1 through 3 and column level 1 of the outline:

```
SHOW.LEVELS(3,1)
```

Related Function

Function	Description
SHOW.DETAIL	Expands or collapses a portion of an outline

SHOW.TOOLBAR

Macro Sheets Only

Equivalent to choosing the Show Toolbars button or the Hide Toolbars button in the Options Toolbars dialog box. Hides or displays a toolbar.

Syntax

SHOW.TOOLBAR(*bar_id,visible,dock,x_pos, y_pos,width*)

Bar_id   is a number or name of a toolbar, or an array of numbers or names of toolbars, corresponding to the toolbars you want to display. For detailed information about *bar_id,* see ADD.TOOL.

Visible   is a logical value that, if TRUE, specifies that the toolbar is visible or, if FALSE, specifies that the toolbar is hidden.

Dock   specifies the docking location of the toolbar.

Dock	Position of toolbar
1	Top of workspace
2	Left edge of workspace
3	Right edge of workspace
4	Bottom of workspace
5	Floating (not docked)

X_pos   specifies the horizontal position of the toolbar.

- If the toolbar is docked (not floating), *x_pos* is measured horizontally from the left edge of the toolbar to the left edge of the toolbar's docking area.

- If the toolbar is floating, *x_pos* is measured horizontally from the left edge of the toolbar to the right edge of the rightmost toolbar in the left docking area.

- *X_pos* is measured in points. A point is 1/72nd of an inch.

Y_pos   specifies the vertical position of the toolbar.

- If the toolbar is docked, *y_pos* is measured vertically from the top edge of the toolbar to the top edge of the toolbar's docking area.

- If the toolbar is floating, *y_pos* is measured vertically from the top edge of the toolbar to the top edge of the Microsoft Excel workspace.

- *Y_pos* is measured in points.

Width   specifies the width of the toolbar and is measured in points. If you omit *width,* Microsoft Excel uses the existing width setting.

Example

The following macro formula displays Toolbar8 as a floating toolbar.

```
SHOW.TOOLBAR("Toolbar8",TRUE,5)
```

Related Function

Function	Description
ADD.TOOLBAR	Creates a new toolbar with the specified tools

SIGN

Determines the sign of a number. Returns 1 if *number* is positive, 0 if *number* is 0, and –1 if *number* is negative.

Syntax

SIGN(*number*)

Examples

```
SIGN(10)  equals 1
SIGN(4-4)  equals 0
SIGN(-0.00001)  equals –1
```

Related Function

Function	Description
ABS	Returns the absolute value of a number

SIN

Returns the sine of the given angle.

Syntax

SIN(*number*)

Number   is the angle in radians for which you want the sine. If your argument is in degrees, multiply it by PI()/180 to convert it to radians.

Examples

SIN(PI()) equals 1.22E–16, which is approximately zero. The sine of π is zero.

SIN(PI()/2) equals 1

SIN(30*PI()/180) equals 0.5, the sine of 30 degrees

Related Functions

Function	Description
ASIN	Returns the arcsine of a number
PI	Returns the value π

SINH

Returns the hyperbolic sine of *number*.

Syntax

SINH(*number*)

The formula for the hyperbolic sine is:

$$SINH(z) = \frac{e^z - e^{-z}}{2}$$

Examples

SINH(1) equals 1.175201194

SINH(-1) equals –1.175201194

You can use the hyperbolic sine function to approximate a cumulative probability distribution. Suppose a laboratory test value varies between 0 and 10 seconds. An empirical analysis of the collected history of experiments shows that the probability of obtaining a result, x, of less than t seconds is approximated by the following equation:

$P(x<t) = 2.868 * SINH(0.0342 * t)$, where $0<t<10$

To calculate the probability of obtaining a result of less than 1.03 seconds, substitute 1.03 for t:

2.868*SINH(0.0342*1.03) equals 0.101049063

You can expect this result to occur about 101 times for every 1000 experiments.

Related Functions

Function	Description
ASINH	Returns the inverse hyperbolic sine of a number
COSH	Returns the hyperbolic cosine of a number
TANH	Returns the hyperbolic tangent of a number

SIZE

Macro Sheets Only

Equivalent to choosing the Size command from the Control menu in Microsoft Excel for Windows version 3.0 or earlier or to changing the size of a window by dragging its border. In Microsoft Excel for the Macintosh version 3.0 or earlier, equivalent to changing the size of a window by dragging its size box. This function is included only for macro compatibility and will be converted to WINDOW.SIZE when you open older macro sheets. For more information, see WINDOW.SIZE.

Syntax

SIZE(*width*,*height*,*window_text*)
SIZE?(*width*,*height*,*window_text*)

SKEW

Returns the skewness of a distribution. Skewness characterizes the degree of asymmetry of a distribution around its mean. Positive skewness indicates a distribution with an asymmetric tail extending towards more positive values. Negative skewness indicates a distribution with an asymmetric tail extending towards more negative values.

Syntax

SKEW(*number1*,*number2*,...)**

Number1,number2... are 1 to 30 arguments for which you want to calculate skewness.

Remarks

- The arguments should be numbers, or names, arrays, or references that contain numbers.

- If an array or reference argument contains text, logical values, or empty cells, those values are ignored; however, cells with the value zero are included.

- If there are less than three data points, or the sample standard deviation is zero, SKEW returns the #DIV/0! error value.

- The equation for skewness is defined as:

$$\frac{n}{(n-1)(n-2)} \sum \left(\frac{x_i - \bar{x}}{s} \right)^3$$

Example

SKEW(3,4,5,2,3,4,5,6,4,7) equals 0.359543

Related Functions

Function	Description
KURT	Returns the kurtosis of a data set
STDEV	Estimates standard deviation based on a sample
STDEVP	Calculates standard deviation based on the entire population
VAR	Estimates variance based on a sample
VARP	Calculates variance based on the entire population

SLIDE.COPY.ROW

Macro Sheets Only

Equivalent to choosing the Copy Row button on a slide show document. Copies the selected slides, each of which is defined on a single row, to the Clipboard.

If this function is not available, you must install the Slide Show add-in macro. For more information, see "Managing Add-in Commands and Functions" in Chapter 4 in Book 2 of the *Microsoft Excel User's Guide*.

Syntax

SLIDE.COPY.ROW( )

Remarks

- SLIDE.COPY.ROW, SLIDE.CUT.ROW, SLIDE.DELETE.ROW, and SLIDE.PASTE.ROW return TRUE if successful, or FALSE if not successful. If the active document is not a slide show or is protected, these functions return the #N/A error value. If the current selection is not valid, these functions return the #VALUE! error value.

- For more information about slide shows, see "Creating a Slide Show with Microsoft Excel" in Chapter 15 in Book 1 of the *Microsoft Excel User's Guide*.

Related Functions

Function	Description
SLIDE.CUT.ROW	Cuts the selected slides and pastes them onto the Clipboard
SLIDE.DEFAULTS	Specifies default values for the active slide show document
SLIDE.DELETE.ROW	Deletes the selected slides
SLIDE.EDIT	Changes the attributes of the selected slide
SLIDE.GET	Returns information about a slide or slide show
SLIDE.PASTE	Pastes the contents of the Clipboard onto a slide
SLIDE.PASTE.ROW	Pastes previously cut or copied slides onto the current selection
SLIDE.SHOW	Starts a slide show in the active document

SLIDE.CUT.ROW

Macro Sheets Only

Equivalent to choosing the Cut Row button on a slide show document. Cuts the selected slides, each of which is defined on a single row, and pastes them onto the Clipboard. For more information, see SLIDE.COPY.ROW.

Syntax

SLIDE.CUT.ROW( )

SLIDE.DEFAULTS

Macro Sheets Only

Equivalent to choosing the Set Defaults button on a slide show document. Specifies the default values for the transition effect, speed, advance rate, and sound on the active slide show document.

If this function is not available, you must install the Slide Show add-in macro. For more information, see "Managing Add-in Commands and Functions" in Chapter 4 in Book 2 of the *Microsoft Excel User's Guide*.

Syntax

SLIDE.DEFAULTS(*effect_num,speed_num, advance_rate_num,soundfile_text*)
SLIDE.DEFAULTS?(*effect_num,speed_num, advance_rate_num,soundfile_text*)

For a description of the arguments, see SLIDE.PASTE. If an argument is omitted, its default value is not changed.

Remarks

- SLIDE.DEFAULT returns TRUE if it successfully changes the default values, or FALSE if you choose the Cancel button when using the dialog-box form. If the active document is not a slide show or is protected, SLIDE.DEFAULT returns the #N/A error value.

- For more information about slide shows, see "Creating a Slide Show with Microsoft Excel" in Chapter 15 in Book 1 of the *Microsoft Excel User's Guide*.

SLIDE.DELETE.ROW

Macro Sheets Only

Equivalent to choosing the Delete Row button on a slide show document. Deletes the selected slides, each of which is defined on a single row. For more information, see SLIDE.COPY.ROW.

Syntax

SLIDE.DELETE.ROW( )

SLIDE.EDIT

Macro Sheets Only

Equivalent to choosing the Edit button in a slide show document. Gives the currently selected slide the attributes you specify.

If this function is not available, you must install the Slide Show add-in macro. For more information, see "Managing Add-in Commands and Functions" in Chapter 4 in Book 2 of the *Microsoft Excel User's Guide*.

Syntax

SLIDE.EDIT(*effect_num,speed_num, advance_rate_num,soundfile_text*)
SLIDE.EDIT?(*effect_num,speed_num, advance_rate_num,soundfile_text*)

For a description of the arguments, see SLIDE.PASTE.

Remarks

- SLIDE.EDIT returns TRUE if it successfully edits the slide, or FALSE if you choose the Cancel button when using the dialog-box form. If the active document is not a slide show or is protected, SLIDE.EDIT returns the #N/A error value. If the current selection is not a valid slide, SLIDE.EDIT returns the #VALUE error value.

- For more information about slide shows, see "Creating a Slide Show with Microsoft Excel" in Chapter 15 in Book 1 of the *Microsoft Excel User's Guide*.

SLIDE.GET

Macro Sheets Only

Returns the specified information about a slide show or a specific slide in the slide show.

If this function is not available, you must install the Slide Show add-in macro. For more information, see "Managing Add-in Commands and Functions" in Chapter 4 in Book 2 of the *Microsoft Excel User's Guide*.

Syntax

SLIDE.GET(***type_num,****name_text,slide_num*)

Type_num is a number specifying the type of information you want.

These values of *type_num* return information about a slide show.

Type_num	Type of information
1	Number of slides in the slide show
2	A two-item horizontal array containing the numbers of the first and last slides in the current selection, or the #VALUE error value if the selection is nonadjacent
3	Version number of the Slide Show add-in macro that created the slide show document

These values of *type_num* return information about a specific slide in the slide show.

Type_num	Type of information
4	Transition effect number
5	Transition effect name
6	Transition effect speed
7	Number of seconds the slide is displayed before advancing
8	Name of the sound file associated with the slide, or empty text ("") if none is specified (in Microsoft Excel for the Macintosh, this includes the number or name of the sound resource within the sound file)

Name_text is the name of an open slide show document for which you want information. If *name_text* is omitted, it is assumed to be the active document.

Slide_num is the number of the slide about which you want information.

- If *slide_num* is omitted, it is assumed to be the slide associated with the active cell on the document specified by *name_text*.

- If *type_num* is 1 through 3, *slide_num* is ignored.

SLIDE.PASTE

Macro Sheets Only

Equivalent to choosing the Paste button in a slide show document. Pastes the contents of the Clipboard as the next available slide of the active slide show document, and gives the slide the attributes you specify.

If this function is not available, you must install the Slide Show add-in macro For more information, see "Managing Add-in Commands and Functions" in Chapter 4 in Book 2 of the *Microsoft Excel User's Guide*.

Syntax

SLIDE.PASTE(*effect_num,speed_num, advance_rate_num,soundfile_text*)
SLIDE.PASTE?(*effect_num,speed_num, advance_rate_num,soundfile_text*)

Effect_num is a number specifying the transition effect you want to use when displaying the slide.

- The numbers correspond to the effects in the Effect list in the Edit Slide dialog box. The first effect in the list is 1 (None).

- If *effect_num* is omitted, the default setting is used.

Speed_num is a number from 1 to 10 specifying the speed of the transition effect.

- If *speed_num* is omitted, the default setting is used.

- If *speed_num* is greater than 10, Microsoft Excel uses the value 10 anyway.

- If *effect_num* is 1 (none), *speed_num* is ignored.

Advance_rate_num is a number specifying how long (in seconds) the slide is displayed before advancing to the next one.

- If *advance_rate_num* is omitted, the default setting is used.

- If *advance_rate_num* is 0, you must press a key or click with the mouse to advance to the next slide.

Soundfile_text is the name of a file enclosed in quotation marks and specifies sound that will be played when the slide is displayed.

- If *soundfile_text* is omitted, Microsoft Excel plays the default sound defined for the slide show document, if any.

- If *soundfile_text* is empty text (""), no sound is played.

- In Microsoft Excel for the Macintosh, *soundfile_text* also includes the number or name of the sound resource to play in the file.

Resource is the number or name of a sound resource in *soundfile_text*.

- This argument applies only to Microsoft Excel for the Macintosh.

- If *resource* is omitted, Microsoft Excel uses the first resource in the file.

- If the file does not contain a sound resource with the specified name or number, Microsoft Excel halts the macro and displays an error message.

Remarks

- SLIDE.PASTE returns TRUE if it successfully pastes the slide, or FALSE if you choose the Cancel button when using the dialog-box form. If the active document is not a slide show or is protected, SLIDE.PASTE returns the #N/A error value. If the Clipboard format is not compatible with the slide show document's format, SLIDE.PASTE returns the #VALUE error value.

- For more information about slide shows, see "Creating a Slide Show with Microsoft Excel" in Chapter 15 in Book 1 of the *Microsoft Excel User's Guide*.

Examples

In Microsoft Excel for Windows, the following macro formula pastes the contents of the Clipboard into the active slide show document. The slide's transition effect is fade, at a speed of 8; it is displayed for five seconds; and Microsoft Excel plays the specified sound file:

```
SLIDE.PASTE(3,8,5,"C:\SLIDES\SOUND\
MACHINES.WAV")
```

In Microsoft Excel for the Macintosh, the formula is:

```
SLIDE.PASTE(3,8,5,"HARD DISK:SLIDES:SOUND:
MACHINE SOUNDS")
```

SLIDE.PASTE.ROW

Macro Sheets Only

Equivalent to choosing the Paste Row button in a slide show document. Pastes previously cut or copied slides onto the current selection. For more information, see SLIDE.COPY.ROW.

Syntax

SLIDE.PASTE.ROW( )

SLIDE.SHOW

Macro Sheets Only

Equivalent to choosing the Start Show button in a slide show document. Starts the slide show in the active document.

If this function is not available, you must install the Slide Show add-in macro. For more information, see "Managing Add-in Commands and Functions" in Chapter 4 in Book 2 of the *Microsoft Excel User's Guide*.

Syntax

SLIDE.SHOW(*initialslide_num,repeat_logical, dialogtitle_text,allownav_logical, allowcontrol_logical*)
SLIDE.SHOW?(*initialslide_num,repeat_logical, dialogtitle_text,allownav_logical, allowcontrol_logical*)

All arguments except *dialogtitle_text* correspond to options and settings in the Start Show dialog box.

Initialslide_num   is a number from 1 to the number of slides in the slide show and specifies which slide to display first. If omitted, it is assumed to be 1.

Repeat_logical   is a logical value specifying whether to repeat or end the slide show after displaying the last slide. If *repeat_logical* is TRUE, the slide show repeats; if FALSE or omitted, the slide show ends.

Dialogtitle_text   is text enclosed in quotation marks that specifies the title of the dialog boxes displayed during the slide show. If *dialogtitle_text* is omitted, it is assumed to be "Slide Show".

Allownav_logical   is a logical value specifying whether to enable or disable navigational keys (arrow keys, PAGE UP, PAGE DOWN, and so on) or the mouse during the slide show. If *allownav_logical* is TRUE or omitted, you can press navigational keys or use the mouse to move between slides; if FALSE, all movement is controlled by the slide show document settings.

Allowcontrol_logical   is a logical value specifying whether to enable or disable the Slide Show Options dialog box during the slide show. If *allowcontrol_logical* is TRUE or omitted, you can press ESC to interrupt the slide show and display the dialog box; if FALSE, pressing ESC stops the slide show but does not display the dialog box.

Tip If you want to display the last slide in a show but don't know its number, use SLIDE.GET(1) as the *initialslide_num* argument.

Remarks

- SLIDE.SHOW returns the values shown in the following table:

Situation	Returned value
The slide show ends normally.	TRUE
You press the Cancel button when using the dialog-box form.	FALSE
The active document is not a slide show or is protected.	#N/A
You interrupt the slide show, and then stop it.	1

- For more information about slide shows, see "Creating a Slide Show with Microsoft Excel" in Chapter 15 in Book 1 of the *Microsoft Excel User's Guide*.

SLN

Returns the straight-line depreciation for an asset for a single period.

Syntax

SLN(*cost,salvage,life*)

Cost   is the initial cost of the asset.

Salvage   is the value at the end of the depreciation (sometimes called the salvage value of the asset).

Life   is the number of periods over which the asset is being depreciated (sometimes called the useful life of the asset).

Example

Suppose you've bought a truck for $30,000 that has a useful life of 10 years and a salvage value of $7500. The depreciation allowance for each year is:

SLN(30000,7500,10) equals $2250

Related Functions

Function	Description
DDB	Returns the depreciation for an asset for a specified period using the double-declining balance method
SYD	Returns the sum-of-years' digits depreciation of an asset for a specified period
VDB	Returns the depreciation of an asset for a specified or partial period using a declining balance method

SLOPE

Returns the slope of the linear regression line through data points in *known_y's* and *known_x's*. The slope is the vertical distance divided by the horizontal distance between any two points on the line, which is the rate of change along the regression line.

Syntax

SLOPE*(known_y's,known_x's)*

Known_y's is an array or cell range of numeric dependent data points.

Known_x's is the set of independent data points.

Remarks

- The arguments should be numbers, or names, arrays, or references that contain numbers.

- If an array or reference argument contains text, logical values, or empty cells, those values are ignored; however, cells with the value zero are included.

- If *known_y's* and *known_x's* are empty or have a different number of data points, SLOPE returns the #N/A error value.

- The equation for the slope of the regression line is:

$$b = \frac{n\Sigma xy - (\Sigma x)(\Sigma y)}{n\Sigma x^2 - (\Sigma x)^2}$$

Example

SLOPE({2,3,9,1,8,7,5},
{6,5,11,7,5,4,4}) equals 0.305556

Related Functions

Function	Description
INTERCEPT	Returns the intercept of the linear regression line
LINEST	Returns parameters of a linear trend
LOGEST	Returns parameters of an exponential trend
PEARSON	Returns the Pearson product moment correlation coefficient
RSQ	Returns the r^2 value of the linear regression line
STEYX	Returns the standard error of the predicted *y* value for each *x* in the regression
TREND	Returns values along a linear trend

SMALL

Returns the *k*-th smallest value in a data set. Use this function to return values with a particular relative standing in a data set.

Syntax

SMALL*(array,k)*

Array is an array or range of numerical data for which you want to determine the *k*-th smallest value.

K is the position (from the smallest) in the array or range of data to return.

Remarks

- If *array* is empty, SMALL returns the #NUM! error value.

- If $k \leq 0$ or if *k* exceeds the number of data points, SMALL returns the #NUM! error value.

- If *n* is the number of data points in *array*, SMALL(*array*,1) equals the smallest value, and SMALL(*array*,n) equals the largest value.

Example

SMALL({3,4,5,2,3,4,5,6,4,7},4) equals 4

SMALL({1,4,8,3,7,12,54,8,23},2) equals 3

Related Functions

Function	Description
LARGE	Returns the *k*-th largest value in a data set
MAX	Returns the maximum value in a list of arguments
MEDIAN	Returns the median of the given numbers
MIN	Returns the minimum value in a list of arguments
PERCENTILE	Returns the *k*-th percentile of values in a range

Function	Description
PERCENTRANK	Returns the percentage rank of a value in a data set
QUARTILE	Returns the quartile of a data set

SOLVER.ADD

Macro Sheets Only

Equivalent to choosing the Solver command from the Formula menu and choosing the Add button in the Solver Parameters dialog box. Adds a constraint to the current problem. For more information about Microsoft Excel Solver, see Chapter 2 in Book 2 of the *Microsoft Excel User's Guide*. For an explanation of constraints, see "Remarks" later in this topic.

If this function is not available, you must install the Solver add-in macro. For more information, see "Managing Add-in Commands and Functions" in Chapter 4 in Book 2 of the *Microsoft Excel User's Guide*.

Syntax

SOLVER.ADD(*cell_ref,relation,formula*)

Cell_ref is a reference to a cell or range of cells on the active worksheet and forms the left side of the constraint.

Relation specifies the arithmetic relationship between the left and right sides, or whether *cell_ref* must be an integer.

Relation	Arithmetic relationship
1	<=
2	=
3	>=
4	Int (*cell_ref* is an integer)

Formula is the right side of the constraint and will often be a single number, but it may be a formula (as text) or a reference to a range of cells.

- If *relation* is 4, *formula* is ignored, and *cell_ref* must be a subset of the By Changing cells.

- If *formula* is a reference to a range of cells, the number of cells in the range must match the number of cells in *cell_ref*, although the shape of the areas need not be the same. For example, *cell_ref* could be a row and *formula* could refer to a column, as long as the number of cells is the same.

Remarks

- The SOLVER.ADD, SOLVER.CHANGE and SOLVER.DELETE functions correspond to the Add, Change, and Delete buttons in the Formula Solver Parameters dialog box. You use these functions to define constraints. For many macro applications, however, you may find it more convenient to load the problem specifications from the worksheet in a single step using the SOLVER.LOAD function.

- Each constraint is uniquely identified by the combination of the cell reference on the left and the relationship (<=, =, or >=) between its left and right sides, or the cell reference may be defined as an integer only. This takes the place of selecting the appropriate constraint in the Formula Solver Parameters dialog box. You can manipulate the constraints with SOLVER.CHANGE or SOLVER.DELETE.

SOLVER.CHANGE

Macro Sheets Only

Equivalent to choosing the Solver command from the Formula menu and choosing the Change button in the Solver Parameters dialog box. Changes the right side of an existing constraint. For more information about Microsoft Excel Solver, see Chapter 2 in Book 2 of the *Microsoft Excel User's Guide*.

If this function is not available, you must install the Solver add-in macro. For more information, see "Managing Add-in Commands and Functions" in Chapter 4 in Book 2 of the *Microsoft Excel User's Guide.*

Syntax

SOLVER.CHANGE*(cell_ref,relation,formula)*

For an explanation of the arguments and constraints, see SOLVER.ADD.

Remarks

- If the combination of *cell_ref* and *relation* does not match any existing constraint, the function returns the value 4 and no action is taken.

- To change the *cell_ref* or *relation* of an existing constraint, use SOLVER.DELETE to delete the old constraint and then use SOLVER.ADD to add the constraint in the form you want.

SOLVER.DELETE

Macro Sheets Only

Equivalent to choosing the Solver command from the Formula menu and choosing the Delete button in the Solver Parameters dialog box. Deletes an existing constraint. For more information about Microsoft Excel Solver, see Chapter 2 in Book 2 of the *Microsoft Excel User's Guide.*

If this function is not available, you must install the Solver add-in macro. For more information, see "Managing Add-in Commands and Functions" in Chapter 4 in Book 2 of the *Microsoft Excel User's Guide.*

Syntax

SOLVER.DELETE*(cell_ref,relation,formula)*

For an explanation of the arguments and constraints, see SOLVER.ADD.

Remarks

If the combination of *cell_ref* and *relation* does not match any existing constraint, the function returns the value 4 and no action is taken. If the constraint is found, it is deleted, and the function returns the value 0. The *formula* argument is not used.

SOLVER.FINISH

Macro Sheets Only

Equivalent to choosing the Finish dialog box that appears when the solution process is complete. The dialog-box form displays the dialog box with the arguments that you supply as defaults. This function must be used if you supplied the value TRUE for the *userfinish* argument to SOLVER.SOLVE. For more information about Microsoft Excel Solver, see Chapter 2 in Book 2 of the *Microsoft Excel User's Guide.*

If this function is not available, you must install the Solver add-in macro. For more information, see "Managing Add-in Commands and Functions" in Chapter 4 in Book 2 of the *Microsoft Excel User's Guide.*

Syntax

SOLVER.FINISH*(keep_final,report_array)*
SOLVER.FINISH?*(keep_final,report_array)*

Keep_final   is the number 1 or 2 and specifies whether to keep the final solution. If *keep_final* is 1 or omitted, the final solution values are kept in the changing cells. If *keep_final* is 2, the final solution values are discarded and the former values of the changing cells are restored.

Report_array   is an array argument specifying what reports to create when Solver is finished.

If *report_array* is	Microsoft Excel creates
{1}	An answer report
{2}	A sensitivity report
{3}	A limit report

Any combination of these produces multiple reports. For example, if *report_array* is {1,2}, Microsoft Excel creates an answer report and a sensitivity report.

SOLVER.GET

Macro Sheets Only

Returns information about current settings for Solver. The settings are specified in the Solver Parameters and Solver Options dialog boxes, or with the other SOLVER functions described in this book.

If this function is not available, you must install the Solver add-in macro. For more information, see "Managing Add-in Commands and Functions" in Chapter 4 in Book 2 of the *Microsoft Excel User's Guide*.

Syntax

SOLVER.GET(*type_num,sheet_name*)

Type_num   is a number specifying the type of information you want.

The following settings are specified in the Solver Parameters dialog box.

Type_num	Returns
1	The reference in the Set Cell box, or the #N/A error value if Solver has not been used on the active document
2	A number corresponding to the Equal To option 1 = Max 2 = Min 3 = Value of
3	The value in the Value Of box
4	The reference (as a multiple reference if necessary) in the By Changing Cells box
5	The number of constraints

Type_num	Returns
6	An array of the left sides of the constraints in the form of text
7	An array of numbers corresponding to the relationships between the left and right sides of the constraints: 1 = <= 2 = = 3 = >= 4 = int
8	An array of the right sides of the constraints in the form of text

The following settings are specified in the Solver Options dialog box:

Type_num	Returns
9	The maximum calculation time
10	The maximum number of iterations
11	The precision (as a decimal number)
12	The integer tolerance value (as a decimal number)
13	TRUE if the Assume Linear Model check box is selected; FALSE otherwise
14	TRUE if the Show Iteration Results check box is selected; FALSE otherwise
15	TRUE if the Use Automatic Scaling check box is selected; FALSE otherwise
16	A number corresponding to the type of estimates: 1 = Tangent 2 = Quadratic
17	A number corresponding to the type of derivatives: 1 = Forward 2 = Central
18	A number corresponding to the type of search: 1 = Quasi-Newton 2 = Conjugate Gradient

Sheet_name   is the name of a document that contains the scenario for which you want information. If *sheet_name* is omitted, it is assumed to be the active document.

SOLVER.LOAD

Macro Sheets Only

Equivalent to choosing the Solver command from the Formula menu, choosing the Options button from the Solver Parameters dialog box, and choosing the Load Model button in the Solver Options dialog box. Loads Solver problem specifications that you have previously saved on the worksheet. For more information about Microsoft Excel Solver, see Chapter 2 in Book 2 of the *Microsoft Excel User's Guide.*

If this function is not available, you must install the Solver add-in macro. For more information, see "Managing Add-in Commands and Functions" in Chapter 4 in Book 2 of the *Microsoft Excel User's Guide.*

Syntax

SOLVER.LOAD(*load_area*)

Load_area   is a reference on the active worksheet to a range of cells from which you want to load a complete problem specification.

- The first cell in *load_area* contains a formula for the Set Cell box; the second cell contains a formula for the changing cells; subsequent cells contain constraints in the form of logical formulas. The last cell optionally contains an array of Solver option values (see SOLVER.OPTIONS).

- Although *load_area* must be on the active worksheet, it need not be the current selection.

SOLVER.OK

Macro Sheets Only

Equivalent to choosing the Solver command from the Formula menu and specifying options in the Solver Parameters dialog box. Specifies basic Solver options. For more information about Microsoft Excel Solver, see Chapter 2 in Book 2 of the *Microsoft Excel User's Guide.*

If this function is not available, you must install the Solver add-in macro. For more information, see "Managing Add-in Commands and Functions" in Chapter 4 in Book 2 of the *Microsoft Excel User's Guide.*

Syntax

SOLVER.OK(*set_cell,max_min_val,value_of, by_changing*)
SOLVER.OK?(*set_cell,max_min_val,value_of, by_changing*)

Set_cell   corresponds to the Set Cell box in the Solver Parameters dialog box.

- *Set_cell* must be a reference to a cell on the active worksheet.

- If you enter a cell, you must enter a value for *max_min_val*. If you do not enter a cell, you must include three commas before the *by_changing* value.

Max_min_val   corresponds to the options Max, Min, and Value Of in the Solver Parameters dialog box. Use this option only if you entered a reference for *set_cell*.

Max_min_val	Option specified
1	Maximize
2	Minimize
3	Match specific value

Value_of   is a number that becomes the target for the cell in the Set Cell box if *max_min_val* is 3. *Value_of* is ignored if the cell is being maximized or minimized.

By_changing   indicates the changing cells, as entered in the By Changing Cells box. *By_changing* must be a cell reference (usually a range or multiple-cell reference) on the active worksheet.

Related Function

Function	Description
SOLVER.SOLVE	Returns an integer value indicating the condition that caused Solver to stop

SOLVER.OPTIONS

Macro Sheets Only

Equivalent to choosing the Solver command from the Formula menu and then choosing the Options button in the Solver Parameters dialog box. Specifies the available options. For detailed information about the Solver command, see Chapter 2 in Book 2 of the *Microsoft Excel User's Guide*.

If this function is not available, you must install the Solver add-in macro. For more informaion, see "Managing Add-in Commands and Functions" in Chapter 4 in Book 2 of the *Microsoft Excel User's Guide*.

Syntax

SOLVER.OPTIONS*(max_time,iterations,precision, assume_linear,step_thru,estimates,derivatives, search,int_tolerance,scaling)*

The arguments correspond to the options in the dialog box. If an argument is omitted, Microsoft Excel uses an appropriate value based on the current situation. If any of the arguments are the wrong type, the function returns the #N/A error value. If an argument has the correct type but an invalid value, the function returns a positive integer corresponding to its position. A zero indicates all options were accepted.

Max_time   must be an integer greater than zero. It corresponds to the Max Time box.

Iterations   must be an integer greater than zero. It corresponds to the Iterations box.

Precision   must be a number between zero and one, but not equal to zero or one. It corresponds to the Precision box.

Assume_linear   is a logical value corresponding to the Assume Linear Model check box and allows Solver to arrive at a solution more quickly. If TRUE, Solver assumes that the underlying worksheet model is linear; if FALSE, it does not.

Step_thru   is a logical value corresponding to the Show Iteration Results check box. If you have supplied SOLVER.SOLVE with a valid command macro reference, your macro will be called each time Solver pauses. If TRUE, Solver pauses at each trial solution; if FALSE, it does not.

Estimates   is the number 1 or 2 and corresponds to the Estimates options: 1 for the Tangent option and 2 for the Quadratic option.

Derivatives   is the number 1 or 2 and corresponds to the Derivatives options: 1 for the Forward option and 2 for the Central option.

Search   is the number 1 or 2 and corresponds to the Search options: 1 for the Quasi-Newton option and 2 for the Conjugate Gradient option.

Int_tolerance   is a decimal number corresponding to the Tolerance box in the Solver Options dialog box. This argument applies only if integer constraints have been defined.

Scaling   is a logical value corresponding to the Use Automatic Scaling check box. If *scaling* is TRUE, then if two or more constraints differ by several orders of magnitude, Solver scales the constraints to similar orders of magnitude during computation. If *scaling* is FALSE, Solver calculates normally.

SOLVER.RESET

Macro Sheets Only

Equivalent to choosing the Solver command from the Formula menu and choosing the Reset All button in the Solver Parameters dialog box. Erases all cell selections and constraints from the Solver Parameters dialog box and restores all the settings in the Solver Options dialog box to their defaults. The SOLVER.RESET function is performed automatically when you call SOLVER.LOAD. For more information about Microsoft Excel Solver, see Chapter 2 in Book 2 of the *Microsoft Excel User's Guide*.

If this function is not available, you must install the Solver add-in macro. For more information, see "Managing Add-in Commands and Functions" in Chapter 4 in Book 2 of the *Microsoft Excel User's Guide*.

Syntax

SOLVER.RESET( )

SOLVER.SAVE

Macro Sheets Only

Equivalent to choosing the Solver command from the Formula menu, choosing the Options button from the Solver Parameters dialog box, and choosing the Save Model button in the Solver Options dialog box. Saves the Solver problem specifications on the worksheet. For more information about Microsoft Excel Solver, see Chapter 2 in Book 2 of the *Microsoft Excel User's Guide*.

If this function is not available, you must install the Solver add-in macro. For more information, see "Managing Add-in Commands and Functions" in Chapter 4 in Book 2 of the *Microsoft Excel User's Guide*.

Syntax

SOLVER.SAVE *(save_area)*

Save_area   is a reference on the active worksheet to a range of cells or to the upper-left corner of a range of cells into which you want to paste the current problem specification.

- If you specify only one cell for *save_area,* the area is extended downwards for as many cells as are required to hold the problem specifications (3 plus the number of constraints).

- If you specify more than one cell and if the area is too small, the last constraints (in alphabetic order by cell reference) or options will be omitted and the function will return a nonzero value.

- *Save_area* must be on the active worksheet, but it need not be the current selection.

SOLVER.SOLVE

Macro Sheets Only

Equivalent to choosing the Solver command from the Formula menu and choosing the Solve button in the Solver Parameters dialog box. If successful, returns an integer value indicating the condition that caused Solver to stop as described in "Remarks" later in this topic. For more information about Microsoft Excel Solver, see Chapter 2 in Book 2 of the *Microsoft Excel User's Guide*.

If this function is not available, you must install the Solver add-in macro. For more information, see "Managing Add-in Commands and Functions" in Chapter 4 in Book 2 of the *Microsoft Excel User's Guide*.

Syntax

SOLVER.SOLVE*(user_finish,show_ref)*
SOLVER.SOLVE?*(user_finish,show_ref)*

User_finish   is a logical value specifying whether to display the standard Finish dialog box.

- If *user_finish* is TRUE, SOLVER.SOLVE returns its integer value without displaying anything. Your macro should decide what action to take (for example, by examining the return value or presenting its own dialog box); it must call SOLVER.FINISH in any case to restore the worksheet to its proper state.

- If *user_finish* is FALSE or omitted, Solver displays the standard Finish dialog box, which allows you to keep or discard the final solution and run reports.

Show_ref   is a macro to be called in place of the Show Trial Solution dialog box. It is used when you want to regain control whenever Solver finds a new intermediate solution value.

- For this argument to have an effect, the Show Iteration Results check box must be selected in the Solver Options dialog box. This can be done manually by selecting the check box, or automatically by calling SOLVER.OPTIONS in your macro.

- The macro you call can inspect the current solution values on the worksheet or take other actions such as saving or charting the intermediate values. It must return the value TRUE with a statement such as =RETURN(TRUE) if the solution process is to continue, or FALSE if the solution process should stop at this point.

Remarks

If a problem has not been completely defined, SOLVER.SOLVE returns the #N/A error value. Otherwise, the Solver application is started and the problem specifications are passed to it. When the solution process is complete, SOLVER.SOLVE returns an integer value indicating the stopping condition:

Value	Stopping condition
0	Solver found a solution.
1	Solver has converged to the current solution.
2	Solver cannot improve the current solution.

Value	Stopping condition
3	The maximum time or iteration limit has been reached.
4	The values do not converge.
5	Solver could not find a feasible solution.
6	Solver stopped at user's request.
7	The linearity condition is not satisfied.
8	Solver encountered an error value.
9	There is not enough memory available.
10	Another session of Microsoft Excel is using Solver.

SORT

Macro Sheets Only

Equivalent to choosing the Sort command from the Data menu. Sorts the rows or columns of the selection according to the contents of a key row or column within the selection. Use SORT to rearrange information into ascending or descending order. For detailed information about the Sort command, see online Help.

Syntax

SORT(*sort_by,key1,order1,key2,order2,key3, order3*)
SORT?(*sort_by,key1,order1,key2,order2,key3, order3*)

Sort_by   is a number specifying whether to sort by rows or columns. Enter 1 to sort by rows or 2 to sort by columns.

Key1   is a reference to the cell or cells you want to use as the first sort key. The sort key identifies which column to sort by when sorting rows or which row to sort by when sorting columns. There are two ways to specify sort keys:

Type of key	Examples
An external reference to the active worksheet.	!B:B or !Price
An R1C1-style reference in the form of text. If the reference is relative, it is assumed to be relative to the active cell in the selection.	"C2" or "C[1]" or "Price"

Order1 specifies whether to sort the row or column containing *key1* in ascending or descending order. Enter 1 to sort in ascending order or 2 to sort in descending order.

Key2, order2, key3, and *order3* are similar to *key1* and *order1*. *Key2* specifies the second sort key, and *order2* specifies whether to sort the row or column containing *key2* in ascending or descending order. *Key3* and *order3* work similarly.

Tip If you want to sort using more than three keys, then sort the data three keys at a time, starting with the least important group of keys and progressing to the most important group, but listing the most important key first within each group. See the second example following.

Examples

To sort the selected rows using columns A, B, and C as the sort keys so that the cells in columns A and B appear in ascending order and the cells in column C appear in descending order:

SORT(1,!$A$4,1,!$B$4,1,!$C$4,2)

The following lines in a macro sort the selected rows in ascending order using columns A, B, C, D, and E as the sort keys.

	A	B	C
13		=SORT(1,!$D$4,1,!$E$4,1)	
14		=SORT(1,!$A$4,1,!$B$4,1,!$C$4,1)	

SOUND.NOTE

Macro Sheets Only

Records sound into or erases sound from a cell note or imports sound from another file into a cell note. This function requires that you have recording hardware installed in your computer, and you must be running Microsoft Windows version 3.0 with Multimedia Extensions 1.0 or later, Microsoft Windows version 3.1 or later, or Apple system software version 6.07 or later.

Syntax 1

Recording or erasing sound

SOUND.NOTE(*cell_ref,erase_snd*)

Syntax 2

Importing sound from another file

SOUND.NOTE(*cell_ref,file_text,resource*)

Cell_ref is a reference to the cell containing a note into which you want to record or import sounds or from which you want to erase a sound.

Erase_snd is a logical value specifying whether to erase the sound in the note. If *erase_snd* is TRUE, Microsoft Excel erases only the sound from the note. If FALSE or omitted, Microsoft Excel displays the Record dialog box so that you can record sound into the note.

File_text is the name of a file containing sounds.

Resource is the number or name of a sound resource in *file_text* that you want to import into your note.

- This argument applies only to Microsoft Excel for the Macintosh.

- If *resource* is omitted, Microsoft Excel uses the first resource in the file.

- If the file does not contain a sound resource with the specified name or number, Microsoft Excel halts the macro and displays an error message.

Remarks

To find out if a cell has sound attached to it, use GET.CELL(47).

Examples

The following macro formula erases the sound, if present, from cell A1 on the active worksheet:

```
SOUND.NOTE(!$A$1,TRUE)
```

The following macro formula displays the Record dialog box so that you can record sound into a note for cell A1 on the active worksheet:

```
SOUND.NOTE(!$A$1)
```

In Microsoft Excel for Windows, the following macro formula imports the sound from a file named CHIMES.WAV into a note for the cell named Doorbell on the active worksheet:

```
SOUND.NOTE(!Doorbell,"C:\SOUNDS\CHIMES.
WAV")
```

In Microsoft Excel for the Macintosh, the following macro formula imports a sound called Chimes from a file named SOFT SOUNDS into a note for the cell named Doorbell on the active worksheet:

```
SOUND.NOTE(!Doorbell,"HARD DISK:SOUNDS:SOFT
SOUNDS","Chimes")
```

Related Functions

Function	Description
NOTE	Creates or changes a cell note
SOUND.PLAY	Plays the sound from a cell note or a file

SOUND.PLAY

Macro Sheets Only

Plays the sound from a cell note or a file. Equivalent to choosing the Note command from the Formula menu and choosing the Play button, or choosing the Note command from the Formula menu, choosing the Import button, and then opening a file, selecting a sound, and choosing the Play button. To play sounds in Microsoft Excel for Windows, you must be running Microsoft Windows version 3.0 with Multimedia Extensions 1.0 or later, or Microsoft Windows version 3.1 or later.

Syntax

SOUND.PLAY(*cell_ref,file_text,resource*)

Cell_ref is a reference to the cell note containing sound that you want to play. If *cell_ref* is omitted, Microsoft Excel plays the sound from the active cell, or from a file if you specify one.

File_text is the name of a file containing sounds. If *cell_ref* is specified, *file_text* is ignored.

Resource is a number or name given as text specifying a sound resource in *file_text* that you want to play.

- This argument applies only to Microsoft Excel for the Macintosh.

- If *cell_ref* is specified, *resource* is ignored.

- If *resource* is omitted, Microsoft Excel uses the first sound resource in the file.

- If the file does not contain a sound resource with the specified name or number, Microsoft Excel halts the macro and displays an error message.

Examples

The following macro formula plays the sound, if any, contained in the note for a cell named Doorbell on the active worksheet:

```
SOUND.PLAY(!Doorbell)
```

In Microsoft Excel for Windows, the following macro formula plays the sound in the file named CHIMES.WAV:

```
SOUND.PLAY(,"C:\SOUNDS\SOFTSNDS.WAV")
```

In Microsoft Excel for the Macintosh, the following macro formula plays a sound called Chimes in a file named SOFT SOUNDS:

```
SOUND.PLAY(,"HARD DISK:SOUNDS:SOFT SOUNDS",
"Chimes")
```

Related Function

Function	Description
SOUND.NOTE	Records or imports sound into or erases sound from cell notes

SPELLING

Macro Sheets Only

Equivalent to choosing the Spelling command from the Options menu. Checks the spelling of words in the current selection. For detailed information about the Spelling command, see online Help.

Syntax

SPELLING(*custom_dic,ignore_uppercase, always_suggest*)

Custom_dic   is the filename of the custom dictionary to examine if words are not found in the main dictionary. If *custom_dic* is omitted, the currently specified dictionary is used.

Ignore_uppercase   is a logical value corresponding to the Ignore Words In Uppercase check box.

If *ignore uppercase* is	Microsoft Excel will
TRUE	Ignore words in all uppercase letters
FALSE	Check words in all uppercase letters
Omitted	Use the current setting

Always_suggest   is a logical value corresponding to the Always Suggest check box.

If *always _suggest* is	Microsoft Excel will
TRUE	Display a list of suggested alternate spellings when an incorrect spelling is found
FALSE	Wait for user to input the correct spelling
Omitted	Use the current setting

Examples

In Microsoft Excel for Windows, the following macro formula checks the spelling of all words in the current selection, except words in all uppercase letters, and suggests alternatives for incorrect spellings:

```
SPELLING("CUSTOM.DIC",TRUE,TRUE)
```

In Microsoft Excel for the Macintosh, the following macro formula checks the spelling of all words in the current selection, except words in all uppercase letters, and suggests alternatives for incorrect spellings:

```
SPELLING("User 1",TRUE,TRUE)
```

Related Function

Function	Description
SPELLING.CHECK	Checks the spelling of a word

SPELLING.CHECK

Macro Sheets Only

Checks the spelling of a word. Returns TRUE if the word is spelled correctly; FALSE otherwise.

Syntax

SPELLING.CHECK(*word_text,custom_dic, ignore_uppercase*)

Word_text   is the word whose spelling you want to check. It can be text or a reference to text.

Custom_dic is the filename of a custom dictionary to examine if the word is not found in the main dictionary.

Ignore_uppercase is a logical value corresponding to the Ignore Words In Uppercase check box. If *ignore_uppercase* is TRUE, the check box is selected, and Microsoft Excel ignores words in all uppercase letters; if FALSE, the check box is cleared, and Microsoft Excel checks all words; if omitted, the current setting is used.

Remarks

This function does not have a dialog-box form. To display the Spelling dialog box, use SPELLING.

Example

The following macro formula checks the spelling of a part name using the main dictionary and a custom dictionary named "PARTS.DIC":

```
=SPELLING.CHECK(PartName,"PARTS.DIC",FALSE)
```

Related Function

Function	Description
SPELLING	Checks the spelling of words in the current selection

SPLIT

Macro Sheets Only

Equivalent to choosing the Split command from the Window menu or to dragging the split bar in the active window's scroll bar. Splits the active window into panes. Use SPLIT when you want to view different parts of the active document at the same time. For detailed information about the Split command, see online Help.

Syntax

SPLIT(*col_split,row_split*)

Col_split specifies where to split the window vertically and is measured in columns from the left of the window.

Row_split specifies where to split the window horizontally and is measured in rows from the top of the window.

If an argument is 0 and there is a split in that direction, the split is removed. If an argument is omitted, a split in that direction is not changed.

Examples

The following macro formula splits the window horizontally after the third row and removes a vertical split, if there is one:

```
SPLIT(0,3)
```

The following macro formula splits the window vertically after the third column and has no effect on horizontal splitting:

```
SPLIT(3,)
```

Related Function

Function	Description
FREEZE.PANES	Freezes or unfreezes the panes of a window

SQRT

Returns a positive square root.

Syntax

SQRT(*number*)

Number is the number for which you want the square root. If *number* is negative, SQRT returns the #NUM! error value.

Examples

```
SQRT(16)  equals 4
```
```
SQRT(-16)  equals #NUM!
```
```
SQRT(ABS(-16))  equals 4
```

SQRTPI

Returns the square root of (*number* * π).

If this function is not available, you must install the Analysis ToolPak add-in macro. For more information, see "Managing Add-in Commands and Functions" in Chapter 4 in Book 2 of the *Microsoft Excel User's Guide*.

Syntax

SQRTPI *(number)*

Number is the number by which π is multiplied.

Remark

If *number* < 0, SQRTPI returns the #NUM! error value.

Examples

SQRTPI(1) equals $\sqrt{\pi}$ or 1.772454

SQRTPI(2) equals $\sqrt{2\pi}$ or 2.506628

Related Functions

Function	Description
PI	Returns the value π
SQRT	Returns a positive square root

STANDARD.FONT

Macro Sheets Only

Sets the attributes of the standard font (or Normal style) for the active worksheet or macro sheet. STANDARD.FONT is included for compatibility with earlier versions of Microsoft Excel. Normally, to define and apply a standard font style, you use the DEFINE.STYLE and APPLY.STYLE functions, which are equivalent to the actions you perform when you change the Normal style definition with the Styles command from the Format menu.

Syntax

STANDARD.FONT*(name_text,size_num,bold, italic,underline,strike,color,outline,shadow)*

Remarks

STANDARD.FONT takes the same arguments as FORMAT.FONT. For more information about the arguments, see FORMAT.FONT. For more information about defining and applying styles, see DEFINE.STYLE and APPLY.STYLE. Also see Chapter 7 in Book 1 of the *Microsoft Excel User's Guide*.

STANDARDIZE

Returns a normalized value from a distribution characterized by *mean* and *standard_dev*.

Syntax

STANDARDIZE*(x,mean,standard_dev)*

X is the value you want to normalize.

Mean is the arithmetic mean of the distribution.

Standard_dev is the standard deviation of the distribution.

Remarks

- If *standard_dev* ≤ 0, STANDARDIZE returns the #NUM! error value.

- The equation for the normalized value is:

$$Z = \frac{X - \mu}{\sigma}$$

Example

STANDARDIZE(42,40,1.5) equals 1.333333

Related Functions

Function	Description
NORMDIST	Returns the normal cumulative distribution
NORMINV	Returns the inverse of the normal cumulative distribution
NORMSDIST	Returns the standard normal cumulative distribution
NORMSINV	Returns the inverse of the standard normal cumulative distribution
ZTEST	Returns the two-tailed P-value of a z-test

STDEV

Returns an estimate for the standard deviation of a population based on a sample given as arguments. The standard deviation is a measure of how widely values are dispersed from the average value (the mean).

Syntax

STDEV(*number1,number2,...*)

Number1,number2,... are 1 to 30 number arguments corresponding to a sample of a population. *Number* can be a reference to a range.

Remarks

- STDEV assumes that its arguments are a sample of the population. If your data represents the entire population, you should compute the standard deviation using STDEVP.

- The standard deviation is calculated using the "nonbiased" or "$n-1$" method.

- STDEV uses the following formula:

$$\sqrt{\frac{n\sum x^2 - (\sum x)^2}{n(n-1)}}$$

Example

Suppose 10 tools stamped from the same machine during a production run are collected as a random sample and measured for breaking strength. The sample values (1345, 1301, 1368, 1322, 1310, 1370, 1318, 1350, 1303, 1299) are stored in cells A2:E3. STDEV estimates the standard deviation of breaking strengths for all the tools.

STDEV(A2:E3) equals 27.46

Related Functions

For a complete list of related functions, see "Statistical Functions" in the third and fourth sections, "Worksheet Functions Listed by Category" and "Macro Functions Listed by Category."

STDEVP

Returns the standard deviation of a population given the entire population as arguments. The standard deviation is a measure of how widely values are dispersed from the average value (the mean).

Syntax

STDEVP(*number1,number2,...*)

Number1,number2,... are 1 to 30 number arguments corresponding to a population. *Number* can be a reference to a range.

Remarks

- STDEVP assumes that its arguments are the entire population. If your data represents a sample of the population, you should compute the standard deviation using STDEV.

- For large sample sizes, STDEV and STDEVP return approximately equal values.

- The standard deviation is calculated using the "biased" or "n" method.

- STDEVP uses the following formula:

$$\sqrt{\frac{n\sum x^2 - \left(\sum x\right)^2}{n^2}}$$

Example

Using the same data from the STDEV example and assuming that only 10 tools are produced during the production run, STDEVP measures the standard deviation of breaking strengths for all the tools.

`STDEVP(A2:E3)` equals 26.05

Related Functions

For a complete list of related functions, see "Statistical Functions" in the third and fourth sections, "Worksheet Functions Listed by Category" and "Macro Functions Listed by Category."

STEP

Macro Sheets Only

Stops the normal flow of a macro and calculates it one cell at a time. Running a macro one cell at a time is called single-stepping and is very useful when you are debugging a macro. Use the STEP function, instead of choosing the Run command from the Macro menu and choosing the Step button, when you want to start single-stepping at a specific line in a macro. For more information about debugging macros, see Chapter 7 in Book 2 of the *Microsoft Excel User's Guide* and the Macro Debugger macro in the Macro Library in online Help.

Syntax

STEP( )

Remarks

- When Microsoft Excel encounters a STEP function, it stops running the macro and displays a dialog box. The dialog box tells you which cell in the macro Microsoft Excel is about to calculate, and what formula is in that cell. You can choose Step to carry out the next instruction; choose Evaluate to calculate part of the formula; choose Halt to interrupt the macro; or choose Continue to continue the macro without single-stepping.

  You can evaluate the formula by holding down the SHIFT key while you click the Step button. You can also choose Step Over to carry out, but not step through, a user-defined function call; choose Pause, to suspend the macro so you can perform other tasks; and choose Goto, to stop the macro and select the cell being evaluated.

- When placed at the beginning of a macro, STEP is equivalent to choosing the Run command from the Macro menu and selecting the Step check box in the Run dialog box.

- You can start single-stepping while a macro is running by pressing ESC in Microsoft Excel for Windows or by pressing ESC or COMMAND+PERIOD in Microsoft Excel for the Macintosh.

- The Single Step dialog box is initially displayed in the lower-right corner of the screen. You can move the dialog box if it's in your way. If you move it, it will remain in the new location until you stop single-stepping.

Related Functions

Function	Description
HALT	Stops all macros from running
RUN	Runs a macro

STEYX

Returns the standard error of the regression. The standard error is a measure of the amount of error in the prediction of *y* for an individual *x*.

Syntax

STEYX*(known_y's,known_x's)*

Known_y's is an array or range of dependent data points.

Known_x's is an array or range of independent data points.

Remarks

- The arguments should be numbers, or names, arrays, or references that contain numbers.

- If an array or reference argument contains text, logical values, or empty cells, those values are ignored; however, cells with the value zero are included.

- If *known_y's* and *known_x's* are empty or have a different number of data points, STEYX returns the #N/A error value.

- The equation for the standard error of the predicted *y* is:

$$S_{y \cdot x} =$$

$$\sqrt{\left[\frac{1}{n(n-2)}\right]\left[n\Sigma y^2 - (\Sigma y)^2 - \frac{\left[n\Sigma xy - (\Sigma x)(\Sigma y)\right]^2}{n\Sigma x^2 - (\Sigma x)^2}\right]}$$

Example

STEYX({2,3,9,1,8,7,5}, {6,5,11,7,5,4,4}) equals 3.305719

Related Functions

Function	Description
INTERCEPT	Returns the intercept of the linear regression line
LINEST	Returns the parameters of a linear trend
LOGEST	Returns the parameters of an exponential trend
PEARSON	Returns the Pearson product moment correlation coefficient
RSQ	Returns the r^2 value of the linear regression line
SLOPE	Returns the slope of the linear regression line

STYLE

Macro Sheets Only

Checks the fonts for a bold and/or italic font and applies it to the current selection in Microsoft Excel for the Macintosh version 1.5 or earlier. If no appropriate font is available, Microsoft Excel finds the most similar font available and formats the selection using that font. This function is included only for macro compatibility. If you want to change a font to bold or italic, use the FORMAT.FONT function. For more information, see FORMAT.FONT earlier in this manual.

Syntax

STYLE*(bold,italic)*
STYLE?*(bold,italic)*

SUBSCRIBE.TO

Macro Sheets Only

Inserts the contents of the edition into the active document at the point of the current selection. Use SUBSCRIBE.TO to incorporate editions published from other documents into your Microsoft Excel worksheets and macro sheets. SUBSCRIBE.TO returns TRUE if successful.

422

Syntax

SUBSCRIBE.TO(*file_text,format_num*)

Important This function is only available if you are using Microsoft Excel for the Macintosh with system software version 7.0 or later.

File_text is the name, as a text string, of the edition you want to insert into the active document. Unless *file_text* is in the current folder, supply the full path of the document. If *file_text* cannot be found, SUBSCRIBE.TO returns the #VALUE! error value and interrupts the macro.

Remarks

- If a single cell is selected, the data from the edition file is placed into as large a range of cells as is required by the data. Data already present in those cells is replaced. If the data is a picture, it is inserted from the upper-left corner of the selected cell.

- If a range of cells is selected, and the range is not big enough to contain the edition data, Microsoft Excel displays a dialog box asking if you want to clip the data to fit the range.

Format_num is the number 1 or 2 and specifies the format type of the file you are subscribing to.

Format_num	Format type
1 or omitted	Picture
2	Text (includes BIFF, VALU, TEXT, and CSV formats)

Examples

The following macro formula subscribes to an edition named CORPORATE LOGO in the current folder. The 1 indicates that the edition is a picture, if available.

```
SUBSCRIBE.TO("CORPORATE LOGO",1)
```

The following macro formula subscribes to an edition in the specified path named SALES HEADING. The 2 indicates that the edition is text, if available.

```
SUBSCRIBE.TO("Hard Disk:Word:Sales
Heading",2)
```

Related Functions

Function	Description
CREATE.PUBLISHER	Creates a publisher from the selection
EDITION.OPTIONS	Sets publisher and subscriber options
GET.LINK.INFO	Returns information about a link

SUBSTITUTE

Substitutes *new_text* for *old_text* in a text string. Use SUBSTITUTE when you want to replace specific text in a text string; use REPLACE when you want to replace any text that occurs in a specific location in a text string.

Syntax

SUBSTITUTE(*text,old_text,new_text, instance_num*)

Text is the text or the reference to a cell containing text for which you want to substitute characters.

Old_text is the text you want to replace.

New_text is the text you want to replace *old_text* with.

Instance_num specifies which occurrence of *old_text* you want to replace with *new_text*. If you specify *instance_num,* only that instance of *old_text* is replaced. Otherwise, every occurrence of *old_text* in *text* is changed to *new_text.*

Examples

SUBSTITUTE("Sales
Data","Sales","Cost") equals "Cost Data"

SUBSTITUTE("Quarter 1,
1991","1","2",1) equals "Quarter 2, 1991"

SUBSTITUTE("Quarter 1,
1991","1","2",3) equals "Quarter 1, 1992"

To replace every occurrence of the text constant named Separator in the cell named CellCont2 with square brackets:

SUBSTITUTE(CellCont2,Separator,"] [")

Related Functions

Function	Description
REPLACE	Replaces characters within text
TRIM	Removes spaces from text

SUM

Returns the sum of all the numbers in the list of arguments.

Syntax

SUM(*number1,number2,...*)

Number1,number2,... are 1 to 30 arguments for which you want the sum.

- Numbers, logical values, and text representations of numbers that you type directly into the list of arguments are counted. See the first and second examples following.

- If an argument is an array or reference, only numbers in that array or reference are counted. Empty cells, logical values, text, or error values in the array or reference are ignored. See the third example following.

- Arguments that are error values or text that cannot be translated into numbers cause errors.

Remarks

You can also enter the SUM function with the Auto-Sum tool on the toolbar. For more information, see "Using Worksheet Functions to Simplify Formulas" in Chapter 5 in Book 1 of the *Microsoft Excel User's Guide.*

Examples

SUM(3,2) equals 5

SUM("3",2,TRUE) equals 6 because the text values are translated into numbers, and the logical value TRUE is translated into the number 1.

Unlike the previous example, if A1 contains "3" and B1 contains TRUE, then:

SUM(A1,B1,2) equals 2 because references to non-number values in references are not translated.

If cells A2:E2 contain 5, 15, 30, 40, and 50:

SUM(A2:C2) equals 50

SUM(B2:E2,15) equals 150

Related Functions

Function	Description
AVERAGE	Returns the average of its arguments
COUNT or COUNTA	Count how many numbers or values are in a list of arguments
PRODUCT	Multiplies its arguments
SUMPRODUCT	Returns the sum of the products of corresponding array components

SUMPRODUCT

Multiplies corresponding components in the given arrays and returns the sum of those products.

Syntax

SUMPRODUCT(*array1,array2,array3,...*)

Array1, array2, array3,... are 2 to 30 arrays whose components you want to multiply and then add.

- The array arguments must have the same dimensions. If they do not, SUMPRODUCT returns the #VALUE! error value.

- SUMPRODUCT treats array entries that are not numeric as if they were zeros.

Example

	A	B	C	D	E	F
1	3	4		2	7	
2	8	6		6	7	
3	1	9		5	3	
4						

The following formula multiplies all the components of the two arrays in the preceding worksheet and then adds the products—that is, $3*2 + 4*7 + 8*6 + 6*7 + 1*5 + 9*3$.

SUMPRODUCT(A1:B3,D1:E3) equals 156

Remarks

The preceding example returns the same result as the formula SUM(A1:B3*D1:E3) entered as an array. Using arrays provides a more general solution for doing operations similar to SUMPRODUCT. For example, you can calculate the sum of the squares of the elements in A1:B3 by using the formula SUM(A1:B3^2) entered as an array.

Related Functions

Function	Description
MMULT	Returns the matrix product of two arrays
PRODUCT	Multiplies its arguments
SUM	Adds its arguments

SUMSQ

Returns the sum of the squares of the arguments.

Syntax

SUMSQ(*number1,number2,...*)

Number1, number2,... are 1 to 30 arguments for which you want the sum of the squares. You can also use a single array or a reference to an array instead of arguments separated by commas.

Example

SUMSQ(3,4) equals 25

Related Functions

Function	Description
SUM	Adds its arguments
SUMPRODUCT	Returns the sum of the products of corresponding array elements

SUMX2MY2

Returns the sum of the difference of squares of corresponding values in two arrays.

Syntax

SUMX2MY2(*array_x,array_y*)

Array_x is the first array or range of values.

Array_y is the second array or range of values.

Remarks

- The arguments should be numbers, or names, arrays, or references that contain numbers.

- If an array or reference argument contains text, logical values, or empty cells, those values are ignored; however, cells with the value zero are included.

- If *array_x* and *array_y* have a different number of values, SUMX2MY2 returns the #N/A error value.

- The equation for the sum of the difference of squares is:

$$SUMX2MY2 = \sum (x^2 - y^2)$$

Example

SUMX2MY2({2,3,9,1,8,7,5}, {6,5,11,7,5,4,4}) equals −55

Related Functions

Function	Description
SUMPRODUCT	Returns the sum of the products of corresponding array elements
SUMX2PY2	Returns the sum of the sum of squares of corresponding values in two arrays
SUMXMY2	Returns the sum of squares of differences of corresponding values in two arrays

SUMX2PY2

Returns the sum of the sum of squares of corresponding values in two arrays. The sum of the sum of squares is a common term in many statistical calculations.

Syntax

SUMX2PY2(*array_x,array_y*)

Array_x　is the first array or range of values.

Array_y　is the second array or range of values.

Remarks

- The arguments should be numbers, or names, arrays, or references that contain numbers.

- If an array or reference argument contains text, logical values, or empty cells, those values are ignored; however, cells with the value zero are included.

- If *array_x* and *array_y* have a different number of values, SUMX2PY2 returns the #N/A error value.

- The equation for the sum of the sum of squares is:

$$SUMX2PY2 = \sum (x^2 + y^2)$$

Example

SUMX2PY2({2,3,9,1,8,7,5}, {6,5,11,7,5,4,4}) equals 521

Related Functions

Function	Description
SUMPRODUCT	Returns the sum of the products of corresponding array elements
SUMX2MY2	Returns the sum of the difference of squares of corresponding values in two arrays
SUMXMY2	Returns the sum of squares of differences of corresponding values in two arrays

SUMXMY2

Returns the sum of squares of differences of corresponding values in two arrays.

Syntax

SUMXMY2(*array_x,array_y*)

Array_x is the first array or range of values.

Array_y is the second array or range of values.

Remarks

- The arguments should be numbers, or names, arrays, or references that contain numbers.

- If an array or reference argument contains text, logical values, or empty cells, those values are ignored; however, cells with the value zero are included.

- If *array_x* and *array_y* have a different number of values, SUMXMY2 returns the #N/A error value.

- The equation for the sum of squared differences is:

$$\text{SUMXMY2} = \sum (x - y)^2$$

Example

SUMXMY2({2,3,9,1,8,7,5}, {6,5,11,7,5,4,4}) equals 79

Related Functions

Function	Description
SUMPRODUCT	Returns the sum of the products of corresponding array elements
SUMX2MY2	Returns the sum of the difference of squares of corresponding values in two arrays
SUMX2PY2	Returns the sum of the sum of squares of corresponding values in two arrays

SYD

Returns the sum-of-years' digits depreciation for an asset for a specified period.

Syntax

SYD(*cost,salvage,life,per*)

Cost is the initial cost of the asset.

Salvage is the value at the end of the depreciation (sometimes called the salvage value of the asset).

Life is the number of periods over which the asset is being depreciated (sometimes called the useful life of the asset).

Per is the period and must use the same units as *life*.

Examples

If you've bought a truck for $30,000 that has a useful life of 10 years and a salvage value of $7500, the yearly depreciation allowance for the first year is:

SYD(30000,7500,10,1) equals $4090.91

The yearly depreciation allowance for the 10th year is:

SYD(30000,7500,10,10) equals $409.09

Related Functions

Function	Description
DDB	Returns the depreciation of an asset for a specified period using the double-declining balance method
SLN	Returns the straight-line depreciation of an asset for one period
VDB	Returns the depreciation of an asset for a specified or partial period using a declining balance method

T

Returns the text referred to by *value*.

Syntax

T*(value)*

Value   is the value you want to test. If *value* is or refers to text, T returns *value*. If *value* does not refer to text, T returns "" (empty text).

Remarks

You do not generally need to use the T function in a formula since Microsoft Excel automatically converts values as necessary. This function is provided for compatibility with other spreadsheet programs.

Examples

If B1 contains the text "Rainfall":

T(B1) equals "Rainfall"

If B2 contains the number 19:

T(B2) equals ""

T("True") equals "True"

T(TRUE) equals ""

Related Functions

Function	Description
CELL	Returns information about the formatting, location, or contents of a cell
N	Returns the value converted to a number
VALUE	Converts a text argument to a number

TABLE

Macro Sheets Only

Equivalent to choosing the Table command from the Data menu. Creates a table based on the input values and formulas you define on a worksheet. Use data tables to perform a "what-if" analysis by changing certain constant values on your worksheet to see how values in other cells are affected.

For information about data tables, see Chapter 1 in Book 2 of the *Microsoft Excel User's Guide*.

Syntax

TABLE*(row_ref,column_ref)*
TABLE?*(row_ref,column_ref)*

Row_ref   specifies the one cell to use as the row input for your table.

- *Row_ref* should be either an external reference to a single cell on the active worksheet, such as !$A$1 or !Price, or an R1C1-style reference to a single cell in the form of text, such as "R1C1", "R[–1]C[–1]", or "Price".

- If *row_ref* is an R1C1-style reference, it is assumed to be relative to the active cell in the selection.

Column_ref   specifies the one cell to use as the column input for your table. *Column_ref* is subject to the same restrictions as *row_ref*.

Examples

Each of the following macro formulas creates a two-input table in the selection on the active sheet using A1 and A2 as input cells:

TABLE(!$A$1,!$A$2)
TABLE("R1C1","R2C1")

If the selection is C3:E5 and the active cell is C3, this macro formula creates a one-input table in the selection using cell B2 as the column-input cell:

```
TABLE(,"R[-1]C[-1]")
```

If cell B2 on the active worksheet is named Size, each of the following macro formulas creates a one-input table in the selection using cell B2 as the row-input cell:

```
TABLE(!Size,)
TABLE("Size",)
```

If cell B2 on the active worksheet contains the text "Size", the first macro formula below sets up a one-input table in the selection using cell B2 as the row-input cell, while the second macro formula sets up a one-input table using a cell named Size as the row-input cell.

```
TABLE(!$B$2,)
TABLE(DEREF(!$B$2),)
```

TAN

Returns the tangent of the given angle.

Syntax

TAN(*number*)

Number is the angle in radians for which you want the tangent. If your argument is in degrees, multiply it by PI()/180 to convert it to radians.

Examples

TAN(0.785) equals 0.9920399

TAN(45*PI()/180) equals 1

Related Functions

Function	Description
ATAN	Returns the arctangent of a number
ATAN2	Returns the arctangent from *x*- and *y*-coordinates
PI	Returns the value π

TANH

Returns the hyperbolic tangent of *number*.

Syntax

TANH(*number*)

The formula for the hyperbolic tangent is:

$$\mathrm{TANH}(z) = \frac{\mathrm{SINH}(z)}{\mathrm{COSH}(z)}$$

Examples

TANH(-2) equals –0.96403

TANH(0) equals 0

TANH(0.5) equals 0.462117

Related Functions

Function	Description
ATANH	Returns the inverse hyperbolic tangent of a number
COSH	Returns the hyperbolic cosine of a number
SINH	Returns the hyperbolic sine of a number

TBILLEQ

Returns the bond-equivalent yield for a Treasury bill.

If this function is not available, you must install the Analysis ToolPak add-in macro. For more information, see "Managing Add-in Commands and Functions" in Chapter 4 in Book 2 of the *Microsoft Excel User's Guide.*

Syntax

TBILLEQ(*settlement,maturity,discount*)

Settlement is the Treasury bill's settlement date, expressed as a serial date number.

Maturity   is the Treasury bill's maturity date, expressed as a serial date number.

Discount   is the Treasury bill's discount rate.

Remarks

- *Settlement* and *maturity* are truncated to integers.

- If any argument is non-numeric, TBILLEQ returns the #VALUE! error value.

- If *settlement* or *maturity* is not a valid serial date number, TBILLEQ returns the #NUM! error value.

- If *discount* ≤ 0, TBILLEQ returns the #NUM! error value.

- If *settlement* > *maturity,* or if *maturity* is more than one year after *settlement,* TBILLEQ returns the #NUM! error value.

Example

A Treasury bill has the following terms:

March 31, 1991 settlement date
June 1, 1991 maturity date
9.14% discount rate

The Treasury bill price (in the 1900 Date System) is:

TBILLEQ(33328,33390,0.0914) equals 0.094151 or 9.4151%

Related Functions

Function	Description
DATE	Returns the serial number of a particular date
TBILLPRICE	Returns the price per $100 face value for a Treasury bill
TBILLYIELD	Returns the yield for a Treasury bill

TBILLPRICE

Returns the price per $100 face value for a Treasury bill.

If this function is not available, you must install the Analysis ToolPak add-in macro. For more information, see "Managing Add-in Commands and Functions" in Chapter 4 in Book 2 of the *Microsoft Excel User's Guide.*

Syntax

TBILLPRICE(*settlement,maturity,discount*)

Settlement   is the Treasury bill's settlement date, expressed as a serial date number.

Maturity   is the Treasury bill's maturity date, expressed as a serial date number.

Discount   is the Treasury bill's discount rate.

Remarks

- *Settlement* and *maturity* are truncated to integers.

- If any argument is non-numeric, TBILLPRICE returns the #VALUE! error value.

- If *settlement* or *maturity* is not a valid serial date number, TBILLPRICE returns the #NUM! error value.

- If *discount* ≤ 0, TBILLPRICE returns the #NUM! error value.

- If *settlement* > *maturity,* or if *maturity* is more than one year after *settlement,* TBILLPRICE returns the #NUM! error value.

Example

A Treasury bill has the following terms:

March 31, 1991 settlement date
June 1, 1991 maturity date
9% discount rate

The Treasury bill price (in the 1900 Date System) is:

TBILLPRICE(33328,33390,0.09) equals 98.43

Related Functions

Function	Description
DATE	Returns the serial number of a particular date
TBILLEQ	Returns the bond-equivalent yield for a Treasury bill
TBILLYIELD	Returns the yield for a Treasury bill

TBILLYIELD

Returns the yield for a Treasury bill.

If this function is not available, you must install the Analysis ToolPak add-in macro. For more information, see "Managing Add-in Commands and Functions" in Chapter 4 in Book 2 of the *Microsoft Excel User's Guide.*

Syntax

TBILLYIELD(*settlement,maturity,pr*)

Settlement   is the Treasury bill's settlement date, expressed as a serial date number.

Maturity   is the Treasury bill's maturity date, expressed as a serial date number.

Pr   is the Treasury bill's price per $100 face value.

Remarks

- *Settlement* and *maturity* are truncated to integers.

- If any argument is non-numeric, TBILLYIELD returns the #VALUE! error value.

- If *settlement* or *maturity* is not a valid serial date number, TBILLYIELD returns the #NUM! error value.

- If *pr* ≤ 0, TBILLYIELD returns the #NUM! error value.

- If *settlement* ≥ *maturity,* or if *maturity* is more than one year after *settlement,* TBILLYIELD returns the #NUM! error value.

Example

A Treasury bill has the following terms:

March 31, 1991 settlement date
June 1, 1991 maturity date
98.45 price per $100 face value

The Treasury bill price (in the 1900 Date System) is:

TBILLYIELD(33328,33390,98.45) equals 9.1417%

Related Functions

Function	Description
DATE	Returns the serial number of a particular date
TBILLEQ	Returns the bond-equivalent yield for a Treasury bill
TBILLPRICE	Returns the price per $100 face value for a Treasury bill

TDIST

Returns the Student's *t*-distribution. The *t*-distribution is used in the hypothesis testing of small sample data sets. Use this function in place of a table of critical values for the *t*-distribution.

Syntax

TDIST(*x,degrees_freedom,tails*)

X   is the numeric value at which to evaluate the distribution.

Degrees_freedom   is an integer indicating the number of degrees of freedom.

Tails   specifies the number of distribution tails to return. If *tails* = 1, TDIST returns the one-tailed distribution. If *tails* = 2, TDIST returns the two-tailed distribution.

Remarks

- If any argument is non-numeric, TDIST returns the #VALUE! error value.

- If *degrees_freedom* < 1, TDIST returns the #NUM! error value.

- The *degrees_freedom* and *tails* arguments are truncated to integers.

- If *tails* is any value other than 1 or 2, TDIST returns the #NUM! error value.

Example

TDIST(1.96,60,2) equals 0.054645

Related Functions

Function	Description
PTTESTM	Performs a paired two-sample Student's *t*-Test for means
PTTESTV	Performs a two-sample Student's *t*-Test, assuming unequal variances
TINV	Returns the inverse of the Student's *t*-distribution
TTEST	Returns the probability associated with a Student's *t*-Test
TTESTM	Performs a two-sample Student's *t*-Test for means, assuming equal variances

TERMINATE

Macro Sheets Only

Closes a dynamic data exchange (DDE) channel previously opened with the INITIATE function. Use TERMINATE to close a channel after you have finished communicating with another application.

Syntax

TERMINATE*(channel_num)*

Important Microsoft Excel for the Macintosh requires system software version 7.0 or later for this function.

Channel_num is the number returned by a previously run INITIATE function. *Channel_num* identifies a DDE channel to close.

If TERMINATE is not successful, it returns the #VALUE! error value.

For information about accessing other applications, see Chapter 3 in Book 2 of the *Microsoft Excel User's Guide.*

Related Functions

Function	Description
EXEC	Starts another application
INITIATE	Opens a channel to another application

TEXT

Converts a value to text in a specific number format.

Syntax

TEXT*(value,format_text)*

Value is a numeric value, a formula that evaluates to a numeric value, or a reference to a cell containing a numeric value.

Format_text is a number format from the Number dialog box in text form. *Format_text* cannot contain an asterisk (*) and cannot be "General". For information about the Number command on the Format menu and a list of the available number formats, see Chapter 7 in Book 1 of the *Microsoft Excel User's Guide.*

Remarks

Formatting a cell with the Number command on the Format menu changes only the format, not the value. Using the TEXT function converts a value to formatted text, and the result is no longer calculated as a number.

Examples

`TEXT(2.715,"$0.00")` equals "$2.72"

`TEXT("4/15/91","mmmm dd, yyyy")` equals "April 15, 1991"

Related Functions

Function	Description
DOLLAR	Converts a number to text, using currency format
FIXED	Formats a number as text with a fixed number of decimals
FORMAT.NUMBER	Formats numbers, dates, and times
T	Converts its arguments to text
VALUE	Converts a text argument to a number

TEXT.BOX

Macro Sheets Only

Replaces characters in a text box or button with the text you specify.

Syntax

TEXT.BOX(*add_text,object_id_text,*start_num, num_chars)

Add_text   is the text you want to add to the text box or button.

Object_id_text   is the name of the text box or button to which you want to add text (for example, "Text 1" or "Button 2"). If *object_id_text* is omitted, it is assumed to be the selected item.

Start_num   is a number specifying the position of the first character you want to replace (or the position at which you want to insert characters if you do not want to replace any). If *start_num* is omitted, it is assumed to be 1.

Num_chars   is the number of characters you want to replace. If *num_chars* is 0, then no characters are replaced, and *add_text* is inserted starting at the position *start_num*. If *num_chars* is omitted, all the characters are replaced.

Examples

The following macro formula replaces the first five characters in a text box named "Text 5" with the text "Net Income":

`TEXT.BOX("Net Income","Text 5",1,5)`

The following macro formula inserts the words "Account Summary for 1991" at the beginning of a text box named "Text 6":

`TEXT.BOX("Account Summary for 1991", "Text 6",1,0)`

Related Functions

Function	Description
CREATE.OBJECT	Creates an object
FORMAT.FONT	Applies a font to the selection
GET.OBJECT	Returns information about an object

TEXTREF

Macro Sheets Only

Converts text to an absolute reference in either A1- or R1C1-style. Use TEXTREF to convert references stored as text to references so that you can use them with other functions, such as OFFSET.

Syntax

TEXTREF(*text,a1*)

Text   is a reference in the form of text.

A1   is a logical value specifying the reference type of *text*. If *a1* is TRUE, *text* is assumed to be an A1-style reference; if FALSE or omitted, *text* is assumed to be an R1C1-style reference.

Remarks

- If you use TEXTREF by itself in a cell, you will get the value contained in the cell specified by *text*, not the reference itself, because references are automatically converted into the contents of the referenced cell.

- If you use TEXTREF as a *reference* argument to a function, Microsoft Excel does not convert the reference to a value.

Tip You can convert a reference to text with REFTEXT, manipulate it with the REPLACE and MID functions, and convert it back to a reference with TEXTREF.

Examples

TEXTREF("B7",TRUE) equals the reference value $B$7

TEXTREF("R5C5",FALSE) equals the reference value R5C5

TEXTREF("B7",FALSE) equals the #REF! error value, because "B7" can't be interpreted as an R1C1-style reference.

The following macro uses REFTEXT to convert the reference returned by SELECTION into text. The SUBSTITUTE function then changes the worksheet name in the reference, and the TEXTREF function in cell B6 converts the text returned by SUBSTITUTE back to a reference, to be used by FORMULA.FILL.

	A	B	C
1	*Names*	*Formulas*	*Comments*
2			
3		ConvertAndFill	
4	OldRef	=REFTEXT(SELECTION())	Gets reference of selection
5	NewRef	=SUBSTITUTE(OldRef,"Sheet1","Sheet2")	Changes document names
6		=FORMULA.FILL("text",TEXTREF(NewRef))	Fills into new reference
7		=RETURN()	

Also see the examples for REFTEXT.

Related Functions

Function	Description
DEREF	Returns the values of the cells in a reference
INDIRECT	Returns a reference indicated by a text value
OFFSET	Returns a reference offset from a given reference
REFTEXT	Converts a reference to text

TIME

Returns the serial number of a particular time. The serial number returned by TIME is a decimal fraction ranging from 0 to 0.99999999, representing the times from 0:00:00 (12:00:00 A.M.) to 23:59:59 (11:59:59 P.M.).

Syntax

TIME(*hour,minute,second*)

Hour is a number from 0 to 23 representing the hour.

Minute is a number from 0 to 59 representing the minute.

Second is a number from 0 to 59 representing the second.

Remarks

Microsoft Excel for Windows and Microsoft Excel for the Macintosh use different date systems as their default. For more information about date systems and serial numbers, see NOW.

Examples

TIME(12,0,0) equals the serial number 0.5, which is equivalent to 12:00:00 P.M.

TIME(16,48,10) equals the serial number 0.700115741, which is equivalent to 4:48:10 P.M.

TEXT(TIME(23,18,14),"h:mm:ss AM/PM") equals "11:18:14 PM"

Related Functions

Function	Description
HOUR, MINUTE, and SECOND	Convert serial numbers into hours, minutes, and seconds
NOW	Returns the serial number of the current date and time

TIMEVALUE

Returns the serial number of the time represented by *time_text*. The serial number is a decimal fraction ranging from 0 to 0.99999999, representing the times from 0:00:00 (12:00:00 A.M.) to 23:59:59 (11:59:59 P.M.). Use TIMEVALUE to convert a time represented as text into a serial number.

Syntax

TIMEVALUE*(time_text)*

Time_text   is a text string that gives a time in any one of the Microsoft Excel time formats. Date information in *time_text* is ignored.

Remarks

Microsoft Excel for Windows and Microsoft Excel for the Macintosh use different date systems as their default. For more information on date systems and serial numbers, see NOW.

Examples

TIMEVALUE("2:24 AM") equals 0.1

TIMEVALUE("22-Aug-55 6:35 AM") equals 0.274305556

Related Functions

Function	Description
DATEVALUE	Converts a date in the form of text to a serial number
HOUR, MINUTE, and SECOND	Convert serial numbers into hours, minutes, and seconds

Function	Description
NOW	Returns the serial number of the current date and time
TIME	Returns the serial number of a particular time

TINV

Returns the inverse of the Student's *t*-distribution for the specified degrees of freedom.

Syntax

TINV*(probability,degrees_freedom)*

Probability   is the probability associated with the two-tailed Student's *t*-distribution.

Degrees_freedom   is the number of degrees of freedom to characterize the distribution.

Remarks

- If either argument is non-numeric, TINV returns the #VALUE! error value.

- If *probability* < 0 or if *probability* > 1, TINV returns the #NUM! error value.

- If *degrees_freedom* is not an integer, it is truncated.

- If *degrees_freedom* < 1, TINV returns the #NUM! error value.

TINV uses an iterative technique for calculating the function. Given a probability value, TINV iterates until the result is accurate to within $\pm 3 \times 10^{-7}$. If TINV does not converge after 100 iterations, the function returns the #N/A error value.

Example

TINV(0.054645,60) equals 1.96

Related Functions

Function	Description
PTTESTM	Performs a paired two-sample Student's t-Test for means
PTTESTV	Performs a paired two-sample Student's t-Test, assuming unequal variances
TDIST	Returns the Student's t-distribution
TTEST	Returns the probability associated with a Student's t-Test
TTESTM	Performs a two-sample Student's t-Test for means, assuming equal variances

TODAY

Returns the serial number of the current date. The serial number is the date-time code used by Microsoft Excel for date and time calculations. For more information about serial numbers, see NOW.

Syntax

TODAY( )

Related Functions

Function	Description
DATE	Returns the serial number of a particular date
DAY	Converts a serial number to a day of the month
NOW	Returns the serial number of the current date and time

TRANSPOSE

Returns the transpose of *array*. TRANSPOSE must be entered as an array formula in a range that has the same number of rows and columns, respectively, as *array* has columns and rows. Use TRANSPOSE to shift the vertical and horizontal orientation of an array on a worksheet or macro sheet. For example, some functions, such as DOCUMENTS, return horizontal arrays. The following formula would return a vertical array from DOCUMENTS:

```
TRANSPOSE(DOCUMENTS())
```

Syntax

TRANSPOSE(*array*)

Array is an array on a worksheet or macro sheet that you want to transpose. *Array* can also be a range of cells.

The transpose of an array is created by using the first row of the array as the first column of the new array, the second row of the array as the second column of the new array, and so on.

Tip In a macro, you can transpose an array and paste only the values contained in the array, using the PASTE.SPECIAL macro function with 3 (values) as the *paste_num* argument and TRUE as the *transpose* argument.

Example

	A	B	C	D
1	1	2	3	
2	4	5	6	
3				
4	1	4		
5	2	5		
6	3	6		

In the worksheet above, when the following macro formula is entered as an array into cells A4:B6:

```
TRANSPOSE($A$1:$C$2)
```
equals the values in A4:B6

Related Functions

Function	Description
CHART.WIZARD	Creates and formats a chart
MDETERM	Returns the matrix determinant of an array
MINVERSE	Returns the matrix inverse of an array
MMULT	Returns the matrix product of two arrays

TREND

Fits a straight line (using the method of least squares) to the arrays *known_y's* and *known_x's*. Returns the *y*-values along that line for the array of *new_x's* that you specify.

Syntax

TREND(*known_y's,known_x's,new_x's,const*)

Known_y's is the set of *y*-values you already know in the relationship $y = mx + b$.

- If the array *known_y's* is in a single column, then each column of *known_x's* is interpreted as a separate variable.

- If the array *known_y's* is in a single row, then each row of *known_x's* is interpreted as a separate variable.

Known_x's is an optional set of *x*-values that you may already know in the relationship $y = mx + b$.

- The array *known_x's* can include one or more sets of variables. If only one variable is used, *known_y's* and *known_x's* can be ranges of any shape, as long as they have equal dimensions. If more than one variable is used, *known_y's* must be a vector (that is, a range with a height of one row or a width of one column).

- If *known_x's* is omitted, it is assumed to be the array {1,2,3,...} that is the same size as *known_y's*.

New_x's are new *x*-values for which you want TREND to return corresponding *y*-values.

- *New_x's* must include a column (or row) for each independent variable, just as *known_x's* does. So, if *known_y's* is in a single column, *known_x's* and *new_x's* should have the same number of columns. If *known_y's* is in a single row, *known_x's* and *new_x's* should have the same number of rows.

- If you omit *new_x's,* it is assumed to be the same as *known_x's.*

- If you omit both *known_x's* and *new_x's,* they are assumed to be the array {1,2,3,...} that is the same size as *known_y's.*

Const is a logical value specifying whether to force the constant *b* to equal 0.

- If *const* is TRUE or omitted, *b* is calculated normally.

- If *const* is FALSE, *b* is set equal to 0 and the *m*-values are adjusted so that $y = mx$.

Remarks

- For information on how Microsoft Excel fits a line to data, see LINEST.

- You can use TREND for polynomial curve fitting by regressing against the same variable raised to different powers. For example, suppose column A contained *y*-values and column B contained *x*-values. You could enter x^2 in column C, x^3 in column D, and so on, and then regress columns B through D against column A.

- Formulas that return arrays must be entered as array formulas.

- When entering an array constant for an argument such as *known_x's*, use commas to separate values in the same row and semicolons to separate rows.

Example

Suppose a business wants to purchase a tract of land in July, the start of the next fiscal year. The business collected cost information that covers the most recent 12 months for a typical tract in the desired area.

	A	B	C	D
1	Month	Price		
2	March	$133,890		
3	April	$135,000		
4	May	$135,790		
5	June	$137,300		
6	July	$138,130		
7	August	$139,100		
8	September	$139,900		
9	October	$141,120		
10	November	$141,890		
11	December	$143,230		
12	January	$144,000		
13	February	$145,290		

When entered as a vertical array in the range C2:C6, the following formula returns the predicted prices for March, April, May, June, and July:

TREND(B2:B13,,{13;14;15;16;17}) equals {146172;147190;148208;149226;150244}

The company can expect a typical tract of land to cost about $150,244 if it waits until July. The preceding formula uses the default array {1;2;3;4;5;6;7;8;9;10;11;12} for the *known_x's* argument, corresponding to the 12 months of sales data. The array {13;14;15;16;17} corresponds to the next five months.

Related Functions

Function	Description
DATA.SERIES	Fills a range of cells with a series of numbers or dates
FILL.AUTO	Copies cells or automatically fills a selection
GROWTH and LOGEST	Are similar to TREND and LINEST, but fit your data to an exponential curve

Function	Description
LINEST	Also calculates a line, but returns the parameters of the line instead of an array of *y*-values

TRIM

Removes all spaces from *text* except for single spaces between words. Use TRIM on text that you have received from another application that may have irregular spacing.

Syntax

TRIM(*text*)

Text   is the text from which you want spaces removed. For information about using text arguments, see "Converting Data Types" in the first section, "About Functions."

Example

TRIM(" First   Quarter Earnings   ") equals "First Quarter Earnings"

Related Functions

Function	Description
CLEAN	Removes all nonprintable characters from text
MID	Returns a specific number of characters from a text string starting at the position you specify
REPLACE	Replace characters within text
SUBSTITUTE	Substitutes new text for old text in a text string

TRIMMEAN

Returns the mean taken by excluding a percentage of data points from the top and bottom tails of a data set. You can use this function when you wish to exclude outlying data from your analysis.

Syntax

TRIMMEAN(*array,percent*)

Array   is the array or range of values to trim and average.

Percent   is the fractional number of data points to exclude from the calculation. For example, if *percent* = 0.2, 4 points are trimmed from a data set of 20 points (20 x 0.2), 2 from the top and 2 from the bottom of the set.

Remarks

- If *percent* < 0 or *percent* > 1, TRIMMEAN returns the #NUM! error value.

- TRIMMEAN rounds the number of excluded data points down to the nearest multiple of 2. If *percent* = 0.1, 10% of 30 data points equals 3 points. For symmetry, TRIMMEAN excludes a single value from the top and bottom of the data set.

Example

```
TRIMMEAN({4,5,6,7,2,3,4,5,1,2,3},0.2)
equals 3.777778
```

Related Functions

Function	Description
AVERAGE	Returns the average of its arguments
GEOMEAN	Returns the geometric mean
HARMEAN	Returns the harmonic mean
MEDIAN	Returns the median of the given numbers
MODE	Returns the most common value in a data set

TRUE

Returns the logical value TRUE.

Syntax

TRUE( )

Remarks

You can enter the value TRUE directly into cells and formulas without using this function. The TRUE function is provided primarily for compatibility with other spreadsheet programs.

TRUNC

Truncates a number to an integer by removing the fractional part of the number.

Syntax

TRUNC(*number,num_digits*)

Number   is the number you want to truncate. For information about using number arguments, see "Converting Data Types" in the first section, "About Functions."

Num_digits   is a number specifying the precision of the truncation. The default value for *num_digits* is zero.

Remarks

TRUNC and INT are similar in that both return integers. TRUNC removes the fractional part of the number. INT rounds numbers down to the nearest integer based on the value of the fractional part of the number. INT and TRUNC are different only when using negative numbers: TRUNC(–4.3) returns –4, but INT(–4.3) returns –5, because –5 is the lower number.

Examples

TRUNC(8.9) equals 8

TRUNC(-8.9) equals –8

TRUNC(PI()) equals 3

Related Functions

Function	Description
CEILING	Rounds a number up to the nearest integer
FLOOR	Rounds a number down, toward zero
INT	Rounds a number down to the nearest integer
MOD	Gives the remainder from division
ROUND	Rounds a number to a specified number of digits

TTEST

Returns the probability associated with a Student's *t*-Test. Use TTEST to determine whether two samples are likely to have come from the same two underlying populations that have the same mean.

Syntax

TTEST(*array1,array2,tails,type*)

Array1   is the first data set.

Array2   is the second data set.

Tails   specifies the number of distribution tails. If *tails* = 1, TTEST uses the one-tailed distribution. If *tails* = 2, TTEST uses the two-tailed distribution.

Type   is the kind of *t*-test to perform.

If *type* equals	This test is performed
1	Paired
2	Two-sample equal variance (homoscedastic)
3	Two-sample unequal variance (heteroscedastic)

Remarks

- If *array1* and *array2* have a different number of data points, and *type* = 1 (paired), TTEST returns the #N/A error value.

- The *tails* and *type* arguments are truncated to integers.

- If *tails* is non-numeric, TTEST returns the #VALUE! error value.

- If *tails* is any value other than 1 or 2, TTEST returns the #NUM! error value.

Example

TTEST({3,4,5,8,9,1,2,4,5},{6,19,3,2,14,4,5,17,1},2,1) equals 0.191996

Related Functions

Function	Description
PTTESTM	Performs a paired two-sample Student's *t*-Test for means
PTTESTV	Performs a two-sample Student's *t*-Test, assuming unequal variances
TDIST	Returns the Student's *t*-distribution
TINV	Returns the inverse of the Student's *t*-distribution
TTESTM	Performs a two-sample Student's *t*-Test for means, assuming equal variances

TTESTM

Macro Sheets Only

Performs a two-sample Student's *t*-Test for means, assuming equal variances. For more information, see "Analyzing Statistical or Engineering Data" in Chapter 1 in Book 2 of the *Microsoft Excel User's Guide*.

If this function is not available, you must install the Analysis ToolPak add-in macro. For more information, see "Managing Add-in Commands and Functions" in Chapter 4 in Book 2 of the *Microsoft Excel User's Guide*.

Syntax

TTESTM(*inprng1,inprng2,outrng,labels,alpha, difference*)

Inprng1   is the input range for the first data set.

Inprng2   is the input range for the second data set.

Outrng is the first cell (the upper-left cell) in the output table.

Labels is a logical value.

- If *labels* is TRUE, then labels are in the first row or column of the input ranges.

- If *labels* is FALSE or omitted, all cells in *inprng1* and *inprng2* are considered data. The output table will include default row or column headings.

Alpha is the confidence level for the test. If omitted, *alpha* is 0.05.

Difference is the hypothesized difference in means. If omitted, *difference* is 0.

Related Functions

Function	Description
PTTESTM	Performs a paired two-sample Student's *t*-Test for means
PTTESTV	Performs a two-sample Student's *t*-Test, assuming unequal variances
TDIST	Returns the Student's *t*-distribution
TTEST	Returns the probability associated with a Student's *t*-Test

TYPE

Returns the type of *value*. Use TYPE when the behavior of another function depends on the type of value in a particular cell.

Syntax

TYPE(*value*)

Value can be any Microsoft Excel value, such as a number, text, logical value, and so on.

If *value* is	TYPE returns
A number	1
Text	2
A logical value	4

If *value* is	TYPE returns
A formula	8
An error value	16
An array	64

Remarks

TYPE is most useful when you are using functions that can accept a variety of different types of data, such as ARGUMENT and INPUT. Use TYPE to find out what type of data was returned by the function.

Examples

If A1 contains the text "Smith", then:

TYPE(A1) equals TYPE("Smith") equals 2

TYPE("MR. "&A1) equals 2

TYPE(2+A1) equals TYPE(#VALUE!) equals 16

TYPE({1,2;3,4}) equals 64

The following macro demonstrates how you can use TYPE to return the type of an argument given to a custom function.

		B	C
1		*Formulas*	*Comments*
2			
3		**Custom Function**	
4		=ARGUMENT("Value",15)	Name and type of argument
5	ArgType	=TYPE(Value)	Gets type of argument
6		=IF(ArgType<>1,RETURN(""),RETURN(Value	Returns argument to function
7		=RETURN()	

Following is the complete formula in cell B6.

=IF(ArgType<>1,RETURN(""),RETURN(Value*3))

Related Functions

Function	Description
GET.CELL	Returns information about the specified cell
IS functions	Return information about the type of information in a cell

UNDO

Macro Sheets Only

Equivalent to choosing the Undo command from the Edit menu. Reverses certain actions and commands. UNDO is available in the same situations as the Undo command. For detailed information about the Undo command, see online Help.

Syntax

UNDO( )

UNGROUP

Macro Sheets Only

Equivalent to choosing the Ungroup command from the Format menu. Separates a grouped object into individual objects. Use UNGROUP to separate a group of objects so that you can format, move, or size one of the objects. For detailed information about the Ungroup command, see online Help.

If the selection is not a grouped object, UNGROUP returns FALSE.

Syntax

UNGROUP( )

Related Function

Function	Description
GROUP	Groups selected objects

UNHIDE

Macro Sheets Only

Equivalent to choosing the Unhide command from the Window menu. Use UNHIDE to display hidden windows. For detailed information about the Unhide command, see online Help.

Syntax

UNHIDE*(window_text)*

Window_text is the name of the window to unhide. If *window_text* is not the name of an open document, an error value is returned and the macro is interrupted. You cannot unhide a window of an add-in document.

Tip You can use UNHIDE to open an embedded chart in order to edit and format it. Use the CLOSE function to close the chart window.

Examples

The following macro formula opens an embedded chart window:

UNHIDE("SHEET1 CHART2")

In Microsoft Excel for Windows, the following macro formula displays the global macro sheet:

UNHIDE("GLOBAL.XLM")

In Microsoft Excel for the Macintosh, the following macro formula displays the global macro sheet:

UNHIDE("GLOBAL MACROS")

Use GET.WINDOW(7,*window_text*) to find out if a specific window is hidden. The following macro unhides all currently hidden documents.

	A	B	C
1	Names	Formulas	Comments
2			
3		**UnhideAllWindows**	Unhides all open windows
4		=SET.NAME("WindowArray",WINDOWS())	Names of open windows
5		=FOR("Counter",1,COLUMNS(WindowArray))	Begins a FOR–NEXT loop
6	WinName	=INDEX(WindowArray,1,Counter)	Returns one window name
7	Hidden	=GET.WINDOW(7,WinName)	Hidden sheet?
8		=IF(Hidden,UNHIDE(WinName))	Unhides hidden sheets
9		=NEXT()	Continues the loop
10		=RETURN()	

Related Functions

Function	Description
GET.WINDOW	Returns information about a window
HIDE	Hides the active window

UNLOCKED.NEXT
UNLOCKED.PREV

Macro Sheets Only

Equivalent to pressing TAB or SHIFT+TAB to move to the next or previous unlocked cell in a protected worksheet. Use these functions when you want to control which cell is active on a protected sheet.

Syntax

UNLOCKED.NEXT( )
UNLOCKED.PREV( )

Related Functions

Function	Description
CELL.PROTECTION	Controls protection for the selected cells
PROTECT.DOCUMENT	Controls protection for the active document

UNREGISTER

Macro Sheets Only

Unregisters a previously registered dynamic link library (DLL) or code resource. You can use UNREGISTER to free memory that was allocated to a DLL or code resource when it was registered. For more information about using the CALL and REGISTER functions, see the Appendix, "Using the CALL and REGISTER Functions." There are two syntax forms of this function. Use syntax 1 when you want Microsoft Excel to unregister a function or code resource according to its use count. Use syntax 2 when you want Microsoft Excel to unregister a function or code resource regardless of the use count.

Syntax 1

UNREGISTER(*register_id*)

Register_id   is the register ID returned by the REGISTER or REGISTER.ID function, which corresponds to the function or code resource to be removed from memory.

Microsoft Excel counts the number of times you register a function or code resource. This number is called the use count. Each time you unregister a function or code resource, its use count is decremented by 1. When the use count equals 0, Microsoft Excel frees the allocated memory.

Therefore, if you register a function or code resource more than once, you must use a corresponding number of UNREGISTER functions to ensure that it is completely unregistered.

Note   Because Microsoft Excel for Windows and Microsoft Excel for the Macintosh use different types of code resources, REGISTER has a slightly different syntax form when used in each operating environment.

Syntax 2a

For Microsoft Excel for Windows

UNREGISTER(*module_text*)

Syntax 2b

For Microsoft Excel for the Macintosh

UNREGISTER(*file_text*)

Module_text or *file_text*   is text specifying the name of the dynamic link library (DLL) that contains the function (in Microsoft Excel for Windows) or the name of the file that contains the code resource (in Microsoft Excel for the Macintosh).

If you use this syntax of UNREGISTER, all functions in the DLL (or all code resources in the file) are immediately unregistered, regardless of the use count.

Examples

Assuming that a REGISTER function in cell A5 of a macro sheet has already run (and has run only once), the following macro formula unregisters the corresponding function or code resource:

```
UNREGISTER(A5)
```

You could also use REGISTER.ID to return the register ID, instead of specifying a cell reference:

```
UNREGISTER(REGISTER.ID("User",
"GetTickCount")
```

Assuming that you have registered several different functions from the USER.EXE DLL of Microsoft Windows, the following macro formula unregisters all functions in that DLL:

```
UNREGISTER("User")
```

Tip If you register a function or code resource, and use the optional *function_text* argument to specify a custom name that will appear in the Paste Function dialog box, this custom name will not be removed by the UNREGISTER function. To remove the custom name, use the SET.NAME function without its second argument, as shown in the following sample macro:

	A	B	C
1	*Names*	*Formulas*	*Comments*
2			
3	AddTicks	=REGISTER("User","GetTickCount","J","GetTicks",,1,9)	
4		=RETURN()	
5			
6			
7	RemoveTicks	=UNREGISTER(B3)	
8		=SET.NAME("GetTicks")	
9		=RETURN()	

Related Functions

Function	Description
CALL	Calls a procedure in a dynamic link library or code resource
REGISTER	Registers a code resource
REGISTER.ID	Returns the register ID of the resource

UPDATE.LINK

Macro Sheets Only

Equivalent to choosing the Links command from the File menu and choosing the Update button with a link selected in the Links dialog box. Updates a link to another document. Use UPDATE.LINK to get the newest information from a supporting document. For detailed information about the Links command, see online Help.

Syntax

UPDATE.LINK(*link_text,type_of_link*)

Link_text is a text string describing the full path of the link as displayed in the Links dialog box. If *link_text* is omitted, only links from the active document to other Microsoft Excel documents are updated.

Type_of_link is a number from 1 to 4 that specifies the type of link to update.

Type_of_link	Link document type
1 or omitted	Microsoft Excel link
2	DDE link
3	Not available
4	Not available

Examples

In Microsoft Excel for Windows, the following macro formula updates the link from the document named SALES.XLS.

```
UPDATE.LINK("C:\EXCEL\SALES.XLS")
```

In Microsoft Excel for the Macintosh, the following macro formula updates the link from the document named SALES EAST.

```
UPDATE.LINK("HARD DISK:EXCEL:SALES EAST")
```

Related Functions

Function	Description
CHANGE.LINK	Changes supporting worksheet links
GET.LINK.INFO	Returns information about a link
OPEN.LINKS	Opens specified supporting documents

UPPER

Converts *text* to uppercase.

Syntax

UPPER*(text)*

Text is the text you want converted to uppercase. For information about text arguments, see "Converting Data Types" in the first section, "About Functions."

Examples

The following macro formula converts the contents of the active cell to uppercase:

```
FORMULA(UPPER(ACTIVE.CELL()),ACTIVE.CELL())
```

The following macro uses UPPER along with the FIND and MID functions to ensure that the state abbreviations are capitalized.

	A	B	C
1	Names	Formulas	Comments
2			
3		UppercaseState	
4	Text	=INPUT("Enter city and state",2)	
5	Comma	=FIND(",",Text)	Gets location of the comma
6	Upper	=UPPER(MID(Text,Comma+1,2))	Converts to uppercase
7		=FORMULA(MID(Text,1,Comma)&Upper,Text)	Replaces "Text" with chars
8		=RETURN()	

Also see the last example for PROPER.

Related Functions

Function	Description
LOWER	Converts text to lowercase
PROPER	Capitalizes the first letter in each word of a text value

VALUE

Converts *text* to a number.

Syntax

VALUE*(text)*

Text is the text enclosed in quotation marks or a reference to a cell containing the text you want to convert. *Text* can be in any of the constant number, date, or time formats recognized by Microsoft Excel. If *text* is not in one of these formats, VALUE returns the #VALUE! error value.

Remarks

You do not generally need to use the VALUE function in a formula since Microsoft Excel automatically converts text to numbers as necessary. This function is provided for compatibility with other spreadsheet programs.

Examples

VALUE("$1,000") equals 1,000

VALUE("16:48:00")-VALUE("12:00:00") equals "16:48:00"–"12:00:00" equals 0.2, the serial number equivalent to 4 hours and 48 minutes.

Related Functions

Function	Description
DOLLAR	Converts a number to text, using currency format
FIXED	Formats a number as text with a fixed number of decimals
TEXT	Formats a number and converts it to text

VAR

Returns an estimate for the variance of a population based on a sample given as arguments.

Syntax

VAR(*number1*,*number2*,...)

Number1,number2,...   are 1 to 30 number arguments corresponding to a sample of a population.

Remarks

- VAR assumes that its arguments are a sample of the population. If your data represents the entire population, you should compute the variance using VARP.

- VAR uses the following formula:

$$\frac{n\sum x^2 - \left(\sum x\right)^2}{n(n-1)}$$

Example

Suppose 10 tools stamped from the same machine during a production run are collected as a random sample and measured for breaking strength. The sample values (1345, 1301, 1368, 1322, 1310, 1370, 1318, 1350, 1303, 1299) are stored in cells A2:E3. VAR estimates the variance for the breaking strength of the tools.

VAR(A2:E3) equals 754.3

Related Functions

For a complete list of related functions, see "Statistical Functions" in the third and fourth sections, "Worksheet Functions Listed by Category" and "Macro Functions Listed by Category."

VARP

Returns the variance of a population given the entire population as arguments.

Syntax

VARP(*number1*,*number2*,...)

Number1,number2,...   are 1 to 30 number arguments corresponding to a population.

Remarks

VARP assumes that its arguments are the entire population. If your data represents a sample of the population, you should compute the variance using VAR.

Example

Using the data from the VAR example and assuming that only 10 tools are produced during the production run, VARP measures the variance of breaking strengths for all the tools.

VARP(A2:E3) equals 678.8

Related Functions

For a complete list of related functions, see "Statistical Functions" in the third and fourth sections, "Worksheet Functions Listed by Category" and "Macro Functions Listed by Category."

VDB

Returns the depreciation of an asset for any period you specify, including partial periods, using the double-declining balance method or some other method you specify. VDB stands for variable declining balance.

Syntax

VDB(*cost*,*salvage*,*life*,*start_period*,*end_period*, *factor,no_switch)*

Cost   is the initial cost of the asset.

Salvage   is the value at the end of the depreciation (sometimes called the salvage value of the asset).

Life   is the number of periods over which the asset is being depreciated (sometimes called the useful life of the asset).

Start_period   is the starting period for which you want to calculate the depreciation. *Start_period* must use the same units as *life*.

End_period   is the ending period for which you want to calculate the depreciation. *End_period* must use the same units as *life*.

Factor   is the rate at which the balance declines. If factor is omitted, it is assumed to be 2 (the double-declining balance method). Change *factor* if you do not want to use the double-declining balance method. For a description of the double-declining balance method, see DDB.

No_switch   is a logical value specifying whether to switch to straight-line depreciation when depreciation is greater than the declining balance calculation.

- If *no_switch* is TRUE, Microsoft Excel does not switch to straight-line depreciation even when the depreciation is greater than the declining balance calculation.

- If *no_switch* is FALSE or omitted, Microsoft Excel switches to straight-line depreciation when depreciation is greater than the declining balance calculation.

All arguments except *no_switch* must be positive numbers.

Examples

Suppose a factory purchases a new machine. The machine costs $2400 and has a lifetime of 10 years. The salvage value of the machine is $300. The following examples show depreciation over several periods. The results are rounded to two decimal places.

VDB(2400,300,3650,0,1) equals $1.32, the first day's depreciation. Microsoft Excel automatically assumes that *factor* is 2.

VDB(2400,300,120,0,1) equals $40.00, the first month's depreciation.

VDB(2400,300,10,0,1) equals $480.00, the first year's depreciation.

VDB(2400,300,120,6,18) equals $396.31, the depreciation between the 6th month and the 18th month.

VDB(2400,300,120,6,18,1.5) equals $311.81, the depreciation between the 6th month and the 18th month using a *factor* of 1.5 instead of the double-declining balance method.

Suppose instead that the $2400 machine is purchased in the middle of the first quarter of the fiscal year. The following macro formula determines the amount of depreciation for the first fiscal year that you own the asset, assuming that tax laws limit you to 150% depreciation of the declining balance:

VDB(2400,300,10,0,0.875,1.5) equals $315.00

Related Functions

Function	Description
DDB	Returns the depreciation of an asset for a specified period using the double-declining balance method
SLN	Returns the straight-line depreciation of an asset for one period
SYD	Returns the sum-of-years' digits depreciation of an asset for a specified period

VIEW.3D

Macro Sheets Only

Equivalent to choosing the 3-D View command from the Format menu, available when a chart is the active document. Adjusts the view of the active 3-D chart. Use VIEW.3D to emphasize different parts of your chart by viewing it from different angles and perspectives. For detailed information about the 3-D View command, see online Help.

Syntax

VIEW.3D(*elevation,perspective,rotation,axes, height%,autoscale*)
VIEW.3D?(*elevation,perspective,rotation,axes, height%,autoscale*)

Elevation   is a number from –90 to 90 specifying the viewing elevation of the chart and is measured in degrees. *Elevation* corresponds to the Elevation box in the 3-D View dialog box.

- If *elevation* is 0, you view the chart straight on. If *elevation* is 90, you view the chart from above (a "bird's eye view"). If *elevation* is –90, you view the chart from below.

- If *elevation* is omitted, it is assumed to be 25.

- *Elevation* is limited to 0 to 44 for 3-D bar charts and 0 to 80 for 3-D pie charts.

Perspective   is a number from 0 to 100% specifying the perspective of the chart. *Perspective* corresponds to the Perspective box in the 3-D View dialog box.

- A higher *perspective* value simulates a closer view.

- If *perspective* is omitted, it is assumed to be 30.

- *Perspective* is ignored on 3-D bar and pie charts.

Rotation   is a number from 0 to 360 specifying the rotation of the chart around the value (z) axis and is measured in degrees. *Rotation* corresponds to the Rotation box in the 3-D View dialog box. As you rotate the chart, the back and side walls are moved so that they do not block the chart.

- If *rotation* is omitted, it is assumed to be 30.

- *Rotation* is limited to 0 to 44 for 3-D bar charts.

Axes   is a logical value specifying whether axes are fixed in the plane of the screen or can rotate with the chart. *Axes* corresponds to the Right Angle Axes check box in the 3-D View dialog box.

- If *axes* is TRUE, Microsoft Excel locks the axes.

- If *axes* is FALSE, Microsoft Excel allows the axes to rotate.

- If *axes* is omitted and the chart view is 3-D layout, *axes* is assumed to be FALSE.

- If *axes* is omitted and the chart view is not 3-D layout, *axes* is assumed to be TRUE.

- *Axes* is TRUE for 3-D bar charts and ignored for 3-D pie charts.

Height%   is a number from 5 to 500 specifying the height of the chart as a percentage of the length of the base. *Height%* corresponds to the Height box in the 3-D View dialog box. *Height%* is useful for controlling the appearance of charts with many series or data points. If *height%* is omitted, it is assumed to be 100.

Autoscale   is a logical value corresponding to the Auto Scaling check box in the 3-D View dialog box. If TRUE, automatic scaling is used; if FALSE, it is not; if omitted, the current setting is not changed.

Example

The following macro formula adjusts the selected 3-D chart so that its elevation angle is 45 degrees, it has a relatively close view of 75, it has no rotation, its axes are free to rotate, and its height is 150% of the length of the base:

```
VIEW.3D(45,75,0,FALSE,150)
```

Related Function

Function	Description
FORMAT.MAIN	Formats a main chart

VIEW.DEFINE

Macro Sheets Only

Equivalent to choosing the Add button from the Views dialog box, which appears when you choose the View command from the Window menu. Creates or replaces a view.

If this function is not available, you must install the View Manager add-in macro. For more information, see "Managing Add-in Commands and Functions" in Chapter 4 in Book 2 of the *Microsoft Excel User's Guide*.

Syntax

VIEW.DEFINE(*view_name, print_settings_log, row_col_log*)

View_name is text enclosed in quotation marks and specifies the name of the view you want to define.

Print_settings_log is a logical value that, if TRUE or omitted, includes current print settings in the view or, if FALSE, does not include current print settings in the view.

Row_col_log is a logical value that, if TRUE or omitted, includes current row and column settings in the view or, if FALSE, does not include current row and column settings in the view.

Example

The following macro formula creates a view called V1 and includes current print, row, and column settings in the view.

```
VIEW.DEFINE("V1",TRUE,TRUE)
```

Related Functions

Function	Description
VIEW.DELETE	Removes a view from the active document
VIEW.SHOW	Shows a view

VIEW.DELETE

Macro Sheets Only

Equivalent to selecting a view and choosing the Delete button from the Views dialog box, which appears when you choose the View command from the Window menu. Removes a view from the active document.

If this function is not available, you must install the View Manager add-in macro. For more information, see "Managing Add-in Commands and Functions" in Chapter 4 in Book 2 of the *Microsoft Excel User's Guide*.

Syntax

VIEW.DELETE(*view_name*)

View_name is text enclosed in quotation marks and specifies the name of the view you want to delete.

Remarks

VIEW.DELETE returns the #VALUE error value if *view_name* is invalid or if the document is protected.

Example

The following macro formula removes the view V1 from the active document.

```
VIEW.DELETE("V1")
```

Related Functions

Function	Description
VIEW.DEFINE	Creates or replaces a view
VIEW.SHOW	Shows a view

VIEW.GET

Macro Sheets Only

Equivalent to displaying a list of views in the Views dialog box, which appears when you choose the View command from the Window menu. Returns an array of views from the active document.

If this function is not available, you must install the View Manager add-in macro. For more information, see "Managing Add-in Commands and Functions" in Chapter 4 in Book 2 of the *Microsoft Excel User's Guide*.

Syntax

VIEW.GET(*type_num,view_name*)

Type_num is a number from 1 to 3 that specifies the type of information to return, as shown in the following table.

Type_num	Result
1	Returns an array of views from the active document or the #N/A error value if none are defined.
2	Returns TRUE if print settings are included in the specified view. Returns FALSE if print settings are not included. Returns the #VALUE! error value if the name is invalid or the document is protected.

Type_num	Result
3	Returns TRUE if row and column settings are included in the specified view. Returns FALSE if row and column settings are not included. Returns the #VALUE! error value if the name is invalid or the document is protected.

View_name is text enclosed in quotation marks and specifies the name of a view in the active document. *View_name* is required if *type_num* is 2 or 3.

Example

The following macro formula returns an array of views from the active document:

```
VIEW.GET(1)
```

Related Functions

Function	Description
VIEW.DEFINE	Creates or replaces a view
VIEW.DELETE	Removes a view from the active document
VIEW.SHOW	Shows a view

VIEW.SHOW

Macro Sheets Only

Equivalent to selecting a view and choosing the Show button in the Views dialog box, which appears when you choose the View command from the Window menu. Shows a view.

If this function is not available, you must install the View Manager add-in macro. For more information, see "Managing Add-in Commands and Functions" in Chapter 4 in Book 2 of the *Microsoft Excel User's Guide*.

Syntax

VIEW.SHOW(*view_name*)
VIEW.SHOW?(*view_name*)

View_name   is text enclosed in quotation marks and specifies the name of a view in the active document.

Remarks

VIEW.SHOW returns the #VALUE error value if *view_name* is invalid or the document is protected.

Example

The following macro formula shows view V1.

```
VIEW.SHOW("V1")
```

Related Functions

Function	Description
VIEW.DEFINE	Creates or replaces a view
VIEW.DELETE	Removes a view from the active document

VLINE

Macro Sheets Only

Scrolls through the active window vertically by the number of rows you specify.

Syntax

VLINE(*num_rows*)

Num_rows   is a number that specifies how many rows to scroll.

- If *num_rows* is positive, Microsoft Excel scrolls down by the number of rows indicated by *num_rows*.

- If *num_rows* is negative, Microsoft Excel scrolls up by the number of rows indicated by *num_rows*.

Related Functions

Function	Description
HLINE	Horizontally scrolls through the active window by columns
HPAGE	Horizontally scrolls through the active window one window at a time
HSCROLL	Horizontally scrolls through a document by percentage or by column number
VPAGE	Vertically scrolls through the active window one window at a time
VSCROLL	Vertically scrolls through a document by percentage or by row number

VLOOKUP

Searches the leftmost column of an array for a particular value, and returns the value in the cell indicated. Use VLOOKUP instead of HLOOKUP when your comparison values are located in a column to the left or right of the data you want to find.

Syntax

VLOOKUP(*lookup_value,table_array, col_index_num*)

Lookup_value   is the value to be found in the first column of the array. *Lookup_value* can be a value, a reference, or a text string.

Table_array   is the table of information in which data is looked up. Use a reference to a range or a range name, such as Database.

- The values in the first column of *table_array* must be placed in ascending order: ..., −2, −1, 0, 1, 2, ... , A–Z, FALSE, TRUE; otherwise VLOOKUP may not give the correct value.

- You can put the values in ascending order by choosing the Sort command from the Data menu and selecting Ascending.

- The values in the first column of *table_array* can be text, numbers, or logical values.

- Uppercase and lowercase text are equivalent.

Col_index_num is the column number in *table_array* from which the matching value should be returned. A *col_index_num* of 1 returns the value in the first column in *table_array;* a *col_index_num* of 2 returns the value in the second column in *table_array,* and so on. If *col_index_num* is less than 1, VLOOKUP returns the #VALUE! error value; if *col_index_num* is greater than the number of columns in *table_array,* VLOOKUP returns the #REF! error value.

Remarks

- If VLOOKUP can't find *lookup_value,* it uses the largest value that is less than or equal to *lookup_value.*

- If *lookup_value* is smaller than the smallest value in the first column of *table_array,* VLOOKUP returns the #N/A error value.

Examples

	A	B	C	D
1	Air at 1 atm pressure			
2	Density	Viscosity	Temp	
3	(kg/cubic m)	(kg/m*s)*1E+05	(degrees C)	
4	0.457	3.55	500	
5	0.525	3.25	400	
6	0.616	2.93	300	
7	0.675	2.75	250	
8	0.746	2.57	200	
9	0.835	2.38	150	
10	0.946	2.17	100	
11	1.09	1.95	50	
12	1.29	1.71	0	

In the preceding worksheet, where the range A4:C12 is named Range:

VLOOKUP(1,Range,1) equals 0.946

VLOOKUP(1,Range,2) equals 2.17

VLOOKUP(1,Range,3) equals 100

VLOOKUP(0.1,Range,2) equals #N/A, because 0.1 is less than the smallest value in column A

VLOOKUP(2,Range,2) equals 1.71

Related Functions

Function	Description
HLOOKUP	Looks in the top row of an array and returns the value of the indicated cell
INDEX	Uses an index to choose a value from a reference or array
LOOKUP and MATCH	Look up values in an array or reference

VOLATILE

Macro Sheets Only

Specifies whether a custom function is volatile or nonvolatile. A volatile custom function is recalculated every time a calculation occurs on the worksheet.

Syntax

VOLATILE(*logical*)

Logical is a logical value specifying whether the custom function is volatile or nonvolatile. If *logical* is TRUE or omitted, the function is volatile; if FALSE, nonvolatile.

Remarks

- VOLATILE must precede every other formula in the custom function except RESULT and ARGUMENT.

- Normally, a worksheet recalculates a cell containing a nonvolatile custom function only when any part of the complete formula in the cell is recalculated. Use VOLATILE(TRUE) to recalculate the function every time the worksheet is recalculated.

- Most custom functions are nonvolatile by default, but custom functions with reference arguments are volatile by default. Use VOLATILE(FALSE) to prevent these functions from being recalculated unnecessarily often.

Example

The following custom function is a volatile version of RANDBETWEEN.

	A	B	C
1	*Names*	*Formulas*	*Comments*
2			
3		**VolRandBetween**	
4		=ARGUMENT("Low",1)	Lower number
5		=ARGUMENT("High",1)	Higher number
6		=VOLATILE()	Makes function volatile
7	RandInteger	=RANDBETWEEN(Low,High)	Computes a random integer
8		=RETURN(RandInteger)	

Related Function

Function	Description
RESULT	Specifies the data type a custom function returns

VPAGE

Macro Sheets Only

Vertically scrolls through the active window one window at a time. Use VPAGE to change the displayed area of a worksheet or macro sheet.

Syntax

VPAGE(*num_windows*)

Num_windows   specifies the number of windows to scroll through the active window vertically. A window is defined as the number of visible rows. If 20 rows are visible in the window, VPAGE scrolls in increments of 20 rows.

- If *num_windows* is positive, VPAGE scrolls down.

- If *num_windows* is negative, VPAGE scrolls up.

Related Functions

Function	Description
HPAGE	Horizontally scrolls through the active window one window at a time
HSCROLL	Horizontally scrolls through a document by percentage or by column number
VLINE	Vertically scrolls through the active window by rows
VSCROLL	Vertically scrolls through a document by percentage or by row number

VSCROLL

Macro Sheets Only

Vertically scrolls through the active document by percentage or by row number.

Syntax

VSCROLL(*position*,*row_logical*)

Position   specifies the row you want to scroll to. *Position* can be an integer representing the row number or a fraction or percentage representing the vertical position of the row in the document. If *position* is 0, VSCROLL scrolls through your document to its top edge, which is row 1. If *position* is 1, VSCROLL scrolls through your document to its bottom edge, which is row 16,384.

Row_logical   is a logical value specifying how the function scrolls.

- If *row_logical* is TRUE, VSCROLL scrolls through the document to row *position*.

- If *row_logical* is FALSE or omitted, VSCROLL scrolls through the document to the vertical position represented by the fraction *position*.

Remarks

- To scroll to a specific row *n,* either use
VSCROLL(*n*,TRUE) or VSCROLL(*n*/16384).
To scroll to row 138, for example, enter
VSCROLL(138,TRUE) or
VSCROLL(138/16384).

- If you are recording a macro and move the scroll
box several times in a row, the recorder only
records the final location of the scroll box, omitting any intermediate steps. Remember that
scrolling does not change the active cell or the
selection.

Examples

The following macro formulas all scroll through the
document to row 8192, halfway down the
worksheet:

```
VSCROLL(8192,TRUE)
VSCROLL(50%)
VSCROLL(0.5,FALSE)
VSCROLL(8192/16384)
```

The following macro goes to a cell, then positions
the cell in the upper-left corner of the window.

	B	C
1	Formulas	Comments
2		
3	PositionCell	
4	=ACTIVATE("Worksheet1")	Switches to a document
5	=FORMULA.GOTO("R400C14")	Goes to a cell
6	=VSCROLL(ROW(ACTIVE.CELL()),TRUE)	Puts active cell at window top
7	=HSCROLL(COLUMN(ACTIVE.CELL()),TRUE)	Puts active cell at window left
8	=RETURN()	

Related Functions

Function	Description
FORMULA.GOTO	Selects a named area or refer-ence on any open document
HLINE	Horizontally scrolls through the active window by columns

Function	Description
HPAGE	Horizontally scrolls through the active window one window at a time
HSCROLL	Horizontally scrolls through a document by percentage or by column number
SELECT	Selects a cell, worksheet object, or chart item
VLINE	Vertically scrolls through the active window by rows
VPAGE	Vertically scrolls through the active window one window at a time

WAIT

Macro Sheets Only

Pauses the macro until the time specified by the
serial number.

Syntax

WAIT(*serial_number*)

Serial_number is the date-time code used by
Microsoft Excel for date and time calculations. You
can give *serial_number* as text, such as "4:30 PM",
or as a formula, such as NOW()+"00:00:04", instead
of as a number. The text or formula is automatically
converted to a serial number. For more information
about *serial_number,* see NOW.

Important WAIT suspends all Microsoft Excel
activity and may prevent you from performing
other operations on your computer. Background
processes, such as printing and recalculation, are
continued.

Remarks

You can use WAIT with NOW to pause a macro for a specified length of time. For example, the following macro formula waits 3 seconds from the time the functions are evaluated:

```
WAIT(NOW()+"00:00:03")
```

Related Functions

Function	Description
ON.TIME	Runs a macro at a specific time
NOW	Returns the serial number of the current date and time

WEEKDAY

Returns the day of the week corresponding to *serial_number*. The day is given as an integer, ranging from 1 (Sunday) to 7 (Saturday).

Syntax

WEEKDAY*(serial_number)*

Serial_number is the date-time code used by Microsoft Excel for date and time calculations. You can give *serial_number* as text, such as "15-Apr-1991" or "4-15-91", instead of as a number. The text is automatically converted to a serial number. For more information about *serial_number,* see NOW.

Remarks

Microsoft Excel for Windows and Microsoft Excel for the Macintosh use different date systems as their default. For more information, see NOW.

Tip You can also use the TEXT function to convert a value to a specified number format when using the 1900 Date System:

```
TEXT("4/16/90","dddd") equals Monday
```

Examples

```
WEEKDAY("2/14/90") equals 4 (Wednesday)
```

If you are using the 1900 Date System (the default in Microsoft Excel for Windows), then:

```
WEEKDAY(29747.007) equals 4 (Wednesday)
```

If you are using the 1904 Date System (the default in Microsoft Excel for the Macintosh), then:

```
WEEKDAY(29747.007) equals 3 (Tuesday)
```

Related Functions

Function	Description
DAY	Converts a serial number to a day of the month
NOW	Returns the serial number of the current date and time
TEXT	Formats a number and converts it to text
TODAY	Returns the serial number of today's date

WEIBULL

Returns the Weibull distribution. Use this distribution in reliability analysis, such as calculating a device's mean time to failure.

Syntax

WEIBULL*(x,alpha,beta,cumulative)*

X is the value at which to evaluate the function.

Alpha is a parameter to the distribution.

Beta is a parameter to the distribution.

Cumulative determines the form of the function. If *cumulative* is TRUE, WEIBULL returns the cumulative distribution function; if FALSE, it returns the probability density function.

Remarks

- If *x, alpha,* or *beta* is non-numeric, WEIBULL returns the #VALUE! error value.

- If $x < 0$, WEIBULL returns the #NUM! error value.

- If $alpha \leq 0$ or if $beta \leq 0$, WEIBULL returns the #NUM! error value.

- The equation for the Weibull cumulative distribution function is:

$$F(x;\alpha,\beta) = 1 - e^{-(x/\beta)^{\alpha}}$$

- The equation for the Weibull probability density function is:

$$f(x;\alpha,\beta) = \frac{\alpha}{\beta^{\alpha}} x^{\alpha-1} e^{-(x/\beta)^{\alpha}}$$

- When *alpha* = 1, WEIBULL returns the exponential distribution with:

$$\lambda = \frac{1}{\beta}$$

Examples

WEIBULL(105,20,100,TRUE) equals 0.929581

WEIBULL(105,20,100,FALSE) equals 0.035589

Related Function

Function	Description
EXPONDIST	Returns the exponential distribution

WHILE

Macro Sheets Only

Carries out the statements between the WHILE function and the next NEXT function until *logical_test* is FALSE. Use WHILE–NEXT loops to carry out a series of macro formulas while a certain condition remains TRUE.

Syntax

WHILE(logical_test)

Logical_test   is a value or formula that evaluates to TRUE or FALSE. If *logical_test* is FALSE the first time the WHILE function is reached, the macro skips the loop and resumes running at the statement after the next NEXT function. If there is no NEXT function in the same column, WHILE displays an error message and interrupts the macro.

For information about WHILE–NEXT loops, see Chapter 7 in Book 2 of the *Microsoft Excel User's Guide*.

Remarks

If you know exactly how many times you'll need to carry out the statements within a loop, in most cases you should use a FOR–NEXT loop.

Example

The following macro illustrates how to use a WHILE–NEXT loop to enclose functions that you want to run repeatedly until a certain condition is met.

	A	B	C
1	Names	Formulas	Comments
2			
3		ExitLoop	
4		=SET.VALUE(Counter,1)	Initializes Counter to 1
5		=WHILE(Counter<10)	Begins WHILE–NEXT loop
6	Counter	=Counter+INT(RAND()*5)	Increments Counter
7		=ProcessCounter(Counter)	Runs subroutine
8		=IF(Counter=8,BREAK())	If Counter = 8, break
9		=NEXT()	Ends WHILE–NEXT loop
10		=RETURN()	Ends the macro

Related Functions

Function	Description
FOR	Starts a FOR–NEXT loop
FOR.CELL	Starts a FOR.CELL–NEXT loop
IF	Specifies an action to take if a logical test is TRUE
NEXT	Ends a FOR–NEXT, FOR.CELL–NEXT, or WHILE–NEXT loop

WINDOW.MAXIMIZE

Macro Sheets Only

Changes the active window from its normal size to full size. In Microsoft Excel for Windows, using WINDOW.MAXIMIZE is equivalent to pressing CTRL+F10 or double-clicking the title bar. In Microsoft Excel for the Macintosh, using WINDOW.MAXIMIZE is equivalent to double-clicking the title bar or clicking the zoom box.

Syntax

WINDOW.MAXIMIZE(*window_text*)

Window_text specifies which window to switch to and maximize. W*indow_text* is text enclosed in quotation marks or a reference to a cell containing text. If *window_text* is omitted, the active window stays the same.

Remarks

WINDOW.MAXIMIZE replaces FULL(TRUE) in earlier versions of Microsoft Excel.

Example

The following macro formula maximizes all windows:

```
WINDOW.MAXIMIZE()
```

Related Functions

Function	Description
WINDOW.MINIMIZE	Minimizes a window
WINDOW.MOVE	Moves a window
WINDOW.RESTORE	Restores a window to its previous size
WINDOW.SIZE	Changes the size of a window

WINDOW.MINIMIZE

Macro Sheets Only

Shrinks a window to an icon. In Microsoft Excel for Windows, using WINDOW.MINIMIZE is equivalent to clicking the minimize button on a document window. In Microsoft Excel for the Macintosh, the minimize feature is not supported.

Syntax

WINDOW.MINIMIZE(*window_text*)

Window_text specifies which window to minimize.

- W*indow_text* is text enclosed in quotation marks or a reference to a cell containing text.

- If *window_text* is omitted, Microsoft Excel minimizes the active window.

Remarks

If a window is already minimized, WINDOW.MINIMIZE has no effect.

Example

The following macro formula shrinks the active window to an icon:

```
WINDOW.MINIMIZE()
```

Related Functions

Function	Description
WINDOW.MAXIMIZE	Maximizes a window
WINDOW.MOVE	Moves a window
WINDOW.RESTORE	Restores a window to its previous size
WINDOW.SIZE	Changes the size of a window

WINDOW.MOVE

Macro Sheets Only

Equivalent to choosing the Move command from the Control menu in Microsoft Excel for Windows or moving a window by dragging its title bar or its icon. Moves the active window so that its upper-left corner is at the specified horizontal and vertical positions. The dialog-box form, WINDOW.MOVE?, is supported only in Microsoft Excel for Windows.

Syntax

WINDOW.MOVE(*x_pos,y_pos,window_text*)
WINDOW.MOVE?(*x_pos,y_pos,window_text*)

X_pos is the horizontal position to which you want to move the window. *X_pos* is measured in points. A point is 1/72nd of an inch.

- In Microsoft Excel for Windows, *x_pos* is measured from the left edge of your workspace to the left edge of the window.

- In Microsoft Excel for the Macintosh, *x_pos* is measured from the left edge of your screen to the left edge of the window.

- If *x_pos* is omitted, the window does not move horizontally.

Y_pos is the vertical position to which you want to move the window. *Y_pos* in measured in points from the bottom edge of the formula bar to the top edge of the window. If *y_pos* is omitted, the window does not move vertically.

Window_text specifies which window to restore.

- W*indow_text* is text enclosed in quotation marks or a reference to a cell containing text.

- If *window_text* is omitted, it is assumed to be the name of the active window.

Remarks

- If the window is minimized, WINDOW.MOVE moves the icon on the workspace. Measurements are relative to the upper-left corner of the workspace and the icon.

- WINDOW.MOVE does not change the size of the window or affect whether the specified window is active or inactive.

- In Microsoft Excel for the Macintosh, if *window_text* is "Clipboard", WINDOW.MOVE moves the Clipboard. The Clipboard must already be available; if it is not available, choose the Show Clipboard command from the Window menu or use the SHOW.CLIPBOARD function before using the WINDOW.MOVE function.

- WINDOW.MOVE replaces MOVE in earlier versions of Microsoft Excel.

Examples

In Microsoft Excel for Windows, the following macro formula places the active window against the upper-left edge of the Microsoft Excel workspace:

```
WINDOW.MOVE(1,1)
```

In Microsoft Excel for the Macintosh, the following macro formula places the active window against the upper-left edge of the screen:

```
WINDOW.MOVE(1,1)
```

Related Functions

Function	Description
FORMAT.MOVE	Moves the selected object
WINDOW.MAXIMIZE	Maximizes a window
WINDOW.MINIMIZE	Minimizes a window
WINDOW.RESTORE	Restores a window to its previous size
WINDOW.SIZE	Changes the size of a window

WINDOW.RESTORE

Macro Sheets Only

Changes the active window from maximized or minimized size to its previous size. In Microsoft Excel for Windows, using WINDOW.RESTORE is equivalent to pressing CTRL+F5 or double-clicking the title bar (or double-clicking the icon if it is minimized). In Microsoft Excel for the Macintosh, using WINDOW.RESTORE is equivalent to double-clicking the title bar or clicking the zoom box.

Syntax

WINDOW.RESTORE(*window_text*)

Window_text   specifies which window to switch to and restore.

- W*indow_text* is text enclosed in quotation marks or a reference to a cell containing text.

- If *window_text* is omitted, Microsoft Excel restores the active window.

Remarks

- If the window is minimized, WINDOW.RESTORE restores the icon to its previous size. This operation is equivalent to double-clicking the icon.

- WINDOW.RESTORE replaces FULL(FALSE) in earlier versions of Microsoft Excel.

Example

The following macro formula restores the active window to its previous size:

```
WINDOW.RESTORE()
```

Related Functions

Function	Description
WINDOW.MAXIMIZE	Maximizes a window
WINDOW.MINIMIZE	Minimizes a window
WINDOW.MOVE	Moves a window
WINDOW.SIZE	Changes the size of a window

WINDOW.SIZE

Macro Sheets Only

Equivalent to choosing the Size command from the Control menu or to adjusting the sizing borders (in Microsoft Excel for Windows) or the sizing box (in Microsoft Excel for the Macintosh) of the window with the mouse. Changes the size of the active window by moving its lower-right corner so that the window has the width and height you specify. WINDOW.SIZE does not change the position of the upper-left corner of the window, nor does it affect whether the specified window is active or inactive.

Syntax

WINDOW.SIZE(*width,height,window_text*)
WINDOW.SIZE?(*width,height,window_text*)

Width   specifies the width of the window and is measured in points. A point is 1/72nd of an inch.

Height   specifies the height of the window and is measured in points.

Window_text   specifies which window to size.

- W*indow_text* is text enclosed in quotation marks or a reference to a cell containing text.

- If *window_text* is omitted, it is assumed to be the name of the active window.

Remarks

- In Microsoft Excel for Windows, an error occurs if you try to resize a window that has already been minimized to an icon or enlarged to its maximum size. You must first restore the window to its original size using the WINDOW.RESTORE formula. For more information, see WINDOW.RESTORE.

- WINDOW.SIZE replaces SIZE in earlier versions of Microsoft Excel.

Example

The following macro formula changes the size of the active window to 250 by 125 points:

```
WINDOW.SIZE(250,125)
```

Related Functions

Function	Description
FORMAT.SIZE	Sizes an object
WINDOW.MAXIMIZE	Maximizes a window
WINDOW.MINIMIZE	Minimizes a window
WINDOW.MOVE	Moves a window
WINDOW.RESTORE	Restores a window to its previous size

WINDOW.TITLE

Macro Sheets Only

Changes the title of the active window to the title you specify. The title appears at the top of the document window. Use WINDOW.TITLE to control window titles when you're using Microsoft Excel to create a custom application.

Syntax

WINDOW.TITLE*(text)*

Text is the title you want to assign to the window. If *text* is omitted, it is assumed to be the name of the document as it is stored on your disk. Empty text ("") specifies no title.

Important WINDOW.TITLE changes the name of the window, not the actual name of the document as it is stored on your disk. To change the name of the document, use the SAVE.AS function.

Remarks

- The window name you create using WINDOW.TITLE will appear on the Window menu, and will be returned by the WINDOWS function, but not by the DOCUMENTS function. You must use the new window name in the ACTIVATE function and the ON.WINDOW function.

- If you use NEW.WINDOW to create new windows on the document, the window title will be restored to its original name.

Example

The following macro formula changes the title of the active window to First Quarter.

WINDOW.TITLE("First Quarter")

Related Function

Function	Description
APP.TITLE	Changes the title of the application workspace

WINDOWS

Macro Sheets Only

Returns the names of the specified open Microsoft Excel windows, including hidden windows. Use WINDOWS to get a list of active windows for use by other macro functions that return information about or manipulate windows, such as GET.WINDOW and ACTIVATE. The names are returned as a horizontal array of text values, in order of their appearance on your screen. The first name is the active window, the next name is the window directly under the active window, and so on.

Syntax

WINDOWS(*type_num,match_text*)

Type_num　is a number that specifies which types of documents are returned by WINDOWS, according to the following table.

Type_num	Returns window names from these types of documents
1 or omitted	All windows except those belonging to add-in documents
2	Add-in documents only
3	All types of documents

Match_text　specifies the windows whose names you want to returned and can include wildcard characters. If *match_text* is omitted, WINDOWS returns the names of all open windows.

Tips

- You can change the output of a horizontal array to vertical with the TRANSPOSE function.

- You can use WINDOWS with the INDEX function to choose individual window names from the array for use in other functions that take window names as arguments.

- You can use the COLUMNS functions to count the number of entries in the array, which is the number of windows.

Examples

If the active window, named SHEET1, is on top of a window named MACRO1:2, which is on top of a window named MACRO1:1, then:

WINDOWS() equals {"SHEET1","MACRO1:2","MACRO1:1"}

For more information, see UNHIDE.

Related Functions

Function	Description
ACTIVATE	Switches to a window
DOCUMENTS	Returns the names of the specified open documents
GET.WINDOW	Returns information about a window
NEW.WINDOW	Creates a new window for an existing worksheet or macro sheet
ON.WINDOW	Runs a macro when you switch to a window

WORKBOOK.ACTIVATE

Macro Sheets Only

Equivalent to double-clicking a document in a workbook contents window. Activates the specified document in a workbook. Also unhides the document if it is hidden, or restores the document if it is minimized.

Syntax

WORKBOOK.ACTIVATE(*sheet_name, new_window_logical*)

Sheet_name　is the name of the document you want to activate within the active workbook. If omitted, the workbook contents window is activated.

New_window_logical is a logical value that, if TRUE, displays the document in a new window just as if you had chosen the New Window command from the Window menu, or, if FALSE or omitted, displays the document at the same size and in the same location as the workbook contents window.

Related Function

Function	Description
WORKBOOK.OPTIONS	Changes the settings of a workbook document

WORKBOOK.ADD

Macro Sheets Only

Equivalent to choosing the Add button on the workbook contents window. Adds one or more documents to a workbook. For more information about workbooks, see "Managing Documents with Workbooks" in Chapter 4 in Book 1 of the *Microsoft Excel User's Guide*.

Syntax

WORKBOOK.ADD(*name_array,dest_book, position_num*)
WORKBOOK.ADD?(*name_array,dest_book, position_num*)

Name_array is the name of a document, or an array of names of documents, that you want to add to a workbook.

Dest_book is the name of the workbook to which you want to add *name_array*. If *dest_book* is omitted, it is assumed to be the active workbook.

Position_num is a number that specifies the position of the document within the workbook.

Examples

In Microsoft Excel for Windows, the following macro formula adds a worksheet named SALES.XLS to the first position in a workbook named DIV2.XLW:

```
WORKBOOK.ADD("SALES.XLS","DIV2.XLW",1)
```

In Microsoft Excel for the Macintosh, the following macro formula adds a worksheet named SALES FOR THE 3RD QUARTER to the first position in a workbook named DIVISION 2:

```
WORKBOOK.ADD("SALES FOR THE 3RD QUARTER",
"DIVISION 2",1)
```

Related Function

Function	Description
WORKBOOK.COPY	Copies one or more documents from their current workbook to another workbook

WORKBOOK.COPY

Macro Sheets Only

In Microsoft Excel for Windows, equivalent to holding the CTRL key while dragging a document from one workbook to another. In Microsoft Excel for the Macintosh, equivalent to holding the OPTION key while dragging a document from one workbook to another. Copies one or more documents from their current workbook into another workbook at the specified position.

Syntax

WORKBOOK.COPY(*name_array,dest_book, position_num*)

Name_array is the name of a document, or an array of names of documents, that you want to copy from one workbook to another.

Dest_book is the name of the workbook to which you want to copy *name_array*. If *dest_book* is omitted, the copy of *name_array* becomes a separate document that is not part of any workbook.

Position_num is a number that specifies the target position for the document within the new workbook. The first position is 1, the top of the document list.

- If *position_num* is specified, Microsoft Excel inserts the copy of the document at the specified position in the workbook.

- If *position_num* is omitted, Microsoft Excel places the document at the last position in the workbook.

- If *dest_book* is omitted, *position_num* is ignored.

Examples

In Microsoft Excel for Windows, the following macro formula copies the unbound worksheet SALES.XLS to position 3 in a workbook named DIV2.XLW:

```
WORKBOOK.COPY("SALES.XLS","DIV2.XLW",3)
```

The following macro formula copies a worksheet named SL2.XLS, which is bound into a workbook named INF.XLW, to the end of a workbook named DIV2.XLW :

```
WORKBOOK.COPY("[INF.XLW]SL2.XLS",
"DIV2.XLW")
```

In Microsoft Excel for the Macintosh, the following macro formula copies the unbound worksheet SALES RESULTS to position 3 in a workbook named DIVISION 2:

```
WORKBOOK.COPY("SALES RESULTS",
"DIVISION 2",3)
```

The following macro formula copies a worksheet named SALES 2, which is bound into a workbook named INFORMATION, to the end of a workbook named DIVISION 2:

```
WORKBOOK.COPY("[INFORMATION]SALES 2",
"DIVISION 2")
```

Related Function

Function	Description
WORKBOOK.MOVE	Moves one or more documents from one workbook to another workbook or to another position in the same workbook

WORKBOOK.MOVE

Macro Sheets Only

Equivalent to dragging a document from one workbook to another workbook or to another position in the same workbook. Moves one or more documents between workbooks or changes a document's position within a workbook. Use WORKBOOK.MOVE to reorder documents within a workbook, move documents between workbooks, or remove documents from workbooks.

Syntax

WORKBOOK.MOVE(*name_array*,*dest_book*, *position_num*)

Name_array   is the name of a document, or an array of names of documents, that you want to move.

Dest_book   is the name of the workbook to which you want to move *name_array*. If *dest_book* is omitted, WORKBOOK.MOVE moves the document out of the workbook and makes it a separate document.

Position_num   is a number that specifies the target position for the document within *dest_book*. The first position is 1, the top of the document list.

- If *position_num* is specified, Microsoft Excel inserts the document at the specified position in the workbook.

- If *position_num* is omitted, Microsoft Excel moves the document to the last position in the workbook.

Examples

In Microsoft Excel for Windows, the following macro formula moves a worksheet named SALES.XLS, which is bound into a workbook named DIV1.XLW, to position 3 of a workbook named DIV2.XLW:

```
WORKBOOK.MOVE("[DIV1.XLW]SALES.XLS",
"DIV2.XLW",3)
```

The following macro formula moves this worksheet to position 8 within the same workbook:

```
WORKBOOK.MOVE("[DIV2.XLW]SALES.XLS",
"DIV2.XLW",8)
```

In Microsoft Excel for the Macintosh, the following macro formula moves a worksheet named SALES RESULTS, which is bound into a workbook named DIVISION 1, to position 3 of a workbook named DIVISION 2:

```
WORKBOOK.MOVE("[DIVISION 1]SALES RESULTS",
"DIVISION 2",3)
```

The following macro formula moves this worksheet to position 8 within the same workbook:

```
WORKBOOK.MOVE("[DIVISION 2]SALES RESULTS",
"DIVISION 2",8)
```

Related Function

Function	Description
WORKBOOK.COPY	Copies one or more documents from their current workbook into another workbook

WORKBOOK.OPTIONS

Macro Sheets Only

Equivalent to selecting the Options button in a workbook contents window. This function operates only when the workbook contents window is active.

Syntax

WORKBOOK.OPTIONS(*sheet_name, bound_logical,new_name*)

Sheet_name   is the name of a document that is part of a workbook.

Bound_logical   is a logical value that specifies whether the document should be bound or unbound. If *bound_logical* is TRUE, Microsoft Excel binds the document; if it is FALSE, Microsoft Excel unbinds the document; if it is omitted, the setting is not changed.

New_name   is the document name to assign to *sheet_name*. If *new_name* is omitted, then the document name is not changed. If *sheet_name* is unbound, then *new_name* must be a valid filename.

Examples

In Microsoft Excel for Windows, the following macro formula binds SHEET3 to the active workbook:

```
WORKBOOK.OPTIONS("SHEET3",TRUE)
```

In Microsoft Excel for Windows, the following macro formula unbinds SHEET2 from the active workbook:

```
WORKBOOK.OPTIONS("SHEET2",FALSE)
```

In Microsoft Excel for the Macintosh, the following macro formula binds SHEET3 to the active workbook:

```
WORKBOOK.OPTIONS("SHEET3",TRUE)
```

In Microsoft Excel for the Macintosh, the following macro formula unbinds SHEET2 from the active workbook:

```
WORKBOOK.OPTIONS("SHEET2",FALSE)
```

Related Functions

Function	Description
GET.WORKBOOK	Returns information about a workbook document
WORKBOOK.SELECT	Selects the specified documents in a workbook

WORKBOOK.SELECT

Macro Sheets Only

Equivalent to selecting individual documents in the active workbook window.

Syntax

WORKBOOK.SELECT*(name_array,active_name)*

Name_array is a horizontal array of text names of documents you want to select. If *name_array* is omitted, no documents are selected.

Active_name is the name of a single sheet in the workbook which should be given the focus when the selection is made. If *active_name* is not in the selection, WORKBOOK.SELECT returns the #VALUE! error value. If *active_name* is omitted, the first sheet in *name_array* is given the focus.

Example

The following macro formula selects three worksheets in the active workbook:

```
WORKBOOK.SELECT({"SALES.XLS","ORDERS.XLS",
"PARTS.XLS"})
```

Related Functions

Function	Description
GET.WORKBOOK	Returns information about a workbook
SELECT	Selects a cell, worksheet object, or chart item

WORKDAY

Returns the serial number date that is the indicated number of working days before or after *start_date*. Working days exclude weekends and any dates identified in *holidays*. Use WORKDAY to exclude weekends or holidays when you calculate invoice due dates, expected delivery times, or the number of days of work performed.

If this function is not available, you must install the Analysis ToolPak add-in macro. For more information, see "Managing Add-in Commands and Functions" in Chapter 4 in Book 2 of the *Microsoft Excel User's Guide.*

Syntax

WORKDAY*(start_date,days,holidays)*

Start_date is a serial date number that represents the start date.

Days is the number of nonweekend and non-holiday days before or after *start_date*. A positive value for *days* yields a future date; a negative value yields a past date.

Holidays is an optional array of one or more serial date numbers to exclude from the working calendar, such as state and federal holidays and floating holidays.

Remarks

- If any argument is non-numeric, WORKDAY returns the #VALUE! error value.

- If *start_date* is not a valid serial date number, WORKDAY returns the #NUM! error value.

- If *start_date* plus *days* yields an invalid serial date number, WORKDAY returns the #NUM! error value.

- If *days* is not an integer, it is truncated.

Examples

WORKDAY(DATEVALUE("01/03/91"),5) equals 33248 or 01/10/91

If January 7, 1991 and January 8, 1991 are holidays, then:
WORKDAY(DATEVALUE("01/03/91"),5,
{33245,33246}) equals 33252 or 01/14/91

Related Functions

Function	Description
EDATE	Returns the serial number of the date that is the indicated number of months before or after the start date
EOMONTH	Returns the serial number of the last day of the month before or after a specified number of months
NETWORKDAYS	Returns the number of whole workdays between two dates
NOW	Returns the serial number of the current date and time

WORKGROUP

Macro Sheets Only

Equivalent to choosing the Group Edit command from the Options menu. Creates a group. For detailed information about the Group Edit command, see online Help.

Syntax

WORKGROUP(*name_array*)
WORKGROUP?(*name_array*)

Name array is the list of open, unhidden worksheets and macro sheets, as text, that you want to include in a group.

- If *name_array* is omitted, the most recently created group is recreated.

- If no group has been created during the current Microsoft Excel session, all open, unhidden worksheets are created as a group.

- Charts cannot be part of a group.

Remarks

WORKGROUP returns the #VALUE! error value and interrupts the macro if it can't find any of the documents in *name_array* or if any of the documents is a chart.

Examples

In Microsoft Excel for Windows, the following macro formula creates a group from the specified worksheets:

```
WORKGROUP({"SALES.XLS","EXPENSES.XLS",
"PROFITS.XLS"})
```

In Microsoft Excel for the Macintosh, the following macro formula creates a group from the specified worksheets:

```
WORKGROUP({"SALES","EXPENSES","PROFITS"})
```

Related Function

Function	Description
FILL.GROUP	Fills the contents of the active worksheet's selection to the same area on all other worksheets in the group

WORKSPACE

Macro Sheets Only

Equivalent to choosing the Workspace command from the Options menu. Use WORKSPACE to change the workspace settings for a document. For detailed information about the Workspace command, see online Help.

Syntax

WORKSPACE(*fixed,decimals,r1c1,scroll, status,formula,menu_key,remote,entermove, underlines,tools,notes,nav_keys,menu_key_action, drag_drop,show_info*)

WORKSPACE?(*fixed,decimals,r1c1,scroll, status,formula,menu_key,remote,entermove, underlines,tools,notes,nav_keys,menu_key_action, drag_drop,show_info*)

Arguments correspond to check boxes and text boxes in the Workspace dialog box. Arguments corresponding to check boxes are logical values. If an argument is TRUE, the check box is selected; if FALSE, the check box is cleared; if omitted, the current setting is not changed.

Fixed   corresponds to the Fixed Decimal check box.

Decimals   specifies the number of decimal places. *Decimals* is ignored if *fixed* is FALSE or omitted.

R1c1   corresponds to the R1C1 check box.

Scroll   corresponds to the Scroll Bars check box.

Status   corresponds to the Status Bar check box.

Formula   corresponds to the Formula Bar check box.

Menu_key   is a text value indicating an alternate menu key, and corresponds to the Alternate Menu Or Help Key box.

Remote   corresponds to the Ignore Remote Requests check box.

Important   Microsoft Excel for the Macintosh requires system software version 7.0 or later for this argument.

Entermove   corresponds to the Move Selection After Enter/Return check box.

Underlines   is a number corresponding to the Command Underline options as shown in the following table.

Note   This argument is only available in Microsoft Excel for the Macintosh.

If *underlines is*	Command underlines are
1	On
2	Off
3	Automatic

Tools   is a logical value. If TRUE, the Standard toolbar is displayed; if FALSE, all visible toolbars are hidden. If omitted, the current toolbar display is not changed.

Notes   corresponds to the Note Indicator check box.

Nav_keys   corresponds to the Alternate Navigation Keys check box. In Microsoft Excel for the Macintosh, *nav_keys* is ignored.

Menu_key_action   is the number 1 or 2 specifying options for the alternate menu or Help key. In Microsoft Excel for the Macintosh, *menu_key_action* is ignored.

Menu_key_action	Alternate menu or Help key activates
1 or omitted	Microsoft Excel menus
2	Lotus 1-2-3 Help

Drag_drop   corresponds to the Cell Drag And Drop check box.

Show_info   corresponds to the Info Window check box.

Related Function

Function	Description
GET.WORKSPACE	Returns information about the workspace

XIRR

Returns the internal rate of return for a schedule of cash flows that is not necessarily periodic.

If this function is not available, you must install the Analysis ToolPak add-in macro. For more information, see "Managing Add-in Commands and Functions" in Chapter 4 in Book 2 of the *Microsoft Excel User's Guide.*

Syntax

XIRR(*values,dates,guess*)

Values is a series of cash flows that correspond to a schedule of payments in *dates*. The first payment is optional, and corresponds to a cost or payment that occurs at the beginning of the investment. All succeeding payments are discounted based on a 365-day year.

Dates is a schedule of payment dates that corresponds to the cash flow payments. The first payment date indicates the beginning of the schedule of payments. All other dates must be later than this date, but they may occur in any order.

Guess is a number that you guess is close to the result of XIRR.

Remarks

- Numbers in *dates* are truncated to integers.

- If any argument is non-numeric, XIRR returns the #VALUE! error value.

- XIRR expects at least one positive cash flow and one negative cash flow; otherwise, XIRR returns the #NUM! error value.

- If any number in *dates* is not a valid serial date number, XIRR returns the #NUM! error value.

- If any number in *dates* precedes the starting date, XIRR returns the #NUM! error value.

- If *values* and *dates* contain a different number of values, XIRR returns the #NUM! error value.

- Microsoft Excel uses an iterative technique for calculating XIRR. Starting with *guess*, XIRR cycles through the calculation until the result is accurate within 0.000001%. If XIRR can't find a result that works after 20 tries, the #NUM! error value is returned.

- In most cases you do not need to provide *guess* for the XIRR calculation. If omitted, *guess* is assumed to be 0.1 (10%).

- XIRR is closely related to XNPV, the net present value function. The rate of return calculated by XIRR is the interest rate corresponding to XNPV = 0.

Example

Consider an investment that requires a $10,000 cash payment on January 1, 1991, and returns $2750 on March 1, 1991, $4250 on October 30, 1991, $3250 on February 15, 1992, and $2750 on April 1, 1992. The internal rate of return (in the 1900 Date System) is:

XIRR({-10000,2750,4250,3250,2750}, {33239,33298,33541,33649,33695},0.1) equals 0.374581 or 37.4581%

Related Functions

Function	Description
IRR	Returns the internal rate of return for a series of cash flows
MIRR	Returns the internal rate of return where positive and negative cash flows are financed at different rates
NPV	Returns the net present value of an investment based on a series of periodic cash flows and a discount rate
RATE	Returns the interest rate per period of an annuity
XNPV	Returns the net present value for a schedule of cash flows

XNPV

Returns the net present value for a schedule of cash flows that is not necessarily periodic.

If this function is not available, you must install the Analysis ToolPak add-in macro. For more information, see "Managing Add-in Commands and Functions" in Chapter 4 in Book 2 of the *Microsoft Excel User's Guide*.

Syntax

XNPV(*rate,values,dates*)

Rate is the discount rate to apply to the cash flows.

Values is a series of cash flows that correspond to a schedule of payments in *dates*. The first payment is optional, and corresponds to a cost or payment that occurs at the beginning of the investment. All succeeding payments are discounted based on a 365-day year.

Dates is a schedule of payment dates that corresponds to the cash flow payments. The first payment date indicates the beginning of the schedule of payments. All other dates must be later than this date, but they may occur in any order.

Remarks

- Numbers in *dates* are truncated to integers.

- If any argument is non-numeric, XNPV returns the #VALUE! error value.

- If any number in *dates* is not a valid serial date number, XNPV returns the #NUM! error value.

- If any number in *dates* precedes the starting date, XNPV returns the #NUM! error value.

- If *values* and *dates* contain a different number of values, XNPV returns the #NUM! error value.

Example

Consider an investment that requires a $10,000 cash payment on January 1, 1991, and returns $2750 on March 1, 1991, $4250 on October 30, 1991, $3250 on February 15, 1992, and $2750 on April 1, 1992. Assume that the cash flows are discounted at 9%. The net present value is:

```
XNPV(0.09,{-10000,2750,4250,3250,
2750},{33239,33298,33541,33649,33695})
equals 2088.918556
```

Related Functions

Function	Description
IRR	Returns the internal rate of return for a series of cash flows
MIRR	Returns the internal rate of return where positive and negative cash flows are financed at different rates
NPV	Returns the net present value of an investment based on a series of periodic cash flows and a discount rate
RATE	Returns the interest rate per period of an annuity
XIRR	Returns the internal rate of return for a schedule of cash flows

YEAR

Returns the year corresponding to *serial_number*. The year is given as an integer in the range 1900–2078.

Syntax

YEAR(*serial_number*)

Serial_number is the date-time code used by Microsoft Excel for date and time calculations. You can give *serial_number* as text, such as "15-Apr-1991" or "4-15-91", instead of as a number. The text is automatically converted to a serial number. For more information about *serial_number,* see NOW.

Remarks

Microsoft Excel for Windows and Microsoft Excel for the Macintosh use different date systems as their default. For more information, see NOW.

Examples

YEAR("7/5/90") equals 1990

If you are using the 1900 Date System (the default in Microsoft Excel for Windows), then:

YEAR(0.007) equals 1900

YEAR(29747.007) equals 1981

If you are using the 1904 Date System (the default in Microsoft Excel for the Macintosh), then:

YEAR(0.007) equals 1904

YEAR(29747.007) equals 1985

Related Functions

Function	Description
MONTH, DAY, WEEKDAY, HOUR, MINUTE, and SECOND	Convert serial numbers into months, days, days of the week, hours, minutes, and seconds
NOW	Returns the serial number of the current date and time
TODAY	Returns the serial number of today's date

YEARFRAC

Returns the year fraction representing the number of whole days between *start_date* and *end_date*. Use YEARFRAC to identify the proportion of a whole year's benefits or obligations to assign to a specific term.

If this function is not available, you must install the Analysis ToolPak add-in macro. For more information, see "Managing Add-in Commands and Functions" in Chapter 4 in Book 2 of the *Microsoft Excel User's Guide.*

Syntax

YEARFRAC(*start_date,end_date,basis*)

Start_date is a serial date number that represents the start date.

End_date is a serial date number that represents the end date.

Basis is the type of day count basis to use.

Basis	Day count basis
0 or omitted	30/360
1	Actual/actual
2	Actual/360
3	Actual/365

Remarks

- All arguments are truncated to integers.
- If any argument is non-numeric, YEARFRAC returns the #VALUE! error value.
- If *start_date* or *end_date* are not valid serial date numbers, YEARFRAC returns the #NUM! error value.
- If *basis* < 0 or if *basis* > 3, YEARFRAC returns the #NUM! error value.
- If *start_date* ≥ *end_date,* YEARFRAC returns the #NUM! error value.

Examples

YEARFRAC(DATEVALUE("01/01/91"), DATEVALUE("06/30/91"),0) equals 0.5

YEARFRAC(DATEVALUE("01/01/91"), DATEVALUE("07/01/91"),3) equals 0.49589

Related Functions

Function	Description
EDATE	Returns the serial number of the date that is the indicated number of months before or after the start date
EOMONTH	Returns the serial number of the last day of the month before or after a specified number of months
NETWORKDAYS	Returns the number of whole workdays between two dates
NOW	Returns the serial number of the current date and time
WORKDAY	Returns the serial number of the date before or after a specified number of workdays

YIELD

Returns the yield on a security that pays periodic interest. Use YIELD to calculate bond yield.

If this function is not available, you must install the Analysis ToolPak add-in macro. For more information, see "Managing Add-in Commands and Functions" in Chapter 4 in Book 2 of the *Microsoft Excel User's Guide.*

Syntax

YIELD(*settlement,maturity,rate,pr,redemption, frequency,basis*)

Settlement is the security's settlement date, expressed as a serial date number.

Maturity is the security's maturity date, expressed as a serial date number.

Rate is the security's annual coupon rate.

Pr is the security's price per $100 face value.

Redemption is the security's redemption value per $100 face value.

Frequency is the number of coupon payments per year. For annual payments, *frequency* = 1; for semi-annual, *frequency* = 2; for quarterly, *frequency* = 4.

Basis is the type of day count basis to use.

Basis	Day count basis
0 or omitted	30/360
1	Actual/actual
2	Actual/360
3	Actual/365

Remarks

- *Settlement, maturity, frequency,* and *basis* are truncated to integers.

- If any argument is non-numeric, YIELD returns the #VALUE! error value.

- If *settlement* or *maturity* is not a valid serial date number, YIELD returns the #NUM! error value.

- If *rate* < 0, YIELD returns the #NUM! error value.

- If *pr* ≤ 0 or if *redemption* ≤ 0, YIELD returns the #NUM! error value.

- If *frequency* is any number other than 1, 2, or 4, YIELD returns the #NUM! error value.

- If *basis* < 0 or if *basis* > 3, YIELD returns the #NUM! error value.

- If *settlement* ≥ *maturity,* YIELD returns the #NUM! error value.

Example

A bond has the following terms:

February 15, 1991 settlement date
November 15, 1999 maturity date
5.75% semiannual coupon
95.04287 price
$100 redemption value
30/360 basis

The bond yield (in the 1900 Date System) is:

`YIELD(33284,36479,0.0575,95.04287,100,` `2,0)` equals 0.065 or 6.5%

Related Functions

Function	Description
NOW	Returns the serial number of the current date and time
PRICE	Returns the price per $100 face value for a security that pays periodic interest

YIELDDISC

Returns the annual yield for a discounted security.

If this function is not available, you must install the Analysis ToolPak add-in macro. For more information, see "Managing Add-in Commands and Functions" in Chapter 4 in Book 2 of the *Microsoft Excel User's Guide.*

Syntax

YIELDDISC(*settlement,maturity,pr,redemption, basis)*

Settlement   is the security's settlement date, expressed as a serial date number.

Maturity   is the security's maturity date, expressed as a serial date number.

Pr   is the security's price per $100 face value.

Redemption   is the security's redemption value per $100 face value.

Basis   is the type of day count basis to use.

Basis	Day count basis
0 or omitted	30/360
1	Actual/actual
2	Actual/360
3	Actual/365

Remarks

- *Settlement, maturity,* and *basis* are truncated to integers.

- If any argument is non-numeric, YIELDDISC returns the #VALUE! error value.

- If *settlement* or *maturity* is not a valid serial date number, YIELDDISC returns the #NUM! error value.

- If $pr \leq 0$ or if *redemption* ≤ 0, YIELDDISC returns the #NUM! error value.

- If *basis* < 0 or if *basis* > 3, YIELDDISC returns the #NUM! error value.

- If *settlement* $\geq$ *maturity,* YIELDDISC returns the #NUM! error value.

Example

A bond has the following terms:

February 15, 1991 settlement date
March 1, 1991 maturity date
99.795 price
$100 redemption value
Actual/360 basis

The bond yield (in the 1900 Date System) is:

`YIELDDISC(33284,33298,99.795,100,2)` equals 5.2823%

Related Functions

Function	Description
DISC	Returns the discount rate for a security
NOW	Returns the serial number of the current date and time
PRICEDISC	Returns the price per $100 face value of a discounted security

YIELDMAT

Returns the annual yield of a security that pays interest at maturity.

If this function is not available, you must install the Analysis ToolPak add-in macro. For more information, see "Managing Add-in Commands and Functions" in Chapter 4 in Book 2 of the *Microsoft Excel User's Guide.*

Syntax

YIELDMAT*(settlement,maturity,issue,rate,pr,basis)*

Settlement is the security's settlement date, expressed as a serial date number.

Maturity is the security's maturity date, expressed as a serial date number.

Issue is the security's issue date, expressed as a serial date number.

Rate is the security's interest rate at date of issue.

Pr is the security's price per $100 face value.

Basis is the type of day count basis to use.

Basis	Day count basis
0 or omitted	30/360
1	Actual/actual
2	Actual/360
3	Actual/365

Remarks

- *Settlement, maturity, issue,* and *basis* are truncated to integers.

- If any argument is non-numeric, YIELDMAT returns the #VALUE! error value.

- If *settlement, maturity,* or *issue* is not a valid serial date number, YIELDMAT returns the #NUM! error value.

- If *rate* < 0 or if *pr* ≤ 0, YIELDMAT returns the #NUM! error value.

- If *basis* < 0 or if *basis* > 3, YIELDMAT returns the #NUM! error value.

- If *settlement* ≥ *maturity,* YIELDMAT returns the #NUM! error value.

Example

A bond has the following terms:

March 15, 1991 settlement date
November 3, 1991 maturity date
November 8, 1990 issue date
6.25% semiannual coupon
100.0123 price
30/360 basis

The yield (in the 1900 Date System) is:

`YIELDMAT(33312,33545,33185,0.0625,` `100.0123,0)` equals 0.060954 or 6.0954%

Related Functions

Function	Description
DATE	Returns the serial number of a particular date
PRICEMAT	Returns price per $100 face value of a security that pays interest at maturity

ZOOM

Macro Sheets Only

Equivalent to choosing the Zoom command from the Window menu. Enlarges or reduces a document in the active window. Use ZOOM when you need to view more cells than would normally fit in the active windows, or fewer cells at a larger size. For detailed information about the Zoom command, see online Help.

Syntax

ZOOM*(magnification)*

Magnification is a logical value or a number specifying the size of the document.

- *Magnification* can be a number from 10 to 400 specifying the percentage of enlargement or reduction.

- If *magnification* is TRUE or omitted, the current selection is enlarged or reduced to completely fill the active window.

- If *magnification* is FALSE, the document is restored to normal 100% magnification.

Related Function

Function	Description
PRINT.PREVIEW	Previews pages and pagebreaks before printing.

ZTEST

Returns the two-tailed *P*-value of a *z*-test. The *z*-test generates a standard score for *x* with respect to the data set, *array,* and returns the two-tailed probability for the normal distribution. You can use this function to assess the likelihood that a particular observation is drawn from a particular population.

Syntax

ZTEST(*array,x,sigma*)

Array   is the array or range of data against which to test *x*.

X   is the value to test.

Sigma   is the population (known) standard deviation. If omitted, the sample standard deviation is used.

Remarks

- If array is empty, ZTEST returns the #N/A error value.

- ZTEST is calculated as follows:

  $$\text{ZTEST}(array, x) =$$

  $$1 - \text{NORMSDIST}\left(\frac{\mu - x}{\sigma \div \sqrt{n}}\right)$$

Example

ZTEST({3,6,7,8,6,5,4,2,1,9},4) equals 0.090574

Related Functions

Function	Description
CONFIDENCE	Returns a confidence interval for a population
NORMDIST	Returns the normal cumulative distribution
NORMINV	Returns the inverse of the normal cumulative distribution
NORMSDIST	Returns the standard normal cumulative distribution
NORMSINV	Returns the inverse of the standard normal cumulative distribution
STANDARDIZE	Returns a normalized value

ZTESTM

Macro Sheets Only

Performs a two-sample *z*-test for means, assuming the two samples have known variances. For more information, see "Analyzing Statistical or Engineering Data" in Chapter 1 in Book 2 of the *Microsoft Excel User's Guide*.

If this function is not available, you must install the Analysis ToolPak add-in macro. For more information, see "Managing Add-in Commands and Functions" in Chapter 4 in Book 2 of the *Microsoft Excel User's Guide*.

Syntax

ZTESTM(*inprng1,inprng2,outrng,labels,alpha, difference,var1,var2*)

Inprng1   is the input range for the first data set.

Inprng2   is the input range for the second data set.

Outrng   is the first cell (the upper-left cell) in the output table.

Labels is a logical value.

- If *labels* is TRUE, then the first row or column of the input ranges contains labels.

- If *labels* is FALSE or omitted, all cells in *inprng1* and *inprng2* are considered data. Microsoft Excel will then generate the appropriate data labels for the output table.

Alpha is the confidence level for the test. If omitted, *alpha* is 0.05.

Difference is the hypothesized difference in means. If omitted, *difference* is 0.

Var1 is the variance of the first data set.

Var2 is the variance of the second data set.

Related Functions

Function	Description
NORMDIST	Returns the normal cumulative distribution
NORMINV	Returns the inverse normal cumulative distribution
NORMSDIST	Returns the standard normal cumulative distribution
NORMSINV	Returns the inverse of the standard normal cumulative distribution
ZTEST	Returns the two-tailed *P*-value of a *z*-test

Using the CALL and REGISTER Functions

This appendix describes the argument and return value data types used by the CALL, REGISTER, and REGISTER.ID functions. Arguments and return values differ slightly depending on your operating environment, and these differences are noted in the data type table.

The *Microsoft Excel 4.0 Software Development Kit* contains detailed information about dynamic link libraries (DLLs) and code resources, the Microsoft Excel application programming interface (API), file formats, and many other technical aspects of Microsoft Excel. It also contains code samples and programming tools that you can use to develop custom applications. To obtain a copy of the *Microsoft Excel 4.0 Software Development Kit*, contact your software supplier or Microsoft Corporation. In the United States, contact the Microsoft Developer Services Team at (800) 227-4679 for more information.

Data Types

In the CALL, REGISTER, and REGISTER.ID functions, the *type_text* argument specifies the data type of the return value and the data types of all arguments to the DLL function or code resource. The first character of *type_text* specifies the data type of the return value. The remaining characters indicate the data types of all the arguments. For example, a DLL function that returns a floating-point number and takes an integer and a floating-point number as arguments would require "BIB" for the *type_text* argument.

The following table contains a complete list of the data type codes that Microsoft Excel recognizes, a description of each data type, how the argument or return value is passed, and a typical declaration for the data type in the C programming language.

Code	Description	Pass by	C Declaration
A	Logical (FALSE = 0, TRUE = 1)	Value	`short int`
B	IEEE 8-byte floating-point number	Value (Windows)	`double` (Windows)
		Reference (Macintosh)	`double *` (Macintosh)
C	Null-terminated string (maximum string length = 255 characters)	Reference	`char *`

Code	Description	Pass by	C Declaration
D	Byte-counted string (first byte contains length of string, maximum string length = 255 characters)	Reference	`unsigned char *`
E	IEEE 8-byte floating-point number	Reference	`double *`
F	Null-terminated string (maximum string length = 255 characters)	Reference (modify in place)	`char *`
G	Byte-counted string (first byte contains length of string, maximum string length = 255 characters)	Reference (modify in place)	`unsigned char *`
H	Unsigned 2-byte integer	Value	`unsigned short int`
I	Signed 2-byte integer	Value	`short int`
J	Signed 4-byte integer	Value	`long int`
K	Array	Reference	`FP *`
L	Logical (FALSE = 0, TRUE = 1)	Reference	`short int *`
M	Signed 2-byte integer	Reference	`short int *`
N	Signed 4-byte integer	Reference	`long int *`
O	Array	Reference	Three arguments are passed: `unsigned short int *` `unsigned short int *` `double []`
P	Microsoft Excel OPER data structure	Reference	`OPER *`
R	Microsoft Excel XLOPER data structure	Reference	`XLOPER *`

Remarks

- The C-language declarations are based on the assumption that your compiler defaults to 8-byte doubles, 2-byte short integers, and 4-byte long integers.

- In the Microsoft Windows programming environment, all pointers are far pointers. For example, you should declare the D data type code as `unsigned char far *` in Microsoft Windows.

- All functions in DLLs and code resources are called using the Pascal calling convention. Most C compilers allow you to use the Pascal calling convention by adding the `pascal` keyword to the function declaration, as shown in the following example:

```
pascal void main (rows,columns,a)
```

- If a function uses a pass-by-reference data type for its return value, you can pass a null pointer as the return value. Microsoft Excel will interpret the null pointer as the #NUM! error value.

Additional Data Type Information

This section contains detailed information about the F, G, K, O, P, and R data types, and other information about the *type_text* argument.

F and G Data Types

With the F and G data types, a function can modify a string buffer that is allocated by Microsoft Excel. If the return value type code is F or G, then Microsoft Excel ignores the value returned by the function. Instead, Microsoft Excel searches the list of function arguments for the first corresponding data type (F or G) and then takes the current contents of the allocated string buffer as the return value. Microsoft Excel allocates 256 bytes for the argument, so the function may return a larger string than it received.

K Data Type

The K data type uses a pointer to a variable-size FP structure. You should define this structure in the DLL or code resource as follows:

```
typedef struct _FP
{
    unsigned short int rows;
    unsigned short int columns;
    double array[1];           /* Actually, array[rows][columns] */
} FP;
```

The declaration `double array[1]` only allocates storage for a single-element array. The number of elements in the actual array equals the number of rows multiplied by the number of columns.

O Data Type

The O data type can be used only as an argument, not as a return value. It passes three items: a pointer to the number of rows in an array, a pointer to the number of columns in an array, and a pointer to a two-dimensional array of floating-point numbers.

Instead of returning a value, a function can modify an array passed by the O data type. To do this, you could use ">O" as the *type_text* argument. For more information, see "Modifying in Place—Functions Declared as Void" later in this appendix

The O data type was created for direct compatibility with FORTRAN DLLs, which pass arguments by reference.

P Data Type

The P data type is a pointer to an OPER structure. The OPER structure contains eight bytes of data, followed by a two-byte identifier that specifies the type of data. With the P data type, a DLL function or code resource can take and return any Microsoft Excel data type.

The OPER structure is defined as follows:

```
typedef struct _oper
{
    union
    {
        double num;
        unsigned char *str;
        unsigned short int bool;
        unsigned short int err;
        struct
        {
            struct _oper *lparray;
            unsigned short int rows;
            unsigned short int columns;
        } array;
    } val;
    unsigned short int type;
} OPER;
```

The *type* field contains one of these values:

Type	Description	Val field to use
1	Numeric	num
2	String (first byte contains length of string)	str
4	Boolean (logical)	bool

Type	Description		*Val* field to use
16	Error: the error values are:		err
	0	#NULL!	
	7	#DIV/0!	
	15	#VALUE!	
	23	#REF!	
	29	#NAME?	
	36	#NUM!	
	42	#N/A	
64	Array		array
128	Missing argument		
256	Empty cell		

The last two values can be used only as arguments, not return values. The missing argument value (128) is passed when the caller omits an argument. The empty cell value (256) is passed when the caller passes a reference to an empty cell.

R Data Type—Calling Microsoft Excel Functions from DLLs

The R data type is a pointer to an XLOPER structure, which is an enhanced version of the OPER structure. In Microsoft Excel version 4.0, you can use the R data type to write DLLs and code resources that call Microsoft Excel functions. With the XLOPER structure, a DLL function can pass sheet references and implement flow control, in addition to passing data. A complete description of the R data type and the Microsoft Excel application programming interface (API) is beyond the scope of this appendix. The *Microsoft Excel 4.0 Software Development Kit* contains detailed information about the R data type, the Microsoft Excel API, and many other technical aspects of Microsoft Excel. For more information, see the introductory paragraphs at the beginning of this appendix.

Volatile Functions and Recalculation

Microsoft Excel usually calculates a DLL function (or a code resource) only when it is entered into a cell, when one of its precedents changes, or when the cell is calculated during a macro. On a worksheet, you can make a DLL function or code resource volatile, which means that it recalculates every time the worksheet recalculates. To make a function volatile, add an exclamation point (!) as the last character in the *type_text* argument.

For example, in Microsoft Excel for Windows, the following worksheet formula recalculates every time the worksheet recalculates:

```
CALL("User","GetTickCount","J!")
```

Modifying in Place—Functions Declared as Void

You can use a single digit *n* for the return type code in *type_text,* where *n* is a number from 1 to 9. This tells Microsoft Excel to modify the variable in the location pointed to by the *n*th argument in *type_text,* instead of returning a value. This is also known as modifying in place. The *n*th argument must be a pass-by-reference data type (C, D, E, F, G, K, L, M, N, O, P, or R). The DLL function or code resource also must be declared with the void keyword in the C language (or the procedure keyword in the Pascal language).

For example, a DLL function that takes a null-terminated string and two pointers to integers as arguments can modify the string in place. Use "1FMM" as the *type_text* argument, and declare the function as void.

Previous versions of Microsoft Excel used the > character to modify the first argument in place—there was no way to modify any argument other than the first. The > character is equivalent to *n* = 1 in Microsoft Excel version 4.0.

For More Information

The following books provide detailed information on financial, statistical, and engineering methods. For a list of these functions by category, choose the Paste Function command from the Formula menu and select a function category, or see "Functions Listed by Category" earlier in this book.

Milton Abramowitz and Irene A. Stegun, *Handbook of Mathematical Functions with Formulas, Graphs, and Mathematical Tables, Tenth Edition*. Washington, D. C.: United States Government Printing Office, 1972.

Jay L. Devore, *Probability and Statistics for Engineering and the Sciences, Third Edition*. Pacific Grove, California: Brooks/Cole Publishing Company, 1991.

Frank J. Fabozzi and Irving M. Pollack, *The Handbook of Fixed Income Securities*. Homewood, Illinois: Business 1 Irwin, 1986.

Hewlett-Packard Company, *HP-12C Owner's Handbook and Problem-Solving Guide*, 1981.

John J. Lynch, Jr. and Jan H. Mayle, *Standard Securities Calculation Methods, Fixed Income Securities Formulas*. New York, New York: Securities Industry Association, 1986.

Robert B. McCall, *Fundamental Statistics for the Behavioral Sciences, Fifth Edition*. New York, New York: Harcourt Brace Jovanovich, Inc., 1990.

W. H. Press, B. P. Flannery, S. A. Teukolsky, and W. T. Vetterling, *Numerical Recipes in C: The Art of Scientific Computing*. New York, New York: Cambridge University Press, 1988.

Robert R. Sokal and F. James Rohlf, *Biometry: The Principles and Practice of Statistics in Biological Research, Second Edition*. New York, New York: W. H. Freeman and Company, 1981.

Marcia Stigum and John Mann, *Money Market Calculations: Yields, Break-Evens, and Arbitrage*. Homewood, Illinois: Business 1 Irwin, 1989.

Index

Numbers

2-D chart *See* Chart

360-day year 95–96

3-D Area command (Gallery menu) 83

3-D Bar command (Gallery menu) 183

3-D chart *See* Chart

3-D Column command (Gallery menu) 183

3-D Line command (Gallery menu) 183–184

3-D Pie command (Gallery menu) 184

3-D Surface command (Gallery menu) 184

3-D View command (Format menu) 447

A

A1 reference style
    changing type in formula 170
    detecting 209

A1.R1C1 function
    described 1
    example of 1, 15

ABS function
    described 1
    examples of 1
    related functions 1

Absolute reference
    changing type in formula 170
    converting
        ABSREF function 2
        FORMULA.CONVERT
            function 170
        REFTEXT function 2, 349
        TEXTREF function 2, 432

Absolute value
    ABS function 1
    IMABS function 228

ABSREF function
    described 1
    example of 2
    related functions 2
    returning references 2
    returning values 2

Access, restricting 104

Access key 355

ACCRINT function
    described 2
    example of 3
    related functions 3

ACCRINTM function
    described 3
    example of 3
    related functions 4

Accrued interest
    ACCRINT function 2
    ACCRINTM function 3

ACOS function
    described 4
    example of 4
    related functions 4

ACOSH function
    described 4
    example of 4
    related functions 4

Action, undoing 441

ACTIVATE function
    described 4
    example of
        Microsoft Excel for the
            Macintosh 5
        Microsoft Excel for
            Windows 5
    related functions 5

ACTIVATE.NEXT function
    described 5
    related functions 6

ACTIVATE.PREV function
    described 5
    related functions 6

Activating a window 4

Activating applications 18
    See also Application, external

ACTIVE.CELL function
    described 6
    example of 6
    related functions 6

Active document *See* Document

Activity, suspending 453

Add Arrow command (Chart menu) 7

ADD.ARROW function
    described 7
    related functions 7

ADD.BAR function
    *Refer also to Book 2 index,
        Microsoft Excel User's Guide*
    described 7
    example of 7
    related functions 7, 104

ADD.COMMAND function
    described 8, 9
    example of 9
    related functions 9

Add Legend command (Chart menu) 252

ADD.MENU function
    described 10, 11
    example of 10
    related functions 11

Add Overlay command (Chart menu) 11

ADD.OVERLAY function
    described 11
    related functions 11

ADD.TOOL function
    described 11
    example of 12
    related functions 12

ADD.TOOLBAR function
    described 13
    example of 13
    related functions 13